Operational Risk Assessment

For other titles in the Wiley Finance series
please see www.wiley.com/finance

Operational Risk Assessment

The Commercial Imperative of a More Forensic and Transparent Approach

Brendon Young and Rodney Coleman

A John Wiley and Sons, Ltd., Publication

Published by   John Wiley & Sons Ltd, The Atrium, Southern Gate, Chichester,
                    West Sussex PO19 8SQ, England

                    Telephone   (+44) 1243 779777

Email (for orders and customer service enquiries): cs-books@wiley.co.uk
Visit our Home Page on www.wiley.com

Other Wiley Editorial Offices

John Wiley & Sons Inc., 111 River Street, Hoboken, NJ 07030, USA

Jossey-Bass, 989 Market Street, San Francisco, CA 94103-1741, USA

Wiley-VCH Verlag GmbH, Boschstr. 12, D-69469 Weinheim, Germany

John Wiley & Sons Australia Ltd, 42 McDougall Street, Milton, Queensland 4064, Australia

John Wiley & Sons (Asia) Pte Ltd, 2 Clementi Loop #02-01, Jin Xing Distripark, Singapore 129809

John Wiley & Sons Canada Ltd, 6045 Freemont Blvd, Mississauga, ONT, L5R 4J3, Canada

Wiley also publishes its books in a variety of electronic formats. Some content that appears in print may not be
available in electronic books.

Library of Congress Cataloging-in-Publication Data

Young, Brendon.
    Operational risk assessment : the commercial imperative of a more forensic and transparent approach / Brendon
Young and Rodney Coleman.
        p. cm.
    Includes bibliographical references and index.
    ISBN 978-0-470-75387-3
    1. Financial risk management.   2. Banks and banking–Risk management.   3. Financial services industry–Risk
management.   I. Coleman, Rodney.   II. Title.
    HG173.Y68 2009
    658.15′5–dc22

                                                                                                    2009005616

British Library Cataloguing in Publication Data

A catalogue record for this book is available from the British Library

ISBN 978-0-470-75387-3 (H/B)

Typeset in 10/12pt Times by Aptara Inc., New Delhi, India
Printed and bound in Great Britain by CPI Antony Rowe, Chippenham, Wiltshire

To my wife, Denise, without whose enduring support and encouragement this book would never have been written – Thank you.
(BY)

To my daughters, Clarissa and Jennifer, a long delayed dedication.
(RC)

Contents

Foreword

Brendon Young and Rodney Coleman's book is extremely timely. There has never been a greater need for the financial industry to reassess the way it looks at risk.

The financial crisis is primarily a product of poor management. During its first inquiry into the financial crisis in late 2007, the Treasury Committee was astounded to discover that managers and directors did not understand the risks their banks were taking, nor the products in which they were investing. I was concerned when the chairman of the UK branch of a leading investment bank came before the Treasury Committee and couldn't explain what a CDO was, despite the fact that his organisation had millions of pounds worth of them on their books.

In an environment of low interest and low yields, our financial system turned to riskier investments to get the high returns it was used to. This was disguised by a flurry of radical innovation in financial products, which disguised and complicated the process, as well as making it difficult to regulate. The opacity of the new markets meant that investors no longer carried out proper due diligence on their investment, and began to rely simply on credit ratings – which themselves turned out to be misleading. But, as we now know, what was happening was fundamentally a monumental failure to assess risk.

The crisis is also a product of insufficient regulation. The near-collapse of Northern Rock in summer 2007 demonstrated this spectacularly. In our report on this collapse in January 2008, the Treasury Committee found that "the current regulatory regime for the liquidity of United Kingdom banks is flawed" and that the FSA demonstrated a "substantial failure of regulation."

The Northern Rock debacle, as well as problems at other major UK banks including RBS and HBOS, can be seen as part of a wider problem. The FSA did not tackle the fundamental weaknesses in Northern Rock's funding model, nor persuade the board to take remedial action, despite identifying clear warning signs during 2007 – such as the bank's rapid growth and falls in its share price. The FSA has told the Treasury Committee that it did not consider it to be within its remit to analyse companies' business models, question their appointments of directors, and so on; there was an assumption that the banks knew best in these areas. In light of the failure of this approach, the FSA has told the Committee that it will adopt a radically different attitude in the future.

Liquidity also became a hot topic following the problems at Northern Rock. We have realised that, despite being one of the major factors affecting our financial stability, liquidity was swept under the carpet. Experts appearing before the Treasury Committee have explained that international efforts to create a liquidity regulation framework failed, and that no national system was devised in its place. The FSA is now working on a new system of liquidity regulation for UK banks.

The financial crisis has demonstrated that regulation needs to be coordinated at the international level. Recently, we have seen authorities in some countries taking a unilateral approach which has undermined stability in the UK. We have also realised that the UK may be host to large branches of foreign banks, which are not regulated by British authorities but which have a very large impact on our financial stability. There is a clear need for an international approach to many of these issues.

The crisis has brought to light many more examples of flaws in our systems of managing risk. For example, the Treasury Committee has questioned credit rating agencies on the conflicts of interest inherent in their business model, and their overarching reliance on quantitative models – even relying on models devised by the banks themselves. As another example, we questioned auditors on whether it was appropriate for them to provide additional services to banks, in addition to the statutory role, and we considered what future role they might have to play in giving assurance to shareholders on a company's risk management processes.

I welcome Brendon Young and Rodney Coleman's call for better, more "forensic" risk management. They are right to draw attention to the current widespread practices of risk management, which rely on comparative assessment and experience, and have allowed risk to become underpriced across the entire industry. Like the emperor's new clothes, those who criticised the new ways in which risk was being 'sliced and diced,' were regarded as Luddites who simply didn't understand. The collective mania apparently extended to the regulator itself, through its 'revolving doors' policy of exchanging staff with the institutions it regulated.

I welcome the attention they draw to the role of institutional investors in ensuring adequate risk management. I have raised concerns about the apparent lack of intervention by non-executive directors in banks such as Northern Rock, RBS and HBOS – many of whom were luminaries of the financial industry, with enormous experience. Clearly, the task of supervising the banks' management must not be left to directors alone. Evidence given to the Committee suggests that many make very little use of their rights as shareholders. In future, they must take on a more active role. Indeed, many other issues which have been unearthed by the crisis, such as executive remuneration, would also benefit from closer involvement of investors.

I welcome this widening of the debate on risk management in the financial industry at this crucial time.

Whilst there has been much debate over the appropriateness of a 'light-touch' regulatory framework, it is clear now that, in the past, we have experienced not light-touch, but 'soft-touch' regulation. Whatever the regulatory system will look like in the future, the days of soft touch regulation are over.

Rt Hon John McFall MP
Chairman, House of Commons Treasury Committee

Preface

The devil is in the detail. Ludwig Mies van der Rohe (1886–1969)

The failure of senior management and analysts to properly understand Operational Risk represents a threat to the financial system.

The strategic significance and sphere of influence of Operational Risk is not widely understood in the banking and financial services industry, particularly at senior management level. Yet losses experienced have been considerable, threatening not only the survival of individual organizations but also undermining stability within the financial system itself. This has been clearly demonstrated by the recent "credit crunch"[1] as well as by other major loss events such as Long Term Capital Management (LTCM) and Enron. Such events have served to identify a number of underlying fundamental weaknesses and, consequently, brought to the fore the need for corrective actions to restore confidence in the system itself.

Loss events impact upon overall wealth creation and world living standards; from an individual bank's perspective loss events threaten reputation and survival.

The true significance of loss events stems from the fact that they have a major impact upon overall wealth creation and global living standards. From an individual bank's perspective, in addition to reducing its capital, significant losses undermine the reputation of the bank, threatening its competitive position and reducing shareholder value. In the light of the recent "credit crunch," shareholders are questioning bank's business models and performance. Consequently, those banks that fail to win shareholder support will be faced with the possibility of takeover or even collapse.

Action will increasingly be taken against individuals as well as organizations.

In the UK, Legal & General Investment Management, which owns approximately 4.5 % of the UK stock market, put considerable pressure on HBOS[2] and both the Chairman and the CEO of Royal Bank of Scotland (RBS),[3] expressing the view that "they have a lot to answer for." In the US, a significant number of senior banking executives have recently been removed, including the heads of Citigroup and Merrill Lynch.[4] Similarly, in Europe, the heads of UBS[5] and Société Générale stepped down, whilst the CEO of Fortis was also forced to resign.

In addition to shareholder pressure, regulatory and legislative action is increasing. Credit Suisse was fined £5.6 million in August 2008, following a trading scandal that cost the bank $2.7 billion. This was the fourth largest fine by the FSA after Shell's £17 million fine for mis-statement of its reserves, Citigroup's £14 million fine for European bond market irregularities, and Deutsche Bank's £6.4 million fine for share issue mishandling. The FSA has indicated that significant fines are likely to become more common and that actions may also be taken against individuals. In June 2008, the FSA warned "We know that taking enforcement action against individuals is a vital part of achieving credible deterrence overall." "So you can expect to see more supervision and enforcement focus on individuals."[6]

Shareholder value and the cost of capital will increasingly be influenced by risk management.

The rating agencies have recognized the importance of risk management and are increasingly adopting an enterprise-wide risk management approach. This requires a more forensic view of risk at all levels, whilst also recognizing the need for a holistic overview, taking into account the importance of correlations and interrelationships.

Similarly, institutional investors are increasingly taking risk into consideration, in particular, "enhanced analytical" risk factors that have the potential to impact upon an organization's longer-term performance and thereby affect shareholder value.

Transparency is essential for the market to work properly.

Unfortunately, esoteric information known and understood only by the few will not bring about wider market changes, no matter how important. Hence, for a more forensic risk-based approach to improve performance and enhance market stability, an increase in the level of transparency is necessary; opaqueness undermines market confidence.

This book promotes a more forensic and transparent approach towards risk management.

This book seeks to promote adoption of a more forensic and transparent approach towards risk management, facilitating a continuous evolutionary approach to change.

The book aims to provide a sound foundation upon which to build an understanding of operational risk (its principles and best practices). Initially, it looks at traditional methods of risk assessment and shows how these have developed into the approaches currently being used. It then goes on to consider some of the more advanced forensic techniques being developed, which will undoubtedly improve the quality of analysis and understanding.

Who the book is aimed at.

This book is aimed at investors and those operational risk professionals who require a sound understanding of the approaches needed to assess the standing of a bank and determine its true potential (i.e. to identify the potential winners and possible losers). It will also be of interest to those various bodies and organizations that make up and influence the overall financial system. A number of recommendations are put forward in order to promote debate. In particular, consideration is given to the efficacy of:

- **institutional shareholder-investors** – who, as owners, have responsibility to their members to bring about change by influencing board thinking, particularly with regard to longer-term considerations;
- **regulators, legislators, and central banks** – who are responsible for maintaining trust in the financial system and ensuring overall financial stability;
- **accountants, auditors, and financial reporting bodies** – who are responsible for ensuring transparency and, in particular, ensuring that a "true and fair view" is provided;
- **rating agencies** – whose current function appears limited merely to providing their fee-paying customers with a properly considered expert opinion regarding the probability of default;
- **insurance companies** – who make possible the transfer of risk (away from those unable or unwilling to accept it) and also assist with the smoothing of earnings;
- **banks** – who owe an ultimate duty of care to their customers[7] – and also to their shareholders.

Although the book is based on the banking sector, it will also be relevant to other sectors.

Whilst the book primarily considers the banking sector, it should be recognized that the principles and techniques apply equally to other financial institutions and government bodies. For instance, the Poynter report into HMRC, commissioned by the UK government and published in June 2008, in effect suggested that HMRC was similar to those banks previously found in the old Soviet states; (i.e. complex, inefficient, with low morale and lacking in appropriate risk management systems) and that HMRC needed to move forward towards becoming a modern financial services organization.

The challenge ahead is to improve efficiency and responsiveness.

Put simply, the challenge over the next decade for competing organizations, in a dynamic global financial industry experiencing rationalization, is to apply more forensic risk management techniques, in order to improve responsiveness, increase efficiency and effectiveness and raise levels of customer service, in pursuit of competitive advantage and long-term survival.

ENDNOTES

[1] The credit crunch is said to have officially started when the markets froze, on 9 August 2007.

[2] HBOS had to make a rights issue for £4 billion. Unfortunately, it was only taken up by approximately 8 % of shareholders.

[3] In April 2008, RBS put forward a £12 billion rights issue following its deteriorating performance and its acquisition of the Dutch bank, ABN Amro. This rights issue was the largest ever launched in the UK.

[4] Merrill Lynch suffered $29 billion of losses on collateralized debt obligations (CDOs) related to the sub-prime credit crunch. The *Financial Times* newspaper reported (on 15 August 2008) that "if UK subsidiary Merrill Lynch International were to continue to generate profits at 2006 levels – a record for the investment banking business – it would pay no UK corporation tax for 60 years."

[5] UBS stated that most of the $42 billion loss suffered by the bank was due to the sub-prime meltdown.

[6] Statement by Margaret Cole, Head of Enforcement, FSA, June 2008.

[7] "Treating Customers Fairly" is a recognized FSA priority.

Acknowledgements

In writing this book we are indebted to many people and organizations who have kindly shared with us their ideas and information.

We would particularly like to thank those people who kindly participated in the research for this book, specifically: Helmut Bauer at Deutsche Bank, James Gifford at U.N. PRI, Dr Jimi Hinchliffe and his colleagues at the FSA, Rob Jones at Standard & Poor's, Colin Melvin at Hermes, Jon Moulton of Alchemy Partners, Krishnan Ramadurai and his colleagues at Fitch Ratings, David Russell of USS, and Sir David Tweedie of the International Accounting Standards Board (IASB).

We would also like to especially thank those former colleagues who have worked with us in the past on various assignments, and who have provided material that has been incorporated into this book in some way. In particular:

- Professor John Sparrow, who contributed material and ideas on control risk self assessment (CRSA) and knowledge management;
- Dr Simon Ashby, who jointly wrote the original research paper submitted to Basel upon which the chapter on insurance and other risk transfer methods is based;
- Professor Norman Fenton and Dr Martin Neil of Agena, who helped to develop our thinking on the practical applications of Bayesian Belief Networks;
- Professor Brian Toft, whose overall contribution is greatly appreciated; his ideas relating to the human aspects of risk management were invaluable;
- Michael Tripp, for his guidance on actuarial views towards advances in the quantification of operational risk;
- Andrew Cunningham, whose insightful comments early on shaped our thinking on the strengths and limitations of ratings and credit rating agencies;
- Samuel Theodore, who kindly provided much information and practical insight into the rating of banks by rating agencies.

We would also like to express our gratitude to the members of the Operational Risk Research Forum (ORRF), whose presentations and participation helped in advancing the boundaries of knowledge. Whilst there are too many to mention in full, we would particularly like to thank: Dr Jeremy Quick, Dr Victor Dowd, Mark Laycock, David Clark, John Thirlwell, Peter Brown, Professor Michael Dempster, Dr Elena Medova, Shirley Beglinger, David Lawrence, and Dr Marcelo Cruz.

Special thanks go to Tom Lewthwaite for his vision in recognizing, early on, the commercial imperative of risk management and for assisting in the establishment of Arthur Andersen's Centre for Operational Risk Research and Education.

We must also thank the directors of the Institute of Operational Risk (IOR) who are endeavoring to establish professional standards. We thank them for their encouragement and hope this book goes some way to meeting their requirements.

We would also like to give special thanks to Rob Hofstede of the Dutch National Bank for his invaluable suggestions and feedback on our early material. The courses we presented there acted as a catalyst for this book.

We are indebted to John Wiley & Sons, Ltd for their help and encouragement. In particular, we would like to thank Caitlin Cornish, Kerry Batcock, and Rachael Wilkie.

About the Authors

Brendon Young, founding president of the Institute of Operational Risk (IOR), is recognized as one of the foremost authorities in the field of risk management. He was global director of Arthur Andersen's operational risk research centre (CORRE), and special advisor to the banking group of Moody's Investors Service. He has advised regulatory bodies and numerous financial institutions. Currently, he is an invited member of the Board for Actuarial Standards (BAS), modeling standards advisory group (part of the Financial Reporting Council).

In 1999, he established the highly acclaimed Operational Risk Research Forum (ORRF), in association with the FSA, academia, and leading financial services firms, with a view to driving forward the boundaries of knowledge in the field of operational risk management. A paper submitted to Basel received an international prize for research excellence. He has lectured widely, and given presentations at places such as the Bank of England, the FSA, Lloyds of London, BaFin, the Dutch National Bank, the OCC, and the New York State Banking Department, amongst many others.

As a venture capitalist, associated with Lazards, he was actively engaged in the risk-based assessment and management of investments. Whilst working in venture capital he developed a strong interest in risk management, which he later pursued in academia and where, as associate dean, he was responsible for research and business development.

He is a chartered management accountant and a chartered engineer, with his early career having been spent in industry with Rolls-Royce aero-engines and Jaguar Cars. Subsequently, he moved into consultancy with PKF and Deloitte's, where he specialized in performance improvement and business development.

Rodney Coleman has been involved with operational risk research for more than 12 years, and is a founding fellow of the Institute of Operational Risk and an Associate Editor of the Journal of Operational Risk. He was an author of the first published academic paper on applying statistical methods to model loss data for quantifying operational risk.

He has been closely associated with the Operational Risk Research Forum since its beginnings, and addressed its meetings at BaFin and the New York State Banking Department. He has given presentations at the Dutch National Bank, the Oprisk Europe Conference, the Institute of Actuaries Actuarial Teaching and Research Conference, the Actuarial Studies in Non-Life Insurance UK meeting, and given seminars extensively in universities in Canada, Italy, Korea, as well as in the UK.

He was until recently a senior lecturer in mathematics at Imperial College London, and there supervised PhD students in finance and operational risk. His own PhD was awarded by Cambridge University. He is a fellow of the Royal Statistical Society and a member of the International Statistical Institute.

Abbreviations

AMA	Advanced measurement approaches
ARE	Asymptotic relative efficiency
ASA	Alternative standardized approach
BBN	Bayesian belief network
BCBS	Basel Commmittee on Banking Supervision
BIA	Basic indicator approach
BIS	Bank of International Settlement
BL	Business line
BU	Business unit
cdf	Cumulative distribution function
CF	Capital factor
CI	Confidence interval
CL	Confidence limit
DFA	Dynamic financial analysis
EI	Exposure indicator
EL	Expected loss
ET	Event type
EVT	Extreme value theory
GEV	Generalized extreme value distribution
GI	Gross income
GPD	Generalized Pareto distribution
IMA	Internal measurement approach
IQR	Inter-quartile range
LDA	Loss data approach
LF	Lower fence (boxplot)
LGE	Loss-given-event
LW	Lower whisker (boxplot)
MLE	Maximum likelihood estimate
MoME	Method of moments estimate
MSE	Mean square error
MTTF	Mean time on test per failure
MVUE	Minimum variance unbiased estimate
NTA	Normal theory assumptions

OpVaR	Operational value-at-risk
OR	Operational risk
Pdf	Probability density function
pmf	Probability mass function
PE	Probability of loss event
POT	Peaks over threshold (method)
P-P	Probability v. probability (plot)
PWM, pwm	Probability weighted moment
Ql, Q2, Q3	First, second and third quartile
QD	Quartile difference
QF, qf	Quantile function
Q-Q	Quantile v. quantile (plot)
RSS	Residual sum of squares
rv	Random variable
SOA	Second order assumptions
TSA	The standardized approach
TTT	Total time on test
UF	Upper fence (boxplot)
UW	Upper whisker (boxplot)
VaR	Value-at-Risk

Part I

The Assessment of Risk and its
Strategic Importance

Introduction

1.1 EXECUTIVE OVERVIEW: RESPONSIVENESS, COMPETITIVE ADVANTAGE, AND SURVIVAL

*It is **not the strongest** of the species that survive, **nor the most intelligent**, but the one most **responsive** to change.* Charles Darwin

Given the advanced nature of the global financial community and its level of complexity it may seem incredible that failures can occur that result in the demise of major financial institutions or even threaten the entire system itself. On a lesser scale, losses due to operational risk events occur on a daily basis in all organizations. Their combined value is without doubt very significant, although difficult to determine since many go unreported. The results of such inefficiencies are a reduction in overall global wealth-creation and associated living standards.

1.1.1 Banking is a highly competitive global industry

Banking is a highly competitive and dynamic industry in which there exists over-capacity. However, disintermediation, product commoditization, and technological advances are resulting in globalization and rationalization. In addition, institutional shareholders are becoming increasingly powerful and demanding growth in shareholder value, both in the short term and longer term. Consequently, for an individual bank, survival and growth have become primary concerns, requiring careful strategic positioning based upon the bank's particular franchise and chosen risk reward profile. It is the flexibility and responsiveness of an organization, its ability to innovate and adapt quickly to change, which assists in creating competitive advantage.

1.1.2 Regulation is necessary but not sufficient[1]

As part of this changing market place, one of the more important developments is the increasing emphasis being placed on transparency, together with a growing recognition of the need for "a more forensic approach" including consideration of longer-term enhanced analytic factors.[2] The dynamic nature of the banking and financial services industry has inevitably resulted in regulation and legislation lagging some way behind market developments. Consequently, the banking and financial services sector is being subjected to more demanding regulatory and legislative requirements, including the introduction of risk-based regulatory capital and a drive towards enhanced market discipline. The New Basel Capital Accord (Basel II) indicates the regulators' desire to promote more effective risk-based management through market forces rather than adopting a wholly prescriptive compliance approach. Whilst regulatory intervention is an important factor, it acts primarily as a catalyst, merely influencing the market's rate of change.[3] In a dynamic competitive environment, leading banks will naturally strive continuously to gain strategic competitive advantage in order to improve their performance and standing.[4]

1.1.3   How well a bank manages operational risk has a direct impact upon competitive advantage

Risk is concerned with volatility in outcomes and the possibility that objectives will not be achieved either in whole or in part. Principally, operational risk[5] is concerned with efficient and effective management;[6] its primary aims being to improve the quality and stability of earnings[7] and reduce the probability of failure, by optimizing risk and improving responsiveness.[8] It is for these reasons that a discipline, which was virtually unheard-of 10 years ago, is now being afforded such prominence. Fundamentally, the commercial imperative[9] of operational risk stems from its potential to impact upon an organization's reputation and ability to do business. Given that in extreme cases operational risk can threaten an organization's survival,[10] it is receiving increasing attention not only from the board of directors of banks but also from the investment community[11] and their service providers (i.e. credit rating agencies) as well as the regulatory and legislative authorities.

Risk assessment is an integral part of informed decision making, influencing strategic positioning, and direction. It is a key differentiator between competing management teams. This is particularly so in the financial services sector where the performance of an organization is inextricably linked to its ability to manage risk. Although it is often rightly stated that not all risks can be quantified, it remains incumbent upon management to determine the impact of possible risk-events on financial statements[12] and to indicate, within stated confidence bounds, the level of variation in projected figures. Consequently, management performance must be assessed in the light of how well the team manages risk and achieves their stated objectives.

1.1.4   A more forensic approach is required to properly understand and manage risk given its dynamic nature

Management action can reduce the level of risk by reducing both the impact and likelihood of a loss event. This requires a detailed understanding of event–cause–effect relationships, together with an expert ability to properly interpret loss data.[13] Breaking risk down into appropriate granular categories is important for analysis and understanding, since different categories can have different loss-distribution curves and different risk drivers. However, it is also important to see how risks react overall – i.e. "the whole can be greater (or less in some cases) than the sum of the parts," depending upon interactions and correlations. Consequently, there is need for both a holistic enterprise-wide risk management approach and detailed forensic analysis.

Since the boundaries of good practice move continuously, there is a need for responsiveness and practical optimization,[14] both within specific business units and for the group as a whole. What is appropriate for a particular organization will change continuously and will be dependent upon its particular circumstances (contingency theory),[15] including such factors as market position and the level of sophistication. Consequently, pursuing best practice quixotically is inappropriate. Risk management must be integrated into the business and involve continuous assessment. Resources must be continuously reallocated to achieve efficiency and effectiveness.

1.1.5   Capital supplements risk management but does not replace it

Capital is considered to be a key factor in a bank's strategy, providing the last line of defense against unexpected losses and thus providing protection for those having dealings with the organization (i.e. investors, depositors, creditors, counterparties, and employees). Furthermore, capital is a prime regulatory consideration, providing protection against systemic risk; banks operating with borderline solvency margins lack the flexibility necessary for dealing with unexpected loss-events. In addition to minimum regulatory requirements, economic capital is necessary to meet the growth and development needs of an organization, in order to maintain and enhance competitive positioning. Economic capital techniques are considered to be of potential importance in risk management and, consequently, their use is increasing. However, it should be noted that the rating agencies have stated that there is no direct correlation between a bank's credit rating and its level of capital,[16] other factors such as earnings potential and liquidity also being of significant influence.

Typically, an increasing level of competition requires companies to take more risk with less capital (all other things being equal). This eventually leads to rationalization within the market. Significant institutional failures in recent years have demonstrated the need for more responsive approaches to risk management and have changed the business environment.[17] As a consequence, credit rating agencies and equity analysts are being asked by investors to take an ever more forensic approach.[18] In general, the market can digest bad news but hates uncertainty and reacts badly to shocks. Investors are fundamentally concerned with the quality and stability of earnings. Unfortunately, as stated previously, risk introduces volatility[19] (both in service levels and earnings) with the impact of risk-events being difficult to predict (as expounded by complexity theory).[20] Uncertainty increases with time, hence investor pressure to concentrate on increasing gains in the short term. Unfortunately, short-termism can adversely affect the overall risk profile. Given that an organization has finite financial strength,[21] the level of risk accepted influences the probability of long-term survival.[22] Analysts and professional investors are therefore increasingly recognizing the need for enhanced analytics.

1.1.6   Adequate and appropriate risk measures are essential

Intercompany comparisons of performance must take into account those companies' differing risk profiles in order to have meaning. A weakness of traditional measures such as return-on-assets (ROA) or free cashflow is their inability to take account of risk. Whilst traditional P/E ratios are forward looking and include an implicit assessment of known risks, they are not based on a forensic technical analysis of an organization. Instead, they are influenced by events known to the market causing movement about a current position rather than an absolute base. In addition, they are heavily influenced by the herd mentality of investor sentiment, leading to timing (market) risk. Consequently, efforts have been made to introduce risk-adjusted indicators such as RAROC (risk adjusted return on capital employed). Techniques such as economic value added (EVA) or cashflow return on investment (CFROI) provide a link to shareholder value as well as providing a clearer basis for choosing between alternatives. A "balanced scorecard" approach facilitates coordinated enterprise-wide risk management. Key performance indicators and key risk indicators (KPIs and KRIs) provide useful early warnings for management, although many practitioners remain sceptical of their predictive capabilities.[23]

In practice, it is often found that banks pursue cost reduction without taking into account possible changes in risk profile.[24] The development of risk management typically comprises three broad stages. The first is concerned with the establishment of sound systems and management controls, with the aim being to prevent the occurrence of losses. This is closely related to a quality-management based approach (Section 26.10).[25] The second stage is concerned with increasing the level of responsiveness – i.e. fine-tuning systems so that where loss-events do occur, their impact can be mitigated by "catching them early." This requires greater understanding of those risks being faced, enabling resources to be efficiently and effectively appropriated in both time and place. The third stage is concerned with attaining competitive advantage through enhanced reputation.

1.1.7   Quantification of risk serves to increase understanding – this is more important than any derived number

Mathematical tools and techniques are naturally becoming an increasingly important part of this more forensic approach and they will inevitably continue to be developed and enhanced over time. Unfortunately, the usefulness of mathematical tools can be constrained by the quality and quantity of data available, with contamination and data shortage being serious limiting factors. The calculation of a regulatory capital charge for operational risk, to a high degree of confidence, means that by definition very little data is available in the tail of the loss distribution curve. Therefore, the margin for error can be very large. Further, even where there is a comparatively large amount of data in the tail Extreme Value Theory (EVT) may fail to be statistically robust and therefore any value calculated must be suspect. Consequently, there is a need to understand the underlying factors influencing extreme events. To overcome the deficiencies of traditional actuarial techniques, other methods such as advanced Delphi techniques, causal modeling, fuzzy logic, and scenario analysis are being applied with varying degrees of success by different organizations. However, it has been argued that, in some cases, extreme loss events may simply be due to random chance[26] and therefore the application of logic-based pattern approaches may be inappropriate.

The rating agencies have stated[27] that quantification has its place; however, truly effective operational risk management will continue to remain primarily underpinned by qualitatively stronger elements such as solid corporate governance, a healthy risk culture throughout the organization, effective operational risk management at all levels, tight procedures and controls, performing technology and, not least, well qualified and honest people. This recognizes the complexity of risk and emphasizes the need for a detailed forensic view, incorporating quantification where appropriate. It also recognizes the importance of considering risk in its entirety.

1.1.8   Corporate governance, social, and environmental issues are of growing importance, particularly to longer-term institutional investors

The importance of sound corporate governance, which is seen by many as the cornerstone of operational risk management, has been acknowledged at an international level by the OECD (Organisation for Economic Co-operation and Development) and the World Bank. Any organization that is recognized as exercising sound corporate governance can expect to attract relatively more financial resources at lower rates. The efficient and effective use of resources enables more to be achieved with less.[28] Similarly, a country having sound legislative and regulatory standards can expect to attract relatively more external investment and consequently see an increase in economic and social standards. There is growing recognition amongst institutional investors that, in order to meet their fiduciary duties and to better align these with broader objectives of society, it is necessary to take account of environmental, social, and corporate governance issues, which can affect the performance of investment portfolios (to varying degrees across companies, sectors, regions, asset classes, and over time). In recognition of the increasing relevance of environmental, social and corporate governance (ESG) issues to investment practices, the United Nations (UN) has given its support to an international group of institutional investors, in the development and promotion of "Principles for Responsible Investment" (PRI).[29]

1.1.9   Transparency is essential for the market to function properly and for crime to be prevented

Transparency is widely recognized as being essential for the market to work effectively; opaqueness undermines market confidence and increasing volatility. Key regulatory and legislative factors influencing the level of transparency are: the New Basel guidelines (particularly Pillar 3 of Basel II) and its European legislative equivalent (the Capital Requirement Directive); the US Sarbanes-Oxley Act; the International Financial Reporting Standards (IFRS), which came into force in 2005; and new accounting standards being developed by the International Accounting Standards Board (IASB). Transparency is seen as a facilitator of competition and efficiency as well as being a barrier to fraud, corruption, and financial crime. Increased transparency, including an improvement in financial disclosure and the quality of financial statements, could markedly improve banking practices and thereby improve investor confidence.

1.2   UNDERSTANDING THE INCREASINGLY COMPLEX AND COMPETITIVE BANKING ENVIRONMENT

The banking industry has experienced unprecedented and accelerating change over the last 20 years. As a result, the banking environment is becoming increasingly complex and competitive.

Traditionally, banking was built upon trust and discretion, epitomized by the monolithic pillars of the great banking halls. Parsimony of disclosed information, which often cloaked substantial hidden reserves, was considered a virtue and helped to instill public confidence. However, traditional banking was, and to some extent remains, an inherently unstable activity, borrowing short and lending long. The banking crises of the late 1980s and early 1990s signalled the need for change, in order to meet the needs of a changing world. Events such as the Asian Crisis, the Russian Default, and the structural problems of the Japanese banks highlighted the weaknesses of a globally interrelated industry and the need for improved risk management. The recent credit crunch (of 2007–2009) has confirmed the need for continuous improvement.

Some of the major changes that have been instrumental in transforming the banking industry, improving its overall soundness and financial stability, are as follows.

1.2.1   Increased regulatory and legislative requirements

In an endeavour to prevent systemic risk, banking regulators from the leading industrialized nations implemented the original Basel Accord in 1988. This required banks to maintain a minimum level of regulatory capital, based on their weighted assets. Unfortunately, the detailed requirements of the Accord led to perverse lending actions, increasing risk. Hence the new Basel Accord (Basel II), which was introduced after much deliberation, attempts to relate regulatory capital to the underlying risks within a particular bank. The Capital Requirements Directive, applicable within the EU, converts the Basel II guidelines into legislation.

The Sarbanes-Oxley Act,[30] although much criticized, has been of significant influence in increasing transparency and developing a risk-aware culture within organizations. Ultimate legal responsibility rests firmly with the chief executive officer and the chief financial officer, who are required to certify that the organization's internal controls are adequate and effective. In addition, the company's external independent auditor is required to attest to management's assessment of internal controls. Whilst the Sarbanes-Oxley Act relates specifically to companies under the jurisdiction of the US Securities and Exchange Commission (SEC), its influence has been much more widely felt. Unfortunately, the Sarbanes-Oxley Act had the perverse effect of initially stopping research into the assessment of operational risk (which had reached an advanced stage) by effectively preventing the rating agencies offering independent operational risk ratings.

1.2.2 Greater transparency

Both the quantity and the quality of information disclosed have increased considerably in recent years. This will assist in improving the quality of banks' balance sheets, through endeavouring to curtail their involvement in excessively risky activities. This will result in an overall improvement in the soundness of the banking industry. However, the International Accounting Standards Board (IASB) acknowledges that there remains much to be done.

Sir David Tweedie,[31] chairman of the International Accounting Standards Board, has stated that there is a need to improve transparency, particularly with regard to high-risk structured investment vehicles that are typically held off-balance sheet. These vehicles are currently used to veil billions of dollars of exposure by global institutions, distorting asset-liability statements and consequently distorting stock prices. Leading institutions such as Citibank and HSBC have already indicated their intentions to include structured investment vehicles on their balance sheets. The IASB has indicated its intention to make this compulsory, possibly through the use of parallel balance sheets.[32] Increased transparency, including better financial disclosure, could markedly improve banking practices and the quality of balance sheets, thereby improving investor confidence.

The third pillar of the new Basel Accord, which is directly concerned with transparency, aims to facilitate the control of risk through use of market forces. It seeks to reinforce the other two pillars of the Accord, which involve regulatory intervention.

The International Financial Reporting Standards (IFRS), which came into force in 2005, have assisted to some extent in further improving disclosure, giving a clearer insight into the financial condition and the earnings capability of individual banks. This has improved cross-boarder comparisons and will facilitate mergers and aquisitions.

1.2.3 Improving Corporate Governance

There has been a growing recognition of the importance of corporate governance over the last 20–30 years. In the UK, this began in earnest in 1991, with publication of the Cadbury Report, following a number of high-profile failures which threatened confidence in the City. In the US, the Sarbanes-Oxley Act came into force in 2002 as a reaction to the loss of investor confidence following the demise of major organizations including Enron, Arthur Andersen, and others. This improved both corporate governance and disclosure.

In recognition of the impact corporate governance can have on the economic development of countries, organizations including the World Bank and the OECD have issued various guidelines.

In February 2006, the Basel Committee on Banking Supervision published a revised paper entitled: "Enhancing Corporate Governance for Banking Organisations." This paper, which sets out eight principles, recognized the sensitivity of banks to ineffective corporate governance.

1.2.4 Deregulation of banking

Deregulation seeks to improve efficiency and effectiveness through creating a level playing field, thus encouraging competition. Deregulation of the banking industry began in earnest in the early 1980s in the US, and shortly afterwards in the UK, with Continental Europe following suit throughout the 1990s. Deregulation has enabled banks to broaden their activities by diversifying into areas where previously they had not been allowed to operate.

In the City of London, the removal of restrictive practice (Big Bang) took place on 27 October 1986.[33] This was an event of profound significance, which resulted in rapid internationalization and cross-sector mergers, leading to the City's current elevated status as the world's largest financial centre for global business. Now there are approximately 260 foreign banks with a presence in the City, and more than 300 foreign firms listed on the London Stock Exchange.

1.2.5 Disintermediation and changing funding structures

The formative phase of disintermediation of assets and savings began in the United States during the 1970s and 1980s. Financial liberalization in the developed countries led to broader and deeper capital markets. This attracted a greater share of savings and loans, which previously had been the preserve of banks.

Levels of disintermediation vary significantly by region. In the US, the level of bank deposits (as a percentage of total financial stock) was 20 % in 2003 (23 % in 1993, 41 % in 1980); in Japan, 37 % in 2003 (40 % in 1993, 48 % in 1980); in the Eurozone, 30 % in 2003 (32.5 % in 1993, 50 % in 1980); in the UK, 27.5 % in 2003 (25 % in 1993, 32 % in 1980).

More recently, particularly in Europe, there had been evidence of reintermediation. Banks had been changing their funding mix (in response to the growing demand for residential, commercial, and public sector loans) issuing bonds, MTNs, and commercial paper in order to grow their loan portfolios. However, the longer-term impact of the credit crunch on these activities has yet to be fully determined.

1.2.6 Commoditization of products

The financial services industry relies upon its ability to innovate, continuously creating new products to meet customers' changing needs, in an endeavour to secure more lucrative margins. However, increasing competitive pressure reduces the period over which a product can achieve above-average returns. Securitization and the increasing use of derivatives have resulted in certain products effectively become commoditized.

1.2.7 Globalization

Banking is a global industry. Rationalization is continuing to take place (with excess capacity being eliminated), as the major players fight to secure their position in a market that, in the future, may be dominated by only a few mega financial institutions with oligopolistic influences.

Traditionally, banks existed to serve their local community and their country of origin, facilitating the creation of wealth and jobs. In countries such as Germany, some sectoral banking organizations retain a strong social *raison d'être*. Unfortunately, this tends to reduce profitability and thus constrain growth. In addition, it can lead to inefficiency, as evidenced in Eastern Europe. With the removal of governmental protectionism, such organizations become vulnerable.

Within emerging market economies[34] the banking sector has experienced a significant influx of global financial institutions. In some countries, such as Poland, the banking industry is now dominated by foreign controlled financial institutions. This has brought all-round benefits by providing expansion and diversification opportunities for international organizations whilst also improving the quality of banking within the host nation. However, it has also brought additional risks. The possibility of cross-border failures is of significant concern to regulators.

In some of the advanced countries, such as Italy, there appears to have been a somewhat nationalistic reaction by governments, who have deliberately sought to promote home banks to international echelons. In contrast, Germany has seen one of its leading banks, Deutsche Bank, substantially move away from its country of origin in its drive towards becoming a truly global bank.

1.2.8   Greater shareholder power

The emergence of transnational investment funds, brought about by savings disintermediation and the pooling of significant levels of institutional and retail savings, has resulted in a greater transfer of power to shareholders. Such investors concentrate on the quality and stability of earnings, requiring continuous growth in shareholder value, with no exceptions and no excuses. This has had a direct impact upon the strategies adopted by banks, with there being a concentration on short-term performance, in some cases at the expense of weakening long-term competitive position.

Those banks with underlying weak performance (i.e. low profitability, volatile earnings, and low growth rates) are unattractive to institutional investors. As a consequence, in the absence of governmental support, they face increasing uncertainty and vulnerability.

1.2.9   Technological developments

Information and communication technology (ICT) has been and will continue to remain a key enabler, facilitating globalization and increasing efficiency. It has made possible the move from local branches to call centres (often now located in low-cost countries,[35] such as India) to the development of E-commerce via the Internet.[36]

Increased processor power and straight-through-processing (STP) methods have substantially lowered the cost of transactions as well as vastly improving the speed of distribution of information. Vast amounts of data can be rapidly processed, with data-mining techniques (enabling patterns in activity to be identified) facilitating the identification of fraud and systems' weaknesses. The ability to identify patterns in customer behaviour and thereby improve customer service (thus preventing reputational risk and degradation of competitive advantage) are of significant importance.

ICT has played an important part in reducing traditional risks; however, it has brought with it other types of risk. In the event of systems down-time, significant losses can result in addition to reputational damage through the loss of customer confidence. Hence systems suppliers place great emphasis on resilience and robustness.

Technology and systems are developing rapidly. Typically, the life of a system is three years; hence there is continuous pressure on banks to replace existing systems, at considerable cost. Unfortunately, new systems are often built on top of older legacy platforms and systems, which can result in inefficiency as well as giving rise to potential failure risk.

1.2.10   Risk management and risk transfer tools

A bank can now structure its risk profile more precisely. The use of new risk management techniques, together with a growing market for risk transfer instruments, has had a profound impact upon bank strategies and resulting balance sheets.

It is interesting to note that development and expansion of the credit risk transfer (CRT) market appears to have been limiting disintermediation, particularly in Europe, with banks having been more willing to increase their corporate loan activities. The CRT market has expanded considerably in recent years. In June 2005, the world market for credit derivatives was estimated to be $12.43 trillion. This represented a 128 % increase compared to the previous year.

Some commentators, including Warren Buffett, have likened derivatives to a time bomb, saying they represent a significant systemic threat to the financial system. However, a Joint Forum study undertaken in 2004,[37] concluded that the notion of credit risk not going away but ending up in the hands of those less able to assess it was ill founded and that there was no evidence of "hidden concentrations." In general, the working group concluded that participants (including nonbanking entities) were aware of the risks and able to properly manage them. The 2007–2009 credit crunch has clearly demonstrated the dangers of not properly understanding risk.

1.3   RISK MANAGEMENT AND STRATEGY – IDENTIFYING WINNERS AND LOSERS

Look not only at the upside potential but look also at the downside risk. Lord Hanson

1.3.1   Introduction

Risk management is an applied management science rather than an exact pure science. As such, it cannot be precisely prescribed. Management expertise and judgement are essential requirements, involving a combination of logic, tacit knowledge, and intuitive forecasting. Given that businesses are constantly changing, risk management is concerned with possible developments whose "actual" manifestation may not be fully and precisely predicted. Survival and growth require responsiveness to change. Professor Gerry Johnson has suggested that rigidity, as enshrined in organizational culture, leads to economic drift, resulting in underperformance by the firm and to its eventual demise (see Figure 1.1). Responsiveness requires sound risk assessment and proactive management.

1.3.2   Strategy

The essence of strategy is competition and the creation and maintenance of competitive advantage. This requires an understanding of the risks an organization faces (both internal and external), its strengths and weaknesses, and its threats and opportunities (SWOT). In theory, the most successful organizations will be those that are well focused (concentrating on their core activities) and who dominate the market sectors in which they operate. Theory also

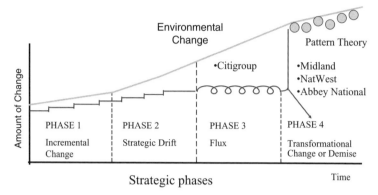

Figure 1.1   Survival and growth requires responsiveness to change.
Source: Professor Gerry Johnson

suggests that a large market share creates a virtuous circle since it leads to lower unit costs and, in turn, to increased sales and hence to increased profits. These profits are then available to develop the next generation of products and services, thus further increasing market share. It is here that brand names and reputation (developed through customer satisfaction) also become important, since branding allows product differentiation, thereby enabling the company to obtain premium prices for its product and services, thus generating higher profits.

Although traditional strategic categorizations – as originally espoused by the Boston Consulting Group (see Figure 1.2) and also by McKinsey – allow broad inferences to be drawn regarding the cash-generative characteristics of individual products or services, no explicit attention is given to the earnings capacity or the total risks associated with the portfolio. Concentration on market share alone is insufficient, since many other factors such as corporate culture, quality of management, technologies and product lifecycles have to be taken into account as they impact upon the risk profile.

It is important to recognize that the organization's chosen risk profile determines the appropriateness of strategies. A high-risk strategy is not of itself a problem providing it offers the appropriate risk-adjusted rate of return and management have the appropriate skills and resources to address the resultant level of volatility. Low risk, low growth strategies can also

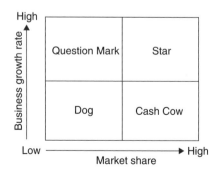

Figure 1.2   Traditional strategic categorizations.

be acceptable (for example, in countries such as Belgium and Germany), provided the bank has an appropriate franchise. However, overly cautious risk strategies and excessive levels of (underutilized) capital will lead to below-par performance and result in a poor rating. It should be borne in mind that a particular risk profile will attract certain types of stakeholders. Consequently, an organization may not be free to readily change its pre-established risk profile.

1.3.3 Market segmentation

Banks can be broadly categorized according to market segmentation and related strategies, as follows:

- global;
- regional and cultural;
- domestic; and
- specialized.

Global

Whilst a number of banks have aspired to become truly global and to offer a full range of services, few – if any – have actually achieved this; the two main players in this sector being Citigroup and HSBC. Instead, several banks have established a global footprint but have restricted their activities depending upon their relative strengths and areas of expertise. Examples of selective global strategies and those banks applying them include:

- retail and business banking – ABN AMRO (now gone);
- consumer finance – BNP Paribas;
- investment banking – Credit Suisse, Deutsche Bank, and UBS;
- direct banking – ING.

Regional and cultural

Several banks with a significant domestic presence have engaged in cross-border activities, partly to overcome limited growth prospects in their home market. Expansion has tended to be into neighbouring countries and other countries where there is a cultural affinity. Examples include:

- Nordic region – Danske Bank, Nordea;
- Baltic states – SEB, Swedbank;
- Central and Eastern Europe – HVB/Bank Austria, Erste Bank, RZB, UniCredito, KBC;
- Latin America – BBVA, Santander.

Cross-border consolidation within the Eurozone was advanced by a number of large transactions, including: HSBC and CCF of France; Santander (Spain) and Abbey (UK) in 2004; ABN AMRO (Netherlands) and Banca Antonveneta (Italy) in 2005; UniCredito and HVB in 2005. Whilst this appears to indicate the way forward, a perfectly level playing field still does not exist, with significant socio-economic cultural and politically nationalistic barriers remaining.

Domestic

A number of large banking groups have adopted a domestically-focused strategy. These include:

* UK – Lloyds TSB, HBOS;
* France – Banque Fédérative du Crédit Mutuel;
* Netherlands – Rabobank;
* Norway – Den Norske Bank ASA;
* Sweden – Svenska Handelsbanken;
* Spain – Banco Popular Español, Caja Madrid, La Caixa;
* Portugal – Caixa Genal de Depósitos;
* Hungary – OTP Bank.

The ability of such groups to maintain their existing strategy in the long term is likely to be tested as globalization continues.

Specialized

A few organizations have adopted a specific business-line strategy. For example, Dexia specializes in public sector lending, with activities in France, Belgium, Germany, Austria, Italy, Spain, and Sweden.

In addition, there remains a considerable number of smaller specialist niche players, such as:

* mortgage banks – in Germany, France, Denmark, etc;
* development banks – in Germany, Austria, Japan, South Africa, etc;
* export finance houses;
* cooperative banks;
* savings banks.

Many of these organizations developed their franchise before deregulation and liberalization of the financial markets. Some have adapted and survived successfully; however, many face a difficult and uncertain future due to competitive forces reducing their market share and margins. Limited resources and a small customer base effectively prevent growth and diversification. In contrast, a number of relatively small specialist investment houses have sprung up in recent years and are currently very profitable, although their longevity has yet to be proved in the face of adverse economic factors.

1.3.4 Mergers and Acquisitions

Organic growth is of key importance. However, organic growth alone can constrain the rate at which an organization develops and can thereby affect its competitive position.

The mergers and acquisitions arena has been described as a marketplace in which competing management teams vie for the right to manage scarce resources by offering alternative corporate strategies. Hence takeovers offer the opportunity to discuss competing ideas on corporate strategy in the public domain and allow shareholders, particularly the large pension funds, to exercise their considerable but often latent powers. Undoubtedly, the intense pressure on public companies to boost earnings per share is a significant influencing factor. Progress towards the establishment of a level playing field and hence creation of a truly global market has also provided an important stimulus.

Given over-capacity and rationalization in the banking industry, mergers and acquisitions are important. Acquisitions enable an organization to grow and develop at a considerable pace. Substantial empires can be created via acquisitions in a relatively short period of time. The takeover of Midland Bank by HSBC and the acquisition of NatWest by Royal Bank of Scotland created significant banking groups. Acquisitions also allow established companies to quickly change direction and reposition themselves when they find their traditional activities are no longer capable of producing the performance demanded by shareholders/owners. In addition to corporate strategic activities, acquisitions are useful at the business development level, where it is necessary to fill in gaps in the organization's product-market profile, or to acquire specialist skills and expertise.

Research has shown that acquisitions often lead to a reduction in the wealth of shareholders of the acquiring company. To succeed in an acquisition attempt, the acquirer company will undoubtedly have to pay a premium to the market price ruling, prior to the approach being made to the target company. This means that it would be cheaper for the shareholders personally to buy the shares of the target company in the marketplace, rather than allowing the acquirer company to do it for them.

Why, then, does the market seem to actively encourage takeovers? Is it simply that it is the market's *raison d'être,* that to survive and create wealth for itself it must do deals? Certainly there is an element of truth in this; however, recent acquisition and merger activity appears to have been based on more sound economic and financial factors. In recent periods the more highly regarded, better-performing organizations have tended to take over less well-run organizations despite the fact that the company being taken over could be considerably larger than the acquirer. This is in contrast to the historical concept of large companies being valued at a premium and tending to take over smaller well-performing organizations. It should be borne in mind that organizations that make acquisitions and fail to perform could find that they themselves become targets.

A fund manager presented with the opportunity of a substantial short-term gain will be under considerable pressure to accept in order to maintain his own rating. Fund managers whose portfolios underperform do not last long. However, evidence shows that, on balance, the market is rational and in the longer-term eventually takes account of fundamental underlying issues.

When considering an acquisition as part of an overall corporate and business development strategy it is necessary to identify clearly how the acquisition will result in added value to the group, how quickly these benefits can be obtained and how the overall risk profile of the group will be affected. Consideration needs to be given to two key criteria: the level of business affinity and the business attractiveness (i.e. market size, growth, profitability, etc) of the target company (see Figure 1.3).

Primarily, there are only two reasons why an acquiring management may be able to extract greater returns from the assets of a business than the previous management team (all other things being equal). Firstly, through greater management ability (combined with entrepreneurial flair), and secondly through synergy (including economies of scale). With regard to synergy there should be a certain amount of scepticism. Synergy is not inherent in a situation; such potential gains come as a reward for management effort. The release of profit potential in an acquisition or merger depends upon the existence of sound management, the depth of management skills

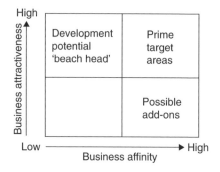

Figure 1.3 Key criteria.

and the level of motivation. Effective hands-on management is essential immediately after an acquisition to ensure that required changes are implemented and the company becomes quickly integrated into the group. It is often found in practice that organizations unused to making acquisitions try to adopt a hands-off approach towards their new charges, often with disastrous consequences.

It is also argued that mergers and acquisitions facilitate diversification. This is based on the idea of portfolio theory, with the objective being to reduce risk by broadening the range of business activities. However, product-market theory suggests that risk increases as the organization moves into new areas in which it is unfamiliar and that diversification represents the highest-risk strategy (see Figures 1.4 and 1.5).

Shareholders expect to see growth in earnings per share each year without fail and with no excuses. Hence if gains from an acquisition are likely to take several years to come through, shareholders are likely to withdraw their support. Investors and rating agencies have long experience of companies making acquisitions in pursuit of esoteric strategies that fail to produce the required growth in shareholder value. The market takes into account the level of risk in an investment. If the risk profile of the company changes due to acquisition, the share price will be adjusted accordingly by the market to reflect this change.

Merger and acquisition activity in the European banking sector was seen in the first half of the 1990s following the banking crisis. It took place again in the late 1990s and the early part of the 2000s as a result of increased focus on strategies aimed at enhancing shareholder value and

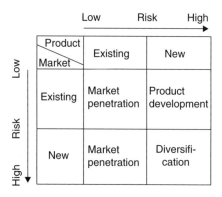

Figure 1.4 Business risk factors.

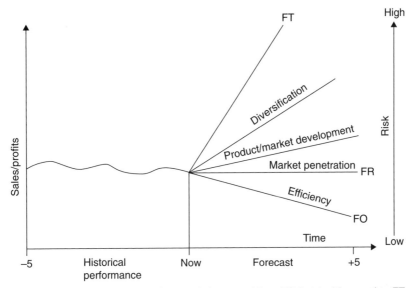

The level of risk increases as the forecast is increased from FO (original forecast) to FT (the target)

The original forecast (FO) is based on the company's continuing as it is with its existing weaknesses.

The revised forecast (FR) assumes an increase in internal efficiency, following a review of existing internal strengths and weaknesses.

Figure 1.5   Gap analysis.
Source: Brendon Young, ORRF

increasing performance efficiency. This resulted in the creation of a number of significantly more powerful groups, including:

- the UK – HBOS (from Halifax and Bank of Scotland); the acquisition of NatWest by the Royal Bank of Scotland; and Barclay's acquisition of the Woolwich;
- France – Crédit Mutuel/CIC, Banque Populaire/Natexis, BNP Paribas, Crédit Agricole/ Crédit Lyonnais;
- Italy – UniCredito, Intesa, Sanpaolo IMI, Capitalia;
- Spain – BBVA, Santander Central Hispano.

And similarly in Austria, Belgium, Norway, Portugal, Sweden, and Switzerland, etc. Also, during this period of activity, rationalization was taking place amongst the numerous smaller financial institutions, including mortgage banks, cooperative banks, savings banks and the state-owned sector.

In Germany, the financial services sector is very fragmented and profitability is low. Rationalization of the cooperative banking sector has been going on for some time. In public sector banking, the removal of state guarantees (in 2005) proved a stimulus. Alignment of the Landesbanken with savings banks is producing more effective regional banking groups. The German mortgage sector is also experiencing consolidation.

In November 2007, the underperforming Dutch bank ABN Amro, a major European bank, was acquired by a consortium led by Royal Bank of Scotland Group plc, (and included Fortis Group NV of Belgium and Santander Central Hispano SA of Spain). At the time, this represented the largest financial services merger in history. Merger and acquisition activities often result in further secondary redistribution of assets to other interested third parties.

More recently (in 2008), as the severity of the credit crunch increased, a growing wave of mergers and acquisition took place. This was actively encouraged by both the US and UK governments (including their central banks and regulators), in an endeavour to avert total collapse of the world's financial system. Initially, in the UK, Northern Rock collapsed and was nationalized. Shortly after, HBOS had to be rescued by Lloyds TSB. In the US, the demise of Bear Stearns was quickly followed by Lehman Brothers. Subsequently, a number of other major financial institutions had to be rescued, including the world's largest insurer (AIG), and major US mortgage institutions, Fannie Mae and Freddie Mac. Similarly, in Europe (as well as other parts of the world), major banks like Fortis experienced severe difficulties. The full impact of the credit crunch, which was initiated by the US sub-prime mortgage crisis, has yet to be determined but will undoubtedly have fundamental repercussions.

Bancassurance

In addition to straight merger and acquisition activity within the banking sector, some integration has taken place between insurance companies and banks. This was brought about with the aim of cross-selling services to a larger combined customer base, thus making better use of the existing channel-to-market infrastructure (branches, staff, customer information, etc) and consequently lowering unit costs. This strategy is more appropriate in Europe where life insurance products are seen as an alternative form of long-term savings. In the UK, the life insurance market is more sophisticated and in the US there are barriers restricting adoption of the bancassurance model. In the early years of the new millenium the insurance industry experienced difficulties when stock markets declined (due to overexposure to the equity markets). This resulted in difficulties for banks associated with insurance companies, since the banks were required to provide capital to meet the resultant shortfall experienced by their insurance company.

1.3.5 Management

There is a widely accepted assertion in Venture Capital that the only thing to consider when evaluating an investment is the quality of management. Excellent management will introduce new products and services at the appropriate time, use resources efficiently and effectively, and develop winning strategies.

Whilst changes in economic conditions create opportunities, business is about people, those with vision and ability. In their book *In Search of Excellence* (profile Business, 2004), Peters and Waterman refer to individuals with the drive, determination and ability to succeed as "champions." Such individuals will undoubtedly continue to drive their organizations forward despite increasing regulation and the ups and downs of the stock market. Personal motivation and ambition are significant influencing factors when assessing the derivation of strategy and the ability to effectively implement it. Mergers and acquisitions are often driven by personal ambition, with economic considerations being secondary. However, management is primarily about leadership, not leaders. Research shows that longer-term success correlates with leadership. Sound leadership creates belief in and commitment to corporate objectives. Weak leadership, on the other hand, leads to blameism, with employees deliberately hiding risks and mistakes, and managers consequently making decisions based on wrong information. High staff turnover, low morale, excessive restrictions, an inability to take preventive action (i.e. responsibility without authority), and excessive levels of pressure to perform, are clear indicators of weakness.

In assessing management it is necessary to take account of many factors, including:

- *The appropriateness of the approach adopted by the Chief Executive.* A dominant chief executive can be appropriate where there is a necessity to bring about change and develop a more responsive organization. However, for a well-performing organization in a developed market, the primary requirement is to create a professional management team and harness their combined skills.
- *The level of experience and ability of senior management.* This can be a particularly serious issue in emerging markets when there is a move away from state influence towards a free market economy. Management may be ill-equipped to cope with the change from political acquiescence to the market demand for transparency combined with the efficient and effective use of resources.
- *The competence and motivation of second tier management.* These are vital considerations when determining the ability of the organization to properly implement its strategies.
- *The existence of a risk-aware culture.* The existence of a culture that recognizes the importance of risk management and control is evidenced by how well risk-based systems and controls are embedded as demonstrated by the use-test.
- *The appropriateness and effectiveness of review and reward schemes.* These must be appropriate for the particular activity being carried out. High levels of pressure, particularly on traders in investment banks, have resulted in significant operational risk losses.

The ultimate tests for management are the ability to achieve acceptable (risk adjusted) financial performance (including growth in earnings per share), to maintain and grow market share, and to maintain and enhance the organization's reputation, whilst also balancing the requirements of other stakeholder groups. These are largely functions of how efficiently and effectively resources have been applied, together with how effectively external threats have been mitigated. In emerging markets, it is important to recognize that the ability to manage may be constrained by ingrained cultural issues (preventing restructuring and the removal of excess labour) together with the level of economic development within the country itself (restricting the use of new technologies and risk management tools).

1.3.6   Identifying winners and losers

Those banking groups that survive prosper and grow in the increasingly competitive and dynamic financial services environment will exhibit many, if not all, of the following qualities:

- a visible and valued brand worldwide, achieved through creation and retention of a satisfied customer base;
- sound corporate governance, culture, and ethics;
- dynamic strategies facilitating responsiveness and resilience;

- a strong and defendable franchise position (i.e. a leading position in retail financial services, including a dominant share of the domestic market together with a strong international market presence);
- high and sustainable recurring earnings – any organization relying upon business-to-business (B2B) activity without a well-established business-to-customer (B2C) activity is likely to have a weak franchise with uncertain earnings;
- provision of a broad range of both banking and nonbanking services, possibly including fund management, bancassurance, pensions, and private banking, as well as Internet and retail banking;
- efficient and effective use of resources, including IT;
- The ability to attract and retain excellent managers having vision and motivation; and
- a sound risk management culture, properly embedded throughout the organization.

A report by the Senior Supervisors Group,[38] into the risk management practices of those firms that performed better in the recent credit crunch, revealed that such firms demonstrated a comprehensive firm-wide view of risk. They often aligned risk management with other functions, including treasury, and were therefore able to enforce more active controls over the organization's consolidated balance sheet, capital, and liquidity requirements. The management team engaged in more effective dialogue across the firm, sharing quantitative and qualitative information more effectively. In particular, they:

- had more dynamic and adaptive risk measurement processes and risk management systems that could rapidly adjust to cater for current circumstances;
- viewed risk exposures from a number of different perspectives, relying upon a wide range of risk measures (both qualitative and quantitative); and
- employed effective stress testing with greater use of scenario analysis.

1.4   CAPITAL – UNDERSTANDING AND ASSESSING ITS IMPORTANCE AND LIMITATIONS

Capital is part of the regulatory tool kit, but only a small part. For most problems capital is not our preferred response. Sir Howard Davies

1.4.1   Historical assessment approaches

The level of equity held by a bank has traditionally been regarded as a measure of financial strength and a protection against moral hazard, since the greater the level of equity capital shareholders (owners) have at risk the more likely they are to ensure the bank is managed prudently. Since margins have historically been thin in banking, high levels of gearing have been necessary in order to generate adequate returns on equity (see Figure 1.6). Prudent management has therefore been necessary since any errors in highly-geared organizations are greatly magnified.

Traditionally, capital strength was measured by two primary ratios: *equity:assets* and *equity:deposits*. In the early 1900s an accepted rule of thumb used in the United States was 1 dollar ($1) of capital to 10 dollars ($10) of deposits. However, this was found to be inappropriate for the period of economic expansion following the Second World War. Consequently, the US Federal Reserve introduced a benchmark figure of 8% for equity-capital to total-assets. The actual level of leverage (which is simply the inverse of the equity-capital to total-assets

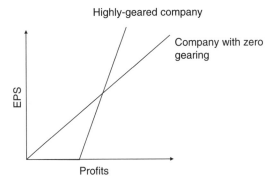

Figure 1.6 Shareholders benefit from rapid growth in Earnings Per Share (EPS) in a highly-geared company, after interest-on-borrowings has been paid. However, in times of stress, a highly-geared company may not be able to meet its obligations as and when they fall due and therefore faces an increased risk of insolvency.
Source: Brendon Young, ORRF

ratio) varies considerably between different countries and banking sectors. Leverage is still widely used in the assessment of banks, particularly in emerging markets where only limited data may be available. However, leverage has serious limitations since it fails to take account of the riskiness of assets. Consequently, as part of the evolutionary development of assessment techniques, rating agencies began comparing equity to loans and to risk assets.[39] Whilst this enabled a bank's static capital strength to be determined, it failed to take account of its resilience as indicated by retained profits (the Internal Growth Rate Of Capital – IGRC).[40] The recognition of the ability of a bank to earn its way out of trouble was an important step forward but unfortunately the IGRC ratio can be subject to large fluctuations and is prone to manipulation (paradoxically, a small equity base can make it easier to achieve a high IGRC ratio). Also, historical performance is not necessarily a good indicator of future performance and survival.

1.4.2   The original Basel Accord

In 1974, the central bank governors of the G10 nations established the Basel Committee on Banking Supervision, partly in response to the collapse of a small undercapitalized German bank (Bank Herstatt), which threatened the stability of the international foreign exchange market.

In 1988, the Basel Committee introduced its Capital Accord, which was originally established for internationally active banks from the G10 countries, but which became adopted as a standard by over 100 countries worldwide. The Accord was primarily prompted by the actions of Japanese and French banks, which were undercutting competitors through operating with what was considered to be unfairly low levels of capital (i.e. undercapitalized). The fundamental aims of the Accord were to strengthen the overall international banking system and to create a level playing field.[41] The Accord introduced a risk-weighted capital adequacy ratio, which was set at an arbitrary 8 % level (see Table 1.1). Prior to the Accord, there had been no accepted definition of what constituted capital from a regulatory perspective and certainly no international benchmark for capital adequacy.

Table 1.1   Risk weighted assets (1988 Basel Accord).

0 % Weightings
- Cash.
- Local currency deposits with central government/central bank.
- Deposits with OECD central governments and central banks (some countries applied a 10 % weighting for short-term instruments and a 20 % weighting for long-term instruments).
- Claims collateralized by cash, by OECD central government securities, or guaranteed by OECD central governments.
- Claims on domestic public sector entities other than the central government and loans guaranteed by such entities.

20 % Weightings
- Claims on or guaranteed by multilateral development banks, or collateralized by the securities of such banks.
- Claims on banks incorporated in the OECD and loans guaranteed by OECD incorporated banks.
- Claims on banks incorporated outside the OECD or guaranteed by such banks having a residual maturity of one year or less.
- Claims on or guaranteed by nondomestic OECD public sector entities.
- Cash items in the process of collection (added following 1998 amendment).

50 % Weightings
- Loans fully secured by mortgages on owner-occupied residential property.

100 % Weightings
- Claims on the private sector.
- Claims on the non-OECD incorporated banks with a residual maturity of over one year.
- Nonlocal currency claims on central governments outside the OECD.
- Claims on private sector commerical companies.
- Fixed assets.
- Real estate and other investments.
- Capital instruments issued by other banks unless deducted from capital.

The Accord originally recognized two[42] categories in its definition of capital:

1. Core (Tier 1) Capital – which included share-capital, retained earnings and equity reserves;
2. Supplementary (Tier 2) Capital – which included other forms of defined capital such as loan loss reserves, subordinated debt and hidden reserves.

The inclusion of supplementary capital gave the impression that banks had more capital available than had been the case under traditional measures. Also, by applying weightings to assets, the total level of assets accepted by the regulators was reduced. These two factors gave a somewhat distorted impression by making the capital-to-assets ratio look stronger than under traditional approaches.

The original Basel Accord represented an important step forward by introducing the concept of regulatory capital adequacy. Whilst the Accord was based on the traditional simple ratio of equity to assets, the major advance was in making this ratio risk based. Through international adoption, it facilitated cross-boarder comparisons. The Accord was very successful in improving capital adequacy and strengthening the international banking system; however, it created perverse incentives for banks due to assets with widely different risk characteristics being equally weighted. This resulted in banks taking on greater risks rather than adopting a more prudent approach as originally envisaged by the Accord. Fundamentally, the Accord encouraged banks to take on higher exposures without requiring them to hold commensurate levels of risk capital. Given that the Accord effectively capped leverage at 12.5%, banks needed to look for higher yielding stock in order to achieve a commercially competitive rate of return on equity. The Accord's broad-brush categorization resulted in sound organizations being lumped together with far less creditworthy corporations that were, of necessity, offering higher yields. Thus banks were induced to make higher yielding loans to less creditworthy customers and to securitize the most secure (but low yielding) loans. Similarly, in order to increase yields banks engaged in interbank lending, with the borrowing bank subsequently lending to riskier domestic corporations. In Thailand this contributed to the "Asian Crisis."[43] Another important criticism of the Accord was that it was unfairly biased in favour of OECD countries, thus preventing creation of a truly level playing field.

1.4.3   Creation of a level playing field

The European Commission has stated that institutions must not have capital requirements imposed on them that are higher than the underlying risks to which they are exposed, as this would run counter to the principle of retaining competitive equality. No institution will be obliged to adopt a more complex approach than is suitable for its capabilities and scale of operation.

The level playing field relationship must be considered both within the EU (between regulated and unregulated institutions, credit institutions and investment firms, and between low impact and high impact firms), as well as between EU and non-EU entities. In particular, prudential regulation must not become so complex that small-scale institutions, whether credit institutions or investment firms, are no longer viable. Consumer interests would be ill served if business activities shifted from regulated to unregulated (or less regulated) firms. Equally, banks and other financial institutions should not be encouraged to engage in regulatory arbitrage. The regulations must not provide loopholes ("capital arbitrage opportunities"), for financial institutions, regardless of their size, to hold insufficient capital in comparison to their risk profile, or to transfer business activities to unregulated parts of their group, since this would damage the interests of depositors and investors. There are many factors influencing competitive equality. Certainly, in a dynamic environment, no simplistic or rigid framework can be expected to be entirely appropriate.

1.4.4   The impact of the new Basel Accord on the level of capital held by a bank

The new Basel Accord (Basel II) sought to overcome the weaknesses of the original Accord by requiring banks to assess the risks they face and the level of capital necessary to protect against those risks, together with encouraging implementation of management actions necessary to mitigate and control the risks retained. The primary aim of the new Basel Accord was to enhance protection of the overall financial system (i.e. avoid systemic risk), by making regulatory capital more risk sensitive. The impact of this could be expected to provide well-managed banks with the opportunity of operating with less regulatory capital than required under the 1988 Basel Accord. But since the regulators wish to maintain the overall level of regulatory capital in the system at existing levels, other banks must expect an increase in their regulatory capital requirement. However, it must be recognized that a bank is not simply a profit maximizer; instead it will seek to optimize its capital requirement. Consequently, banks will continue to hold capital in excess of the regulatory minimum in order to inspire confidence (i.e. avoid reputational risk) and facilitate business development, as well as fulfilling the aspirations of owners together with meeting obligations to depositors and other creditors. Whilst Basel II has acted as a catalyst and indeed represents a significant advance in the discipline of risk management, the size of regulatory capital is of relatively little importance from an analyst's perspective, although the associated management actions certainly are important. It has yet to be seen whether transparency, as required under Pillar 3 of the new Accord, will assist in making regulatory capital a useful indicator. However, it is highly likely that regulators from different countries will apply regulatory capital differently, thus reducing its usefulness from the point of view of cross-border comparisons.

1.4.5   Is capital the solution to risk?

Whilst Chairman of the FSA, Howard Davies stated that with regard to the new Basel Accord, *Capital is part of the regulatory tool kit, but only a small part. For most problems capital is not our preferred response.*

Capital is certainly a protection against risk events. However, an increase in capital will not of itself reduce risk; only management action can do that. By holding a larger amount of capital, a bank will be able to withstand greater losses than would otherwise be the case. However, excess capital will reduce financial performance, as expressed by return on capital employed (ROCE) or its risk-adjusted equivalents (RAROC or RORAC), and thereby impact upon a bank's competitiveness.

1.4.6   Credit rating agency view

It is a widely held misconception, inadvertently perpetrated by the regulators, that the level of capital held by a bank indicates its strength and therefore defines its credit rating. In fact, there is no direct correlation between capital and the rating assigned by the credit rating agencies. It is important to realize that capital on its own does not determine the longer-term strength of an organization. This is not to diminish the importance of capital but to indicate that, whilst it is necessary, capital on its own is not sufficient. For example, consider a bucket in which there is a hole: eventually it will run dry no matter how big the bucket or how small the hole; it needs to be continuously filled. Hence, the level of capital held by a bank is important to meet immediate needs but in the longer term the level of sustainable earnings (i.e. the minimum rate of generation of new capital) becomes an increasingly important consideration, as does leakage due to unexpected risk events. Also, liquidity (i.e. the immediate access to funding – or water in the above example – when needed) is an important consideration.

1.4.7   Defining regulatory, actual, and economic capital

Despite the complexity, the essential aims are simple: to devise a set of rules that create a better fit between regulatory and economic capital; and to create incentives for banks to assess their own risks, and need for capital, more accurately and systematically than before. Howard Davies, FSA, March 2001

Different organizations use differing definitions of capital. Therefore, the relationship between regulatory capital, actual balance sheet capital, and economic capital, needs to be clearly understood:

- Regulatory capital is the minimum amount of capital a bank is required to hold under the new Basel Accord (Basel II) taking into account its particular risk profile. Regulatory capital is an artificial construct prescribed by the regulators to meet their stated objectives, including the prevention of systemic risk to the overall banking system. Regulatory capital can be considered as the cost to a bank of remaining in business.[44]

- Balance sheet capital is the actual capital that a bank is using to run its business activities. Research by the Bank of England has shown that banks typically hold an amount well in excess of the regulatory capital minimum (11.6% on average). However, the actual level can vary considerably between different countries and different banks.
- Economic capital is the amount of capital a bank should have to run its business activities taking into account the risks it is taking and its growth strategy (i.e. its risk profile). The importance of economic capital stems from its ability to act as *a tool to integrate all risks into one consistent and comprehensive risk measure.*

Economic capital methodologies vary considerably from firm to firm. However, in essence they all seek to achieve at least two basic objectives: firstly, to compare the actual capital shown in the balance sheet to the economic capital requirement (i.e. gap analysis); secondly, to calculate the return on economic capital. This provides a risk-adjusted performance measure for assessing individual business units as well as for assessing the group as a whole.

1.4.8 Internal Capital Apportionment Process (ICAP)

In Europe, many larger banking groups have adopted the Internal Capital Apportionment Process and, indeed, in certain organizations the methodology has become quite advanced. ICAP is a management control methodology that seeks to allocate capital to business units and business lines according to their individual intrinsic level of risk. It therefore enables the bank to more precisely tailor its risk profile through calculation of a risk-adjusted return on capital for each activity. The importance of ICAP stems from the ability it gives management to better control the quality and stability of earnings.

1.4.9 Uses of economic capital methodologies

The level and structure of a bank's capital, together with its earnings potential, are useful indicators of its level of resilience and its ability to respond to change. Economic capital methodologies can be used to allocate capital and to control risk, leading to:

- Improved measurement of performance, facilitating more effective risk reporting to senior management.
- More informed decision-making, enabling the risk profile to be more precisely defined.
- Comparison of risk returns, so that capital can be transferred in order to optimize performance.
- Risk assessment of business development opportunities, including mergers, acquisitions, and divestment opportunities, as well as assessment of new product/market and diversification proposals.
- Greater accountability for the management of risks.
- Determination of appropriate staff compensation and motivation schemes.
- Better indication of risk concentrations.
- Determination of correlation and diversification benefits.
- Reconciliation of financial accounts to the risk profile, allowing determination of volatility and therefore of the quality and stability of earnings for the group as a whole.

1.4.10   Assessing factors influencing the economic capital requirement

There is no single deterministic value for economic capital; instead, the requirement will lie within a probabilistic range. Indeed, in a dynamic business environment the economic capital requirement will change continuously. As with critical path analysis, when one key activity varies, both the critical path and capital requirement change. In assessing the appropriateness of the level of risk capital held by an organization, there are a number of factors that need to be assessed, including:

- **The quality of management** – It has been said that "no amount of capital can save an ill-managed bank."[45]
- **Risk transfer facilities** – The existence and use of risk transfer instruments, such as securitisation, insurance and catastrophe bonds, enables a bank to more precisely price risk and define its risk profile.
- **Asset type and quality** – To meet any calls resulting from losses, assets will need to be liquidated within an acceptable period of time. Where asset quality is such that the full value may not be realized (either immediately or in the future), particularly in times of stress, then a higher level of capital will be required.
- **Quality and stability of earnings** – The faster a bank can regenerate funds to replenish losses resulting from unexpected events the less capital it will need to hold.
- **Liquidity issues** – Banks tend to fail for liquidity reasons rather than poor asset quality or insolvency. Factors such as the availability of support from the parent group, external support from commercial organizations (e.g. back-up lines and swing lines[46]) and the realistic possibility of central bank support, need to be taken into account.

1.4.11   The importance of capital in different markets

In emerging markets volatility is greater and therefore capital is more important than in developed economies. However, there is a tendency for banks in emerging markets to rely too heavily on funding from the interbank market, which can be both expensive and volatile. The Turkish bank crisis of 1994 was exacerbated by overreliance on syndicated funding from foreign banks.

In Japan, the stock market crash of 1990 resulted in the disappearance of a significant amount of hidden reserves[47] held by Japanese banks as part of their regulatory capital. This threatened their very survival and, consequently, government/regulatory intervention was required in order to maintain confidence and prevent systemic risk.

1.4.12   Methodology for determining the amount of risk capital required

The generally accepted approach for determining the risk capital requirement involves a combination of the following methodologies, which are discussed in more detail later in this book:

- **Control Risk Self Assessment (CRSA)** – This involves (tacit) assessment by management of the main risk challenges and their associated controls.
- **Data collection and analysis** – Loss events (and also near misses) need to be recorded in a loss-register and the data analyzed for trends, patterns, and correlations.

- **Modeling** – This is used to determine the risk capital requirement at a chosen confidence level.[48] Some financial organizations are now using stochastic models and dynamic financial models to address the issue of risk integration.
- **Stress testing** – This involves determining the impact (on the model) of extreme events, whether experienced by the organization itself or by others or simply by varying parameters.
- **Scenario analysis** – This is concerned with the assessment of events that have not happened but against which the organization needs to protect itself (e.g. terrorism and war, pandemics, IT meltdown, etc).
- **Use test assessment** – This involves continuous evaluation in order to quickly identify any changes that could lead to an increased level of risk and result in the requirement for additional capital. Key indicators and dynamic financial analysis modeling may be used.

Where data are available, risk capital can be quantified using various statistical techniques, including:

- Taking actual loss data, ordered by size, and simply selecting a chosen percentile. This is commonly referred to as the simple VaR (Value at Risk) approach.
- Taking actual loss data and fitting a mathematical distribution curve to the tail of the loss distribution (basic Extreme Value Theory methodology).
- Using a simulation approach, where a large number of samples are taken from the existing small amount of data. These samples are then ordered by size and the value for a chosen percentile used (simulation VaR).
- Fitting a mathematical distribution curve to simulation data.
- Combining external loss data, actual data and simulation data, then applying the VaR approach.
- Applying the mathematical distribution curve approach to the combined actual data, simulation data and external data.

The appropriateness of the method chosen depends upon a number of factors such as the availability, quantity, completeness and accuracy of data, together with the resources available, computational ease and technical expertise. Given the shortage of loss data, particularly in the tail of the distribution, there is need to carry out stress testing and scenario analysis on the models developed in order to determine robustness. Important factors to take into consideration include:

- loss recognition (whether there was a single loss at a given point in time or a gradual loss build-up over a period).
- the time period over which data is collected.
- the minimum size of losses recorded (below which events are ignored).

It should be noted that, since it is not possible to accurately predict the future, there can be no correct answer for the amount of capital to be held, only a level of prudence compared to previous experience and future expectations.

ENDNOTES

[1] It is not universally accepted that regulatory intervention is necessary. Indeed, it is widely considered that such intervention has the propensity to produce procyclicality. Free-market economists argue that, in theory, regulatory intervention allows poor management to survive, thus rewarding them for excessive risk taking, but by so doing punishes good management, putting them at a competitive

disadvantage. However, the argument makes strong tacit assumptions about existing types of regulatory intervention rather than proposing possible alternatives. In essence, it appears simply to be an argument for management change through shareholder activism, which has an important (additional, not alternative) place. Free-market economists also argue, correctly, that depositor protection schemes have a perverse effect in that they effectively remove the risk from depositors, thereby encouraging them to seek those financial institutions taking greater risks and offering higher rewards. However, the theories of free-market economics ignore social issues such as the destruction of social capital and the impact upon the lives of people; put simply, it takes time to redistribute capital and retrain people who may be relatively immobile (both physically and mentally). The destruction of the UK's industrial base in the 1980s, which dramatically reduced the level of diversification in the economy, provides clear evidence of the risk of unforeseen consequences.

[2] See www.enhancedanalytics.com

[3] In fact, Basel II has been a main driver in the speed of development of Operational Risk.

[4] Commerzbank Group 2005 Risk Report, page 93: *"We believe that considerable value leverage for further boosting the Group's earnings performance over the next few years lies in the claim to 'being the benchmark in risk control and management,' ... The importance of highly-developed risk management was also confirmed in an international benchmarking study last year, where it is seen as the most significant challenge to successful business management for internationally competitive banks. ... We share this view and are confident that we can achieve further major breakthroughs in risk control and management during this decade. ... This will prove highly positive for the market positioning of the Commerzbank Group."*

[5] The Basel Committee on Banking Supervision simply defines Operational Risk as: *the risk of loss resulting from inadequate or failed internal processes, people and systems or from external events.*

[6] Operational risk involves taking a forensic approach to the assessment and management of risk.

[7] From a regulatory perspective, the aim is to prevent systemic risk rather than to protect any one particular organization.

[8] An important secondary aim is ensuring regulatory and legislative compliance. Less sophisticated organizations may actually regard this as being the most important objective.

[9] Operational Risk:
- increases volatility;
- threatens the existence and long-term survival of the organization;
- increases the cost of capital;
- strategically weakens an organization in respect to its competitors.

[10] As evidenced by Barings, Enron, Andersen's, etc.

[11] *"An important scientific innovation rarely makes its way by gradually winning over and converting its opponents: What does happen is that the opponents gradually die out."* Max Planck.

[12] Profit & Loss, Cashflow Forecast, and Balance Sheet.

[13] It is recommended that loss data includes near misses.

[14] However, risk optimization should not be construed as acceptance of compromised quality standards. In a changing business environment, what is considered to be optimal at a particular point in time will not necessarily be so in the future.

[15] Contingency theory states that there is no one correct solution or course of action but that what is appropriate at a given point in time depends upon the prevailing circumstances of the situation.

[16] *Rating Methodology: An Analytical Framework for Banks in Developed Markets*, Moody's Investors Service, April 1999, p. 36.

[17] Barings Bank, ENRON, etc.

[18] The need for a forensic approach to risk management was clearly emphasized by the catastrophic failure of the Challenger space shuttle due to an O-ring failure. Similarly, in the financial services industry, rogue trader events have resulted in very significant losses, out of all proportion to the number of people involved (often only one individual person).

[19] The Sharpe ratio, which compares return with volatility of return, is commonly used for financial portfolio analysis, although it can be applied more widely.

[20] Complexity has been defined as a measure of the variety of states in a system (Beer, S. (1970). Managing Modern Complexity. In Committee on Science and Astronautics, US House of Representatives, The Management of Information and Knowledge.; Ashby, W.R. (1973). Some peculiarities of complex systems. *Cybernetics Medicine* **9**, 1–8.). Complexity increases as the number and variety

of elements and relationships within the system increase. Complexity becomes greater as the level of predictability and understanding of the system as a whole decreases (McCarthy, I.P. (1995). Manufacturing Classification: Lessons from Organisational Systematics and Biological Taxonomy. *Journal of Manufacturing Technology Management* **6**, 37–49.). The emergent behaviour of the system as a whole becomes difficult to predict, even when subsystem behaviour is readily predictable. Small changes in inputs or parameters may produce large and unexpected changes in output behaviour.

[21] Financial strength can be defined as capital plus earnings capability.

[22] This can be very well demonstrated by the simple *gambler's ruin* model.

[23] Research by Citigroup indicated no direct link between key indicators and actual losses experience. See: http://www.terrapinnfinancial.com/faculty.aspx?ID=19; http://db.riskwaters.com/public/showpage.html?page=flagships_opriskadvisory_speakers

[24] The FSA stated in February 2003: *"In the current difficult climate, some firms may be tempted to cut back on investment in back office systems. This would be extremely short sighted."* In imposing a fine for what was described as serious failings following implementation of a new computer system, the FSA said the particular bank had demonstrated *"inadequate controls and a lack of staff training"* and that these actions had exposed the bank to increased risk of fraud.

[25] E.g. Six Sigma.
Leading figures in the field of total quality management include: Edwards-Deming, Crosby, et al.

[26] *Nassim Nicholas Taleb. Fooled by Randomness – The Hidden Role of Chance in Life and the Markets.* ISBN: 1-58799-184-5.

[27] Moody's Analytical Framework For Operational Risk Management of Banks, January 2003.

[28] However, not all banks accept that efficient use of resources is a necessary primary goal. This is based upon their view that banks are not simply profit maximizers but have an important social responsibility.

[29] The Principles are available on http://www.unpri.org/principles/

[30] The Sarbanes-Oxley Act was signed into US law on 30 July 2002, in response to a number of high profile corporate scandals, including Enron, WorldCom, Adelphia, Global Crossings, etc. The purpose of the Act, as stated in the introduction to the US Senate Committee Report, is: "to improve quality and transparency in financial reporting and independent audits and accounting services for public companies, to create a Public Company Accounting Oversight Board, to enhance the standard-setting process for accounting practices, to strengthen the independence of firms that audit public companies, to increase corporate responsibility and the usefulness of corporate financial disclosure, to protect the objectivity and independence of securities analysts, to improve Securities and Exchange Commission resources and oversight."

[31] Sir David Tweedie stated: *"What we don't want to do is haul things onto the balance sheet that are not really yours, nor do we want things flying off a balance sheet you have problems with. It's getting the line drawn properly."*

[32] The IASB proposal is to have parallel balance sheets that would explain off-balance sheet vehicles in detail and reconcile the figures with those on the main balance sheet.

[33] Big Bang involved the ending of the discount house monopoly on issuing government securities and the liberalization of the London Stock Exchange. Changes at the Stock Exchange involved merging the functions of the jobber (who dealt in stocks and shares) and the broker (who mediated between the jobber and the public), introducing negotiated commission rates, and allowing foreign banks and financial companies to own British brokers/jobbers, or themselves to join the London Stock Exchange.

[34] Emerging market economies include: Central and Eastern Europe, the Middle East, Africa, Latin America, and Asia-Pacific.

[35] Referred to as "off-shoring."

[36] This transformation is often referred to as "from bricks to clicks".

[37] Report of the Joint Forum on Credit Risk Transfer (BIS), Credit Risk Transfer, October 2004.

[38] Senior Supervisors Group, Observations on Risk Management Practices During the Recent Market Turbulence, 6 March 2008.

[39] Capital: risk assets is defined as Total Shareholders' Equity divided by [Total Assets − (Cash + Government Securities + Fixed Assets)].

[40] The Internal Growth Rate Of Capital (IGRC) can be defined as the retained earnings (after dividends paid to shareholders) as a percentage of shareholders' equity.

[41] Page 279 footnote 6, Golin Basel Committee on Banking Supervision, "International Convergence of Capital Measurement and Capital Standards" [The 1988 Basel Accord], June 1988. *"Two fundamental*

objectives lie at the heart of the Committee's work ... firstly ... to strengthen the soundness and stability of the international banking system; and secondly that the framework should be ... fair and have a high degree of consistency in its application to banks in different countries with a view to diminishing a source of competitive inequality among international banks." Section 3.

[42] An amendment to the Accord in 1996, designed to accommodate Market Risk, introduced Tier 3 capital. This is a form of short-term subordinated debt designed to support market risk exposure in trading and treasury activities.

[43] The East Asian Financial Crisis (also referred to as the IMF crisis) started in July 1997 in Thailand and South Korea with the financial collapse of Kia Motors. The crisis affected currencies, stock markets, and other asset prices in several East Asian countries. Indonesia, South Korea, and Thailand were the countries most affected. There is no concensus on the causes of the crisis; however, some of the key events are as follows:

- East Asia attracted almost half of total capital inflow to developing countries prior to the crisis, due to high growth rates of 8–12 % GDP, in the late 1980s and early 1990s.
- The economies of Southeast Asia in particular maintained high interest rates, attracting foreign investors seeking high returns. This hot money produced a dramatic increase in asset prices.
- Thailand, Indonesia and South Korea had large private current account deficits. Pegged exchange rates encouraged external borrowing and led to excessive exposure to foreign exchange risk in both the financial and corporate sectors.
- In the mid-1990s the US economy recovered from a recession. In order to prevent inflation the US Federal Reserve Bank raised interest rates. This made the US a more attractive investment destination relative to Southeast Asia.
- The US dollar, to which many Southeast Asian nations' currencies were pegged, rose, making exports from these nations more expensive and thus less competitive.
- Southeast Asia's export growth slowed dramatically in the spring of 1996, resulting in a deterioration of their current accounts.
- Western investors started losing confidence in the securities of developing economies after the Mexican peso crisis of 1994. This led to a withdrawal of investments.

The IMF has been criticized for encouraging the developing economies of East Asia to adopt the policies of "fast track capitalism." This involved liberalizing the financial sector and elimination of restrictions on capital flows; maintaining high domestic interest rates in order to suck in portfolio investment and bank capital; and pegging currencies to the dollar in order to reassure foreign investors against currency risk.

Since those governments and businesses that had taken out loans in US dollars found themselves unable to pay, the IMF offered multi-billion dollar rescue packages to enable these nations to avoid default. However, the IMF's support was conditional on a series of drastic economic reforms involving structural adjustment packages (SAP). The SAPs required crisis nations to cut government spending and reduce deficits; to allow insolvent banks and financial institutions to fail; and to aggressively raise interest rates.

[44] Under the original 1988 Basel Accord, the regulatory capital figure was 8% of risk-weighted assets.

[45] Walter Bagehot.

[46] A "Back-Up Line" is a general liquidity support facility whereas "Swing Line" refers to a small facility designed to provide immediate and temporary support in a foreign jurisdiction.

[47] As a concession to the Japanese regulators, Japanese banks were allowed to count up to 45% of their hidden reserves as part of their capital adequacy.

[48] Basel II specifies a 99.9 % confidence level for operational risk regulatory capital.

2

The Importance of Corporate Governance

Good governance is an aid to good performance. Sir Adrian Cadbury.

2.1 DEFINING CORPORATE GOVERNANCE

Corporate governance is defined as *the method by which a company is directed and controlled.* It relates to the formal interface between the board of directors and the owners of the company. It also determines the relationship between other stakeholders and the company. Consequently, corporate governance is concerned with accountability and involves reconciling conflicting aims, taking into account movements in the balance of power between the various stakeholder groups.

2.2 UNDERSTANDING THE IMPORTANCE OF CORPORATE GOVERNANCE AND ETHICS

Corporate governance is a key element in the assessment of management and leadership (see Appendix 2.A). As such, it is considered an important determinant in the overall rating process. Since corporate governance provides the over-arching framework under which leadership operates it must, of necessity, be a board priority. The responsibility of the board of directors is to provide leadership and to engender an ethical culture; corporate governance without ethics is bankrupt. Consideration must therefore be given to the differing cultures and legislative frameworks of the countries in which the organization operates.

The influence of corporate governance is experienced at two levels:

- At a global macro level, the economic importance of corporate governance stems from its ability to create confidence in the financial system. It facilitates economic growth, allowing organizations to attract low cost, long-term, patient capital from global financial markets. Consequently, corporate governance has emerged as a major international issue.
- At the micro level, for an individual organization the main issues are accountability, stability, performance and customer care.[1]

There have been a number of surveys suggesting that fund managers and analysts believe corporate governance is an important consideration in the investment decision and that investors are prepared to pay a premium for those companies having sound corporate governance profiles.[2] This premium varies depending upon the particular country. One survey suggests that, in developing countries where corporate governance legislation and guidelines are less well developed, an organization having a sound corporate governance profile could expect to achieve a confidence premium of 20 % or possibly more.

A study carried out in the United States[3] concluded that: *Although the results do not prove causation, corporations with active and independent boards appear to have performed much better in the 1990s than those with passive non-independent boards.* Whilst these results may not stand the test of academic rigour due to the complexity of issues involved, intuitively the generality of the results appears compelling. Sound corporate governance principles and practices should ensure the board and its members are of high quality. This should result in reduced risk and enhanced transparency, leading to an improvement in the quality and stability of earnings together with a lower cost of finance, thereby improving the overall competitive position of the organization.

In determining the appropriateness of corporate governance in a particular organization, it is important not to simply adopt a check-list approach to assessment. Experience shows that there is no single right corporate governance model and blind appliance of "best practice" does not guarantee best performance, neither does chief executive remuneration bear a direct relationship to shareholder return. It is the calibre of the individual board members and how they coalesce as a competitive team that determines performance.

Under the Anglo-Saxon system (adopted by the UK, America, Canada, and Australia), underperformance is dealt with by the market. Resources are transferred to those managers considered most successful, via the mechanism of mergers and acquisitions. This system has the advantage of firmly placing power in the hands of shareholders. However, whilst this may seem to meet the requirements of performance and accountability, unfortunately, it does so in a somewhat costly and disruptive manner, which may not always be the most appropriate.

The replacement of executive directors through actions that threaten both the competitive position of the organization and shareholder value may be considered excessive. It is for this reason that shareholder activism, promoted by the big institutional investors such as CalPERS, Teachers, and Hermes, is becoming an increasingly important alternative and, in the UK in particular, has received government endorsement. However, it should be borne in mind that economic growth and profitability can mask corporate weakness. It has been said that the seeds of future crises are sown in times of plenty, when diligence lapses, and providers of funds no longer keep an eye on where their money is going; hence the need for greater forensic understanding and sound risk management practices.

2.3 INTERNATIONAL ORGANIZATIONS AND THEIR ACTIVITIES

On an international level, there have been four main organizations promoting corporate governance initiatives, aimed at promoting economic growth and reducing the deleterious sapping effects of corruption.

2.3.1 OECD

In 1998 the OECD developed a set of high-level corporate governance principles intended to assist governments in improving their legal, institutional and regulatory frameworks. These principles are embodied within the following five key sections:

1. the responsibilities of the board;
2. the rights of shareholders;
3. the equitable treatment of shareholders;
4. the role of stakeholders; and
5. the requirement for disclosure and transparency.

The principles were also intended to provide guidance for organizations, stock exchanges and investors. They were the first intergovernmental attempt to establish a high-level set of internationally accepted standards for benchmarking corporate governance. They were not intended as a substitute for any individual governmental or private sector initiative but sought to provide an over-arching framework. The principles recognized the importance of legal and cultural differences between different countries. They also recognized the need to take into account the needs of different stakeholder groups. The principles state that organizations should respond positively to environmental and social standards and the expectations of the communities in which they operate. The importance of business ethics is also addressed.

The OECD's Business Sector Advisory Group on Corporate Governance emphasized that corporate governance should be a private sector initiative. However, it also stated that governments have a responsibility to provide a regulatory framework that allows investors and enterprises to adapt to the continuously evolving business dynamic. The Advisory Group recognized that there is no static or ideal solution that could be adopted by every country and every company: *Experimentation and variety should be expected and encouraged within the limits of credible regulations, emphasising fairness, transparency, accountability and responsibility*. In April 2004, the OECD revised its *Principles of Corporate Governance* in response to requests to do so following a number of high profile breakdowns in corporate governance.

The OECD principles constitute one of the Financial Stability Forum's[4] 12 key standards for sound financial systems.

2.3.2   The World Bank

In 1999 The World Bank published a report entitled *Corporate Governance: A Framework for Implementation*. The report put forward a framework for corporate governance reform, taking into account the widely differing business environments (political, economic, social, and regulatory) around the world. The aim of the World Bank was to promote corporate governance on a global scale with a view to assisting emerging market economies in particular.

2.3.3   The Commonwealth Code

The Commonwealth Code of Corporate Governance shares similar aims with the World Bank initiative and has put forward 15 principles aimed at assisting Commonwealth countries.

2.3.4   United Nations Convention against Corruption

In December 2005, the United Nations Convention against Corruption, which established a global legal framework for sustainable progress against corruption, came into force. The Convention seeks to accelerate the retrieval of stolen funds, to encourage action by banking centres against money laundering, to allow nations to pursue foreign companies and individuals that have committed corrupt acts on their soil, and to prohibit bribery of foreign public officials.

2.4   THE BASEL PAPER ON CORPORATE GOVERNANCE FOR BANKS

In February 2006, the Basel Committee on Banking Supervision published a revised[5] paper entitled *Enhancing Corporate Governance for Banking Organisations*. This paper recognized the importance of the financial intermediation role of banks in the economy, and the degree of sensitivity of banks to ineffective corporate governance. The paper set out the following eight principles:

- **Principle 1:** Board members should be qualified for their positions, have a clear understanding of their role in corporate governance and be able to exercise sound judgement about the affairs of the bank.
- **Principle 2:** The board of directors should approve and oversee the bank's strategic objectives and corporate values that are communicated throughout the banking organization.
- **Principle 3:** The board of directors should set and enforce clear lines of responsibility and accountability throughout the organization.
- **Principle 4:** The board should ensure that there is appropriate oversight by senior management consistent with board policy.
- **Principle 5:** The board and senior management should effectively utilize the work conducted by the internal audit function, external auditors, and internal control functions.
- **Principle 6:** The board should ensure that compensation policies and practices are consistent with the bank's corporate culture, long-term objectives and strategy, and control environment.
- **Principle 7:** The bank should be governed in a transparent manner.
- **Principle 8:** The board and senior management should understand the bank's operational structure, including where the bank operates in jurisdictions, or through structures, that impede transparency (i.e. "know your structure").

2.5   COUNTRIES: THEIR DIFFERENT REQUIREMENTS AND EXPERIENCES

Corporate governance varies between different countries, depending upon culture, legislation, and experience. Those countries where there is a strong reliance upon equity funding and well established stock markets, tend to be at the forefront of developments, whilst those countries having protective funding structures, such as Germany and a number of other European countries, have tended to be more prosaic in their approach. There is, however, broad agreement on the need for transparency and management openness, together with timely, accurate, and appropriate reporting.

Within the different countries, different bodies have been responsible for promoting standards of corporate governance:

- in Spain the government was the main driving force;
- in France it was companies themselves;
- in the Netherlands it was the investment community; whilst in
- Hong Kong, the accountancy profession took the lead;
- in the United States, Canada and Australia it has been a combination of business, financial, regulatory, and legislative initiatives; whilst in
- the UK it has tended to be the financial services sector, encouraged by government.

2.5.1   Europe

The European Union has a propensity to eschew legislation in favour of guidelines and accepted best practice. Currently, there are in excess of 40 different corporate governance codes in Europe.[6] However, whilst these may differ in detail, they tend to be very similar in principle. As a consequence, a move towards standardization has been muted for many years.

In November 2002, the Jaap–Winter Committee submitted recommendations to the European Commission. Amongst the recommendations proposed were:

- inclusion of a corporate governance statement in the published accounts of companies;
- disclosure of individual directors' salaries and bonuses;
- the opportunity for shareholders to discuss and vote on calculations of directors' salaries and bonuses;
- a majority of audit committee members to be independent;
- electronic voting at annual general meetings to be available for shareholders not present;
- a requirement for institutional shareholders to disclose their stance and support.

2.5.2   United Kingdom

In the United Kingdom, in 1991, following the failure of a number of prominent organizations, there was concern that confidence in the City of London as a major financial centre could be threatened. As a result, the Financial Reporting Council set up the Committee on the Financial Aspects of Corporate Governance. The resulting document, known as the Cadbury Report, has been widely regarded as the definitive report on corporate governance and the foundation stone upon which to build.

The original primary aim of the Cadbury Report was to address the inadequacy of published accounts in revealing the extent of problems faced by distressed companies. However, following the subsequent failure of BCCI Bank and the Maxwell affair, the remit of the Committee was widened to include corporate governance.

Sir Adrian Cadbury, chairman of the committee, stated that in his view, . . . *there is no single right corporate governance model and that the best approach is to start from whatever system is in place and to seek ways of improving it. In this search for improvement, every country can learn from the experience of others.*

Since the Cadbury Report, there have been a number of initiatives in the UK, including:

- the Greenbury Report (1995), which concentrated on financial disclosures;
- the Hampel Report (1999), which formally recognized that corporate governance was not a box-ticking exercise and placed emphasis on flexibility and performance;
- the Turnbull Report (2000), which advanced understanding and disclosure through requiring identification of significant risks and their impact upon company objectives. The Turnbull Report was adopted by the London Stock Exchange (LSE) and resulted in the Combined Code applying to all LSE-listed companies.
- The Myners Report (2001), which promoted institutional shareholder activism. The UK Government indicated its intention to introduce legislation if the financial services industry failed to respond adequately;
- the Higgs Committee, which investigated the role and responsibilities of non-executive directors and their impact upon performance. This related to earlier conclusions drawn by the Bank of England, from its experience in rescuing distressed major organizations. The Bank had found that the prime causes of corporate disasters were often attributable to weaknesses within the board and the failure to appoint sound non-executive directors;
- the Smith Report, which was published (in 2003, following Enron *et al.*) to clarify the role and responsibilities of the audit committee and to reinforce the independence of the auditor. It was incorporated into the revised UK Combined Code on Corporate Governance, and a separate document, *The Smith Guidance on Audit Committees*, was published to assist

boards in implementing the Code and to also assist audit committee directors in carrying out their role. In October 2006, a committee was established, and consultation began on potential risks arising from characteristics of the market, including the possible exit of one of the Big 4 audit firms. A revised version of the Smith Guidance is due to be published in 2008.

2.5.3   United States

US standards of good corporate governance call for a board with a substantial majority of its directors to be clearly independent from the company and its senior managers. This means that, in general, two-thirds of directors should have no financial ties, except through their director fees and stock ownership.

It is considered that equity ownership should be significant in relation to a director's net worth, since this can assist in aligning the interests of directors with shareholders.

The National Association of Corporate Directors recommends that a CEO should serve on no more than two other boards, and that a full-time professional director should serve on no more than six boards. It is now considered reasonable to expect a member of a large company board to devote 150 hours or more a year to a directorship, and to devote considerably more in time of crisis.

Sarbanes-Oxley Act

The Sarbanes-Oxley Act, which came into force during July/August 2002, was a reaction to the loss of investor confidence following the demise of Enron and other major organizations including Andersens, WorldCom and Tyco.

The spirit of the Act, which seeks to raise standards of corporate governance and transparency, initially found widespread approval. However, since it has significant implications for organizations outside the boundaries of the United States, it has been strongly criticized, particularly in Europe where a heavy legislative approach is considered inappropriate.

The size of the Act, with regard to the matters covered, is considerable. However, some of the key points contained in the Act are:

- the Directors are required to demonstrate that they have put in place processes that prove the company's accounts are not misleading;
- the Chief Executive Officer and the Chief Financial Officer are required to provide quarterly sworn statements certifying the truth of the company's accounts. If they are found to have filed false accounts they can be jailed for up to 120 years and fined $5 million;
- where accounts have to be restated, executives will be required to forfeit bonuses;
- loans by non-US companies to directors and executives are prohibited;
- the audit committee is to be comprised entirely of independent persons;
- the company must disclose all off-balance-sheet transactions, such as special purpose vehicles;
- protection is provided for corporate whistle blowers.

The administrative and legislative burden of the Sarbanes-Oxley Act has led to listing arbitrage, resulting in a weakening of the competitive position of the US stock exchange. Consequently, the Act is expected to face amendment.

United States Sentencing Commission – Corporate Sentencing Guidelines

In addition to the Sarbanes-Oxley Act, in the United States it is necessary to have regard for the requirements of the corporate sentencing guidelines of the United States Sentencing Commission.[7] These require the court to determine, amongst other things, whether or not:

- facilities were in place to enable an employee to report any issues without fear of recrimination;
- employees were adequately trained to required competence levels;
- comprehensive audits and investigations were carried out.

Companies that have shown serious endeavours to comply with these guidelines have tended to receive significantly reduced fines.

2.6 BOARD STRUCTURES

In some countries, particularly in Europe, there is a two-tier board structure comprising (1) the supervisory board, and (2) the executive board. This contrasts with the unitary system, favoured by the UK and the US, which consists of a single board but includes independent non-executive directors. A third structure which appears to be developing is the establishment of an additional level – the active institutional investor – the aims of which are to increase performance and transparency whilst optimizing risk.

2.7 SHAREHOLDER ACTIVISM AND EXTRA-FINANCIAL ISSUES

Significant levels of funds are accruing in the hands of big institutional investors; a process that will undoubtedly continue over time. In the US over 50 % of all publicly held equity is controlled by the top 100 fiduciary institutions, with a similar level of ownership concentration existing in the UK. Hence the old approach of selling underperforming shares is considered less appropriate, particularly for tracker funds and large investors whose activities could shift the share price.

In order to increase fund performance there has been a move towards shareholder activism. A further development is the establishment of funds that deliberately seekout underperforming companies and invest with the intention of bringing about change. These investment funds are tending to produce their own corporate governance codes, which may be written into investment contracts. Such funds often invest on an international level and thus assist in raising the standards of corporate governance globally.

Many of these institutions are major pension funds (e.g. CalPERS, CalSTRS, USS, TIAA-CREF and Caisse de Dépôt et Placement du Quebec). They tend to adopt a long-term "universal owner" perspective, with portfolio considerations being holistic in nature rather than simply being based upon the sum of the performances of individual companies.

There is growing recognition of the rise of the "financially intermediated society" involving "universal ownership" and "fiduciary capitalism," where multiple "agency chains" exist, resulting in "capitalism without owners."[8]

Institutions such as USS and Hermes clearly recognize that, being large institutional investors with diversified portfolios, their performance is dependent to a significant extent upon the overall performance of the economy. These institutions are overtly aware that externalities generated by portfolio firms impact upon other portfolio firms. The cost of any negative externalities adversely affects the total portfolio; in general, externality costs exceed individual company benefits.

As corporate governance has increased in maturity, its scope has extended to include Extra-Financial Issues (EFI) that affect long-term performance and economic value. EFIs tend to be qualitative in nature, and relate to externalities not well captured by the market but which can lead to reputational risk and a reduction in stakeholder value. They include environmental and social issues, such as employment standards, human resource management issues, executive motivation, and climate change issues.

The UN Principles of Responsible Investment (PRI),[9] launched in April 2006, which explicitly refer to the "universal owner" hypothesis, provide a framework to assist investors. The Principles seek to address major environmental, social, and corporate governance (ESG) issues considered to be beyond the scope of individual firms or industry sectors. These include climate change, globalization, workplace health and safety, health care, and pharmaceuticals issues.

Similarly, the formation of the Enhanced Analytics Initiative,[10] the Investor Network on Climate Risk in the US, and the Institutional Investor Group on Climate Change in the UK represent important developments.

It is important to recognize that "responsible investment" is directly focused on performance, not non-commercial socio-ethical considerations. Responsible investment is economically driven and takes a longer-term view. In contrast, hedge funds and other forms of private equity investment, which often appear completely opaque, are fuelled by institutional investors' search for alpha factor performance. Unfortunately, this may undermine possible long-term generic growth referred to as enhanced beta factor performance.

Long-term, sustainable, economy-wide performance criteria influence the underlying performance of investments and must therefore be managed, particularly given that they may also severely affect an institution's ability to meet its fiduciary obligations over the longer term. It is now widely accepted that trustee fiduciary duty includes consideration of holistic portfolio performance from a "universal owner" perspective.[11]

2.8   ASSESSING GOVERNANCE, BRIBERY, AND CORRUPTION

There is growing awareness of the influence that corruption has on world stability. Corruption is closely correlated with poverty. Consequently, bribery is regarded as an unacceptable business strategy. Indicators of governance, bribery, and corruption are therefore increasingly being used both by rating agencies, institutional investors, and aid agencies.

2.8.1   Worldwide governance indicators

Measuring governance is complex, and requires consideration of many factors. Shlomo Yitzhaki, Professor of Economics at the Hebrew University and Director of Israel's Central Bureau of Statistics has stated: *Until the mid-nineties, I did not think that governance could be measured. The Worldwide Governance Indicators have shown me otherwise ... It constitutes the state of the art on how to build periodic governance indicators which can be a crucial tool for policy analysts and decision-makers benchmarking their countries. Uniquely, it publicly discloses the aggregated and disaggregated data, as well as the estimated margins of error for each country. It definitely sets a standard for transparency in data.*

The Worldwide Governance Indicators, produced by the World Bank, measure six components of good governance:

1. *Voice and Accountability* – measuring political, civil, and human rights.
2. *Political Stability and Absence of Violence* – measuring the likelihood of violent threats to, or changes in, government, including terrorism.
3. *Government Effectiveness* – measuring the competence of the bureaucracy and the quality of public service delivery.
4. *Regulatory Quality* – measuring the incidence of market-unfriendly policies.
5. *Rule of Law* – measuring the quality of contract enforcement, the police, and the courts, including judiciary independence, and the incidence of crime.
6. *Control of Corruption* – measuring the abuse of public power for private gain, including petty and grand corruption (and state capture by elites).

Research[12] shows that countries such as Russia, China, and Bangladesh have serious problems with regard to corruption. Whilst the regulatory quality ratings of the United States and the UK are good, they are, perhaps surprisingly, not the best, ranking behind New Zealand, Australia, Denmark, and Switzerland. It is interesting to note that countries such as Italy and Greece receive relatively poor ratings in comparison to other developed countries.

The Director of Global Governance at the World Bank Institute, Daniel Kaufmann, has stated that good governance matters for development: *A country that improves in governance gets three times more income per capita in the long term. The indicators show that when governance is improved by one standard deviation, incomes rise about three-fold in the long run, and infant mortality declines by two-thirds. There are similar results in terms of improved literacy and improved competitiveness.*

2.8.2 Corruption Perceptions Index (CPI)

The Corruption Perceptions Index is produced by Transparency International, a non-governmental organization devoted to combating corruption. The first CPI survey was produced in 1995 and now covers around 180 countries. This index indicates the overall level of corruption as perceived by country analysts and business people. It is derived from a composite survey of 16 different polls from 10 independent institutions. Ratings range from 10 (perfectly clean) to 0 (highly corrupt).

The index has been criticized for being subjectively based and therefore merely measuring perception; business practices considered acceptable in one country being regarded as bribery and corruption in another (e.g. political donations, tipping, and gifts). Since the index is based on polls it is considered less reliable for countries where there are fewer independent information sources.

Longer-term analysis[13] indicates that over the past decade, although corruption has decreased significantly in countries such as Bulgaria, Colombia, and Estonia, in higher-income countries such as Canada and Ireland there has been a marked increase, indicating the need to continuously strive to maintain a climate of integrity. The most highly-rated countries in the 2007 survey were New Zealand, Finland, and Denmark with an index rating of 9.4. In the same survey, the UK was ranked number 12 with a CPI of 8.4, and the USA was ranked number 20 with an index rating of 7.2.

Transparency International, has stated: *Corruption isn't a natural disaster, it is the cold, calculated theft of opportunity from the men, women and children who are least able to protect*

Table 2.1   Corruption Perception Index.

Country rank	Country	2007 CPI score*
1	Finland	9.4
	New Zealand	9.4
	Denmark	9.4
4	Singapore	9.3
9	Canada	8.7
11	Australia	8.6
12	United Kingdom	8.4
16	Germany	7.8
17	Ireland	7.5
	Japan	7.5
19	France	7.3
20	USA	7.2
41	Italy	5.2
143	Russia	2.3

*(Transparency International 2007)
Source: Transparency International. Reproduced by permission of Transparency International.

themselves. Leaders must go beyond lip service and make good on their promises to provide the commitment and resources to improve governance, transparency and accountability. The responsibility for preventing corruption rests with both the supply-side (those offering bribes) and the demand-side (the recipients).

2.9   KEY CONSIDERATIONS

2.9.1   Legislation or guidelines

The appropriateness of legislation is a matter of some conjecture in the field of corporate governance. Legislation can set definitive rules and provide a means of prosecuting those who breach these rules. The Enron affair has demonstrated the need for appropriate (and adequately enforced) legislation. However, legislation comes at the expense of flexibility, which can lead to economic drift and a reduction in competitiveness. Offset against this is the gain in investor confidence necessary to enable the financial markets to work effectively. Thus legislation is a matter of balance and needs to be supported by an ethical culture. It is the role of guidelines to assist in creating this ethical culture.

In principle, legislation should not reduce the rigorousness of audits nor deter investigations by individual directors (in fulfilment of their duties) because of to the possibility of legal action. Disclosure of problems should lead to appropriate mitigation of legislative or regulatory action.

Separation of the roles of chairman and CEO

The two primary responsibilities of the chairman are (1) to ensure that the organization maintains an adequate external focus, and (2) to build the board into an effective team. The chairman therefore has a facilitating and mentoring role. In contrast, the Chief Executive Officer is a paid employee of the company and is charged with implementing the strategy determined by the board in an efficient and effective manner. There is debate over the efficacy of combining these roles.

The Australian Working Group recommends: *Except where special circumstances exist, the roles (of Chairman and CEO) should be separate.* However, in the United States there is a tendency to combine these roles in order to obtain strong leadership and direction. France adopts a similar approach.

It is interesting to note that in the UK, the FSA itself combined these roles under Howard Davies. The Government recommended the same approach for the Office of Fair Trading. However, the London Stock Exchange Combined Code requires separation for listed companies.

Assessment of board members

As part of the drive for improved performance by institutional investors, increasing attention is being paid to the assessment of the board and its individual members. In particular, consideration is being given to the appropriateness of the composition of the board, the steps being taken to improve performance, and the means of measuring and reporting efficiency and effectiveness.

The Canadian corporate governance code somewhat forcefully states: *Every board of directors will have in place some mechanism for, at least annually, assessing the performance of the CEO. Good governance requires the board to also have in place a mechanism for assessing its own effectiveness as a board and for assessing the contribution of individul directors.*

Non-executive directors

As part of the assessment of the board, institutional investors take into consideration the degree of independence of individual non-executive directors and their level of skills. The value of non-executive directors derives from their contribution to and oversight of:

• committees, including the audit, remuneration, and nomination committees;
• the strategic direction of the organization (including mergers and acquisitions);
• the assessment of executive management performance;
• resolution of potential conflicts of interest; and
• transparency and reporting.

Non-executive directors cannot guarantee the accuracy of financial information. However, they have a key role in ensuring that the reports and accounts do give a true and fair view. They must be aware of the risks faced by the organization and must seek independent professional advice where appropriate. Non-executive directors need to ensure that consideration is given to the longer-term performance of the company, with a view to protecting and enhancing shareholder value and resolving potential conflicts with other stakeholders. They have a responsibility for promoting transparency, so that the market can arrive at an informed view.

Fundamentally, the role of the non-executive director should be seen as one of providing advice, guidance and mentoring. It should not involve policing and second guessing management, nor should it be seen as a back-stop for failures by other market participants.

Auditors

Auditors (both internal and external) have a responsibility for putting all directors on alert. The auditors therefore require the right to request a meeting, and to report without fear or favour directly to the non-executive directors. This meeting, which needs to exclude the chairman, should be chaired by the senior independent non-executive director (SID).

2.10   CONCLUSIONS

The overarching aim of corporate governance is to deliver enhanced and sustainable performance, both at an individual organizational level and globally. It should be recognized that companies are always going to fail since that is the nature of competition. However, sound corporate governance enables a flexible and more responsive approach, facilitating change. To quote Sir Adrian Cadbury: *Good governance is an aid to good performance.*

APPENDIX 2A

CORPORATE GOVERNANCE QUESTIONNAIRE
   This questionnaire provides a framework for corporate governance, culture and ethics, by identifying the key areas to be considered and the main underlying issues. It is based upon accepted best practice and draws on various codes and legislation from around the world.
   However, it should be recognized that there is no one right solution to the issue of corporate governance.

Board Structure and Performance
1. Are the roles of the chairman and the CEO separated and if not why not?
2. Is there a balance between non-executive directors (NEDs) and senior management?
3. Does the board have all the skills it requires (multiple lenses of perception)?
4. Is a succession plan in place?
5. How is the performance of the board as a whole, and each member individually, regularly and thoroughly evaluated?

Non-executive Directors (NEDs)
1. Are non-executive directors:
    a. competent – how is this determined;
    b. professionally qualified;
    c. independent – how is this determined?
2. How many directorships does each NED hold?
3. Are the roles and responsibilities for each NED specified in writing?
4. Who is responsible for appointing NEDs and monitoring their performance?
5. Is there a NED on the risk committee?

Executive Directors (Senior Managers)
1. Who determines the senior management remuneration?
2. What shareholdings and other benefits have been granted (or could be granted) to each member of the senior management team? Are these shown separately in the published accounts?
3. Is there a main board director directly responsible for risk?
4. Is there a risk committee? Is it chaired by a main board director?
5. Are senior management (executive directors) excluded from the audit committee?

6. Is each director professionally competent to hold the position of director? Does each director actively take part in a continuous professional development (CPD) programme?
7. Do any of the directors hold any other external directorships and, if so, why and how many?

Stakeholders
1. Do all shareholders have the right to take forceful action? Are there any shareholders who actively promote corporate governance (e.g. CalPERS, Hermes, etc)?
2. How are the interests of stakeholders (other than shareholders) taken into account?
3. Are there any limitations imposed on proxy voting (including unreasonable financial costs)?
4. Are there any shareholders with substantial shareholdings or other significant influence?
5. Are minority shareholders represented on the board?

Auditors
1. Who appoints the auditors and to whom do they report? Are senior management excluded from this process?
2. Do the auditors provide any additional services? If so, why?
3. How long have the auditors been in place? Is it longer than five years? When will they be replaced?
4. Is there another audit firm appointed to provide an overview (second opinion) and a watching brief?

The Governance Framework
1. Who reviews the corporate governance framework (e.g. the audit committee)?
2. How is the effectiveness of the board as a whole validated, and that of individual members including the Chief Executive Officer?
3. Have the board taken any measures to prevent takeovers (i.e. poison pills)?
4. What restrictions exist on voting and are these appropriate? Is there a policy of *one share one vote*?
5. How often does the board of directors meet and is this appropriate?
6. Does each member of the board receive full information? Is this information comprehensive and appropriate, clear (not opaque), timely, and accurate?
7. How is corporate governance treated – i.e. as an important separate issue, dealt with by a special committee or is it considered to be just a minor part of the board's responsibilities?
8. Are all directors at liberty to obtain independent professional advice in the furtherance of their duties?

Management
1. How does the organization guard against perfunctory management?
2. Are managers set clear and measurable objectives? Do they have the opportunity to determine these objectives?
3. How are managers motivated?
4. Do all managers receive regular ongoing training to maintain and further develop their competence level? Is the level of competence assessed?
5. Does the organization operate an upward assessment system?
6. Is there a whistle blowing system in place? Can it be used without fear of recrimination?
7. What management style is encouraged in the organization?

ENDNOTES

[1] The FSA regards "Treating Customers Fairly" as an ongoing priority. It has developed a culture framework, enabling supervisors to identify how a firm's culture impacts upon customers. http://www.fsa.gov.uk/pubs/other/tcf_culture.pdf

[2] See:
Newell R. and Wilson G. (2002). A Premium for Good Corporate Governance, *The McKinsey Quarterly*, Number 3.
McKinsey, Global Investor Opinion Survey 2002. (www.mckinsey.com/practices/ CorporateGovernance/index.asp)
Millstein, Ira M. (1998). *Corporate Governance: Improving Competitiveness and Access to Capital in Global Markets,* Brookings Institute.

[3] Millstein, I.M. and MacAvoy, P. W. (1997). *The Active Board of Directors and Performance of the Large Publicly Traded Corporations*, Columbia Law.

[4] The Financial Stability Forum (FSF) brings together senior representatives of national financial authorities (e.g. central banks, supervisory authorities and treasury departments), international financial institutions, international regulatory and supervisory groupings, committees of central bank experts and the European Central Bank. Mr Mario Draghi, Governor of the Banca d'Italia, chairs the FSF in a personal capacity. The FSF is serviced by a small secretariat housed at the Bank for International Settlements in Basel, Switzerland. It was first convened on 14 April 1999 (for more details see http://www.fsforum.org/about/history.htm).

[5] The first paper, having the same title, was published in September 1999.

[6] The European Commission, *A Comparative Study of Corporate Governance Codes in the EU Member Nations,* Survey undertaken by Weil, Gotshal & Manges LLP (www.weil.com).

[7] United States Sentencing Commission, *Corporate Sentencing Guidelines* (www.ussc.gov/guidelin).

[8] Hawley, J. and Williams, A. (2000). *The Rise of Fiduciary Capitalism, University of Pennsylvania Press.*

[9] UN Principles of Responsible Investment:
  1. We will incorporate ESG issues into investment analysis and decision-making processes.
  2. We will be active owners and incorporate ESG issues into our ownership policies and practices.
  3. We will seek appropriate disclosure on ESG issues by the entities in which we invest.
  4. We will promote acceptance and implementation of the Principles within the investment industry.
  5. We will work together to enhance our effectiveness in implementing the Principles.
  6. We will each report our activities and progress towards implementing the Principles.

[10] Enhanced Analytics Initiative: www.enhancedanalytics.com

[11] See the report prepared for UNEP-FI by Freshfield, Brukhaus and Deringer entitled *A Legal Framework for the Integration of Environmental, Social and Governance Issues into Institutional Investment.*

[12] Kaufmann, Daniel, Kraay, Aart and Mastruzzi, Massimoh (2008). Governance Matters VII: Aggregate and Individual Governance Indicators, 1996–2007 World Bank Policy Research Working Paper No. 4654; available at SSRN: http://ssrn.com/abstract=1148386

[13] Long-term analysis of the CPI has been carried out by Prof. Dr. Johann Graf Lambsdorff, University of Passau, Germany.

3

Fundamental Assessment

One bank's operational risk is another bank's credit risk. Anon

3.1 INTRODUCTION

Risk assessment methodologies have advanced considerably in recent years. This chapter seeks to provide an understanding of traditional analysis techniques developed by the banking industry over many years and to identify the need for a more robust forensic approach. Initially it focuses on fundamental analysis and identifies the relationship between credit, market and operational risk. Consideration is then given to the development of more predictive techniques used to assess risk and determine the likelihood of failure. Finally, consideration is given to the requirements of the Enhance Analytical Initiative (EAI) being driven by major institutional investors.

3.2 THE FUNDAMENTAL RELATIONSHIP BETWEEN CREDIT RISK, MARKET RISK, AND OPERATIONAL RISK

Traditionally, banks were primarily concerned with credit risk. Banks are well accustomed to assessing the risk of lending to clients. In general, a bank will not lend unless it is satisfied that there is a high probability of the loan being repaid in accordance with the agreed terms of the loan, and without recourse to security (i.e. the proposal generating surplus cashflow). Whilst a bank will often want to take collateral, it is well recognized that this is not expected to be called. When assessing the standing of a client, the traditional approach is to consider both past and present performance together with future predictions. The confidence level for the future takes account of the character and capability of the client. As can be seen, the assessment methodologies used became progressively more thorough.

- **CCC**: The first methodology, known as the 3 Cs, simply looked at the Capital, Character, and Capability of the borrower and their business.
- **PARTS**: Lloyds Bank and TSB Bank advanced the assessment by adding other elements, using Purpose, Amount, Repayment, Terms, Security.
- **PARSERS**: Midland Bank (now HSBC) used Personality, Amount, Repayment, Security, Expenditure, Remuneration, Services.
- **CAMPARI**: Barclays used Character, Ability, Means, Purpose, Amount, Repayment, Insurance.
- **CAMPARI & ICE**: NatWest (now part of RBS) went further, adding Interest, Charges, and Extras.

The main problems with these methodologies are that they tend to be subjective and value laden. Consequently, the results are not perfectly reproducible, different managers possibly deriving different conclusions. However, such methodologies, which adopt an inspection and selection approach, proved relatively successful in reducing the risk from individual failures (*credit risk*). By also adopting a portfolio approach, the risk of overexposure to a particular sector could also be reduced (*market risk*).

In traditional banking activities, margins are thin and therefore high levels of leverage are essential in order to achieve the necessary return on shareholders' capital (ROE) demanded by the market. Consequently, given their comparatively low levels of equity, banks are also predisposed to risk resulting from the impact of large loss events (*operational risk*). This innate vulnerability means that interbank activity has the potential to create *systemic risk*.

3.3   EXTERNAL ASSESSMENT FRAMEWORKS

A financial organization needs to take cognizance of external requirements, such as those emanating from the regulators, rating agencies, and other significant bodies. In assessing a bank it is important for the analyst to be clear about what is trying to be achieved. The three primary questions to be addressed are:

1. Currently, what is the appropriate value of the bank's shares, based on its earnings, now and in the future? This is the domain of the equity analyst.
2. What is the ability of the bank to survive in the medium/long term? This is the concern of the credit rating analyst.
3. Does the bank pose a threat to the financial system? This is the primary concern of regulators.

3.3.1   Equity analysis

There are two approaches to equity analysis: technical analysis and fundamental analysis.

Technical analysis attempts to determine the appropriate timing for buying or selling a company's shares, taking into account the collective sentiment and psychology of the market. It considers movements in overall market prices, seeking to identify patterns and resistance levels (see Figure 3.1).

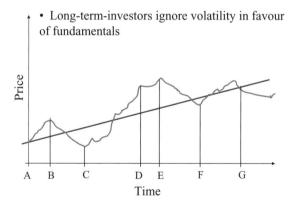

Figure 3.1   Long term v. short term market trends.

Note: The slope is determined from point of purchase to point of sale. The rate of gain also takes into account the holding period.

Souce: Brendon Young, ORRF

Fundamental analysis is regarded as the primary tool for longer-term investors. It seeks to arrive at a conclusion about the share price based on consideration of a number of factors affecting the quality and stability of earnings, including competitive advantage, management quality, strategy, and business environmental factors. The equity analyst is concerned with indicators derived from historical information, primarily contained in the published accounts. To be more specific, traditionally the key area of interest was the earnings line of the income statement, the aim being to determine an assessment of the expected growth in earnings per share (EPS).

For the equity analyst, one of the main indicators is the return achieved on shareholders' equity (ROE). Increasing the level of gearing can increase this; however, doing so increases the level of risk. In other words, return is directly proportional to risk (see Table 3.1).

Table 3.1   Relationship between ROE and ROA.

1. Gearing (G) $= \frac{A}{E}$ Therefore A $= E \times G$

2. ROA $= \dfrac{NPAT}{A}$

3. ROE $= \dfrac{NPAT}{E}$

4. Hence ROA $= \dfrac{NPAT}{E \times G} = \dfrac{ROE}{G}$

5. ROE $=$ ROA $\times$ G

Hence, to increase ROE simply increase gearing.
Source: Brendon Young, ORRF

3.3.2   Credit analysis

Credit analysis takes a longer-term view, being primarily concerned with the overall soundness and ability of the bank to withstand adverse business conditions as well as the impact of risk events. The rating agencies claim to "look through the cycle."

Often the credit analyst has access to the management of the company and consequently the information is more accurate, up-to-date, and forensic in nature.

3.3.3   Regulatory analysis – and the CAMEL framework

Under the new Basel Accord the regulators have access to certain detailed confidential information and will be aware of significant weakness in a bank. This will be reflected in the capital charge. However, the regulators do not take a commercial view when carrying-out their analysis, therefore the information obtained from the regulator is currently of limited value to the market.

CAMEL

The historical, universally accepted approach to assessing the fundamental creditworthiness of a bank was developed by US bank examiners and is known as CAMEL. This has been further developed and refined over the years in the light of experience. The acronym identifies five key elements said to determine the standing and robustness of a bank. Whilst all factors can be analyzed using techniques such as ratio analysis, trend analysis and peer group comparisons, it is also necessary to use qualitative assessment, particularly when assessing management where subjective judgement is essential. The relative importance assigned to the different CAMEL elements will vary depending upon the primary objective and views of the analyst concerned, although typical weightings are indicated below.

C: Capital Adequacy (typical weighting: 20 %)
Capital adequacy refers to the appropriateness of the level and type of funds available to absorb shocks and survive adverse trading conditions that could lead to a significant diminution of asset value and result in liquidity problems.

The original Basel Accord (Basel I) defined the Capital Adequacy Ratio in terms of different risk weightings assigned to different asset types. In addition to shareholders' funds (i.e. equity, retained earnings, and equity reserves), other items such as subordinated debt, general loan loss provisions, and hidden reserves were taken into account.

The capital cushion represents the first line of defense. Once this is exhausted, a bank is technically insolvent. However, it may continue to trade if it has appropriate external support providing access to adequate resources.

A: Asset Quality (typical weighting: 25 %)
Asset quality denotes the extent to which earning assets are continuing to perform in accordance with the terms upon which the funds were advanced or invested. Earning assets are comprised of those loans included in the loan portfolio and those assets included in the investment portfolio (i.e. fixed income securities and equity investments), together with any off-balance sheet items. Poor asset quality is exposed in times of economic downturn. This results in the bank having to increase its loan–loss reserves, thus reducing its profits and also requiring the write-off of irrecoverable loans, thus reducing regulatory capital.

M: Management (typical weighting: 25 %)
Evaluation of the quality of management (including its plausibility, competence and motivation) is an essential part of the assessment process. However, by its very nature, this is largely a subjective undertaking. Although the overall financial performance resulting from implementation of the strategy developed by management is clearly quantifiable, other factors (such as corporate governance, culture, ethics, and competitive positioning) are less so.

In a dynamic competitive business environment, management teams compete for the right to manage scarce resources. This is even more so the case where, as in banking, the industry is global and is undergoing rationalization and consolidation.

It is interesting to note that the characteristics of sure-footedness, commended by the regulators, may to some extent be at odds with demands of the market, which requires growth in earnings per share year-on-year, without excuse. Pressure to perform is said to have contributed in part to the collapse of Enron, Worldcom, and Parmalat.

E: Earnings (typical weighting: 10 %)
Quality and stability of earnings are important factors in that they enable a bank to earn its way out of trouble, build its reserves, and further develop its business. In countries such as Belgium and Germany a bank may have a strong franchise, giving it stability of earnings but

the level of those earnings (profitability) will be markedly behind banks operating in the UK and the United States where margins are significantly higher. Thus, whilst the Belgium bank may be stable, it will have difficulty in attracting new capital. Hence it will lack the ability to develop and grow unless it diversifies into countries offering better quality of earnings.

L: Liquidity (typical weighting: 20 %)
A bank needs sufficient funds to meet its liabilities as and when they fall due. A lack of liquidity is the proximate cause of many bank failures. It is the primary responsibility of the Asset-Liability Committee (ALCO) to ensure that the bank has timely and certain (unrestricted) access to required funding.

3.4   CREDIT RATING AGENCIES' APPROACH: THE 7 PILLARS

The traditional assessment methodology adopted by credit rating agencies is comprised of three separate activities:

1. **a business risk assessment** in which all operating divisions are reviewed, with factors such as the quality of management, strategy, and competitive position being considered;
2. **a financial risk assessment**, which includes a review of the financial history of the organization together with an assessment of the future projections, in addition to comparison with 60–80 industry average ratios;
3. **an overall assessment** by the risk committee, which before awarding its final rating index considers the strength of the organization in comparison to its peers, together with the potential impact of external factors.

A similar system is adopted by the venture capital industry, where risk assessment is signified by the required internal rate of return (IRR) on investment together with the stringency of the applied terms and conditions.

A comparison of ratings available from the three main agencies is shown in Table 3.2. Often it is erroneously assumed that ratings are based statistically on the number of standard deviations from the norm. Whilst a quantitative approach may appear logical, ratings remain subjective and value laden rather than quantitatively determined.

The analysis of the creditworthiness of a financial institution, complex and dynamic as it is, has traditionally been based on seven fundamental interrelated pillars[1]:

1. operating environment;
2. ownership and governance;
3. franchise value;
4. recurring earning power;
5. risk profile;
6. economic capital allowance;
7. management priorities and strategies.

Criticisms of the credit rating agencies

The inability of the credit rating agencies to identify serious problems sufficiently early has been severely criticized. Events such as the Thai Baht devaluation (which sparked the Asian crisis) and the Enron, Worldcom, and Parmalat scandals (which significantly contributed to

Table 3.2   Rating scale equivalencies.

STANDARD & POOR'S		MOODY'S		FITCH	
Short Term	Long Term	Short Term	Long Term	Short Term	Long Term
Investment grade ratings					
	AAA		Aaa		AAA
	AA+		Aa1		AA+
A - 1+	AA	P - 1	Aa2	F1+	AA
	AA-		Aa3		AA-
A - 1	A+		A1	F1+	A+
	A		A2		A
A - 2	A-	P - 2	A3	F2	A-
	BBB+		Baa1		BB+
A - 3	BBB	P - 3	Baa2	F3	BBB
	BBB-		Baa3		BBB-
Speculative grade ratings					
	BB+		Ba1		BB+
B	BB		Ba2		BB
	BB-		Ba3	B	BB-
	B+		B1		B+
	B		B2		B
	B-	Not prime	B3		B-
	CCC+		Caa1		CCC+
C	CCC		Caa2	C	CCC
	CCC-		Caa3		CCC-
	CC		Ca		CC
	C		C		C
D	D			D	D

the demand for further legislation in the US, resulting in the Sarbanes-Oxley Act) seriously dented public confidence.

In 1997, the Head of Sovereign Ratings at Fitch IBCA admitted: *We've all been behind the curve on Korea. We were all too focused on how low Korea's external debt was as a proportion of export receipts, so we underestimated the danger of a Korean default on its short term debt.*

In April 1997, three months prior to the Thai Baht devaluation, S&P somewhat mistakenly stated: *People say, in Mexico, when the currency crashed, there was a financial crisis involving the government, so why can't that happen in Thailand? The answer is very simple. Because the fiscal position and financial position of Thailand is fundamentally different from that of Mexico.*

Table 3.3   Average cumulative default rates for corporates by holding period (1920–1999)

	1 Year %	10 Years %	20 Years %
Aaa	0.00	1.09	2.38
Aa	0.08	3.10	6.75
A	0.08	3.61	7.47
Baa	0.30	7.92	13.95
Ba	1.43	19.05	30.82
B	4.48	31.90	43.70
Investment-grade	0.16	4.85	9.24
Speculative-grade	3.35	25.31	37.74
All corporates	1.33	11.49	17.79

Source of data: Moody's

With regard to Enron, the rating agencies continued to rate it as being suitable for investment purposes up to four days before the company filed for bankruptcy.

In contrast, in 2003 the rating agencies were accused by telecommunications companies of precipitating a crisis in the sector by cutting ratings too hastily.

In summary, the main criticisms levied at the rating agencies are:

- **Fallibility**: A rating is merely an opinion. Whilst this may be true, it belies the level of detailed knowledge and understanding possessed by the rating agencies. Complexity and probability mean that not every result can be accurately predicted, although on balance the trend may be correct.
- **Bad faith**: It has been questioned whether rating agencies risk reputational damage by favouring fee-paying banks. Some have also commented that unsolicited ratings are morally wrong. The provision of additional consultancy services by certain rating agencies is considered by some to be a conflict of interest.
- **Timeliness**: It has been claimed that ratings are primarily lagging indicators and therefore do not properly serve their purpose. The rating agencies claim that in looking through the cycle, short-term volatility is merely noise and therefore not relevant to longer-term investors.
- **Market reference**: Ratings do not respond sufficiently to the market, with bond spreads appearing more in tune with the market than do credit ratings.[2]
- **Anti-competitive practices**:[3] The international credit ratings industry is an oligopoly effectively dominated by three companies: Moody's, Standard & Poor's and Fitch. Hence, price is not determined by the market. Since bond issuers require a recognized rating, this essentially bars the growing number of local agencies in Europe, China, and India, who are effectively excluded from the world stage.

The high number of failures, the size and impact of those failures, and the increasing sophistication of financial markets has led to recognition of the need to take a more forensic risk-based approach.

3.5   MOODY'S OPERATIONAL RISK ASSESSMENTS – TOWARDS A MORE FORENSIC APPROACH

After stating that its focus on operational risk for banks was becoming more central in the overall fundamental analysis of rated institutions, Moody's Investors Service published a paper in January 2003 entitled: *Moody's Analytical Framework For Operational Risk Management Of Banks.*

The framework presented in that paper adopts a holistic approach to risk management and is based on the premise that, fundamentally, management is concerned with consideration of four interrelated areas:

1. leadership;
2. organizational efficiency and effectiveness;
3. external factors; and
4. performance and reporting.

The framework recognizes that, when assessing any business, a primary consideration is the quality of management and its leadership capability. Ultimately, the success of management can be determined from the results achieved, which are a function of how efficiently and effectively the various resources have been applied. However, given that a business is an open socio-technical system, which interacts intimately with the outside environment, consideration also has to be given to how well external threats have been mitigated and managed.

Under the four primary areas, a number of key issues are identified for discussion purposes, the assessment process being "a journey of discovery rather than a detailed checklist of requirements." Contingency and complexity paradigms indicate that there is no single "right" solution in a dynamic, constantly changing business milieu, although pattern theory and benchmarking enable identification of the more successful solutions.

3.5.1 Leadership

The quality of management and leadership is considered to be a key factor in determining the rating of a bank. The primary areas to consider include:

- corporate governance;
- culture;
- ethics; and
- strategy.

In addition, at a more detailed level, consideration needs to be given to such issues as the level of professional competency, the appropriateness and impact of motivational factors, avoidance of a "blame culture," and the linking of personal objectives to corporate strategic objectives.

3.5.2 Organizational efficiency and effectiveness (see Figures 3.2 & 3.3)

Some of the key issues to consider include:

- completeness and effectiveness of the operational risk framework (including its link to the organizational structure);
- development stages reached;
- key risks, drivers, controls, and priorities;
- data, quantification, and modeling; and
- validation and verification.

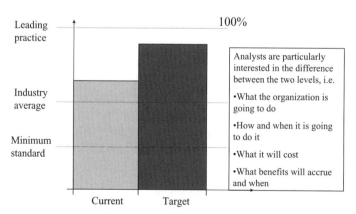

Figure 3.2   Operational risk assessment.
Source: Brendon Young, ORRF

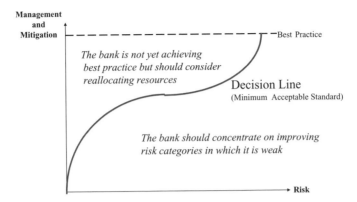

Figure 3.3   Benchmarking, risk prioritization, and resource allocation.
Source: Brendon Young, ORRF

3.5.3   External factors

Consideration should be given to:

- contingency planning;
- outsourcing; and
- insurance and risk transfer.

3.5.4   Performance and reporting

Performance is clearly the ultimate indicator of success but this has a time element (short-term success can be achieved at the expense of long-term gains). It can also impact upon competitive strategic positioning. Whilst the quality and stability of earnings are key considerations, other areas to consider include:

- reporting and transparency;
- rating assessments;
- stakeholder assessments; and
- reputational assessment.

3.6   THE REGULATORY APPROACH – DEVELOPMENT OF THE ARROW FRAMEWORK

In April 2003, the Basel Committee on Banking Supervision stated: *An improved capital adequacy framework is intended to foster a strong emphasis on risk management and to encourage ongoing improvements in banks' risk assessment capabilities. The Committee believes this can be accomplished by closely aligning banks' capital requirements with prevailing modern risk management practices, and by ensuring this emphasis on risk makes its way into supervisory practices and into market discipline through enhanced risk and capital related disclosures.*

3.6.1   The FSA's ARROW Framework[4]

The ARROW[5] regulatory framework (Advanced Risk-Response Operating FrameWork) is the methodology used by the UK Financial Services Authority (FSA) to identify and assess risks within the financial institutions under its supervision that may pose a threat to its statutory objectives. In addition, ARROW provides a means of informing the FSA of emerging risks and other trends within the industry. Overall, the ARROW initiative has proved to be successful both for the FSA and the supervised firm, helping to embed risk knowledge and improve risk management practices.

The FSA adopts a risk orientated, non-zero failure approach to supervision. It has stated: . . . *although the idea that regulation should seek to eliminate all failures may look superficially appealing, in practice this would impose prohibitive costs on the industry and consumers. Consumers benefit from healthy, competitive markets, where different firms try to meet their needs. . . .*[6]

ARROW I Framework

Under the original ARROW[7] framework the identification of risks involved determining:

1. where risks could arise; and
2. which statutory objectives could be compromized.

The framework identified and described 45 separate risks (referred to as risk elements). Whilst it is clearly useful to be aware of what the regulators are seeking to identify, it should be remembered that not all risks can be predetermined and, indeed, this is particularly the case with extreme events. Under the restricted definition of operational risk used by the FSA, operational risk was shown as a risk element, within which the following issues were assessed (see Appendix 3.A):

- risk appetite;
- exposure from people;
- exposure from processes and systems;
- exposure from change;
- exposure from firm structure; and
- risk mitigation.

In the ARROW I framework risk was initially broken down into two categories: business risk, and control risk. Business risk was then subdivided into four categories, whilst control risk was subdivided into five (referred to as risk groups):

Business Risk

1. Strategy;
2. Market, credit, insurance underwriting, and operational risk;
3. Financial soundness;
4. Nature of customers/users and products/services.

Control Risk

1. Treatment of customers;
2. Organization;
3. Internal systems and controls;
4. Board, management and staff;
5. Business and compliance culture.

The table given in Appendix 3.B shows the detailed scoring matrix used, identifying the risk groups and separate risk elements.

ARROW II Framework

In 2006, the ARROW II[8] risk model replaced the original ARROW framework. Under the revised ARROW framework, risks are measured on the basis of their impact and probability; each being assessed using a four-point score – i.e. low, medium-low, medium-high, or high. The scores are used to prioritize risks and determine the regulatory action required together with the level of resources necessary. Qualitative factors, such as the number of consumers affected and the level of harm likely to be suffered, are also taken into account when determining impact.

With regard to probability (being the probability of harm to regulatory objectives), firstly, consideration is given to the gross risk before any mitigating effects from controls (referred to as business risk). The quality of controls is assessed separately. Probability is assessed using a framework consisting of 10 "high-level" risk groups, which are further subdivided into "risk elements," of which there are 52 in total (see Appendix 3.C) covering both business risks and control risks. The 10 risk groups are:

1. Environmental risks
2. Customers, products and markets
3. Business process risks
4. Prudential risks
5. Customers, products, and markets controls
6. Financial and operating controls
7. Prudential risk controls
8. Control functions
9. Management, governance, and culture
10. Capital and liquidity

Of these, items 2, 8, 9 and 10 are currently regarded as core areas, and therefore assessed in all cases.

The ARROW II risk model

The ARROW II risk model has three fundamental risk categories. These relate to the intrinsic business risks that the firm elects to bear when determining its risk profile, i.e. risks associated with:

1. interactions with retail customers and market counterparties. This may be broadly characterized as the firm's "front office;"
2. the firm's internal processes; and
3. the financial soundness of the firm (prudential risk).

These risks influence regulatory driving factors such as oversight and governance, which determine the level of supervision required. Excess capital and liquidity are considered to be mitigants available to absorb prudential risks.

Scores are produced using both horizontal and vertical aggregation (as shown in Figure 3.4).[9] Horizontal aggregation produces a score for the net risk after controls and mitigants (subdivided into scores for the three areas: (1) customer treatment and market conduct, (2) operating risks, and (3) financial soundness), whilst vertical aggregation gives average scores for (1) business risk, (2) direct controls, and (3) oversight and governance.

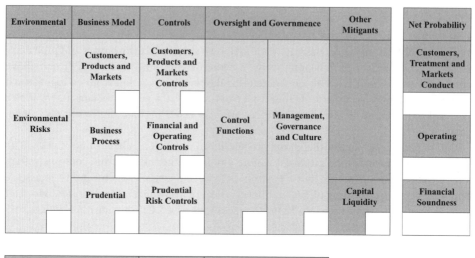

Environmental	Business Model	Controls	Oversight and Governmence	Other Mitigants	Net Probability
Environmental Risks	Customers, Products and Markets	Customers, Products and Markets Controls	Control Functions	Management, Governance and Culture	Customers, Treatment and Markets Conduct
	Business Process	Financial and Operating Controls			Operating
	Prudential	Prudential Risk Controls		Capital Liquidity	Financial Soundness

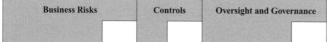

Business Risks	Controls	Oversight and Governance

Figure 3.4 Arrow II risk model.

Oversight and governance are considered to be the most important controls within the ARROW framework. These high-level activities are comprised of functions including internal audit, compliance and risk management.

The ARROW II model can be adjusted to reflect the regulatory risk appetite by adjusting the following parameters:

1. impact thresholds;
2. sector weightings;
3. aggregation;[10]
4. risk group weightings; and
5. core areas.

3.7 ENHANCED ANALYTICS

Major investment institutions, such as USS and Hermes, are increasingly adopting a more forensic approach towards risk management and extra-financial issues (EFI), with a view to gaining an enhanced and more realistic financial perspective. Such factors are now considered by some to have an increasing influence, with around 80 % of value being related to important but difficult to quantify areas such as stakeholder capital, corporate governance, human capital, environment factors, and reputational risk. From a "universal owner" perspective, such factors are important because they influence long-term performance and also have a portfolio-wide impact.

Currently, efforts are being made to determine the significance of such externalities and their related interactions. This involves the development of appropriate methodologies and financial analysis techniques, with a view to incorporating metrics into a more holistic assessment. Research in this area has been actively encouraged by such professional bodies as the Enhanced Analytics Initiative (EAI),[11] which includes asset managers and asset owners, having total assets under management of approximately €1.9 trillion. EAI member institutions allocate a minimum of 5 % of their brokerage commissions towards research into extra-financial issues, thus stimulating the provision of buy-side data by providing a commercial incentive for those research houses producing more comprehensive, innovative, and differentiated research. The Enhanced Analytics Initiative also has the advantage of providing reputational benefits for recognized research providers.

The evaluation of EFI research reports is undertaken half-yearly, using the following criteria:

1. Scope of extra-financial issues covered.
2. Overall presentation and originality, including the user-friendliness, originality and transparency of research outputs.
3. Investment relevance of sector and issue analysis; i.e.
   - thoroughness of top-down analysis;
   - quantitative modeling of sector impacts; and
   - allocation to both long-term and short-term horizons.
4. Comparative company analysis, i.e.
   - analysis of EFI impacts on company-specific investment value drivers;
   - integration into stock valuation; and
   - ranking of companies, integration of EFI analysis in stock recommendations.
5. Coverage of research universe.

3.8 MEASURING CUSTOMER SATISFACTION AND LOYALTY

Banks are increasingly seeing customer satisfaction as an important factor in gaining competitive advantage. High levels of customer satisfaction can lead to greater customer loyalty. Loyal customers are likely to purchase additional services and to recommend their bank to others. In a highly competitive market, customer satisfaction and customer loyalty are key factors affecting growth in both revenue and margins, and hence profitability.

Whilst the importance of measuring customer satisfaction is becoming widely recognized, as yet there is no generally accepted methodology. Customer satisfaction can be regarded as an indicator of past performance and, as such, on its own it is generally considered a poor indicator of changing consumer attitudes,[12] whereas customer loyalty is considered to have future relevance and value. Together they offer an indication of those banks that can be expected to be future winners and losers. The credit rating agencies have certainly recognized the significance of stability arising from loyal customers remaining with a bank during times of stress (referred to as customer stickiness).

One particular approach for assessing the predisposition of customers towards a bank involves categorizing the customers, as follows:

- **A loyal advocate** – the customer believes the bank acts in the best interests of the customer at all times and the customer will therefore remain with the bank during times of stress. The customer will act as a net promoter and positively recommend the bank to others.
- **An apathetic user** – the customer may indicate superficial satisfaction with the service received but will have no intention of purchasing further products/services from the bank.
- **An agnostic switcher** – the customer will always seek alternative quotations from competitors.

Some have advocated use of a single indicator of customer satisfaction based on a net promoter assessment, citing its simplicity and relevance. However, others have questioned the value of a single indicator, stressing the importance from a management perspective of adopting a more forensic approach.

What are the factors that would move a customer from one category to another? The Institute of Consumer Service (ICS) UK customer satisfaction index takes into account 20 factors that UK consumers consider their main priorities. In contrast, the assessment carried out by J. D. Power,[13] a global marketing information services firm, is based on only six areas of consideration:

1. transactions;
2. account openings/product offerings;
3. fees;
4. account statements;
5. problem resolution; and
6. convenience.

Given the range of approaches used to determine customer satisfaction, interpretation of results can prove difficult and requires considerable skill. For example, Barclays Bank achieved second place in the UK customer satisfaction index produced by the Institute of Customer Service. However, shortly afterwards it was ranked last in a similar study conducted by J. D. Power.

Historically, rather than adopting a customer-centric view, banks have tended to adopt a product/service approach, which has been reinforced by the increasing level of market segmentation within retail financial services. Fragmentation means that there is no single measure that is universally applicable. Unfortunately, a product/service approach tacitly assumes a stable world and therefore fails to properly recognize political, environmental, social, and technological changes, which serve to influence public/customer opinion. It also fails to take into account customers' changing attitudes in times of stress and uncertainty.

With regard to regulatory initiatives, in the UK the FSA has recently introduced a "treating customers fairly" initiative to replace the previous voluntary banking code, which stood for 15 years.

APPENDIX 3.A

ARROW I

FSA, The Firm Risk Assessment Framework, February 2003, p. 47

Operational Risk Assessment

Risk Group **Market, Credit and Operational Risk (Business Risk)**	**Risk Element** **6. Operational Risk**

The risks arising from the type and nature of operational risk involved in the firm's activities. These include direct or indirect loss resulting from inadequate or failed internal processes, people and systems or from external events (note: operational risk in relation to the control environment is assessed within the relevant control sections).

Risk appetite
- Nature of operational risk culture and scale of risk (conservative vs aggressive)
- Tolerance and thresholds for impact on financial resources and/or reputation
- Fit with strategic direction
- Degree to which risk appetite reflects standards and values of board

Exposures from people
- Management awareness of operational risk exposures
- Appropriateness of training and supervision of staff for nature of business and strategy
- Appropriateness of personnel policies
- Resource profile (e.g. number of employees, permanent/temporary staff ratio, staff turnover)

Exposures from processes and systems
- State and suitability of manual and automated processes and systems given the complexity and volume of transactions
- Frequency and impact of process and system failures (e.g. customer/user complaints, regulatory fines, system downtime, reconciliation breaks and processing and documentation errors)
- Effects of process and systems failures on market, credit and insurance risk systems and controls, or other regulatory requirements

Exposures from change
- Extent of environmental change (new technologies, legal framework, structure of markets etc)
- Extent of new staff, counterparties and suppliers
- Extent of new or significant changes to existing processes and systems
- Extent of new or significant changes to existing products and business activities
- Presence of significant corporate activity (e.g. acquisitions, mergers and disposals)

Exposures from firm structure
- Relationships and interdependencies between departments and staff
- Complexity of business structure (e.g. multiple or remote locations, numerous legal entities and interdependencies on group companies)
- Reliance on and complexity of outsourcing arrangements

Risk mitigation
- Insurance coverage

APPENDIX 3.B

ARROW I

The FSA's, Firm Risk Assessment Framework, February 2003, Annex 4

Detailed probability scoring matrix

Risk Groups	Risk Elements	Financial Failure (RTOs 1 & 8)	Misconduct and Mismanagement	Consumer Understanding (RTOs 7 & 12)	Incidence of Fraud or Dishonesty (RTOs 3 & 13)	Incidence of Market Abuse (RTOs 3, 10 & 14)	Incidence of Money Laundering (RTOs 3 & 15)	Market Quality (RTOs 4 & 11)
Strategy	Quality of Strategy	L	L	N/A	L	L	N/A	L
	Nature of Business	L	L	N/A	L	L	N/A	L
Strategy Score		**L**	**L**	**N/A**	**L**	**L**	**N/A**	**L**
Strategy Score - OVERRIDE								
Market, Credit, Insurance Underwriting and Operational Risk	Credit Risk	L	N/A	N/A	L	N/A	N/A	L
	Insurance Underwriting Risk	L	L	N/A	N/A	N/A	N/A	N/A
	Market Risk	L	N/A	N/A	N/A	N/A	N/A	L
	Operational Risk	L	L	L	L	L	L	L
	Litigation/Legal Risk	L	N/A	N/A	L	N/A	N/A	L
Market, Credit, Insurance Underwriting and Operational Risk Score		**L**	**L**	**L**	**L**	**L**	**L**	**L**
Market, Credit and Op Risk - OVERRIDE								
Financial Soundness	Adequacy of Capital	L	L	N/A	L	L	L	L
	Liquidity	L	L	N/A	L	L	L	L
	Earnings	L	N/A	N/A	L	L	L	L
Financial Soundness Score		**L**	**L**	**N/A**	**L**	**L**	**L**	**L**
Financial Soundness - OVERRIDE								
Nature of Customers/Users and Products/Services	Type of Customer and/or User/Member	N/A	L	L	L	N/A	L	L
	Sources of Business and Distribution Mechanisms	N/A	L	L	L	L	L	L
	Types of Products/Services	N/A	L	L	L	L	L	L
	Market Efficiency	N/A	N/A	L	L	L	N/A	L
	Proper Markets	N/A	N/A	L	N/A	N/A	N/A	L
Customers, Products/Services, Score		**N/A**	**L**	**L**	**L**	**L**	**L**	**L**
Customers, Prod/Serv Score - OVERRIDE								

Risk Group	Risk Elements	Financial Failure (RTO ≤ 1 & 8)	Misconduct and Mismanagement (RTOs 2 & 9)	Consumer Understanding (RTOs 7 & 12)	Incidence of Fraud or Dishonesty (RTOs 3 & 13)	Incidence of Market Abuse (RTOs 3, 10 & 14)	Incidence of Money Laundering (RTOs 3 & 15)	Market Quality (RTOs 4 & 11)
Treatment of Customers/Users	Sales Force Training & Recruitment	N/A	L	L	N/A	N/A	N/A	N/A
	Basis of Remuneration of Sales Force	N/A	L	L	L	N/A	N/A	N/A
	Financial Promotion	N/A	L	L	N/A	N/A	N/A	N/A
	Accepting, Advising and Reporting to Customers/Users	N/A	L	L	N/A	N/A	N/A	L
	Dealing and Managing	N/A	L	L	L	L	N/A	L
	Security of Customer/User Assets	N/A	L	L	L	N/A	N/A	L
	Disclosure/Adequacy of Product Literature	N/A	L	L	N/A	N/A	N/A	N/A
	Membership Arrangements	L	N/A	L	L	L	N/A	L
Treatment of Customers/Users Score		**L**	**L**	**L**	**L**	**L**	**N/A**	**L**
Treatment of Customers/Users - OVERRIDE								
Organisation	Clarity of Legal/Ownership Structure	L	N/A	N/A	L	L	N/A	L
	Jurisdiction/Characteristics of Controllers/Group Entities	L	N/A	N/A	L	L	L	L
	Relationship with the Rest of the Group	L	L	N/A	L	L	L	L
Organisation Score		**L**	**L**	**N/A**	**L**	**L**	**L**	**L**
Organisation OVERRIDE								
Internal Systems and Controls	Risk Management	L	L	L	L	L	N/A	L
	Policies, Procedures & Controls	L	L	L	L	L	N/A	L
	Management Information	L	L	L	L	L	N/A	L
	IT Systems	L	L	L	L	L	N/A	L
	Financial and Regulatory Reporting and Accounting Policies	L	N/A	N/A	N/A	N/A	N/A	N/A
	Compliance	L	L	L	L	L	L	L
	Internal Audit	L	L	L	L	L	L	L
	Outsourcing/Third Party Providers	L	L	L	L	N/A	N/A	L
	Professional Advisors	L	L	N/A	L	L	N/A	N/A
	Business Continuity	L	L	L	N/A	N/A	N/A	L
	Money Laundering Controls	N/A	N/A	N/A	N/A	N/A	L	N/A
	Market Cleanliness	N/A	L	N/A	L	L	L	L
	Settlement Arrangements	L	N/A	N/A	N/A	N/A	N/A	L
Internal Controls Score		**L**	**L**	**L**	**L**	**L**	**L**	**L**
Internal Controls - OVERRIDE								
Board, Management and Staff	Corporate Governance	L	L	L	L	L	L	L
	Allocation and Definition of Management Responsibilities	L	L	L	L	L	L	L
	Quality of Management	L	L	L	L	L	L	L
	Human Resources	L	L	L	L	L	L	L
Board, etc. score		**L**	**L**	**L**	**L**	**L**	**L**	**L**
Board, etc - OVERRIDE								
Business and Compliance Culture	Relationship with Regulators	L	L	L	L	L	L	L
	Cultural Issues and Business Ethics	L	L	L	L	L	L	L
Controls Culture Score		**L**	**L**	**L**	**L**	**L**	**L**	**L**
Controls Culture Score - OVERRIDE								

Note: Intersections which are shaded out are not generally applicable. However, there may be cases where they are indeed applicable, and therefore all shaded boxes are subject to manual override if it is felt that they are relevant.

APPENDIX 3.C
ARROW II

The FSA's Risk-Assessment Framework, 2006, Appendix 4, Annex 1, pp. 54 and 55

Business Risk Elements

	Risk Groups		Risk Elements
1	Environmental Risks	1	Economic Environment
		2	Legislative/Political Environment
		3	Competitive Environment
		4	Capital Market Efficiency
2	Customers, Products & Markets	5	*Institutional Client/Counterparty Characteristics*
		6	*Retail Customer Characteristics*
		7	*Institutional Product/Market Characteristics*
		8	*Retail Product Characteristics*
		9	*Distribution Channels*
		10	*Conflicts of Interest*
3	Business Process Risks	11	Litigation/Legal Risk
		12	People Risk
		13	IT Systems
		14	Other Business Process Risks
		15	Structure & Ownership
4	Prudential Risks	16	Credit Risk
		17	Market Risk
		18	Operational Risk
		19	Liquidity Risk
		20	Insurance Underwriting Risk
		21	Element 2 Risks
		22	Element 3 Risks
		23	Element 4 Risks

Italics = core area

Control risk elements

	Risk Groups		Risk Elements
5	Customers, Products & Markets Controls	21	Accepting Customers
		22	Sales Process & Product Development
		23	Post Sale Handling of Customers/Counterparties
		24	Market Conduct Controls
		25	Membership Arrangements for RIEs
		26	Conflict of Interest Management
6	Financial and Operating Controls	27	Clearing and Settlement Arrangements
		28	Financial Controls
		29	IT Security and Controls
		30	Policies, Procedures and Controls
		31	Human Resources Controls
		32	*Security of Client Assets or Client Money*
		33	Business Continuity Planning
7	Prudential Risk Controls	34	Credit Risk Controls
		35	Market Risk Controls
		36	Operational Risk Controls
		37	Liquidity Risk Controls
		38	Insurance Risk Controls
		39	Element 2 Controls
		40	Element 3 Controls
		41	Element 4 Controls
8	*Control Functions*	42	*Compliance*
		43	*Internal Audit*
		44	*Enterprise-wide Risk Management*
9	*Management, Governance and Culture*	45	*Culture & Management*
		46	*Corporate Governance*
		47	*Relationship with Regulators*
		48	*Strategic Planning*
		49	*Relationship with Rest of Group*
10	*Capital & Liquidity*	50	*Adequacy of Capital*
		51	*Adequacy of Liquidity*
		52	*Adequacy of PII*

Italics = Core area

ENDNOTES

[1] Moody's Investors Service, *Rating Methodology – Bank Credit Risk (An Analytical Framework for Banks in Developed Markets)*, April 1999.

[2] To overcome this problem KMV incorporates market data into its model.

[3] In December 2004, the International Organization of Securities Commissioners (IOSCO) issued a code of conduct intended to guarantee the reliability and independence of credit rating agencies. It took the view that there would be sufficient market pressure on the rating agencies to abide by this voluntary code and therefore further regulation was not necessary. In March 2005, the Committee of European Securities Regulators (CESR) issued a report that considered whether the IOSCO code should be enforced by EU regulation. CESR viewed the oligopolistic nature of the market as a natural part of its function and credibility. The report concluded that regulation would not necessarily increase competition but in fact could erect further barriers to entry. In the US, credit rating agencies have to be registered with the Securities and Exchange Commission (SEC) as Nationally Recognized Statistical Rating Organizations (NRSRO). In June 2006, the SEC adopted rules to implement the Credit Rating Agency Reform Act (the "Rating Agency Act") enacted on 29 September 2006.

[4] The reader should be aware that information relating to the ARROW Framework and associated diagrams were correct at the time of printing but may not reflect current FSA practices/policies.

[5] ARROW is now a registered trademark.

[6] Reasonable Expectations: Regulation in a Non-zero Failure World, September 2003.

[7] The Firm Risk Assessment Framework, FSA, February 2003.

[8] The FSA's Risk Assessment Framework, FSA, August 2006.

[9] The FSA's Risk Assessment Framework, 2006, Appendix 1, p. 41.

[10] Aggregation – how aggressive the model is when aggregating the scores across rows and down columns. A more aggressive model will yield a greater dispersal of scores.

[11] Enhanced Analytics Initiative: www.enhancedanalytics.com

[12] Essor, B. *Building Stronger Customer Relationships*, Forrester Research.

[13] J.D. Power is a member of the McGraw-Hill group of companies (as is Standard & Poor's).

4

An Introduction to Risk and Default Analysis

4.1 PREDICTING SOUNDNESS

In this chapter, consideration is given to some of the more important stages in model development that have led up to the creation of today's advanced operational risk models. Expressed simply, operational risk models take a detailed internal (forensic) view of an organization whilst credit risk models take an external view. Clearly, both types of model should arrive at the same conclusion regarding the level of soundness of an organization (although internal models may also give an assessment of the level of responsiveness and flexibility, which impact upon shareholder value[1]). Certainly, the rating agencies are working in this direction and are seeking to enhance their assessment of internal risk systems and models.

Development of failure prediction models began in earnest in the late 1960s. Initially, these were relatively simple models based on financial ratios, their aim being merely to predict bankruptcy. Unlike current advanced risk models, these early models lacked any formal structure or understanding necessary for determining the level of soundness of an organization. Such weaknesses were recognized at the time by a number of researchers, including Ohlson,[2] who commented on the limitations of models that merely gave a binary result of either fail or non-fail:

> ... real world problems concern themselves with choices which have a richer set of possible outcomes. No decision problem I can think of has a payoff space which is partitioned naturally into the binary status bankruptcy versus non-bankruptcy.... Most of the analysis should simply be viewed as descriptive statistics... which may, to some extent, include estimated prediction error-rates... no "theories" of bankruptcy or usefulness of financial ratios are tested.

Wilcox[3] and others also commented on the lack of a conceptual framework and the limited amount of available data preventing the emergence of any useful generalization. Whilst solvency is clearly an important consideration, it is in fact the resultant outcome of a number of risk drivers. An organization with high fixed costs, achieving low profitability, and experiencing erratic cash flows will clearly be at risk of default. In determining the soundness of an organization a range of factors need to be considered, including the quality of management, the competitive position and franchise value of the organization and its quality and stability of earnings. Buzzell and Gale[4] amongst others, have discussed the link between strategy and performance, identifying the correlation between return-on-investment (ROI) and factors such as market share, perceived product quality, and capital intensity. An organization having a strong strategic market position will have a higher probability of achieving above average returns on investment and therefore enhancing its solvency, whereas weak organizations are less likely to achieve industry average returns and are therefore more likely to experience financial distress.

4.2   ARGENTI'S A-SCORE: CAUSES OF BUSINESS FAILURE

In 1976, Argenti[5] developed a non-statistical model (the A-score shortlist) that identified the main causal factors of business decline. Another factor, organization structure, was regarded as a related contributor (driver) of high costs and a lack of control. Poor management and a lack of financial control stood out as the most frequent causes of financial decline. The model gives a points score, where a score of 25 or above indicates danger, particularly if the score in the "Mistakes" section is 15 or more or the "Defects" section score is 10 or over.

Defects

Autocratic chief executive	8
Chairman and chief executive combined	4
Passive board	2
Unbalanced skills, especially over-technical	2
Weak finance director	2
Poor management depth below board level	1
No budgetary control	3
No cash flow plans, or no cash flow updating	3
No reliable costing system	3
Poor response to change, unawareness of business environment	15
Total for Defects	**43**
Danger mark for Defects	**10**

Mistakes

High debt gearing	15
Overtrading (inadequate equity base)	15
Big project in relation to business size	15
Total for Mistakes	**45**
Danger mark for Mistakes	**15**

Symptoms

Financial signs, e.g. Z-score warning signs	4
Creative accounting, especially changes to previous policy resulting in increased stock values, lower depreciation, and capitalization of R&D or repairs/maintenance	4
Non-financial signs, including deterioration in product quality/service, premises and morale	3
Terminal signs	1
Total for Symptoms	**12**
Total overall maximum possible	**100**
Danger mark overall	**25**

4.3   STATISTICAL FAILURE PREDICTION MODELS

Statistical failure prediction models fall into four categories, depending upon the approach taken:

1. univariate analysis;
2. multi-discriminant analysis (MDA);
3. conditional logit regression analysis; and
4. gambler's ruin approach.

4.3.1   Beaver's univariate model

William Beaver was one of the early pioneers in the field of bankruptcy prediction. He evaluated a number of financial ratios[6] and concluded that one univariate – Cash-flow: Total Debt – was the best predictor of bankruptcy. This ratio appeared to work reasonably well over a period up to five years before failure. Beaver's approach was to consider a business as a reservoir of liquid assets, which was continuously being replenished by cash inflows and drained by cash outflows.

It is interesting to contrast the approach adopted by Beaver to that currently employed by the rating agencies, who calculate a wide range of ratios in an effort to assess specific factors determining financial strength.

4.3.2   Altman's multi-discriminant analysis (Z-score) model

Edward Altman[7] built on the work of Beaver and sought to develop a model that would overcome the potential problem of individual ratios giving conflicting indications.[8] The significance of Altman's model was that it enabled the *level* of solvency of a firm to be determined (referred to as its "Z-score"). This score can be used to infer the probability of default and hence the default rate. Altman found that firms having a Z-score greater than 2.99 were solvent, whilst those having a Z-score below 1.81 were bankrupt.

Altman's model uses a linear discriminant analysis approach (Section 26.8) and was originally comprised of five ratios representing liquidity, solvency, profitability, leverage, and asset turnover, respectively. It was arranged in the following form:

$$Z = 1.2X_1 + 1.4X_2 + 3.3X_3 + 0.6X_4 + 0.999X_5$$

where: X_1 = working capital/total assets; X_2 = retained earnings/total assets; X_3 = earnings before interest and taxes/total assets; X_4 = market value of equity/book value of total liabilities; and X_5 = sales/total assets.

The original Z-Score model was developed in 1968 and at the time proved to be very accurate, correctly predicting bankruptcy in 94 % of cases. It was based on a sample of 66 US manufacturing companies. A matched pair analysis was carried out, with the 33 firms in the bankruptcy group being taken from those companies that filed for bankruptcy under the United States Bankruptcy Act between 1946 and 1965.

Altman subsequently revised the model to minimize potential specific industry effects related to asset turnover. Hence a new variable (net book worth/total liabilities) was introduced to replace variables X_4 and X_5.

The Altman Z-Score model remains widely used by practitioners to predict corporate bankruptcy. However, as Sheppard[9] has indicated, despite its success, the model does have some significant weaknesses. Firstly, it assumes that the variables in the sample data are normally distributed; however, if this assumption is incorrect then the predictors selected may be inappropriate. Secondly, the model has a linear specification, although as Saunders[10] points out "the path to bankruptcy may be highly nonlinear."

Ratio analysis has been challenged as an analysis technique. Whilst it can indicate areas requiring investigation it does not provide answers (only questions). Altman stated:

> ... *academicians seem to be moving toward the elimination of ratio analysis as an analytical technique in assessing the performance of the business enterprise. Theorists downgrade arbitrary rules of thumb (such as company ratio comparisons) widely used by practitioners. Since attacks on the relevance on ratio analysis emanate from many esteemed members of the scholarly world, does this mean that ratio analysis is limited to the world of 'nuts and bolts'? Or, has the significance of such an approach been unattractively garbed and therefore unfairly handicapped? Can we bridge the gap, rather than sever the link, between traditional ratio analysis and the more rigorous*

*statistical techniques, which have become popular among academicians in recent years? Along
with our primary interest, corporate bankruptcy, I am also concerned with an assessment of ratio
analysis as an analytical technique.*

4.3.3   Ohlson's logit model

The one-year prediction model developed by Ohlson in 1980 is generally considered to
have represented the next generation of financial distress prediction models, adopting a more
complex approach based on *"multiple lenses of perception."* It remains widely regarded and
is considered to be one of the leading models of its type. It is often cited by researchers who
use an O-Score, calculated using Ohlson's original coefficients from Model 1, as a benchmark
proxy for financial distress. Begley *et al.* (1996)[11] and Hillegeist,[12] together with others, have
commented on the model's predictive accuracy.

The model adopts the practice of using multiple variables to more fully capture the significance of a particular financial issue:

- In the case of **liquidity**, the model uses both *working capital-to-total assets* and *current
  liabilities-to-current assets.*
- For **profitability** in addition to *net income-to-total assets*, the model employs a discrete
  variable (INTWO), which is assigned the value of 1 if net income was negative for the last
  two years or 0 otherwise. In addition, net income is also scaled.
- The level of **solvency** is determined by *total liabilities-to-total assets* (TL/TA) plus the use
  of a discrete variable (OENEG) that takes the value of 1 if owners' equity is negative or
  0 otherwise.
- The significance of the **size** of an organization is captured using two variables: the *log of
  total assets* scaled by the GDP deflator (SIZE), and *funds from operations-to-total liabilities*
  (FFO/TL).

4.3.4   Zavgren's refined logit model

Since the original works of Beaver and Altman, many more traditionally based failure prediction models have been developed, virtually all being either matched-pair multi-discriminate
models or logit[13] models. Efforts have largely been concentrated on refining the variables in
order to improve their predictive ability. The use of more powerful and robust statistical packages has greatly assisted the process. The underlying tacit assumption made in these models
is that the future will be the same as the past.

In 1985, Zavgren[14] developed a model using logit analysis in order to refine Altman's model,
correcting for the problem of assumed normal distribution. Given its use of logit analysis,
Zavgren's model is generally considered to be more robust.[15] One of the advantages of logit
analysis is that it provides a probability assessment of failure, which could be considered as
an assessment of the effectiveness of management (i.e. the greater the probability of failure
the weaker the management).

Logit analysis began to replace muti-discriminant analysis from the late 1980s,[16] and
discrete hazard regression (which is similar to the single-period logit methodology) gradually
became the preferred method during the 1990s.

Research subsequently found that neural networks performed similarly and could therefore
be used in conjunction with logit analysis to provide supporting confirmation.[17]

4.3.5   Wilcox's gambler's ruin approach

Wilcox[18] also adopted Beaver's reservoir concept, although he applied it differently. In 1976 he derived the probability of failure of firms using what is known as the "gambler's ruin" approach. Under this approach, bankruptcy is said to occur when the net liquidation value (NLV) of a company becomes negative (i.e. when total liabilities exceed the total value of assets assuming liquidation values).

Clearly, the NLV varies constantly from period to period, being increased by cash inflows and decreased by cash outflows, defined by Wilcox as "adjusted cash flow."

Wilcox used the gambler's ruin approach to demonstrate that the probability of financial distress is dependent upon:

1. the initial level of funds (NLV) available to prevent ruin;
2. the amount of net cashflow received (positive "adjusted cash flow"); and
3. volatility (i.e. the level of adjusted cash flow "at risk" each period), referred to by Wilcox as the size of the bet.

In explaining the relevance and applicability of his model, Wilcox stated:

> The **inflow rate** ... can be increased through a higher average return on investment. However, having a major impact here usually requires long-term changes in strategic position. This is difficult to control over a short time period except by divestitures of peripheral unprofitable businesses ... The average **outflow rate** is controlled by managing the average growth rate of corporate assets. Effective capital budgeting ... requires resource allocation emphasizing those business units which have the highest future payoff. ... The size of **the bet** is the least understood factor in financial risk. Yet management has substantial control over it. Variability in liquidity flows governs the size of the bet. This variability can be managed through dividend policy, through limiting earning variability and investment variability, and through controlling the co-variation between profits and investments ... True earnings smoothing is attained by control of exposure to volatile industries, diversification, and improved strategic position.

4.3.6   Vinso's enhanced gambler's ruin model

Others who adapted a gambler's ruin approach to bankruptcy prediction include Santomero[19] and Vinso.[20] Whilst the statistics underlying gambler's ruin models may appear complex, in general they lack the conceptual framework of business failure sought by Wilcox and Argenti. Vinso did, however, begin to move in this direction.

Vinso supported Wilcox in his emphasis on cash flow but also identified the need to take into account the organization's debt capacity, stating: ... debt capacity, if available ... must be included as the firm can use this source without being forced to confront shareholders, creditors, a third party or a bankruptcy court ... debt holders or other creditors will force reorganization if a firm is unable to meet contractual obligations because working capital is too low and the firm cannot obtain more debt. He also recognized the need to differentiate between fixed and variable costs, stating: ... earnings come to (the) firm from revenue(s) ... less the costs incurred in producing (the revenues). There are two types of costs to be considered: variable, which change according to the stochastic nature of the revenue sources, and fixed costs, which do not vary with revenue but are a function of the period. So, revenue less variable costs ... can be defined as variable profit, which is available to pay fixed costs.

Vinso further enhanced the gambler's ruin model by developing a safety index, used to predict the point in time when ruin is most likely to occur (referred to as "first passage time"). The model takes into account the variability of "expected contribution margin amounts."

4.4   CREDIT RISK MODELS

It is often said that one bank's operational risk is another bank's credit risk – i.e. a bank that experiences an operational risk event may ultimately default on its obligations, thus causing a credit risk event at a counter-party bank. Clearly, a bank making a loan would like full and detailed information about the borrower in order to properly assess the risk. Unfortunately, due to a lack of transparency this is unlikely to be the case, particularly if the lending bank is merely a junior participant in a syndicate. Given the lack of internal forensic information, credit risk models have adopted alternative approaches.

Taking an operational risk assessment of a bank and comparing it to its external credit rating can be compared to the practice adopted by external auditors when conducting an audit of a computer system. Firstly, the auditors carry out an audit *around* the system, then they audit *through* the system. One method is a check on the other. In comparison, a credit risk assessment can be considered the external assessment around the system, whilst an operational risk assessment can be considered as the internal forensic view through the system. Transparency, as required by Pillar 3 of Basel II, should ultimately lead to operational risk assessments informing credit risk assessments, thus making the market better informed and more responsive.

Whilst it is not the intention to examine credit risk in any great detail in this chapter, it is, instructive to look at some of the modeling approaches used. The traditional approach to credit risk management is to set tolerances for exposure, by category and by specific obligor – expressed simply, "don't put all your eggs in one basket." The categories used may include those defined by regulatory bodies and credit rating agencies as well as those of particular interest to an individual bank, such as country, currency, and corporate governance index.

The more sophisticated approaches to credit risk involve use of models that take account not only of the credit quality of the counterparty but also the resultant portfolio exposure. Banks may also use internal capital allocation as an internal management charge in order to take account of the price of credit risk.

From a modeling perspective, credit risk can be defined as Expected Loss (EL), which is expressed as a function of three variables:

1. **Default Rate (DR)**: defined as how likely or how often a firm will default.
2. **Loss In the Event of Default (LIED)**: defined as the current market value of an asset, adjusted for any costs that would be incurred, any recoveries achieved, and any collateral realized.
3. **Potential Credit Exposure (PCE)**: defined as a measure of exposure an asset might have if a default occurs at sometime in the future.

It is written as:

$$EL = DR \times LIED \times PCE$$

Unfortunately, this traditional credit risk model has a number of weaknesses. Default Rates can be volatile, rather than constant as assumed in the model. Also, the distribution of default rates is, in fact, highly asymmetric. The risk of credit rating downgrade migration is ignored in the model. Correlation and portfolio effects are also ignored.

4.4.1 Default rate

From a modeling and operational risk perspective, the Default Rate is of particular interest. The four methods typically used to assess this are:

1. **Subjective judgement.** This is the traditional approach used by credit risk officers. It relies on their expertise, including intimate knowledge of the client and the market. The approach suffers from subjectivity and resultant inconsistency. However, as part of a credit risk management system it can add additional sensitivity and responsiveness not always available with statistical models alone.
2. **External ratings.** This approach is based on the default ratings produced by the main credit rating agencies (Moodys, S&P and Fitch) and other knowledge vendors. The probability of default for a particular rating category is applied to all creditors in that category.
3. **Internal ratings.** The internal ratings based (IRB) approach, as defined by Basel II, allows a bank to establish its own ratings methodology. This must be consistently applied and must employ a basic set of risk factors, possibly incorporating external credit ratings. Examples of credit scoring models, include those of Altman and Ohlson, are discussed above.
4. **Models.** Fundamentally, there are two types of model to consider:
   - the asset-based option model (e.g. the Merton 1974 model, and the KMV model); and
   - the actuarial sudden default model (e.g. the CreditRisk+ model).

4.5   MERTON'S 1974 MODEL

In 1974, Robert C. Merton[21] proposed a model for assessing the credit risk of a company based on treating the company's equity as a call option on its assets. Fundamentally, the model relates credit risk to the capital structure of the firm.[22] It assumes the firm issues two single forms of security – equity and debt – with the equity receiving no dividends and the debt being a pure discount bond repayable in the future at a promised time T. If at time T the value of the firm's assets exceeds the debt D then the whole debt can be repaid in full. Whereas, if the assets are not sufficient to fully meet the debt, then the firm defaults, with the creditor receiving an amount equal to the value of the assets but with the equity shareholder getting nothing.

The value of the firm's equity E at time T is the asset value A at time T less the original debt D at time 0. It is expressed as:

$$E(T) = \max[A(T) - D(0), 0].$$

The model assumes the value of the firm's assets follow a lognormal diffusion process with a constant volatility.

Merton's model has a number of limitations:

1. The assumption that the firm's debt financing consists of a zero-coupon debt with a single maturity date is in practice likely to be an oversimplification.
2. The Black & Scholes (1973)[23] simplifying assumptions, adopted by Merton, are questionable in the context of corporate debt.

3. The firm's value is not directly observable, which makes assigning values to it and its volatility problematic. The volatility of equity is not a particularly good proxy for asset volatility.

4.6   THE KMV MODEL

One of the most successful commercial derivatives of the Merton (1974) Asset Value Model is that developed by Moody's KMV. This provides an expected default frequency (EDF), which can be used as an estimate of the default rate (DR). It is therefore a forward-looking measure of the probability of actual default. As with the Merton (1974) model, the KMV model relates the observable value of equity to the theoretical call value. It relies almost exclusively on externally available market information, rather than taking a detailed internal forensic approach to risk.

The model is based on a firm's:

- capital structure;
- current asset value; and
- volatility of returns on assets.

It assumes the firm has a capital structure comprised of equity, preferred convertible shares, long-term perpetual debt, and short-term cash-equivalent debt.

KMV has built up a substantial database, which shows that in actual practice firms default when their asset value is at a level between total liabilities and short-term debt (referred to by KMV as the *default point*).

The main weaknesses of the KMV approach are:

- subjective estimation of the input parameters is required;
- the assumption of normality of asset returns is required to construct theoretical expected default frequencies (EDFs);
- account is not taken of the different types of long-term bonds, factors such as seniority, collateral, or convertibility being ignored; and
- the EDFs of private firms have tended to be calculated using comparable quoted company data (compared on the basis of accounting data). However, KMV is building a significant private company database.

4.7   CREDITRISK+

In contrast to the option-type models mentioned previously, actuarial models use mathematical techniques applied widely in the insurance industry to model sudden default by an obligor.

CreditRisk+[24] is one of the best-known statistical actuarial sudden default models. It makes no assumptions about the causes of default; instead, it is based on a portfolio approach to modeling credit default risk. It takes into account information relating to size and maturity of an exposure together with the credit quality and systematic risk of an obligor.

This approach is similar to that taken by market risk management, where no attempt is made to model the causes of market price movements. The CreditRisk+ model considers default rates as continuous random variables and incorporates the volatility of default rates in order to capture the uncertainty in the level of default rates. Often, background factors, such as the state of the economy, may cause the incidence of defaults to be correlated, even though there is no causal link between them. The effects of these background factors are incorporated into the CreditRisk+ model through the use of default rate volatilities and sector analysis, rather than using default correlations as explicit inputs into the model.

The CreditRisk+ model does not take into account the possible loss in value resulting from a credit rating downgrade.

4.8   PORTFOLIO CREDIT RISK MODELS

Credit risk models that also take into account the risk of downgrade (migration risk) as well as default risk include: CreditMetrics, by J. P. Morgan; Portfolio Manager, by Moody's KMV; and CreditPortfolioView, by McKinsey. However a detailed review of these models is outside the scope of this book. Interested readers are advised to refer to other texts.[25]

4.9   INTERNAL OPERATIONAL RISK MODELS

The development of operational risk models, including expert systems, has been strongly influenced by the requirements of Basel II. Whilst the regulators have wisely avoided being overly prescriptive in what remains a developing and complex area, they have set some important requirements. In particular, to meet qualifying criteria for an Advanced Measurement Approach (AMA), four basic elements must be included:

1. internal data;
2. external data;
3. scenario analysis; and
4. factors reflecting the business environment and internal control systems.

Whilst there is no accepted measurement methodology, the approaches adopted by AMA banks tend to be broadly similar. Although there are differences in emphasis, a bank will need to consider the past, present, and future.

4.9.1   Past: historical LDA approach (see Figure 4.1)

Those banks emphasizing the past use standard statistical and actuarial modeling techniques to analyze historical data in order to find underlying risk trends. The basic tacit assumption is that the future will strongly mirror the past. The Industry Technical Working Group (ITWG)[26] has stated that those banks adopting this approach: *believe that loss data is the most objective risk indicator currently available, which is also reflective of the unique risk profile of each financial institution.*[27] However, the ITWG also recognized that internal loss data has some inherent weaknesses. Being backward looking, the methodology will not be responsive to changes in the risk and control environment, and where data is not available in sufficient quantity then a reasonable assessment of exposure will become difficult. Banks using this approach include: Citigroup, JP Morgan Chase, Deutsche Bank, BNP Paribas, Credit Lyonnaise, Royal Bank of Scotland, ING, ABN Amro, Bank Intesa, San Paolo IMI, Sumitomo Mitsui, and the Bank of Montreal, amongst others.

The Loss Distribution Approach AMA model, outlined by the ITWG in Figure 4.1, shows how consideration is given to the past, present and future. The model has three stages:

Stage 1 is concerned with establishing a credible set of historical data, from which an aggregate loss distribution curve can be generated. Firstly, internal loss data is analyzed

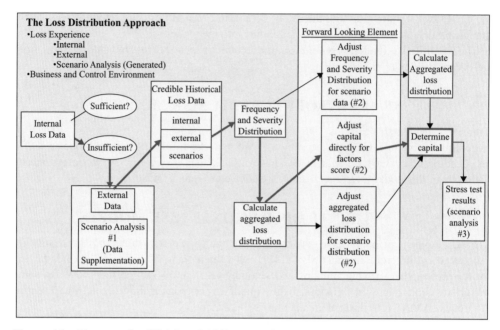

Figure 4.1 Elements of an LDA-based AMA approach.
Source: Industry Technical Working Group (ITWG), reproduced with permission.

to see if there is sufficient data. Where this is not the case, it is supplemented by external loss data and other generated data. Once a credible dataset has been established, frequency and severity curves are determined for the various risk categories. An aggregate loss distribution curve is then generated.

Stage 2 adds a forward-looking element to the analysis. Firstly, the frequency and severity distributions are adjusted using scenario analysis. Secondly, the capital required is directly adjusted to take account of the assessment of the business and control environment. Thirdly, adjustment is made to the aggregated loss distribution in order to take account of the scenario distribution. The capital requirement is then determined (at the 99.9 % confidence level).

Stage 3 concerns stress testing, to determine the robustness of the model. Typically, this involves the use of scenario analysis to consider possible extreme events and their likely impact given occurrence.

4.9.2 Present: control risk self assessment scorecard approach (see Figure 4.2)

This approach concentrates on risk drivers and controls using scorecards and questionnaires, which effectively act as expert systems, to assess the quality of the internal control environment and the level of exposure to specific risk drivers. Capital allocation, based on RDCA (Risk Drivers and Controls Approaches) outputs, is used to provide behavioral incentives for improving risk management. The emphasis is on direct relevance. However, to rely on the present at the exclusion of the past and future would imply that a tacit assumption was being made that the business environment was dynamic and, therefore, the past was largely irrelevant plus the future could not be determined with any real degree of accuracy. Banks using this

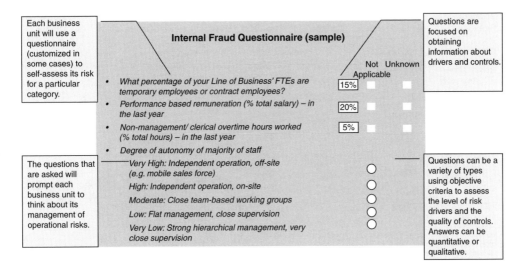

Figure 4.2   Example of an RDCA questionnaire. The questionnaire probes for information on risk drivers and quality of controls within each risk category.
Source: Industry Technical Working Group (ITWG), reproduced with permission.

approach include: Australia & New Zealand Banking Group, Bank of New York, HBOS, and Mellon Bank.

The top-down allocation of group economic capital takes account of a number of factors. Risks are categorized according to type (taking account of the recommended Basel categories) and then weighted. Answers to questions are scored, with a typical scoring system ranging from 1 (optimal) to 10 (sub-optimal). All questions are then weighted in comparison with one another to indicate their "relative importance." Sizing factors are used to take account of the size of the business unit and the relative level of risk it presents. For example, headcount (or full-time equivalents) may be used as a scaling factor for two similar departments of different size. In practice, sizing may require the use of multiple organizational characteristics.

4.9.3   Future: scenario approach (see Figure 4.3)

Banks that concentrate on the future seek to identify the probability and impact of possible future events in an attempt to be broadly prepared for whatever may happen – i.e. a business continuity approach is adopted through the use of scenario analysis. Banks employing this approach include: Dresdner Bank, Fortis, UFJ Holdings, HBOS, RBOS, Barclays, Lloyds TSB, CSFB, Banc Intesa, and Euroclear.

4.10   COMMERCIALLY AVAILABLE OPERATIONAL RISK SYSTEMS AND MODELS

A significant proportion of banks appear to have developed their own internal operational risk expert systems and models. Whilst initial research by ORRF would appear to suggest that there are approximately 150 firms offering operational risk software solutions, closer analysis

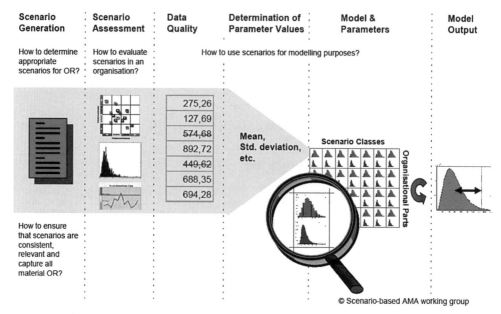

Figure 4.3 Scenario-based AMA approach – overview of concept.
Source: Industry Technical Working Group (ITWG), reproduced with permission.

shows that these are often fragmented partial solutions. Some of those worthy of investigation include offerings from: Algorithmics (Fitch), HSBC Operational Risk Consultancy, Raft Radar (Financial Objects plc), Methodware, and Agena, although others may be equally educational and practically capable depending upon the requirements and sophistication of the user.

Given the complexity of operational risk, solutions are often subdivided into various modules, which can in some cases be interlinked to provide an enterprise-wide solution. Such a system may include the following modules:

- loss data register;
- quantification (LDA and EVT);
- CRSA – Control Risk Self Assessment;
- scenario analysis;
- key indicators and balance scorecard;
- systems analysis audit;
- professional competency;
- causal analysis modeling; and
- dynamic financial analysis.

ENDNOTES

[1] For an introduction to this subject, see:
Myers, S.C. (1977). Determinants of Corporate Borrowing, *Journal of Financial Economics* **5**, 147–175.
Copeland, T. and Antikarov, V. (2001). *Real Options: A Practitioner's Guide*, New York: Texere LLC.

[2] Ohlson, J.A. (1980). Financial Ratios and the Probabilistic Prediction of Bankruptcy. *Journal of Accounting Research*, 109–131.

[3] Wilcox, J.W. (1973). A Prediction of Business Failure Using Accounting Data, *Journal of Accounting Research*, **11**, 163–179.

[4] Buzzell, R.D. and Gale, B.T. (1987). *The PIMS Principles Linking Strategy to Performance*. New York: The Free Press.

[5] Argenti, J. (1976). *Corporate Collapse*, Maidenhead: McGraw-Hill.

[6] Beaver identified 30 ratios concerning profitability, liquidity and solvency. These were applied to 79 matched pairs of bankrupt/nonbankrupt firms.

[7] Altman, Edward I. (1968). Financial Ratios, Discriminate Analysis and the Prediction of Corporate Bankruptcy. *The Journal of Finance*, 589–609.

[8] Cook, R.A. and Nelson, J. L. (1998). A Conspectus of Business Failure Forecasting. (12 April 1998).

[9] Sheppard, Jerry Paul. (1994). The Dilemma of Matched Pairs and Diversified Firms in Bankruptcy Prediction Models. *The Mid-Atlantic Journal of Business*, **11:2**, 9–25.

[10] Saunders, A. (1999). *Credit Risk Measurement: New Approaches to Value at Risk and Other Paradigms*. New York, John Wiley & Sons Inc.

[11] Begley, J., Ming, J. and Watts, S. (1997). Bankruptcy Classification Errors in the 1980s: An Empirical Analysis of Altman's and Ohlson's Models, *Review of Accounting Studies*.

[12] Hillegeist, S.A., Keating, E.K., Cram, D.P. and Lundstedt, K.G. (2004). Assessing the Probability of Bankruptcy. *Review of Accounting Studies* **9**, 5–34.

[13] Logit and probit come from regression modeling of binary responses (zero-one events). The logit is the logarithm of the odds ratio of the probability of getting one result with respect to the other, i.e. $f(p) = \log\{p/(1-p)\}$, where p is the probability of a response, is a logistic curve. The probit curve is the quantile function for the normal distribution. Usually, in medicine, p is a function $p(x)$ of the dose and $p(x)$ is the probability of a reaction. See also Section 18.4.6.

[14] Zavgren, C. V. (1985). Assessing the Vulnerability to Failure of American Industrial Firms: A Logistic Analysis. *Journal of Business Finance and Accounting*, **12:1**, 19–45.

[15] Lo, A.W. (1986). Logit Versus Discriminant Analysis: A Specification Test and Application to Corporate Bankruptcies. *Journal of Econometrics*, **31**, 151–178.

[16] Stickney, C.P. (1996). *Financial Reporting and Statement Analysis, 3rd edition*. Texas: The Dryden Press.

[17] Altman, E.I. Marco G. and Varetto F. (1994). Corporate Distress Diagnosis: Comparisons Using Linear Discriminant Analysis and Neural Networks (the Italian Experience). *The Journal of Banking and Finance*. **3**, 505–29.

[18] Wilcox, J.W. (1971). A Gambler's Ruin: Prediction of Business Failure Using Accounting Data, *Sloan Management Review*, **12**, 1–10.
Wilcox, J.W. (1976). The Gambler's Ruin Approach to Business Risk, Sloan Management Review.

[19] Santomero, A.M. and Vinso, J.D. (1977). Estimating the Probability of Failure for Commercial Banks and the Banking System. *Journal of Banking and Finance*, **2**, 185–205.

[20] Vinso, J.D. (1979). A Determination of the Risk of Ruin, *Journal of Financial and Quantitative Analysis*. **14:1**, 77–100.

[21] Merton, Robert C. (1974). On the Pricing of Corporate Debt: The Risk Structure of Interest Rates. *Journal of Finance*, **29**, 449–470.

[22] The **Merton Model** is also referred to as the **Asset Value Model**. Merton anticipated the model in 1970, and he actively supported the work of Black and Scholes, who proposed it in their seminal paper on option pricing: Black, F. and Scholes, Myron S. (1973). The Pricing of Options and Corporate Liabilities, *Journal of Political Economy* **81**, 637–654.

[23] Black, F. and Scholes, M. (1973). The Pricing of Options and Corporate Liabilities. *Journal of Political Economy* **81**, 637–654.

[24] Credit Suisse Financial Products (1997). CreditRisk+, A Credit Risk Management Framework. http://www.csfb.com/institutional/research/assets/creditrisk.pdf.

[25] Crouhy M., Galai D. and Mark R. (2000). A Comparative Analysis of Current Credit Risk Models, *Journal of Banking and Finance* **24**, 59–117.

[26] The Industry Technical Working Group (ITWG) was a small group of operational risk practitioners, formed in 2000 from financial institutions around the world, who were interested in developing and sharing practical new ideas for the quantification of operational risk.

[27] Basel Committee on Banking Supervision Risk Management Group: Conference on Leading Edge Issues in Operational Risk Measurement, 29 May 2003 http://www.newyorkfed.org/events/banking/2003/con052903.

5
Control Risk Self Assessment (CRSA) – A Behavioural Approach to Risk Management

5.1 INTRODUCTION

Competitiveness through continuous improvement, innovation, and adaptability promotes responsiveness to change, the importance of which was highlighted by Charles Darwin. Businesses are constantly changing; therefore, there is need to continually visualize alternatives. In such an environment, rigid structures are found to be inappropriate, leading to inefficiency and underperformance; hence, the assumption of singular best-practice is to be avoided. Organizational practice is not singular and should not be imposed; an organizational structure cannot be optimized. The need is for many self-determined and empowered business units rather than one rigidly controlled monolith. The requirement is for distributed intelligence, contained within communities of practice.

Risk management is continuing to evolve through greater risk awareness. Current good practice standards will undoubtedly become outdated. Therefore systems and controls need to be continuously reviewed for relevance, being simplified and minimized wherever possible. There is evidence of risk management theorists and practitioners continuously seeking to align the level of assurance their approach can provide with their appreciation of risk awareness and organizational behaviour.[1]

Risk management is exhibiting parallels with quality management, with a progressive move away from policing and post event checking (involving a constant search for appropriate measurements and controls), towards recognition of the importance of ownership of risk.

Control Risk Self Assessment (CRSA) seeks to capture and apply the expert knowledge resident within an organization to the assessment and control of risks. It is a proactive approach to operational risk management, seeking to embed a risk-aware culture throughout the organization. The focus of Control Risk Self Assessment is on relevance, with responsiveness to change being a primary consideration.

Whilst CRSA is largely a qualitative, behavioural-science based approach to risk management, it can be supported and enhanced by quantitative tools where appropriate. The methodology concentrates on risk drivers and controls using scorecards and questionnaires – which effectively act as non-rigid expert systems – to assess the quality of the internal control environment and the level of exposure to specific risk drivers. Consequently, CRSA can lead to greater understanding of operational risk exposures, through surfacing tacit assumptions, and capturing knowledge resident within the organization. This increases internal transparency. Hence it enables development of a focused "road-map" for improving risk management, which can be reinforced by behavioral incentives including the allocation of capital to different strategic business units and business lines, based on their assessment "scores."

CRSA is a well-established methodology that is widely used, with varying degrees of success, in many industries, including banking and particularly auditing. It has been taken to a high degree of sophistication by some. The original development is accredited to the Gulf Oil Company of Canada which, in 1987, introduced a "facilitated meeting" self-assessment approach, and subsequently went on to develop the methodology over a 10 year period. Whilst others had used related approaches previously, these were not applied in such a formalized and sophisticated manner.

5.2   ADVOCATES

Those banks advocating the use of Control Risk Self Assessment as a methodology towards meeting the Basel II requirements for an advanced measurement approach (AMA) for operational risk, include:

- Australia New Zealand Bank (ANZ);
- Halifax Bank of Scotland (HBOS);
- Bank of New York; and
- Mellon Bank.

5.3   DEFINING CONTROL RISK SELF ASSESSMENT

CRSA has been defined as "a process which allows individual line managers and staff to participate in reviewing existing controls for adequacy (both now and in the predicted future) and recommending, agreeing and implementing improvements (modifications, additions or elimination of existing controls)."[2]

Similarly, CIPFA (the Chartered Institute of Public Finance and Accountancy) has defined CRSA as "a formalized documented and committed approach to the regular fundamental and open review by managers and staff of the strength of control systems designed and operated to achieve business objectives and guard against risk within their sphere of influence".[3]

The values and principles incorporated in CRSA recognize involvement (i.e. "participation") of line management and staff (i.e. "communities of practice"), in deep and searching reviews and reappraisals (i.e. "committed," "fundamental," "open," and "systematic" reviews), through exploration, reflection and action (i.e. "evaluating," "recommending," "agreeing" and "implementing"), to take account of the fluid nature of organizational configuration in value creating activities (i.e. "spheres of influence").

5.4   BENEFITS AND LIMITATIONS OF A CRSA APPROACH

In summary, the primary benefits accruing from successfully implementing a Control Risk Self Assessment methodology are:

- alignment of corporate and business unit objectives;
- an improvement in the management and control of risks;
- ownership of risks and controls, leading to continuous improvement;
- the capture of knowledge within the organization, enabling challenge of tacit assumptions;
- assistance in improving competence levels (providing relevant action-based education and training);

- fostering teamwork and communication; and
- improving responsiveness, providing early identification of potential risks.

The successful implementation of a CRSA methodology requires commitment and understanding from management at all levels, including senior management. In the early part of the new millennium the Bank of England, with support from external consultants, attempted to introduce a CRSA system. Unfortunately, the project failed to meet expectations, with consequential results.

The main limitations to CRSA are:

- An open and supportive organizational culture is required. Where this is not the case, participants may feel threatened. Consequently, information obtained may not be entirely accurate and teamwork may not be effective.
- The effort and costs involved can be considerable. These are often underestimated.
- The information must be continuously updated. This can lead to fatigue and decay. Individuals often give the same answer as they gave last time.
- Skilled individuals with expert knowledge are required to facilitate the elicitation workshops.
- A broad range of skills is required to properly challenge any assumptions and assertions and to avoid group-think.
- The methodology must clearly demonstrate how it is adding value. Given the considerable effort involved in implementing and maintaining the system, if it is not successfully embedded and used as an essential part of the management and control process, it will gradually be abandoned.

5.5 RESIDUAL RISKS

Controls seek to reduce risks to an acceptable level; they do not seek to completely eliminate risk. The resultant residual risk represents the risk profile of the organization, which requires approval by senior management. Residual risk can be regarded as the probability of an organization not achieving its objectives.

Risks relate to an organization's comparative strengths, weaknesses, threats, and opportunities. These change constantly. Consequently, management must continuously review and revise the organization's objectives and residual risk profile in the light of new information available.

5.6 METHODOLOGY

In outline, the CRSA process involves the following stages:

- **Preparation and planning.** The preparation and planning process involves determining the objectives, scope, timing, and outputs required from the workshops. In addition, information may need to be obtained and prepared concerning current recognized industry best practice, weaknesses identified by internal audit reports, and proposed developments, together with regulatory and legislative requirements. Where necessary, training programmes may need to be held to ensure everyone participating is fully aware of the process and what is required of them.

- **Participants.** The primary participants are those who are identified as owners of the key objectives, risks and controls. In addition, those with relevant expert knowledge may also be asked to participate (i.e. members of the risk function, internal audit, IT, compliance, etc.).
- **Tools and techniques.** Various tools and techniques will be required in order to: record outputs of facilitated meetings; provide easy interrogation of information; consolidate the information into reports; and to monitor the progress of implementation.
- **Facilitation.** Workshops need to be facilitated by experienced experts. The approach adopted will vary depending upon the culture of the organization. This may need to be ascertained by prior research during the preparation and planning stage. Where the culture is supportive and reinforcing, participants can be expected to give candid responses that can then be examined. Where this is not the case, greater reliance will need to be placed upon anonymous responses to questionnaires and external reviews from the internal auditing function.
- **Validation.** Validation is concerned with comparing the outputs from facilitated meetings to what has been experienced in the past and to what external experts expect. Validation is particularly important with regard to high impact risks and areas where residual risk remains high. A considerable degree of validation should have taken place as part of the facilitated workshop activities, through the surfacing and challenging of tacit assumptions. However, a final separate test for realism is still necessary. The validation team may include representatives from various supporting staff functions such as the group risk function, internal audit, legal and compliance, IT, etc.
- **Reporting.** The final reports emanating from the CRSA process represent agreed action plans, which should link into and form part of the organization's overarching corporate plans (i.e. giving a "balanced scorecard").
- **Continuous monitoring.** To ensure the organization achieves its objectives (both on time and within budget) and adheres to its chosen risk profile, continuous monitoring is necessary by the business units and control functions (e.g. group risk function, internal audit, etc).

5.7 TYPES OF MEETING

Fundamentally, facilitated meetings can have four primary aims, these being, to address:

1. **Objectives**. Objectives influence the strategy to be pursued, which in turn determines the structure of the organization. Objectives need to be cascaded down throughout the organization and any incompatibilities and risks identified. Consideration needs to be given to the impact of not meeting any objectives.
2. **Risks**. Consideration has to be given to the risks faced by the organization, the level of residual risks remaining after application of controls (i.e. the risk profile of the organization) and the potential correlation between risks.
3. **Controls**. The adequacy and continuing appropriateness of controls need to be considered. Consideration needs to be given to both the probability and impact of control failures. Correlation and "fail-safe" issues should also be considered.
4. **Process**. The aim is to ensure that the processes and systems are compatible with the organizational structure and that they are efficient and effective. Consideration needs to be given to the level of flexibility and responsiveness, with a view to avoiding ossification.

The qustionnaire probes for information relating to the level of risk drivers
and quality of controls within each risk category.

Each business unit will use a questionnaire (customized in some cases) to self-assess its risk for a particular category.	**Internal Fraud Questionnaire (sample)**		Questions are focused on obtaining information about drivers and controls.
		Not Applicable Unknown	
	• What percentage of your Line of Business' FTEs are temporary employees or contract employees?	15% ☐ ☐	
	• Performance based remuneration (% total salary) – in the last year	20% ☐ ☐	
	• Non-management/ clerical overtime hours worked (% total hours) – in the last year	5% ☐ ☐	
	• Degree of autonomy of majority of staff		
The questions that are asked will prompt each business unit to think about its management of operational risks.	Very High: Independent operation, off-site (e.g. mobile sales force)	○	Questions can be a variety of types using objective criteria to assess the level of risk drivers and the quality of controls. Answers can be quantitative or qualitative.
	High: Independent operation, on-site	○	
	Moderate: Close team-based working groups	○	
	Low: Flat management, close supervision	○	
	Very Low: Strong hierarchical management, very close supervision	○	

Figure 5.1 Example of a Risk Drivers and Control Assessment (RDCA) questionnaire.
Source: Industry Technical Working Group (ITWG), reproduced with permission.

The purpose of any meeting will determine its structure. In practice, interrelationships mean that more than one objective at a time may need to be addressed.

5.8   QUESTIONNAIRES AND WEIGHTINGS

Questionnaires specifically designed to reflect a business unit's unique operational risk profile typically consist of a series of weighted, risk-based questions (see Figure 5.1). Applied weightings reflect the relative importance of individual risks to particular business units; hence response scores may not be linear. Responses are assessed in order to determine the level of acceptability and the stage of advancement, whether leading edge, follower, or laggard.

5.9   RESOURCE ALLOCATION

Rather than merely responding to risk events, CRSA encourages management to proactively strengthen controls, thus reducing the probability of loss (see Figure 5.2).

Capital charges can be used to encourage business units to respond to changes in their risk profile. Since these charges are formulaically determined they have the benefit of being fully transparent as well as risk sensitive.

5.10   LOSS DATA

Analysis of internal loss data enables risk drivers to be identified and evaluated. Historical data can also be used to validate assessments and check their completeness. However, the control environment existing at the time of historical losses needs to be compared to the current control environment. Near misses can also provide useful information regarding

If you don't properly assess risk, you can waste resources, and may still not have solved the problem.

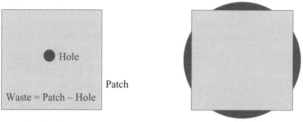

Potential Problem
The hole may grow larger than the patch,
or further holes may appear elsewhere

Remaining problem
The hole and the patch are the same size
but wrongly allocated

It is necessary to determine three things:	
1. The size and shape of the hole	(how bad is it?)
2. The growth rate of the hole	(is it getting worse?)
3. The size and shape of the patch	(what can be done? – is it adequate and appropriate?)

Figure 5.2   Representation of risk and resource allocation (consider water escaping through a hole).
Source: Brendon Young, ORRF

the robustness of systems. With regard to external loss data, this can be useful for considering
potential causal factors and the level of robustness of the organization to these.

5.11   DETERMINATION OF CAPITAL REQUIREMENT

Under the CRSA approach, the capital requirement for operational risk is determined by
comparing the outputs obtained from a number of different approaches, including:

- **Top-down**. Determination of the total capital requirement, of which a part is then apportioned
  to operational risk. The reasons for the level of apportionment chosen need to be clearly
  articulated.
- **Bottom-up**. Assessment of the level of capital required for each risk type and each business
  unit.
- **Benchmarking**. Peer group comparisons of both the level of capital and the apportionment
  percentages. The reasons for any variations need to be clearly identified.
- **Historical loss data**. Quantification using the Loss Distribution Approach (LDA) and Extreme Value Theory (EVT) at the chosen percentile (99.9 % being required by Basel II for
  regulatory capital).
- **Simplified basel factors**. Application of the standardized approach, defined by Basel II.

The emphasis placed on the different approaches can vary from organization to organization,
with the level of capital considered appropriate being chosen rather than precisely determined.
Under the CRSA approach it is essential to ensure that the capital charge is accepted by line
management and used within the business to reflect the risk profile of the various business
units.

The distribution of capital is initially made on a top-down basis. Within each business
unit, the CRSA assessments identify both the risk profile and the appropriate risk scalars for
each risk category. These form the basis for the distribution of capital to individual business

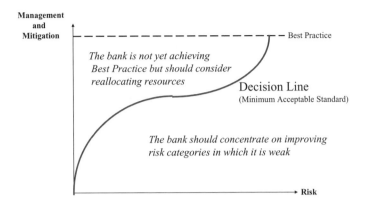

Figure 5.3   Benchmarking, risk prioritization and resource allocation.
Source: Brendon Young, ORRF

units. The final allocation of initial capital is determined by negotiation between business line management and the group risk function.

Once having determined the initial capital requirement for the organization and allocated it appropriately, all future amounts are determined on a bottom-up basis by considering direct changes to the risk profile for each business unit (see Figure 5.3). Such changes result in corresponding changes in risk scores and scalars, which lead to either an increase or decrease in risk capital for the business unit concerned, and by consolidation to a change in the total capital requirement for the organization as a whole.

5.12   DEVELOPING AND REFINING THE SYSTEM

When initially developing the methodology, the primary focus should be on inculcating responsiveness and appropriateness. Excessive precision in the initial measurement of risk should be avoided; a key strength of the CRSA approach is its ability to improve as it evolves.

Reviews of the methodology, including questionnaires, response choices, weightings, and key indicators should be undertaken on a regular basis in order to capture emerging risks resulting from changes in the business mix, possibly due to the introduction of new products and new business lines. As part of this review, consideration should be given to the appropriateness of existing behavioural incentives. The focus should be on new risks and those representing a threat to the business due to inadequate controls identified by unacceptable assessment scores.

External data can be useful for considering the effects of changes in the external business environment, for stress testing, and for formulating future scenarios. Changes in leading practices employed by competitors need to be taken into account.

5.13   ACHIEVING AND MAINTAINING CREDIBILITY
AND APPROPRIATENESS

Senior management acceptance and continued support for the CRSA approach, including the concept of allocating capital to the business units as a behavioural motivator, is essential. Similarly, involvement of the business units in developing and maintaining the CRSA system is necessary to ensure their buy-in. The extent to which the system is perceived to assist and add value to the management process, rather than simply creating additional administrative effort, will determine its ultimate success. To meet the "use-test," as required by the regulators, the system must be seen to be an integral part of day-to-day management.

Linking behavioral incentives to changes in capital encourages managers to attempt to continuously and actively reduce operational risk. This may be achieved in a number of ways, including linking management performance to indicators such as risk adjusted return on capital (RAROC) and economic value added (EVA).

To ensure the system does not degenerate over time, one particularly effective approach is to require the management team from one business unit to assess another business unit or, alternatively, validate the assessment. A more mature variation of this approach is to establish assessment teams having a mix of members drawn from various business units, possibly with the exclusion of the member from the particular business unit to be assessed. This creates an element of competition, particularly if salaries, bonuses, and promotional career prospects are affected. In addition, such an approach also assists with individual development and training. Management rotational practices are regarded as an important way of preventing internal fraud and mismanagement in banking. Degeneration of the system can occur due to employees seeking to cover up errors or near misses rather than disclosing them. This is particularly the case where an organization adopts a blame culture. Degeneration can also occur where management do not perceive any benefits in the methodology and therefore simply give the same responses to the assessment as given in previous periods.

5.14   VALIDATION

Validation of both initial and on-going assessments is essential. Independent reviews can be achieved by involving experts drawn from those support functions outside the direct-line business units, such as internal audit, compliance, IT, business continuity, and any other independent risk-related functions. Experts external to the organization, having experience of current leading-edge good practice, should also be used to provide an independent objective view.

5.15   AUDITING

CRSA is a technique that has been embraced by the auditing profession. It assists with validation of assessments and action plans through providing greater understanding of risks and their controls. However, CRSA should not be seen as a substitute for more fundamental auditing practices, which remain essential. The Institute of Internal Auditors (IIA)[4] has stated that self-assessment can augment the auditing process. The information generated on internal control may be: *A positive influence on the control environment within an organization by raising control consciousness and achieving buy-in of members.* The IIA supports the use of self-assessments to:

- increase the scope of coverage of internal control reporting during a given year;
- target audit work by reviewing high risks and unusual items noted in the results; and
- increase the effectiveness of corrective action by transferring ownership to operating employees.

Basel has recognized the need for sound practices in the management of operational risk and has also acknowledged the essential role of auditing. However, Basel has stated that the internal audit function should remain separate from the operational risk function. The fundamental role of the internal audit function is to provide a service to management, assisting them to properly fulfill their responsibilities by evaluating and making recommendations regarding the adequacy of, and adherence to, the risk-management systems and controls. However, this restriction does not prevent the internal audit function having a significant involvement in the CRSA process. This involvement may include conducting training in the CRSA process, providing data and other relevant information, facilitating workshops, and producing reports of the outcomes. Clearly, the level of involvement of the internal audit function will be determined by the sophistication of the risk management function. Even where the auditors' involvement is minimal, the CRSA output still serves to assist the auditing process by providing validation and information on proposed future developments.

5.16   THE RELATIONSHIP BETWEEN RISK MANAGEMENT AND KNOWLEDGE MANAGEMENT

There are strong parallels between a Control Risk Self Assessment (CRSA) approach towards risk management and knowledge management.[5] CRSA is dependent upon knowledge; knowledge management seeks to ensure that the knowledge in play within an organization's sphere of operation is appropriate for its purposes. This entails examining the organization's objectives, the risks it faces, the processes it employs, and the effectiveness of its controls. All these factors shape the requirement, the creation, and the flow of knowledge, which need to be considered at different levels (i.e. strategic, tactical, operational) in order to determine sufficiency and appropriateness (i.e. the organizational knowledge "capability"). Put simply, CRSA and the management of knowledge, when combined, can prove effective for the identification and control of risks, particularly those associated with human behaviour.

5.17   AETIOLOGY OF KNOWLEDGE MANAGEMENT

The management of knowledge stems from several underlying ancestral concepts of management. Fundamentally, when considered in a broad holistic way, knowledge management explores and highlights the integrative synergies between human beings, information systems, and business processes.

Human thinking.   Knowledge management can be said to lie upon an evolutionary path that includes recognition of the value of job enrichment and empowerment;[6] teamwork (Fisher and Fisher, 1997);[7] reflection in action (Schon, 1991);[8] and management as facilitation (Schein, 1999).[9] In essence, this is a path that has sought to recognize and manage the contribution of human thinking.

Systems-based embedded knowledge.   Knowledge management is also partly the product of a parallel set of developments, which include knowledge-based expert and decision support systems (Turban, 1988);[10] systems thinking (Senge, 1990);[11] and business process reengineering (Hammer and Champy, 1993).[12] Effectively, this approach has sought to embed knowledge within organizational systems (particularly those that are computer based).

Innovation and responsiveness.   Knowledge management can also be seen to have evolved in part from definitions of competitiveness that address knowledge creation processes (Nonaka and Takeuchi, 1995);[13] organizational learning (Moingeon and Edmondson, 1996);[14] operational management of continuous business improvement (Deming, 1986);[15] strategic management of core competency (Prahalad and Hamel, 1990);[16] and uncertainty management and adaptivity (Stacey, 1992).[17] This path has sought to emphasize the importance of innovation and adaptive responsiveness.

The particular emphasis that researchers and consultants place upon these contributory facets of knowledge will vary partly with their own personal understanding and experience (e.g. Sveiby, 1997;[18] Davenport and Prusak, 1998;[19] Stewart, 1998;[20] Ruggles and Holtshouse, 1999;[21] Malhotra, 2000[22]).

5.18   AVOIDING OSSIFICATION

Ossification occurs because organizations fail to recognize and act upon changes in the business environment. Unfortunately, many managers cling to the illusion of security based upon maintenance of the status quo. However, the knowledge and practices that enabled an organization to compete efficiently and effectively in the past may not be sufficient now or relevant in the future.

5.18.1   People issues

There is evidence to suggest that managers with a strong belief in control (i.e. those emphasizing strict adherence to policies and procedures) may adopt a different approach towards risk management than managers who emphasis flexibility (i.e. those seeking to develop knowledge and skills within communities of practice; Sparrow and Bentley, 2000[23]). There is clear evidence of the value a degree of diversity in teams can bring (Wiersema and Bantel, 1992). The value of "creative abrasion" (Eisenhardt et al., 1997) and "task conflict" (Simons and Peterson, 2000[24]) in organizations has also been recognized. The alternative approach towards maintaining competitiveness is based upon the learning capability of a firm (Boisot, 1995[25]). This requires a number of interrelated adaptive characteristics (Denton, 1998[26]), referred to as an alternative inquiry system (Malhotra, 2000[27]).

5.18.2   Issues relating to processes and systems

A majority of knowledge projects address improvements in specific business processes (Applehans, et al., 1999[28]). These operational improvements can benefit from specific teams exploring limitations in current practices and agreeing ways forward to enhance knowledge processes. Braganza et al., (1999)[29] suggested the classification of knowledge projects according to their contribution to innovation, distinguishing between projects that:

- produce efficiency benefits to the firm;
- enhance the relative performance of the business in its sector;
- exploit a new opportunity for the firm, giving it competitive advantage in its industry; and
- explore possible innovations.

5.18.3   Strategic issues

It has been said that "strategy determines structure and structure determines systems." The knowledge and skills needed for effective technical systems developments are computing related, but there is evidence to suggest that broader leadership and symbolic actions are important (Earl and Feeny, 2000[30]). Knowledge management also requires consideration of a number of business development issues. These can include processes of analysis (both qualitative and quantitative) that aid decision making concerning alternative reconfigurations of knowledge processes, together with related alterations in organizational structure, systems, incentives, and culture.

Strategic aspects of knowledge capability have been considered in terms of strategic vulnerability (e.g. Hall and Andriani, 1999[31]) and strategic capability (e.g. Bowander and Miyake, 1999[32]). It has been argued that organizations need to manage uncertainty less through predictive modeling but instead more through greater adaptability and flexibility in order to roll with the punches (Stacey, 1992; see endnote 17). The hardwiring of business senses and processes may jeopardize the flexibility and adaptability of an organization (Ansoff and McDonnell, 1990[33]).

5.19 MANAGING RISK WITHIN COMMUNITIES OF PRACTICE

The fundamental importance of human behaviour inherent within risk management is overtly demonstrated by the need to integrate risk management into personal practice. Designing socio-technical systems that work in the absence of human considerations is clearly incongruous. This has long been recognized within computer systems design (Blackler and Oborne, 1987[34]). However, historically, the emphasis was on building-in human considerations (i.e. developing artificial intelligence) rather than promoting active human interaction. Knowledge management theory and practice recognizes the limitations of such a restrictive approach. Communities of practice need to continuously develop their own systems and practices in order to remain responsive to current and future requirements.

The considerations that communities of practice need to address will vary depending upon the particular role and setting. One approach that can be used to gain insight into different practices is to consider variations in effectiveness. This can be achieved through comparing and contrasting:

- generally accepted good practice;
- alternative practices (possibly within other divisions or those used by competitors); and
- practices applied when a system is subject to stressors.

In considering the benefits derived from communities of practice developing and managing their own risk-management approaches, consideration needs to be given to three aspects of human behaviour that can prove problematic:

1. individual productive behaviour;
2. workgroup productive behaviour; and
3. counter-productive behaviour.

5.19.1 Individual productive behaviour

Task conflict has been associated with enhanced group decision quality and increased acceptance of decisions (Fiol, 1994[35]) because of the value of giving "voice" to a diversity of perspectives. On the other hand, relationship conflict (the perception of personal animosities and incompatibility) is dysfunctional (Jehn, 1995[36]). What is needed is sufficient trust to enable open discussion (Simons and Peterson, 2000; see endnote 24) and yet avoid the development of unquestioning practices (e.g. group-think; Aldag and Fuller, 1993[37]) or cozy mutual accommodation (Argyris, 1986[38]). The frequency, stability, and form of interactions between "players" in work situations are changing in line with the changing work environment.

Uncertainty capability (Sorrentino *et al.*, 1995[39]), skills of interaction (Dunnette, 1998[40]), and the management of relationship characteristics (e.g. trust, commitment and compatibility; Hutt *et al.*, 2000[41]) have all been found to be significant in a modern collaborative context. Effective management of innovation has been argued to be a key factor for organizations in the modern business environment (Boisot, 1995; see endnote 25). It seems clear that individuals (Tullett, 1995[42]) and work teams need to manage their own (Anderson and West, 1998[43]) and collaborative (Sparrow and Goodman, 1999[44]) innovation behaviour in order to secure effective development of new practices. Failure to adapt may be one of the major risks facing modern business. There is increasing recognition of the value of understanding innovation potential (Patterson, 1999[45]).

5.19.2   Work-group productive behaviour

Knowledge management also involves the ongoing and concurrent development of the ability of participants to work together effectively. Organizational development considerations include: group processes (Hartley, 1997)[46]; individual reflection and learning practices (e.g. Schon, 1991; see endnote 8); team and organizational learning processes (Isaacs, 1993[47]); and the means to develop the learning capability (Jones, 1996[48]) of one's community of practice to have the ability to contain diversity of a sufficient order to forestall ossification and promote "repetitive questioning, interpretation and revision of assumptions" (Malhotra, 2000, p.10; see endnote 27).

5.19.3   Counter-productive behaviour

Counter-productive behaviour, which deliberately attempts to reduce the effectiveness of the organization or a work group, is a prime risk driver. Counter-productive behaviour can include: placing additional burden upon work-group members through individual lateness (Koslowsky *et al.*, 1997[49]); absence (Farrell and Stamm, 1988[50]); labour turnover (Maertz and Campion, 1998[51]); aggression (Neuman and Barron, 1997[52]); sabotage and theft (Spector, 2000[53]); Failure to address such behaviour can result in its tacit reinforcement. In contrast, within tighter and closer work groups there is far less evidence of "social loafing" (Latane *et al.*, 1979[54]). Common themes identified throughout counter-productive behaviour are feelings of inequity (unfairness) and frustration (lack of control) due to the inability to bring about change (Greenberg, 1990;[55] Chen and Spector, 1992[56]), An effective community of practice may be more able to surface and address such issues than larger, "anonymous" organizational groupings.

5.20   FLEXIBILITY AND RESPONSIVENESS

In the existing dynamic business environment, management activity is characterized by an increasing pace of radical and unforeseen change (Nadler *et al.*, 1995[57]) requiring a greater intellectual contribution from employees (Wilson, 1996[58]). In an uncertain business environment, managers need the ability to continually visualize alternatives. This requires tolerance of ambiguity, given that management approaches cannot be precisely related to clear outcomes. Reality is a world of possible developments whose potentials need to be understood but whose "actual" manifestations are uncertain. Insight into how others perceive evolving situations and the development of competencies relevant to these possible outcomes is essential. Johnson[59]

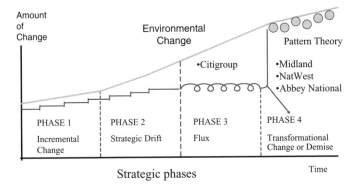

Figure 5.4   Survival and growth requires responsiveness to change.
Source: Professor Gerry Johnson, reproduced with permission of Pearson Education Ltd.

has spoken about the dangers of strategic drift as experienced by Midland Bank, NatWest, and Abbey National, prior to their take-overs. (see Figure 5.4).

Sparrow (1998)[60] suggests that "management by perception" is an approach towards management and decision-making involving a fundamental acceptance of the role of knowledge in a dynamic environment. A realization of the plurality of ways that different participants "perceive" (interpret and act upon) situations is necessary.

Within organizations, the relative reliance upon management skills, policies, and procedures and employee team activities can vary considerably. Organizations have different preferred configurations for these resources – i.e. unique approaches to "event management" (Smith and Peterson, 1988[61]). Very large organizations, such as HSBC, tend to place greater emphasis on compliance and conformity. In contrast, a knowledge management emphasis within an organizational construct can enable discrete "communities of practice" to effectively manage their development and responsiveness.

Managers and communities of practice require the competencies and tools necessary to see more complete sets of options. Organizational structures need to be sufficiently flexible and responsive in order to accommodate diverse perceptions of situations and their possible manifestations. This requires acceptance that organizational practice is not something singular that can be designed and imposed. It is the acceptance that uncertainty as conceived in chaos theory (Stacey, 1992; see endnote 17) cannot be best managed using a single predictive account (and an associated "optimized" organizational configuration). The power of creativity and adaptation comes from unleashing "distributed intelligence" implicit within an organization. This facilitates action in teams as "communities of practice" (Hendry *et al.*, 1995[62]) to review current and prospective situations, to reflect upon current practices, and to continually evolve more appropriate practices and "shared understanding" (Smircich, 1983[63]) in an ongoing "sense-making" responsive process (Weick, 1995[64]).

5.21   THE LIMITATIONS OF ENFORCED BEST PRACTICE

Knowledge management requires the application of multiple lens of perception for decision making and action. It is an active process involving consideration of the knowledge in play within any particular setting and the implications of reconfiguration. The role of cognition in work has been recognized: *more and more jobs now require mental, not manual skills, involving the processing of information and the creation of knowledge* (Wilson, 1996, p. 20; see endnote 56). Indeed: *organizations are becoming more knowledge intensive and this is matched by the significant occupational growth of knowledge worker groups* (Scarbrough, 1996, p. 8[65]). Moreover, knowledge is itself increasingly the product of: *repeated configuration of human resources in flexible, essentially transient forms of organization rather than solely the product of specific "disciplines"* (Gibbons *et al.*, 1994, p. 9[66]).

Attempts to analyze and document systems (e.g. ISO 9000) and to align human resources with business strategy (e.g. Investors in People) implicitly acknowledge "knowledge work," but unfortunately attempt to define the "singular" means through which outcomes sought by the defined objectives are secured. *The productivity of workers' minds and the quality of mental work*, however, *lies quite beyond the direct control of managers – and yet most senior managers cling to the illusion of control* (Wilson, 1996, p. 21; see endnote 56).

The knowledge that enables organizations or business units to operate to best practice standards today will undoubtedly date and decay over time. Organizations need to develop practices that support effective knowledge renewal and flow. Unfortunately, there is evidence to suggest that many business operations fail to ensure that the right people have the right information at the right time (Applehans, *et al.*, 1999; see endnote 28) or that service delivery and knowledge access technologies are simply not up to date (Coen and Hoogenboom, 1997[67]).

Managing knowledge is a holistic process. Studies of effective knowledge projects have indicated the importance of aligning the necessary elements of a system (i.e. technologies, practices, culture, reward systems). Pattern Theory suggests that an accumulative series of smaller projects may enable organizations to maintain alignment more readily than with a single "big bang" implementation. Narrow IT-based approaches have frequently experienced implementation difficulties, whilst diffuse organizational developments involving cultural change programmes (e.g. knowledge sharing) can lack focus.

Organizations need to ensure that there are processes whereby individuals can reflect upon their own and others' understanding of issues. This may include consideration of the relevance of external loss data. The success of a particular operation results from the actions of the system as a whole. It is not that each element in the system has the same understanding. Rather, the system succeeds because of the unique contribution that stems from the personal understanding that each participant brings. The importance of eliciting and sharing the perspectives held by different players has been widely demonstrated. The knowledge in play in any particular setting is not bounded by neat departmental or organizational circumscriptions. Value creation involves a wide spectrum of players in its co-production, (Wikstrom and Normann, 1994[68]) including customers, suppliers, partners, and networks, in fluid configurations.

Sparrow (2000[69]) proposed a framework based on lenses of perception (see Figure 5.5) that facilitates consideration of the many subtle and deep aspects that contribute to an individual's decisions and actions, such as skills, tacit feel, values and mood. He found that the effective management of knowledge has four components that can be managed at three levels, through three sets of developments.

The effectiveness with which organizations "sense" their environment differs. Ansoff and McDonnell (1990; see endnote 33) identified a number of key factors that affect the information available to managers and their ability to understand and use it. Studies of organizational practices have revealed limitations in the take-up of possible sources of learning (Bryson and Daniels, 1998[70]) and the effectiveness of flows or connections between individuals, groups, and organizations (Kim, 1993;[71] Sparrow *et al.*, 1998[72]). Thus, "best practice" is too simplistic a notion given complexity (both internal and external) and a dynamic business environment.

3 types of thinking (x), 5 kinds of mental material (y), 2 forms of thought (z)

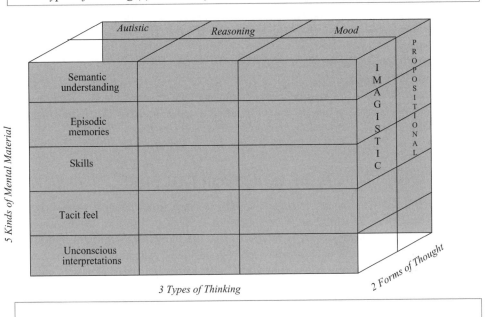

Not all risks can be quantified

Figure 5.5 Lenses of perception.
Source: Professor John Sparrow. Reproduced from *Knowledge in Organizations: Access to Thinking at Work* by John Sparrow with permission from Sage Publications.

5.22 BENCHMARKING AND STRESS TESTING HUMAN FACTORS

Whilst reviews of the effectiveness of practices used by others can be valuable, unfortunately, this may promote undue conformity (and inhibit creativity and initiative) by standardizing task definition, measurement, and control (Bartlett and Ghoshal, 1995[73]). Systematic contrasting of the approaches used by different individuals, groups, and organizations can enhance understanding (Isaacs, 1993; see endnote 46) if carried out in a non-defensive manner (Sparrow and Bushell, 1997;[74] Denton, 1998; see endnote 26). It can, however, be the learning that comes with adverse experience that can be the most salient (Kolb 1984[75]). The problems that ensue when a system is stretched or subject to excessive stressors can be established by considering the resultant strain reactions. Here, communities of practice need to adopt a holistic approach, considering the socio-technical system as a whole and exploring those features (including some of the deeper human factors and dynamics) that may lead to stress events together with any resultant limitations in anticipatory capability (i.e. using double-loop learning[76] and event-cause-effect analysis).

An example of an exploration of strain might be analysis of individual human performance that is considered to be below acceptable levels. Work groups need to explore their approach towards analysis of job demands (Morgeson and Campion, 1997[77]). Factors to consider may include their appreciation of likely future developments (e.g. working increasingly with others; Dunnette, 1998; see endnote 40); the bases for judgment such as 360 degree feedback (Baldwin and Padgett, 1993[78]); the appropriateness of their personnel selection practices (Smith *et al.*, 1989[79]), and the ability of their training and development processes to address organizational, job, and individual development needs (Goldstein, 1993[80]). Hesketh (1997)[81] has commented upon the need to develop broad transferable skills, in order to reduce constant retraining within a framework of lifelong learning.

More acute aspects of human behaviour might include stressors implicit within design features of a job (e.g. role ambiguity and role conflict; Fried *et al.*, 1998[82]) or failure to address other associated strain reactions (e.g. burnout; Cordes and Dougherty, 1993[83]).

5.23   REASONS FOR FAILURE

Toft[84] has stressed that "where organizations fail to learn from disasters, history is likely to repeat itself." Indeed, whilst some organizations learn from disasters, evidence suggests that others certainly do not. This is referred to as the "failure of hindsight and absence of foresight." Effective risk management requires considered reflection, which may involve analysis of personal, group, organizational and collaborative practices. Disasters are socio-technical in nature; often it is organizational issues that manifest themselves as technical failures. *"In many ways this is not surprising since it is people who conceptualize, design, develop, construct, operate and maintain both the physical and organizational systems which sometimes fail so catastrophically."* (see Section 8.2.3).

Where communities of practice apply knowledge management initiatives, such as CRSA, human-related risks may be more effectively assessed and controlled. However, such an approach is not a panacea for all risks or risk management. Evidence suggests that work groups may resist the duties and responsibilities that go with enriched jobs. Consideration needs to be given to issues concerning education (understanding and approval of such practices), organization (alterations to specializations that have traditionally been performed), management (fears of loss of control over operations, etc.) and employees (fear of new challenges). Attempts to manage human risk by those external to the community of practice (i.e. by "outsiders") have been found to be lamentable failures. However, the opportunity for reducing risk afforded by human risk being managed explicitly by communities of practice is clear.

ENDNOTES

[1] Lilley, M. and Saleh, O. (1999). Making Risk a Rewarding Business. *Internal Auditing*, 18–20.

[2] Outram, R. (1997). The Cost of Catastrophe: Different Approaches to Assessing and Controlling Business Risk. *Internal Auditing*, 12–13.

[3] See: CIPFA (1997). It's a Risky Business: The Auditors. Role in Risk Assessment and Risk Control. London: CIPFA.

[4] The Institute of Internal Auditors. (1998). Professional Practices Pamphlet 98-2: A Perspective on Control Self-Assessment.

[5] Wade, K. and Wynne, A. (1999). *A Control Self Assessment for Risk Management and Other Practical Applications*. Chichester: John Wiley and Sons Ltd.

[6] Fairclough, G. (1994). *Creative Compartments: A Design for Future Organisation*. Adamantine Press.

[7] Fisher, K. and Fisher, M.D. (1997). *The Distributed Mind: Achieving High Performance Through the Collective Intelligence of Knowledge Work Teams*. Amacom.

[8] Schon, D.A. (1991). *The Reflective Practitioner: How Professionals Think in Action*. Aldershot: Avebury.

[9] Schein, E. (1999). *Process Consultation Revisited: Building the Helping Relationship*. Reading, MA: Addison-Wesley.

[10] Turban, E. (1988). *Decision Support and Expert Systems: Managerial Perspectives*. New York: Macmillan.

[11] Senge, P.M. (1990). *The Fifth Discipline: The Art and Practice of the Learning Organisation*. London: Century Business.

[12] Hammer, M. and Champy, J. (1993). *Reengineering the Corporation*. Nicholas Brealey.

[13] Nonaka, I. and Takeuchi, H. (1995), *The Knowledge-Creating Company*. New York: Oxford University Press.

[14] Moingeon, B. and Edmondson, A. (Eds) (1996). *Organizational Learning and Competitive Advantage*. London: Sage.

[15] Deming, W.E. (1986). *Out of the Crisis*. Cambridge University Press.

[16] Prahalad, C. and Hamel, G. (1990). The Core Competency of the Corporation. *Harvard Business Review*.

[17] Stacey, R. (1992). *Managing Chaos*. London: Kogan Page.

[18] Sveiby, K.E. (1997). *The New Organizational Wealth: Managing and Mesauring Knowledge-Based Assets*. Berrett Koehler.

[19] Davenport, T.H. and Prusak, L. (1998). *Working Knowledge: How Organizations Manage What They Know*. Boston, MA: Harvard Business School Press.

[20] Stewart, T. (1998). *Intellectual Capital*. Nicholas Brealey.

[21] Ruggles, R. and Holtshouse, D. (1999). *The Knowledge Advantage: Leveraging Knowledge into Marketplace Success*. Capstone Publishing.

[22] Malhotra, Y. (Ed.) (2000). *Knowledge Management and Virtual Organizations*. Idea Group Publishing.

[23] Sparrow, J. and Bentley, P. (2000). Decision Tendencies of Entrepreneurs and Small Business Risk Management Practices. *Risk Management: An International Journal*. 17–26.

[24] Simons, T.L. and Peterson, R.S. (2000). Task Conflict and Relationship Conflict in Top Management Teams: The Pivotal Role of Intragroup Trust. *Journal of Applied Psychology* **85:1**, 102–111.

[25] Boisot, M. (1995). Is Your Firm a Creative Destroyer? Competitive Learning and Knowledge Flows in the Technological Strategies of Firms. *Research Policy* **24**, 489–506.

[26] Denton, D.K. (1998). Blueprint for the Adaptive Organisation. *Creativity and Innovation Management* **7:2**, 83–91.

[27] Malhotra, Y. (2000). Knowledge Management and New Organization Forms: A Framework for Business Model Innovation. *Information Resources Management Journal* **13:1**, 5–14.

[28] Applehans, W. Globe, A. and Laugero, G. (1999). *Managing Knowledge: A Practical Web-Based Approach*. Reading, MA: Addison-Wesley.

[29] Braganza, A. Edwards, C. and Lambert, R. (1999). A Taxonomy of Knowledge Projects to Underpin Organizational Innovation and Competitiveness. *Knowledge and Process Management* **6:2**, 83–90

[30] Earl, M. and Feeny, D. (2000). How to be a CEO in the Information Age. *Sloan Management Review*. **14:2**, 11–23.

[31] Hall, R. and Andriani, P. (1999). Managing Knowledge in an Innovative Environment. In: CBI/IBM (Eds) *Liberating Knowledge*. London, Caspian Publishing.

[32] Bowander, B. and Miyake, T. (1999). Japanese LCD Industry: Competing through Knowledge Management, *Creativity and Innovation Management* **8:2**, 77–99.

[33] Ansoff, H.I. and McDonnell, E. (1990). *Implanting Strategic Management*. 2nd edn. Hemel Hempstead: Prentice Hall.

[34] Blackler, F. and Oborne, D. (Eds) (1987). *Information Technology and People*. Leicester: British Psychological Society.

[35] Fiol, C.M. (1994). Consensus, Diversity and Learning in Organizations. *Organizational Science* **5**, 403–420.

[36] Jehn, K.A. (1995). A Multimethod Examination of the Benefits and Detriments of Intragroup Conflict. *Administrative Science Quarterly* **42**, 530–557.

[37] Aldag, R.J. and Fuller, S.R. (1993). Beyond Fiasco: A Reappraisal of the Groupthink Phenomenon and a New Model of Group Decision Processes. *Psychological Bulletin* **113**, 533–552.

[38] Argyris, C. (1986). 'Skilled Incompetence'. Reprinted in: The Logic of Business Decision Making, *Harvard Business Review* **64:5**, 74–79.

[39] Sorrentino, R.M., Holmes, J.G., Hanna, S.E. and Sharp, A. (1995). Uncertainty Orientation and Trust in Close Relationships: Individual Differences in Cognitive Style. *Journal of Personality and Social Psychology* **68:2**, 314–327.

[40] Dunnette, M.D. (1998). Emerging Trends and Vexing Issues in Industrial and Organizational Psychology. *Applied Psychology: An International Review* **47**, 129–153.

[41] Hutt, M.D., Stafford, E.R., Walker, B.E. and Reingen, P.H. (2000). Defining the Social Network of a Strategic Alliance. *Sloan Management Review* **41**, 51–62.

[42] Tullett, A.D. (1995). The Adaptive-Innovative (A-I) Cognitive Styles of Male and Female Project Managers: Some Implications for the Management of Change. *Journal of Occupational and Organisational Psychology* **65**, 177–184.

[43] Anderson, N. R. and West, M.A. (1998). Measuring Climate for Work Group Innovation: Development and Validation of the Team Climate Inventory. *Journal of Organizational Behavior* **19:3**, 235–258.

[44] Sparrow, J. and Goodman, F. (1999). Small Business Considerations in Collaboration upon Crime Management. *Security Journal* **13**, 21–31.

[45] Patterson, F. (1999). *Manual for the Innovation Potential Indicator*. Oxford: Oxford Psychologists Press.

[46] Hartley, P. (1997). *Group Communication*. London: Routledge.

[47] Isaacs, W.N. (1993). Dialogue, Collective Thinking and Organizational Learning. *Organizational Dynamics* **22:2**, 24–39.

[48] Jones, S. (1996). *Developing a Learning Culture: Empowering People to Deliver Quality. Innovation and Long-Term Success*. London: McGraw-Hill.

[49] Koslowsky, M., Sagie, A., Krausz, M. and Singer, A.D. (1997). Correlates of Employee Lateness: Some Theoretical Considerations. *Journal of Applied Psychology* **82**, 79–88.

[50] Farrell, D. and Stamm, C.L. (1988). Meta-analysis of the Correlates of Employee Absence. *Human Relations* **41**, 211–227.

[51] Maertz, C.P. and Campion, M.A. (1998). 25 years of Voluntary Turnover Research: A Review and Critique. In: C.L. Cooper and I.T. Robertson (Eds) *International Review of Industrial and Organizational Psychology*. Chichester: John Wiley & Sons Ltd., pp. 40–81.

[52] Neuman, J.H. and Baron, R.A. (1997). Aggression in the Workplace. In: R.A. Giacolone and J. Greenberg (Eds) *Antisocial Behavior in Organizations*. Newbury Park, CA: Sage, 37–67.

[53] Spector, P.E. (2000). Productive and Counterproductive Employee Behavior. In: *Industrial and Organizational Psychology 2nd edn*. New York: John Wiley and Sons Inc. 233–245.

[54] Latane, B., Williams, K. and Harkins, S. (1979). Many Hands Make Light the Work: The Causes and Consequences of Social Loafing. *Journal of Personality and Social Psychology* **37**, 822–832.

[55] Greenberg, J. (1990). Employee Theft as a Reaction to Underpayment Inequity: The Hidden Cost of Paycuts. *Journal of Applied Psychology* **5**, 561–568.

[56] Chen, P.Y. and Spector, P.E. (1992). Relationships of Work Stressors with Aggression, Withdrawal, Theft and Substance Use: An Exploratory Study. *Journal of Occupational and Organisational Psychology* **65**, 177–184.

[57] Nadler, D.A., Shaw, R.B. and Walton, A.E. (Eds) (1995). *Discontinuous Change: Leading Organizational Transformation*. San Fransisco: Jossey-Bass.

[58] Wilson, D.A. (1996). *Managing Knowledge*. Oxford: Butterworth-Heinemann.

[59] Professor Gerry Johnson is at Lancaster University Management School. He is most famous for his book *Exploring Corporate Strategy* which he wrote with Scholes (Johsonson, G., Scholes, K. and Whittington, R. (2007). *Exploring Corporate Strategy*. FT/Prentice Hall.

[60] Sparrow, J. (1998). *Knowledge in Organizations: Access to Thinking at Work*. London: Sage.

[61] Smith, P.B. and Peterson, M.F. (1988). *Leadership, Organizations and Culture: An Event Management Model*. London: Sage.

[62] Hendry, C., Arthur, M.B. and Jones, A.M. (1995). *Strategy through People: Adaptation and Learning in the Small–Medium Enterprise*. London: Routledge.

[63] Smircich, L. (1983). Concepts of Culture and Organizational Analysis. *Administrative Science Quarterly* **28**, 339–368.

[64] Weick, K. (1995). *Sensemaking in Organizations*. Thousand Oaks, CA: Sage.

[65] Scarbrough, H. (Ed.) (1996). *The Management of Expertise*. Basingstoke: Macmillan.

[66] Gibbons, M., Limoges, C., Nowotny, H., Schwartzman, S., Scott, P. and Trow, M. (1994). *The New Production of Knowledge: The Dynamics of Science and Research in Contemporary Societies*. London: Sage.

[67] Coen, R. and Hoogenboom, M.C. (1997). *Web-Enabled Applications Programmed on the Net: How to Become a Web-Enabled Enterprise*. New York: McGraw Hill.

[68] Wikstrom, S. and Normann, R. (1994). *Knowledge and Value: A New Perspective on Corporate Transformation*. London: Routledge.

[69] Sparrow, J. (2000). Knowledge Management in Small Firms. *Knowledge and Process Management* **8**, 3–16.

[70] Bryson, J.R. and Daniels, P.W. (1998). Traded and Untraded Knowledge and Expertise Interdependencies Between SMEs. In: *Proceedings of the 21st National Small Firms Policy and Research Conference*. Durham University Business School, 18–20 November 1998.

[71] Kimm. D.H. (1993). The Link between Individual and Organizational Learning. *Sloan Management Review*. Fall, 37–50.

[72] Sparrow, J., Zetie, S. and Bushell, M. (1998). Organizational Learning in Small Firms: Implications for Supporting Knowledge Management. In: *Proceedings of the 21st National Small Firms Policy and Research Conference*. Durham University Business School, 18–20 November 1998.

[73] Bartlett, C.A. and Ghoshal, S. (1995) Changing the Role of the Top Management: Beyond Systems to People. *Harvard Business Review*. May–June, 132–142.

[74] Sparrow, J. and Bushell, J. (1997). Personal Business Advisers Models and Organizational Learning in Business Links. In: M. Ram, D. Deakins and D. Smallbone (Eds) *Small Firms: Enterprising Futures*. London: Paul Chapman Publishing, 136–147.

[75] Kolb, D.A. (1984). *Experiential Learning*. Englewood Cliffs, NJ: Prentice-Hall.

[76] See: Argyris, C. (1999). *On Organizational Learning*, 2nd Ed., Oxford, UK: Blackwell. Double-Loop Learning Theory (as espoused by Argyris and Schön) is concerned with solving complex problems that are not precisely structured – i.e. problems that can change as problem-solving advances. This requires examination of changes in underlying assumptions, including values, behaviours, and leadership factors. Double-loop learning can improve effective decision-making and provide greater understanding of risk. An important element of the theory is improving effectiveness by bringing into congruence an individual's espoused theory and their actual "theory-in-use" (what they actually do). The four basic steps in the Action Learning process are:

(1) discovery of "espoused" and "theory-in-use;"
(2) invention of new meanings;
(3) production of new actions;
(4) generalization of results.

Argyris and Schön made a significant contribution towards learning theory by introducing to the experiential learning cycle the concept of learning by reflecting upon "theory-in-action." In contrast, Dewey (1933), Lewin (1948, 1951), and Kolb (1984), postulated that learning stems from making a mistake and reflecting upon it – i.e. learning by trial and error.

[77] Morgeson, F.P. and Campion, M.A. (1997). Social and Cognitive Sources of Potential Inaccuracy in Job Analysis. *Journal of Applied Psychology*. **82**, 627–655.

[78] Baldwin, T.T. and Padgett, M.Y. (1993). Management Development: A Review and Commentary. In C.L. Cooper and I.T. Robertson (Eds) *International Review of Industrial and Organizational Psychology*. Chichester: John Wiley & Sons Ltd., 35–38.

[79] Smith, M., Gregg, M. and Andrews, D. (1989). *Selection and Assessment: A New Appraisal*. London: Pitman.

[80] Goldstein, I.L. (1993). *Training in Organizations: Needs Assessment, Development and Evaluation*, 3rd edn. Monterey CA: Brooks-Cole.

[81] Hesketh, B. (1997). Dilemmas in Training for Transfer and Retention. *Applied Psychology: An International Review* **46**, 317–339.

[82] Fried, Y., Ben-David, H.A., Tiegs, R.B., Avital, N. and Yeverechyahu, U. (1998). The Interactive Effect of Role Conflict and Role Ambiguity on Job Performance. *Journal of Occupational and Organizational Psychology*, **71**, 19–27.

[83] Courdes, C.L. and Dougherty, T.W. (1993). A Review and an Integration of Research on Job Burnout. *Academy of Management Review*. **18**, 621–656.

[84] Toft, B. (1999). *Learning From Disasters: A Management Approach*. Perpetuity Press.

6

Data and Data Collection

6.1 THE IMPORTANCE OF DATA

Data collection and analysis are essential steps in gaining a better, more informed understanding of the losses incurred by an organization and its exposure to risk. Historically, risk assessment lacked rigour and was overly reliant upon management intuition. Certainly, Einstein could not have envisaged the phenomenon of light bending when passing near a large object simply by looking at data; this required intuition to the extent of genius. However, data plays a vital role in allowing a proposition to be tested and either confirmed or rejected. Data is the trace effect of a risk event. Risk *events* result from *causes,* and give rise to *effects.* Complexity stems from interaction (of people, systems and processes, and external events – see Figure 6.1) and the fact that an *event* may have multiple *causes* and multiple *effects* (see Figure 6.2), and may also be correlated with other *events.*

To simply collect all available data in the hope that it may prove useful at some future point in time is of questionable value. Data that is available may not be sufficient or appropriate and may be wrongly categorized. Historically, risk data were only partially collected by banks and the data in the financial accounts were often in an unusable format. Prior to the new Basel recommendations, Deutsche Bank had collected several years' of data but was unable to recategorize it due to the sheer volume of data and the time and costs that would have been involved. Collecting the right data and correctly analyzing it is essential in achieving an understanding of the relationship between an event, its cause(s), and its effect(s). Basically, it is necessary to know both the size of the loss incurred (its severity or impact) and how often that particular type of loss has occurred (its frequency). However, complexity means that this is unlikely to be adequate, with management requiring additional information for control purposes. Whilst, historically, departmental managers maintained records for control purposes, these were often kept for private use only. Where a blame culture prevailed, losses were more likely to be deliberately hidden and near misses simply ignored. Consequently, historical losses tended to be somewhat opaque, possibly understated and, probably, higher than necessary given that loss severity can be significantly influenced by the speed and appropriateness of management action.

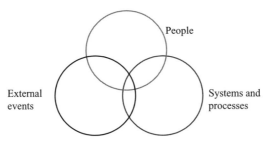

Figure 6.1 Risk sources. Complexity and chaos come from interaction.
Source: Brendon Young, ORRF

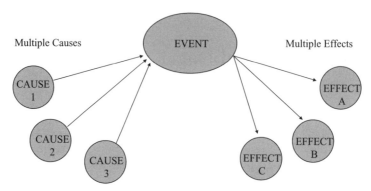

Figure 6.2 What data are being collected: (events, causes, effects).
Source: Brendon Young, ORRF

6.2   THE REGULATORY PERSPECTIVE

From a regulatory perspective a bank must track internal loss data. This is considered to be an essential prerequisite to the development of a functioning credible operational risk-management system.[1] A bank's internal loss data must be comprehensive, with all material activities and exposures from all appropriate sub-systems and geographic locations being captured.[2] Whilst Basel II does not explicitly state that a bank should collect information about near misses or opportunity costs, there is an expectation that consideration is given to these issues. In addition, Basel II states that a bank's operational risk measurement system must use relevant external data.

The new Basel Accord adopts a three-pillar approach to the assessment of operational risk capital: Pillar 1 is concerned with a minimum capital charge; Pillar 2 allows an upward variation to the capital charge through a supervisory review process; Pillar 3 then introduces transparency, facilitating control through market forces.

Pillar 1 of the new Basel Accord puts forward three approaches for determining the minimum regulatory capital requirement for operational risk, based upon the level of risk management sophistication:

1. the Basic Indicator approach.
2. the Standardized approach.
3. the Advanced Measurement approach.

The *Basic Indicator* approach simply assumes the operational risk regulatory capital charge to be a fixed proportion (the alpha value) of the gross income for the whole organization. One of the basic difficulties that has caused concern is the lack of sensitivity to risk of gross income, which Basel has proposed as a proxy for operational risk.

The *Standardized* approach is based on the concept of a "universal bank" with eight business lines. The issue of "granularity" arises due to Basel specifying the risk categories to be used for analyzing data under the Standardized approach, which is seen by the regulators (although not necessarily the banking industry) as a stepping stone between the Basic Indicator approach and the Advanced Measurement approach. The aim of the Standardized approach is to encourage firms to improve their operational risk management, firstly by collecting data and, secondly, analyzing it by particular business line and risk category. Unfortunately, the business lines and risk types specified by the regulators, although having been determined through consultation, are considered by some to be inappropriate. Some of these business lines are extremely broad, covering activities that look very different when considered in terms of their operational risk exposure (i.e. a business line may include a range of activities that have widely different levels of risk). Under the Standardized approach the regulatory capital charge for each business line is a set proportion (the beta value) of the gross income.

The *Advanced Measurement* approach allows the particular institution to determine its own capital requirement (subject to a minimum floor) based upon its own loss data and modeling methodology.

6.3 SOURCES AND LIMITATIONS OF DATA

The four primary sources of operational risk data are: internal data; external data; scenario generated data; and data related the business environment. When collecting and analyzing data, there are a number of limitations that need to be taken into consideration, as indicated below. It is important to remember that the accuracy of data will limit the accuracy of any model, since a model cannot have a greater degree of accuracy than the data from which it is derived.

6.4 NOT ALL DATA WILL BE RECORDED

A particular loss event may be considered insignificant from a management perspective and therefore ignored. However, this can lead to possible distortion of the loss distribution curve.

It should also be recognized that a particular type of loss will have its own distribution curve, and therefore the size of a single loss event will not give a true indication of the potential risk to the business from that risk type. Where an organization implements a loss collection threshold, all lower-level data will simply be disregarded. It is important to be aware of the particular risk type and its potential since a single, seemingly insignificant, loss event may indicate weaknesses in the system and be an early warning of a potential extreme tail event. This concept is well understood by the accounting profession, which recognizes the importance of precise reconciliation, with accounts being balanced to the last penny.

In addition to actual losses, consideration also needs to be given to meta-data such as near misses, unexpected gains, and opportunity costs:

- By their very nature, near misses are difficult to quantify and therefore often go unrecorded. However, a near miss is as much a signal of weakness as an actual loss event. Whilst current practice in this area varies, in general near-miss data is not used for risk quantification purposes but to identify risk trends, evaluate the adequacy of management controls and determine resilience.
- Similarly, unexpected gains should be recorded and their causes investigated.
- With regard to opportunity costs, the primary purpose is to further enhance management's understanding of risk exposure in relation to the determination of a bank's chosen risk profile, where alternative options exist. This is somewhat of an esoteric economics technique and is not widely used in practice.

6.5   DIFFERENCES IN APPROACH LEAD TO VARIATIONS IN CAPITAL REQUIREMENT

The integrity and comprehensiveness of operational risk data can directly affect the outcome of a bank's assessment of capital adequacy. As a result, Basel II prescribes standards that must be satisfied, although in some areas it provides opportunities for alternative interpretations. As previously stated, it is necessary to establish the size of a loss event (its impact) and also the date when the event occurred, with a view to determining the frequency of occurrence for the loss type. However, this may not be straightforward since differences in approach can cause variations in the loss distribution curve, resulting in uncertainty regarding the appropriate level of capital to hold.

6.6   GROSS OR NET LOSSES

In determining the size of a loss event there is some variation in practice between banks. Basel II requires a bank to record the gross loss incurred. Additionally, any recoveries also need to be recorded. In many banks, a recovery period is specified, during which any recoveries received are netted-off against the gross loss figure. It is this net figure that is recorded in the loss database. Where full recovery is received, a bank may not record the event as a loss but rather as a near miss. Another approach involves estimating the probability of recovery. Where the probability is very high, even though the recovery period is outside the norm, netting may be considered appropriate. However, accounting standards require prudence. Given that the amounts involved can be large, particularly in the case of money transfers, differences in practice can result in significant variations in capital requirements.

6.7   DATE OF LOSS

When a loss event is discovered immediately, its date of occurrence is known precisely. However, if the loss takes place over a period and is not discovered until some time later then the situation becomes more complex. An extreme example is the Sumitomo copper scandal in which the chief copper trader, Yasuo Hamanaka, carried out fraudulent trading activities over a period of approximately 10 years (up to 1995), resulting in a loss to the bank estimated to be in the order of US$ 2.6 billion.

In cases where the *date of occurrence* is not clear, the *date of discovery* may be used; alternatively, where litigation is involved, either the *accounting date* or the *date upon which the case was settled* may be used. In actual practice, all approaches are found in use, although the *date of occurrence* is the one preferred. The date of discovery has the potential disadvantage of suddenly introducing a very large loss into the dataset, causing distortion and indicating the immediate need for greater capital when in actual fact this may not be the case, particularly where corrective management action has already been taken or where the loss occurred gradually over a period. In litigation cases, it is often considered that early recognition may adversely prejudice the final outcome, hence the approached favoured in practice is to use the date of final settlement, although accounting standards may alter this to the accounting date.

Whilst the new Basel Accord requires banks to collect information about the date of the event, it is not prescriptive other than requiring information to be commensurate with the size of the gross loss amount.[3] This may lead to differences in practice amongst banks, making comparisons more difficult and leading to differences in calculated capital requirements.

6.8   DAMAGE TO PHYSICAL ASSETS

Damage to physical assets was specifically identified by Basel as a risk category. Currently, there are three methods in general use for determining the risk impact.

1. Accounting standards require the use of book value, which is calculated to be the actual purchase price less depreciation. This is often regarded as an underestimate of the true impact.
2. To reflect the fact that the asset may no longer be available in its original form (possibly due to technological advancement) or at its original cost (partly due to inflation), the replacement cost may be considered more appropriate (i.e. the current market value). However, the new asset may have a life longer than one accounting year, hence this is regarded as an overestimate.
3. A more realistic approach, which reflects the actual impact of the risk event, may be the amount by which the economic value of the asset is impaired. This would include the cost of repair or partial replacement plus the loss in income. Whilst this approach may seem more appealing, it lacks precision and therefore leaves room for divergence in results.

6.9   ALLOCATION OF CENTRAL LOSSES ACROSS BUSINESS UNITS

Basel states that a bank must develop specific criteria for assigning losses arising from an event in a centralized function (e.g. an information technology department) or an activity that spans more than one business line.[4] Any banking or non-banking activity which cannot be readily mapped into the business line framework, but which represents an ancillary function to an activity included in the framework, must be allocated to the business line it supports. If more than one business line is supported through the ancillary activity, an objective mapping criteria must be used.[5]

In practice, the favoured method for dealing with a loss affecting several business lines is to allocate the entire loss to that business line for which the impact is greatest. This has the advantage of simplicity but lacks appropriateness. From a management perspective, this method can lead to the capital allocation process being discredited.

An alternative approach involves allocating the loss on a prorata basis across all those business lines affected. Unfortunately, this approach can lead to distortion since the apportioned loss amount shown in each business line may not reflect the actual impact of the loss event.

6.10   BOUNDARY ISSUES BETWEEN OPERATIONAL RISK, CREDIT RISK, MARKET RISK, AND OTHER RISKS

The distinctions between the different types of risk are not always clear at the boundaries, with definitions varying between banks. Consequently, since Basel II has included different approaches for calculating the capital requirement for different risk types, a bank can vary its overall regulatory capital requirement by reclassifying its risks or, rather, different banks may have different capital requirements despite having identical risk profiles.

With regard to the definition of operational risk, from a regulatory perspective Basel II[6] includes legal risk but excludes strategic and reputational risk. Whilst this definition is widely accepted, some banks have, for sound commercial reasons, decided to adopt a different definition having different inclusions and exclusions,[7] thus direct comparison may not always be possible. Basel has not defined strategic risk or legal risk. Hence, a bank can reduce its regulatory capital requirement through omitting certain large losses that it has chosen to categorize as either strategic or legal.

With regard to the boundary between operational risk and credit risk, Basel states: *Operational risk losses that are related to credit risk and have historically been included in banks' credit risk databases (e.g. collateral management failures) will continue to be treated as credit risk for the purposes of calculating minimum regulatory capital under this framework. Therefore, such losses will not be subject to the operational risk capital charge.*[8] By arbitraging from credit risk to operational risk, a bank adopting the AIRB approach for credit risk and the Standardized approach (TSA) for operational risk could reduce its capital requirement. Conversely, by arbitraging from operational risk to credit risk, a bank adopting an Advanced Measurement approach (AMA) for operational risk and a FIRB for credit risk could reduce its capital requirement.

In the case of credit card fraud, losses can be substantial; hence, capital requirements can vary significantly depending upon the method adopted. The simple approach is to treat all losses as operational risk losses. However, some banks have adopted a more informative approach, separating out external fraud and treating it as operational risk, whilst treating other forms of credit card fraud as credit risk.

With regard to the boundary between operational risk and market risk, Basel is relatively clear, stating: *Operational risk losses that are related to market risk are treated as operational risk for the purposes of calculating minimum regulatory capital under this framework and will therefore be subject to the operational risk capital charge.*[9] Accepted practice within the banking industry is to treat losses caused by traders who violate limits as operational risk rather than market risk, for regulatory capital purposes.

6.11   EXTREME EVENTS DO NOT LEND THEMSELVES TO DETECTION BY DATA ANALYSIS

Clearly, for low frequency/high impact losses there will be few data points. Extreme events data are in short supply, leading to high levels of uncertainty. In the case of extreme, long tail, catastrophic failure events, it is not possible to obtain a realistic, quantitative, probabilistic appraisal given the high levels of uncertainty. The numerical probabilities make the event appear unlikely and therefore possibly outside the scope of normal management action.[10]

6.12   THE SMALL SAMPLE PROBLEM (OVERREPRESENTATION AND UNDERREPRESENTATION)[11]

Since extreme events are by definition, rare, it follows that if an extreme event is contained in a small sample of data it must be overrepresented. Each large loss event (such as a major fraud) will distort the shape of the fitted distribution. Conversely, if there is no extreme event in a small sample of data then this sample is not truly representative. Clearly, no evidence of risk is not evidence of no risk. Consequently, it is not possible to precisely model a heavy tail distribution through data fitting. This is true for all models given the paucity of data. Any inferences drawn from the data must therefore be inherently unreliable, particularly in the tail of a loss distribution curve.

6.13   THE PAST IS NOT NECESSARILY A GOOD PREDICTOR OF THE FUTURE

Although it may seem intuitively sensible to increase the period over which data is collected in order to increase the number of data points, unfortunately this does not help and in fact can cause distortion. Current data cannot be assumed to be the same as historical data or future data. Consequently, long data series cannot automatically be assumed to improve estimation. Where an organization has experienced a significant loss event, it is likely that changes will be made in order to reduce the possibility of reoccurrence. For a dynamic organization operating in a dynamic global economy, historical data may no-longer be relevant and therefore possibly misleading. In such conditions, probabilistic uncertainty is high.[12]

6.14   INFLATION AND CURRENCY VARIATIONS LIMIT THE USE OF HISTORICAL DATA

It is an accounting convention that costs be recorded at their historical level – i.e. their actual value at the time they were incurred. Over time, this information becomes less meaningful due to inflation and currency variations. Hence, direct comparisons between historical and current loss values can be misleading, although information on quantity and type may still be relevant (all other things being equal).

6.15   ERROR AND ACCURACY

Increasing the number of observations does not reduce the error in sampling. In 1756 the mathematician, Reverend Thomas Bayes, stated: *Now that the errors arising from the imperfection of the instrument and the organs of sense should be thus reduced to nothing or next to nothing only by multiplying the number of observations seems to me extremely incredible. On the contrary the more observations you make with an imperfect instrument the more it seems to be that the error in your conclusion will be proportional to the imperfection of the instrument made use of . . .*

Clearly, given personal bias in qualitative assessments, error and inaccuracy become significant factors. This is of relevance with regard to home-host issues in Pillar 2 of the new Basel Accord.

6.16   EXTERNAL DATA IS NOT READILY TRANSFERABLE FROM ONE ORGANIZATION TO ANOTHER

Data from one organization will not necessarily be relevant to another since each will have its own culture, people, systems, metrics, and taxonomy. External events, which may change with time, contribute to the overall risk environment, and will impact differently on different firms.[13] Management and supervision are key differentiators. The essence of good management is the ability to identify risks early and take prompt corrective action in order to minimize losses. Hence, a well-managed organization can expect to have fewer losses and those losses relatively smaller (all other things being equal) than those incurred by a poorly managed company with inadequately trained staff.

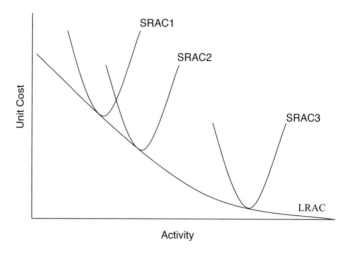

Figure 6.3   SRAC (Short Run Average Cost) and LRAC (Long Run Average Cost) curves.
Source: Brendon Young, ORRF

6.17   DATA IS NOT READILY SCALEABLE

As an organization grows and develops, and adapts to the changing business environment, it will expand some business activities, reduce or eliminate others, and take on new ones. In a global industry an international organization can expect to undergo changes in both its home and host countries. Consequently, its structure will change (including its fixed costs and variable costs) as will the risks it faces. Hence, data is not readily scaleable. Clearly, scaling data between totally different organizations is extremely difficult.

A business unit will have an organizational structure determined by the appropriate Short Run Average Cost curve (SRAC) for the level of business being conducted. In the future, activity levels may change. Small changes will result in movement along the particular SRAC curve. However, significant movements in activity will result in major organizational changes, and a move to a different SRAC curve positioned further along the Long Run Average Cost curve (LRAC) (see Figure 6.3). Hence, a moment's reflection will reveal that a significant change in competitive position can result from a movement in the level of activity both in the short term and long term.

6.18   EMERGENT PROPERTIES

Holistic systems have additional emergent properties and consequently are greater than the mere sum of their component parts. Components assembled into an aeroplane acquire the additional property of flight. Similarly, television parts acquire the additional ability to provide images and sound.

Originally, economic theory recognized two primary factors of production: capital and labour, later, technology was included. Subsequently, it was recognized that a fourth factor (profound knowledge) existed, and it was this that led to differentiation, enabling one organization to outperform another through the ability to make better use of resources.

A firm will have its own culture, reputation, and organizational knowledge. As an entity, a bank will have additional emergent properties; hence, it is not possible to simply sum risk assessments from the individual constituent business units. Correlation and diversification need to be taken into account.

6.19   RISK TYPES AND CAUSES

There are five types of risk, each with different loss distribution characteristics. In gaining an understanding of a particular risk (i.e. its probability of occurrence, likely impact, and distribution) it is essential to establish the fundamental category to which the risk belongs. A widely, accepted approach in risk management is to first identify the major (i.e. top 10) risks faced by an organization. Whilst this approach may indeed be useful,[14] it is often based on a lack of understanding of the nature of risk (see Figure 6.2). Consequently, those risks having a high severity but which have not yet been experienced or are difficult to predict (low probability) may often be ignored.

The five risk types are:

1. **People risks.** There are two types of risk resulting from the actions of people:
   (a) those due to deliberate wilful action by an employee or external persons (e.g. fraud or malicious damage);
   (b) those due to normal adaptive human behaviour (e.g. errors due to fatigue).
2. **Systems and process risks.** Systems and process-based risks will be of an inherent nature and therefore the recurrence of losses will be unavoidable in the absence of change to the system itself. This type of risk will produce a clear loss distribution signature.
3. **External events.** External events may lead to systemic losses; it is these that regulatory capital seeks to avert. External factors can be expected to impact differently on different organizations.
4. **Randomness.** A major loss may be totally random in nature. Such risks are unique, totally unpredictable and nonrecurring. Consequently, data analysis will not indicate the probability of the next event nor its magnitude. If present in the data, random events lead to distortion of an organization's overall loss distribution curve. Because of their uniqueness, random events are sometimes treated as a separate risk class, and referred to as black swans.[15] However, they will be part of the three previous fundamental risk types.
5. **Cumulative interactive risks.** A catastrophic loss event may result from the accumulation and interaction of a number of lesser errors and weaknesses (from all or any of the above classes). It is unlikely that data alone will indicate the possibility of this type of risk.

6.20   ACTIONS BY PEOPLE

The complexity of human behaviour prevents the actions of people being predicted with certainty. Personal characteristics such as ethics, loyalty, drive, and commitment are important factors. The wants, needs, and motivations of individuals change over time due to changes in personal circumstances and experiences. Given the level of uncertainty associated with human behaviour in general and individual action in particular, it is not possible to precisely predict and quantify all potential errors. Many errors are simply the result of normal adaptive learning, and can be considered as the cost of human advancement. (Grose, 1987;[16] Reason, 1990;[17] Elms and Turkstra, 1992;[18] Waring, 1992).[19]

Deliberate wilful actions – such as fraud, corruption, and financial crime – can prove very difficult to discover. In its various guises, financial crime represents a serious risk to all businesses and is said to be increasing. In the UK, for example, the National Criminal Intelligence Service has identified fraud as one of the most serious risks that companies face and has indicated that it may represent between 2 % to 5 % of turnover for most organizations. Unfortunately, fraud is notoriously difficult to detect, and around 75 % of fraudulent acts are only discovered by chance. Auditing alone has not proved effective in detecting fraud. There is some evidence to suggest that the volume of fraudulent events increases in times of economic down-turn. Research by Citigroup and others suggests that for credit card fraud there is a clearly definable loss distribution curve. This is not necessarily the case for other forms of financial crime. In one Scandinavian country, where cash transactions take place openly, minor bank robbery (snatching) is accepted as normal and is statistically predictable.

In certain types of banking activity, such as trading, where there is considerable pressure on individuals to perform, there is a tendency towards financial crime. Perfunctory management only serves to exacerbate the situation, as was seen in the Barings Bank and Allied Irish Bank cases. Performance-related pay, including annual bonuses, is also considered to have an increased impact upon the level of risk.

The primary defences against financial crime are considered to be an ethical culture and vigilant management.

6.21   SYSTEMS AND PROCESS-BASED LOSS EVENTS

A well-performing system will have a clearly defined and stable loss distribution curve. However, where an organization is experiencing an unacceptable level of loss events it will inevitably make changes to its processes and systems in order to improve performance (i.e. improve responsiveness and resilience).[20] Unfortunately, changes to a process or system render historical loss data no longer relevant.

Quality and reliability of systems and processes is an area that is well understood and well advanced, particularly in the computing and manufacturing industries. All systems and processes are designed to operate within given confidence bounds, in that the output will not be precise but will be within acceptable tolerances. In engineering, a component is manufactured to a given size plus or minus an acceptable standard error (say 1 cm + or −0.001) and in a batch of components only a small amount will fall outside this tolerance (say one component in one million). Similarly in banking, when processing transactions, there will inevitably be failures but these should only be within predetermined limits. Reducing the number of failures would require changes to the system itself. Proponents such as Edwards-Deming, Crosby, et al.[21,22] made considerable advances in the area of total quality management (TQM) and continuous improvement. This led to a virtual revolution in the manufacturing industry in the 1970s, resulting in Japanese dominance of the automotive related industries by firms such as Toyota, Honda, and Kawasaki. TQM enabled them to significantly reduce costs and increase quality, thereby increasing their market share. Probably the most well-known methodology in the field of world-class manufacturing and management is *Six Sigma*, developed by Motorola. Various banks, including J.P. Morgan, have tried this methodology, but with limited success.

In the early 1980s, Ford sought to improve the performance of its accounts payable operation by reducing its headcount from 500 to 400, thus reducing costs by 20 %. However, Mazda (with whom Ford had an association) was performing the same task with only five people.

Techniques such as "straight through processing" (STP) and "parallel systems processing" can greatly improve performance and reduce loss events.

6.22   EXTERNAL EVENTS

External events fall into two categories: firstly, those events suffered by other (similar) organizations; and secondly, external events that have not yet happened but which pose a real threat to the business environment or the organization itself.

Basel II states that a bank's operational risk measurement system must use relevant external data (either public data and/or pooled industry data), especially when there is reason to believe that the bank is exposed to infrequent, yet potentially severe, losses. These external data should include data on actual loss amounts, information on the scale of business operations where the event occurred, information on the causes and circumstances of the loss events, or other information that would help in assessing the relevance of the loss event for other banks. A bank must have a systematic process for determining the situations for which external data must be used and the methodologies used to incorporate the data (e.g. scaling, qualitative adjustments, or informing the development of improved scenario analysis). The conditions and practices for external data use must be regularly reviewed, documented, and subject to periodic independent review.[23]

6.22.1   Events suffered by other (similar) organizations

The initial reason for considering using external data obtained from other similar organizations, was to overcome the serious problem of a paucity of internal loss data (particularly in the tail of the loss distribution curve). The extent to which external data is of use depends upon the particular type of loss. For example, credit card loss data appears to be similar across different organizations. However, certain other types of data are not readily transportable, due to timing and organizational differences. It is generally recognized that external data may be of use when considering scenario analysis but can lead to distortion if incorporated with a bank's internal loss data. The accuracy and completeness of external data need to be carefully examined.

External loss data is available from both industry consortia and commercial sources. The Operational Riskdata eXchange Association (ORX)[24] is possibly the most well-known industry consortia (see Table 6.1). In the UK, the British Bankers Association offers its GOLD consortia database. There is also a banking industry consortia initiative in Italy. With regard to commercially-available databases, there are two types: those using publicly-available data (e.g. Algorithmics and SAS); and those created by insurance companies from their claims databases (e.g. AON and Willis). Clearly, databases using publicly-available information (i.e. obtained from newspapers and trade journals, etc) are vulnerable to a number of constraints such as: not all losses being recorded; the actual size of losses not being accurately determined, particularly where losses occur over a long period of time; and losses being differently categorized by different sources. Insurance databases have a more restricted scope being based solely on claims, although these may go back many years. AON claims to have a database comprising approximately 10 000 settled insurance claims. The main advantage of insurance databases is that the size of the loss event is based on the actual amount paid out.

ORX is attempting to establish universally accepted loss-data standards by creating a platform for the secure exchange of high-quality anonymous operational risk loss data. ORX was originally founded in January 2002 by 12 banks; there are now approximately 36 members

Table 6.1 Sample of ORX Loss Database Report.

ORX REF ID	OWN DATA	REGION	EL-L2	BL-L2	GROSS LOSS	DIRECT RECOVERY	NET AFTER DIRECT RECOVERY	INDIRECT RECOVERY	NET AFTER ALL RECOVERY	DATE OF OCCURENCE	DATE OF DISCOVERY	DATE OF RECOGNITION	CREDIT AND/OR MARKET RISK	EVENT STATUS
60611	N	North America	BL0301	EL0102	100 828	100 828	0	0	0	08-Jan-02	19-Mar-02	19-Mar-02	N	Unchanged
8208	N	Western Europe	BL0101	EL0701	29 179	8.203	20 976	0	20 976	20-Mar-02	20-Mar-02	20-Mar-02	N	Unchanged
3495	N	Western Europe	BL0204	EL0701	23 997	0	23 997	0	23 997	07-Jan-02	10-Jan-02	14-Mar-02	N	Unchanged
21792	N	Other	BL0201	EL0701	22 000	11 701	10 299	0	10 299	13-Aug-02	31-Aug-02	31-Aug-02	Y	Unchanged
1643	N	Western Europe	BL0204	EL0701	22 250 426	22 250 426	0	0	0	18-Jan-02	09-Sep-02	02-Oct-02	N	Updated
56166	Y	North America	BL0901	EL0201	20 978	0	20 978	0	20 978	29-Jul-02	29-Jul-02	29-Jul-02	N	Unchanged
1789	N	Western Europe	BL0301	EL0403	2069 560	2056 048	44 501	0	44 501	12-Jul-02	15-Jul-02	15-Jul-02	N	Unchanged
7496	N	Western Europe	BL0201	EL0703	549 259	0	549 259	0	549 259	05-Feb-01	05-Feb-01	14-Jul-03	N	Unchanged
16880	N	Western Europe	BL0202	EL0701	561 811	0	461 811	100 000	461 811	31-Mar-04	31-Mar-04	31-Mar-04	N	Updated
56442	Y	North America	BL0301	EL0201	23 681	0	23 681	0	23 681	03-Feb-03	03-Feb-03	10-Apr-03	N	Unchanged
13462	N	North America	BL1001	EL0501	28 372 822	688 035	27 684 787	0	27 684 787	29-Aug-05	29-Aug-05	29-Nov-05	N	New
14460	N	North America	BL0201	EL0402	42 103 583	0	42 103 583	0	42 103 583	01-Jan-99	01-Apr-03	29-Feb-04	N	Updated

Source: ORX. Reproduced with permission.

from 12 countries. Since its formation, ORX has developed a database of approximately 51 500 operational risk losses, each over €20 000 in value, totalling in excess of €15 billion. In addition, nine Spanish member banks have created a regional database having a loss threshold of €3000.

ORX collects data quarterly using a standard format, which takes into account the Basel II requirements. Each loss is characterized according to the following primary attributes:

- Reference ID number (member generated)
- Business Line (Level 2) Code
- Event Category (Level 2) Code
- Country (ISO Code)
- Date of Occurrence
- Date of Discovery
- Date of Recognition
- Credit-related
- Gross Loss Amount
- Direct Recovery
- Indirect Recovery
- Related event (Ref ID)

Data is initially prepared, tested, and validated by individual members, who are required to attest to its accuracy and completeness prior to submission. Members are also required to provide explanations of any anomalies in the data supplied. To assist in scaling, ORX requires members to submit their gross income for each business line. In order to increase the number of scaling factors, it is proposed to also use expenses and assets. Future plans include taking causation into account.

Every member of ORX receives the entire anonymized database (see below) containing every loss together with the associated standard characteristics. The name of the originating bank is withheld and a regional identifier substituted for the country.

6.22.2   Potential external events, which pose a real threat to the business environment or the organization itself

External events are outside the control of management. However, through business continuity management (BCM), an organization can prepare for various eventualities or the derivatives thereof. Such events may include war, terrorism, and civil unrest, epidemics, systems failures (including hacking), and organized crime. Scenario analysis enables an organization to estimate the potential impact of such events. However, this clearly represents little more than a best-guess estimate. Events such as these are extreme in nature. Their inclusion with actual loss data will corrupt that data and distort the loss distribution curve. This will lead to a higher capital requirement than would otherwise be the case, although, its adequacy and appropriateness will remain in doubt. The fundamental question is how far wrong such estimates can be before they become meaningless, or even possibly threatening to the competitiveness of the organization. Given the nature of such serious events, it is highly likely that clustering and correlation may occur, possibly resulting in the whole being greater than the sum of the parts.

On a lesser scale, an organization will need to take account of other changes in the business environment that could impact upon its risk profile and thus require modification to the strategy being pursued.

6.23 RANDOM EVENTS

Random events are by definition unpredictable and unique, occurring at any time, without warning. Hence, analysis of historical loss data cannot be expected to yield totally meaningful results. If random events are present in the data, they will distort the loss distribution curve.

It is complexity that leads to randomness. Random events are the result of the multitude of variables in the real world, making it impossible to completely predict the outcome of all interactions. The philosophical example often quoted is that of a butterfly flapping its wings in Beijing, ultimately leading to a hurricane in New York.

Despite complexity and uncertainty, it may appear possible to identify recurring patterns in the data. Given the ability of computers to analyze vast quantities of data, patterns and correlations that may not be immediately obvious to the human observer may be identified. However, it is a well-known phenomenon that patterns can be indicated where in reality there is no actual relationship – i.e. a false positive. For example, if 100 people are asked to select which box they want out of a choice of 100 identical Christmas boxes, it is likely that some boxes will be chosen more than once, and therefore some will not be chosen at all. (Note that for all boxes to be picked once only there is one chance in 10 to the power of -200, i.e. there is one chance in 100 of a person picking a particular box and this probability (1/100) must be multiplied 100 times since there are 100 people. If this example is repeated but with the boxes that are not chosen being removed, eventually one box will be chosen, despite the fact that it looks identical to all others. Note that we have made no assumption about its contents, which could have been totally void.) The example can be likened to television talent shows, which explains why the winner may quickly vanish into obscurity. Similarly, cancer clusters may be apparent from data in some regions, where in actual fact there is no problem. Consequently, human interpretation of the outcomes remains essential. Randomness may not appear random.

With regard to investment funds, randomness brings into question the ability of the fund manager, certainly in the short term and to some extent in the longer term. Where someone is promoted on their ability to make the right choice it is possible that randomness can lead to a person being elevated beyond their true ability. The performance of an investment fund may simply be due to randomness; bonuses based on short-term performance are therefore questionable. Portfolio theory suggests that a "fund of funds" investment strategy should reduce risk; however, randomness reveals a potential weakness in this approach.

With regard to management, contingency theory states that, given complexity, the most appropriate form of control is dependent upon the contingencies of the situation at any point in time. Consequently, there is no one best overall solution or management style. Responsiveness is essential but may be fraught with danger given randomness. Some historical rules existing within an organization may simply be the result of their survival through randomness.

6.24 ACCUMULATION OF ERRORS AND WEAKNESSES

Historically, human error was regarded as the primary cause of failure, with responsibility being assigned to a particular individual (a "blame the pilot" approach). A more enlightened approach recognized the importance of latent organizational factors (involving a "no blame" analysis-based approach). However, if incorrectly applied, this approach can lead to the primary causal factor always being regarded as management incompetence (a "blame the manager" culture). A more balanced approach (see Figure 6.5) involves consideration of both the current active errors and the latent organizational conditions (which are always present but remain

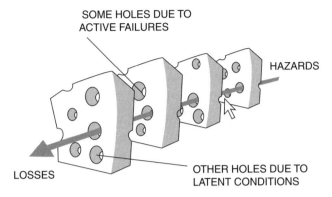

Figure 6.4   The Swiss cheese model.
Source: Professor James Reason, reproduced with permission.

dormant until triggered).[25] It should be recognized that active errors might be the result of a defective system. However, active errors may also be independent of and more important than inherent latent factors. Often, the causal relationship between active errors and distant latent conditions can prove tenuous, with many latent conditions appearing inconsequential in a pre-event scenario. From a management perspective, some latent conditions may be very difficult to control and may require considerable time and expense to ameliorate.

The widely accepted approach to investigation of major loss events is the accident causation model (known as the Swiss cheese model), propounded by Professor James Reason (see Figure 6.4). The model assumes the existence of several preventive layers between the initial spark event and the final occurrence of a catastrophic loss. Such a loss occurs when all levels of control fail simultaneously – i.e. when "holes" in all the cheese layers align (note that in a dynamic business system the holes themselves may change over time).

This has effectively become the de facto standard model for accident investigation, having been endorsed by organizations such as the International Civil Aviation Organization and

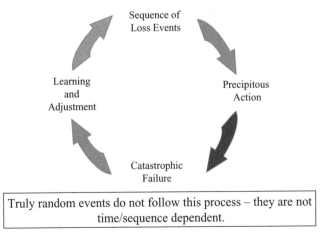

Figure 6.5   Systematic catastrophic-risk process.

accepted by many other industries including the chemical, nuclear and energy industries. However, whilst the Swiss cheese model is a powerful theoretical construct, the approach has a number of limitations that prevent its universal applicability. Unfortunately, it fails to take account of all five fundamental risk types. Rigid concentration on the identification of latent conditions can obscure the importance of active errors, which may be dominant factors in their own right and not merely symptoms of inherent systems weaknesses. In recognition of this, Reason stated: *The pendulum may have swung too far in our present attempts to track down possible errors and accident contributions that are widely separated in both time and place from the events themselves.*[26] With regard to prevention, Reason stated: *Maybe we are reaching the point of diminishing returns.*[27]

6.25   GRANULARITY

The loss distribution curve is comprised of data from the many different types of loss, each with different curve characteristics, collected from all business units within the organization. Where loss data are simply aggregated or too broadly defined, there is the possibility of concealing low impact events behind large ones. The loss database (risk register) should therefore allow separate analysis for each business unit and for each loss type. The degree of granularity required reflects the extent to which losses need to be disaggregated in order to enable individual loss types to be identified and their particular curve characteristics determined. However, it should be recognized that, whilst granularity increases understanding, unfortunately, it can also conceal the effects of correlation.

With regard to regulatory requirements, the new Basel Accord states: *A bank's risk measurement system must be sufficiently "granular" to capture the major drivers of operational risk affecting the shape of the tail of the loss estimates.*[28]

Work carried out by the Risk Management Group of Basel into operational risk granularity, resulted in development of an 8×7 matrix, categorizing risks by business line and event type (Table 6.2). Basel states that, in order to assist in supervisory validation, a bank must be able to map its historical internal loss data into the relevant level 1 supervisory categories (defined in Annexes 8 and 9) and to provide these data to supervisors upon request. The bank must document objective criteria for allocating losses to the specified business lines and event types. However, it is left to the bank to decide the extent to which it applies these categorizations in its internal operational risk measurement system.[29] From a regulatory perspective, standardization assists with benchmarking, and can be used to identify those

Table 6.2   Loss data analysis.

Basel identifies 8 business lines and requires losses to be analyzed over 7 event classifications:

Business lines	Loss event types
1. Corporate Finance	1. Internal Fraud
2. Trading & Sales	2. External Fraud
3. Retail Banking	3. Employment Practices & Workplace Safety
4. Commercial Banking	4. Clients, Products & Business Practices
5. Payment & Settlement	5. Damage to Physical Assets
6. Agency & Custody Services	6. Business Disruption & System Failures
7. Assessment Management	7. Execution, Delivery & Process Managements
8. Reatail Brokerage	

banks posing a threat to the regulatory objectives. However, in seeking to determine a standard methodology for the categorization of operational risks, it is important that a bank is not forced to adopt an approach that may be antithetical to its own internal risk control mechanism. Consequently, there are no requirements for a bank to map its internal loss data on an ongoing basis into the standard 8 × 7 matrix.

In practice, there is considerable diversity amongst banks regarding their approach to data classification and granularity. This is partly influenced by the differences in view between regulators, which varies from country to country.

Some banks have developed their own matrix for classifying operational risk losses, whilst others use the standard Basel 8 × 7 matrix. Some choose to ignore the issue altogether, instead using a single loss distribution curve for the whole enterprise. However, this approach tacitly assumes that all losses have the same probability of occurrence (i.e. they have identical statistical distributions) and that the losses are independent (i.e. there is no correlation). Such an approach is indeed a simplification of the real world. A more sophisticated approach involves establishing a set of models, possibly covering each business unit and each loss type. Some banks have chosen to go beyond this. Alternative approaches involve analysis of losses by client rather than product or concentration on causes rather than events. The level of granularity will obviously be limited by a paucity of data.

6.26 VALIDATION AND ADJUSTMENTS

Validation refers to the method of assessing the integrity and comprehensiveness of both the data itself and the data collection process. Validation is essential to ensure that the data upon which management decisions are made are reliable and appropriate. A bank must be able to tie its risk estimates to its actual loss experiences. Hence the actual loss data must be sound and must cover a sufficient period of time.[30] Given that data need to be comprehensive, a bank must be able to justify the exclusion of any activities or exposures (both individual and in combination), which would have a material impact on overall risk estimates.[31] Given its importance, validation forms an essential part of compliance both for Basel II and the Sarbanes-Oxley Act; internal and/or external auditors being required to perform regular reviews.

Data integrity and comprehensiveness are certainly two of the main concerns regarding emerging practices in the banking sector. In particular, reliance upon self-assessment techniques and voluntary loss reporting by employees may result in flawed data due to employee self interest.

Moody's assessment of Dresdner Bank is instructive. In its operational risk assessment prepared in October 2004, Moody's stated that Dresdner Bank seems to have made substantial efforts to overcome the subjective flaws in the standard OR (operational risk) tools. Verification is more rigorous than seen at other institutions: clear attention is being paid to verification of estimates of potential loss magnitudes and to "ownership" of losses. Processes are mapped end-to-end, with entries to the loss event register being made by all managers of the various departments comprising the overall process. Losses are assigned or apportioned to the departments responsible. The next level of management is automatically informed by electronic alerting, as is the risk control department. In all cases, assessments are checked by the central risk control function for consistency, particularly against those completed by owners of similar processes in other business lines or functions. After the risk control department is satisfied with the responses, these are further presented for verification to the reporting manager of the process owner. A final stage of "quality" or "relevance" assurance lies in the review by internal audit of the self-assessments.

ENDNOTES

[1] Basel II, paragraph 670.

[2] Basell II, paragraph 673, 2 bullet).

[3] Basel II, paragraph 673, 3 bullet.

[4] Basel II, paragraph 673, 4 bullet.

[5] Basel II, Annex 8, paragraph (b).

[6] Operational risk is defined as the risk of loss resulting from inadequate or failed internal processes, people and systems or from external events. This definition includes legal risk, but excludes strategic and reputational risk. Basel II, paragraph 644.

[7] The original industry definition of operational risk was simply *everything except credit risk and market risk*.

[8] Basel II, paragraph 673, fifth bullet.

[9] Basel II, paragraph 673, sixth bullet.

[10] See:

Lewis, H., Budnitz, R.J., Kouts, H.J., von Hippel, F., Lowenstein, W. and Zachariasen, F. (1978). Risk Assessment Review Group Report to the US Nuclear Regulatory Commission. Los Angeles, CA: Nuclear Regulatory Commission.

Collingridge, D. (1980). *The Social Control of Technology*. Milton Keynes: Open University Press.

Pidgeon, N.F. (1988). Risk Assessment and Accident Analysis. *Acta Psychologic* **68**, 355–68.

Funtowicz, S.O. and Ravetz, J.R. (1990). *Uncertainty and Quality in Science for Policy*. Dordrecht: Kluwer.

ACSNI (Advisory Committee on the Safety on Nuclear Installation Group on Human Factors) (1991). *Second Report: Human Reliability Assessment – A Critical Overview*. London: HMSO.

[11] Any data outliers should be the subject of individual examination. It may be the result of an error in the data or an indication of serious weakness.

[12] Toft, B. and Reynolds, S. (1997). *Learning from Disasters: A Management Approach*. Perpetuity Press.

[13] See:

Fiering, M. and Wilson, R. (1983). Attempts to Establish a Risk by Analogy. *Risk Analytics*, **3,** 3.

Reason, J. (1985). Predicting Human Error in High-risk Technology. Lecture to BPS Annual Conference, Swansea, March 1985.

[14] "Our main interest must be in the changeable and controllable." (Reason, 1997; see endnote 19).

[15] Taleb, N.N. (2004). *Fooled by Randomness: The Hidden Role of Chance in Life and in the Markets*, 2nd ed. Thomson Texere.

[16] Grose, V.L. (1987). *Managing Risk: Systematic Loss Prevention for Executives*. Englewood Cliffs, NJ: Prentice Hall.

[17] Reason, J. (1990). *Human Error.* NY: Cambridge University Press.

[18] Elms, D.G. and Turkstra, C.J. (1992). A Critique of Reliability theory. In: D. Blockley (Ed.) *Engineering Safety*. McGraw-Hill: pp. 427–445.

[19] Waring, A. (1992). Developing a Safety Culture. *The Safety & Health Practitioner;* April 1992.

[20] "Systems-Accidents have their primary origins in the fallible decisions made by designers and high-level (corporate or plant) managerial decision makers." (Reason, 1990, *Human Error*, p. 203).

[21] Edwards Deming, W. (2002). *Out of the Crisis*. MIT Press. See also: Life History of Deming: http://en.wikipedia.org/wiki/W._Edwards_Deming

[22] Crosby, P. (1997). Quality is Free. NY: McGraw-Hill. See also: http:// www.enotes.com/management-encyclopedia/quality-gurus

[23] Basel II, paragraph 674.

[24] Operational Riskdata eXchange Association (ORX): www.orx.org

[25] "The extent to which they are revealed will depend not so much upon the 'sickness' of the system, but on the resources available to the investigator." Reason, 1997; see endnote 19, p. 236.

[26] Reason, J. (1997). *Managing the Risk of Organizational Accidents*, Aldershot: Ashgate, p. 234.

[27] Reason, J. (2003). Aviation Psychology in the Twentieth Century: Did we Really Make a Difference? 2003 Australian Aviation Psychology Symposium, 1–5 December 2003, Sydney.

[28] Basel II, paragraph 669(c).

[29] Basel II, paragraph 673, bullet 1.

[30] Basel II, paragraph 672 'Internally generated operational risk measures used for regulatory capital purposes must be based on a minimum five-year observation period of internal loss data, whether the internal loss data is used directly to build the loss measure or to validate it. When the bank first moves to the AMA, a three-year historical data window is acceptable . . .

[31] Basel II, paragraph 673.

7

Data Analysis, Quantification, and Modeling

This chapter seeks to give an understanding of the fundamentals of data analysis, quantification, and modeling. Part II of this book gives a more detailed appreciation of the techniques involved.

7.1 ANALYZING DATA

If data is extracted from the loss-database and represented graphically on a time-severity diagram, the result would be a long chart with data points scattered on it in an apparently random manner, as shown in Figure 7.1. Clearly, this is of little use. The task is therefore to analyze this data in such a way that meaningful information can be derived. Initially, no assumptions are made about the data; any possible properties, such as risk type, correlation or originating business unit, are ignored.

If all the data for a particular period, say one year, are placed in order of magnitude, this would simply give a long line of data-points, since it is unlikely that any two loss events would have exactly the same value (to the last penny). However, by grouping the data into size bands, some interesting and potentially useful results start to emerge. The severity-frequency histogram obtained can be expected to show that there are many more smaller losses than larger ones, and the significance (absolute and relative frequency) of each grouping can be revealed, as shown in Figure 7.2.

However, it is important to recognize that there is no relationship between the different columns of the histogram. In other words, by knowing the number of losses in one column it is not possible to determine the number of losses in any other column. The diagram is therefore said to be discontinuous. It is also important to recognize that only historical data are being considered and the diagram is not trying to predict the future. Obviously, the sum of all the losses represents the total loss incurred by the organization during the particular period of time under consideration. Over a different period a different sum would no doubt be obtained, but the general distribution shape of the severity-frequency graph would be expected to be similar.

In order to improve the loss distribution diagram, the mid-point of each column can be calculated and a straight line drawn from the mid-point of one column to the mid-point of the next, as shown in Figure 7.3. If the columns are sufficiently narrow, the line diagram approximates to a continuous curve. Clearly, this requires a significant amount of data. Although a useful curve has been obtained, there is still no direct (continuous) relationship between the size of a loss (the independent variable, X) and its frequency of occurrence (the dependent variable, Y). In other words, although it is possible to choose a particular category of loss size and read from the graph its frequency of occurrence, it is not possible to take this information and derive the frequency of occurrence of a different loss size. To do this, a formula is required that expresses the relationship between X and Y. In actual fact, no such perfect relationship will exist in reality due to the occurrence of random events and the changing nature of relationships over

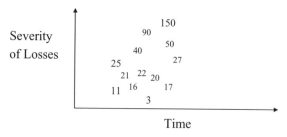

Figure 7.1   Modeling severity.
Source: Rodney Coleman

time, as discussed in the Chapter 6. However, it is often possible to find curves (continuous mathematical expressions) that match the data very closely over a given range.

The problem with fitting a continuous curve through discontinuous data is that the curve is unlikely to fit well over the entire data range. In particular, towards the extreme tail end of the curve (where there are only a few large-sized losses occurring very infrequently) the shortage of data makes it difficult to fit a continuous curve with any real degree of certainty (accuracy). In other words, it becomes unsafe to use the curve at the extreme to determine the size of rare events.

7.2   EMPIRICAL DISTRIBUTIONS

The most simplistic approach is to assume that the historical data fully prescribes the discrete probability distribution. The use of empirical distributions is becoming increasingly popular where there is sufficient historical data and there has been a period of continued stability (i.e. relationships have remained constant over the period). Empirical distributions are easy to use and require no limiting assumptions to be made by the analyst/modeler. However, if they are used to indicate what will continue to occur, then a tacit assumption is being made that the future will be the same as the past, which may be true in the short term but may be less so as time increases.

7.3   THEORETICAL PROBABILITY DISTRIBUTIONS – WHY IS IT NECESSARY TO COMBINE SEPARATE CURVES FOR FREQUENCY AND SEVERITY?

In the absence of sufficient historical data, an alternative to using an empirical distribution, is to assume a probability model represented by a theoretical probability density function.

In line with standard actuarial practice, Basel II requires the loss distribution curve to be constructed from a combination of two separate models (one for frequency and the other for severity). It is assumed that the frequency and severity of losses vary independently. Whilst this reasoning may be perfectly correct, it in no way invalidates the construction of an empirical severity–frequency curve, given sufficient data. However, it should be recognized

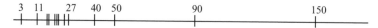

Figure 7.2   Losses shown in Figure 7.1 ordered by size.
Source: Rodney Coleman

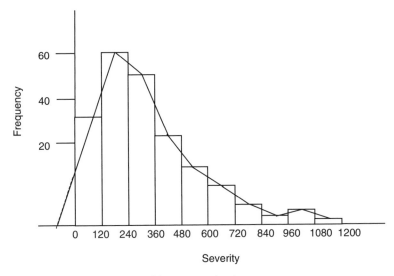

Figure 7.3 Distribution of loss events: histogram and polygon.
Source: Brendon Young and Rodney Coleman

that some management actions will affect just the severity of losses (e.g. wearing a seatbelt in a car) whilst others will affect just the frequency (e.g. better trained employees making fewer errors). Some actions, such as the introduction of straight-through-processing (STP) systems, will affect both; changing the complete loss distribution curve for the particular business unit concerned and thus rendering previous loss data inappropriate.

In an x–y graph, x is the independent variable and y is the dependent variable. In other words, x can assume any chosen value. By using a graph with a continuous curve the single value of y related to a particular value of x can be read off. The difference between this simple type of graph and that for severity–frequency (impact–likelihood) is that in the latter case both factors (x and y) are variable.

7.4 CHOOSING APPROPRIATE CURVES

In the absence of complete and comprehensive data, which prevents the use of empirical distributions, the analyst/modeler must choose appropriate parametric distributions for both severity and frequency.

There are a wide number of curves to choose from and it is here that the analyst's skills become important in determining their adequacy and appropriateness. It should be recognized that curves are simply being matched to the data. No assumptions are being made about the underlying causes of the losses.

Curves typically used to represent severity distributions (see also Chapter 19) include:

- normal (Gauss)
- lognormal
- inverse normal (Wald)
- exponential
- Weibull
- Pareto (Zeta)

- gamma
- Cauchy
- beta
- Rayleigh

Those curves used to represent frequency distributions (see also Chapter 19) include:

- Poisson
- negative binomial
- binomial
- hypergeometric
- geometric
- Polya-Aeppli (Poisson – geometric)

7.5   TESTING THE "GOODNESS OF FIT"

If empirical distributions are used there is clearly no need to test for "goodness of fit." However, with assumed parametric distributions the "goodness of fit" between the data and the chosen distribution is a prime consideration.

For severity distributions, the primary methods are:

- human observation;
- least-squares method;
- quantile-quantile (Q-Q) plots; and
- formal tests, including
  - Kolmogorov-Smirnov;
  - Anderson Darling;
  - Mann's test (for Weibull).

The same tests, where appropriate, can be used for frequency distributions. In addition, the formal chi-square test (Section 18.5.1) can be used for general distributions.

7.6   CHARACTERISTICS (MOMENTS) DEFINING A DISTRIBUTION CURVE

To appreciate "goodness of fit" it is necessary to be aware of the basic characteristics of data that are used to model a distribution curve. The four primary characteristics (known as *moments*) are:

1. mean[1] (the data average, denoted $\bar{x}$);
2. standard deviation[2] (the root mean square deviation of the data from its mean, denoted s);
3. skewness[3] (a scaled mean cubed deviation from the mean, denoted $\widehat{\beta_1}$);
4. peakedness (kurtosis)[4] (a scaled mean fourth power deviation from the mean, denoted $\widehat{\beta_2}$).

7.7   COMBINING THE SEVERITY AND FREQUENCY CURVES USING MONTE CARLO ANALYSIS

Having confirmed the adequacy of fit for both the severity and frequency distributions, the next step is to combine them in order to produce a loss distribution curve. Typically, this is done using Monte Carlo simulation. Fundamentally, this involves taking a random sample from the

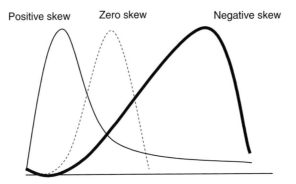

Figure 7.4 Skewness.
Source: Brendon Young and Rodney Coleman

severity curve and then a random sample from the frequency curve. This gives one point on the combined loss distribution graph (having coordinates *s1, f1*). This process is repeated a large number of times (say 10 000) until a robust loss distribution curve is produced.

Monte Carlo simulation is a powerful tool for risk analysis. A range of Monte Carlo-based simulation approaches has been developed and such computer-based programs are now ubiquitous. However, there are a number of potential limitations to bear in mind. Research into decision psychology indicates that experts are prone to overconfidence, overestimating the probability of occurrence of a forecasted outcome, and applying ranges that are too narrow to reflect the true uncertainty. Thus Monte Carlo simulation models have a tendency to underestimate the level of uncertainty and therefore the level of risk. In practice, it is also found that many users of Monte Carlo simulations rely entirely on the results generated without bothering to compare them against empirical observations; no criteria of acceptability being determined.

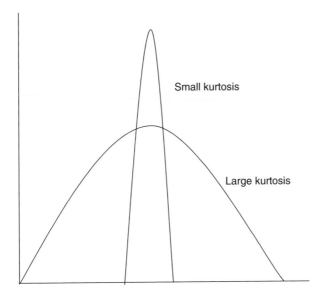

Figure 7.5 Peakedness.
Source: Brendon Young and Rodney Coleman

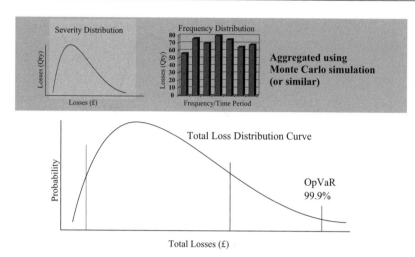

Figure 7.6   Total loss distribution produced from combination of severity distribution and frequency distribution.
Source: Rodney Coleman

7.8   EXTREME VALUE THEORY (EVT)

In practice, it is found necessary to distinguish between the main body of a distribution (where there is a relatively large amount of data) and the tail of a distribution (where there are few extreme losses). A different distribution curve will be necessary for the extreme tail. Extreme Value Theory (EVT) is a statistical technique for modeling the potential impact of rare events in the tail of the loss distribution using asymptotic theory. EVT allows an effective tail estimation to be obtained without making any particular assumptions regarding the shape of the tail.

There have been claims that EVT extrapolates extreme past events in order to try and predict the future. This is incorrect. EVT does not predict the future; it merely indicates the probability

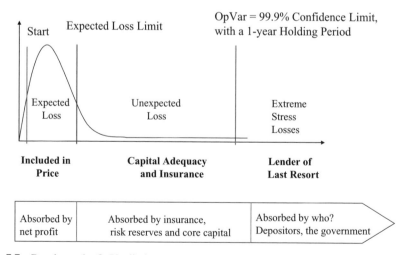

Figure 7.7   Basel sets the OpVar limit.
Source: Brendon Young

1. Minimum Cut-off Level
(Peaks over Threshold – POT)

2. Maximum Value for each Period
(Distribution of Period Maxima)

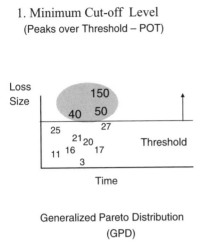

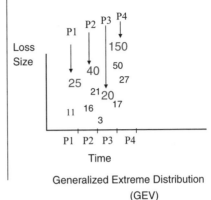

Generalized Pareto Distribution
(GPD)

Generalized Extreme Distribution
(GEV)

Figure 7.8   Extreme Value Theory.
Source: Rodney Coleman

of the occurrence of an extreme event. Such an event may never occur, although there is a possibility, however small, that it could. EVT will not tell you when, where, or why an extreme event will occur; it will merely give you an indication of the probabilities of such an event at chosen confidence levels. It may seem intuitively obvious that if extreme events have happened then they are representative of the open system (i.e. the business and its environment) and could therefore happen again. Indeed, a larger outlier must almost certainly be possible. EVT simply attempts to quantify this probability.

EVT was originally developed to determine the required height of dams following the severe floods in 1953 which resulted in the deaths of approximately 1800 people in Holland and many others elsewhere. It has subsequently been widely used in reliability theory (i.e. the probability of a nuclear meltdown; the probability of a catastrophic failure of a plane in flight, etc), and in various industries including computing, telecommunications and insurance (i.e. the probability of large insurance claims).

In selecting the data, there are two approaches. In the method known as Peaks Over Threshold (POT), only those loss events over a subjectively chosen threshold boundary are used. In the method known as Block Maxima, a sequence of periods are considered, and the largest event from each period is taken to provide the dataset to be evaluated. It should be recognized that, with small samples, the inclusion (or exclusion) of a single extreme operational risk event could significantly influence the shape of the tail and therefore the results obtained. Hence with small samples it can be seen that the model might not be accurate. Resampling techniques, including the bootstrap and jackknife methodologies (Section 26.6), can be used to reestimate parameters in order to determine their level of variation. The jackknife methodology involves recalculations of the parameter with all but one of the observed data values. In the bootstrap methodology, each estimate is based on a random sample of the same size taken with replacement from the data. Resampling techniques are based on the Central Limit Theorem, which fundamentally states that the value of a parameter derived from a sample will be approximately normally distributed about the true value for the parameter.

The most appropriate curves for use in EVT modeling are the Generalized Pareto Distribution (GPD) for POT data, and the General Extreme Value (GEV) distribution for Block Maxima.

The parameters relating to these curves which need to be determined are the shape, the scale, the location, and the distribution of standardized extremes. These parameters are estimated using the following methods: moments, probability weighted moments (PWM), and maximum likelihood (ML).

As yet, there is no formal method for testing the "goodness of fit" for EVT. The Kolmogorov-Smirnov test lacks power, whilst Q-Q and other diagnostic plots require skilled interpretation.

7.9   INTERPRETING THE RESULTS – THE ADEQUACY OF REGULATORY CAPITAL IS DIFFICULT TO DETERMINE

Unfortunately, there is a considerable amount of subjectivity involved in selecting the most appropriate curves and in determining the methodologies for fitting those models. This can lead to a wide variation in the results obtained, as shown in Figure 7.9, taken from the case study of Section 24.1.

From Table 24.1, the range of the four fitted quantiles (y-axis, in units of $1000) is 264 at the 95% confidence level, 1852 at the 99% level, and a massive 14 857 at the 99% level. Each is a close fit up to the 95% point, but the gap between highest and lowest at 99% is nearly $15 m. Figure 7.9 shows the largest observed loss to be at the 99.2% level. Thus the difficulty in complying with the Basel II requirements is obvious.

7.10   THE CAUSES OF RISK MEASUREMENT ERROR

Errors – or rather, variations – in measuring risk arise from a whole range of factors, including:

- the size of individual losses being incorrectly determined (including misallocation and timing errors);
- data shortage issues (including omissions and augmentation errors);
- model choice error (including incorrect parameter setting and poor fitting);
- model instability (arising from changes in frequency and severity relationships); and
- use of excessively high quantiles (where model robustness no longer applies).

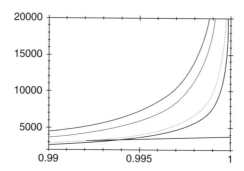

Figure 7.9   High confidence levels are not possible at the extremes (i.e. at the 99.9% quantile, different models give widely different answers – which one is correct?)
Source: Rodney Coleman

Subjectivity is involved in virtually every stage of the quantification process and leads to variation in results. With regard to loss data capture, subjectivity arises in assigning a loss (in part or in whole) to operational risk, to an event type, and to a particular event. Data augmentation, using external data, simulated data or near misses, also involves subjectivity, as does data censoring (i.e. ignoring data below a chosen threshold limit).

Model risk arises from two primary factors: firstly, from selecting inappropriate models for the data range being analyzed; and secondly, from parameter uncertainty. In analyzing the data it is the role of management to decide where the boundaries lie between expected, unexpected, and stress losses. It is most unlikely that a model that fits the main body of the data will also be appropriate for extreme values. In general, model risk increases with complexity and correlation dependencies.

7.11   MODEL VALIDATION, BACK TESTING, AND STRESS TESTING[5]

The validation of internal models used in determining capital adequacy, through back testing and stress testing, is essential and, indeed, is a fundamental regulatory requirement. Many violations of a model would imply that a bank is riskier than expected and therefore the model is inadequate. In contrast, a model that is too conservative will result in excess regulatory capital being held.

Fundamentally, back testing involves taking historical data and seeing how well they relate to model predictions.[6] Clearly, the historical data points that are of most interest are the extremes which have been experienced. However, as discussed previously, the inadequacies of historical operational risk data, particularly the shortage of extreme data and the extent to which the data are truly representative, limit the effectiveness of back testing.

Stress testing[7] can assist in overcoming some of the problems encountered with using historical data. Factors within the model can be given various selected values (including extremes) and the resultant impacts examined. Stress testing can include simply moving a parameter by a chosen significant amount, and it can incorporate external extreme data and also include the results from scenario analysis[8] and business continuity planning. It should be recognized that stress testing, whilst being a powerful diagnostic tool, only indicates the impact of a selected event, not its frequency. In general, stress testing ignores any correlation between variable stress factors.

It is important to ensure that a bad model is not being accepted or, indeed, that a good model is not being rejected. There are several tests and statistical techniques that can be of assistance:

- Testing to determine if there is any clustering of that data not matching the model. Statistically, this can be tested by the extremal index, using either the mean cluster size approach or the blocks approach.
- Testing to see if the size (impact value) of those data points that do not match the model is nevertheless still within acceptable boundaries. The Crnkovic-Drachman Q-Test[9] can be used to compare the CDF (cumulative distribution function) of the model with the latest actual impact data sample distribution function from measurements made on the P-P plot.
- Testing to see if the frequency of violations is acceptable. The Kupiec test[10] can be used to compare the violations ratio (number of exceptions to total sample size) with the confidence level.
- Testing to ensure that the capital requirement predicted by the model is not excessively different to actual ongoing experience (i.e. the business is not under- or over-capitalized).

Priority/ Rating	OpRisk Type	Loss Distribution Curves
1		
2		
3		
4		
5		
6		
7		
8		
9		
10		
Other		

Figure 7.10 Risk disaggregation: each risk category should have its own distribution curve – and this should be reviewed for each business unit.

Whilst essential, model validation[11] can be computationally demanding and extremely time consuming. The process needs to be properly constructed and should not simply be a one-off ad hoc occurrence. Model sign-off should be a board responsibility. Internal audit should regularly monitor the continuing adequacy of models.

It is not unusual for a model to represent the risk appetite of the board and for the businesses to adjust their operational risk management practices accordingly, with any model violations indicating areas requiring management attention.

7.12   LOSS DATA IS COMPRISED OF MANY DIFFERENT RISK TYPES, HENCE THE NEED FOR GRANULARITY

As discussed previously, the data used to construct the loss distribution curve are in fact comprised of many different loss types. Therefore, each column (or grouping) will consist of different quantities from each risk type. A further, more granular, analysis of data involves examining each risk type and its particular loss distribution curve. This can be extended to each business unit, as considered appropriate.

The fundamental challenge is in determining the dependence structure between the different cells[12] and the resultant impact.

7.13   RISK ASSESSMENT REQUIRES BOTH QUANTITATIVE AND QUALITATIVE METHODS

From a management perspective, understanding event-cause-effect relationships is important. In reality, such relationships can be complex, not necessarily constant or linear. Where a new system is introduced, losses will gradually decline as employees gain experience (known as the "learning curve effect") and may then remain relatively constant. Where new technology is introduced a "bath-tub" distribution may be experienced: losses gradually decrease during the "burn-in" period, remain relatively constant during the "useful-life" period, and finally increase again during the "burn-out" period.

In order to properly understand risk, it is necessary to adopt an approach based on "multiple lenses of perception." Risk assessment requires a balancing of both quantitative and nonquantitative (qualitative) methods. Quantification allows decisions to be made more rationally and openly, with assumptions and logic being explicitly displayed. It exposes underlying tacit assumptions and tests empirical views concerning the size and importance of losses. As such, it can lead to greater efficiency and effectiveness with regard to the control and allocation of resources. However, not all risks can be quantified; therefore, it is also necessary to use qualitative risk assessment approaches, which capture and employ inherent knowledge and expertise. Whilst quantification can indeed represent a significant step forward, it should be recognized that the enhancement of knowledge and understanding is often more important than the derivation of any absolute figure.

Typically, regulators from both the financial and nonfinancial sectors seek a single figure for risk assessment despite the fact that it is not possible to identify and quantify all risks. Risk theory, which is well advanced in other sectors such as the nuclear, chemical, and aerospace industries, indicates that:

- Quantifiable risks can be significantly influenced by nonquantifiable factors. Where such factors are better (or worse) than average, risk will be reduced (or increased) relative to the assessed level, but the actual amount may be indeterminate.
- Statistical theory states that it is not safe to predict losses far beyond the range for which data are available.
- Whilst important, mathematical modeling techniques (such as OpVar)[13] provide a simplified view of a complex situation; and therefore have limitations which need to be clearly appreciated to prevent misinterpretation. Their applicability needs to be constantly evaluated, given the changing financial environment.[14]
- Risk assessment processes are subjective and value laden. Organizational culture, internal political pressures and individual interpretation of company guidelines can lead to bias. Therefore, risk cannot be precisely defined and unambiguously measured in objective terms. Given the subjective nature of risk, individual perceptions need to be calibrated through benchmarking against referenced experiences.[15]
- The complexity of human behaviour prevents errors being prespecified and reduced to a simple numerical representation. With regard to the actions of people, these cannot be predicted with certainty. The wants, needs and motivations of individuals change with time and circumstances. Given the level of uncertainty associated with human behaviour in general and individual action in particular, it is not possible to predict and quantify all potential errors.[16]
- Organizations are open socio-technical systems and as such have an infinite number of ways of failing. Therefore, it is not possible to undertake a risk analysis of an organization and specify a complete set of failure modes. Accidents do not only result from poor average condition but also, more specifically, from particular instances usually involving abnormalities. It may be less important to assess risk on the assumption of achievement of a good industry standard of management and operational standards, but on the probability of failure of that assumption.[17]
- Holistic systems have additional emergent properties and are thus greater than the sum of the parts. A firm will have its own culture, reputation, and organizational knowledge. As an entity, a bank will have additional properties; hence it is not possible to simply sum risk assessments from individual constituent business units.

7.14   THE RISK ANALYSIS AND MODELING CONTINUUM

There is a continuum of methods available for analyzing and modeling risk. These range from the use of empirical distributions where there is sufficient data existing to fully define the probability distribution, through to methods relying on expert assessments, such as control

DATA ANALYSIS		MODELING		QUALITATIVE ANALYSIS TECHNIQUES
Empirically Distributions	Loss Data Analysis (LDA)	Neural Networks and Artificial Intelligence		Control Risk Self Assessment (CRSA)
	Extreme Value Theory	Causal Analysis		Business Continuity Management (BCM)
Data Mining	Regression Analysis	Bayesian Belief Networks		Scenario Analysis

Figure 7.11   Methods to analyze and model risk.
Source: Brendon Young, ORRF

risk self assessment (CRSA). In between these two polar approaches are various modeling techniques which seek to combine and interpret whatever quantitative and qualitative information is available. In particular, Bayesian Belief Networks (BBNs) seek to provide a more forensic, quantified view of causality.

It is unlikely that one method alone will prove entirely effective in assessing and understanding risk; consideration needs to be given to the past, the present, and the future. The appropriateness of any method will be dictated by the circumstances and objectives; each method requires different analytical skills and experience. In general, as the business environment becomes more dynamic and complex there is a move from historical analysis towards scenario analysis, as illustrated Figure 7.12.

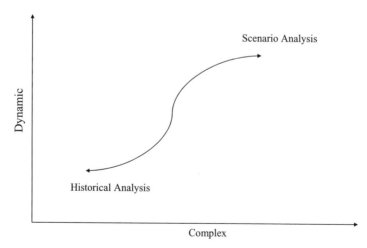

Figure 7.12   Complex–dynamic business environment analysis.
Source: Brendon Young, ORRF

It should be remembered that any model is merely a simplification of the real world and as such is subject to various limitations and uncertainties, including:

- data quality and completeness;
- the quality of expert judgements;
- parameter risk, resulting from uncertainty;
- variability, due to randomness of outputs (process error); and
- how well the model fits reality (model risk).

In developing a model it is important to be clear about its objectives and to minimize its complexity,[18] including limiting the number of parameters to a minimum (referred to as the principle of parsimony).

7.15   STOCHASTIC MODELING AND STOCHASTIC DIFFERENTIAL EQUATIONS (SDE)

In general, a stochastic process will have an underlying trend or pattern but, in addition, it also exhibits an element of randomness. Therefore, instead of only one deterministic outcome, a stochastic process may have many possible outcomes. These may be described by a probability distribution.

Stochastic modeling is a useful method for quantifying risks, providing probabilistic analysis is possible. However, it should be recognized that not all factors of uncertainty lend themselves to probabilistic analysis.

In financial engineering, stochastic differential equations (SDEs) are used to model the behavior of complex systems whose output cannot be precisely determined (e.g the rate of operational risk loss events, stock exchange movements, exchange rates, and the rate of insurance claims).

A differential equation is an equation which contains differential coefficients,[19] defining some property common to a family of curves. The solution of a differential equation is obtained by eliminating these differential coefficients. For example, in solving an nth order[20] differential equation, n successive integrations must be carried out. Since each integration introduces an arbitrary constant, the final solution will therefore contain n arbitrary constants. The *general solution* is the equation of any member of the family, and contains arbitrary constants (i.e. $y = 2x + c$ is the *general solution* of $dy/dx = 2$), whilst a *particular solution* is the equation of one specific member of the family (i.e. $y = 2x + 2$ is the *particular solution* obtained when $y = 4$ and $x = 1$).

Thus an SDE can be defined as an equation containing differential coefficients in which one or more of the terms is stochastic, thus producing a solution that is of necessity also stochastic.

With regard to rating assessments, the rating agencies specifically seek to identify those key factors in which a change would result in a change in the rating awarded to the organization. The difficulty arises in determining the rate of change that will sufficiently alter the risk profile to warrant a rating change. The situation is further complicated by the fact that the organization operates in a dynamic financial environment.

7.16   REGRESSION EQUATIONS

A regression equation is a model of a variable expressed in terms of its drivers or causal variable factors. Early examples in risk analysis were the failure prediction models developed by Beaver and Altman, as discussed previously. Within operational risk management, regression equations may consist of a number of key risk indicators and key performance indicators. Regression equations can be used to provide dynamic information on those factors underlying a specific risk.

7.17   QUANTIFYING EXPERT TESTIMONY

Where data are not readily available, probability estimates can be obtained through expert testimony. A simple direct approach is to ask an expert to assess the probability of an event occurring. However, behavioral science research indicates that such direct questions produce unreliable responses due to personal bias resulting from differences in knowledge, experience, and personal risk aversion. The "near-far" effect can often result in an individual attributing a higher probability estimate to an event that has recently occurred than would otherwise be justified. It is for this reason that simply asking experts to prioritize risks is of limited value. Decision and risk analysts have developed a number of methods to deal with these problems, including the *Preference Among Bets* approach, the *Relative Likelihood* approach, and the *Probability Distribution Estimation* approach.

7.17.1   Preference Among Bets

Under the *Preference Among Bets* approach an expert is asked to choose between two alternatives. These alternative outcomes are gradually adjusted until the expert is indifferent to the result (i.e. the probable outcomes are considered to be of equal value).

Events must be clearly and unambiguously defined. For example, rather than asking the probability of an event occurring, it is more precise to ask what is the probability of an event of a given value occurring in a given time frame.

To increase the accuracy of estimation it is advisable to ask the expert to estimate the probability of an event occurring and the probability of the event not occurring. Clearly, the sum of the probability plus its complement should total to 1. In practice, however, this may require several iterations to achieve.

7.17.2   Relative Likelihood

The *Relative Likelihood* methodology requires the expert to indicate whether the probability of an event occurring is more likely, less likely, or equally likely than the occurrence of a known event of known probability (the reference event).

7.17.3   Probability Distribution Estimation

This method seeks to more precisely define the properties of a random quantity and thus reduce its uncertainty. In particular, the aim is to attempt to define the full probability distribution. This is particularly appropriate for operational risk where there are a number of different risk types (Basel defines a 7×8 matrix), all having their own distribution curves.

7.18   CAUSAL ANALYSIS

A further, more forensic, approach is to decompose a risk into conditional causal factors taking account of event-cause-effect relationships. The probabilities and impacts relating to the underlying factors can then be considered. This approach can facilitate greater understanding of complex situations. It should be recognized that an event might have multiple causes and multiple effects.

Causal analysis allows input from functional domain experts and practitioners, accommodating both qualitative and quantitative data. As such, it can make use of other techniques, such as control risk self assessment (CRSA), scenario analysis, and business continuity management, as well as data analysis techniques.

Given its importance, causal analysis is considered in greater depth in Chapter 8.

7.19   CONCLUSIONS AND RECOMMENDATIONS

Data analysis, quantification and modeling require considerable analytical skills. At the moment these still appear to be in relatively limited supply.

The Basel confidence level requirement of 99.9 % for operational risk seems excessive and unjustifiable. Greater robustness could be achieved by choosing multiples of a lower quantile, or a combination of quantiles such as the 95 % and 99 % confidence limits.

A limited model choice for regulatory operational risk capital may be appropriate (i.e. possibly just the GEV or GPD). A particular choice of model within these classes, together with any estimation method, should be allowed as long as the model fit can be justified. This would assist in creating wider experience in the methodology and its interpretation.

Data analysis and quantification are necessary but not sufficient. Multiple lens of perception are necessary to properly understand and assess risk in a dynamic environment.

ENDNOTES

[1] Mean: the average.

[2] Standard deviation: This is a measure of the spread. It is calculated by taking the average value (mean) and measuring the amount that each value (all of them) is away from the mean. Since some differences will be below the mean and some will be above, it is necessary to square the values in order to get rid of the minus signs. Then it is a matter of summing all the squared values, calculating the average, then taking the square root.

[3] Skewness: This is a measure of distortion. It can be defined as the distance (i.e. the number of standard deviations) that the mode is from the mean. This is a dimensionless parameter, known as Pearson's definition of skewness. Note: The mode is the most frequently occurring value. $Skewness = (mean - mode)/(standard\ deviation)$.

[4] Peakedness (kurtosis): This indicates the nature of the spread of values around the mean. A distribution with a sharp peak in the middle is said to have a small kurtosis.

[5] See: Klugman, S., Panjer, H. and Wilmot, G. (2008). Loss Models. New York: John Wiley & Sons Inc.

[6] Back Testing involves taking an historical dataset and comparing the outputs predicted by the model to those events that actually occured. This may be repeated for datasets from several different periods. Whilst back testing provides an indication of the predictive capability of a model, it is of limited value in a dynamic environment.

[7] Stress Testing enables identification of those parameters in a model that have the greatest impact upon output results i.e. those factors that cause the greatest uncertainty or variability.

[8] Scenario analysis is concerned with varying a number of parameters at the same time in order to simulate a particular potential exceptional/extreme event (e.g. a market crash). Models based on stable conditions will be of limited ran at rates of 15 % to 20 % during the late 1970s to early 1980s.

[9] Crnkovic, C. and Drachman, J. (1996). Quality Control. Risk 9, 139–143.

[10] Kupiec, P. (1995). Techniques for Verifying the Accuracy of Risk Management Models. Journal of Derivatives 7, 41–52.

[11] Model validation is concerned with determining whether or not a model is "fit for purpose." This is a subjective process based on how well a model complies with predetermined checks. Reproducibility is an important validation check. If outputs cannot be reproduced then model stability is questionable. The relationship between inputs and outputs cannot therefore be determined.

[12] See:

Powosjowski, M.R., Reynolds, D. and Tuenter, J.H. (2002). Dependent Events and Operational Risk. *Algo Research Quarterly* **5(2)**, 65–73.

Chavez-Demoulin, V., Embrechts, P. and Neslehova, J. (2005). Quantitative Models for Operational Risk: Extremes, Dependence and Aggregation. *Journal of Banking and Finance* **30(10)**, 2563–2658.

Bocker, K. and Kluppelberg, C. (2007). *Multivariate Models for Operational Risk*. ERM Symposium.

[13] Value-at-Risk is defined as the value of the expected loss, at a chosen confidence level, for a particular time period. The Basel Committee has indicated that, under the advanced measurement approach (AMA), it will require a 1-year holding period and a 99.9 % confidence level. As stated previously, high confidence levels are difficult to establish given relatively few extreme data points.

[14] See:

Lewis, H., Budnitz, R.J., Kouts, H.J., von Hippel, F., Lowenstein, W. and Zachariasen, F. (1978). Risk Assessment Review Group Report to the US Nuclear Regulatory Commission. Los Angeles, CA: Nuclear Regulatory Commission.

Pitblado, R.M. and Slater, D.H. (1990). Quantitative Assessment of Process Safety Programs. Internal company document. Technica Inc., 335 East Campus Blvd, Columbus, OH43085.

Elms, D.G. and Turkstra, C.J. (1992). A Critique of Reliability. In: D. Blockley (Ed). *Engineering Safety*. London: McGraw-Hill, pp. 427–45.

Toft, B. (1996). Limits to the Mathematical Modeling of Disasters. In: C. Hood and D.K.C. Jones (Eds). *Accident and Design: Contemporary Debates in Risk Management*. London School of Economics and Political Science: UCL Press.

[15] See:

Otway, H. and Pahner, P. (1980). Risk Assessment. In: J. Dowie and P. Lefrere (Eds). *Risk and Chance: Selected Readings*. Milton Keynes: Open University Press, pp. 140–168.

Douglas, M. and Wildavsky, A. (1982). *Risk and Culture: An Analysis of the Selection of Technological Dangers*. Berkeley, CA: University of California Press.

Shrader-Frechette, K.S. (1991). Reductionist Approaches to Risk. In: D.G Mayo and R.D Hollander (Eds). *Acceptable Evidence: Science and Values in Risk Management*. New York: Oxford University Press.

Reid, S.G. (1992). Acceptable Risk. In: D. Blockley (Ed). *Engineering Safety*. London: McGraw-Hill, pp. 138–66.

Pidgeon, N., Hood, C.C., Jones, D.K.C., Turner, B.A. and Gibson, R. (1992). Risk Perception. In *Risk: Analysis, Perception and Management*, The Royal Society.

Slovic, P. (1992). Perception of Risk: Reflections on the Psychometric Paradign. In: S. Krimsky and D. Golding (Eds). *Social Theories of Risk*. West Point, CT: Praeger.

[16] See:

Grose, V.L. (1987). *Managing Risk: Systematic Loss Prevention for Executives*. Englewood Cliffs, NJ: Prentice Hall.

Reason, J. (1990). *Human Error*. New York: Cambridge University Press.

Elms, D.G. and Turkstra, C.J. (1992). A Critique of Reliability. In: D. Blockley (Ed). *Engineering safety*. London: McGraw-Hill, pp. 427–45.

Waring, A. (1992). Developing a Safety Culture. *The Safety & Health Practitioner* **10(4)**, 42–44.

[17] Tweeddale, H.M. (1992). Balancing Quantitative and Non Quantitative Risk Assessment. *Trans. Chem E.* **70**. Part B.

[18] See for example: Derman E. (1996). Model Risk. *Risk* **9:5**, 139–145.

[19] A differential equation is an equation containing any differential coefficients such as dy/dx or $d2y/dx2$.

[20] The order of a differential equation is determined by the highest differential coefficient present – i.e. $d^n y/dx^n$ would be an nth order differential equation.

8

Causal Analysis

8.1 INTRODUCTION

One of the main problems encountered within operational risk management is the difficulty in quantifying the information available in order to properly assess risk. Much of the knowledge contained within an organization is qualitative in nature and as such does not lend itself readily to quantification. Indeed, as stated previously, not all information can be quantified. In addition, traditional quantitative techniques have significant limitations. It should be recognized that statistical techniques such as Loss Data Analysis (LDA) and Extreme Value Theory (EVT) completely ignore causality. However, causal analysis is a key factor in adopting a more forensic approach.

From a management perspective, determining the cause of an event is essential. Toft[1] has stated that where organizations fail to learn from disasters, history is likely to repeat itself. In practice, it is often found that there is a tendency to treat the *effect* (outcome) rather than the underlying *cause*. Frequently, this is due to a lack of understanding (see Figure 8.2). Dr Edwards Deming demonstrated[2] that adjusting a system or process without profound knowledge and understanding can result in a loss of control and increased volatility.

The pressure to take action, and to be seen to be doing so, can often be overwhelming and can result in deleterious actions that worsen the situation. One senior executive of a New York bank decided to address a well-recognized problem experienced by bank tellers: that of cash balances at the end of the day not matching the accounting records. The approach adopted by the senior executive was simply to issue a zero-tolerance edict, stating that any teller who failed to reach the required standard within three months would be dismissed. This resulted in all the problems disappearing, to the delight of the senior executive and his board colleagues. Unfortunately, only the effect had been addressed, not the underlying causes. The problem persisted but was hidden from senior management by the tellers simply operating an undisclosed pooling system. Given that the original system was already in-balance and operating within capability, only fundamental changes to the system itself could have reduced variation and volatility. It is incorrect to assume that performance can be improved simply by the action of inspection, with defectives merely being identified and rejected. Auditing is not management.

Former Soviet leader Mikhail Gorbachev blamed the Chernobyl nuclear disaster on the workers at that plant. Similarly, a gas pipeline blast was also blamed on the laxness of workers. In fact, these events resulted from a combination of people–systems related factors. Blaming all faults on workers or, indeed, on management usually demonstrates a lack of understanding of the event-cause-effect relationship.

At the origin, causality reveals that all events are due to one (or a combination) of three fundamental causes: people, systems and processes, and external events (as shown in Figure 8.1). An event can have multiple effects and can result from multiple causes (see Figure 8.2). It is this interactive multiplicity that leads to complexity.

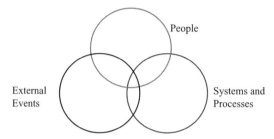

Figure 8.1 Complexity and chaos come from interaction.
Source: Brendon Young, ORRF

8.2 HISTORY OF CAUSALITY

Causality as a concept can be traced back to Aristotle, who stated: *All causes of things are beginnings; that we have scientific knowledge when we know the cause; that to know a thing's existence is to know the reason why it is.* Aristotle's thinking had a significant influence on the subsequent development of causal theories. However, theoretical debate appears to have added little to enlightenment, it having proved impossible to find a definition of causality that is unambiguous and applicable in all cases. Philosophers have identified a number of difficulties in establishing theories of causality.[3]

David Hume (1711–1776),[4] a Scottish philosopher, historian, and economist, put forward in his publication, *Treatise of Human Nature*, views that were considered revolutionary at the time, concerning causality, the problem of induction, and the distinction between fact and value. Hume criticized dogmatic rationalism as being sterile, and stated that: *Since only demonstrative reason can give us judgements having certainty, and since demonstrative reason can never tell us anything about the world, the attempt to have certain knowledge of the world is doomed to failure from the beginning. If we restrict ourselves to certain knowledge we will never know anything other than the relations of our own ideas.*

Hume argued that causes are inferred from observation of effects, whereas Kant (1724–1804) believed that people already possess innate assumptions relating to causes. Cheng[5] attempted to reconcile both these views, based on the theory that individuals interpret observations of

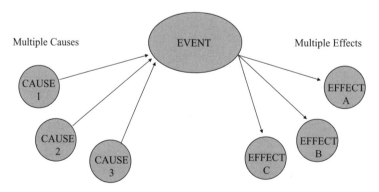

Figure 8.2 What data are being collected: (events, causes, or effects).
Source: Brendon Young, ORRF

events by employing a basic belief that causes have the power to generate (or prevent) effects, thus inferring cause-effect relationships.

The mathematician and physicist, Max Born (1882–1970) described three assumptions in the definition of causality:

1. "Causality postulates that there are laws by which the occurrence of an entity **B** of a certain class depends on the occurrence of an entity **A** of another class, where the word entity means any physical object, phenomenon, situation, or event. **A** is called the cause, **B** the effect."
2. "Antecedence postulates that the cause must be prior to, or at least simultaneous with, the effect."
3. "Contiguity postulates that cause and effect must be in spatial contact or connected by a chain of intermediate things in contact."

However, "relativity and quantum mechanics have forced physicists to abandon these assumptions as exact statements of what happens at the most fundamental levels, but they remain valid at the level of human experience."[6]

8.2.1   Probabilistic causation

Both Mellor[7] and Suppes[8] have defined causality in terms of a cause preceding and increasing the probability of the effect. Whilst a deterministic relationship requires that *if A causes B, then A must always be followed by B*, in practice, it is often found that the relationship between *A* and *B* is not perfect (i.e. a one-to-one mapping does not exist). Therefore, probabilistic causation states that *A probabilistically causes B if the occurence of A increases the probability of B*.

As stated previously, correlation does not imply causation. However, the possible existence of causal relationships among variables can be deduced from covariance analysis. Inference algorithms can be used to search among variables for possible causal structures, with those where the observed correlations are weak being discarded. The result of the analysis is a set of possible causal relations, which can then be tested for reasonableness. Causal direction can be determined by applying the assumption that a cause precedes its effects. Though not proving causality, time-lines increase the level of confidence in the direction and therefore the nature of causality

8.2.2   The counterfactual approach

David Kellogg Lewis (1941–2001) proposed the use of counterfactual statements to examine causality. The counterfactual approach has proved to be important in the study of medicine. For example, the experimental group (i.e. those receiving treatment) is used to demonstrate *"if X is present, then Y is present"* (i.e. if the patient receives treatment the disease will disappear). Whereas the control group (i.e. those not receiving treatment) allows testing of the proposition that *"if X does not occur, neither will Y"* (i.e. if a patient does not receive treatment then the disease will not disappear). Hence causality can be established using a counterfactual approach.

8.2.3 Mapping *necessary* or *sufficient* causes

Causes can be classified as being either *necessary* or *sufficient*.

If x is a necessary cause of y, then the existence of y necessarily implies the existence of x. However, the existence of x does not imply that y will result.

If x is a sufficient cause of y, then the existence of x must indicate the existence of y. However, the existence of y does not mean that x exists.

Where causes are both necessary and sufficient:

If x is a necessary and sufficient cause for y, then the existence of x implies the presence of y. Also, the presence of y implies the existence of x.

8.3   MAPPING CAUSALITY

In order to understand causality it is often helpful to draw a simple graphical representation, often referred to as a mind map. The various causal factors are shown as circles (referred to as "nodes") and the relational links between them shown as adjoining lines (sometimes referred to as "arcs"). The analysis can go down to as many levels as considered appropriate (see Figure 8.3).

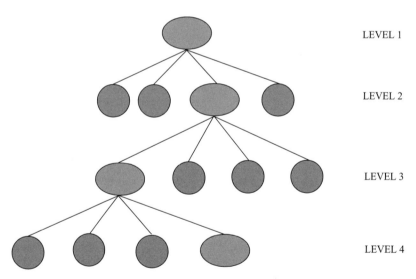

Figure 8.3   Causal analysis and mind maps.
Source: Brendon Young, ORRF

8.3.1   Towards quantification

Having gained an understanding of causal analysis, the next step is to attempt to quantify the information using both historical data and expert opinion, with a view to estimating probabilities.

Figure 8.4 illustrates two simple decision trees. To interpret these and the relationship between events and their probabilities we need some notation.

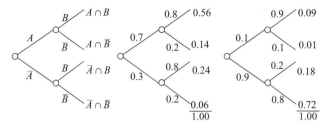

Figure 8.4 Three decision trees, the first shows the set of choices, the second gives their probabilities showing events A and B to be independent, and the third shows probabilities for which A and B are dependent on each other.
Source: Brendon Young, ORRF

Notation	We say	An example of what we mean
A		Ms A passes her banking exam
$\bar{A}$	not A	Ms A fails her banking exam
B		Mr B passes his banking exam
$\bar{B}$	not B	Mr B fails his banking exam
$A \cap B$	A and B	Both pass
$B \cap A$	B and A	Both pass
$A \cap \bar{B}$	A and not B	A passes and B fails
$\bar{A} \cap B$	not A and B	A fails and B passes
$\bar{A} \cap \bar{B}$	not A and not B	Both fail
$A \cup B$	A or B	One or other or both pass
$P(A)$	the probability of A	the probability of A passing
$P(\bar{A})$		the probability of A not passing
$P(A\|B)$	the probability of A given B	the probability of event A occuring given that the event B is known to have occured

This last one, $P(A|B)$, expresses the strength of the causal relationship and is known as the conditional probability of A given B, central to the probabilistic modeling for events.

Clearly we have the relationships:

- $P(\bar{A}) = 1 - P(A)$
- $P(\bar{A}|B) = 1 - P(A|B)$
- $P(A) = P(A \cap B) + P(A \cap \bar{B})$
- $P(A \cap B) + P(A \cap \bar{B}) + P(\bar{A} \cap B) + P(\bar{A} \cap \bar{B}) = 1$

In the first of the probability trees, we have the information that $P(B|A) = 0.8$ and $P(B|\bar{A}) = 0.8$, so the probability of B occuring does not depend on whether A does or not. This supplies the definition of independence.

- For two events A and B, if $P(A|B) = P(A)$ then A and B are independent.

In the second of the probability trees, and Figure 8.8, we have that:

- $P(A \cap B) = P(A) \times P(B|A)$.

This supplies the definition of conditional probability:

$$P(A|B) = \frac{P(A \cap B)}{P(B)}, \tag{8.1}$$

provided that $P(B)$ is non-zero, since obviously if B cannot occur, we cannot be given that is has.

- If A and B are independent, $P(A \cap B) = P(A) \times P(B)$.

It is a classic error to assume independence when is not appropriate to do so.

This kind of simple decision tree is useful for modeling chains of causal events, where the events unfold in a single direction. However, among other things, a decision tree cannot handle the backward propagation of evidence. That is, it cannot help analysts to link a consequence back to its underlying cause. And the traditional decision tree does not allow for the specification of common causes – i.e. multiple consequences arising from the same (parental) causal event(s).

8.3.2 Causal modeling techniques

Two of the most common causal modeling techniques used to identify the risk of failure (faults) within a system or process, are Fault Tree Analysis (FTA) and Failure Modes and Effects Analysis (FMEA). FMEA and FTA can be used to complement one another. FMEA can be used as a "bottom-up" tool, whereas FTA is better suited for "top-down" analysis. It should be recognized that FMEA is not able to discover complex multiple failure modes or to indicate expected failure intervals for a particular failure mode.

Fault Tree and Event Tree Analysis

Fault Tree Analysis (FTA) is concerned with the investigation of a selected undesirable effect, which forms the starting point (known as the "root" or "top" event) of a logic tree graph. Each potential cause of the effect is then added to the tree, forming a series of logic expressions (branches). Any path through the tree is referred to as a "cutset," with the shortest path being called the "minimal cutset." Where available, probabilities can be added throughout the tree and hence the risk of failure, calculated for each cutset.

Event Trees adopt a similar directed graphical approach to that of Fault Trees; however, an Event Tree begins with an initiator (e.g. a component failure or loss of critical supply), rather than an effect. The tree then graphs further possible related events, leading to identification of a series of final effects, whose probabilities can then be calculated.

Two of the most renowned analysis programes of these types are:

- SAPHIRE,[9] developed by the Idaho National Laboratory. This is used by the US Government to evaluate the safety and reliability of nuclear reactors, the Space Shuttle, and the International Space Station; and
- CAFTA, developed by the Electric Power Research Institute (EPRI). This is used by virtually all US nuclear power plants and by the majority of US and international aerospace manufacturers.

Failure Mode and Effects Analysis (FMEA)

Failure Mode and Effects Analysis (FMEA) is a detailed forensic methodology used to assess the risk of failure of a process or system. FMEA starts at the conceptual design stage and continues throughout the product life-cycle. The basic approach involves considering each element within a system and identifying the consequences of its failure, using the following three criteria:

- impact or severity (S);
- probability or likelihood of occurance (P);
- inability of controls to detect it (D).

Details of the risks identified and their controls are documented to assist in continuous improvement.

The methodology was originally developed by the US military in 1949 and was subsequently used in the Apollo space missions. FMEA is now widely used in the manufacturing and design industries. In the 1980s the methodology was famously used by Ford to eliminate design faults associated with fuel tanks.[10]

FMEA can be used to establish management priorities regarding risk mitigation actions. The overall rating is known as the *Risk Priority Number (RPN)* or *SOD Number* and is simply the product of Severity (S), Occurrence (O), and Detection (D) rankings. A simple FMEA scheme could have a scoring system ranging from 1 (lowest risk) to 10 (highest risk), for each of the three criteria. The overall ratings obtained can be used to prioritize all potential risks.

Within the banking industry, HSBC Consultants use a simple causal analysis system for operational risk, based on a project management approach. This involves documenting the existing processes and their controls, then identifying possible areas of weakness that increase the level of risk to the organization.

8.4   THE BAYESIAN APPROACH

The importance of the Bayesian approach to the estimation of probability is that it allows the estimate to be updated and improved in the light of new additional information. With regard to terminology, the probability of an event before the new information is received is known as the *prior* probability; the probability afterwards is referred to as the *posterior* probability. In the absence of no other information a rational person will assume that information based on the past will be a good indicator of the future. However, in the light of new information, that person may want to revise their belief about what the future could be like. This may be due to numerous factors such as: changes in the credit ratings of counterparties; regulatory and legislative changes; political, social, and environmental changes, etc. Where the business environment is changing fast then the new, *sample*, information may be a better indicator of the future. From Figures 8.5 and 8.6, it can be seen that the resultant posterior belief lies somewhere between the historical prior belief and the sample likelihood. Where a person is confident in their beliefs (i.e. the past is a good indicator of the future because the rate of change is infinitesimally small), then posterior belief will be the same as the prior belief. However, where the person has uncertain beliefs about the future (i.e. because the rate of change is rapid, and there is a high degree of complexity), the posterior belief will tend towards the sample likelihood.

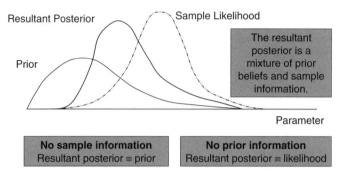

Figure 8.5   Priors, likelihoods, and resultant posteriors.
Source: Brendon Young, ORRF

8.4.1   Proof of Bayes' Formula

The mathematical theory underpinning Bayesian Belief Networks (BBNs) was introduced by the Reverend Thomas Bayes (1702–1761) around 250 years ago (see Figure 8.7). Bayes set out his theory of probability in "Essay Towards Solving a Problem in the Doctrine of Chances." This was published in the *Philosophical Transactions of the Royal Society of London* in 1764, after his death.

Suppose, for a particular bank, that 10 % of its risk team are members of ORRF. Of those who are, 90 % are classed as high performers. Only 20 % of those who are non-members of ORRF are viewed as high performers. If the bank is to appoint its head of risk at random from the high performers, what is the chance that a member of ORFF would be chosen?

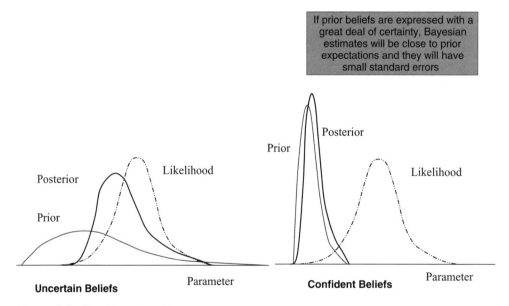

Figure 8.6   The effect of confidence.
Source: Brendon Young, ORRF

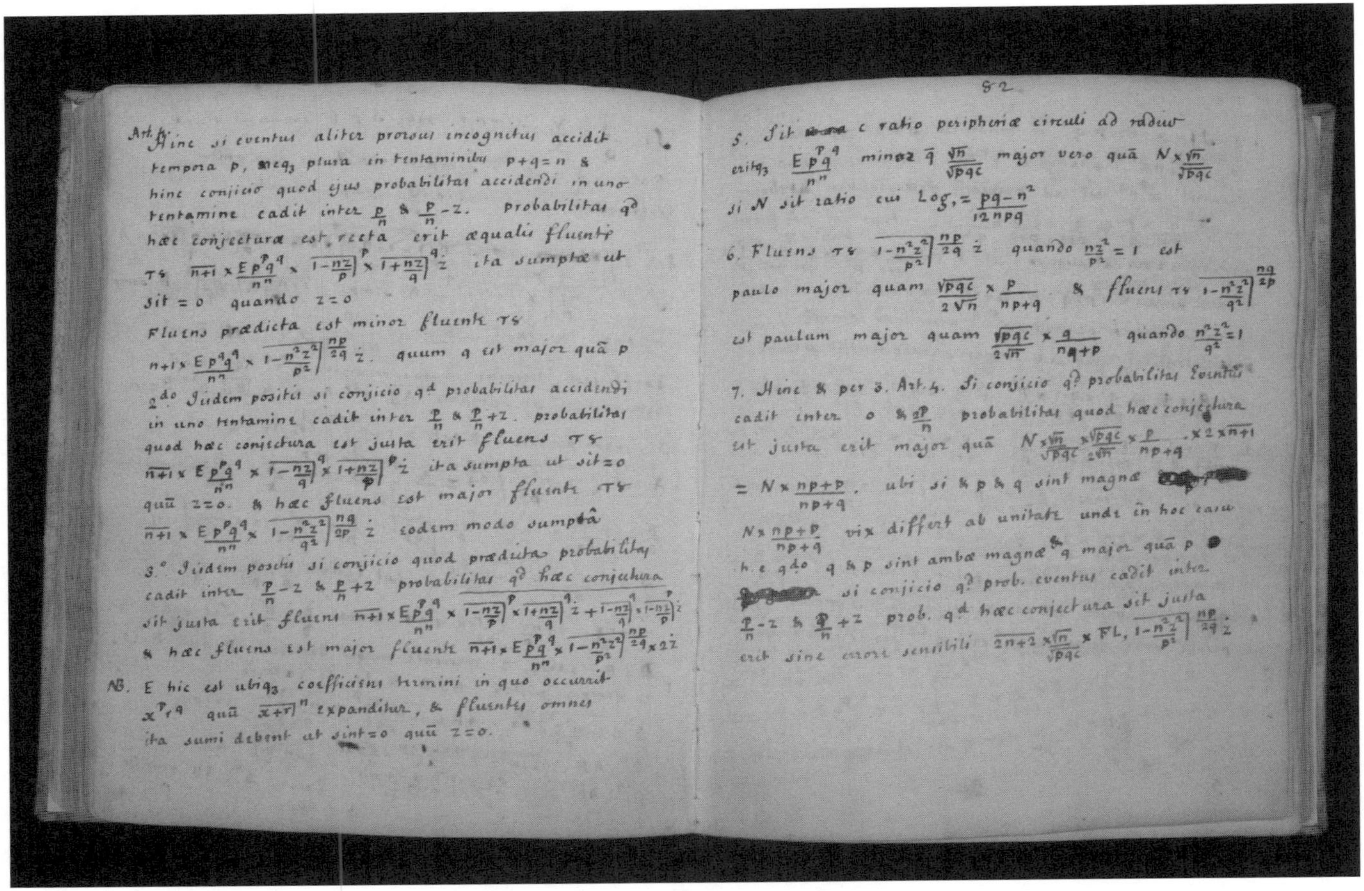

Figure 8.7 Pages from Bayes' notebook. Reproduced with permission from the Faculty of Actuaries and the Institute of Actuaries.

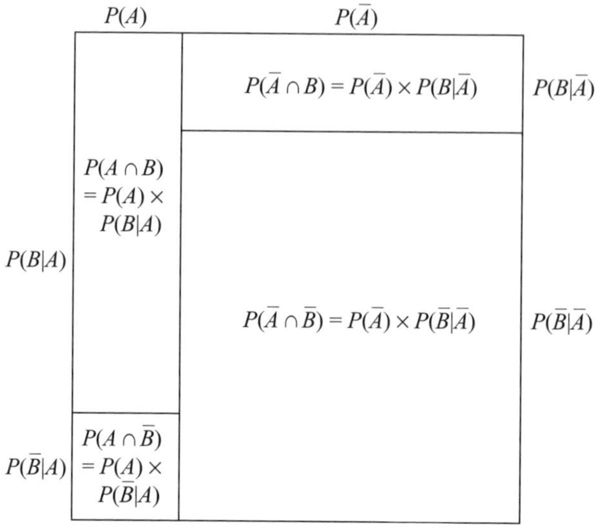

Figure 8.8 Areas represent the calculations of joint probabilities of A and B from a decision tree.
Source: Brendon Young, ORRF

Let A be membership and B be high performing. We have the information that $P(A) = 0.1$, that $P(B|A) = 0.9$, and that $P(B|\overline{A}) = 0.2$. This is the information given in the second probability tree of Figure 8.4. From the tree we have that $P(B) = P(A \cap B) + P(\overline{A} \cap B) = 0.09 + 0.18 = 0.27$, and $P(A|B) = P(A \cap B)/P(B) = 0.09/0.27 = 1/3$.

This is the inverse probability of reverse causality that Bayes formula gives: obtaining $P(A|B)$ from $P(B|A)$.

By taking Equation 8.1 and substituting for Pr(a V b) from Equation 8.2:

$$\Pr(a\,|\,b) = [\Pr(a) \times \Pr(b\,|\,a)]/\Pr(b)$$

This can be rearranged into the more useful and commonly seen form of Bayes' formula:

$$\Pr(a\,|\,b) = \Pr(b\,|\,a) \times \frac{\Pr(a)}{\Pr(b)}$$

8.4.2   Implications of Bayes' Formula

The importance of this expression is that it allows reverse mapping. It states that if you know **b** given **a** then you can determine **a** given **b**. This is one of the strengths of BBNs. It is possible to move both forwards and backwards through a Bayesian Belief Network – i.e. propagation is directionally independent. Although the probability of one factor in the net may not be known it can be estimated from others. Also, the probabilities of the various factors can be updated in the light of additional information – i.e. the net can learn over time.

In contrast, the traditional probability diagram is unidirectional – i.e. it is not possible to move from the end back to the beginning. It should be noted that, whilst the arcs (directional arrows) in a Bayesian network can be reversed, simply by applying the Bayesian expression, in the case of causality this is not possible – i.e. causality is directionally dependent (unidirectional).

8.4.3   Putting BBNs into practice

The essence of Bayesian probability theory is that it offers a means of reassessing probabilities in the light of additional information.

The approach requires construction of a causal network – i.e a Bayesian Belief Network (BBN).[11] The two major problems for a risk analyst seeking to build a Bayesian Belief Network are:

1. determining the activity/event nodes and establishing the relationship between the nodes; and
2. obtaining realistic probability estimates for each node.

A simple BBN graph is shown in Figure 8.9. Complexity often dictates the need to construct discrete subnets and subsequently conjoin them. The following diagram (see Figure 8.10) shows a BBN made up of four subgraphs. For clarity, the mathematical apparatus has not been added to this network. In practice, each of the nodes would contain the state of the variable that it represents and a conditional probability table (CPT), as shown in Figure 8.11. The CPT may contain historical data, expert opinion, or a combination of these. Both continuous and discrete loss distribution curves can be incorporated, using Monte Carlo simulation techniques to generate values. Hence the model is not restricted to any predetermined conjugate probability distributions. These are families of prior distributions chosen for their mathematical tractability, rather than for their representation of one's elicited personal prior belief.

Two major advances have greatly simplified the creation of complex networks. Firstly, standard modules of frequently-occurring nodes and arcs (idioms) have been identified.[12] This means that most BBNs can now be substantially constructed from combinations of a handful of idioms. Secondly, it is no longer necessary to identify all of the probability estimates in a network. In practice, it is only the probability estimates at the "boundaries" of the network that

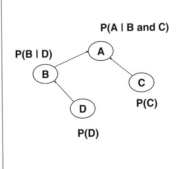

Figure 8.9   Bayesian Belief Nets (BBNs).
Source: Brendon Young, ORRF

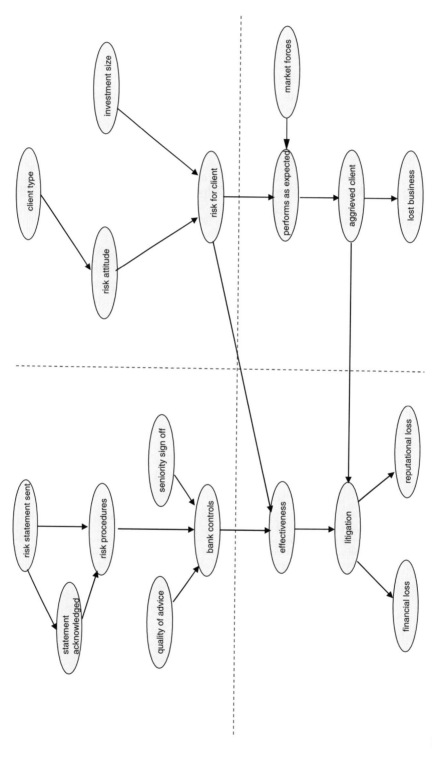

Figure 8.10 A full BBN: Comprised of four subnets.
Source: Brendon Young, ORRF

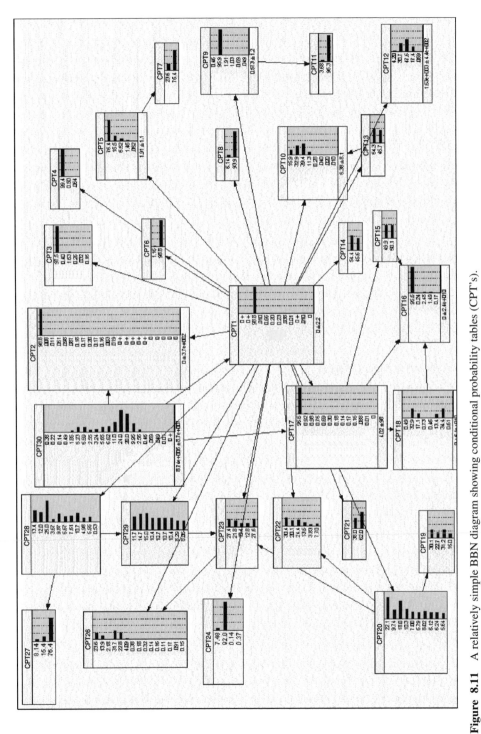

Figure 8.11 A relatively simple BBN diagram showing conditional probability tables (CPT's).

need to be determined. The remaining values can then be extrapolated automatically using an elicitation process.

Having constructed the BBN, the model can be compiled using appropriate propagation algorithms. Bayes' theory was of limited practical use until relatively recently, when break-throughs were made in the development of efficient propagation algorithms.[13] Tools incorporating these algorithms have subsequently been developed, allowing analysts to create very large and complex models.[14]

8.4.4 BBNs and correlation

Correlation remains the subject of much debate among operational risk practitioners. In general it assumes that the frequency and severity of loss events are independent. However, in practice this may not be the case over the entire data range. For example, poor control systems and weak management can be expected to increase both the frequency and severity of fraudulent events (i.e. the cause is common to both event-frequency and event-severity, hence frequency and severity are correlated, although not necessarily linearly). Fenton *et al.* have suggested that under independence, the VaR measure may be optimistic: ". . . when F and S are dependent we get a longer tail than when they are independent."[15]

For most organizations, a detailed correlation review of the institution's portfolio of operational risks would prove prohibitively difficult and expensive. Many variables in the operational risk environment are non-numerical and therefore not readily analyzed in terms of correlation. An alternative approach may be contingency analysis, since the tables created through the analysis represent estimates of a CPT (conditional probability table).

It can be argued that, by definition, the output of BBN modeling indicates the level of correlation between each of the variables, whether the nodal linkages are subjectively or objectively identified. Changing nodes and linkages in a BBN-based software program provides a means of testing the strength of any possible dependency. It therefore follows that BBNs could be useful in correlation analysis.

8.4.5 Uses of BBNs

Over the last few years, BBNs have been applied to a wide variety of problems, including those where very high levels of reliability and safety[16] are required, such as:

- determination of software reliability;
- detection and tracking of terrorist activity;[17]
- establishment of the probability of innocence or guilt of a defendant in a court trial;
- medical diagnosis (involving development of expert systems);
- diagnosis of space shuttle propulsion systems (VISTA by NASA/Rockwell); and
- situational assessment of nuclear power plants.

A more commonly encountered example is the Microsoft Office Assistant,[18] of which BBNs form the basis.

To date, one of the largest known models constructed is a decision-support system for improved reliability predictions of prototype military vehicles, developed for the Ministry of Defense.[19] This model contains several million nodes.

8.4.6   BBNs and their application to operational risk in financial institutions

While the use of BBNs is relatively advanced in industries such as computing and software engineering, it remains in a state of comparative infancy within the financial services sector. A number of issues arise out of the relative complexity of banking systems. In particular, it would in most cases be necessary to create a number of sub-networks rather than one single network that attempts to bring together all products and customers. One large South African national bank (ABSA) has already implemented a BBN model capturing its operational risk profile. A number of Italian banks have also made good progress. Those practitioners and academics familiar with the technique have said that BBNs could prove to be appropriate for such tasks as:

- validating and quantifying self-assessment reviews (CRSAs);
- supporting capital computation and allocation;
- providing early warning of bank failures; and
- providing structural forensic analysis underpinning risk rating assessments.[20]

8.4.7   Some limitations to BBNs

BBNs are investigative in nature, seeking to analyze causes. This is in contrast to traditional actuarial statistical techniques, which focus on the analysis of loss data (effects). Consequently, BBNs can be complex and require considerable expertise to construct. Since the business environment is dynamic, a BBN must be regularly maintained and constantly validated in order to correctly incorporate changes, both internally and externally. This can prove costly. BBN models represent a subjective view of reality; hence there can be no one uniquely correct model. Consequently, rigorous validation and testing are necessary. Subjectivity in the assessment of risk, as in control risk self assessments (CRSA), means that results are not readily reproducible, thus casting doubt on the outputs. Eliciting sufficiently accurate and meaningful probability estimates from domain experts can be difficult, although there are significant advantages in surfacing and challenging tacit knowledge. Inaccurate data can significantly reduce the value of the initial outputs from the model; however, BBNs can learn and thus their accuracy can be improved over time.

8.5   SUMMARY

Causal analysis is essential in improving management's understanding of the risks faced by an organization and thereby enabling appropriate action to be taken. Unfortunately, traditional actuarial statistical techniques ignore causality. Toft has indicated that, given a failure of hindsight and foresight, risk events are likely to be repeated. Edwards-Deming has highlighted the need for profound knowledge in order to improve performance.

Considerable advances have been made in recent years within the field of causal analysis, with sophisticated tools and software programs now available. Many sectors such as computing and software, aerospace, and the nuclear industries are well advanced in the area of causal risk analysis. However, with a few notable individual exceptions, the banking industry has been slow to embrace what is available.

A more forensic approach has been ushered in within the banking and financial services sector, by regulatory and legislative enactments such as Basel II, CAD III, MiFID, Sarbanes-Oxley, etc. Similarly, criticism of the rating agencies has resulted in their investigation into ways of adopting a more forensic and quantifiable methodology. These events represent manifestations of advances in knowledge and understanding, with operational risk management being seen as an important development in engendering greater understanding and confidence. It seems inevitable that causal analysis will eventually become more widespread in the banking and financial services sector, given its ability to improve understanding and thus reduce risk and volatility whilst also improving efficiency and effectiveness.

ENDNOTES

[1] Toft B. and Reynolds S. (2005). *Learning From Disasters – A Management Approach*. Perpetuity Press.

[2] Using his funnel experiment.

[3] There are many different views of causality. The *deterministic* view assumes a universe that is simply a chain of events following one after another, governed by cause-effect relationships, with there being no such thing as free will. Sometimes it is argued that the chain does not go backwards in time, but instead moves outwards towards eternity. Such ideas lead to causality theories such as the doctrine of responsibility assumption. One of the classic arguments for the existence of God is based on the premise that every natural event is the result of a cause. If this is so, then the events that caused the present events must have had causes, and they must also have had causes, and so forth. Since the chain is endless the hypothesis of an "actual infinite" is recognized. If the chain does have an initial causal event then it must be a supernatural cause at the start of the universe (i.e. a creation by God), possibly including the Big Bang Theory.

[4] http://www.humesociety.org/.

[5] Cheng, P.W. (1997). From Covariation to Causation: A Causal Power Theory. *Psychological Review* **104**, 367–405.

[6] Sowa J.F. (2000). *Processes and Causality*. http://www.jfsowa.com/ontology/causal.htm.

[7] Mellor, D.H. (1995). *The Facts of Causation*. London: Routledge.

[8] Suppes, P. (1970). *A Probabilistic Theory of Causality*. Amsterdam: North-Holland Publishing Company.

[9] SAPHIRE *(Systems Analysis Programs for Hands-on Integrated Reliability Evaluations)* is a probabilistic risk and reliability assessment software tool developed for the US Nuclear Regulatory Commission (NRC) by the Idaho National Laboratory. It can handle large fault trees, having up to 64 000 basic events and gates. Models explicitly capturing dynamic or time-dependent situations are not available in current versions.

[10] In April 1974, the Center for Auto Safety petitioned the National Highway Traffic Safety Administration to recall the Ford Pinto model due to a flaw in the design of the fuel tank strap. This defect made the vehicle prone to fire in the event of a moderate-speed rear end collision. The petition submitted was based upon the reports of attorneys regarding three deaths and four serious injuries in such accidents. On 9 June 1978, Ford Motor Company finally agreed to recall 1.5 million Ford Pinto and 30 000 Mercury Bobcat sedan and hatchback models for fuel tank design defects. The action was the result of investigations by the National Highway Traffic Safety Administration's Office of Defect Investigations (Case # C7-38).

[11] A BBN is a directed acyclical graphical representation model consisting of nodes, which represent variables, and arrows (arcs), which represent probabilistic dependencies between variables. See Jensen, F.V. (1996). *An Introduction to Bayesian Networks*. UCL Press.

[12] See www.agena.co.uk

[13] See: Speigelhalter, D.J. and Cowell, R.G. (1992). *Learning in Probabilistic Expert Systems*. Oxford: Oxford University Press, pp. 447–465.
Lauritzen, S.L. and Speigelhalter, D.J. (1988). Local Computations with Probabilities on Graphical Structures and their Application to Expert Systems [With Discussion]. *J. R. Stat. Soc. B* **50:2**, 157–224.
Pearl, J. (1988). *Probabilistic Reasoning in Intelligent Systems*. Palo Alto, CA: Morgan Kaufman.
Pearl, J. (1986). Fusion, Propagation and Structuring in Belief Networks. *Artificial Intelligence*, **29**, 241–288.

[14] See www.hugin.dk.

[15] Neil, M. Fenton N. and Tailor, M. (2005). *Using Bayesian Networks to Model Expected and Unexpected Operational Losses*, Risk Analysis, Vol. 25, No. 4, 2005.

[16] Fenton, N.E. et al. (1998). Assessing Dependability of Safety Critical Systems Using Diverse Evidence. *IEE Proceedings Software Engineering*, **145(1)**, 35–39.

[17] Pattipati, K. Willett, P. Allanach, J. Tu, H. and Satnam Singh, S. (2006). *Hidden Markov Models and Bayesian Networks for Counter-Terrorism*. Published online: 20 September 2006. Online ISBN: 9780471786566, Copyright © 2006 the Institute of Electrical and Electronics Engineers, Inc.

[18] Heckerman, D. (1995/6). A Tutorial on Learning Bayesian Networks. Technical Report MSR-TR-95-06; Microsoft Research.
Heckerman, D., Geiger, D. and Chickering, D.M. (1995). Learning Bayesian Networks: The Combination of Knowledge and Statistical Data. *Machine Learning* **20(3)**, 197–243.
Heckerman, D., Mamdani, A. and Wellman, M. (1995). Real-world Applications of Bayesian Networks. *Communications of the ACM* **38(3)**.

[19] TRACS (Transport Reliability Assessment & Calculation System): Overview, 1999, DERA project, E20262, http://www.agena.co.uk/tracs/index.html.

[20] ORRF is actively engaged in this field.

9

Scenario Analysis and Contingency Planning

At times, the world can look so complex and unpredictable that it becomes hard to make decisions. Scenario building is a discipline for breaking through this barrier. Ged Davis, Managing Director, Centre for Strategic Insight, World Economic Forum

9.1 INTRODUCTION

Scenario analysis is a methodology that seeks to provide a forward-looking approach to risk management. It is concerned with "being prepared" for possible types of events rather than trying to accurately predict the future. Scenario analysis facilitates the identification and analysis of high-impact risks, which may not have happened previously but where there is a possibility of occurrence in the future (e.g. terrorism, failure of integrated computer and telecommunications systems, natural disasters, severe economic volatility, etc). In order to provide a comprehensive assessment of the external business environment, scenario analysis often uses a detailed analysis approach, such as "PESTEL."[1]

With regard to quantification, in practice it is often found that data generated from scenario analysis are used to help supplement insufficient historical loss data, with scenario outputs being included within the (LDA) loss-distribution curve. However, the correctness of this practice is mathematically questionable. Combining two totally different data sets does not improve the overall quality of the data but instead leads to data corruption, resulting in the outputs being at best questionable.

In practice, scenario analysis often incorporates contingency planning and business continuity management. Contingency planning is primarily concerned with robustness (i.e. the ability to withstand high-impact, low-frequency, long-tail events). This is carried out to ensure controls and measures are put in place in order to address potential problems of the kind identified during the analysis stage. A record of these plans and controls, together with accountability, provide an auditable record of organizational preparedness and management capability.

9.2 HISTORICAL DEVELOPMENT

Scenario analysis has its origins in war and can be traced back to Sun Tzu,[2] a renowned 6th century BC Chinese military strategist. However, the Second World War proved to be the major catalyst for the study of complex systems. Industry quickly adopted and further developed these techniques, with organizations such as The Rand Corporation, Shell, and IBM being in the vanguard of development, together with academic institutions such as the Hudson Institute and Stanford University Research Institute (SRI).

In the 1950s the Rand Corporation developed the Delphi technique,[3] which became widely adopted in the 1970s as part of formal planning techniques. This involves seeking the views of a range of experts from different fields and, through a process of iteration, arriving at a consensus opinion.

The world economic recession of the 1970s, which was due to the oil embargo caused by the Yom Kippur war, resulted in considerable uncertainty. Consequently, scenario analysis became widely used by major corporations, with the US corporation, General Electric, being considered the leader in the field. It adopted a top-down approach and used various techniques including the Boston Consulting Group's formulaic growth-share matrix (Boston Box), which became the most widely-used strategic analysis tool of its time.

Large losses suffered by major corporations in the 1980s resulted in a change in approach – towards one of cost cutting, including retrenchment and downsizing. Simplistic formulaic approaches were blamed by some for exacerbating the precipitous decline of a number of major US corporations and, as a result, forward planning fell out of favour in *the realization by mainstream managers that they did not have the answers*.[4] Against this background, in 1985 Michael Porter introduced the concept of fundamental forces acting upon an organization, in which scenarios were considered important for understanding trends and carrying out stress analysis. During this period, other scenario techniques were introduced, including intuitive logistics (used by Shell and SRI International), trend-impact analysis, and cross-impact analysis.

In the 1990s there was a move towards value and growth, taking into account increasing complexity and possible future turbulence.

Since the early part of the new millennium, scenario analysis has been seen as an important approach to risk management, requiring the adoption of a more forensic approach. It is also seen as being important from a management development perspective for establishing a shared vision and providing a learning environment for increasing professional competence.

Scenario analysis has moved from predicting the future (i.e. a single solution approach) as proposed by the Delphi technique, to the recognition of complexity, with the need to determine a credible and coherent set of possible future outcomes (probability universe). Whilst trend analysis remains important for assessing the credibility of future estimates, scenario analysis seeks to also address those events that could upset trends (i.e. unexpected long-tail, extreme events). In addition, cross-impact and correlation analysis attempts to identify and analyze those forces acting on an organization, which may interact and produce a result greater than the sum of the parts.

Scenario analysis can be regarded as a methodology for dealing with complexity. Ackoff[5] identified three levels of complexity:

1. **Mess.** A mess is a complex issue, which is neither well defined nor precisely structured. Given the existence of a mess, it is not obvious what the actual problem is that needs to be addressed. Indeed, a mess may be an interaction of many problems.
2. **Problem.** A problem is a clearly formulated and well-defined issue. However, its solution is not singular. A problem may have many different, potentially viable solutions, depending upon values attributed to its multiple variables. Thus the most appropriate solution may vary over time, depending upon such factors as availability of funding, technology, and competitor action.
3. **Puzzle.** A puzzle is a clearly defined and precisely structured problem having a single correct solution that is entirely determinable.

Scenario analysis attempts to assess complex nonquantifiable situations that can have more than one outcome depending upon a number of variables. In effect, scenario analysis seeks to analyze a mess and structure it into a collection of related but clearly-defined problems and puzzles, with the aim of finding acceptable solutions to particular scenarios which may manifest themselves in the future. However, caution needs to be exercised: *One of the greatest mistakes that can be made when dealing with a mess is to carve off part of the mess, treat it as a problem and then solve it as a puzzle – ignoring its links with other aspects of the mess.*[6]

9.3 MORPHOLOGICAL ANALYSIS

In order to structure and investigate complex muti-dimensional, nonquantifiable situations, astrophysicists[7] developed a technique known as morphological analysis. This is a method for structuring and analyzing problems that contain nonresolvable uncertainties where a judgemental approach is essential. It is now used in many scientific disciplines where structural relationships are more important than straight quantification. In particular, it has been used for threat assessment, future studies, policy analysis, and strategy modeling (Coyle *et al.*, 1994; Pidd, 1969; Rhyne, 1995; Ritchey, 1997, 2006).[8]

Morphological analysis was specifically developed to turn a mess into a collection of structured problems. This is achieved by developing an input-output model, in which variables are defined, the conditional states of each variable determined and tested against those for each other variable, and a credible possible universe identified against which hypotheses can be evaluated and alternative solutions generated.

Morphological analysis does not have the same spatial restrictions as traditional topological analysis, which is usually limited to three-dimensional variables, the x-axis, y-axis, and z-axis (although embedded and rotational axes are possible). In contrast, morphological analysis does not have restrictions regarding the number of variables.

9.4 MODEL DEVELOPMENT

Morphological analysis involves two main stages: an analysis phase and a synthesis phase. However, in practice, model development is an interactive process. It should be remembered that a model is, of necessity, a simplification of the real world (reality having an infinite number of variables) but that a relatively small number of variables, if carefully selected and defined, can provide a robust understanding of a complex mess or problem. When developing the initial model it is often advisable to limit the number of variables to between 5–10, with more variables being added later as required. However, the initial model may still give rise to a very large total universe, possibly consisting of several million configurations. For example, a total universe having 10 variables, each of which is able to assume 10 separate and discrete values (states), will have 10 to the power of 10 possible configurations. Fortunately, it is possible, through use of computer-aided analysis,[9] to quickly reduce the size of the total universe (usually by around 90 %) through selecting limiting criteria. Having considered the consistency of conditions, it is often found necessary to reformulate parameters, either combining or subdividing them as appropriate. Morphological models have the advantage of being adaptable. They can be gradually improved over time in the light of further knowledge and experience.

9.4.1 The analysis phase

The overall aim of the analysis phase is to identify the main parameters (variables). An important part of the analysis involves determining the overall boundaries of the mess. Having identified the main variable parameters, it is then necessary to determine the possible states for each variable. Ideally, the conditional range (states) for each parameter should be mutually exclusive, with no overlapping or coexistence between different possible states of a variable parameter. The overall process is iterative, with the parameters and their conditions typically being reevaluated and revised or replaced many times.

9.4.2 The synthesis phase

The synthesis phase serves three purposes, allowing:

1. concepts and terminology to be clearly defined and agreed;
2. the creation of dialogue between knowledge specialists and participants, thus enabling tacit knowledge to be surfaced and underlying assumptions to be challenged; and
3. the credible universe (solution space) to be prescribed.

Whilst the initial analysis phase produces a total morphological universe having a large number of configurations, many will have logical and empirical contradictions. The synthesis phase enables a significant number of these to be discarded by considering the consistency between different pairs of parameters. This is achieved by judging the possibility of joint existence of conditions – i.e. "is condition 1 for parameter X consistent with condition 2 for parameter Y?" (say). This is repeated on a paired-parameter basis for all possible combinations of paired conditions. From this analysis, a cross-consistency matrix can be produced identifying the possible credible universe. Consistency can be determined by applying a simple tick/cross (consistent/nonconsistent) assessment although, in practice, a more detailed scale may be found more illuminating and preferable.

9.4.3 Using the model

Having defined the credible universe (solution space) it is possible to select a particular parameter condition and find all the solutions that contain the required condition. This is achieved by selecting the particular parameter condition as input, fixing it, and viewing the resultant surviving solution space. It is a property of the morphological universe that any independent variable can be selected as the fixed driver. Indeed, when investigating complex problems it may be necessary to select multiple drivers (e.g. risk type, location, and loss limit). In this way the model can be used to perform detailed sensitivity analysis.

9.5 MANAGEMENT AND FACILITATION

Traditionally, scenario analysis was conducted in a somewhat unstructured manner, typically involving a small group of subject matter experts using brainstorming techniques (often referred to as a BOGSAT methodology). The main problem with this approach is that it is not comprehensive, so that serious gaps in the analysis can result. However, the approach can prove useful as a starting point for identifying the main parameters for use in a more detailed and structured analysis. Given the complexity of morphological analysis, expert facilitation is often necessary.

From a management perspective, there has been a move away from the simple BOGSAT methodology towards intuitive logics, where the aim is to embed scenario analysis within the organization, changing the line-management mind-set towards anticipation of problems and identification of risks. The concept of scenario analysis often appears opaque to line managers whose priorities tend to be short term and whose focus is quite precise, being based on key indicators, budgets, and quarterly forecasts. Analyzing and preparing for risks that are extremely unlikely to occur may initially appear to be wasteful in terms of time and resources. However, it is important for the organization to be cognisant of early warning indicators. This requires a move from forecasting to foresight, with consideration being given to the consequences of current actions and the impact of possible future events.

Scenario analysis can be used at both the macro and micro levels, using top-down and bottom-up approaches. In practice, micro-level scenarios can be time consuming and are unlikely to provide information relevant to the extreme tail of a loss distribution.

Scenario analysis can facilitate the generation of benefits in the form of risk mitigation actions, often without the need for establishment of a risk quantum.

9.6   RELATIONSHIP BETWEEN SCENARIO ANALYSIS AND QUANTITATIVE TECHNIQUES

Quantitative techniques such as Loss Data Analysis and Extreme Value Theory are now recognized as important tools within the field of risk management. However, forecasts based on historical data and current trends can be misleading in a dynamic, changing business environment. It should be recognized that a forecast is merely one probability in a plethora of possible solutions. Other techniques, such as causal modeling, can prove useful in increasing understanding. However, complex situations (i.e. a mess) cannot be precisely delineated and may be nonreducible. In such cases, given the need for judgemental perceptions, morphological analysis techniques are required. Following structuring of a mess, traditional quantification techniques may prove appropriate for further, more forensic, analysis of the constituent parts.

9.7   VALIDITY AND REPEATABILITY

In any model it is essential to ensure that the data used is valid and that the results obtained are repeatable. Given the need for subjective judgement in scenario analysis, both validity and repeatability are difficult to achieve. Empirical evidence suggests that different experts, when presented with the same data, may arrive at different conclusions. However, this is no reason for discounting scenario analysis, since it can greatly assist understanding and insight. It is essential that all assumptions are recorded and properly challenged, that any data used are carefully examined using different lenses of perception, and that internal data are compared against various sources of external data.

9.8   APPLICATION OF SCENARIO ANALYSIS TO RISK MANAGEMENT WITHIN BANKS

The Industry Technical Working Group (ITWG) of Basel, which was responsible for evaluating scenario analysis, stated: *experience has found that the process can yield invaluable insight into risk and mitigation, and provide quantitative input into capital calculations that can be used with a certain degree of confidence in concert with other inputs. The primary set of issues related to scenario analysis is the inherently subjective nature of the process. However, some techniques have been identified to attempt to reduce the subjectivity and increase the repeatability. Overall, the quality of results that have been generated confirms scenario analysis as a key tool for operational risk management.*[10]

Scenario data can be used independently. However, in practice, it is often found that scenario data are combined in some way with historical data. Given the shortage of loss data, particularly in the tail of the loss distribution curve, banks have sought to supplement historical data with that generated from scenarios. As stated previously, whilst this may seem sensible from a practical viewpoint, the methodology lacks mathematical correctness. Datasets from different environments (timeframes) lack compatibility; therefore, the validity of combining them is questionable. Historical data can provide a sound factual base upon which to build; however, the underlying tacit assumption is that there will be no changes in either the business or internal control environments. Scenario analysis seeks to overcome the problem of the past not being truly representative of the future by taking a forward-looking view. The question therefore arises of the need to amend historical data (possibly through weighting) to reflect the future environment. The efficacy of such action is questionable given that it can result in 'reality lost'. In a dynamic, changing environment, judgement becomes essential; however, judgement involves probability and therefore should not be represented singularly as fact.

In practice, there are a number of approaches adopted by banks with regard to the use of scenario analysis for operational risk management. These include:

1. directly estimating the capital requirement from scenarios alone;
2. incorporating scenario data into the historical LDA (Loss Distribution Analysis) distribution;
3. producing a combined distribution from historical data and scenarios;
4. modifying historical data; and
5. stress testing risk types.

9.8.1 Directly estimating the capital requirement from scenarios alone

Clearly, if sufficient risk types are considered, it is possible to produce an aggregate distribution curve derived solely from scenarios, from which an initial capital requirement can be determined. For a particular risk type, the severity distribution and frequency distribution derived from scenarios are combined by use of a convolution technique, such as Monte Carlo simulation, in order to give a loss distribution curve. This process is repeated for each risk type. All the curves are then combined, again using a convolution technique. This scenario-derived distribution curve can then be compared for reasonableness to that generated from historical data. The approach has the advantage of not mixing two dissimilar datasets and is therefore not open to the charge of data corruption.

9.8.2 Incorporating scenario data into the historical LDA distribution

This is the simplest and most widely-used approach, with the aim of generating enough data points to provide a sufficiently comprehensive LDA curve.

The data point to be added to the LDA curve is represented by the expected value (E). For example, consider the case of a particular risk type that has a potential severity distribution of X1, X2, and X3 under scenarios 1, 2, and 3 respectively, and that the relative frequency-densities weightings are P1, P2 and P3 respectively. The potential event therefore has an expected loss of $E = X1^*P1 + X2^*P2 + X3^*P3$, the sum of each X multiplied by its corresponding P.

Since the analysis is concerned with potential events, rather than actual ones, the future outcome is uncertain and is therefore expressed as a probability distribution. Hence three primary loss scenarios need to be considered:

1. the expected loss;
2. the unexpected loss; and
3. the extreme (catastrophic) loss.

Mathematically, it is usual to consider the quartiles of a distribution, although more (including the 99.9 % quantile) can be selected as appropriate.

The methodology involves selecting a list of risk types (typically, the level-2 risk categories specified by Basel), then estimating their severities and frequencies for each of the range of scenarios (i.e. estimating the expected value for each risk type). This requires expert judgement, provided by business unit managers, risk managers, and technical experts, who need to take account of assessments of the future business and internal control environments as well as considering the appropriateness of historical loss data, both internal and external.

9.8.3 Producing a combined distribution from scenarios and historical data

A more sophisticated approach to the one described above involves use of simulation instead of expected value.

This methodology involves combining the scenario-generated distribution curve with the historical LDA curve, using a convolution technique such as Monte Carlo simulation, thus giving an aggregate loss distribution curve.

9.8.4 Modifying historical data

Another approach found in practice is the use of scenario data to modify historical data. The aim is to overcome the degradation in relevance of historical data over time, thus providing a more forward-looking model.

The methodology involves modifying both the frequency and severity distributions. With regard to frequency, the weighted average value of historical data (for either a business line or risk type) is multiplied by the estimated scenario frequency. For severity, the mean loss for historical data may be scaled by the average loss generated from scenario analysis. Weightings may be further amended by judgement, to take account of the degree of confidence in the different types of data. The modified frequency and severity curves are then combined in the usual way using a convolution technique.

9.8.5 Stress testing risk types

Scenario analysis can be particularly useful when carrying out stress testing. The analysis is concerned only with those extreme events that could appear in the tail of the loss distribution.

There are two commonly used methodologies, similar to those described above:

1. adding extreme data points to the LDA curve; and
2. varying parameter values.

Adding extreme data points to the LDA curve

With this approach, members of the risk review team are asked to identify *those risks that keep them awake at night*. In particular, they are asked to estimate the circumstances under which the specific event might occur and its impact given occurrence. Each data point is then simply added to the loss database for use in determining the LDA curve.

Varying parameter values

This approach assumes that the total risk is comprised of a summation of independent risks (i.e. those identified by Basel, say) and that for simplicity correlation is ignored.

Business experts are required to estimate for each risk type, the frequency of losses that could be expected to occur within selected severity ranges (histogram buckets). In addition, the stress loss is estimated and the circumstances determined in which it could be expected to occur. Frequency and severity distributions are then modeled, as usual using convolution techniques.

To determine the significance of the different risks, each in turn is taken to its stress value, whilst the other risks remain held at their expected values, the effect on the model being noted.

9.9   EXTERNAL BUSINESS ENVIRONMENT ASSESSMENT

It is essential for an organization to be aware of risks presented by the external business environment and to take appropriate management action in order to mitigate the potential impact of those risks. Indeed, such an assessment is a regulatory requirement. As discussed previously, an important part of the work of the credit rating agencies involves assessment of the external business environment, together with the level of preparedness of an individual firm.

The framework for understanding the external environment can be regarded as a number of layers that together comprise the strategic position of the organization (similar to the layers of an onion).

- **The first stage** is concerned with the nature of the environment: whether it is static and predictable or dynamic and complex.
- **The second stage** addresses those macro environmental factors likely to impact upon an organization's performance or development. This analysis is traditionally concerned with PESTEL factors.
- **The third stage** seeks to identify those key forces influencing the immediate competitive environment. Here, Porter's five forces analysis[11] can prove useful.
- **Stage four** considers the competitive position of the organization. This can be achieved through:
  - competitor analysis, which addresses the strengths and weaknesses of the organization in comparison to its competitors;

- market segment analysis, which assesses the relative attractiveness of the different market sectors;
- comparative attractiveness assessment, which relates the competitive standing of the organization in the different market segments; and
- strategic grouping, which involves identifying and analyzing the different types of strategies being pursued by competitors and those organizations adopting each particular strategy (e.g. global, regional, domestic, specialized).

This enables those important factors influencing the performance of the organization to be determined and the opportunities it has to be identified. The analysis takes into account the resources available to the organization, the relative competences it possesses, and the restrictions or advantages of its home base. It is important to relate opportunities and threats to risks, including the potential impact on volatility in both earnings and liquidity.

Risk and uncertainty increase as complexity and the rate of change increase. In a stable business environment (noncomplex-static), historical data are appropriate to use when forecasting the future. As the environment becomes more dynamic and complex (see Figure 9.1), an organization needs the ability to adapt rapidly to change. Whilst competitive advantage may be easier to obtain in a complex-dynamic environment, it may be more difficult to retain. Complexity may require decentralization.

The increasing move towards globalization is being driven by a number of factors. For instance, the needs of customers are converging in a number of markets. This provides opportunities in the form of a larger market and lower unit costs in the areas of overheads and product development. This can be particularly so in the financial services sector. Differences in the cost of labour and the relative strength of currencies has put pressure on organizations to relocate their activities to low-cost areas such as India and the Far East, since to do otherwise would put them at a competitive disadvantage. Political changes over the last 20 years have resulted in trading nations encouraging free markets. This has been further reinforced by regulatory, legislative, and technical standardization. As a result of these changes, competition has increased and with it further globalization.

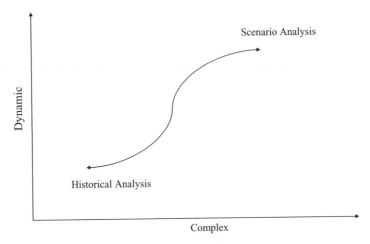

Figure 9.1   Complex-dynamic business environment analysis.
Source: Brendon Young, ORRF

There are inherent reasons why some countries are more competitive than others and, similarly, why certain industries are more competitive.[12] The City of London is an example of competitive advantage resulting from an innovative high-skill base with interrelated business activities in close proximity to one another, in a trading nation espousing free trade. Porter has argued that one of the main reasons for success can be the extent of competitive rivalry. In such a situation the domestic modus operandi can yield competitive advantages that can be exploited internationally. Hence competition and a level playing field are to be encouraged. Conversely, protectionism reduces the extent to which global strategies can be pursued and leads to an increase in costs and lower national and global economic wealth creation.

In a complex dynamic environment such as the financial services sector, predicting the longer-term future with any degree of accuracy is impossible. Hence it is appropriate to apply scenario analysis with a view to investigating alternative possible futures.

9.10   SHELL GLOBAL SCENARIOS TO 2025

Shell is recognized as a market leader in the use of scenarios. Its global scenarios[13] for the period up to 2025 are illuminating. They take account of profound changes in the business environment, which have been brought about by such events as acts of terrorism (e.g. 9/11) and corporate scandals (e.g. Enron). A consequence of these changes has been an increase in the complexity of interactions between market participants, the state, and society. The resulting sense of insecurity and the crisis of trust in market integrity have led to a greater role for the state in ensuring national security and maintaining confidence in the financial system and other markets. This has, to some extent, acted to the detriment of globalization, leading to a rethink of the previously-accepted concept; "There Is No Alternative" (TINA) to new technological advances, market liberalization, increased standardization, and hence further globalization.

The Shell global scenarios consider three types of driving force, which may be in conflict. These are:

1. market incentives, where efficiency is the prime objective;
2. regulatory and coercive forces, where the objective is security; and
3. community demands, whose objective is social cohesion.

The trade offs needed to reconcile these forces are analyzed using a "Trilemma Triangle," assuming three global scenarios or "possible futures" (see Figure 9.2).

9.10.1   Open doors

The first global scenario, Open Doors, assumes the market provides "built-in" solutions to the crises of security and trust. It is a pragmatic future that emphasizes transparency, corporate governance, and voluntary best practice, with efficiency being paramount. In this world, ratings are important; reputation and its protection is key.

9.10.2   Low trust globalization

Low trust globalization assumes the absence of market solutions to the crisis of security and trust. It is a legalistic world in which compliance with ever-changing intrusive rules and the need to manage complex risks are key challenges. Uncertainty leads to short-term portfolio optimization.

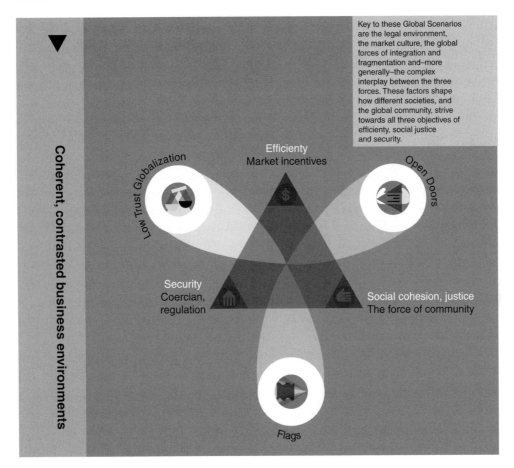

Key to these Global Scenarios are the legal environment, the market culture, the global forces of integration and fragmentation and–more generally–the complex interplay between the three forces. These factors shape how different societies, and the global community, strive towards all three objectives of efficienty, social justice and security.

Figure 9.2   Global scenarios.

9.10.3   Flags

The third, Flags, assumes a nationalistic fragmented approach to security and trust. Community values and security are emphasized at the expense of efficiency, with globalization being held back. In this world, there are conflicts over cultural values, religion, legislation, and regulation. Political interference exists and national champions may be regarded as being beyond the law. Hence market/country risk is a prime consideration.

Although the Trilemma analysis takes as its starting point the three global scenarios, it is not limited to these extremes. In fact, the methodology facilitates consideration of a broad set of possible and plausible futures, which involve complex tradeoffs between the three competing forces. Shell has moved from a three-year scenario cycle to an annual one, enabling regular monitoring of these forces and the identification of risks.

In considering the global scenarios it is necessary to see how they may play out in the different regions of the world and what impact different regions may have on others. Key questions to consider include:

1. Will the US continue to adopt a leadership role? In addition to its financial and military strength, the US has been playing a central role in determining global legal and regulatory matters. To what extent may this change?
2. What influence will the European approach, of mutual recognition together with a more decentralized view of global integration, have? To what extent will this bring about political change within the greater Europe and beyond?
3. How will the economic growth of China, currently fueled by cheap labour, market size, and increasing technological advancement, impact upon global competition? To what extent will China be held back by political and governance issues?
4. To what extent will the Middle East threaten global security and energy supplies?
5. How far will India succeed in fulfilling its potential for economic growth?
6. How will Africa develop and what impact will this have? What will be the financial cost and the outcome of issues such as the struggle against AIDS, poverty and war?
7. How will the world deal with an increase in population that is forecast to rise by 25 % over 20 years? What will be the significance of migration?

9.11 CONCLUSIONS

Whilst the future cannot be predicted with certainty, scenario analysis enables an organization to be prepared and thus become more responsive in its approach.

An organization that is open to change is much more likely to survive and thrive than one that is continually chasing events. Good scenarios are ones that explore the possible, not just the probable – providing a relevant challenge to the conventional wisdom of their users, and helping them prepare for the major changes ahead. Jeroen van der Veer, Chief Executive, Shell.

ENDNOTES

[1] PESTEL is an acronym for Political, Economic, Social, Technical, Environmental, and Legislative. These are considered to be the main external factors, although others may be added.
[2] Sun Tzu (544BC–496BC) wrote *The Art of War*, an immensely influential book on military strategy. Sun Tzu did not advocate war; instead, he put forward a set of philosophies on how to strategically avoid war during times of conflict and yet still remain in control. Sun Tzu was a contemporary of Confucius.
[3] The technique is named after the ancient Greek oracle at Delphi.
[4] Kleiner, A. (1996). *The Age of Heretics*. NY: Doubleday. "The stage was now set for the great managerial event of the late 1970s and early 1980s: the realization by mainstream managers that they did not have the answers. In 1978, Chrysler lost $ 205 million. General Electric, Kodak, Xerox, General Foods, all saw their market share drop precipitously."
[5] Ackoff, R. (1974). *Re-designing the Future*. NY: John Wiley & Sons Inc.
[6] Pidd, M. (1969). *Tools for Thinking*. Chichester: John Wiley & Sons Ltd.
[7] Zwicky, F. (1969). *Discovery, Invention, Research – Through the Morphological Approach*. Toronto: The Macmillan Company. Professor Fritz Zwicky developed the general "morphological" methodology in order to structure and investigate the total set of relationships contained in multi-dimensional, nonquantifiable, complex astrophysical problems. The term "morphology" is derived from the classical Greek word "morphe," meaning shape or form. Thus morphology is the study of the shape of an object (either physical or mental), including how the constituent parts coalesce to create the whole entity.

[8] See:

Coyle, R. G., Crawshay, R. and Sutton, L. (1994). Futures Assessments by Field Anomaly Relaxation. *Futures* **261**: 25–43.

Pidd, M. (1969). *Tools for Thinking*. Chichester: John Wiley & Sons Ltd.

Rhyne, R. (1995). Field Anomaly Relaxation – The Arts of Usage. *Futures* **27**: 6, 657–674.

Ritchey, T. (1997). Scenario Development and Risk Management using Morphological Field Analysis. In: *Proceedings of the 5th European Conference on Information Systems*, Vol. 3. Cork: Cork Publishing Company, pp. 1053–1059.

Ritchey, T. (2006). Problem Structuring using Computer-Aided Morphological Analysis. *Journal of the Operational Research Society*, Special Issue on Problem Structuring Methods, **57**, 792–801.

[9] Without the use of computers the number and range of parameters would be greatly limited (Rhyne, 1995; see endnote 8, Coyle *et al.* (1994) see also endnote 8). Also see Johansen, I. (1996). Planning for Future Conflict: A Morphological Approach. In: A. Woodcock and D. Davis (Eds). *Analytical Approaches to the Study of Future Conflict*. Clemensport, NS: Canadian Peacekeeping Press.

[10] Basel Committee on Banking Supervision Risk Management Group (2003). Conference on Leading Edge Issues in Operational Risk Management, held at the Federal Reserve Bank of New York, 29 May 2003.

[11] Porter M. E. (1980). *Competitive Strategy: Techniques for Analyzing Industries and Competitors*. Free Press.

[12] Porter M. E. (1990). *Competitive Advantage of Nations*. London: Macmillan.

[13] http://www-static.shell.com/static/aboutshell/downloads/our_strategy/shell_global_scenarios/exsum_23052005.pdf

10
Dynamic Financial Analysis

It is not only improvement in the average that is important but the avoidance of unwanted extremes.

10.1 INTRODUCTION

The business environment is dynamic; organizations are subject to forces that result in continuous change. Consequently, rating agencies and investment analysts expect management to demonstrate that not only are performance results in line with expectations but also that the future projections are realistic, with key risk factors having been identified and their possible impact upon volatility carefully assessed.

Whilst the financial impact of different strategies can be identified through the use of scenario analysis, scenarios tends to be deterministic in nature – i.e. a different scenario will give a completely different result. The requirement, therefore, is for a probabilistic financial model with the ability to properly reflect change, now and in the future, taking account of the key threats to the organization.

Dynamic Financial Analysis (DFA) is a well-established, practical modeling approach, which lends itself to the investigation of operational risk.[1] It is widely used within the actuarial profession and the insurance sector.[2] The term "Dynamic Financial Analysis (DFA)" refers to a variety of simulation models and techniques, integrated into one holistic, multivariate, dynamic simulation model. The integrated model may be either deterministic – which assumes that there is only one possible answer – or probabilistic – in which a range of outcomes is possible. A structured holistic model will tend to be more flexible and more readily adaptable to change if it is comprised of a number of submodels.

DFA seeks to model the reactions of an organization in response to a large number of interrelated risk factors, with a view to analyzing the impact of alternative decisions on an organization's bottom line. In particular, DFA provides a structured methodology for evaluating and better controlling an organization's risk profile. It enables determination of a more robust level of capital to support the risk profile accepted by the organization. Specifically, DFA enables an organization to gain a more informed understanding of both the risks and opportunities under a range of scenarios, and thus determine those alternatives that add the greatest marginal benefit.

From an operational risk perspective, the aim is to explore a range of possible outcomes using stochastic simulation techniques, with a view to evaluating alternative mitigation and control proposals, and thus prioritize actions. A DFA model can take into account loss event distributions (both historical and assumed) together with the associated costs, cashflow implications, and capital requirements. The impact of possible extreme events can be investigated, as can the possible effects of correlation and diversification. Since risk distributions can be relatively easily combined, DFA enables an enterprise-wide overview to be taken (which can include credit and market risk), thus facilitating more informed decisions.

10.2   BACKGROUND

DFA grew out of scenario planning work pioneered by the Rand Corporation. British and Finnish working groups investigating insolvency in the insurance industry later adopted the methodology.[3] Their work recognized the limitations of static, backward-looking accounting reports and records when attempting to assess future liquidity in a changing environment.

Historically, the improvement in modeling capability can be seen to have resulted from four separate stages of development:

1. **Traditional financial budgeting.** This is based on one set of assumptions about the future. It therefore merely gives one possible deterministic outcome (see Figure 10.1).
2. **Sensitivity analysis and stress testing.** The next generation of models used "what-if" analysis to undertake sensitivity analysis and stress testing. In addition to the expected outcome, the best and the worst cases were also identified (see Figure 10.2).
3. **Stochastic modeling.** Rather than being limited to fixed values and results, stochastic modeling takes into account probability and enables a range of possible outcomes to be considered (see Figure 10.3).
4. **Dynamic modeling.** By incorporating feedback loops and decision theory, a model can take into account management responses and thus adapt to changing situations. This allows alternative decisions to be evaluated and the range of outcomes compared under each decision path (see Figure 10.4).

Analysis using DFA differs from classical scenario testing of business plans in the number of scenarios used and the level of complexity of the holistic model. DFA is more forensic. DFA allows a large number (many thousands) of scenarios to be generated stochastically and probability distributions of key variables determined, with these then being applied to complex interrelationships.

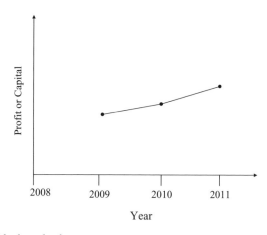

Figure 10.1   Annual budgeted value.

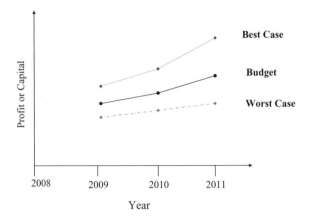

Figure 10.2   Sensitivity and stress-test boundaries.

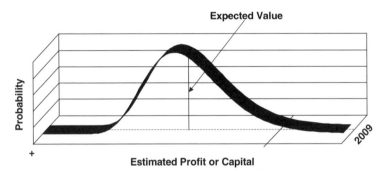

Figure 10.3   Stochastic model.

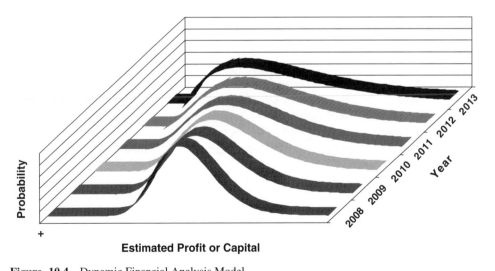

Figure 10.4   Dynamic Financial Analysis Model.

10.3   THE GENERALIZED DFA FRAMEWORK

The generalized DFA framework is comprised of the following six fundamental elements:

- **Parameterization.** Suitable parameters for the model are needed in order to produce sensible scenarios.
- **Scenario generation.** A large number of scenarios[4] are produced, showing the relational behaviour between all risk factors. This involves the use of stochastic models, employing Monte Carlo[5] simulation.
- **Holistic modeling.** The company's model is comprised of a number of parameters under the control of management. The variability of these parameters is recorded for each scenario.
- **Analysis and presentation.** Sophisticated analysis and presentation facilities are necessary to extract information from the large number of Monte Carlo simulation outputs. Statistical analysis, graphical methods, and drill-down analysis techniques can be used.
- **Strategy formulation.** A strategy can be considered to be comprised of a set of values for those parameters under the control of management.
- **Control and optimization.** The outputs are used to adjust the strategy until the parameters are optimized. The aim is to set values for those parameters under the control of management, with a view to maximizing value.

10.4   DFA METHODOLOGY

Although there is no single correct approach regarding the application of DFA to the investigation of operational risk, a suggested methodology involves the construction of several different models, which are then compared and contrasted under different scenario conditions:

- **Implicit model.** Firstly, an implicit model is constructed using historical data, containing all operational risk loss events. This model acts as a reality check.
- **Adjust historical data – remove operational risks.** Next, those operational risks to be modeled explicitly are identified and the historical data adjusted accordingly to remove them.
- **Zero-base model.** A second, simple zero-base model is then constructed with all the explicit operational risks removed. This model represents, theoretically, what the organization could achieve if all operational risks were reduced to zero. It should be noted that no additional charges are included for the increased level of risk management that would be required in practice. Although this model is somewhat simplistic, by comparing it to the first implicit model an initial indication of the impact of operational risk can be obtained.
- **Model operational risks separately.** The operational risk types identified are modeled explicitly, taking and adjusting historical data to reflect the current control environment, as briefly discussed below.
- **Explicit model.** A third, explicit, model is created by taking the zero-base model and adding in the explicitly modeled operational risks. This explicit model is compared to the first implicit model and any differences in output considered.
- **Revise historical operational risk data.** The explicitly modeled operational risks are reevaluated to reflect future expectations and controls. In practice, external data may also be incorporated, once suitably adjusted.
- **Revised explicit model.** A fourth model is then created, using the revised explicit operational risks. The impact of future proposals can thus be evaluated.

- **Use scenario analysis.** Where relevant, the models are evaluated under various scenarios and stress-test conditions, and their outputs compared.

10.5   DATA CONSIDERATIONS

Historical loss data may no longer be relevant since the causes of those losses may have been mitigated, either wholly or in part. Loss events of an extreme nature will have less discernable recurring loss patterns. Consequently, spiked volatility may be introduced into performance curves. Such low-frequency/high-impact events lead to distortion of historical loss data distributions. The extent to which extreme events can be reduced depends upon their causes. Those resulting from the accumulation of lesser errors can be prevented or significantly reduced by risk management actions and controls (i.e. "breaking the chain"); similarly, those due to the deliberate wilful actions of employees or people external to the organization can be reduced in frequency, and possibly size if caught early. However, totally random nonrecurring events require an organization to be prepared, resilient and responsive. Data is discussed in more detail in an earlier chapter.

10.6   AGGREGATION, CORRELATION, AND DIVERSIFICATION

The model needs to encapsulate all of those risks accepted by the organization. However, simple aggregation is unlikely to be appropriate. Model development requires a sound understanding of the dependency between risks. DFA techniques enable assumptions regarding linkages between risk drivers, diversification, and correlation to be evaluated. It is important to identify and determine these interactions otherwise the model will generate meaningless output results.

Risk diversification can reduce the level of risk-based capital an organization needs. However, risks are rarely completely independent and dependency between risks reduces the benefits of diversification. The regulators do not fully recognize the benefits of diversification because, in their experience, the actual benefits realized are often less than those predicted by models, especially across different risk types.[6]

Correlation between risks is not constant but may vary over time. Neither is correlation necessarily constant over the whole range of data. In times of stress, if one thing goes wrong then everything else may also go wrong at the same time. Thus linear dependency models can give misleading results and underestimate the level of risk-based capital needed to support the business in stress situations. From a banking perspective, major catastrophes can lead to losses in multiple business units.

In general, dependency is modeled through linear correlation. However, as indicated above, dependency is not always linear. In such situations, copulas can prove useful. Whilst sufficient data may not be available to estimate the copulas, it is still possible to incorporate expert opinion.

10.7   LIMITATIONS OF DFA MODELS

1. **The model may be incomplete.** Dynamic Financial Analysis is a models-based approach and, as with all models, the quality of the output is dependent upon the quality and quantity of data together with the soundness of the assumptions made, both overtly and tacitly.
2. **The model may be incorrectly specified.** In practice, models used in dynamic financial analysis often lack theoretical soundness and robustness. Many simplifying assumptions

may be made. Management therefore needs to be aware of the limitations of the model. Models with feedback loops may indicate a relatively low level of risk because of a built-in assumption that management action will be taken to mitigate and minimize risk. However, this assumption may be incorrect in actual practice. A model that is incorrectly specified will fail in its purpose. The failure of Long Term Capital Management (LTCM) was due to model failure, and the failure of management to recognize its limitations.

3. **Complexity can lead to model risk.** Extremely large and complex models with many variables can be difficult to use. They rely on complex software tools and require a large amount of computing power, although this is becoming less of a problem as computer technology continues to advance. Model risk can be high because of the large number of variables. Additionally, a holistic model may be comprised of many individual modules. Whilst these modules may prove acceptable when used independently they may produce unrealistic results when combined.

4. **Scenarios may no longer be appropriate.** Strategic assumptions are a fundamental part of the underlying logic, which affects the architectural structure of the model. Where the model has many decisions incorporated into its logic, flexibility can be compromised.

5. **The model may become obsolete.** It is important to test the results obtained and validate the reasonableness of assumptions to ensure that the logic of the model is still appropriate given an ever-changing environment, both internally and externally. Often the insights gained from analytical efforts may be more significant than the accuracy of the outputs obtained from the model.

6. **Models can be costly and require a high level of interpretational skill.** DFA models are often complex and require a high level of interpretational skill. DFA requires a significant ongoing investment in time and effort. Hence, the decision to use the methodology should not be viewed as insignificant.

10.8   OUTPUTS AND ANALYSIS

The *raison d'être* of Dynamic Financial Analysis is the evaluation and optimization of risk. This requires both financial and analytical outputs, including: financial statements (P&L, cashflow, balance sheet); statistical information and representations; and database analyses.

An important element of DFA is solvency testing – i.e. determining the amount of capital an organization will require given the level of risk to which it is exposed (its risk appetite). However, rather than simply treating capital as a reservoir, consideration needs to be given to cashflow and the ability of the organization to meet its commitments as and when they fall due. With regard to potential loss events, in addition to modeling frequency and severity it is also necessary to model the uncertainties involved within the resultant cashflow process (i.e. the cashflow implications of a loss event may be felt over a long period).

Since dynamic models contain feedback loops, the volume of data produced can be overwhelming. Diagnostic capabilities including drill-down facilities are therefore essential in order to enable the major drivers to be identified. The correct interpretation of this data and accurate communication of the information are important considerations.

10.9   THE FUTURE

Adopting a dynamic approach to risk management enables losses to be minimized through prompt corrective action and for risks to be more tightly controlled, in line with the risk

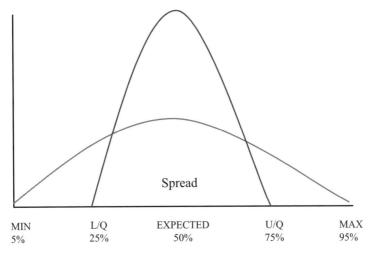

MIN   L/Q   EXPECTED   U/Q   MAX
5%   25%   50%   75%   95%

Figure 10.5 Earnings diagram (pictorial only – not mathematically correct).
Source: Brendon Young, ORRF

appetite of the organization. The distribution spread of losses can be reduced and contained within set bounds (as shown in Figure 10.5).

In addition, improved risk management can lead to enhanced efficiency and effectiveness, resulting in improved performance (as shown in Figure 10.6).

Consequently, the volatility of earnings can be reduced (as shown in Figure 10.7) and the level of performance can be raised above the minimum required amount (as shown in Figure 10.8).

Whilst fully integrated risk management in the banking industry may currently be more of a vision than a reality, there is certainly a trend in this direction. The Board of Actuarial Standards (BAS), which is part of the Financial Reporting Council (FRC) is in the process

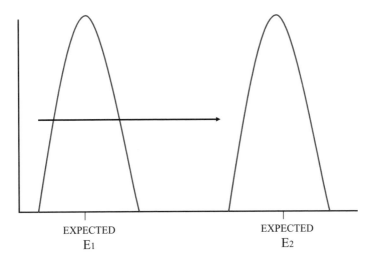

EXPECTED   EXPECTED
E1   E2

Figure 10.6 Performance improvement.
Source: Brendon Young, ORRF

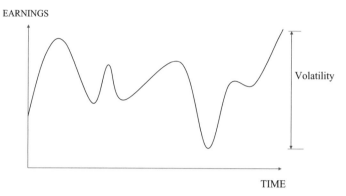

Figure 10.7   Reduce volatility.
Source: Brendon Young, ORRF

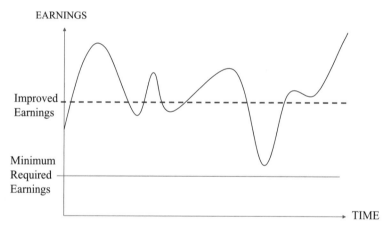

Figure 10.8   Increase required earnings above minimum level.
Source: Brendon Young, ORRF

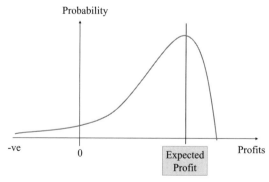

Figure 10.9   Profit is not singular.
Source: Brendon Young, ORRF

of developing new actuarial modeling standards.[7] It has recognized that profit (and similarly, cashflow and capital) is not singular and that there exists a need for credible probability distributions upon which users of actuarial information can confidently rely.

Regulators and rating agencies are increasingly using DFA. Financial advisors use it in support of mergers, acquisitions, and business divestment decisions. Consequently, it is likely that DFA will become more widely used in the assessment and analysis of operational risk. This will further aid concentration on market value maximization, through the adoption of a more forensic approach.

ENDNOTES

[1] Tripp, M.H. *et al.* (2004). Quantifying Operational Risk in General Insurance Companies. GIRO Working Party, Institute of Actuaries.

[2] One of the main proponents of DFA is the research committee of the Casualty Actuarial Society (CAS), http://www.casact.org/research/drm/.

[3] An amalgam of both the UK and Finnish approaches is presented in detail in: Daykin, C.D., Pentikainen, T. and Pesonen, M. (1994). *Practical Risk Theory for Actuaries*. London: Chapman & Hall.
The work of the Finnish working party is summarized in: Pentikainen, T. (1988). On the Solvency of Insurers. In: J.D. Cummins and R.A. Derrig. (Eds), Classical Insurance Solvency Theory, Kluwer Academic Publishers, p. 1–49.
The work of the United Kingdom working party was reported in two papers: Coutts, S. and Devitt, R. (1989). The Assessment of the Financial Strength of Insurance Companies – Generalized Cash Flow Model. In: J.D. Cummins and R.A. Derrig. (Eds), Financial Models of Insurance Solvency. UK: Kluwer Academic Publishers, pp. 1–37; Daykin, C.D. *et al.*, (1989). The Solvency of a General Insurance Company in Terms of Emerging Costs, In: J.D. Cummins and R.A. Derrig (Eds), *Financial Models of Insurance Solvency*. UK: Kluwer Academic Publishers, pp. 87–151.

[4] A scenario can be regarded as a set of assumptions relating to a group of variables.

[5] For a comprehensive description of Monte Carlo methods refer to: Fishman, G. (1996). *Monte Carlo: Concepts, Algorithms, and Applications*. Heidelberg: Springer.

[6] Basel Committee on Banking Supervision, The Joint Forum, Trends in risk integration and aggregation, August 2003.

[7] Structure of new BAS standards (and implications for adopted GNs): Consultation Paper, April 2008; http://www.frc.org.uk/images/uploaded/documents/Consultation%20Paper%20on%20Structure%20 of%20New%20BAS%20Standards%20final.pdf.

11

Enterprise Risk Management

11.1 INTRODUCTION

The financial markets can digest bad news but they hate uncertainty and abhor shocks. The *raison d'être* of enterprise risk management (ERM) is to enhance shakeholder value through reducing uncertainty and increasing the quality and stability of earnings, by taking a holistic view of both risks and opportunities. Enterprise risk management is concerned with creation of value for all stakeholders, and involves the protection of both tangible and intangible assets, through the effective management of uncertainty.

The Casualty Actuarial Society's Committee on Enterprise Risk Management has defined ERM as: ... *the discipline by which an organization in any industry assesses, controls, exploits, finances, and monitors risks from all sources for the purpose of increasing the organization's short- and long-term value to its stakeholders.*[1]

Enterprise risk management still remains widely regarded by many as more of a theoretical concept than a practical approach to risk management, with few if any organizations having embraced its requirements totally. However, the credit rating agencies now consider it to be an important contributory factor when determining the rating to be awarded. Susan Schmidt Bies, a member of the Board of Governors of the US Federal Reserve, has also stated that, in her opinion: *Enterprise Risk Management is essential for improving risk management practices within the banking sector, and as a consequence it should be an integral part of the activities of any bank irrespective of size, ... although, it should be recognized that there is no single solution suitable for all banks.*[2]

In the past, organizations have adopted a defensive stance towards risk. There is now a growing recognition that informed risk taking is a means of achieving competitive advantage. An organization that improves its responsiveness and flexibility can adopt a more aggressive stance. ERM recognizes the value-creating potential of risk management. There is an increasing ability to tailor an organization's risk profile. In addition to avoiding or minimizing risk, risk can be transferred or actively pursued and exploited. It is now considered a direct responsibility of senior management, as evidenced by the creation of the position of Chief Risk Officer (CRO) in many organizations. Whilst regulatory and legislative requirements concerning transparency and market discipline will be of catalytic importance, the primary driving forces will continue to be competitive advantage and market rationalization. The trend towards enterprise risk management can be expected to increase as the ability to manage risk increases. This has resulted in recognition of the strategic importance of enterprise risk management.

ERM focuses directly on a firm's objectives and the possible threats to the achievement of those objectives. A strategic view is taken, with objectives being cascaded down throughout the organization. Management at all levels is thus made overtly aware of the challenges and risks faced. Responsiveness and continuous improvement are inherently required. ERM involves defining the risk appetite of the enterprise (i.e. deciding which risks to accept and the appropriate level for those risks) given the desired stakeholder value to be created.

An important aspect of ERM is determination of the link between measures of risk and measures of overall organizational performance. In general, ERM measures address two specific areas of an organization's risk profile:

1. **Solvency.** These measures address the "tail" of the probability distribution with a view to determining capital requirements. Consequently, they are of particular concern to regulators, rating agencies, and customers. In addition to the level of risk capital, the determination of solvency also requires liquidity to be taken into account.
2. **Performance.** These measures are concerned with determining the level of volatility around the mean of the probability distribution of performance. They are of interest to shareholders and analysts who are particularly concerned with the quality and stability of earnings.

Whilst many of the constituent parts of ERM have long been practised by organizations, it is only over the last 10 years that there has been a growing recognition of the need to manage all risks holistically, taking account of their interactions. Even risks which on their own do not appear to represent a great threat to an organization may, if combined with other risks, pose a major threat.

11.2   ERM FRAMEWORKS

Currently, the two most important ERM frameworks are those developed by COSO and RIMS. Both provide a methodological approach to the holistic determination of risk and its management.

11.2.1   The COSO framework

Enterprise risk management was brought to prominence by the publication in 2004 of a document entitled *Enterprise Risk Management – Integrated Framework*, which resulted from a three-year study commissioned by the US Committee of Sponsoring Organizations of the Treadway Commission (COSO).[3] The project was influenced by events such as Long Term Capital Management (1998), Enron (2001), and the 9/11 terrorist attacks (2001). It is against this background that the need for a widely-accepted risk management framework was envisaged. Public confidence had been significantly affected by the tremendous losses resulting from these high profile events.

One of the primary aims of the COSO framework was to provide a benchmark for organizations to continuously assess their risk management processes on an enterprise-wide basis. In particular, the framework sought to establish a common risk language and definitions, to provide direction and guidance, and provide criteria for evaluating risk management effectiveness. The key concepts addressed, included:

- an ERM philosophy;
- risk appetite; and
- a portfolio view of risk.

The ERM framework, which incorporates the previously-issued COSO *Internal Controls – Integrated Framework*, recognized the need for flexibility, allowing organizations to implement those components most appropriate to their particular business model.

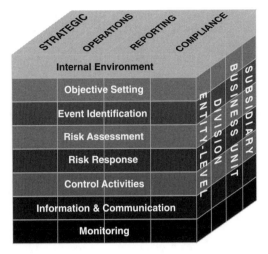

Figure 11.1 COSO ERM framework.
Reproduced by permission of the AICPA.

The COSO definition of enterprise risk management

COSO defined enterprise risk management, broadly, as: . . . *a process, effected by an entity's board of directors, management and other personnel, applied in strategy setting across the enterprise, designed to identify potential events that may affect the entity, and manage risk to be within its risk appetite, to provide reasonable assurance regarding the achievement of entity objectives.*[4]

Components comprising the COSO ERM framework

The basic principle behind the COSO ERM framework shown in Figure 11.1 is that an organization can be hierarchically subdivided into various entities and that each entity will have certain set objectives to achieve. COSO has stated that ERM should be regarded not as a serial process, but rather as a multi-directional iterative process in which the various components can and do influence one another. Each objective is evaluated against the eight components identified below:

1. **Internal environment.** This component is concerned with corporate governance, culture, ethics, and risk appetite. It establishes the tone of the organization, as decided by the board of directors, and determines the risk consciousness of all employees.
2. **Objective setting.** Objectives flow from the mission and vision of the organization. The process of setting objectives involves ensuring objectives are properly aligned with the risk appetite.
3. **Event identification.** Having set the objectives it is necessary to identify those events (both internal and external) that have the potential to impact upon the achievement of objectives. In addition to identifying risks, it is necessary to identify positive opportunities, which need to be looped back into the objective-setting and strategy processes.
4. **Risk assessment.** Risks have to be assessed using qualitative and, where possible, quantitative methods to determine their likelihood and impact. Risks may be assessed both individually and by category.

5. **Risk response.** Management needs to consider various alternative responses to risk (i.e. fully accepting, totally avoiding, partially reducing, or sharing risk), taking account of cost–benefit considerations, with a view to reducing residual risk and maintaining it within acceptable tolerance bounds.

6. **Control activities.** In order to ensure that responses to risk are properly executed, policies and procedures need to be implemented throughout the organization.

7. **Information and communication.** Communication of information, in the right form and at the right time, is essential for effective risk management. This requires that appropriate information, both internal and external, flows throughout the organization both vertically and horizontally.

8. **Monitoring.** Continuous monitoring of the ERM system is required to ensure it remains appropriate for the needs of the organization and the various business units and departments.

Objectives, risk appetite, risk tolerance, and capabilities

ERM requires the establishment of a shared vision of risk management. This vision, which may be aspirational, provides purpose and focus and is given substance through the establishment of objectives, which express directly what is to be accomplished.

Objectives   The COSO framework identifies four separate but potentially overlapping categories of objectives, which are defined as follows:

- **strategic objectives:** high level goals, aligned with and supporting the organization's mission;
- **operations objectives:** concerned with effective and efficient use of resources;
- **reporting objectives:** concerned with reliability of reporting; and
- **compliance objectives:** concerned with compliance with applicable laws and regulations.

Another objective, *safeguarding of resources,* which is often encountered in practice, was also identified but not specifically included as a separate category within the framework.

Risk appetite   Risk appetite is determined by a number of factors, including objectives, strategy, resource allocation, risk tolerances, and risk management capabilities, all serving to influence the chosen risk appetite. Expressed simply, risk appetite reflects the board's view of the world, driving strategic choice through determining the risks to be taken and those to be avoided.

Risk appetite is defined by COSO as: *The amount of risk, on a broad level, an entity is willing to accept in pursuit of value. . . . A company with a high-risk appetite may be willing to allocate a large portion of its capital to such high-risk areas as newly emerging markets. In contrast, a company with a low risk appetite might limit its short-term risk of large losses of capital by investing only in mature, stable markets.*

Risk appetite is strategic in nature, relating to the portfolio of business activities. It sets bounds for opportunity seeking and provides a counter to the pressures for performance.

Risk tolerance   Performance is subject to variability. Risk tolerances set the boundaries for performance variability, determining how much variability the organization is willing to accept as it strives to achieve its business objectives, in pursuit of creation of stakeholder value.

Risk tolerance is defined by COSO as: *The acceptable level of variation relative to achievement of a specific objective....*

In determining risk tolerance it is necessary to take into account:

1. **Variability in expected returns.** This recognizes the need to consider the minimum levels of earnings and cashflow required to meet commitments to stakeholders. The possible impact of default due to variability needs to be assessed.

2. **Susceptibility to extreme events.** This addresses the issue of how susceptible the organization is to: extreme (low frequency, high impact) events such as major business interruption, possibly due to terrorism or IT and telecommunications systems failures; substantial loss of physical assets, possibly due to financial crime; catastrophic health and safety issues; systemic contagion; and reputational damage. The new Basel Accord requires banks to take into consideration such extreme events and to hold an appropriate level of capital against them.

3. **Inconsistency with the desired risk appetite.** In addressing high-risk issues such as the need to engage in acquisitive growth or the development of in-house software systems for risk-sensitive areas, the organization needs to consider whether or not it wants to be involved in these types of activities, and the extent to which they are consistent with its risk appetite.

Capabilities   One of the key aims of enterprise risk management is to gradually enhance and extend risk management competency throughout the organization, continuously improving capabilities, with a view to creating stakeholder value.

The board must be aware of the key risks faced by the organization, how those risks are being managed and who is responsible for their management. The board will also be interested in knowing of the existence of any significant gaps in risk management capabilities plus the actions being taken to close those gaps. The COSO ERM framework can be used to assist in benchmarking the organization's risk management capability.

The goal is to design and implement well-defined capabilities for assessing, managing, and monitoring risk and deploying those capabilities on an enterprise-wide level. This involves, firstly, assessing risk and developing responses, then designing and implementing appropriate risk management and reporting systems. Once the risk management vision and related objectives, together with the risk appetite and risk tolerances, have been determined it is then necessary to assess the required risk management capabilities. Capability is derived from a combination of competent well-motivated and honest employees, guided by appropriate policies and procedures, working within defined systems and processes, supported by relevant and timely reports and indicators.

Regulatory and legislative requirements

In developing the COSO framework, consideration was given to various legislative and regulatory requirements together with other existing standards and frameworks, including: the Australian and New Zealand Risk Management Standard 4360; the ISO/IEC Standardization Guide for International Organizations; and the South African King Report on Corporate Governance. However, there are no regulatory or legislative requirements specifying the use of the COSO ERM framework. Whilst the Institute of Internal Auditors (IIA) is a member of COSO and is supportive of the ERM framework, it does not mandate its use.[5]

The framework can be useful in assisting organizations to meet a number of guidelines and requirements, including:

- **Basel II.** The new Basel Accord requires banks to specifically report on operational risk management.
- **Sarbanes-Oxley Act.** Under this act the CEO and CFO of US publicly-traded corporations are required to ensure that their statements are soundly based. This requires the existence of an appropriate framework to assist certifying officers in discharging their responsibilities with regard to Section 302 (quarterly certification) and Section 404 (annual assessment). Many corporations have opted to use the COSO framework. In 2007, the Public Company Accounting Oversight Board (PCAOB), created by the SOX Act to oversee the auditors of public companies, placed additional emphasis on risk assessment. SOX compliance may be considered a sound platform from which to develop a more broadly-based ERM framework.
- **The Combined Code and Turnbull Guidelines.** Companies incorporated in the UK and listed on the London Stock Exchange are required to report to shareholders on a number of corporate governance issues.
- **The US PATRIOT Act.** This is concerned with anti-money-laundering and requires the existence of a "know your customer" framework.
- **Gramm-Leach-Bliley Act.** This act requires financial institutions to safeguard and preserve the privacy of "non-public" customer information.
- **New York Stock Exchange (NYSE).** *While it is the job of the CEO and senior management to assess and manage the company's exposure to risk, the audit committee must discuss guidelines and policies to govern the process by which this is handled. The audit committee should discuss the company's major financial risk exposures and the steps management has taken to monitor and control such exposures.*[6] A mandatory requirement of the NYSE is the existence of an internal audit function, whose purpose is to provide the audit committee as well as general management with ongoing assessments of the adequacy of the company's risk management system.
- **Kon Trag Legislation.** In Germany, large companies are required to establish and maintain risk management supervisory systems and to report to shareholders.

COSO took the view that the ERM framework was a broad strategically-based framework that would serve to identify key risks. But other more specific and detailed frameworks (such as COBIT, ISO 17799, BITS, NITS Special Publication 800-53 and ITIL) should then be used, where appropriate. COSO did not attempt to reconcile its framework with others, instead taking the view that such actions would be outside the scope of the project. However, COSO did address the issue of how its Internal Controls framework (issued in 1992) would relate to its ERM integrated framework. The ERM document[7] pointed out that roles and responsibilities had been expanded to give a focus on risk management, with areas such as risk management philosophy, risk culture, risk appetite, and risk tolerances being added.

Limitations and criticisms of COSO

Whilst the COSO Enterprise Risk Management Integrated Framework may have tacit regulatory and legislative support, there are many in both Europe and the US who consider the framework to be overly prescriptive and process driven. Such criticisms should not be entirely unexpected given the framework's strong accounting-based antecedence.

The COSO ERM framework adopts a "management by objectives" (MBO) approach to risk management. Unfortunately, this gives rise to incongruity. Management by objectives is a rigid hierarchical approach whereas modern risk management is a dynamic approach that recognizes the need for responsiveness and flexibility, given a complex business environment (both internal and external). When considering the COSO framework, it should be borne in mind that, in reality, it is not possible to predetermine all risks and that complexity limits a system from being optimized.

The COSO definition states that ERM must be applied *across the enterprise, at every level and unit, and includes taking an entity-level portfolio view of risk*. It also states that implementation must be linked to business strategy. Unless all these stringent conditions are met, then the framework implemented cannot be classified as truly ERM-compliant.

COSO pointed out that human error and deliberate actions, including fraud and sabotage, prevent the board and management from having absolute assurance regarding the achievement of objectives.

Although not a panacea, the COSO ERM framework may be considered a useful benchmark, amongst others.

11.2.2   The RIMS Risk Maturity Model[8]

The Risk Maturity Model for Enterprise Risk Management, developed by the US-based Risk and Insurance Management Society Inc. (RIMS), seeks to determine the extent to which enterprise risk management is embedded within the organization and is leading to enhanced performance.

Fundamentally, the RIMS methodology is based upon the assessment of the following seven key factors. A "maturity level" score is determined for each factor, with the overall ERM level of maturity being signified by the weakest attribute.

1. **Culture.** This is concerned with the level of senior management commitment to ERM and the resultant culture engendered within the organization. Consideration is given to the degree of integration and communication between various departments, including internal audit, information technology, compliance, and risk management.
2. **Process.** The extent to which ERM is embedded into business processes is assessed. Consideration is given to the identification, assessment, evaluation, mitigation, and monitoring of risks, together with consideration of the degree to which both qualitative and quantitative methods are used to support one another.
3. **Risk appetite.** Determination of risk appetite involves defining what risks are acceptable to the organization, together with their levels of tolerance or variation. Consideration is given to how effectively risk appetite has been positively defined and communicated throughout the organization via policies, procedures, and guidelines.
4. **Root cause analysis.** Root cause analysis is concerned with "event-cause-effect" analysis, with a view to improving management understanding of risk drivers and control weaknesses, thus facilitating appropriate risk management action.
5. **Risk identification and assessment.** This involves determining how effective the organization is at collecting and analyzing historical risk data. Consideration is also given to the capture and use of tacit expert knowledge throughout the organization. An ERM approach to the identification, analysis, and assessment of risks includes the determination of dependencies and correlations on an enterprise-wide basis.

6. **Performance management.** This is concerned with assessing how well the organization implements its strategy and achieves its performance objectives, taking account of uncertainties.
7. **Business resiliency and sustainability.** This involves evaluating how ERM effectively enhances resiliency and sustainability. Consideration is given to factors such as supply chain disruptions, vendor and distribution dependencies, market pricing volatility, and cash flow and liquidity issues.

RIMS now offers online facilities, providing guidelines and best practice information for developing and evaluating enterprise risk management programmes. The *Risk Maturity Assessment* provides a real-time score of a client's risk programme, evaluated against 25 key characteristics, whilst the *RIMS Risk Maturity Model* can then be used to benchmark this assessment.

11.3   ERM MODELING

The two general classes of stochastic risk models typically used within enterprise risk management are *statistical analytic models* and *structural simulation models*.

11.3.1   Statistical analytic models

Statistical models are based simply on the observed values of random variables. They facilitate observation of correlations between risks but ignore any causal relationships. The principal advantage of a statistical approach is the ease with which the model can be parameterized, using existing historical data. However, as previously discussed, statistical methods are dependent upon the existence of sufficient and relevant data.

Analytic models require determination of a restrictive set of assumptions and probability distributions contained within a set of equations. Their advantage is the relative ease and speed with which output results can be calculated.

11.3.2   Structural simulation models[9]

Structural models explicitly capture the causal relationships between inputs and outputs, using both expert opinion and data to derive the cause/effect relationships. The principal advantages of a structural approach over statistical methods are the ability to examine the underlying causes driving output results, and the ability to evaluate the effects of possible alternative management actions.

Simulation methods involve performing a large number of computer-generated runs in order to gradually move towards a solution. Such methods can accommodate complex relationships and are less dependent upon simplifying assumptions such as standardized probability distributions. These models can be either deterministic or stochastic in nature.[10]

Causal relationships can change over time, and under different conditions they may alter significantly, particularly under conditions of stress. Complexity may indicate the need to construct a simplified model in modular form.

11.4   RISK CORRELATION AND INTEGRATION

A primary reason for adopting a holistic enterprise risk management approach is to determine the impact of the interrelationships between risks. This can be achieved directly, using a covariance matrix to express dependencies. However, estimation of covariances can be difficult from a practical consideration since the number of estimates rises proportionately with the square of the number of risks considered. An alternative approach is to use a structural simulation model incorporating the interrelationships between risks and the cause/effect input/output dependencies. The structural linkages have the effect of preventing the generation of random variable sets that are unrealistic relative to each other, regardless of correlation accuracy. Rather than being separate factors requiring estimation, it should be recognized that the correlations between risks are an emergent property of the structural simulation model – i.e. an output.

In addition to aiding with the understanding of correlation, structural simulation models can also be used to provide a robust ranking of risks. This involves considering the impact of each risk on key performance indicators (KPI), and thus determining the marginal contribution from each risk towards the overall risk profile of the organization. Technically, this can be achieved by isolating each risk in turn, changing the input from stochastic to deterministic, and analyzing the effect on KPI probability distributions.

ENDNOTES

[1] www.casact.org/research/erm.

[2] Susan Schmidt Bies: speech entitled: A Supervisory Perspective on Enterprise Risk Management. Address to the Annual Convention of the American Bankers Association, 17 October 2006.

[3] COSO is a voluntary private sector body established in 1985 to support the National Commission on Fraudulent Financial Reporting. It exists to improve the quality of financial reporting through promotion of business ethics, effective internal controls and corporate governance. Its sponsoring organizations are: The Institute of Internal Auditors (IIA); The American Institute of Certified Public Accountants (AICPA); the Institute of Management Accountants; the American Accounting Association (AAA); and Financial Executives International (FEI). In 1992, COSO produced a document entitled *Internal Controls – Integrated Framework*. This is the main framework used within the United States (and elsewhere) to comply with Section 404 of the Sarbanes-Oxley Act. The Internal Controls Framework is now an integral part of the Enterprise Risk Management – Integrated Framework.

[4] Enterprise Risk Management – Integrated Framework, Executive Summary, September 2004, Page 2. www.coso.org/Publications/ERM/COSO_ERM_ExecutiveSummary.pdf.

[5] IIA Standard 2110.A2 requires a broad risk assessment aligned with the COSO framework.
IIA Standard 2010.A1 requires the internal audit function to carry out an annual risk assessment.

[6] NYSE Listing Standards Part 7d (http://www.nyse.com/pdfs/finalcorpgovrules.pdf).

[7] Appendix C.

[8] http://www.rims.org/Content/NavigationMenu/ERM/Risk_Maturity_Model/RMM.htm.

[9] Dynamic Financial Analysis (DFA) refers to a particular class of structural simulation models designed to generate financial pro-forma projections.

[10] Deterministic (expected): Deterministic models calculate the *expected* outcomes for a given set of inputs – i.e. a single input value leads to a single output value.
Stochastic (probabilistic): With stochastic models, variability in inputs gives rise to variability in outputs. A deterministic model can be transformed into a stochastic model by treating certain inputs as variables with probability distributions. The output from the model will then also be in the form of a probability distribution.

12

Insurance and Other Risk Transfer Methods

12.1 INTRODUCTION

The Basel Committee for Banking Supervision and the European Commission have recognized the role that insurance can play in mitigating the financial impact of a bank's operational losses. However, the banks themselves have to date been slow to realize the potential of insurance as a mitigant for operational risk. The regulators have also raised a number of concerns about the use of insurance by banks.

This chapter addresses the extent to which banks could consider insurance as a viable mitigant for the financial consequences of operational risk. Insurance is a valuable risk transfer tool that can be used to mitigate the financial impact of risks. In a highly competitive environment, outsourcing risk to insurers can increase a bank's performance by smoothing its cash flows and preventing financial catastrophes. Additionally, insurance can provide a variety of valuable risk management services that can enable a bank to more precisely tailor its risk-reward profile. Although there remain some issues that may attenuate the potential of insurance, these should not be considered insurmountable.

12.2 BACKGROUND

The potential of insurance as an operational risk management tool has been recognised by the Basel Committee, who have stated with regard to insurance: *in principle, such mitigation should be reflected in the capital requirement for operational risk.* However, *it is clear that the market for insurance of operational risk is still developing* and that banks *should recognize that they might, in fact, be replacing operational risk with a counterparty risk.* The Committee pointed out a number of potential problems with operational risk insurance and other forms of outsourcing. These can be summarized as follows:

- The insurance industry is not sufficiently well capitalized. A bank that is transferring risk may be better capitalized than the accepting insurance company.
- Blanket cover is not available. There are many different contracts for different elements, which do not fit together sufficiently well. This leads to uninsured gaps or inefficient overlaps.
- Limiting conditions and exclusion clauses lead to doubt regarding payment in the event of failure.
- Delays in payment could result in serious damage to the claimant.
- It is difficult to determine the true economic value of insurance purchased in the absence of sufficient and appropriate data.
- Insurance may lead to moral hazard.
- Systemic risk may be increased in the event of claim payment default.

Thus, it would appear that, although Basel is prepared to consider insurance as a mitigant for operational risk, there are a number of issues that need to be addressed by the users. Basel has stated that outsourcing *does not relieve the bank of the ultimate responsibility for controlling risks that affect its operation.* As such it has recommended that the banks *should adopt policies to limit risks arising from reliance on an outside provider.*

12.2.1   The role of insurance: risk transfer or risk mitigation?

One important issue that needs to be clarified is the extent to which insurance can be viewed as a risk mitigation technique. In particular, it is important to understand that risk transfer devices such as insurance are not designed to control risk and as such may not always provide a reliable means to mitigate risk.[1]

Risk transfer

The primary role of insurance is to allow the financial impact of a particular risk or combination of risks to be transferred from one party to another. More formally, insurance can be defined as a contractual agreement between two parties, the insured and the insurer. The basis of this agreement is that the insurer agrees to finance certain prespecified but random losses in return for the payment of a regular premium by the insured. Thus insurance effectively converts uncertainty into certainty.

The act of risk transfer does not in itself provide a means for controlling risk (i.e. avoiding, preventing or reducing the actual event.[2] It simply transfers the financial impact of certain prespecified losses to another party.[3] The firm that transfers the risk is then reliant upon the insurer to provide compensation and advice in the event of loss. In short, risk transfer is effectively a financing decision.

Risk mitigation

Fundamentally, risk mitigation is about alleviating the impact of risk. As such, risk mitigation tools help a firm to avoid or actively manage the probability of loss and lessen the amount of damage (financial or otherwise) experienced when a loss event does occur. To the extent that insurance reduces the financial consequences of loss it can be viewed as a means to mitigate risk.[4] The value of insurance as a risk mitigation tool will depend upon the ability of an insurer to:

- improve the quality and cost effectiveness of a bank's risk management programme by providing tangible benefits and controlling insurability problems; and
- reduce the gaps within a bank's risk management programme.

12.2.2   Historically, where have we come from and what has changed?[5]

Insurance is a well-established risk management tool that has been used by the banking sector for many decades to provide protection within three main areas: legal liability; crime; and property damage. Peril-specific policies offered by insurance companies include:

- **Fidelity/bankers blanket bond:** designed to protect an employer against dishonesty or default on the part of an employee as well as fraud and forgery. In addition, it may cover on-premises losses such as office damage, in-transit losses, counterfeit currency, and some forms of trading losses;

- **electronic computer crime:** this provides cover against computer failure, viruses, data transmission problems, forged electronic funds transactions, etc;
- **professional indemnity:** this typically covers liabilities to third parties for claims arising out of employee negligence while providing professional services (e.g. investment advice) to clients;
- **directors' and officers' liability:** this covers the personal assets of directors and officers against the expenses that might be incurred due to legal actions arising from the performance of their duties;
- **employment practices liability:** this covers liabilities that might arise due to breaches in employment law, such as harassment, discrimination, breach of contract, etc;
- **non-financial property:** this covers the usual range of property risks (fire, weather damage, etc);
- **unauthorized trading:** this is a relatively new product that offers financial protection against unauthorized trading that was either concealed or falsely recorded;
- **general and other liability:** public liability, employer's liability, motor fleet, etc;

Increasingly, a number of multi-peril basket insurance products are also being offered to the banking sector, such as organizational liability insurance which is a limited multi-peril product that covers losses arising from internal and external fraud, rogue trading, and many other forms of general liability.[6] One possible advantage of multi-peril insurance products is that they may provide a bank with more comprehensive cover, thereby helping to eliminate any gaps or overlaps that might exist between peril-specific products. Moreover, by allowing insurers to take into account correlations across losses, the price of a basket product may be lower than the sum of the equivalent peril-specific products.[7] However, basket products present a number of underwriting challenges, which may restrict demand for them.

Finally, it should be noted that many Western countries, including the UK and US, seek to protect policyholders from risks faced by banks (both operational and nonoperational) by requiring banks to purchase depositor protection insurance. Such schemes are usually government run. In the UK, the Deposit Protection Scheme was originally designed to provide partial cover against losses that arise out of bank insolvency. The scheme is financed on a compulsory basis by the banking industry (each bank paying a flat fee), but is effectively controlled by the state.[8]

The primary advantage of a deposit insurance scheme is that when all else has failed (bank management, regulators, auditors, etc) it acts as a failsafe for depositors against the adverse effects of bank insolvency. In addition, the use of depositor protection schemes provides regulators with the option to refuse to bail out ailing deposit taking institutions, in particular if they are small or new.[9] Thus, deposit insurance is not linked to specific causes; instead, all that is required is the total failure of the bank to trigger the payment of compensation. This means that, for small depositors at least, the banks are already in effect purchasing fully comprehensive (although not full cover) all-risks insurance. Indeed, as far as most consumers are concerned, all that matters is the safety of their deposits. Thus, deposit insurance provides much of the financial security they need. Obviously, this leaves other stakeholders "unprotected."

Unfortunately, the provision of full-cover deposit protection insurance does have problems. The high rate of Savings and Loans failures in the US in the 1980s has been attributed to the use of non-experience rated, full-cover deposit protection schemes.[10] The primary reason for this is moral hazard. In the case of deposit protection insurance, moral hazard is manifested as the incentive for insured depositors to place their funds in banks that take large risks in an attempt to offer high returns.[11] Depositors are drawn towards high-risk organizations because the repayment of their deposit is guaranteed by the state.

Whilst full cover may not be appropriate, the need for an adequate and acceptable level of depositor protection was clearly indicated by the Northern Rock event. Panic by depositors caused a run on the bank resulting in its effective failure. To prevent systemic risk, the UK government nationalized Northern Rock, and fully guaranteed deposits.

Private depositor protection insurance has been suggested[12] as an interesting solution to the problem of moral hazard. They argue that the private provision of depositor protection insurance (through either an independent insurance company or a mutual) is superior to a government scheme. This is due to the monitoring and enforcement skills together with financial penalties employed by private insurers.

The value maximizing insurance decision

As with any risk management tool, managers should only purchase insurance if it adds value to their organization. Whilst value is a hard concept to define, it is usually taken to mean the long-term value of the firm to its owners (i.e. the value of equity). As such, a common proxy for a firm's value is its share price.[13]

In theory, the purchase of insurance should achieve the same basic outcome as holding capital – i.e. the provision of funds to finance losses. The question then is, why should the value maximizing bank purchase operational risk insurance when it could simply use its own funds to finance losses? This question becomes particularly meaningful for the quoted banks since their shareholders should be able (at least in theory) to diversify away, at low cost, the effects of most insurable risks by holding a large portfolio of shares from many different companies. As such, the purchase of insurance should at best add nothing to the returns of these shareholders.[14] Moreover, if the presence of insurability problems – coupled with the need for an insurer to cover its costs and make a profit – are considered, the purchase of an insurance contract might actually seem to lower the value of a firm. In fact, it is quite usual for a policyholder to pay a premium that exceeds the expected level of loss in any given year.

The answer to the question of why a value maximizing bank should purchase operational risk insurance lies in an insurer's ability to offer benefits that are too costly for a bank to replicate in-house. A bank needs to understand these benefits and assess whether they are sufficient to outweigh any of the associated costs of insurance. Effectively, this comes down to understanding the comparative advantages in risk bearing and risk management that are possessed by an insurer and the bank that is considering purchasing insurance.[15] For example, most banks will probably find that they possess a comparative advantage in managing the day-to-day (i.e. high frequency, low impact) risks that are present in their business. Indeed, such risks are often termed business risks, since they are a normal part of any firm's operations. In contrast, a bank will probably prefer to transfer some of its less common, larger impact risks to an insurer. This is because insurers are not only skilled in managing and underwriting many such risks, but also have a large pool of resources to finance losses.

Unfortunately, it is difficult to make general predictions about the value of operational risk insurance. This is because the precise benefits of insurance and many of the potential insurability problems associated with operational risks will depend upon the particular circumstances of the bank.

The main theoretical benefits of insurance

The benefits of insurance can be grouped into two main categories: pooling benefits and risk management benefits. These benefits reflect the comparative advantages that an insurer may possess in risk bearing. A bank that purchases insurance should then be able to exploit these comparative advantages to increase the quality and cost effectiveness of its own risk management programme.

Pooling benefits

An insurer's ability to pool both the resources and risks of many similar policyholders allows it to exploit a statistical theory known as the law of large numbers (a weaker version of the central limit theorem). The law of large numbers helps an insurer to not only predict and therefore price the risks of its policyholders more accurately, but also to ensure that it has sufficient funds to pay claims.[16]

In terms of pooling resources, the law of large numbers states that an insurer's resources for paying claims will tend to grow at a faster rate than the deviation of pooled losses from the expected value, as the number of identical and independent insured risks becomes large. For a very large pool of insured risks, the probability that an insurer can pay all claims will approach (but never quite get to) 100 %. Put simply, the pooling of resources means that an insurance company is able to use the premiums that it receives from the many policyholders that it insures but which do not experience losses in order to pay the claims of those few that do. In short, the losses of the few are borne by the premiums of the many. Consequently, an insurer requires less capital and can therefore provide a form of finance at advantageous rates.

In terms of pooling risks, the law of large numbers implies that the average loss per insured risk will tend to fall close to the true expected loss, as the number of homogeneous (or at least similar) and independent insured risks becomes large (e.g. compare tossing a coin once to tossing it 100 times). Thus, the more similar risks an insurance company insures in a given pool, the more confident it can become about the level of losses that should arise. By pooling similar risks, insurance companies are therefore able to better predict the expected level of claims over a given time period, effectively replacing risk for virtual certainty.

A further issue related to the concept of pooling is that most insurance companies will offer more than one product and as such will operate multiple risk pools. This allows insurance companies to effectively create a pool of pools in which it can exploit the benefits of diversification. For example, an insurance company might use the profits earned from one particular pool of risks to subsidize the losses of another. As such, even where the losses on a particular line exceed the value of its allocated pool of funds, a diversified insurance company will be able to cross-subsidise, using funds from elsewhere.

The net benefits for a bank, resulting from an insurer's ability to pool resources/risks and also diversify risk, are:

1. **Cash flow smoothing.** Large unexpected operational losses can have a negative impact on cash flow where they exhaust internal capital (assuming any has been allocated). The purchase of operational risk insurance, however, may allow a bank to mitigate this risk.

   Through pooling, an insurer is able to offer policyholders the chance to pay a known premium in return for a guarantee that they will be compensated in the event that certain prespecified losses occur. For many banks, this means that the purchase of operational risk insurance could provide a way for them to substitute the possibility of random fluctuations in their cash flows (due to large or unexpected operational losses) for a certain premium. This reduction in cash flow fluctuations may then yield numerous benefits for a bank in the form of improved quality and stability of earnings that in turn help raise its market value.

The benefits of cash flow smoothing have been well researched, both theoretically and empirically,[17] although nothing has been done to relate this to operational risk in banking. Researchers have identified a number of costs that can be associated with cash flow fluctuations, including:

- demands from risk-averse stakeholders such as employees, managers without stock options, and consumers. Risk-averse stakeholders dislike their income being related to a firm's random cash flows. As such, they may demand additional compensation from the firm (possibly in the form of higher wages or interest payments);
- the potential for agency conflicts between shareholders and creditors, resulting in creditors refusing to advance further credit and raising the interest rate;
- the forfeiting of valuable investment opportunities.

2. **Avoidance of catastrophes.** Theoretically, insurance can be used to finance very large operational losses that threaten the solvency of a bank. Such losses would be very difficult (if not impossible) to finance using internal capital.

Large operational losses can lead to both financial distress and even bankruptcy. Obviously, both of these states have a significant effect on the value of a firm to its stakeholders. Where an organization experiences financial distress it can expect to find that there is a reduced demand for its products. This problem may be particularly acute in the banking sector since consumers will be very reluctant to invest in a bank that is showing signs of potential bankruptcy. A firm in financial distress is also likely to experience difficulty in obtaining credit and may lose key personnel.[18] In the event of bankruptcy, there will be a further diminution in value due to the loss of tax credits and investment opportunities, together with additional expenses, including professional fees.[19]

Risk management benefits

Although most banks will have a degree of in-house expertise in operational risk management, an insurer may well have a far greater wealth of resources and expertise in this area, gained from access to a wide range of clients in various sectors. A bank that transfers its operational risks to an insurer can utilize these resources and expertise, appropriating the following benefits:

1. **Real service efficiencies.** The core business of every insurer is assessing, financing, and controlling risk. Thus large insurance companies may have a comparative advantage over all but the largest banks in terms of access to good quality data, experience, and economies of scale. As such, a bank may find it more cost effective to outsource certain elements of its risk management programme to an insurance company. In particular, insurers may offer loss adjustment and assessment services together with legal advice, as well as administrative services such as the payment of claims.[20]

2. **Monitoring.** It is possible that particular stakeholder groups, including consumers, governments, and shareholders, will require a bank's managers to invest more in operational risk management than they might otherwise wish to do. These stakeholders, though, may find it both difficult and expensive to monitor the behaviour of management and ensure compliance. One possible solution to this problem is for stakeholders to demand the

purchase of insurance and then effectively use the insurer to perform the monitoring role.[21] A good example of a company that has exploited the monitoring role of insurance is British Petroleum.[22]

Insurance companies are skilled in monitoring and constraining the opportunistic behaviour of managers. Firstly, since insurers are specialist information gatherers they may be able to collect and accurately process information at a relatively low cost. Secondly, by agreeing to indemnify a firm in the event of certain specified losses, insurers possess a strong vested interest in ensuring that such losses are mitigated. Thirdly, insurance companies have remedies to ensure compliance, including raising premiums, limiting or cancelling cover, raising retention levels or taking legal action against either the firm or its directors and employees.

It is important to note that the monitoring activities of insurers effectively support the functioning of market forces. Risk is a commodity like any other that can be traded. Problems can arise when certain stakeholder groups, like managers, attempt to exploit their position and expose other stakeholders to risks for which they are not being properly compensated.

It has been argued that the correction of market forces is a key regulatory role and, therefore, the presence of an efficient insurance market could be regarded both as a support and a substitute for regulation.[23,24]

12.2.3   The insurability of risk[25]

Although most risks can be insured for a price, some prove easier to insure than others. Thus, in order to assist in understanding why certain operational risks may prove difficult to insure, the main factors that are said to influence insurability are outlined below.[26]

It should be borne in mind that these factors merely represent the desirable characteristics of an insured risk. Indeed, most of the risks that are actually insured, whether operational in nature or not, do not possess all of these characteristics. In fact, insurance companies are very adept at dealing with the insurability challenges that some risks present. For example, a few years ago it would have been difficult for a bank to obtain $50 million in broad form, professional indemnity insurance, yet now such cover is readily available. Furthermore, as computer technology and underwriting techniques develop, the ability of insurers and brokers to overcome limiting factors and meet the insurance requirements of the banking industry should continue to advance.

Large numbers of similar policyholders

Within any one line of insurance an insurer requires a sufficiently large number of similar policyholders in order to both fund and accurately predict losses (see the section above on pooling).

Where an insurer is unable to acquire a large number of similar policyholders, it runs the risk that the premiums charged will not reflect the losses incurred, leading to undesirable fluctuations in profits and cash flows and, in extreme cases, insolvency of the insurer.

Correlated risks

Another obstacle to efficient pooling is where risks are correlated with each other, giving rise to the possibility that a significant number of policyholders could all make claims at the same time. Such a run on claims could potentially prove catastrophic for an insurer. Failure of the insurer could result in a sudden increase in client exposure and, where there are multiple outstanding claims, increase the level of systemic risk. Obviously, though, an insurer that has diversified across multiple geographic markets and/or product lines would be much less exposed to this problem.

Past loss data used to predict the future

The insurance industry uses loss data from the past in order to predict the future. In the absence of such data the insurer runs the risk that the premiums charged will be either too high, thus deterring purchasers, or too low, leading to losses. Moreover, even if available, historical data are of limited use in a dynamic environment where risks are constantly changing.[27]

One way in which insurers respond to lack of loss data is to specify artificial cover limits. The aim is to limit the losses that an insurer can sustain to a known amount. However, the net result is that cover may be restricted to inadequate levels.

It should be noted, however, that insurers are very experienced in the collection of data. Moreover, they already have a lot of data on operational risk, which reduces the possibility of small policy limits. For example, policy limits on some liability policies are already in the region of $1 billion.

Losses of a definite amount – attributable by time, place and cause

Insurance is a form of contingent financing. As such, the obligations of an insurer to finance the losses of a policyholder are only triggered if certain prespecified events occur. This approach works well where both the policyholder and the insurer are fully aware of the nature of the losses (known perils) that are to be included in a contract. In contrast, where the consequences, time, place, and causes of a loss are not fully known, the effectiveness of insurance can be significantly reduced.

The main issue is that insurers naturally do not want to be held liable for losses that have not been factored into their premium calculations (although when this does occur, an insurer may well pay such a claim if it turns out to be valid). As a result, insurers will generally word policies very carefully in order to exclude risks that are not definite in amount, time, place or cause. Necessarily, this will limit the scope of any available cover. In addition, since some insurance policies may rely on potentially imprecise wordings to describe which losses are insured, disputes over claims are possible. This could lead to delays in the payment of claims.

It is important to note, however, that disputes are not necessarily the fault of the insurer. Disputes may well be initiated or intensified by the insured, especially when they have un-realistic expectations over either the type of losses that are covered in their policy or the amount of the claim. Indeed, the best policies are usually those that have been drawn up with the mutual involvement of both the insured and the insurer. In addition, disputes over most standard insurance contracts are relatively short-lived since the wordings of such contracts will already have been heavily tested in the courts.

Accidental

An insured loss is considered wholly fortuitous when the actions of a policyholder have not been a causal factor in its occurrence. As such, fortuitous losses are unintentional.

Where an insured loss is not entirely fortuitous there is the potential for moral hazard. Moral hazard occurs because the purchase of insurance insulates policyholders from the financial consequences of their losses and reduces their incentive to invest in loss control activities. This produces a problem for both insurance companies and society, as the level of losses will then be higher than predicted.

Although moral hazard is a very real problem, insurers are experienced in preventing it. In fact, very few insured losses are wholly fortuitous and, as such, the potential for moral hazard is a common factor in most insurance contracts. One popular solution is for an insurance company to monitor the loss control activities of its policyholders (either ex-ante or ex-post). Another is to demand that the policyholder pay a certain amount of any loss (perhaps by using an excess).

Not catastrophic for the insurer

Unexpectedly large losses or unexpected runs of smaller losses may threaten the solvency of an insurer. Of course, such losses are extremely unlikely where each of the previous conditions of insurability have been met.[28] Moreover, losses that are potentially catastrophic for an individual insurer can usually be either reinsured with a larger insurer or co-insured with a number of similarly sized insurers. Reinsurance and co-insurance provide insurers with the effective means to manage their exposure to catastrophic losses. In fact, the use of reinsurance and co-insurance has helped to protect insurers from some very large and unexpected losses, such as Hurricane Andrew, which cost the insurance industry an estimated $18.3 billion, compared to a maximum expected loss of $8 billion.[29] There are, however, some problems with reinsurance, which are discussed later.

12.2.4 The bank's operational risk insurance decision

In order to assess whether it is worth transferring operational risks to an insurer, a bank needs to identify exactly what the relative benefits of insurance are, and assess whether they outweigh the associated costs. The optimum amount of operational risk insurance can then be determined by comparing the marginal benefit of an increase in insurance cover against its marginal cost.

Insurance and the cost of capital

One way to represent a bank's insurance decision is to compare the cost of insurance against the cost of capital. In short, a bank will only buy insurance to finance its operational losses if the cost of doing so is cheaper than using its own internal capital or cheaper than the rate at which the bank can raise capital in the market place.

The differences between banks

Whether a bank decides to purchase operational risk insurance will depend on its own particular circumstances. These circumstances will determine both the scale of any potential benefits and the extent of particular insurability problems. Key issues include:

1. **Bank size.** Whether a bank is large or small can have a major impact on its insurance decision. Differences arise because bank size affects the scale of many of the insurance benefits and insurability problems that were outlined above.

It is difficult to say whether large or small banks have the most to gain from insurance. Small banks will generally have much less capital and free cash flow and may as a result be much more vulnerable to operational losses than a large bank. In addition, a small bank will often not have the spread of risks or the level of resources needed to replicate the pooling and risk management benefits of insurance.[30] In contrast, the largest banks should be able to replicate many of the pooling and risk management benefits of insurance.

Despite being able to replicate many of the functions of insurance a large bank might still want to use insurance to protect its earnings from less common, larger impact operational risks, especially where such events could damage investor confidence or lead to a takeover. For larger, less common risks an insurer (pooling the risks of multiple banks) is almost always likely to be able to achieve greater pooling benefits than an individual bank. In addition, a large bank may also find it cost effective to outsource the day-to-day administration of some of its more common smaller risks to an insurer, especially when the insurance market for such risks is competitive. This strategy, of outsourcing the management of small-impact risks, has been adopted by British Petroleum.[31]

2. **Risk types and risk profile:** Basel has acknowledged that the level and types of risk found in different product lines may vary. These differences are also likely to impact on the insurability of the risks associated with particular product lines (due to the availability of data or the scale of losses, for example). Thus, in addition to affecting its capital charge, the risk profile of a bank is also likely to influence the availability of good quality, cost effective, operational risk insurance cover.

3. **Time horizons of managers/shareholders:** The benefits of insurance often take time to materialize. In fact, a bank that cancels an insurance policy is likely to be better off in the short run, since it will save money on its premium payments. This saving, though, may be somewhat temporary, especially if the bank experiences a loss in the near future.

   Whether a bank is prepared to go through the immediate expense of paying a premium for insurance cover, which is only likely to provide benefit in the long run, depends on the time horizons of its managers and shareholders.[32] Where managers and shareholders have a short time horizon they are less likely to purchase insurance. However, those managers and shareholders with longer-term horizons will be much more inclined to purchase insurance.

4. **Attitudes of stakeholders towards risk:** In general, the more risk averse a bank's stakeholders are, the more they are likely to want the bank to purchase insurance. There is already some empirical evidence to suggest that the presence of risk-averse stakeholders may influence a bank's risk management strategy.[33]

5. **Credit rating:** The higher a bank's credit rating, the lower will be the cost of debt finance. As such, a bank with a good credit rating may decide to finance its losses through the use of debt, rather than insurance. This does, however, presuppose that credit will be made available to a bank that has just experienced a large loss that it could have insured.[34]

12.2.5   The alternatives to insurance[35]

In addition to internal capital and insurance there are other potential risk financing alternatives. Three of the main alternatives are briefly considered below.

Mutual self-insurance pools

Self-insurance pools are arrangements in which participating firms mutually agree to insure one another. For example, a number of banks might agree to finance the cost of their operational-risk losses by simply pooling their resources and paying claims as they occur. Typically, each bank would provide some initial capital along with a yearly premium to fund claims and ongoing administration costs.

If run properly, a mutual self-insurance pool could enable firms to exploit many of the pooling and risk management benefits of insurance, whilst minimizing any associated insurability problems. Indeed, the main theoretical advantage of a mutual self-insurance pool is that it is run for the benefit of its members. As such, there is not the conflict that may exist in some insurance companies between policyholders and shareholders. This means that a mutual pool might allow firms to finance, in a cost-effective manner, those risks that the insurance industry declines or for which insurance premiums are considered to be excessive. Furthermore, there is no reason why the underwriting capacity of a mutual could not be strengthened through the purchase of reinsurance.

Discussions have taken place in the past between a number of banks, with involvement from the British Bankers Association, regarding the establishment of a mutual insurance company for the industry. Unfortunately, there are two main problems with such self-insurance pools: the possibility of adverse selection and the danger of moral hazard. An additional negative factor is that in a competitive environment it is possible that a bank might decide not to risk its capital to save a rival. This is particularly likely when the ensuing operational loss could be attributable to poor judgement by the management of the distressed competitor or inadequate investment in risk management.

Securitization

Cruz (1999)[36] has already discussed the possibility that securitization could act as a substitute for operational risk insurance. The advantages of securitization are linked to the fact that it provides banks with the potential to transfer operational risk to investors in the global capital markets. Therefore, compared to insurance, the scope for risk spreading and the availability of financial resources are much greater, thereby reducing counterparty risk and increasing cover limits.

One possible means of securitizing operational risk is via issuing a bond similar to catastrophe bonds. For example, a bank could issue a bond whose value is related to certain prespecified operational losses. The purchaser of the bond would expect to receive a high yield. However, if one of the operational events described in the bond occurred, the purchaser would lose some or all of the principal and interest.

Finite risk plans

Finite risk plans are a form of insurance–banking hybrid. These plans are self-financing programmes that involve the formal participation of some external agent. In effect, a firm sets up a bank account that is managed by the external agent. The contract between the firm and the external agent is usually for a period of 3–5 years.

Finite risk plans usually work in the following way:

- the policyholder capitalizes its account through the payment of premiums;
- the external agent deals with the administration of the account (e.g. premium calculations, claims management, etc);
- The external agent may provide some excess insurance to cap the policyholder's losses. A common arrangement is for the policyholder and agent to share any losses that exceed the

value of the account, with the policyholder bearing the greater percentage of these losses (say 80/20);

- the external agent may also guarantee a line of credit to the policyholder in the event that losses cause the account to become empty;
- at the end of the contract any remaining capital is returned to the policyholder, less the external agent's fees.

Finite risk plans allow a firm to spread losses over time. This is in contrast to insurance where losses are spread over policyholders. Spreading the cost of losses over time could allow a bank to achieve the cash flow smoothing benefits of insurance. In addition, by utilizing the risk management skills of an external agent, the real service efficiencies provided by an insurer may also be achieved. Finite risk plans are, however, controversial with some critics suggesting that their benefits are illusory.[37] Finite risk plans merely provide a way of structuring the financing of retained risks and do not involve risk mitigation or transfer. As such, they are not a perfect substitute for insurance. For example, it is hard to see how it would be possible to amortize a large 1-in-50 or 1-in-1000 year loss in an efficient way using the payments made into a finite risk plan that only runs for 5–10 years.

12.3 FINDINGS

12.3.1 Where are the gaps and overlaps in what is currently available?

As stated previously, most traditional insurance products are offered against a limited set of known perils, with each policy setting forth the conditions that apply and the types of losses that are excluded. This has led some to conclude that there are too many gaps and overlaps between insurance policies. However, many working in the insurance industry believe that this perception is somewhat unfair.

One key issue is that insurance markets are far from static. As "new" risks are discovered, insurance companies will often respond by either including them in a product that already exists or by formulating a new product (e.g. unauthorized or "rogue" trader insurance). In addition, insurers are increasingly offering multi-peril basket insurance policies that group together a basket of various standard policies. As such, there are now products that eliminate many of the perceived gaps and overlaps in operational risk insurance.

12.3.2 What are the key issues and potential limiting factors?

There are a number of issues that could adversely affect the extent to which insurance could be used as a mitigant for operational risk. Many of these issues are the direct result of violations in the theoretical principles of insurability, considered above.

Capitalization

The capitalization of some of the largest insurers – such as Allianz, Munich Re, and Swiss Re – rivals that of the largest banks. However, the problem is not the absolute level of capital available but the ability of an individual insurer to access that potential. Operating independently, even a large insurance company might struggle to provide comprehensive cover for all of a bank's operational risks at a level that met the requirements of the banking sector or regulators. Obviously, though, an insurer that has good access to the reinsurance and coinsurance markets would be able to offer much higher levels of cover.

Withdrawal

Related to capitalization is the possibility that an insurer may stop supplying operational risk insurance to the banking sector if it was to suffer very high losses. This problem is likely to be particularly acute during the developmental phase of new basket operational risk insurance products. This is because, in the event of a large loss, there would be pressure within the insurance company to close its operational risk business unit, particularly where losses sustained greatly exceeded premiums, possibly for many years to come.

However, this is more of a transient issue since any gap left in the market could be expected to be filled by other participants. Indeed, the rapid withdrawal and entry of firms is a common characteristic of many developing markets and is often taken as evidence of healthy competition (where inefficient firms are replaced by more efficient ones).

Reinsurance

It is standard practice within the insurance industry for an insurer to lay off part of the risks it has underwritten to a reinsurer (or coinsurer), who may in turn lay off a part of that risk to another reinsurer (and so on). This is a long established and highly effective practice that enables non-specialist reinsurers to increase the capacity of specialist insurers in a variety of insurance market sectors. This practice also helps to spread risk and mitigate the problem of catastrophic losses.

Critics of this practice have, however, suggested that reinsurance creates a lack of transparency within the insurance market and can result in circularity.[38] A bank making an operational risk insurance claim is therefore dependent upon the weakest link. This can result in the following issues.

- The slowing down of a claim payment, since an insurer or reinsurer may only be willing or able to meet its obligation after it has secured funds from the immediate reinsurer in the chain. In some circumstances, though, a reinsurer may have recourse to a precedent, which states that it need only pay out once the insurer has paid the claim. This can lead to liquidity problems for the insurer.
- The addition of further terms and conditions to the original insurance contract. As such, it is possible that a reinsurance company might refuse to pay a claim that is technically covered under the original contract.
- The creation of potential counterparty risks with reinsurers that may not be known to the bank itself. Should a reinsurer fail, though, the bank would still have legal recourse against its original insurer. However, if this insurer were to fail, the bank would have no recourse against the reinsurer.
- A concentration of risk with an unknown counterparty, which might be unacceptable on a known basis.

It is, however, true to say that reinsurers provide some of the highest rated security in the insurance industry. Insurers would argue that reinsurance plays a major role in reducing volatility and adds stability to the insurance process. For example, the chance that an 'A' rated reinsurer would fail is considered to be almost insignificant.

Limiting conditions and exclusion clauses

Even with the broadest multi-peril basket products, the need to specify the basis of an insurance risk transfer is inevitably going to involve a number of limiting conditions and exclusion clauses. As such, it is unlikely that insurance will ever provide a complete solution to the mitigation of operational risks (if it did, then insurance could effectively replace capital). Limiting conditions and exclusions clauses are, however, much less of a problem when they are well understood and accepted by both the insurer and the insured.

Policy language

Many banks argue that insurance policy language is complicated and frequently archaic. In addition, banks and insurance companies can use different terminology and definitions to classify risks. However, the wording of many modern policies are scripted in negotiation with banks and their brokers.

Delays in payment

Delays in claim payment could represent a serious problem in the case of very large losses that threaten the financial stability of the claimant. Delays are most likely to arise where the insured and insurer fail to agree on the amount, time, place, and cause of loss or where a peril is covered by more than one insurance policy (placed with multiple insurers) as this can lead to disputes over responsibility. As such, both the insurer and the insured may cause delays.

There are ways round the problem of delays in payment. One simple solution is to use clearer policy language. Another is to offer claimants the option of receiving an up-front payment for a loss before the validity of any claim has been investigated fully. However, this approach does have its problems and associated costs. One problem is the possibility that the policyholder may either refuse or simply be unable to pay back the up-front payment. Another is that by providing immediate finance an insurer could lose several months (or even years) of investment income. As such, this feature is only likely to be a practical proposition for select firms (i.e. those that can not only pay for it, but also demonstrate their ability to repay up-front payments as required).

Financial enhancement ratings (FER) have been developed by Standard & Poors as a supplement to their security ratings. The FER are designed to test the commitment of an insurance entity to pay first and then to only dispute a claim payment if there has been a clear breach of the contract. FER ratings provide both the regulators and the banks with a professional assessment of the probability of non-payment. Such ratings could encourage prompt payment and thereby reduce regulatory concerns.

Adverse selection

Adverse selection occurs where it is difficult for an insurer to properly assess the risks related to a particular client. One possible consequence of this is that the insurer will charge identical premiums to all policyholders. As such, insurance will have the greatest appeal to those banks that have a higher than average chance of incurring a loss. Consequently, the client that poses the greatest risk will buy a disproportionate amount of insurance (at too low a price) and thus threaten the viability of the insurer's portfolio. High-risk banks will exhibit a preference for insurance, as they will be able to avoid compromising their internal capital resources.

Adverse selection can be a costly problem for insurers and may even threaten the provision of certain products. However, adverse selection can be avoided if risks are properly distinguished and a commensurate premium charged. The new Basel regulatory framework, with its emphasis on data collection and good management, should assist in correcting any adverse selection tendencies. In addition, it should be noted that insurers are already very experienced in assessing the risks of clients and correcting adverse selection problems.

Moral hazard

With regard to moral hazard, one view is that insurance could result in the insured bank reducing its level of diligence and not adopting a continuous improvement policy towards the management of operational risks, since part of the derived benefit would pass to the insurer. An alternative view is that insurance would lead to improvements in operational risk management. This is because insurers are only likely to consider providing insurance to banks that adopt high standards of operational risk management and will then undertake on-going due diligence investigations. Moreover, in the event of failure due to non-compliance, the insurer would be expected to pursue legal remedies against the directors and employees as considered appropriate.

The potential for moral hazard will obviously vary between different banking organizations. For example, it has been suggested that moral hazard may be more of a problem with smaller banks (who have less money to invest in risk management) and those with fundamental cultural issues (such as BCCI or Barings). In addition, the type of insurance product may influence the scope for moral hazard. For example, the scope for opportunism may be greater for multi-peril basket products, especially when they offer cover against currently unknown or nonquantifiable risks. This is because it is hard to monitor the performance of a bank in managing an operational risk when this risk is not properly understood in the first place.

A common way to reduce the likelihood of moral hazard is to specify a comparatively high minimum attachment point (i.e. a deductible). This leaves a substantial burden with the insured and thus provides them with a strong incentive to manage risk. In addition, insurers have considerable experience in monitoring the behaviour of an insured, so are often able to prevent moral hazard from occurring in the first place.

Systemic risk

Although the management of systemic risk is a primary concern for regulators, it does not concern the banks nearly as much. This is because the regulatory authorities are expected to take appropriate action in cases where there is the potential for systemic risk (as with Long Term Capital Management, US Savings & Loans, and the 2007–08 credit crunch). As such, an individual bank is unlikely to perceive any benefit from insuring against systemic risk.

Insurers are also not particularly concerned about the problem of systemic risk. However, problems for insurers could arise where banks adopt similar operational systems that could all fail concurrently (leading to a string of operational risk insurance claims).[39] In addition, the trend amongst banks towards outsourcing certain functions such as payment systems to a very small number of external firms creates the possibility of an industry-wide failure.

It has been argued that the purchase of insurance could actually increase the possibility of systemic risk if the insurer (or its reinsurance chain) was undercapitalized. In this case, a substantial claim from one or a number of banks may cause the insurer to fail and leave other banks in the same portfolio exposed. Clearly, it is a matter for bank management (and perhaps the regulators), to be fully satisfied with the ability of an insurer to accept the risk they have transferred. Moreover, the fact that the insurance industry is highly regulated, coupled with the work of the rating agencies, means that this scenario is unlikely to occur.

Granularity and linearity

Operational risk is often merely a collective name for a mixed bag of risks. In an effort to achieve better understanding and control, efforts have been made to prescribe these risks in a more precise way by identifying common characteristics and causes (granularity). Taken to an extreme, this can lead to one risk event being completely and uniquely described. However, this is clearly of little use for statistical predictive purposes. Given that most operational losses are caused by the complex interaction of various preconditions, it is highly unlikely that a particular type of risk event will exhibit a one-dimensional (linear) characterization. Insurance relies on a loss event being attributable to a specific cause. However, it is much harder to assign probabilities to events that are the result of a combination of several causal factors.[40]

Data and risk classification

Data is vital to the efficient functioning of insurance; data facilitates the quantification of risk and consequently allows the proper pricing of insurance products. However, data on operational risk is limited, particularly for extreme tail events. Efforts are being made to correct this problem with data collection being undertaken in a variety of quarters (e.g. the banks, insurers, rating agencies, industry associations, and the regulatory authorities).

Of particular interest are the external loss databases that have been established. The benefits of initiatives like these are that they should increase the availability of operational risk information and help in the creation of a standardized approach towards the classification and demarcation of operational risks. However, external data needs to be used with caution as it is not always readily transportable in time and place,[41] especially when it is aggregated or where it is used to provide information on low frequency events. This is because many operational risks, especially low frequency ones, may be a direct consequence of the individual attributes of particular banks (as in the case of Barings).[42] Moreover, given the dynamic nature of the banking industry, even when data is recorded accurately and comprehensively its "shelf life" can be short.

Data adjustment techniques

Unfortunately, databases tend to misrecord the more extreme (low frequency/high severity) loss events. By definition, where such an event has occurred it is overstated and where absent it is understated. In practice, some of the rarer types of risk events may not yet have occurred, whilst those that have may be under recorded, possibly due to deliberate attempts to hide embarrassment or because the full scale of the loss is difficult to determine, particularly in the short term. Consequently, where databases are used, it may be considered necessary to adjust the resulting distributions for the misrecording of large losses. Several methods, such as the Delphi technique and causal modeling, can be used to partially correct for limitations of database techniques, as well as providing insight into risk quantification and control methods.

Differences in data requirements

A loss event can be considered to have three fundamental elements: the event itself; its cause; and its effect. Insurers are primarily interested in the financial effect, whereas banks are more concerned with the cause given that their aim is to mitigate and manage risk. As a consequence, there is a difference between the data held by insurers and that being collected in bank databases. To properly prescribe and understand risk it is necessary to consider both the severity of the event and its frequency of occurrence (i.e. impact and likelihood) as well as its probable cause. It should be remembered that an event could have multiple causes and multiple effects.

Risk classification

It is also important to recognize that some operational risks are difficult to classify. For example some elements of operational risk could also be classified as market risk or credit risk. Where such distinctions are not made ex ante this could lead to disputes with insurers. Such disputes are particularly likely with basket products, where the risks included in a policy may not be completely specified.

Quantification and risk assessment[43]

A further issue related to the availability and accuracy of data is quantification. Plentiful amounts of data are needed if an insurer is going to quantify a risk accurately and hence properly calculate insurance premiums. Moreover, even where data is available, an insurer will need to process it correctly in order to ensure accuracy in depicting the operational risk exposures of individual banks.

Clearly, the measurement of risk is an essential part of insurance. However, where risk depends on the unique characteristics of a firm or the actions of management, pure statistical assessment becomes unreliable.[44] One way round this is to adopt those techniques used by risk-rating agencies, which typically consist of three separate activities:

- a business risk assessment in which all operating divisions are reviewed, with factors such as the quality of management, strategy and competitive position being considered;
- a financial risk assessment, which includes a review of the financial history of the organization together with an assessment of the future projections, in addition to comparison of 60–80 industry average ratios;
- an overall assessment by the risk committee, which also considers the potential impact of external factors before awarding the final rating index.

A similar system is adopted by the venture capital industry, with quantification signified by the required internal rate of return on investment, which is then enhanced by the applied terms and conditions.

Loss distribution curve[45]

Deciding which operational losses could and should be insured is far from straightforward. What action a bank decides to pursue and what cover an insurer can sensibly underwrite will depend upon their particular circumstances.

Operational losses can be classified according to their probability of occurrence and the severity of their outcomes. However, it should be noted that the severity of loss is a relative concept that is influenced by the size of a bank.

High-frequency low-severity losses[46]

In general, banks manage higher frequency/lower severity operational risks in-house, since such losses are predictable and more efficiently managed internally. Where such losses are a function of the system, quality control requires continuous management.[47] In fact, high frequency/low severity losses are often termed expected losses and are built into the cost of a product, and charged to the Profit & Loss account. However, some banks may decide to transfer some of their high frequency/low severity losses to an insurer. This may be due to the outsourcing benefits of insurance, tax deductibility of premiums, or simply because insurance cover for such risks is comparatively cheap.[48]

Low to medium frequency and medium to high severity

The most active market sectors for operational risk insurance are expected to be those encompassing the low to medium frequency and medium to high severity losses. It was thought that many banks could appropriate significant cash flow smoothing and risk management benefits from purchasing insurance for such risks. In addition, provided that insurance companies have access to the necessary loss data and have appropriate levels of capitalization, such risks should not prove difficult to insure.

Catastrophic – very low frequency and very high severity losses

The potential pooling benefits of insuring catastrophic risks are likely to be considerable, especially if the purchase of insurance can protect a bank from the costs of financial distress or bankruptcy. However, despite these benefits, catastrophic losses may at times present an underwriting challenge, since they are potentially unique and could even be solvency-threatening for an insurer. This is not to say, though, that catastrophic losses are uninsurable. In particular, a catastrophic loss for a small- or medium-sized bank should not prove catastrophic to a large, well-capitalized insurance company. Moreover, with proper reinsurance arrangements, it is unlikely that the failure of even a large bank would lead to the collapse of the insurance sector.

It should be remembered, though, that catastrophic insurance cover could be expensive. In addition, a certain amount of catastrophic risk can be passed on to both shareholders (whose expected returns will generally reflect such risks) and the tax authorities (since the loss of profits caused by a catastrophic loss means that less corporation tax will be paid).[49] Indeed the general view of those banks questioned was that only a limited level of cover against low frequency/high severity risk was desirable.

Latent losses

Latent losses develop gradually over time. In fact, it is possible for a latent loss to remain hidden for years before being discovered. A simple example of a latent loss would be gradual, unseen pollution that manifests after many years of development. Problems then arise for an insurer because it may have long since stopped holding reserves against claims from "expired" policies. Moreover, additional difficulties arise where a bank has switched insurers, since there may now be a problem in identifying which of its previous insurers should be responsible for paying a claim against a latent loss.

Traditional peril-specific insurance policies purchased by the banks deal with latency by providing coverage on a "losses discovered" or "claims made" basis. This means that the policy incurring the claim is the one that is in force when the bank discovers a particular latent loss. The advantage of "claims made" policies is that they have allowed insurers to deal with the problem of specifying the time of occurrence for a latent loss. However, the nature of "claims made" policies means that a bank must continue to purchase cover if it is to remain protected from latent losses that could manifest in the future.

12.3.3   The alternatives to insurance

Mutual self-insurance pools

Discussions have taken place between a number of banks, with involvement from the British Bankers Association, regarding the establishment of a mutual insurance company for the industry. In order to be cost effective, mutual self-insurance pools usually require a large number of contributors. However, most bank executives believe their bank to be better run than the competitors; therefore, it is unlikely that a bank would risk its capital on the operational failures of a rival.

Securitization

Currently, securitization appears to have limited potential. One key reason for this is that many investors (except perhaps insurance companies) are simply not ready for such unconventional investment products. In addition, there is still insufficient data on low frequency operational losses to properly price bonds. The net result of this is likely to be that investors would demand too high a rate of return on these instruments to make them cost effective.

Finite risk plans

Finite risk plans are controversial and are by no means a perfect substitute for insurance. It is important to remember that finite risk plans merely provide a way of helping a bank to structure the financing of its retained risks and do not involve the transfer of risk. Some critics suggest that their benefits are illusory.[50]

12.4   CONCLUSIONS AND RECOMMENDATIONS

12.4.1 Regulators

The relationship between insurers, risk-rating agencies, and the regulators

Regulation can only be justified when market weaknesses cannot be corrected in a cost-effective manner by other less invasive means. The assessment of banks and their operational risk activities could be transferred, at least in part, to market participants. One possible polar model is for the regulators to simply set the coral bounds and leave the monitoring and to some extent the day-to-day "enforcement" of these bounds to risk–rating agencies and insurance companies. This could create an environment in which market forces are encouraged to function efficiently and effectively.

Insurance companies have a vested interest in encouraging banks to adhere to and improve their risk mitigation activities. In addition, they have the skills to undertake detailed on-going assessment and monitoring of operational risks within banks. Similarly, external independent assessments of banks are already provided by risk-rating agencies.[51] The regulators should concentrate their efforts on creating an environment in which these participants are encouraged to improve their monitoring and control capabilities.

Systemic risk

Given the continuing move towards globalization, consideration needs to be given to systemic risk. Systemic events, which violate the principles of insurance, are seen to be the responsibility of the regulatory authorities and, as such, outside the scope of individual banks or insurers. However, this view is not entirely satisfactory, since it is beholden upon an individual bank to ensure that the decisions it takes (e.g. outsourcing decisions) do not cause it to become overly exposed to systemic risk, or indeed to create systemic risk (as with the 2007–08 credit crunch).

12.4.2   Insurers

For the insurance industry the main conclusions and recommendations are as outlined below.

The traditional, peril-specific approach

The traditional bottom-up approach to insurance, which is based on provision of cover for known perils, is tried and tested, and has much to commend it. This approach is in line with the theoretical concept of pattern theory,[52] akin to democracy, where overall direction tends to result from the outcome of myriad separate projects.

However, the traditional bottom-up approach to new product development can be rather reactive. It is, therefore, necessary for the insurance industry to consider the limitations of this approach in a dynamic industry such as banking. In particular, a reactive approach may allow unforeseen gaps in cover to appear over time due to changes in technology, knowledge, and the economic environment.

New product development in operational risk insurance

In addition to the proven peril-specific approach to operational risk insurance, there are a number of other routes that could be considered for development.

One alternative is simply to substitute current peril-specific products with a single multi-peril basket product. Such a product would have the advantage of eliminating overlaps between product lines. In addition, it may be possible to offer broader levels of cover than before, thereby filling in some of the gaps (whether perceived or actual) that may exist with established products. However, the basket approach is also potentially less flexible (since it removes a bank's ability to select which risks it wants to insure) and can present additional underwriting problems (such as moral hazard and the unavailability of data).

Another possible route might be to develop an umbrella insurance policy designed to complement existing peril-specific products. A policy of this type could be used to provide broad cover at a higher attachment point than current peril-specific policies. This would help to protect banks from any major unforeseen problems, which will naturally occur in a dynamic environment subject to constant change. It might also make it easier for an insurer to underwrite any unknown risks since the high attachment point should help to minimize moral hazard.

Portfolio considerations

Portfolio considerations are becoming increasingly important to insurers. Therefore, insurers are evaluating the interaction of the risks they underwrite in relation to their portfolio as a whole, rather than simply considering each contract separately, on its individual merits. In general, it is considered that a bank's operational risk is uncorrelated with other types of risk and therefore its inclusion in an insurer's portfolio would reduce the capital requirement compared to a bank retaining all the operational risk itself.

Alternative risk – transfer mechanisms

Although the alternative risk-transfer market (e.g. securitization, etc.) remains in a very early stage of development with regard to operational risk, it should not be overlooked by the insurance industry. As the level of operational risk data increases, the viability of alternative risk-transfer tools is likely to increase.

The alternative risk-transfer market, including finite risk insurance, is developing new techniques to handle hard-to-quantify risks. These include the introduction of contingent capital on the occurrence of the insured event as well as allowing repayment out of future profits. The insurer takes the risk that there may not be sufficient profits in future. A variation on the theme of contingent capital would be the issue by a bank of a particular class of preference shares specifically to meet regulatory capital requirements. Such shares could prove of interest to insurance firms as well as other investors. Undoubtedly, alternative risk transfer (ART) techniques will be increasingly considered as a means to finance capital requirements for bank operational risk.

The demand for operational risk insurance

Although pro-active product development has been undertaken by a small number of leading insurers, the longer-term level of demand for these new products remains unclear. Previously, insurance companies have responded to perceived market needs only to find that there was virtually no demand for these new products (e.g. Rogue Trader Insurance).

At the moment, demand seems somewhat muted and may remain so without further support from the regulators.

Standard documentation

There is a recognized need within the industry to move towards standardized documentation. Such standardization could help to reduce the possibility of disputes and provide reassurance to the regulators that insurers will pay out for proven operational losses. It would also assist in the development of alternative risk products (since standardized products could be commoditized and offered to a wider market via securitization). However, care does needs to be taken, as too much standardization could stifle new product development and impact upon the efficient functioning of the market. In addition, the ever-changing and evolving nature of insurance, which is necessary to meet clients' needs, means that it is difficult to draw up fully standardized policy documents for insurance products.

12.4.3   Banks

Insurance and shareholder value

When purchasing insurance, a bank should focus on how this will contribute towards shareholder value, rather than simply basing its decision on cost. Insurance can enhance shareholder value by:

* smoothing a bank's cash flows;
* preventing financial catastrophes;
* assisting with monitoring and control; and
* providing cost-effective risk management advice.

It is important to note that simply trading insurance for a reduced capital charge will not necessarily lead to an increase in shareholder value (especially when the opportunity cost of holding capital is low). The purchase of insurance must be justified on the grounds that it offers services that the firm cannot replicate in-house, at least in a cost-effective way.

Insurance as a device for monitoring and control

A bank should emphasize to its stakeholders the role that insurance can play as a monitoring and control tool. As stated above, the purchase of insurance by a bank can often be taken as a credible signal that a bank is committed to risk management. This is because the active use of insurance requires the bank to:

* be aware of the risks it is facing;
* think carefully about which risks it wants to retain and which it wants to transfer (i.e. properly and overtly define its risk profile);
* discuss with an insurer the risk control tools it will maintain; and
* accept external monitoring and investigation by the insurance company.

Insurance and competitive positioning

From a strategic perspective, insurance allows a firm to focus on those areas of its business in which it has a core competency. This is because insurance provides a mechanism for a bank to outsource those aspects of its risk management function in which an insurer has a comparative advantage. In a competitive industry like banking the need to consider the strategic and tactical implications of insurance is paramount.[53]

The location of the insurance manager

In a number of banks the insurance manager is positioned outside the group risk function. This can result in a lack of coordination between the risk management and insurance decisions of a bank. In particular, it may lead to an overemphasis on the cost of insurance, with inadequate consideration being given to insurance as a shareholder value-enhancing activity.

Data collection and the loss distribution curve

As part of its insurance decision, a bank should take into account the frequency and severity of its losses. In so doing it is helpful to subdivide losses into the following three categories:

- high severity, low frequency;
- low to medium frequency, medium to high severity; and
- catastrophic.

Which of these three categories a bank chooses to insure will depend on its own particular circumstances and the prevailing conditions of the insurance market.

ENDNOTES

[1] Williams, C., Smith, M. and Young, P. (1998). *Risk Management and Insurance.* 8th ed. New York: Mc-Graw Hill International, pp. 259–260.

[2] Williams, C., Smith, M. and Young, P. (1998). *Risk Management and Insurance.* 8th ed. New York: Mc-Graw Hill International, p. 11.

[3] For example the purchase of fire insurance does nothing to stop a fire from occurring, nor does it help to reduce the amount of damage that a fire might cause.

[4] Oldfield, G. and Santomero, A. (1997). Risk Management in Financial Institutions. *Sloan Management Review* **39:1**, 33–46.

[5] History of new product development in the insurance industry – response from ORRF Insurance Working Group:

> *Although not a new development, the insurance industry has historically reacted to new development in advance of the loss experience becoming available. This means that new insurance products can be developed in advance of data becoming available in the operational risk field. A good example of that is in the aviation field where new technological advances totally change the risks and so past data become obsolete. Actuaries and underwriters and other experts work together to estimate rates, which are then adjusted in the light of experience. The introduction of jet aircraft in the 1950s and 1960s were covered even though loss experience was poor. Consequently there was considerable apprehension when wide-bodied jets were introduced in the early 1970s. Here experience was good. Satellites had mixed results and a much more sophisticated approach has now been adopted to ensure continuity of coverage.*

[6] Although it should be noted that some "traditional" insurance products (such as the banker's blanket bond) also offer quite broad levels of cover in their own right.

[7] Culp, C. (2001). *The Risk Management Process: Business Strategy and Tactics.* New York: John Wiley & Sons Inc. p. 562.

[8] Hadjiemmanuil, C. (1996). *Banking Regulation and the Bank of England.* London: LLP. p. 562.

[9] See Note 8.

[10] Karels, G. and McClatchy, C. (1999). Deposit Insurance and Risk-Taking Behaviour in the Credit Union Industry. *Journal of Banking and Finance* **23**, 105–134.

[11] See Note 8.

[12] Kane, E. and Hendershott, R. (1996). The Federal Deposit Insurance Fund that Didn't Put a Bite on U.S. Taxpayers. *Journal of Banking and Finance* **20**, 1305–1327.

[13] Doherty, N. (1985). *Corporate Risk Management: A Financial Exposition.* New York; McGraw-Hill; and Doherty, N. (2000). *Integrated Risk Management: Techniques and Strategies for Reducing Risk.* New York: McGraw-Hill.

[14] Main, B. (1982). Business Insurance and Large, Widely Held Corporations. *The Geneva Papers on Risk and Insurance*. **7:24**, 237–247; and Mayers, D. and Smith, C. (1982). On the Corporate Demand for Insurance. *Journal of Business* **55:2**, 281–296.

[15] Stultz, R. (1996). Rethinking Risk Management. *Journal of Applied Corporate Finance* **9:3**, 8–24.

[16] Williams, C., Smith, M. and Young, P. (1998). *Risk Management and Insurance*. 8th ed. New York: Mc-Graw Hill International. pp. 274–276.

[17] Of particular relevance is the work of authors like Mayers and Smith (1982) and Main (1982) – see Note 14 Doherty (1985, 2000 – see Note 13). See also Froot, K., Murphy, B., Stem, A. and Usher, S. (1995). *The Emerging Asset Class: Insurance Risk*. A Special Report by Guy Carpenter & Co., Inc. pp. 235–1).

[18] Shapiro, A. and Titman, S. (1985). An Integrated Approach to Corporate Risk Management. *Midland Corporate Finance Journal* **3**, 41–56.

[19] See Note 14.

[20] Doherty, N. and Smith, C. (1993). Corporate Insurance Strategy: The Case of British Petroleum. *Journal of Applied Corporate Finance* **16**, 4–15. Also see Note 14.

[21] Holderness, C. (1990). Liability Insurers as Corporate Monitors. *International Review of Law and Economics* **10**, 115–129.

Grillet, L. (1992). Corporate Insurance and Corporate Stakeholders: I. Transactions Cost Theory. *Journal of Insurance Regulation* **11:2**, 232–251.

Skogh, G. (1989). The Transactions Cost Theory of Insurance: Contracting Impediments and Costs. *Journal of Risk and Insurance* **56**, 726–732.

Skogh, G. (1991). Insurance and the Institutional Economics of Financial Intermediation. *The Geneva Papers on Risk and Insurance: Issues and Practice* **16:58**, 59–72.

[22] See Note 20.

[23] Katzman, M. (1985). *Chemical Catastrophes: Regulating Environmental Risk Through Pollution Liability Insurance*. IL: Richard D. Irwin, Inc.

Freeman, P. and Kunreuther, H. (1996). The Roles of Insurance and Well-Specified Standards in Dealing with Environmental Risks. *Managerial and Decision Economics* **17**, 517–530.

[24] Response from ORRF Insurance Working Group: *The report implies that regulators use market forces to do their job for them. Market forces may weed out the weak and so fulfil a quasi regulatory role. Incidentally, I don't believe either banks or insurers are compensated for their risks. That's where the market has a key (and probably perverse) role in that it tends to drive price down, even below apparent economic levels.*

[25] Recent thoughts on capital in insurance – response from ORRF Insurance Working Group: *New thinking on risk and capital in insurance will be helpful in developing banking operational products. Insurers are increasingly looking at risk across the whole portfolio. This means that operational risk needs to be evaluated in relation to the portfolio as a whole and not on a stand-alone basis. Since bank operational risk is probably not correlated with other insurance risks, the capital requirements for risks transferred to insurers are likely to be significantly less than if left in concentrated form in banks provided that the amounts are not too large. This is likely to mean that insurance is part but not the whole solution. It is not necessary for insurers to write large amounts of business in order to balance their books. Insurers divide pricing risk into two aspects: statistical risk or law of large numbers and parameter risk or uncertainty as to the true cost of the risk. Parameter risk is likely to be the biggest source of risk initially for insurers and they are likely not to want to underwrite very large sums in relation to their capital until they have a clearer understanding of the parameters. On the other hand, the uncorrelated nature of the risk will encourage many insurers to write small amounts. These two factors would suggest that there should be an active market though it may take some time to develop fully.*

Increasingly insurers are differentiating between shareholder capital and regulatory capital. Shareholders and stakeholders (with whom regulators are concerned) have very different risk profiles. Stakeholders cannot diversify. This means that spreading the risk widely will reduce the cost of capital from a shareholder perspective. This is also likely to encourage the use of insurance as a partial solution to funding the capital requirements of banking operational risk.

[26] Schmidt, J. (1986). A New View on the Requisites of Insurability. *Journal of Risk and Insurance*, **53**, 320–329. See also Williams et al. (1998), Note 1.

[27] Young, B. (2000a). Data Days. *Futures & OTC World* **348**, (May), 24–25.

[28] See Note 26.

[29] Butler, D. AON Group Limited, Financial Institutions and Professional Risks (2000). The Role of Insurance in Operational Risk Mitigation. Bank Treasury Operational Risk Conference, London, 27–28 September 2000.

[30] See Williams *et.al.* (1998), Note 1.

[31] See Doherty, N. and Smith, C. (1993). Corporate Insurance Strategy: The Case of British Petroleum. *Journal of Applied Corporate Finance*, **6**, 4–15.

[32] See Mayers, D. and Smith, C. (1982). On the Corporate Demand for Insurance. *Journal of Business* **55**:2, 281–296.

[33] Schrand, C. and Unal, H. (1998). Hedging and Co-ordinated Risk Management: Evidence from Thrift Conversions. *Journal of Finance* **53**:3, 979–1013.

[34] See Doherty (2000) for a good discussion of the use of debt as a risk-financing tool (Note 13).

[35] Alternative Risk Transfer Mechanisms – Response from ORRF Insurance Working Group: *The alternative risk transfer market, including finite risk insurance, is developing new techniques to handle hard to quantify risks. These include the introduction of contingent capital on the occurrence of the insured event as well as allowing repayment out of future profits. The insurer takes the risk that there may not be sufficient profits in future. Undoubtedly these techniques will be used in some instances to finance capital requirements for bank operational risk. This is written up in much more detail in a paper written for the EU Commission by JP Ryan of Towers Perrin and is available on the EU Commission web site.*

[36] Cruz, M. (1999). Taking Risk to Market. *Risk, Special Report on Operational Risk*, 21–24.

[37] Williams, C., Smith, M. and Young, P. (1998). *Risk Management and Insurance*. 8th ed. New York: Mc-Graw Hill International. pp. 305–307.

[38] Not everyone in the industry would agree with this view. Response from ORRF Insurance Working Group: *With regard to the risks of reinsurance (unknown counterparty failure), the bullet points greatly exaggerate the issue. There is no instance of any direct claim due from a "regular" insurer – maybe a captive may have had an issue – failing to be met because of reinsurer problems. After all, the insurer is well aware – it is a standard hazard – that if there is a problem with the reinsurance he is on for the original gross claim.*

[39] For example the banking industry's widespread reliance on computing technology created an industry-wide operational risk with the year 2000 problem.

[40] Linearity implies that $Y = mx + c$ (the equation of a straight line). Currently, given the dearth of information available, linearity is the assumption being made by the regulators. However, there should be a move away from linearity (basic indicator approach) to nonlinearity (Internal Measurement and Loss Distribution Approaches) in time, as more information comes to hand and the relationships begin to crystallize.

[41] See Note 27.

[42] Waring, A. and Glendon, I. (1998). *Managing Risk*. Thomson Business Press.

[43] Risk Modeling – Response from ORRF Insurance Working Group: *The development of operational risk-modeling capabilities will enhance both the banks' and the regulatory bodies, capabilities to quantify capital requirements. Development of databases, as covered in the main body of the report, are very helpful. Development of insurance products will also supplement this process of data collection as insurance companies build up their databases. However, there are considerable dangers in just relying on databases for these types of risk. In particular, the real problem is the low frequency/high severity nature of the risk, which means that some of the potential losses may not yet have occurred – e.g. a computer virus destroying several bank computer systems simultaneously. Furthermore, the fact that these types of loss tend to be embarrassing for the banks concerned means that operational risk losses that have occurred may not be reported or may be understated. Consequently there is a tendency for such databases not to be complete and therefore understate the tail of the distribution.*

Consequently firms, such as my own, prefer to rely on several methods in order to correct for these problems. Methods such as Delphi techniques and causal modeling are required to remedy defects of database techniques as well as providing greater insights into the quantification and control of operational risk. Where databases are used, it is necessary to adjust the resulting distributions for the under -recording of large losses. Fortunately, these techniques have been developed by actuaries to deal with a number of similar insurance problems. As these are beginning to be applied to banking operational risk, significant progress can be anticipated in the near future.

Apart from facilitating the pricing of insurance, these techniques can be used to evaluate the impact of insurance packages, whether these are all risk contracts or single or multi-peril. Modeling a bank's exposure before and after insurance is an effective way of evaluating the contribution of insurance to meeting the capital requirements.

[44] Young, B. (2000b). Developing a Standard Methodology for Operational Risk: A Market Value Maximisation Approach. Risk-Waters OpRisk Conference 2000; and Young, B. (1999). Raising the Standard. *Operational Risk: Risk Special Report.* 10–12.

[45] Response from ORRF Insurance Working Group: *With regard to distribution curves, your split of high/low is fine, but against a distribution curve we are going to have to work out things like time horizons and confidence intervals to establish where high, low, etc fit on the curve. Incidentally, is it really worth somebody insuring for catastrophic loss? The answer depends on where on the curve you drop a line called catastrophic. I think this point ought to be made.*

[46] Response from ORRF Insurance Working Group: *High frequency/low severity losses are often termed expected losses and are built into the cost of a product, and charged to the Profit & Loss account. It has been argued that under such circumstances, there is no need to subject these high frequency/low severity losses to a regulatory capital charge (i.e. they do not hit absorption capability).*

[47] Deming, W. Edwards (1988). *Out of Crisis.* Cambridge: Cambridge University Press.

[48] Further discussion of this issue can be found in Doherty and Smith (1993) – see Note 20.

[49] For more on all these issues see Doherty and Smith (1993) – see Note 20.

[50] See Williams *et al.* (1998) – Note 1.

[51] Young, B. (2003). Moody's Analytical Framework for Operational Risk Management of Banks.

[52] Johnson, G. (2000). Organisational Culture and Strategy. Presentation to the Sixth Meeting of the Operational Risk Research Forum, 18 May 2000.

[53] See Note 7.

Observed Best Practices and Future Considerations

13.1 INTRODUCTION

Prior to 26 February 1995[1] operational risk was virtually unheard of. Since then, the rate of development has been quite astonishing.[2] Despite this progress, however, considerable diversity remains, with very few organizations able to claim to be operating at the level of "best practice."[3]

Previous chapters have endeavoured to give an indication of how the key elements of "best practice" have been derived. This chapter looks at some observed "best practices" and comments upon them. Although it is clearly not possible to address all issues and to assess every observed practice, consideration is given to the main challenges currently facing the industry.

Historically, banks relied primarily upon internal control mechanisms, overseen by internal and external auditing activities. Whilst these remain fundamentally important, it is recognized that a more forensic, risk sensitive approach is now required to cope with increasing complexity. At the beginning of the millennium, operational risk management was very much in the genesis of its development. Consequently, the regulatory authorities, which were the initial drivers of change, chose to adopt an open approach illustrated by the expression "let a thousand flowers bloom." The new Basel Accord (Basel II) provides substantial flexibility which in turn has produced considerable diversity. Banks have therefore been able to develope approaches that are "fit for purpose," rather than being totally constrained by regulatory compliance.[4]

The Basel II Accord Implementation Group for Operational Risk (AIGOR) has stated that a narrowing of the range of practices can be expected to occur as those practices determined to be unacceptable are identified; thus, as a consensus gradually emerges there will be greater consistency in the assessment of AMA practices.[5] Undoubtedly, for banks of any size and scope, sound operational risk management requires a strong risk-aware internal control culture and framework, involving:

- board commitment;
- sound management;
- professionally competent, well motivated, and honest staff;
- appropriate and effective management information and reporting systems;
- contingency planning; and
- independent verification and validation.

However, considerable variations in practice can be found within these areas. Hence, in attempting to identify future winners and losers it should be remembered that not all winners will currently be operating at the level of "best practice"; however, the probability is that in the longer term those that survive and prosper will not be significantly dispersed from it. That said, relatively few banks are expected to adopt an AMA approach unless there are clearly demonstrable economic benefits and competitive advantages in doing so, or unless compelled by their regulators, as in the US.

A recent report by the Senior Supervisors Group[6] found that, during the 2007 credit crunch, some firms were able to identify and evaluate the risks faced approximately one year before the crisis occurred. Consequently, they were able to implement appropriate risk-management plans while it was still practical and not prohibitively expensive to do so. The report, which sought to identify those risk-management practices that worked well in the crisis and those that did not, concluded that the better-performing firms: *demonstrated a comprehensive approach to viewing firm-wide exposures and risk, sharing quantitative and qualitative information more effectively across the firm and engaging in more effective dialogue across the management team. . . . They had more adaptive (rather than static) risk measurement processes and systems that could rapidly alter underlying assumptions to reflect current circumstances; management also relied on a wide range of risk measures to gather more information and different perspectives on the same risk exposures and employed more effective stress testing with more use of scenario analysis.*

The approach towards risk management chosen by a bank is influenced by such factors as its size and sophistication together with the nature and complexity of its activities. In addition, existing limitations, particularly in the areas of data, quantification, and modeling, have placed constraints on the solutions developed by many organizations. Consequently, some practitioners regard "best practice" as an inappropriate and somewhat emotive term. Despite this, there are some clear indications that what may be regarded as "best practice" (or alternatively, "sound practice")[7] is starting to emerge, as stated above and discussed in more detail below. Indeed, Sound Practices Principle No. 1 requires the board of directors to regularly review its operational risk framework and to assess it against industry "best practice."[8]

Failure to properly manage operational risk can result in a misstatement of an organization's risk profile and expose it to potentially significant losses.[9] In assessing an organization, the analyst's skill lies in determining how existing practices compare to "best practice" and the extent to which current practices are appropriate for the organization, both now and in the future; consideration being given to how much work the organization needs to do to maintain its competitive position. Determining the quality and stability of earnings and the probability of default is a relatively skilled task, with the analyst seeking to identify those key risk factors that could change the rating. Where transparency becomes opaque, default becomes more difficult to predict. This happens naturally over time but can also be due to deliberate action, as evidenced in the Enron case. Deviations from "best practice" are a useful early warning of potential future problems. The extent to which these factors are important depends upon the flexibility and responsiveness of the organization, together with its underlying level of cultural honesty which is indicated substantially by its degree of transparency.

13.1.1 An organization's definition of "operational risk" indicates its level of understanding

The term "operational risk" has a variety of meanings within the banking industry. In its most general form, operational risk can be considered as a subset of "other risks," with "other risks" being defined as all risks other than credit risk, market risk, and interest rate risk.[10]

Unfortunately, something that cannot be positively defined cannot be precisely measured or properly assessed. Therefore, as part of its work relating to the development of a minimum regulatory capital charge for operational risk, the Basel Committee adopted the following definition, which was originally proposed by the Institute of International Finance (IIF) and at the time was beginning to find favour within the banking industry: *operational risk is . . . the risk of loss resulting from inadequate or failed internal processes, people and systems or from external events. . . . The definition includes legal risk but excludes strategic and reputational risk.*[11]

For comprehensive internal control purposes, the Risk Management Group (RMG) of the Basel Committee on Banking Supervision recognized the importance of allowing banks to choose their own definitions of operational risk. The Committee stated: *. . . banks should seek to manage* **all** *significant banking risks, and supervisors will review them as part of the Supervisory Review Process (Pillar 2) of the new Basel Capital Accord."*[12]

From an analyst's perspective, reviewing a bank's definition of operational risk provides the first insight into its depth of thinking and level of development. Where the standard regulatory definition has been accepted and adopted, it is important to understand the extent to which this is truly appropriate. Obviously, for reasons of completeness and for comparative peer assessment purposes, the analyst will want to know if there are any restrictions or limitations (i.e. exclusions such as business risk and reputational risk; inclusions such as legal risk). However, it should be remembered that it is not possible to predetermine all risks.

Research indicates that most major organizations include legal risk within their definition of operational risk. Some also include reputational risk, although very few attempt to quantify the level of business lost through reputational damage.

13.1.2   Capital is not a panacea

Economic capital methodologies are widely expected to prove an important development in the discipline of operational risk. The accurate assessment and allocation of risk-based economic capital across an organization can assist in identifying those businesses lines that are genuinely profitable. This should lead to an increase in transparency and, ultimately, to an increase in shareholder value. Consequently, leading banks are putting considerable efforts into developing economic capital assessment frameworks. Clearly, failure to properly assess the level of capital for operational risk can produce a distorted view of a bank's overall risk profile and lead to perverse incentives.

With regard to regulatory capital, this is regarded as a very poor indicator of the strength of a financial institution. As discussed in previous chapters, the assumptions made regarding the shape of the loss distribution curve – together with the paucity of data in the tail of the loss distribution – give rise to the possibility that similar organizations can have widely different assessments of regulatory capital. Whilst the regulators cannot meaningfully challenge these technical assessments, under Pillar 2 of the new Basel Accord they can decide upon the level of regulatory capital they consider most appropriate for a particular bank. Whilst this gives flexibility, it is not entirely satisfactory since regulators in different countries may view risk differently.

In assessing capital adequacy, it should be borne in mind that the rating agencies have clearly stated that the level of capital held by a bank does not directly determine its credit rating; capital is not a panacea.

13.1.3   The "Use Test"

The "Use Test," as stipulated by the new Basel Accord, requires that the operational risk framework integrates the operational risk-measurement system into the bank's day-to-day risk-management processes. The output must be integral to monitoring and controlling the bank's operational risk profile. In addition, as an incentive for improving operational risk management throughout the firm, operational risk capital must be allocated to all major business units.[13]

It is widely accepted that active monitoring can quickly detect risks and assist in correcting deficiencies in policies, processes, and procedures, thus significantly reducing the potential frequency and severity of operational risk events. However, the main issues that banks have with respect to the "Use Test" are the breadth of the requirement, and the ability to demonstrate adequately to supervisors that the framework is properly integrated and used rather than established only for regulatory purposes.

With regard to incentives, it is found that in practice banks apply these differently. Some banks, such as Deutsche Bank, decide upon the capital allocation level depending upon the reaction they are trying to invoke in a particular business unit. This may not necessarily relate directly to the level of risk within a particular business line but does act as a strong management incentive to bring about change. Since similar banks may calculate completely different capital requirements (depending upon the modeling methodology used), direct capital allocation may not fully meet the need to demonstrate appropriateness and benefit.

In contrast, a number of banks are in the process of developing transparent risk metrics in order to enable business managers to determine ex ante how their proposed actions will translate into capital allocation. Thus by taking account of the inherent level of risk and the proposed risk-mitigating actions, it is argued that managers will be able to assess the benefits resulting from reduced capital allocation and cost savings due to a reduction in operational risk exposure.

13.1.4   Enterprise-wide risk management (ERM) can change a firm's rating

The rating agencies are beginning to place considerable emphasis on enterprise-wide risk management (with some using models for the assessment). As an indication of the significance of this, in November 2006 S & P upgraded Manulife from AA to AAA, with an "excellent" ERM assessment being cited as one of the main reasons for the firm achieving a higher standing.

Following the Enron scandal in December 2001, and the subsequent investigation into the efficacy of the rating agencies by the SEC, the rating agencies themselves recognized the importance of identifying risks more quickly (and to be seen to be doing so). As a result, greater emphasis has been placed on conducting a more forensic analysis in three interrelated areas – corporate governance, risk management, and financial reporting – with the move towards holistic enterprise-wide risk management (ERM) being a key development.

There is now a growing recognition that ERM facilitates the value-creating potential of risk management through increasing the ability of an organization to tailor its overall risk profile. In addition to avoiding or minimizing risk, risk can be transferred or actively pursued and exploited. Informed risk taking is a means to achieving competitive advantage. An organization that improves its responsiveness and flexibility can adopt a more aggressive stance.

The trend towards ERM can be expected to increase as the ability to manage risk, and thus tailor an organization's risk profile, increases. Whilst regulatory requirements concerning transparency and market discipline will be of catalytic importance, the primary driving forces will be competitive advantage and market rationalization.

13.1.5 Reputational risk needs to be actively managed

Damage to a bank's image can have major impact on public opinion and therefore on its ability to attract and retain customers, thus directly affecting its revenue-generating capability, its credit rating and, indeed, its ability to remain in business. Reputational risk is not merely a resultant of other risk events; it needs to be actively managed. Although Basel II does not require regulatory capital to be held against reputational risk, some banks have started to actively manage it and, indeed, some are attempting to quantify it.

In general, analysts take the view that a sound reputation feeds through to enhanced performance. Investors expect and, through shareholder activism, demand that companies be well managed. A company must demonstrate sound financials and strong performance, with no excuses. Where a company's reputation is damaged, the immediate reaction from analysts and investors is to remove any uncertainty, which invariably necessitates the removal of senior management and possibly the transfer of ownership to another organization having a more highly regarded management team. Generally, there is little support for a tainted board to conduct any detailed investigations into failures; instead, the incoming management is expected to bring about sweeping changes. Research indicates that once a firm loses its reputation it is very difficult indeed for it to regain its former standing. Klein and Leffler[14] have shown, through game theory, that once a company is perceived to have reduced the standard of its products or services it will no longer be able to sell a higher quality offering. Rather than attempting to regain its former standing, financially it will instead be better for the company to accept its new market position and concentrate on selling lower quality products or services. Whilst a company may to some extent improve its tarnished reputation over time, it is virtually impossible for a management team to do so.

Historically, reputational risk was something that the investor relations function dealt with ex post, with the aim of limiting any decline in financial stakeholder confidence. Investors were primarily concerned with financial performance and financial strength. However, investors' attitudes and understanding have developed, with investment attractiveness now being influenced by a more comprehensive range of factors which serves to define the reputation of the board and senior management team. Besides the level and accuracy of earnings forecasts, other influencing factors include corporate governance, culture and ethics, transparency, and communications.

Given the importance of reputational risk, overall responsibility for it rests firmly with the board of directors who must ensure the existence of a clear policy. Given the complexity of reputational risk, which often cuts across many functions, some banks have formed a special subcommittee, chaired by a main board director. Typically, this subcommittee will include the head of risk management. Other approaches found in practice simply include expanding the responsibilities of existing committees. With regard to management and reporting, whilst a small number of banks have investigated the possibility of having a separate dedicated control function for reputational risk, in general this is considered an unnecessary complication. Instead, responsibility may typically be delegated to the operational risk function. However, the possible emergence of an enterprise-wide risk management function in leading banks may see reputational risk reassigned accordingly.

Whilst the ability to quantify reputational risk with any sensible degree of accuracy is currently very questionable, it should be recognized that quantification efforts can lead to greater understanding and thus to better management and resource allocation.

There are numerous examples of the impact of reputational damage on firms. One of the most famous is the Arthur Andersen affair. This formerly well-managed leading international firm of accountants was felled by its involvement in the Enron scandal. Although the shredding of information relating to Enron only took place in a small part of the firm and involved a very few number of employees, its impact served to destroy the entire firm.

More recently, in Italy, Banca Italease suffered serious reputational damage in March 2007, due to the implication of its Chief Executive Officer, Massimo Faenza, in the Danilo Coppola affair. Coppola was charged with fraudulent bankruptcy, money laundering, and embezzlement; Banca Italease announced potential client losses of €600 million. Following investigation by the Italian market regulator, Consob, the Bank of Italy dismissed the entire board of Banca Intalease on the grounds of negligence. On 14 August 2007, Moody's downgraded Banca Italease from Baa3 to Ba1.

In the UK, in September 2007, Northern Rock bank approached the Bank of England for support as "lender of last resort." Northern Rock had adopted a high-risk strategy of repackaging mortgages, using funds obtained from the international money market. Unfortunately, this funding source evaporated due to problems in the US sub-prime market. The lack of UK public confidence in the financial services system, which has been eroded to a fragile level over many years, resulted in the first run on a bank in the UK in 140 years. The impact was such that the Governor of the Bank of England, Mervyn King, found his personal position threatened. In order to prevent imminent systemic failure, the Governor was forced to override previous rules and guidelines regarding not supporting failing banks and only providing limited depositor protection (originally implemented to prevent moral hazard on the part of depositors), thus setting important precedents for the future of the UK financial system. However, the fear remained that there were many other financial services firms, including at least one leading UK bank, affected by imprudent lending to the sub-prime market both in the UK and the US. Unfortunately, the difficulty in determining where the risk actually resided resulted in the financial services industry being likened to players in a game of "pass the parcel." Such uncertainty threatens systemic risk, thus highlighting the importance of transparency and sound reputational standing.

13.1.6   Customer loyalty is a future indicator

Customer loyalty influences profitability and stability, and is therefore considered to be an important indicator of expected future performance. The development and maintenance of loyalty is also seen as important, given changes in the way customer services are being provided (away from personal interaction at branches towards more remote Internet and telephone banking). As a consequence, many leading banks regularly conduct market research, either directly or indirectly, to determine the current level of customer satisfaction and the extent to which customers are positively predisposed towards promoting the bank.

Various research studies into the European banking sector have indicated that a relatively high level of customer satisfaction exists (typically in excess of 70 % in the UK, France, Germany, Holland, and Sweden, with only Italy recording less than 40 %). However, when questioned about loyalty, only 12 % of customers claim to sufficiently trust their bank to provide other investment products. Similarly, research in the US indicates that less than 25 % of customers would act as advocates for their primary bank. Whilst these findings are interesting in that they indicate a relatively low level of trust in the banking system as a whole, the results do in fact hide significant variations between individual banks.

A pan-European study by Forrester Research[15] identified Sparda, a German mutual bank, as the leading customer-centric bank, with the Austrian Raiffeisen Bank also highly rated. In general, the findings indicated that those banks with their roots in the mutual movement scored more highly, although the German operation of Citibank also performed well. In the UK, a separate study[16] found the Nationwide Building Society to be the leading customer-centric performer.

Crédit Agricole, a leading French mutual, with 39 locally run caisses and approximately 16 million customers, has been carrying out customer satisfaction and customer loyalty surveys for approximately 20 years. The survey, which contains 40 questions, is sent out annually to half a million customers. Crédit Agricole seeks to build trust and loyalty by getting to know the customer (including greeting them by name when they visit their branch) and providing them with a proactive service.

In 2007, HSBC – which has approximately 120 million customers – sought to extend its commitment to being "the world's local bank" by linking part of the pay of its Chief Executive, Mike Geoghegan, to the level of customer satisfaction achieved.

Customer loyalty is influenced by the culture of an organization and the extent to which cutomers are treated fairly. Culture influences management and staff behaviour towards customers. The FSA has indicated that it considers "treating customers fairly"[17] to be one of its key ongoing priorities and from December 2008 it is included as part of the ARROW assessment.

13.2 GOVERNANCE AND MANAGEMENT

Corporate governance is a primary area of consideration for the analyst. It relates not only to the way in which the board of directors discharges its responsibilities but also to the culture and ethics of the organization.

Currently, governance structures are evolving as the discipline of operational risk itself continues to evolve. Therefore, whilst this is an area of considerable importance, it is also one in which there is considerable scope for variation.

In the United States, reforms are under way in an endeavour to improve governance structures. Traditionally, significant power is concentrated in the hands of one person, who holds the role of both chairman and Chief Executive. In addition, a number of interlocking board relationships may exist. This contrasts to the UK approach (developed in the aftermath of the BCCI, Maxwell, Polly Peck, and Barings scandals) where emphasis is placed on separating the roles of CEO and chairman. Currently, only around 20 % of US companies adopt this approach, although this is expected to increase as a result of pressure from institutional investors.

Within the banking sector, the Basel Committee has engaged in a number of initiatives in an attempt to improve governance. In particular, in February 2006 Basel published a document entitled *Enhanced Corporate Governance for Banking Organizations*, which set out eight fundamental principles.[18]

13.2.1 Responsibility rests firmly with the board

The board of directors is ultimately responsible for ensuring the financial soundness and stability of the bank. This involves:

- ensuring a risk aware culture exists within the organization;
- approving and periodically reviewing the organization's operational risk strategy;

- defining, endorsing, and reviewing the operational risk appetite (ORA);
- approving the framework for managing operational risk;
- ensuring senior management are accountable and carry out their risk management responsibilities; and
- ensuring proper verification and validation of the adequacy of controls and the appropriateness of the reporting systems.

In February 2003, the Risk Management Group of the Basel Committee on Banking Supervision issued a sound practices paper, which espoused 10 principles (these are given in Appendix 13.1 at the end of this chapter). In essence, the board of directors needs to be fully aware of all major operational risks facing the bank. The board needs to have a clear understanding of the specific characteristics of each risk together with the extent to which each risk can be controlled (mitigated and managed). The board should also appreciate the interrelationships between risks and the possibility for these to lead to catastrophic loss.

In practice, the level of board commitment to operational risk varies considerably. This is influenced by the extent to which operational risk is perceived as a serious threat to the organization as a whole. In the case of HSBC, the view originally taken by the board was that, being a global player, the organization was "too big to fail." HSBC is tightly controlled through rigid adherence to its policies and procedures, laid out in the company manual. These are reinforced by a strong internal audit function. Any operational risk event anywhere in the bank should therefore be contained (i.e. it should not become systemic or promote reputational damage), and consequently would not prove to be significant in comparison to the organization's resources as a whole. In contrast, a number of leading internationally active banks perceive risk management as being fundamentally important in properly managing and controlling their businesses as well as being a way of gaining competitive advantage. Banks such as J.P. Morgan have been in the vanguard of risk-management development in its various forms. The extent to which these polar contrasting views are true in practice is debatable.

It has been said that some organizations have chosen to move at their own pace and consequently have deliberately sought to fend off the regulatory authorities. Others, such as Standard Chartered Bank, have taken the view that they can buy-in any expertise needed at a later date should it prove necessary. Consequently, for them, pursuing an advanced measurement approach (AMA) is inappropriate at this point in time. For those claiming competitive advantage, the rating agencies have sought to identify any gains in bottom-line performance. Some analysts have said that claiming competitive advantage has more to do with enhancing reputational standing, in order to improve share price and facilitate growth through acquisition. In contrast, there are examples of well-controlled organizations failing to achieve performance results acceptable to the market (e.g. ABN AMRO) and therefore becoming targets for possibly less well-run but more ambitious organizations. Here, Charles Darwin's comment regarding strength and intelligence versus responsiveness seems apt. The economic processes of rationalization and globalization will undoubtedly continue to produce unbundling and repackaging.

13.2.2 Senior management has responsibility for implementation

Senior management is responsible for implementing the operational risk strategy approved by the board of directors. Effective risk management enables a bank to more precisely tailor its risk profile. This involves developing policies, processes, and procedures for the management of operational risk relating to all products and activities. In addition, senior management must ensure that, before any new products or processes are introduced, the operational risk inherent in them is properly assessed. However, in practice, although senior management retains overall responsibility for the management of risk throughout the bank, banks actually delegate significant levels of authority and accountability to business unit management for the control of operational risk within their specific area.

Whilst the relevant principles of sound practice are widely understood and accepted, it has been found that where there are subsidiary banks, matters can sometimes be less clear. In particular, senior management at the parent may not have a clear understanding of the operational risks and controls within the subsidiary. Similarly, regulators have found that in some cases senior management at subsidiary banks do not always have sufficient understanding of the parent bank's governance and control procedures. Research by the rating agencies has shown that these problems increase where the subsidiary is less advanced than the parent, or where the subsidiary line management and control personnel are not sufficiently fluent in either the language of the parent or the "lingua franca" of the enterprise. Geographically remote operations, particularly in emerging markets, were in some cases found to be of particular concern, although the Allied Irish Bank (AIB) case proves the generality of the point.

13.2.3   Professionally competent, well motivated, and honest people are essential

Truly effective operational risk management has been acknowledged by the rating agencies as requiring well-qualified and honest people.[19] This applies both to employees and contract staff.

In the UK, from a regulatory perspective the trend with regard to training and competence, as in other areas, has been away from a prescriptive approach based upon detailed rules and requirements towards a more principles-based approach. Section 5.1.2 of the FSA Handbook,[20] states that: *A firm's systems and controls should enable it to satisfy itself of the suitability of anyone who acts for it. This includes assessing an individual's honesty and competence.* The FSA's *Training & Competence Handbook*[21] states that a firm's commitments to training and competence should be that:

a. its employees are competent;
b. its employees remain competent for the work they do;
c. its employees are appropriately supervised;
d. its employees' competence is regularly reviewed; and
e. the level of competence is appropriate to the nature of the business.

The importance of well-qualified and honest people stems in part from the fact that it is people who determine the culture and ethics of an organization. These fundamental factors can prove almost impossible to change, particularly in the short term. Certainly, cultural and ethical incompatibility can limit the effectiveness of growth by preventing effective implementation, particularly where mergers and acquisitions are involved.

In the case of BCCI bank, which was recognized as having a thoroughly corrupt culture, it is interesting to note that the employees successfully sued the liquidators under contract law because they could not get other jobs, resulting in the award of stigma damages.[22] Other important areas of legislation in the Human Rights Act give employees:

- a right to fair trial (*Article 6*);
- a right to privacy and family life (*Article 8*);

- freedom of expression (*Article 10*);
- the right to join trade unions (*Article 11*); and
- freedom from discrimination (*Article 14*).

Some banks use a technique known as "360 degree" feedback, which allows employees to provide feedback by assessing management. This can be particularly useful in surfacing and capturing cultural and legislative issues.

Research[23] has shown that organizations can be inherently prone to errors. This is particularly the case with traders, where aggressive compensation schemes – used to motivate individuals – can lead to excessive risk taking. Where a blamist culture exists, errors may well be hidden, thus preventing organizational learning.[24] Such a culture can promote bullying, which may be used to hide fraud. For example, the "Ludwig" Report[25] into the Allfirst–Allied Irish Bank case, states: *Another pattern of Mr Rusnak's behavior at the bank was his temper and bullying behavior . . . his berating of the back-office and . . . threatening to have back-office employees fired.* The report goes on to comment that Mr Rusnak's manager adopted a hands-off management style and did not display an adequate appreciation of signals that there were serious issues behind front-and back-office friction. The report also comments that, moreover, the back-office perceived a management bias in favour of traders when back-office issues arose, since the traders were the ones making money for the bank.

Fraud has been identified by Basel as one of the main risk categories and is thought to be growing. It is said that four out of five frauds are committed by an organization's own staff, particularly management.

Most leading banks are attempting to provide their own in-house operational risk training, primarily for lower level staff. However, more senior staff are expected to be fully conversant with the new Basel regulations and other country-specific regulatory and legislative requirements, such as Sarbanes-Oxley (Section 404). Some banks, such as Lloyds TSB, have their own "university." Other organizations, such as the Dutch National Bank, have used internationally renowned external experts to assist in developing and delivering leading-edge programmes.

Despite the recognized importance of employing competent and honest people, until quite recently there were few professional bodies providing professional development in the area of operational risk. Limited examinations and qualifications are now provided by august bodies such as the Society of Actuaries, the Securities & Investments Institute, and the Institute of Risk Management, together with other associations in the financial services sector such as GARP[26] and PRMIA.[27] In 2004, the Institute of Operational Risk was founded, thus firmly establishing operational risk as a discipline in its own right. These developments should assist in promoting "best practice" and fostering greater transparency, which in turn should help to obviate the need for additional regulation and legislation.

13.2.4   Management structure and responsibilities

The authority and key responsibilities in relation to internal governance and risk management need to be clearly defined. This is particularly so with regard to the board of directors and senior management. Basel considers that failure to properly define these areas could lead to gaps and overlaps in areas of responsibility, resulting in inefficiencies and possibly leading to losses.

Basel also considers that failure by the board of directors and senior management to become adequately and actively engaged in operational risk can lead to adoption of narrowly focused, compliance-oriented approaches, which tend to be less effective in managing holistic enterprise-wide risk exposures. In order to meet AMA requirements, a bank must satisfy the regulators that, as a minimum: *[i]ts board of directors and senior management, as appropriate, are actively involved in the oversight of the operational risk management framework. ...* [28]

Whilst the need for active involvement is widely accepted, there remains some confusion amongst banks as to what constitutes "active involvement" and how this can be adequately demonstrated for compliance purposes. In addition, where a bank has a subsidiary, there is uncertainty about how the "active involvement" requirement applies to the subsidiary's board and senior management. This can be further confused by the approach to operational risk adopted by a subsidiary compared to the parent. [29]

Assessments by the board and senior management of the level of understanding and active involvement in operational risk management are critical areas of ongoing attention for regulators and rating analysts alike.

13.2.5 Reviewing the risk management environment and framework

The board of directors and senior management should continuously review the risk-management environment and revise the operational risk framework accordingly, in order to ensure that all material operational risks are identified and adequately controlled. In practice, it is found that many banks have chosen to delegate responsibility for the oversight of operational risk to a subcommittee.

Where a bank aspires to AMA recognition, which can in itself be regarded as "best practice," a proactive and responsive approach is a minimum requirement. [30] Basel II requires the operational risk-management system to be conceptually sound and implemented with integrity, with sufficient resources being allocated to all the major business lines and control functions, including internal audit. In addition, Basel [31] requires the operational risk framework to incorporate incentives for improving operational risk management, including allocation of operational risk capital to all major business lines. This is now widely accepted as sound practice.

13.2.6 Operational risk appetite (ORA) and operational risk tolerance (ORT)

The board of directors is responsible for determining the strategy for the organization. This should clearly define the organization's operational risk appetite (ORA) together with the operational risk tolerances (ORT) and how the bank intends to keep risks within these limits.

Operational risk appetite can be defined in terms of the types and levels of risk an organization is prepared to accept, depending upon its particular skills and the resources available to properly control those risks (i.e. given our expertise, what businesses do we want to be in). The appetite chosen will clearly be less than the level at which the loss would be dangerous or unacceptable. The ratio between the unacceptable level and the declared appetite can be referred to as the "factor of safety."

Operational risk tolerance refers to the level of variation considered acceptable around the operational risk appetite. For example, an operational risk appetite may be set at a level of 20 with a tolerance of plus or minus 5%. This may be directly compared to engineering, where the optimum size (appetite) of a component is defined together with its acceptable range (tolerance). To manufacture a component to an exact size with zero tolerance can be prohibitively expensive. Hence, consideration has to be given to the level of variation that will still leave the component "fit for purpose" (i.e. usable). In general, the greater (larger or wider) the tolerance, the lower the cost of production. Similarly in banking, reducing the number of losses can require significant investment in people, processes, and systems.

This leads on to the concept of "fail-safe." Consideration needs to be given to the consequences of a control failing. In particular, both impact and probability of failure need to be considered. When a control fails it is important that this does not lead to an unacceptable level of loss. As discussed previously, Professor James Reason has used the Swiss cheese diagram to explain how an accumulation of smaller losses can lead to a catastrophic event. Where Bayesian Belief Networks (BBN) are employed, the effect of a control failure can be quantified (estimated) and its likely overall significance determined.

Currently, operational risk appetite and tolerance are not clearly understood concepts within the banking sector. Consequently, efforts are being made to advance knowledge and understanding in this area. Many, including some of the more sophisticated organizations, often use the terms "appetite" and "tolerance" interchangeably. The terminology is often more an expression of the culture and the degree of formality within the organization together with the level of development of operational risk management.

In 2006, the UK Financial Services Authority set up a small working group comprised of both regulators and practitioners (primarily from investment banks and large retail banks) to articulate present understanding and to review existing practices used in setting an operational risk appetite.[32] The findings from this limited research suggested that, although not a regulatory requirement, *articulating an ORA, either explicitly or implicitly, may provide an important mechanism for demonstrating compliance with the general SYSC requirements*[33] *and/or the "use" test.*

In practice, a number of approaches to ORA are found. These range from those banks who have not directly considered operational risk appetite at all to those where ORA has been clearly defined and overtly expressed. A common approach is one where the ORA is considered to be the residual risk remaining after the application of controls. Confusion occurs where this residual risk is referred to as "tolerable operational risk" and sometimes even "operational risk tolerance." Some banks argue that operational risk appetite is a misnomer given that it refers to risks such as fraud and systems failures, which are not wanted at all but are unavoidable.

The involvement of the board of directors in determining the operational risk appetite is widely recognized as being important. Where considered appropriate, the board may be supported in its deliberations by the group risk function and the internal audit function. Whilst the overall process is generally accepted to involve defining, challenging, reviewing and managing the ORA, the emphasis placed on the different aspects by the board varies depending upon the culture and internal control environment of the organization. In general, the operational risk appetite is defined and approved by the board of directors, on a group-wide basis. In some cases the operational risk appetite is determined using a bottom-up approach, with the board adopting a challenging role and having overall authority and responsibility for final approval. Clearly, an approach employing both top-down and bottom-up techniques, as with traditional corporate planning and budgeting, may seem advisable since it facilitates greater flexibility and responsiveness.

In line with the concept of defining the overall strategy and expressing this in terms of objectives, which are then cascaded down to different levels of management, an organization's ORA can be defined at different levels, using appropriate indicators. At board level the emphasis is on volatility of earnings, capital requirements, and reputational considerations, whereas senior management are concerned with the identification of risks and the management and control of their potential impact. At lower levels of management, ORA may be expressed in terms of control limits and key indicators (KPI/KRI). A number of firms have already, either overtly or tacitly, expressed their ORA in this hierarchical manner. Where a tacit approach is taken, the ORA is embedded within the overall operational risk framework.

Validation remains in its infancy with regard to operational risk appetite. Some firms have attempted to use the loss data distribution curve, whilst others have employed more subjective assessments relating to the impact and likelihood of risks. Some firms concentrate on controls whilst others emphasize quantifiable limits and thresholds. Validation is an area that is expected to improve as ORA becomes better understood and more transparent.

13.2.7 The central operational risk function

There are a number of different organizational structures currently in existence regarding the reporting lines of the central operational risk function. These depend upon the size and sophistication of the organization and its country of origin. However, despite these variations, it is accepted "best practice" that the board of directors must be fully aware of the risks faced by the organization and the adequacy of the controls relating to those risks.[34] In particular, Principle 5 of the Basel Sound Practices paper states: *Banks should implement a process to regularly monitor operational risk profiles and material exposures to losses. There should be regular reporting of pertinent information to senior management and the board of directors that supports the proactive management of operational risk.*

In virtually all major European banks the central operational risk function has responsibility for aggregating operational risk reports for senior management on an enterprise-wide basis, in addition to being responsible for determining the operational risk methodologies and tools used throughout the group.

13.2.8 Operational risk specialists within business units and central staff functions

It is widely accepted best practice for business units to be the owners of risks and therefore for business unit managers to be responsible for the control of those risks. Each level of management is responsible for the appropriateness and effectiveness of policies, procedures, processes, and controls within its purview. In line with this concept, operational risk specialists are typically located in each business unit and therefore report directly to the business unit head. It is also typical to see operational risk specialists located in large central staff functions such as IT and Finance. In many organizations, operational risk specialists also have dotted responsibility to the central operational risk function, although this is not universal. However, in organizations that are relatively small or where operational risk expertise is less advanced, the central operational risk function may adopt a direct control approach rather than an advisory one. Moody's has stated: *it is evident that in a number of firms a more directed or centralized approach is more appropriate. In these cases Moody's views it to be more appropriate for OR managers at business units to report directly to the central OR function, and to take full charge for implementing OR tools and controls for the business.*[35] Such cases include those where there are high levels of staff turnover, short-term perspectives, and potential communication difficulties (due to distance, language, or culture).

13.2.9 The operational risk function needs to be independent

A lack of independence by the operational risk function can compromise integrity, professional judgement, and impartiality. Therefore, Basel has stated[36]: *The bank must have an independent operational risk management function that is responsible for the design and implementation of the bank's operational risk management framework. The operational risk management function is responsible for*

- *codifying firm-level policies and procedures concerning operational risk management and controls;*
- *for the design and implementation of the firm's operational risk measurement methodology;*
- *for the design and implementation of a risk-reporting system for operational risk;*
- *and for developing strategies to identify, measure, monitor and control/mitigate operational risk.*

Consequently, many leading banks have established an independent central operational risk-management function at group level. Typically, this function reports to the Chief Risk Officer, who has responsibility for the oversight of all risks. The Chief Risk Officer may be a board member as well as being a member of senior management, depending upon the bank's country of origin.

In a minority of cases, usually where the central operational risk group coexists in a risk silo containing other risk groups (such as market risk), the head of department reports to the Chief Risk Officer.

In a few cases the central operational risk function reports to a subcommittee, which is chaired by a director of the board (who may be an executive or non-executive). This subcommittee may have representatives from other functions such as compliance, legal and IT, treasury, etc. It appears that this practice is an emerging trend, resulting from the move to rationalize overlapping activities and provide a coordinating risk-management forum enabling risks to be viewed on an enterprise-wide basis.

In contrast, some smaller organizations consider risk oversight to be part of the Chief Finance Officer's remit; risk management being treated as an extension of management accounting.

13.2.10   The independent challenge function

It is emerging sound practice to have an independent challenge function responsible for verification and validation. However, the way in which this is achieved varies from bank to bank. The most widely adopted approach is for the internal audit function to report to the board of directors on the level of independence of the operational risk function and the extent to which the policies and procedures specified by the board of directors and senior management are effectively being implemented. Both the internal and external audit functions have important contributions to make in ensuring the existence of a comprehensive operational risk-management programme.[37] Basel states: *The bank's operational risk management system must be well documented. The bank must have a routine in place for ensuring compliance with a documented set of internal policies, controls and procedures concerning the operational risk management system, which must include policies for the treatment of non-compliance issues.*[38]

With regard to verification of the timeliness, accuracy, and relevance of risk and audit reports, responsibility resides firmly with senior management, who may draw upon feedback and assistance from external sources such as regulatory supervisors and independent consultants. The regulators have indicated that in their view the issue of validation will require increasing attention, both by banks and supervisors, as bank-wide economic capital assessment methodologies continue to be developed. Some financial organizations have established a separate enterprise-wide risk management function to provide independent verification and validation and to ensure that a more holistic integrated approach towards the assessment and management of risk is taken.

A recent survey[39] showed that three main challenges currently being faced are:

- risk reports throughout the enterprise not being properly aligned or coordinated, leading to gaps and overlaps, thus limiting leverage and effectiveness;
- organizations not properly concentrating on the most important areas of risk, due to limitations in the risk assessment processes together with shortages of required specialist skills and expertise;
- directors and senior management becoming overwhelmed by the sheer volume and disparity of risk reports from across the enterprise.

13.2.11   Information flow to senior management

The ability of a firm to respond quickly to events is significantly influenced by the flow of timely, accurate, and appropriate information to senior management. Hierarchical organization structures can result in the filtering, distortion, and delay of information transmitted to senior management. A recent supervisory review found a significant variation in the overall quality of information between different organizations. In those organizations that performed better than others in the recent credit crunch, senior management were well informed and actively involved at an early stage. In some cases, organizational layers were removed as the crisis developed in order to improve senior management communication and involvement. It was also found that those firms with silo structures tended to compartmentalized information and thus failed to share information across the organization. This resulted in different business units making decisions in isolation. Those better performing firms tended to involve senior management, business unit management, and specialist management (including the treasury function), often on an equal basis, sharing both qualitative and quantitative information more effectively. Such firms gained a significant timing advantage and thereby reduced the level of losses that would otherwise have been experienced. Those firms that experienced more substantial problems tended to rely on inflexible information systems based on inappropriate assumptions, producing information that was neither accurate nor timely.

13.3   QUANTIFICATION AND ASSESSMENT

In the light of Basel II, significant effort has been devoted by the banking industry to the development and integration of qualitative and quantitative risk-management methodologies for the determination of capital adequacy. However, significant diversity in application remains. It should be recognized that many banks do not have a fully articulated comprehensive AMA framework and, indeed, such a sophisticated approach may prove practical for only a relatively small number of major banks. Best practice will therefore be determined by what is appropriate, given the organization's size, sophistication, and stage of development.

13.3.1   There is broad agreement on fundamental best practice methodologies

It is broadly agreed within the banking industry that best practice consists of a combination of methodologies that takes into account the past, present, and future:

- **Past**. Statistical analysis (LDA) techniques, including extreme value theory (EVT), which look at historical data (i.e. what happened in the past) with a view to unbundling losses and gaining a more forensic appreciation of the types of risks, their causes and characteristics, and their inter dependencies over time.

- **Present**. Control risk self assessment (CRSA) is a well-established qualitative behavioral science approach that seeks to capture the knowledge and expertise of employees within the business.
- **Future**. Scenario analysis takes a forward-looking view. It does not seek to accurately predict the future but instead envisions and examines a number of possible futures, seeking to determine the organization's appropriate responses given the potential risks and opportunities.

13.3.2   Considerable diversity exists with regard to integration

Whilst these techniques are broadly accepted, there is considerable diversity with regard to their application and integration. The fundamental dilemma is in determining the level of reliance to be placed on the outcome from each method, given that they inevitably produce different answers. Some banks have decided to concentrate on the historical loss data approach since this is factual and therefore provides a sound base. Others have recognized the limitations of historical data and have sought to supplement it with external data. From a true mathematical perspective this represents data corruption; similarly, attempting to predict outside the data range is beyond the scope of mathematics. It is at this point that it can be said the determination of capital adequacy moves from a science to a practical art form for which there is no right answer, only a view that appears acceptable to reasonable and well-informed people. Some banks are using statistical techniques to determine an initial overall capital figure, then using qualitative techniques to allocate the capital to business lines and adjusting it over time. Some banks are concerned about the subjectivity inherent within qualitative techniques and have therefore limited the extent to which statistical derived capital requirements are adjusted.

In contrast, some banks rely almost entirely on quantitative techniques, using historical data where appropriate to challenge assumptions and to assist in determination of causal relationships. Qualitative methodologies often employ tools such as scorecards to convert qualitative assessments into quantitative metrics, thus enabling the allocation of economic capital to business lines, taking account of risk and performance.

13.3.3   Key indicators provide insight into a bank's risk position

Key indicators are widely used in the banking industry and provide insight into a bank's risk position. As mentioned previously, the Risk Management Association (RMA) has carried out research into this area and has identified several thousand indicators currently in use. Such indicators include, for example, the number of errors and omissions, staff turnover rates, absenteeism, systems breaks, etc. The key challenge for any bank is to identify an appropriate set of operational risk indicators. Consideration needs to be given to the importance and weighting applied to each indicator and the extent to which variation occurs across different business lines. It is also necessary to consider correlation, both within and across business lines and risk types. Threshold limits are typically set for each indicator and/or group of indicators (see Figures 13.1 and 13.2).

Some of the leading banks have developed sophisticated sets of indicators that link to business plans and cascade down to individual performance targets.

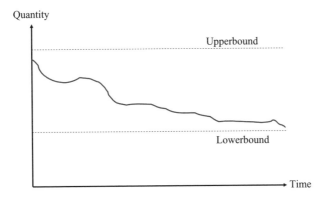

Figure 13.1   KRI control bounds: The difficulty is in determining the appropriate bounds.
Source: Brendon Young, ORRF

13.3.4   Traditional audit based assessment approaches remain appropriate

Risk mapping is a traditional audit based assessment technique that is well established and widely used. It can assist in risk management by revealing areas of weakness and assisting in prioritizing management action. It involves mapping the activities of a business unit then identifying risks by type within the process. The main drawback to this technique is the considerable effort involved in initially mapping all the processes. This can be exacerbated where processes change frequently.

13.3.5   Knowing the relationship between different risks

As Professor J. Reason has pointed out, many catastrophic events are a result of an accumulation of smaller, apparently individually insignificant events. Consequently, it is important to understand the relationship between risks. In contrast, it has been argued that it is most unlikely that all risks will happen at exactly the same time and therefore simply summing the total value of potential risk events will grossly exaggerate the required level of capital. As a result, leading banks are currently exploring the interrelationships of risks using copulas. Unfortunately, this is a complex area and one where work is still at a relatively early stage. There are numerous types of copula, each with different properties. The challenge is therefore

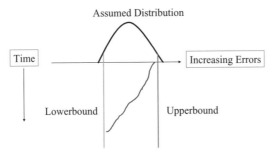

Figure 13.2   Statistical relevance.
Source: Brendon Young, ORRF

to determine the properties of each in order to enable the most appropriate to be selected. This work is further complicated by the considerable amount of data needed to properly estimate the properties. It should also be borne in mind that relationships between risks may not be constant over the full range or remain stable over time.

13.3.6   A 99.9 % confidence level is unrealistic

Basel II stipulates that a confidence level of 99.9 % is required for operational risk. Many have remarked that catering for a once in a 1000-year event is at best challenging if not somewhat absurd. From a statistical point of view, the two fundamental difficulties in measuring operational risk are subjectivity and the very limited amount of data available. These represent major obstacles. The asymptotic nature of the loss distribution curve at extreme confidence levels means that the regulatory capital figure determined is unreliable and very sensitive to any assumptions made. One key assumption is that all data points are independent with no correlation existing, which in practice is unlikely to be true. Consequently, similar banks may end up with completely different capital charges, thus undermining the level playing field principle. The question needs to be asked, how can a 99.9 % quantile from a small sample of often poor-quality data provide a sound base for setting operational risk capital?

Greater robustness with regard to setting operational risk capital could be achieved by selecting a quantile estimation of (say) 95 % and applying a very much larger multiplier. A different question by the regulators may have produced a more realistic and robust outcome. As the rating agencies have pointed out, capital is not a panacea.

13.3.7   Limiting model choice

Currently, model selection and interpretation appear to be areas of weakness with regard to the tail of the loss distribution approach. Therefore, a limited choice of models might be appropriate for regulatory operational risk capital, possibly restricted to the generalized extreme value distribution (GEV) or the general Pareto distribution (GPD). This would allow the industry to gain greater and more focused experience in the methodology and the interpretation of results.

13.3.8   A model is a simplification of the real world

It is not possible to fully prescribe all risks and their interrelationships; therefore, a model is merely a simplification of the real world.

In developing a model, the aims and objectives must be clearly and unambiguously stated. Consideration also needs to be given to materiality and proportionality. An item is regarded as material if its omission or misstatement could significantly alter the output of the model and thereby influence the decisions of users. Proportionality is concerned with the benefits derived from improving the quality (accuracy) of the model compared to the resources and capabilities required to do so (i.e. cost-benefit analysis). In general, the principle of parsimony requires that the number of parameters included in a model be strictly limited to only those which are absolutely necessary.

The results derived from a model need careful interpretation. The collapse of Long Term Capital Management (LTCM) resulted (in part) from the failure of the model to take account of changed business and economic conditions. Consequently, it is necessary to be aware of the underlying assumptions made and the extent to which these assumptions will fail to apply in changing conditions.

In a recent survey related to the credit crunch, it was found that those firms which performed less well tended to apply a mechanistic approach, accepting outputs without challenge. A number of firms highlighted the importance of reviewing assumptions and scenarios, at both the firm and desk level, as business conditions evolved. Senior management has a vital role to play in exercising critical judgement and applying multiple lenses of perception.

13.3.9   Complexity requires models to be subdivided

In practice, modeling can become extremely complex, particularly where dynamic financial analysis (DFA) and causal modeling are involved. Complex models limit management oversight. Errors and omissions become difficult to detect and the appropriateness of the model becomes more difficult to determine. Consequently, consideration needs to be given to appropriately subdividing large models into clearly defined components whose integrity and outputs can be verified.

13.3.10   A more forensic approach requires consideration of causality

In order to effectively manage and control risk it is necessary to take a more forensic approach with a view to understanding causality (i.e. event-cause-effect relationships). The need for a more forensic approach has been recognized in part by the new Basel Accord, which has specified a granular (7×8) matrix for categorizing loss events. Unfortunately, loss analysis can be complicated by the fact that an event can have multiple causes and multiple effects. In practice, it has been observed that banks often treat the effects of an event rather than its underlying causes. However, it is now widely accepted that a major loss event is the result of a number of smaller weaknesses combined with a trigger event. The Swiss cheese diagram shows a series of layers (which can be considered as control levels) each having holes in them. A failure occurs when all the holes line up (i.e. all the control layers fail at once). In theory, failure can be quantified by identifying all the holes in the various control layers and determining their probability of occurrence. A small number of leading banks are taking these concepts and applying Bayesian Belief Networks (BBNs) to them.

13.4   CONTINGENCY AND BUSINESS CONTINUITY

13.4.1   Resilience is affected by a broad range of external factors

Contingency and business continuity management (BCM) is concerned with ensuring the resilience of an organization to any (major) eventuality. It is beginning to be seen, by those leading organizations adopting an enterprise-wide approach to risk management, as a fundamental element within the risk-management process.

The basic aim of business continuity management is to ensure that adequate planning exists to maintain continuity of service to customers, and to protect the organization's reputation and its value to stakeholders.

Originally, BCM was almost exclusively concerned with the resilience of computer systems and the adequacy of IT disaster recovery plans. However, it now encompasses a much broader range of considerations, including:

- crime, terrorism, and war;
- climate change issues (including colder winters, hotter summers, hurricanes, and flooding, etc);

- diseases (such as AIDS and the potential Asian flu pandemic);
- energy and natural resources shortages (including utility outages, as experienced in southern California);
- economic development issues (including the rapid industrialization of China, India, and other Asia countries);
- social migration;
- legislative and regulatory changes; and
- financial contagion.

Consciousness of the threats from major external risks has been heightened in recent years by a number of high profile events. In particular, on Friday 10 April 1992, a terrorist bomb destroyed the Baltic Exchange in the City of London. A year later, the Bishopsgate[40] bomb in the City of London contributed to a crisis in the financial services industry, including the near collapse of one of the world's leading insurance markets, Lloyd's of London. Another major attack on London's financial centre took place in 1996, when terrorists detonated a bomb in Canary Wharf. All these attacks resulted in death and serious injury. However, by far the most devastating terrorist attack on a financial centre took place in New York on 11 September 2001, when two passenger aircraft were deliberately flown into the twin towers of the World Trade Center, killing many thousands of people and threatening the survival of many firms.[41] There has been numerous other high profile attacks around the world, many of which are linked through funding from international terrorist organizations, which appear to have infiltrated certain parts of religious and political society. Consequently, such threats could undoubtedly continue for generations and, indeed, there is no clear end in sight.

Natural disasters also represent very significant threats. A flu pandemic is considered by experts to be inevitable at some time in the future, given the virus's ability to mutate rapidly into new strains. Certainly, the avian flu threat has caused considerable reaction and the World Heath Organization[42] is continuously monitoring the threat of an influenza pandemic, including coordinating the global response to human cases of H5N1 avian influenza.

13.4.2   The FSA's BCM benchmarking exercise

In the UK, the FSA has conducted a major benchmarking exercise, involving over 60 leading financial services firms, all of whom were asked 1000 questions on business continuity management (BCM). Also in the UK, the Tripartite Authorities (HM Treasury, the Bank of England, and the Financial Services Authority) have established the Financial Sector Continuity website[43] as an information centre about continuity planning specifically for the financial services industry. In addition, further information is available from the Business Continuity Institute (BCI) and the British Standards Institute (BSI), who have published guidelines on business continuity management.

13.4.3   The relationship between business continuity management (BCM) and operational risk management (ORM) is not well understood

Individually, both BCM and ORM are well understood but the relationship between them is not. Operational risk management is concerned with frequency and impact whereas BCM is concerned with time and impact. The significance of this is that the measurement of risk in terms of frequency and impact may not be sufficient, since where a service (mission critical activity) is interrupted it is necessary to determine how long it will take to restore that service (recovery time objective) and what level of resources will be required to reach an acceptable default functionality standard (recovery point objective).

13.4.4   Academic reseach on the application of statistical models for BCM

Since business continuity management is primarily concerned with the management of external (high impact, low frequency) tail events, there is very little data available for quantification purposes. However, academic work is currently taking place to determine how statistical models can be used to define the timeframe for the recovery activity and to analyze interruptions within the context of business continuity management. This work includes examining how the survival model for proportional risks, called the Cox model, together with Bayesian Networks, can be used.

13.4.5   Conclusion

All leading firms now have well developed business continuity plans in place. However, complacency must be avoided, since risk in its various guises is dynamic. Regulators and analysts must therefore seek confirmation that plans are regularly updated and tested for effectiveness.

It should be recognized that business continuity management is likely to prove more effective in dealing with extreme events than holding large amounts of capital. However, clearly, the two are not mutually exclusive.

13.5   INFORMATION TECHNOLOGY

13.5.1   Technology has facilitated development of the global financial community

Information and communication technology (ICT) has facilitated the development of the banking and financial services sector, transforming it into an efficient global industry. Its importance should therefore not be underestimated. Further technological developments will undoubtedly continue to have a significant impact. Technology has facilitated the restructuring of organizations and enabled the transfer of activities, such as call centres, to lower-cost locations. Technology has also enabled the processing of vast quantities of data and the rapid transfer of information, which has greatly helped in the identification, assessment, management, and mitigation of risk.

13.5.2   Risks are becoming more complex

However, information and communication technologies have brought with them other risks. The increasing level of sophistication is resulting in activities becoming ever more complex, thus changing the risk profiles of banks. With increased reliance being placed upon integrated systems, there is greater potential to transform previously minor risks into systems risks or even systemic risks.[44]

E-commerce, although offering an important channel to market, also brings with it significant potential risks that are likely to increase in importance and sophistication. Currently, credit card fraud is well understood and to date quite predictable statistically, with losses conforming to a known loss distribution curve. However, in November 2007, the UK Information Commissioner, Richard Thomas, addressed a House of Commons committee to ask for additional powers to tackle data protection breaches following an investigation into the Internet sale, by fraudsters, of thousands of bank details. The initial investigation was carried out by *The Times* newspaper, which reported that it had been able to freely download banking information relating to 32 individuals, including a High Court Judge. *The Times* also reported that there were over 100 websites offering to sell UK bank details (including account numbers, PINs, and security codes), with one website offering to sell 30 000 British credit card numbers for £1 each.[45]

Studies by the Ponemon Institute indicate that such data breaches have served to undermine public confidence and begun to change consumers' purchasing behaviour. Gartner analysts have found that in the US many consumers no longer open emails from individuals or companies they do not know or have not previously dealt with. In addition, approximately a third of consumers have deliberately reduced their level of expenditure via the Internet. This could have potentially serious consequences for online banking, particularly if a bank suffers reputational damage.

13.5.3   The emerging market in software flaws

There is increasing concern over the criminal exploitation of the legal "white market," which is concerned with the identification of weaknesses in software products. Whilst some software flaws are bought and sold over the Internet for many thousands of dollars, criminals are now able to buy for just a few dollars software and malware that will enable them to commit cyberfraud. There is no longer any need for these criminals to be IT or software experts. Indeed, a whole industry has developed which effectively supports criminal activity. Writers of software are currently legally freely able to sell their products without enquiring into its intended use. Thus criminals can buy, rent, or specifically commission the software they require. Tools such as PINCH and MPack[46] keep subscribers up to date with the latest vulnerabilities discovered in software products. Such information can enable criminal users to steal personal details such as bank account information or blackmail the vendor of the affected software. In August 2007, MPack was allegedly used in a cyber-attack on the Bank of India. This attack originated from the infamous Russian Business Network (RBN). Companies such as Tipping-Point (which is owned by 3Com) and iDefense (which is owned by Verisign) identify vulnerabilities and write computer code to deal with zero-day exploits,[47] with the aim of preventing criminals gaining backdoor access to customers' systems.

In January 2006, a Microsoft exploit was sold via the Internet for $4000 and later used to send bogus emails claiming to have insider information in an attempt to inflate share prices.

13.5.4   The real threat of cyber-warfare

International industrial espionage and cyber attacks on infrastructure are currently estimated to cost businesses and consumers billions of dollars a year. A report commissioned by McAfee, with input from organizations such as NATO, the FBI, the UK Serious Organized Crime Agency, and leading academics,[48] states that cyber-warfare and cyber-crime represent the biggest threats to security over the next decade and that future attacks will become ever more sophisticated.

Senior vice president of McAfee Avert Labs, Jeffrey Green, stated: *Cyber-crime is now a global issue ... It has evolved significantly and is no longer just a threat to industry and individuals but increasingly to national security.* About 120 countries are thought to be developing the ability to use the Internet as a weapon. There are signs that intelligence agencies already routinely probe other states' networks looking for weaknesses, and are developing new techniques which are growing in sophistication every year. Those areas particularly at risk include financial institutions and financial markets, government computer networks, utilities, and aviation facilities.

China has openly stated in a white paper that "informationized armed forces" are an important part of its military strategy. James Mulvenon, director of the Centre for Intelligence and Research in Washington, has stated: *The Chinese were first to use cyber-attacks for political and military goals.* China is considered to be at the forefront of cyber-warfare and is thought to have been responsible for attacks in the United States, Australia, New Zealand, India, and Germany. Consequently, the US government objected to the sale of 3Com to a Chinese organization with government connections.

Cyber-attacks on both government and commercial websites in Estonia in April and May 2007 appear to have originated from Russia, although the state has denied any involvement. NATO stated: *The complexity and coordination seen was new ... There were a series of attacks with careful timing using different techniques and specific targets.* Many thousands of websites employing millions of computers were affected in attacks aimed at crippling the computer-based infrastructure. It is thought that 99 % of these attacks may well have gone undetected.

EU Information Society commissioner Viviane Reding said in June 2007 that what happened in Estonia was a wake-up call. NATO has recognized the need for "urgent work" to improve defences, with all of its 26 members having been subject to attacks. The threat is now considered so serious that NATO has directed at least 10 of its agencies to engage in activities to provide protection against such incidents. In the US an anti-cyber-warfare unit has recently been established having 40 000 people. In the UK, The Centre for the Protection of National Infrastructure has described the threat posed by cyber-warfare as "enormous."

13.5.5   Protecting the individual

In the UK, there has been a call for banks and government to do more to protect individuals from fraud. It has been suggested that banks need to control transfers more carefully and should make efforts to spot patterns, in addition to limiting transfers of confidential information to other "trusted" recipients such as gas companies.[49]

A House of Lords report[50] on personal Internet security has stated that the current assumption, that end-users should be responsible for security, is inefficient and unrealistic: *The steps currently being taken by many businesses trading over the Internet to protect their customers' personal information are inadequate. The refusal of the financial services sector in particular to accept responsibility for the security of personal information is disturbing, and is compounded by apparent indifference at Government level.*

The report recognizes that efforts to promote best practice are currently hampered by a lack of commercial incentives for the industry to make products secure. It recommends that the UK government introduce legislation to establish the principle that banks should be held liable for losses incurred as a result of electronic fraud. In general, it also recommends that the UK government explore, at a European level, the introduction of the principle of vendor liability within the IT industry.

The report goes on to state: *We further believe that a data security breach notification law would be among the most important advances that the United Kingdom could make in promoting personal Internet security. . . . As a corollary to the development of an online reporting system, we recommend that the Government review as a matter of urgency their decision to require online frauds to be reported to the banks in the first instance. We believe that this decision will undermine public trust in both the police and the Internet. It is essential that victims of e-crime should be able to lodge a police report and have some formal acknowledgement of the fact of a crime having been committed in exchange. We see no reason why such reports should not be made online, processed and forwarded to the banks automatically.*

13.5.6   What actions are leading banks currently taking?

Whilst banks may inevitably be behind the curve with regard to preventing new criminal activities, considerable efforts are being expended by leading banks to implement sophisticated security systems.

In Brazil, which has one of the most advanced on-line banking systems, secure Internet websites are used together with a multiple PIN approach. One PIN is used to log-on to the site whilst another PIN is used to perform the transaction. A further one-time PIN or password may be used to provide additional security. European and US banks are also increasingly using higher security systems involving a multiple PIN approach. A more recent approach, which is proving very successful in some European countries, is the use of fingerprint recognition, giving very high levels of security whilst also obviating the need for customers to remember PIN numbers and passwords.

13.6   INSURANCE AND OTHER RISK TRANSFER OPTIONS

13.6.1   The potential of operational risk insurance

Insurance was originally thought to have a considerable role to play as a mitigant for operational risk loss events, particularly with regard to providing protection against those more extreme events towards the tail of the loss distribution. Banks have been using insurance to cover a number of peril-specific operational risk loss types for many years and, as such, the insurance industry has accumulated a considerable amount of existing claims data. Consequently, the extension to a broader, more inclusive, operational risk insurance product initially seemed a natural development, merely filling in the gaps and removing overlaps. Yet despite the efforts of some of the most talented teams at firms such as Swiss Re, AON, and Chubb, who created some innovative products in attempting to meet the needs and overcome the concerns of both the banking industry and the regulators, these products have failed to gain widespread acceptance.

From an insurance perspective, providing cover for the more extreme operational risks looked to be attractive. A regular revenue source could be created; claims should be very few, and probably many years away (since Basel II requires a *once in a thousand years* confidence level). In addition, the probability of moral hazard should be very low for events that could threaten the very existence of an organization. With regard to capacity, the use of reinsurance would ensure sufficient funding was available and further lower the risk to any one insurer.

13.6.2   Have regulators effectively killed operational risk insurance in its genesis?

Unfortunately, the regulators expressed concerns at a very early stage about the use of insurance as a set-off against regulatory capital. Regulators are particularly concerned about liquidity and certainty. Where a bank suffers a major loss event it will need access to funds immediately. However, full payout by the insurer is uncertain and the claim may take several years to be resolved. The regulators expressed profound concern over such opaqueness, which could be further exacerbated by the underlying risk differing from the description contained in the insurance policy.

Whilst these concerns may have been justified, they effectively served to undermine confidence in the development and use of operational risk insurance at a critical point in its development. Although the regulators were minded initially not to accept insurance as a set-off against regulatory capital, they eventually decided in favour of allowing its use by AMA banks only. This has had the effect of dramatically reducing the size of the potential market from 20 000 banks to probably a mere 50 banks worldwide.

In addition, the regulators have placed particularly onerous requirements on each AMA bank to justify its use of insurance. The FSA consultation paper, dated February 2006, CP 06/3, entitled *Strengthening Capital Standards 2*, states: *As part of the AMA application, we are asking firms to explain their approach to using insurance under AMA. . . . A firm should be able to justify to us how the insurance it uses to mitigate its operational risk exposures is appropriate and relevant for its business.* With regard to the calculation of risk mitigation, Rule 678 of the new Basel Accord requires the calculation to reflect *the bank's insurance coverage in a manner that is . . . consistent with the actual likelihood and impact of loss used in the bank's overall determination of its operational risk capital.*

Some have interpreted this to mean that an AMA bank must construct and contrast three separate models:

1. a traditional LDA model, using internal historical data, external data and scenarios;
2. a revised model capturing "internal control factors that can change its operational risk profile";[51]
3. a further model, refined to take account of the mitigating effects of insurance. (This model would require independent expert opinion on the probability of recovery, together with level and timing of any recovery.)

A further difficulty is the apparent conflict between regulatory requirements and legal restrictions. The regulators require that an insurance policy may not preclude cover due to supervisory actions. In the case of a failed bank the policy must allow for the recovery by the liquidators of expenses and damages incurred prior to bankruptcy. Indeed, this will be the case under policy run-off. However, after the event, where a liquidator continues to run the business or puts it into liquidation, a different activity under different management is said to exist, to which the original insurance policy does not apply. Where a bank has been engaged in wilful wrongdoing, insurance cover ceases to apply, since acts that are illegal and/or criminal are deemed to be against the public interest. Consequently, a bank cannot be indemnified against such acts since it is a legal requirement that the perpetrators suffer the consequences of their actions.

13.6.3   Banks want a simple all-embracing product

From a banking perspective, insurance has historically been purchased on a peril-specific basis by the bank's own insurance department, which traditionally has been completely autonomous from the operational risk management function. However, Basel II has brought recognition of the need for a more holistic enterprise-wide view, which includes the integration of operational risk insurance. Consequently, banks have sought a simple all-embracing insurance product for operational risk, although the desire for each bank to tailor such a product to meet its own specific requirements can be problematic.

13.6.4   Insurers want economically viable products having clearly defined responsibilities

Insurers want economically viable products having clearly defined responsibilities. In order to accurately price cover, insurers need to precisely determine the bounds of their responsibilities. In addition, when seeking to settle a claim an insurer must determine:

1. whether the bank has suffered any actual loss and, if so, the precise amount of that loss;
2. whether all the loss is covered by the policy or whether any exclusions apply;
3. whether there has been any contributory negligence by the bank.

For lines of business where there is relative certainty (such as business interruption, property, and natural catastrophe), capacity is readily available and claims settlements can be prompt. However, the opposite may be the case where uncertainty exists (i.e. with Bankers Blanket Bond, Directors & Officers insurance, and Personal Indemnity insurance).

In an attempt to meet the requirements of banks, insurers have made efforts to link the Basel risk categories to existing peril-specific insurance products. This has led to discussions concerning standardization of products and contract wording, although final agreement continues to remain ellusive. Standardization could help in reducing payout times and increasing available capacity. By increasing the attractiveness of operational risk insurance products to all banks, rather than just those pursuing AMA recognition, the law of large numbers would apply, thus making insurance feasible. It is thought that there would need to be 500–1000 participating banks for an operational risk insurance market to work properly.

13.6.5   Other risk transfer methods

In an endeavour to overcome the, as yet apparently insurmountable, problems with operational risk insurance, banks have been looking at other risk transfer methods. A number of the leading banks have again considered the possibility of establishing a mutual insurance company. Consideration is also being given to operational risk derivatives, akin to credit derivatives used to provide mitigation in the credit book. Ideas regarding operational risk derivatives have been around in the academic literature for some years.[52] However, whilst the market for catastrophe bonds has developed substantially, the market for operational risk bonds has yet to do so.

The regulators have stated that a similar level of standards should apply to risk transfer mechanisms as to insurance products.

13.7   TRANSPARENCY

Transparency remains an issue of concern despite legislative and regulatory actions (such as Pillar 3[53] of the new Basel accord, the Sarbanes-Oxley Act, and Accounting Standard IFRS 7), all of which are effectively designed to enhance market knowledge and restore investor confidence. The triumvirate determining investor confidence comprises: the board of directors, who is responsible for corporate governance; the external auditors, who are responsible for ensuring "a true and fair view"; and the rating agencies, who provide an informed independent assessment of the standing of the firm (i.e. its risk of default).

13.7.1   Published accounts are failing to give meaningful insight

With regard to financial reporting, in the UK there is growing concern that published accounts are increasingly becoming regulatory filings rather than providing meaningful insight into future performance. According to a report published by KPMG in October 2007,[54] some of the City's leading institutional investors are calling for improvements. KPMG Chairman, John Griffith-Jones, stated: *With financial statements increasing in length and complexity, there is clearly a need to ensure that there is consistency and transparency in the way that information is presented.*

13.7.2   Probability, impact and time to recovery

All the leading banks now provide considerable information with regard to risk management, both in their published accounts[55] and on a privileged basis to credit rating analysts. However, the difficulty for the analyst is in determining the significance of the actions taken in reducing risks and increasing competitive advantage. Much of this information does not lend itself readily to quantification, given its complexity. However, efforts are being made by academics, rating agencies, and also banks themselves to apply scientifically robust techniques that provide a more informed feel for probability, impact, and time to recovery.

13.7.3   Investors do not know where the risks lie

In December 2007, the Association of British Insurers (ABI) called on banks to improve their disclosures relating to off-balance-sheet funding vehicles, stating: *We need much greater clarity of what is on, what is off and what has the potential to come back on the balance sheet.* These comments were prompted, in part, by the actions of some banks following the credit crunch, initiated by difficulties in the US sub-prime (housing) market. In particular, HBOS took action to prop up its Grampian fund; similarly, HSBC provided funding of around £17 billion to bail out two vehicles, Cullinan and Asscher. Whilst such actions may have been appropriate, investors' concerns stemmed from difficulties in seeing where underlying risks actually resided.

The KPMG report also noted that, although investors required greater transparency and consistency, 70 % of respondents considered that the "principles-based" approach to accounting and reporting, adopted by the UK, was preferable to the US rules-based approach. However, it is interesting to note that the EU may be moving in a different direction to the UK, since it is currently considering the implementation of a rules-based approach similar to Sarbanes-Oxley.

13.7.4   Performance considerations are being subverted by regulatory and legislative requirements

A key current concern amongst banks is the extent to which regulatory and legislative requirements subvert performance considerations. Unfortunately, regulatory requirements concentrate attention upon extreme tail events. However, investors are more concerned about the performance of a business, with extreme risks being considered as normal acceptable risks for the particular type of investment (for which an appropriate margin is taken).

Standard and Poor's has stated: *It is important to note that compliance with regulatory standards is often insufficient. In fact, an excessive compliance culture may belie a weak risk-management culture. This is because a compliance approach to risk management usually means that the firm has negligent self-assessment and prioritization of risks and risk management activities, leaving those roles to the regulator.*[56]

ENDNOTES

[1] The date when Barings Bank collapsed due to the rogue actions of Nick Leeson.

[2] This was initially fuelled by regulatory and legislative actions in response to public and investor uncertainty, following a number of high-profile failures.

[3] Certainly, a herd mentality appears to exist within the banking sector, which seems to dictate the need to operate at an acceptable distance behind the leading-edge. But this is only part of the reason.

[4] In the UK, the Financial Services Authority (FSA) has adopted a principles based, rather than a rules based, approach to regulation.

[5] AMA (2006). *Observed Range of Practices in Key Elements of Advanced Measurement Approaches;* BIS. October 2006.

[6] Senior Supervisors Group, Observations on Risk Management Practices during the recent Market Turbulence, 6 March, 2008.

[7] "Best Practice" is transient and refers to current leading-edge practices. It is most appropriate for leading internationally active organizations. Best practice may not be appropriate for all banks in all situations at all times, as explained by Contingency Theory. For second-tier banks it is more likely to be aspirational. "Sound practice," on the other hand, is more permanent and enduring. Whilst it is worthy it is not necessarily the most advanced. "Sound practice" may be necessary but not sufficient (e.g. internal auditing is regarded as "sound practice" but for "best practice" it needs to be risk sensitive).

[8] Basel Committee on Banking Supervision; BIS (2003). *Sound Practices for the Management and Supervision of Operational Risk.* Page 6; paragraph 15.

[9] Basel Committee on Banking Supervision; BIS (2003). *Sound Practices for the Management and Supervision of Operational Risk.* Page 3; paragraph 10.

[10] Basel Committee on Banking Supervision; BIS (2001). *Sound Practices for the Management and Supervision of Operational Risk.* Page 2, paragraph 5.

[11] *International Convergence of Capital Measurement and Capital Standards* (known as Basel II); §644; June 2006; http://www.bis.org/publ/bcbs128.pdf.

[12] Basel Committee on Banking Supervision; BIS (2001). *Sound Practices for the Management and Supervision of Operational Risk.* Paragraph 5.

[13] Basel II, paragraph 666(b); see Note 11.

[14] Klein, Benjamin and Leffler Keith B., (1981). The Role of Market Forces in Assuring Contractual Performance. *The Journal of Political Economy* **89:4**, 615–641.

[15] Condon, Chft, Bennelt, M., Giordanelli, A. and Ensor, B. (2006). *Building Stronger Customer Relationship.* Forrester Research Inc.

[16] Dunnhumby (2007). *Customer Centricity: Discovering what Consumers Really Think of Customer Services.* The study assessed the level of service of 59 UK companies, including Virgin Mobile, Zurich car insurance, Tesco supermarket, and the Abbey bank.

[17] FSA (2007). Treating Customers Fairly – Culture. (http://www.fsa.gov.uk/pubs/other/tcf_culture.pdf).

[18] Basel Corporate Governance Principles:

Principle 1: Board members should be qualified for their positions, have a clear understanding of their role in corporate governance and be able to exercise sound judgment about the affairs of the bank.

Principle 2: The board of directors should approve and oversee the bank's strategic objectives and corporate values that are communicated throughout the banking organization.

Principle 3: The board of directors should set and enforce clear lines of responsibility and account-ability throughout the organization.

Principle 4: The board should ensure that there is appropriate oversight by senior management con-sistent with board policy.

Principle 5: The board and senior management should effectively utilize the work conducted by the internal audit function, external auditors, and internal control functions.

Principle 6: The board should ensure that compensation policies and practices are consistent with the bank's corporate culture, long-term objectives and strategy, and control environment.

Principle 7: The bank should be governed in a transparent manner.

Principle 8: The board and senior management should understand the bank's operational structure, including where the bank operates in jurisdictions, or through structures, that impede transparency (i.e. "know-your-structure").

[19] Moody's Investors Service.(June 2002). *Bank Operational Risk Management – More than an Exercise in Capital Allocation and Loss Data Gathering*; Special Comment: p. 4.

[20] FSA Handbook, *Senior Management Arrangements, Systems and Controls*, SYSC 5.1.2; http://fsahandbook.info/FSA/html/handbook/SYSC/5/1

[21] FSA Handbook, T and C 1.2.1, Commitments, (http://fsahandbook.info/FSA/html/handbook/TC/1/2)

[22] Malik v BCCI [1997] ILR 606.

[23] The reader is referred, in particular, to research carried out at London Business School by Paul Willman and Emma Soane.

[24] Bennett, S. (2001). *Human Error – by Design*. Perpetuity Press. Toft, B. and Reynolds S. (2005). *Learning from Disasters – A Management Approach*. Perpetuity Press.

[25] Report to the Boards of Allied Irish Banks, plc, Allfirst Financial Inc. and Allfirst Bank concerning currency trading losses: 12 March 2002.

[26] Global Association of Risk Practitioners (GARP).

[27] Professional Risk Managers' International Association (PRMIA).

[28] Basel II, paragraph 664; see Note 11.

[29] The reader is referred to background comments from Basel: Principles for the Home-host Recognition of AMA Operational Risk Capital; January 2004; (http://www.bis.org/publ/bcbs106.htm)

[30] Basel II, paragraph 664; see Note 11.

[31] Basel II, paragraph 666; see Note 11.

[32] Operational Risk Expert Group; UK Financial Services Authority. *Operational Risk Appetite*; 3 April 2007.

[33] SYSC 4.1.1, 4.1.2 and 7.1.16 respectively, after 1 November 2007.

[34] See Sarbanes-Oxley; Section 404.

[35] Moody's Investors Service. (2004). *Emerging Best Practices for Operational Risk Management at European Banks*.

[36] New Basel Accord; paragraph 666(a).

[37] The role of internal and external audit is described in the Basel paper entitled *Internal Audit in Banks and the Supervisor's Relationship with Auditors*; August 2001.

[38] Basel II, paragraph 666(d); see Note 11.

[39] Ernst & Young. (2007). *Managing Risk across the Enterprise: Building a Comprehensive Approach to Risk*.

[40] Video of the City of London bombing in Bishopsgate by the IRA on 24 April 1993. (http://news.bbc.co.uk/player/nol/newsid_6730000/newsid_6730000/6730055.stm?bw=nb&mp=rm&news=1&ms3=8&ms_javascript=true&bbcws=2).

[41] Videos of the 9/11 terrorist attacks: http://uk.youtube.com/watch?v=_ZWElC-Qsb4&feature=related/; http://uk.youtube.com/watch?v=cddIgb1nGJ8&feature=related.

[42] http://www.who.int/csr/disease/avian_influenza/en/.

[43] http://www.fsc.gov.uk/.

[44] One of the most famous systemic loss events was the failure of the German bank, Bank Hersatt, on 26 June 1974. Due to insolvency, Bank Herstatt failed to make payments on the US dollar legs of foreign exchange transactions despite the fact that it had already received the Deutschmark payments relating to the transactions. As a result, in order to prevent any recurrance of such settlement risk, the global banking industry implemented a global continuously linked settlement (CLS) system.

[45] *The Times*, Monday 3 December 2007.

[46] MPack is a PHP-based malicious software (malware) kit originally developed by hackers in Russia in December 2006. MPack is sold commercially (costing $500–1 000). It comes with technical support and regular updates of those software vulnerabilities exploitable. New exploits cost approximately $50–150 depending upon the severity of the exploit. The scripts and executables can be made undetectable by antivirus software.

[47] A zero day exploit is defined as computer code that exploits a vulnerability in a software program for which a rectification patch has not yet been developed.

[48] McAfee Virtual Criminology Report. (2007). *Cybercrime: The Next Wave.*

[49] Ref: Dr Richard Clayton, Cambridge University

[50] House of Lords, Science and Technology, Fifth Report, on Personal Internet Security, 24 July 2007.

[51] Rule 676, Basel II.

[52] See in particular, Cruz, M. G. (2002). *Modeling, Measuring and Hedging Operational Risk.* Chichester: John Wiley & Sons Ltd.

[53] Information regarding Pillar 3 is available on the FSA website: http://www.fsa.gov.uk/Pages/About/What/International/basel/info/pill3/index.shtml.

[54] *KPMG's Survey of Leading Investors.* KPMG UK Financial Services. October 2007.

[55] It is up to each firm to determine the most appropriate disclosure medium (e.g. website or annual report) and location of publication. If Pillar 3 disclosures are not included in one location, the firm must indicate where they can be found.

[56] Standard and Poor's; Ratings Direct; Request for comment: enterprise risk management analysis for credit ratings of nonfinancial companies; 15 November 2007.

APPENDIX 13.1: SOUND PRACTICES FOR THE MANAGEMENT AND SUPERVISION OF OPERATIONAL RISK

In February 2003, the Risk Management Group of the Basel Committee on Banking Supervision issued a sound practices paper containing the following 10 principles:

Developing an appropriate risk management environment

Principle 1: The board of directors should be aware of the major aspects of the bank's operational risks as a distinct risk category that should be managed, and it should approve and periodically review the bank's operational risk management framework. The framework should provide a firm-wide definition of operational risk and lay down the principles of how operational risk is to be identified, assessed, monitored and controlled/mitigated.

Principle 2: The board of directors should ensure that the bank's operational risk management framework is subject to effective and comprehensive internal audit by operationally independent, appropriately trained and competent staff. The internal audit function should not be directly responsible for operational risk management.

Principle 3: Senior management should have responsibility for implementing the operational risk management framework approved by the board of directors. The framework should be consistently implemented throughout the whole banking organization, and all levels of staff should understand their responsibilities with respect to operational risk management. Senior management should also have responsibility for developing policies, processes and procedures for managing operational risk in all of the bank's material products, activities, processes and systems.

Risk management: Identification, assessment, monitoring and mitigation/control

Principle 4: Banks should identify and assess the operational risk inherent in all material products, activities, processes and systems. Banks should also ensure that before new products, activities, processes and systems are introduced or undertaken, the operational risk inherent in them is subject to adequate assessment procedures.

Principle 5: Banks should implement a process to regularly monitor operational risk profiles and material exposures to losses. There should be regular reporting of pertinent information to senior management and the board of directors that supports the proactive management of operational risk.

Principle 6: Banks should have policies, processes and procedures to control and/or mitigate material operational risks. Banks should periodically review their risk limitation and control strategies and should adjust their operational risk profile accordingly using appropriate strategies, in light of their overall risk appetite and profile.

This paper refers to a management structure composed of a board of directors and senior management. The Committee is aware that there are significant differences in legislative and regulatory frameworks across countries as regards the functions of the board of directors and senior management. In some countries, the board has the main, if not exclusive, function of supervising the executive body (senior management, general management) so as to ensure that the latter fulfils its tasks. For this reason, in some cases, it is known as a supervisory board. This means that the board has no executive functions. In other countries, the board has a broader competence in that it lays down the general framework for the management of the bank. Owing to these differences, the terms "board of directors" and "senior management" are used in this paper not to identify legal constructs but rather to label two decision-making functions within a bank.

Principle 7: Banks should have in place contingency and business continuity plans to ensure their ability to operate on an ongoing basis and limit losses in the event of severe business disruption.

Role of supervisors

Principle 8: Banking supervisors should require that all banks, regardless of size, have an effective framework in place to identify, assess, monitor and control/mitigate material operational risks as part of an overall approach to risk management.

Principle 9: Supervisors should conduct, directly or indirectly, regular independent evaluation of a bank's policies, procedures and practices related to operational risks.

Supervisors should ensure that there are appropriate mechanisms in place, which allow them to remain apprised of developments at banks.

Role of disclosure

Principle 10: Banks should make sufficient public disclosure to allow market participants to assess their approach to operational risk management.

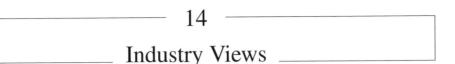

14

Industry Views

Time is the friend of the wonderful company, the enemy of the mediocre. Warren Buffet

This chapter is based upon fundamental research conducted by ORRF during the period February to June 2008. Discussions were held with a number of leading organizations accredited with influencing thinking and driving change, including rating agencies, fund managers, regulators, and other influential bodies. In particular, we would like to thank Helmut Bauer at Deutsche Bank, James Gifford at UN PRI, Dr Jimi Hinchliffe and his colleagues at the FSA, Rob Jones at Standard & Poor's, Colin Melvin at Hermes, Jon Moulton of Alchemy Partners (Venture Capital), Krishnan Ramadurai and his colleagues at Fitch Ratings, David Russell of USS, and Sir David Tweedie of the International Accounting Standards Board (IASB). The views presented are an amalgam of those received and therefore should not be attributed to any one person or firm. However, a number of papers are referenced at the end of the chapter which give further information regarding the specific views of particular organizations.

14.1 THE EFFECTIVE OWNERS OF COMPANIES (I.E. THE LARGE PENSION FUNDS AND INSURANCE COMPANIES) DO NOT APPEAR TO BE TAKING SUFFICIENT ACTION TO PREVENT EXCESSIVE RISK TAKING. WHAT NEEDS TO BE DONE?

Improvements in risk management begin with sound corporate governance. Over the last 15 years or so we have seen a number of important advances in corporate governance, particularly in the UK. This began with the Cadbury Report in 1992, which is as relevant today as it was when first written. The Higgs Report, which was produced in 2003, rightly stated: *Corporate governance provides an architecture of accountability – the structures and processes to ensure companies are managed in the interests of their owners. But architecture alone does not deliver good outcomes.* Higgs clearly recognized that good corporate governance is about people. The report identified the fundamental need to separate the roles of chairman and Chief Executive, focusing on the conditions and behaviors necessary for a non-executive director to be fully effective.

More recently we have seen the Woolf Review calling for the board of directors to take greater responsibility for ethical conduct. The review was undertaken in 2007 in response to the BAE–Saudi Arabia al-Yamamah arms deal affair, in which the High Court ruled that the Serious Fraud Office (SFO) had acted unlawfully in ending its investigation into alleged fraudulent payments. Woolf recommended that a company should be as open and transparent as possible in communicating all its activities and that an independent external audit of ethical business conduct (together with the management of reputational risk) should be carried out at regular intervals. The review went on to recommend that a board's corporate responsibility committee and internal audit function should ensure that standards of ethical behaviour are properly communicated and embedded throughout the organization. It stated that members of the senior executive team and heads of business units have a personal and collective responsibility to demonstrate high standards of ethical business conduct, which should be reflected in performance appraisals and remunerations.

There have been a number of studies into corporate governance, including one produced recently by the Association of British Insurers (ABI), most of which have concluded (although some have proved inconclusive) that a well-governed company ultimately performs better than a poorly-governed one. Deutsche Bank has also done some useful work in this area. However, there is still a long way to go in determining how best to quantify improvements.

In our view, as long-term investors, long-term performance and success is determined by a combination of a company's governance structure together with an active and constructive dialogue with its shareholders. Identifying areas where performance could be improved is only part of the role of active, interested, and involved shareholders. Constructive dialogue on a wide range of issues, including management oversight and encouragement of governance changes where necessary, are important. Being effectively perpetual investors, we share a common goal with the company, that of increasing its value. Hence we seek to work closely with a company in which we invest, where this can add value. It should be recognized that those factors that determine the most appropriate and effective governance structure are likely to change over time, between markets and sectors, thus a responsive approach is required. As such, an assessment of the governance quality of a particular company, based on simplistic objective criteria will, at best, be somewhat unreliable. For these reasons we have developed a diversified, experienced team.

Going forward, we believe that there will be need for greater cooperation between institutional investors, acting in concert, in respect of corporate governance and active shareholder engagement. As universal owners, we are concerned about issues (such as fraud, corruption, money laundering, tax evasion, environmental, and social issues) that ultimately destroy long-term corporate value.

14.2   HOW IMPORTANT DO YOU THINK "EXTRA-FINANCIAL ENHANCED ANALYTICS" FACTORS ARE?

The fundamental importance of "extra-financial enhanced analytics" is that consideration is given to those longer-term factors that could significantly change the structure of an industry. For example, the sale of fish at relatively low prices has resulted in high levels of demand, causing the seas' fish stocks to collapse, reaching dangerously low levels and threatening the extinction of some species, thus threatening the world's fishing industry.

The United Nations' "principles for responsible investment" (PRI) initiative was launched in April 2006. Currently there are approximately $13 trillion of funds signed up to the principles, representing approximately 10 % of global capital markets. The principles are applicable for large diversified investors, holding relatively large stakes in companies, where as a consequence divestment is impractical; an approach based on engagement, rather than screening and stock avoidance, is therefore considered more appropriate. We expect the importance of "responsible investment" to grow as awareness grows. The significance of green issues and global warming are now well understood by the investment community and the general public. The investment community also understands the significance of corruption, although this still remains an issue at government level, particularly in the defense industry.

The Enhanced Analytics Initiative (EAI) is designed to encourage analysts to take longer-term factors into account by allocating at least 5 % of brokerage commissions to "extra-financial" research. We view the allocation of commissions as a fundamental part of our fiduciary duty to protect and manage our clients' assets. A significant proportion of the value of a company can be accounted for by extra financial and intangibles factors, especially over the longer term.

A corollary of enhanced analytics is pro-active investor action ("active ownership"), which is seen as a means of bringing about those changes necessary to properly develop markets and to protect the "factors of production," with a view to ensuring the longer-term value of investments.

14.3   THE PRESSURE TO PERFORM, FROM ANALYSTS, IS OFTEN SAID TO BE A CONTRIBUTORY FACTOR TO FRAUDULENT EVENTS SUCH AS ENRON. WHAT CAN BE DONE TO IMPROVE THE QUALITY OF REPORTING AND THE ACCURACY OF FORECASTING?

There is, indeed, significant pressure on companies to hit targets from the market as a whole. Hence we should not be surprised when occasionally this leads to deliberate misreporting. Market pressure is essential to ensure that companies continue to perform efficiently and effectively and thus remain competitive. The consequences of the absence of such pressure is demonstrated by the performance of state-owned banks and organizations, who often lack responsiveness and whose performance is usually significantly behind commercial rivals.

Quarterly targets currently tend to drive how managers think. Research has shown that managers will give up long-term goals to meet analysts' short-term requirements. In our view, as long-term investors, quarterly targets are an irrelevance and potentially a dangerous distraction. It should be recognized that accounting losses are not necessarily realized economic losses but in the case of banks real capital is needed to meet accounting losses.

In our view, companies need to better explain how they make their money and the risks involved in each activity. For example, HSBC is a huge conglomerate making money in many different ways. More information does not necessarily mean better information. The difficulty is in determining what is relevant and significant.

Whilst some research analysts picked up on the sub-prime crisis quite some time before it developed into the credit crunch, the market as a whole did not recognize its significance until much later. Transparency and communication are essential.

A forecast is a function of risk and uncertainty. More accurate forecasts would require a world with less uncertainty. Forecasts are merely a statement of the most likely (expected) outcome. Consequently, there is a probability that the forecast will not occur. Since this is well recognized, companies give forecasts that they expect to comfortably beat. Unfortunately, they do not give risk-based probability distributions.

An approach put forward by the International Centre for Pensions Management (based at the University of Toronto) involves allocating to a portfolio manager a pot of money and then also giving the manager a risk budget. The portfolio manager is required to make a suitable risk-adjusted return on the funds invested. This approach is currently being considered and used by a number of organizations, including the Ontario Teachers' Pension Fund.

14.4 THE CREDIT RATING AGENCIES ARE OFTEN CRITICIZED FOR THEIR INABILITY TO SPOT PROBLEMS EARLY. (A) TO WHAT EXTENT IS THIS CRITICISM JUSTIFIED? (B) WHAT HAVE THE CREDIT RATING AGENCIES DONE TO IMPROVE THEIR ABILITY TO PREDICT POSSIBLE LOSS EVENTS EARLIER?

We fully recognize the need to continuously improve the rating process and better serve the markets. For these reasons we have issued a range of papers seeking the views of the market on a number of issues, including:

- governance: ensuring integrity of the rating process;
- analytics: enhancing the quality of ratings and opinions;
- information: providing greater transparency and insight to market participants;
- education: more effectively educating the marketplace about credit ratings and rated securities;
- enterprise risk management: providing a forward-looking, structured framework to evaluate management.

With regard to defaults, there are always early warning signs, usually available after the event. However, they are less easy to identify beforehand. All companies will exhibit some undesirable characteristics at different points in time. This does not mean they will go on to default. One of the difficulties in predicting failure is the speed at which a problem can "morph" into a full-blown disaster.

The credibility and reputations of the rating agencies rest upon their ability to accurately estimate the probability of default. It is important to recognize the difference between probability and certainty. Even for a triple-A rated institution there is no certainty that it will not default on its obligations, although the probability will be very low. However, even if such a firm did default this would not, on its own, indicate that the rating was wrong. That is the nature of statistics and uncertainty. Ratings are designed for use by "informed" investors – i.e. professional investors having a portfolio of investments under management. Ratings should not be viewed like an all-or-nothing win/lose bet on a single horse.

Default analysis over the last 20+ years has shown that defaults tend to be due to a number of factors, not necessarily all under the control of the specific organization itself. For example, the demise of Northern Rock in September 2007, which resulted from the company having an insufficiently responsive business strategy, was precipitated by the credit crunch stemming from the US sub-prime mis-selling fiasco, and was then further exacerbated by inept UK government/political interference resulting in nationalization. The UK financial services sector may ultimately prove to have been damaged by the UK government's attempt to limit transparency through preventing public scrutiny under the Freedom of Information Act, in conflict with the new Basel Accord.

14.5 THERE APPEAR TO BE DIFFERENCES BETWEEN WHAT A CREDIT RATING AGENCY PROVIDES AND WHAT SECURITIES ANALYSTS AND INVESTORS WANT. WHY IS THIS?

Fundamentally, the market wants certainty about the future. Unfortunately, this is not possible and, obviously, never will be. Reward relates to risk! Fund managers dislike discontinuous unexpected downgrades. Such events instantly reduce the value of investments and do not provide sufficient opportunity to rebalance portfolios. Investors, therefore, want stable transparent ratings that "look through the cycle" and reflect the underlying fundamentals.

Whilst investors want early warnings of potential problems, it is often said that such warnings have the propensity to become self-fulfilling prophecies. Certainly, such warnings can increase the level of volatility and thus increase uncertainty in the market. For this reason we remain sceptical about the inclusion of stock or bond prices in the information used to determine ratings. It should be recognized that credit ratings indicate the probability of default in the medium term (i.e. within the next 12 or, in some cases, 18 months). Ratings are intended to provide a stable signal of "fundamentally derived" credit risk. To assist clients the rating agencies do issue early warnings, such as putting a bank on negative watch, although this does not indicate it will fail. We also provide longer-term outlooks.

We recognize that investors would like a default distribution for each rating category and a clearly defined mathematical relationship between the different rating categories. However, this is unrealistic. It should be recognized that the rating is ordinal not co-ordinal. The rating agencies do not specify the probability of default for a rating; it can change over time depending upon the business environment. The rating is a holistic overview of the assessments of the various subcategories (i.e. the seven pillars of analysis), in which qualitative factors may dominate. It is not quantitatively derived from the probability of default.

14.6 IS A MORE FORENSIC APPROACH TOWARDS RISK ASSESSMENT AND RATING NECESSARY OR DO YOU THINK THAT COMPLEXITY AND CHAOS LIMIT THE EXTENT TO WHICH RISK CAN BE DECONSTRUCTED AND ACCURATELY ASSESSED?

To rate risk you need to properly understand it; causality is important. This requires a granular assessment, with the level of analysis undertaken being dependent upon the type of risk and its potential impact. Currently, the rating agencies are evaluating whether the market would benefit from traditional credit ratings being complemented by analysis and benchmarking of non-default risk factors. Research is being undertaken into how these risks could be effectively and consistently assessed and measured with a view to supporting predictive analysis. At the moment risk is not well understood by the market; the credit crunch has identified many weaknesses.

14.7 HOW IMPORTANT IS ENTERPRISE RISK MANAGEMENT (ERM) TO THE RATING PROCESS?

Events have shown that it is no longer acceptable to simply consider risks as existing in isolated silos. A holistic enterprise-wide approach, which takes into account correlation factors, is essential. We now treat ERM as an analytical risk factor in its own right. It is analyzed by assessing the following five sub-elements:

- culture;
- risk controls;
- strategic risk management;
- emerging risks; and
- models.

These first two elements were previously assessed as part of the traditional analysis approach. However, in 2005 we enhanced our analysis and introduced the three other elements.

We initially conducted ERM assessments in the insurance sector in October 2005, and expanded it to the banking sector about six months later. The possibility of evaluating ERM in the "corporates" sector is also being considered. Some of the leading insurers, such as AXA and ING, have now leapfrogged some banks by taking a top-down approach, using holistic models. The recent upgrades of Allianz and Munich Re were influenced in part by the quality of their approach to enterprise-wide risk management.

With regard to the final sub-element of ERM (models) we have been using factor-based risk adjusted capital models for over 10 years. These are now in their fourth generation and are beginning to be replaced by economic capital models. Over the next 12 months we expect to start blending our models with those of the firm being rated but only where ERM is assessed as being excellent or strong.

14.8   DO YOU USE MODELS TO QUANTIFY OPERATIONAL RISK AND CAPITAL ADEQUACY?

- How useful do you think models are?
- Do you think Bayesian Belief Models have a role to play in determining causality and the interaction between risk elements?
- Do you think dynamic financial analysis can be linked to enterprise risk management

Modeling remains very much in its infancy with regard to operational risk, there being no consensus as yet. Models are necessary but not sufficient. Unfortunately, where models are used, common sense can sometimes go out of the window; the regulatory requirement for a 99.9 % confidence level for OpVaR being a case in point. We have found that at this confidence level the statistical LDA/EVT models are not stable. Small changes in assumptions can result in similar banks having significantly different capital requirements.

Clearly, models need to be as accurate as sensibly possible but it must be recognized that too much detail can become unmanageable. This places limits on the level of granularity. Different banks will have different requirements and will therefore use different models. In assessing a particular bank's model we are more interested in the underlying cultural approach and the related assumptions made rather than the results obtained. Currently, with regard to operational risk, we do not believe that quantitative skills and experience are sufficiently high in the banking sector to put any great reliance on operational risk modeling.

Whilst modeling is a natural part of improving the assessment and quantification of risk, in our view modeling must not take over. Models support and inform the judgement of management rather than drive decisions. We do not view favourably slavish devotion to models and tools. Checks and balances are an art, not a science.

14.9   MODELS THAT USE MARKET DATA ARE CLAIMED BY SOME TO BE BETTER PREDICTORS THAN TRADITIONAL CREDIT RATING AGENCY METHODS

- What lessons can be learned from a market-based approach?
- What value does such an approach have from a risk management perspective?

Investors can sensibly use both market-based assessments and credit ratings. Neither is a hybrid of the other.

We are aware of some of the claims made by organizations providing market-based assessments, such as Moody's KMV. However, we remain sceptical. Assessment of the probability of default needs to be based on underlying fundamental factors, not short-term market movements. Ratings are intended to look through the cycle and provide a stable signal of fundamentally derived credit risk. On the tradeoff between accuracy and stability, ratings offer stability through providing predictable rating changes that are clearly signalled in advance. Additional information, such as rating history, outlooks, and watch-lists, also provide rating signals.

With market-based assessments the tacit assumptions being made are that if an organization has weaknesses then these will be evidenced in the past and present performance results. With regard to the future, the market will have factored known expected changes into the current market price. Therefore, as an investor, there is no need to investigate any further. The fundamental argument is that good managers will outperform the market in which they operate. However, extreme tail events, for which Basel requires banks to hold regulatory capital, are most unlikely to be evident in the historical and current pricing data. Experience also shows that if something appears to be too good to be true then it probably is. So, interpretation and assessment are key necessities in our view.

14.10   WHAT LEVEL OF LOSS OR RISK WOULD TRIGGER A DOWNGRADE?

Clearly, a significant reduction in the capital base would represent a serious concern, but the extent to which this would result in a ratings downgrade would also be dependent upon other factors such as: the ability of the firm to earn its way out of trouble and rebuild its defenses in an acceptable period of time; its access to liquidity and the strength of its arrangements with other financial institutions (swing-lines); and above all, the quality of its senior management and their strategy. Risk is always present, the judgement is if it is properly understood by the board of directors and is being appropriately managed.

14.11   WHAT ANALYSIS IS DONE INTO THE REASONS FOR DEFAULT, AND WHAT DOES THIS ANALYSIS SHOW?

We produce an annual report of defaults and transitions, providing significant detail on past ratings performance. This report is made freely available. It is our intention to provide quarterly updates in the future.

14.12   SHOULD CREDIT RATING AGENCY ANALYSTS BE GIVEN SMALLER PORTFOLIOS IN ORDER FOR THEM TO DEVOTE MORE TIME TO THE ANALYSIS OF EACH COMPANY, OR WOULD THE COSTS BE PROHIBITIVE?

Professional investors often view rating agencies as their forensic agent in the analytical process. They want rating agency analysts to have smaller portfolios in order for them to devote much more time to in-depth "forensic" analysis, resulting in the publication of in-depth research. In view of this, rating agencies have taken action to optimize analysts' loads in both high grades and speculative grades in order to intensify surveillance, deepen analysis, and increase research cover.

The level and depth of analysis clearly depends upon the size and sophistication of a particular bank – i.e. whether it is a complex global bank with sophisticated risk assessment and reporting requirements or a simple mono-line bank.

14.13   SHOULD SPECIALISTS BE EMPLOYED TO CARRY OUT MORE FORENSIC ANALYSIS AND, IF SO, WHAT SPECIALISTS ARE REQUIRED?

The more proactive fund managers are increasingly developing their own specialist expertise, particularly with regard to "enhanced analytical factors." In addition, specialist research organizations are increasingly being used to improve understanding of factors that could have a significant long-term impact upon sustainability and strategy.

14.14   THE RATING AGENCIES ARE IN A PRIVILEGED POSITION IN THAT THEY RECEIVE CONFIDENTIAL INFORMATION ABOUT A FIRM, WHICH HAS THE EFFECT OF ADDING CREDIBILITY TO THEIR RATINGS AND STATEMENTS

- Should the rating agencies require higher levels of confirmation from a firm (i.e. due diligence checks)?
- Who should be responsible for such due diligence (e.g. the ratings agency itself or the external auditors, or others)?

A rating is simply a rating agency's opinion of a company and its probability of default in a given time frame. This opinion is based upon the information provided to us. We do not have the power to compel a company to provide information and, indeed, full information, in the format required, is not always forthcoming. In this respect, the rating agencies differ significantly from external auditors.

It is often said that the rating agencies should audit the auditors. This is unrealistic. The information that a company provides should give a "true and fair view." Indeed, it is the role of the auditors, supported by legislation and accounting standards, to ensure this is so. However, we do not simply take on face value the information provided to us. We actively question the assumptions made by the auditors in drawing up the published accounts. We also actively question the company's management. However, our approach is not a forensic one and should not be confused as such. Instead, we seek to take a holistic overview of the soundness of a firm.

It should be recognized that auditing is based upon statistical sampling and cannot be expected to uncover all problems such as fraud. With regard to the need for auditing the auditors, in France this problem has been addressed by requiring companies to have two sets of auditors.

If there is doubt about the honesty and reliability of the information provided by a company then the integrity of its board of directors and the senior management team is brought into question. Current auditing and legislative standards, such as Sarbanes-Oxley, require a statement to be made by the auditors regarding the soundness of the published accounts.

The role of the rating agencies is to carefully assess all relevant information available and provide clients with a considered expert opinion. The credibility attributed to a rating is derived from the analytical capability of the rating agency. This is based upon the rating agency's ability to draw upon substantial knowledge about the particular firm, the market of which it is part, and the countries in which it operates. For this reason, the opinion of the rating agency is considered to be the best professional opinion available at the time. However, anyone who thinks they can accurately predict the future is simply deluding themself.

14.15   IS IT POSSIBLE FOR THE RATING AGENCIES TO HIGHLIGHT CONCERNS ABOUT A PARTICULAR FIRM, TO THE MARKET, WITHOUT PRECIPITATING A CRISIS?

We are taking a more forensic approach to our analysis with a view to identifying potential problems earlier. Where we have concerns about a firm in the short term (i.e. over the next six months) we indicate this to the market by putting the firm on "negative watch." We also provide a longer-term outlook (covering a period of about 18 months). Our aim is to provide a smooth transition, thereby avoiding excessive volatility that could result in the destruction of investor capital.

Where cases of serious fraud and corruption suddenly come to light, we are duty bound to take these factors into account and report accordingly to the market. In such cases there could inevitably be a step change in the rating of the firm concerned, resulting in higher levels of volatility until uncertainty is removed and the market adjusts accordingly.

Whilst some investors have argued that downgrades become self-fulfilling prophecies due to the impact on market access, in fact a downgrade is the result of detailed fundamental analysis. The information is only released to the market once it has been discussed and properly verified with the directors of the firm concerned.

14.16   SHOULD THE RATING AGENCIES BE GIVEN THE OPPORTUNITY, OR INDEED BE REQUIRED, TO DISCUSS IN CONFIDENCE ANY CONCERNS THEY MAY HAVE ABOUT A PARTICULAR FIRM WITH THE REGULATORS?

It has been argued by some that in exchange for their recognized privileged status, rating agencies should be required to discuss in confidence with the regulators any concerns they have about a particular firm. Whilst this may appear to offer greater market stability, there are a number of other factors that need to be taken into consideration. Firstly, this would require the rating agencies not to inform the market of any sensitive information in their possession. This is fundamentally against the *raison d'être* of rating agencies. Secondly, rating agencies are not agents of the regulators but are, instead, independent organizations that exist to provide a service (i.e. an independent professional opinion) to their clients (i.e. those firms that are paying a fee to be rated). Thirdly, such covert action could be considered to be in conflict with the principle of transparency as enshrined in Pillar 3 of the Basel II Accord.

However, this issue remains open to debate and revolves around the perceived role of the rating agencies. Increasingly, legislators and investors want rating agencies to look behind the issuer's financial accounting information in order to discover the underlying economic reality. US senator Joe Lieberman stated: *Rating agencies have authority over companies comparable to the FDA. The FDA doesn't let a drug go onto the market until they've gone over all sorts of investigations to guarantee it's safe. We've asked rating agencies to play a similar role with regard to corporations.*

14.17 IS LITIGATION LIKELY TO BECOME AN INCREASING PROBLEM, WITH THE POSSIBILITY OF INVESTORS SUING WHERE INFORMATION LATER PROVES TO BE INACCURATE AND MISLEADING?

In an increasingly litigious society it seems almost inevitable that investor litigation will increase. For example, institutional shareholders held a significant proportion of shares in Northern Rock (NR). The day prior to nationalization, NR shares were trading at 90 p each; upon nationalization the shares became worthless. This is tantamount to stealing from shareholders by the UK government. It could be regarded as the fiduciary duty of institutional shareholders (i.e. pension funds) to seek justifiable compensation. However, we do not consider speculative hedge funds have the same legitimate claim.

With regard to the US sub-prime housing crisis, the US City of Cleveland indicated its possible intention to take legal action against those banks involved, including HSBC and RBS amongst others. The FBI is also carrying out investigations into wrong-doing.

14.18 DO YOU THINK THAT GREATER TRANSPARENCY, AS PROPOSED BY THE THIRD PILLAR OF BASEL II, WILL BRING THE BENEFITS ENVISAGED BY THE REGULATORS, OR IS TRANSPARENCY SOMEWHAT OF AN ILLUSORY CONCEPT?

Pillar 3 is potentially a significant step forward but its form and shape are still debatable. Transparency is a very important concept for the functioning of a free market (with a level playing field). The market only works properly if information is communicated efficiently and effectively, thus facilitating responsive action. For example, with regard to long-term enhanced analytic factors there is little point in one fund manager having this information at the exclusion of all others. In our view there is a need to further educate investors. Consequently, we are putting more effort into this.

We believe there can be few arguments against transparency. But despite its importance, transparency has many powerful opponents and is regarded by some as a mixed blessing since it can lead to increased volatility. For this reason, some banks are seeking ways of limiting disclosure. There has also been a reduction in the number of companies providing quarterly reports (although it should be noted that quoted US companies are still required to provide such reports).

In the UK it is interesting to note that, with regard to transparency, the government has recently given the Bank of England powers to undertake covert intervention into banks. It has also exempted the recently-nationalized Northern Rock bank from disclosure under the Freedom of Information Act. Similarly, where a proactive fund manager has concerns about the strategy (together with the associated risks) being pursued by a particular firm, it will clearly not want this information made public until after discussions are complete. Whilst a fund manager may make a company aware of how it intends to vote with regard to a particular motion, it will only inform the market some time after the event.

14.19   A FUNDAMENTAL REQUIREMENT OF EXTERNALLY AUDITED ACCOUNTS IS TO PROVIDE SHAREHOLDERS WITH A "TRUE AND FAIR VIEW." HOWEVER, BANKS HAVE BEEN DELIBERATELY CONCEALING IMPORTANT INFORMATION AFFECTING THE LEVELS OF RISK FACED. THIS HAS BROUGHT INTO QUESTION THE VALUE OF THEIR AUDITED ACCOUNTS, THE INTEGRITY OF EXTERNAL AUDITORS (WHO ARE IN FACT PAID BY THE BANK BEING AUDITED), THE APPROPRIATENESS OF PRACTICES SUCH AS THE USE OF OFF-BALANCE-SHEET ACTIVITIES, AND THE RELEVANCE OF MARK-TO-MARKET ("FAIR VALUE") VALUATIONS IN A TIME OF HIGH MARKET UNCERTAINTY

a. How can audited accounts be improved to meet the requirements of long-term institutional investors?
b. Can audited accounts ever be expected to provide sufficient risk-related information upon which rating agencies can rely when determining their ratings?

In the UK, the FSA has warned that in the current market conditions there may be a divergence between what is required for valuations in financial statements, and what needs to be considered under the prudent valuation principles laid out in the Basel II banking capital rules. The Institute of International Finance (IIF) has also cautioned that mark-to-market valuations may create distortions. However, Hugo Banziger, Chief Risk Officer at Deutsche Bank, has stated that marking-to-market is an absolutely necessary tool for managing risk and that Deutsche Bank is completely supportive of the concept. Nout Wellink, Chairman of the Basel Committee on Banking Supervision, has stated that valuation approaches for complex trading assets have been a destabilizing factor over the course of the credit crisis. Market participants have a notable lack of confidence in firms' disclosure of exposures to structured products, the processes for valuing positions, and the timely and accurate recognition of losses.

How can audited accounts be improved to meet the requirements of long-term institutional investors?

The answer to this question lies in the promotion of principle-based global accounting standards. The purpose of accounting is to present financial information that is useful for investors, creditors, and other users of financial statements. While accounting standards do not create the economic situation of a company, a bank or other entities, their purpose when implemented and applied correctly is to ensure that financial statements provide investors and other users with the information that they need to make well-informed economic decisions. The credit crisis has shown that it is impossible to account for and anticipate all developments in the marketplace. That is why principle-based global standards are crucial. It is harder to defeat a well-crafted principle than a specific rule that financial engineers can by-pass. Carefully crafted and well-applied principles help to eliminate the need for anti-abuse provisions and provide the transparency that investors need if they are to have confidence in the market and make their decisions.

While we have achieved a lot over the past few years to strengthen the principles in our standards and achieve international convergence, there are still some important areas where more work needs to be done. Two examples are the standards on pensions and leases.

Under IAS 19 (Employee Benefits), not only is the change in the value of a pension fund not correctly reflected in the financial statements but also the annual cost of pensions charged against annual income is offset by the estimated long-term return on the assets in the fund rather than the actual return on the fund. Some of these estimated returns have been huge. In the United States from 2000 to 2004, the income statements of the top 500 companies recorded these estimated returns at $498 billion while the actual return amounted to only $197 billion. In other words, $301 billion of non-existent income flowed through the profit and loss accounts of the top 500 American companies over a period of five years.

Accounting For Leasing is another topic that requires our (IASB's) attention. Hardly any aircraft currently appear on an airline's balance sheet. This is because most aircraft are leased, and IAS 17 (Leases) divides leasing into two types: operating leases and capital/finance leases in which (broadly speaking) the asset is owned for almost its entire life. At present, aircraft fall into the operating leases category because they are leased for a certain period. However, in most cases the airline is committed to annual payments over the next seven years and the amount payable over that time is written into the lease contract. Thus the definition of a liability is met (the airline has an obligation which can be measured reliably and from which it cannot escape). The balance sheet should, therefore, show as a liability (being the present value of the payments that have to be made) and an asset (being the rights to the aircraft for the same period). These would not be trivial figures. The volume of leasing in 2006 amounted to $634 billion (and this was for only one year). Most of it, like the aircraft, was off balance sheet.

Can audited accounts ever be expected to provide sufficient risk-related information upon which rating agencies can rely when determining their ratings?

The answer to this question is both yes and no. The role of accounting is to provide evidence of the current financial situation of a company – no more and no less. We must strive to ensure that this goal is achieved if the standards are applied and implemented correctly. In that respect accounting is only one input, however important, in the rating agencies' work. The example of Northern Rock bank in the United Kingdom made this clear. About a year ago we released new disclosure rules in IFRS 7 (Financial Instruments: Disclosures) to enhance the quality of disclosures. These new disclosure rules were developed with the assistance of bank supervisors and the private sector. As a result of IFRS 7, the short-term funding risks associated with Northern Rock bank in the United Kingdom were set out in their annual accounts and hence visible for all interested parties.

However, that is not to say that there is no need for improvement. Deciding whether there has been adequate information will always be a retrospective exercise and there will always be room for improvement. We have to observe markets closely and learn from past experience. That is why we are assessing IFRS 7 to see whether it has been effective in the current crisis and if there is a need for additional disclosure requirements in relation to fair value measurement. This is also the reason why, in the projects on derecognition and consolidation, we are examining the accounting for off-balance-sheet vehicles. Clarifying the circumstances when it is appropriate for an entity to remove an asset from its balance sheet and when an entity should combine its financial statements with those of another entity (including special purpose entities and structured investment and securitization vehicles) will help regulators and other users of accounts to improve their risk assessment.

14.20   WHAT FURTHER CHANGES DO YOU THINK ARE NECESSARY TO IMPROVE THE STABILITY AND CREDIBILITY OF THE FINANCIAL SYSTEM? FOR EXAMPLE:

- Do you think that Basel II places too much emphasis on capital adequacy as a solution to risk? If so what else is required?
- Do you think that SOX is limited and, if so, why?
- Do you think that the EU's legislative approach is appropriate or that it is somewhat ossifying?

Basel II is a good starting point; fundamentally, it is what all banks should be doing. The concentration on risk-based capital by Basel II has facilitated a move towards economic capital frameworks, which we view as positive. However, Basel II has a number of weaknesses. For example, it ignores many of the business risks historically identified, by researchers such as Argenti, as being the fundamental causes of failure. Consequently, Basel II is expected to be revised in due course, taking account of Solvency II. In reality, Basel II was designed for major globally active banks. Unfortunately, this can lead to problems when less advanced banks try to adopt these guidelines. At the moment there are big issues with banks in emerging markets. For them, an advanced measurement approach (AMA) for operational risk is clearly inappropriate, due to data problems. Whilst the simpler standardized approach is more appropriate, this may result in a higher regulatory capital requirement. Similarly, the AMA approach is inappropriate for German banks where a structural problem exists within the banking system (obviously, this excludes the major internationally active German banks, such as Deutsche Bank).

The Sarbanes-Oxley Act was widely regarded as a knee-jerk reaction by the US government, aimed at restoring investor confidence following the Enron crisis. It has been widely criticized since its introduction, mainly for its simplistic but exhaustive tick-box approach, which is somewhat lacking in vision.

Fundamentally, the European Union took the Basel guidelines and turned them into legislation. This makes revision a more difficult process and as a result could lead to increased rigidity, although the Lamfalussy process seeks to reduce this potential problem.

14.21   WHAT ARE THE MAJOR CHALLENGES CURRENTLY FACING THE SECTOR? WHAT CHANGES DO YOU THINK ARE NECESSARY AND WHAT IS PREVENTING THEM?

There are a number of challenges currently facing the financial services sector, and the banking sector in particular. The difficulty is in identifying which of these could lead to a full-blown crisis. Certainly, it is unlikely that the next crisis will be due to those factors that caused previous ones, although lessons are not always well learnt as we have seen from the recent SocGen fiasco. Greed, corruption, and fraud are always likely to be in existence, to varying degrees, and in various guises.

The current financial system, given occasional governmental intervention, does appear to work and indeed has managed to cope with preventing full-blown meltdown from incidents such as Long Term Capital Management (LTCM), Enron, and more recently, the credit crunch. However, the question is, at what cost? There is no doubt that we could certainly do better.

14.21.1   Reduced stability

Currently, we are seeing increased market volatility and greater uncertainty, due to a number of factors, including:

- mark-to-market valuations;
- hedge fund activities;
- exotic instruments (e.g. collatoralized debt obligations), whose underlying risks are not fully understood;
- activities by monolines; and
- short-term financial reporting.

14.21.2   Concerns relating to regulatory actions

Unfortunately, the current credit crisis appears to have encouraged greater regulatory activity. In Europe there is ongoing discussion about a single European regulator, which appears to be gaining momentum. However, this requires convergence towards a common culture and philosophy and as yet there is still a long way to go. We must be careful not to create a monster.

The primary role of the regulators is to protect investors and protect the market. In our view, they have clearly failed on both counts. The FSA's comment, that Northern Rock would probably have failed anyway, brings into question the purpose of the regulator if it is not to prevent such catastrophes and promote stability. What is particularly concerning is that the FSA allegedly knew of the problem with Northern Rock some 12 months before the bank crashed.

14.21.3   Knowledge and understanding of risk

In our view, risk is not always well understood by firms or by the market and, therefore, not properly priced. Increasingly, there are calls from investor groups for special audits of risk management and control systems. Currently, intense pressure is being placed on directors, particularly those involved with audit and risk oversight committees, in the wake of the credit crunch. We believe that knowledge and understanding of risk could be improved by:

- Financial reporting – improving granularity with a view to enabling the revenues being earned from different business activities to be related to the risks being taken.
- Transparency – actively encouraging transparency and reducing resistance to it. However, care and consideration need to be given to the issue of "who is being protected from what."
- Reducing the "free rider" problem – encourage users to pay for research used rather than simply relying upon that provided by the rating agencies (which is paid for by those being rated).
- Unbundling – separating out broker services with a view to improving the quality of their research.

14.21.4   Investor horizons

With regard to investment activity, short-termism remains a problem. For example, where an investment executive thinks a stock is going to perform well they will go overweight. Alternatively, they will go underweight where stocks are expected to underperform, and indeed the investment executive will actually then want the company to fail. However, this action is counter to the requirements of large long-term investors, such as pension funds, for whom divestment is not a realistic option given the likely impact on the share price together with the risk of not holding a fully diversified portfolio. Long-term investors, therefore, require investment executives to maintain a balanced portfolio; however, they also require the management of the underperforming company to be brought to account. We are working towards getting a more balanced view by encouraging analysts and investment executives to take longer-term factors into consideration.

14.21.5 Corporate governance

We are continuously seeking to drive forward improvements in corporate governance, including enhanced responsiveness. Two areas of concern at the moment are:

1. lack of acceptance of default proxy voting (DPV);
2. some remaining resistance to corporate governance best practices, including separation of the role of chairman and Chief Executive.

Default proxy voting (DPV) is closely associated with proactive investor action and is seen as potentially one of the most powerful developments in the corporate governance sphere. It is currently being considered by proxy voting firms such as ISS and its subsidiary IRRC. However, at the moment the US Securities and Exchange Commission (SEC) are opposing DPV on the grounds that it is too operational. As a consequence, companies under the jurisdiction of the SEC can ask for the outcome of DPV to be set aside.

In the UK it is now widely accepted that the roles of chairman and Chief Executive should be split, with only a few notable exceptions such as Marks & Spencer (M&S) taking a contra view. However, this is not the case in the United States. The quality of corporate governance in the US is less homogeneous. Whilst some of the leading examples of corporate governance are to be found in the US there are also some serious areas of concern. For example, institutional investors cannot remove board members by voting against them; instead, they can only withhold their vote. This contrasts with the UK where there are three options: to vote for, against, or abstain. It is practically impossible to get access to board members in the US, which is concerning since directors are supposed to represent shareholders. Surprisingly, however, access to management is given instead. In the UK, institutional investors have easy access to board members and, therefore, are able to develop a value adding dialogue with them. Unfortunately, in the US it is necessary to put forward a shareholder resolution, thus effectively preventing constructive dialogue.

REFERENCES

Hermes

The Hermes Principles: What shareholders expect of public companies – and what companies should expect of their investors.
Corporate Governance and Performance – The Missing Links.
A brief review and assessment of the evidence for a link between corporate governance and performance.
Hermes Corporate Governance Principles.

Fitch Ratings

Global Bank individual ratings transition and failure study: 1990–2006.
Fitch Ratings Definitions http://www.fitchratings.com/corporate/fitchResources.cfm?detail=1.

Standard & Poor's

Descriptions of new actions to strengthen ratings process and better serve markets. http://www2.standardandpoors.com/spf/pdf/media/Leadership_Action_Details.pdf.

http://www2.standardandpoors.com/portal/site/sp/en/us/page.topic/ratings_capital_model/2,1,5,0,0,0,0,0,0,6,3,0,0,0,0,0.html – This link relates to S&P's own capital adequacy model. It includes the Excel spreadsheet used in Europe and technical specifications.

http://www2.standardandpoors.com/portal/site/sp/en/us/page.article/3,3,3,0,1148451189876.html – This is S&P's annual default and transition analysis.

http://www2.standardandpoors.com/portal/site/sp/en/us/page.article/3,2,2,0,1148449517749.html – This summarizes S&P's ERM criteria.

http://www2.standardandpoors.com/portal/site/sp/en/us/page.article/3,2,2,0,1148447231986.html – This discusses S&P's plans for economic capital analysis.

http://www2.standardandpoors.com/portal/site/sp/en/us/page.topic/ratings_fs_ins/2,1,5,0,0,0,0,0,0,6,2,0,0,0,0,0.html – Finally this is S&P's criteria book, which provides an overview of the whole rating process and puts the other documents in context.

Deutsche Bank

Global Corporate Governance Research, "Beyond the Numbers – Corporate Governance in Asia and Australia," March 2006.

Global Corporate Governance Research, "Beyond the Numbers – Corporate Governance in Europe," March 2005.

Global Corporate Governance Research, "Beyond the Numbers – UK Corporate Governance Revisited," July 2005.

Global Corporate Governance Research, "Beyond the Numbers – Corporate Governance in the UK," February 2004.

Global Corporate Governance Research, "Beyond the Numbers – Corporate Governance in South Africa," October 2004.

Global Corporate Governance Research, "Beyond the Numbers – Corporate Governance: Unveiling the S&P500," August 2003.

15

Summary, Conclusions, and Recommendations

15.1 INTRODUCTION

Despite the sophistication of the banking and financial services sector, the importance of operational risk, particularly from a strategic perspective, is not widely understood. This has been clearly demonstrated by the current credit crunch, whose impact has yet to be fully determined. However, when criticizing the current financial system it should be borne in mind that, notwithstanding its failings, the system has managed to survive a number of major threats to its existence including the Asian crisis, Long Term Capital Management (LTCM), and Enron. Although the main structural components of the financial system (i.e. the key participants) are already in existence, there appears to be a need for greater synergy between them in order to meet current and future market requirements. This chapter puts forward a number of conclusions and recommendations with a view to promoting debate and thereby facilitating appropriate change. In particular, consideration is given to key risk issues facing the following primary participants:

- **Institutional shareholder-investors.** As owners, they are responsible (to their members and the wider community) for bringing about change by influencing board thinking, particularly with regard to longer-term ESG (environmental, social, and corporate governance) considerations.
- **Regulators, legislators, and central banks.** They are responsible for maintaining trust in the financial system and ensuring overall financial stability.
- **Accountants, auditors and financial reporting bodies.** They are responsible for ensuring transparency and, in particular, ensuring that a "true and fair view" is provided (opaqueness undermines confidence).
- **Rating agencies.** Currently, their function is merely to provide their customers with a properly considered opinion regarding the probability of default. However, much more is expected of them by the wider community.
- **Insurance companies.** These make possible the transfer of risk (away from those unable or unwilling to accept it) and can also assist with the smoothing of earnings.
- **Banks.** Banks owe an ultimate duty of care to their customers – and also to their shareholders.

The banking and financial services industry is complex and dynamic in nature. Consequently, a commitment to innovation and improvement is necessary, with a view to driving forward the boundaries of knowledge and increasing understanding of risk. This requires on-going constructive dialogue between institutional investors/shareholders, the rating agencies, the regulators, and the banks themselves, amongst others. Whilst regulatory requirements are of catalytic importance, the primary driving forces are competitive advantage and resultant market rationalization.

It may seem surprising that the financial services industry, whose *raison d'être* is to transfer risk to those better able to accept and manage it, appears not to properly understand risk itself. Currently, rather than being based upon forensic analysis of fundamental factors, the assessment of risk tends to rely upon comparative assessment and experience. Unfortunately, comparative assessment allows the creation of financial bubbles. In addition, experience, which is based upon an underlying tacit assumption that the future will be the same as the past, is likely to prove inappropriate or, at best, inadequate in a dynamic environment. Hence there is need for a more forensic approach, which takes into consideration longer-term enhanced analytical factors that impact upon overall performance, including flexibility, resilience, and, ultimately, survival.

The recent credit crunch represents a clear example of the failure to understand risk and the consequences of such failure.[1] It is concerning that the major financial institutions did not understand the products being sold and their associated risks or even know where those risks lay. Similarly, it is concerning that the rating agencies were not able to properly assess the risks. The great disappointment is that the regulators did not ensure that proper protection was put in place to prevent systemic risk and to safeguard those who unwittingly bought products which they did not understand. Unfortunately, this crisis has resulted in the destruction of significant levels of both social and economic capital. It is interesting to observe that the US City of Cleveland filed a lawsuit, which may act as a test case, against 21 investment banks, with a view to recovering several hundred million dollars, resulting from lost taxes due to property devaluations and costs incurred in boarding up and demolishing abandoned houses. Certainly, the destruction of social capital is antithetical to the values of long-term institutional investors.

15.2   INSTITUTIONAL SHAREHOLDER-INVESTORS

As owners, institutional shareholder-investors have a fundamental and pivotal role to play in bringing about change within the financial system. It is for them to ensure that all other players carry out their responsibilities efficiently and effectively.

For professional investors, the expression "caveat emptor" very much applies. It is incumbent upon such investors to ensure that they have sufficient information upon which to base their decisions. Failure to do so could be regarded as professional incompetence.

Since very large long-term investors are restricted in their divestment options regarding underperforming investments, it is important for them to take a proactive stance towards encouraging management to improve performance. This necessarily includes taking account of long-term enhanced analytical factors. A few leading organizations, such as Hermes, the Universities Superannuation Scheme (USS), and the California Public Employees' Retirement System (CalPERS), are already successfully applying a proactive "board enhancement" approach. In our view, these organizations – along with others such as the United Nations Principles for Responsible Investment (UNPRI) – are to be applauded for their efforts in advancing the understanding and application of risk management.

Evidence suggests that in the short-term the market does not base its decisions on fundamentals but instead adopts a herd mentality. However, in the longer term the market is rational, although this may involve sharp corrections. The management of a large pension fund therefore needs to be subdivided, with part of the fund responding to short-term factors whilst a significant portion is allocated to long-term investments that ignore short-term volatility and respond only to longer-term fundamentals.

Institutional shareholder-investors have a duty to actively encourage those companies in which they invest to increase transparency. Transparency is important to make the market fully aware of fundamental longer-term enhanced analytical factors and to ensure prices properly reflect such factors. This information, therefore, needs to be included in the company's published accounts or, if a separate expert report is commissioned, then this needs to be readily and freely available on the company's website. In our view, it seems appropriate that the cost of providing such information should be borne by the company for the benefit of all shareholders, thus avoiding the "free-rider" problem and a non-homogeneous market.

15.3   REGULATORS, LEGISLATORS, AND CENTRAL BANKS

The regulators have an important role to play in enforcing market discipline and in bringing about necessary market changes, which individual firms acting alone or in concert could not achieve. However, at the moment, the regulatory framework is overly complex and in need of simplification.[2] An increase in regulatory and legislative ossification must be avoided. A plethora of initiatives that are ill thought through are, at best, distracting.

In principle, the fundamental role of the regulator is to decide whether a particular bank should be allowed to operate in its market and which services that bank should be allowed to offer. If the regulator does not think the bank is fit and proper and does not have the required expertise together with the necessary risk control capabilities, then that bank should not be granted a license. Obviously, continuous regulatory review and assessment are essential to ensure that the particular bank continues to meet the required standards. This necessitates clearly defined standards supported by a series of appropriate key indicators and triggers. To avoid ossification, indicators and triggers need to be flexibly interpreted.

It has been mooted that the regulators should issue bank ratings akin to those issued by the rating agencies. However, it should be noted that even the rating agencies have great difficulty with this process, particularly when faced with potential disaster scenarios, which are the ones the regulators are primarily interested in. In our view, it is unrealistic to expect the regulators to duplicate the very formidable skills and expertise of the rating agencies. Instead, the regulators should indicate what information they require the rating agencies to provide. This would establish a minimum level of required analysis and disclosure, and thus link with the transparency requirements of the new Basel Accord (i.e. Pillar 3).

In the UK, control and oversight of banks has been divided between the FSA, the Bank of England, and HM Treasury. Unfortunately, this has produced a fragmented regulatory system that appears incapable of responding efficiently and effectively to a crisis, as clearly demonstrated by the Northern Rock event. In our view, a single oversight body (as seen in the US, Canada, and Belgium) with sufficient powers to intervene quickly and decisively is essential. This body needs to be informed, although not restricted, by a broadly based advisory group drawn from other key market participants, including accountants and financial reporting bodies, shareholders and investment managers, rating agencies, insurance companies, and banking representatives. Previously, when consulting on proposals, the FSA and the Bank of England have drawn advisors from too narrow a universe.

In the UK there has been significant criticism of the FSA for its failure to properly supervise the failed (nationalized) Northern Rock bank. Indeed, in an internal report the FSA accepted responsibility for this mishandling. Unfortunately, in apportioning blame (some of which may have been deserved) the report appears to have missed a number of salient points. It is, in fact, very difficult to identify a firm that will go on to fail, before the event. It should be recognized that many in the City (including those with privileged access, such as the rating agencies and institutional investors, also failed to identify the seriousness of the situation until it was too late. In our view, the regulators should not hold themselves out as experts; this is not their role and serves only to undermine their credibility. External risk experts should be commissioned to undertake detailed investigations, rather than the FSA attempting to carry out this work itself. This is not to imply that the regulators are without competence but that the cost of replicating existing skills readily available in the market may be unacceptably high. Fundamentally, the primary role of the regulators is to create the right control environment. The FSA already has the powers to request an investigation of a bank, although the existing powers may need to be widened. Indeed, we understand that the UK government is currently investigating this issue. For reasons of transparency, once the FSA has discussed its findings with the bank's board of directors and agreed appropriate actions, the institutional owners and other shareholders should be given a copy of the external report (since they are the owners), as should the rating agencies. Whilst a period of delay may be appropriate, this should be strictly limited.

In the US, the UK and a number of other countries, the central banks appear to have readopted their traditional role of "lender of last resort," as evidenced during the recent credit crunch. It should be recognized that regulatory support exists primarily to prevent systemic risk. As a fundamental principle, badly-managed firms should be allowed to fail. However, it is clearly inappropriate for a bank to hold very high levels of capital against extreme events since this would weaken its performance, growth, and development. Hence it would seem sensible for the central banks to provide a guarantee of support to those banks considered too strategically important or too big to be allowed to fail. Such a guarantee would improve the credit rating of those banks concerned and thus reduce their cost of capital. Consequently, these banks should be required to pay a premium to the government for the guarantee. This would have the effect of reducing shareholder gains rather than taking wealth from the voting public at large. An alternative would be to effectively establish a central insurer that would be aware of all the risks covered, their size and where they were residing. Such support should not be universal but should apply only to more extreme risk, which may well be outside the scope of management (i.e. unfortuitous black swans).

In Europe there are ongoing moves towards the establishment of a central regulator. In our view this is based upon unrealistic expectations of what regulation can achieve. To date, the Basel Committee has accomplished a considerable amount through voluntary coopera-tion. This should be built upon rather than abandoned. Basel identifies sound supervisory and regulatory practice from which agreed standards emerge, with national authorities then estab-lishing appropriate legislation. This appears to have achieved a significant degree of regulatory consistency internationally. Although a central European regulator may further improve stan-dardization, it poses the threat of becoming an uncontrollable monolith. Whilst standardization is to be applauded, this should not be at the expense of flexibility and dynamic innovation. For example, a single European regulator could threaten the existence of the City of London as the world's leading financial centre.

15.4   ACCOUNTANTS, AUDITORS, AND FINANCIAL REPORTING BODIES

Auditing has a vital role to play with regard to ensuring confidence and transparency. However, at present, the inability to rely upon published accounts undermines their primary purpose and represents a disservice to users.

Before confidence has a stable base upon which to rebuild, there are a number of key issues that need to be addressed, including:

1. **conflicts of interest**–auditors are paid by the firms they audit;
2. **accountability**–auditors need to be held accountable; SOX has shown a possible way forward;
3. **risk management**–at the moment, this is poorly understood and inadequately dealt with;
4. **fair value accounting**–this allows better comparisons between companies;
5. **off-balance-sheet activities**–residual responsibility has to be recognized;
6. **political influences**–financial standards need to be internationally acceptable;
7. **principles versus rules**–these should not be considered mutually exclusive.

15.4.1   Conflicts of interest

It is widely, although incorrectly, considered that the primary purpose of auditing is to play a policing role. Without the auditors' imprimatur on the banks' accounts the financial system cannot operate. Audited accounts are expected to be "accurate" and to give an open and transparent view of a company. Indeed, the market punishes opaqueness. Whilst published accounts exist to give users "a true and fair view" of the standing of a firm, the preparers of accounts and their auditors are often faced with a number of alternative interpretations and methods of valuation. Consequently, accounts are not precise statements of fact but instead represent the result of subjective judgements. This can produce considerable variation. It should be remembered that it is the role of the Chief Financial Officer to present the company in its best light. Hence, users have to adopt a cautious approach when reviewing accounts. In addition, the financial constraint (i.e. the audit fee) imposed by the organization being audited limits the depth and effectiveness of the audit process. The fact that auditors are paid by the firm they are auditing represents a potential conflict of interest (note: although the audit committee is supposed to prevent such conflicts, its independence is not absolute).

15.4.2   Accountability

The rating agencies and investors need to be able to rely upon published accounts. However, given the inadequacies of current financial accounting standards and the limitations of the auditing process, rating agencies and institutional investors do not have a sufficiently sound base from which to carry out their own due diligence. We believe that the auditors should report to the audit committee and that this committee should be comprised of shareholder and rating agency representatives (amongst others), to the total exclusion of any influence from company senior executives. At the moment, the Smith Guidance,[3] which forms part of the UK Combined Code, recommends that the board of directors makes appointments to the audit committee[4] and that the delegated authority of the audit committee is derived from the board of directors.

We also believe that where financial accounts are found to be significantly misleading the rating agencies and institutional investors should have the right to take legal action against the auditors. This is likely to have a number of consequences. For example:

- the costs of an audit would increase significantly, and these costs would ultimately be borne by existing shareholders;

- a bank would probably need to have a second tier auditor (to audit the auditor) as in France;
- there is a danger that initially there would be information overload as companies and auditors attempt to disclose everything with a view to protecting themselves.

However, the resultant gains could ultimately prove considerable, since auditors would need to identify and properly assess potential risk factors (together with the adequacy of controls). Sarbanes-Oxley legislation has already made a significant move in this direction.

15.4.3   Risk management

In our view, the International Accounting Standards Board (IASB) and the US Financial Accounting Standards Board (FASB) need to work more closely with the banking regulators and legislators, with a view to enhancing risk management reporting and thereby improve transparency. Currently, it is difficult to properly interpret the findings of a risk report and express these in the form of actions that the board of directors needs to take.

Risk management in the banking sector is currently governed primarily through compliance with the new Basel Accord guidelines, with financial reporting being strongly influenced by Sarbanes-Oxley legislation. Unfortunately, reporting under Sarbanes-Oxley is often regarded as little more than a box-ticking exercise. Whilst reporting the past is difficult, developing models and assessing possible future outcomes (scenarios) is even more complex, requiring considerably more judgement. However, long-term institutional investors and rating agencies are primarily interested in fundamentals rather than factors that merely affect short-term volatility. This requires a proper understanding of risk management and related probability distributions (it should be remembered that a profit forecast needs more than a single value description).

15.4.4   Fair-value accounting

Currently, there is much debate around the issue of fair-value (mark-to-market) accounting. The fundamental idea is to base price on what a willing buyer would be prepared to pay a willing seller (i.e. current market price). The approach is said to give financial analysts greater confidence in the numbers being produced and to enable better comparisons to be drawn between companies. Whilst short-term volatility is increased, through accentuating both good and bad news, supporters claim that it actually gives a more realistic picture of the true situation: companies have nowhere to hide; fair-value accounting increases transparency.

Current financial reporting requirements relating to financial instruments are recognized as being overly complex. Many users of financial statements find IAS 39 (Financial Instruments – Recognition and Measurement) and the related GAAP requirements difficult to understand, interpret and apply. This complexity is created by the many ways in which financial instruments are measured and how unrealized gains and losses are reported. Both the IASB and the US FASB are of the view that the best long-term solution is to adopt a "fair value" (mark-to-market) methodology.[5] The IASB has stated:

> A long-term solution to address such measurement problems is to measure in the same way all the types of financial instruments within the scope of a standard for financial instruments. Fair value seems to be the only measure that is appropriate for all types of financial instruments. However, there are issues and concerns that have to be addressed before the boards can require general fair value measurement. It might take a long time to resolve all the issues and concerns.... Many of the rules, associated with measuring financial instruments in different ways, could be eliminated. A single measurement attribute for all types of financial instruments would also

facilitate comparisons between entities and between accounting periods for the same entity.... There are some concerns and issues associated with fair value measurement of financial instruments. The main concerns are:

a. *volatility of earnings arising from changes in fair value;*
b. *presentation of unrealized gains and losses in earnings.*

In addition, greater use of fair value might result in more complexity (e.g. the difficulty in disaggregating changes in fair value into components). The IASB acknowledges that it will need to undertake work on presentation and disclosure issues before it can introduce a general fair value measurement requirement for financial accounts.

Whilst a number of politicians in the US and the UK called for the suspension of mark-to-market accounting during the credit crisis, a letter from the Centre for Audit Quality, addressed to members of the US Congress stated: *The principles of mark to market accounting are rooted in the fundamental virtue of transparency and are central to informed market decisions and efficient allocation of capital.... In our view, investor confidence would be undermined by efforts designed to mask the actual value of financial assets at a given point in time.*

15.4.5   Off-balance-sheet activities

The off-balance-sheet activities of banks have resulted in a lack of transparency and a loss of market confidence. Fundamentally, this issue is concerned with risk and control, and is an area where financial accounting standards need to be improved. Where a bank has control of an asset, this has to be shown on its balance sheet. However, with a structured vehicle, an investment vehicle or a special purpose vehicle it may be difficult to see where control lies. In fact, control may be split between many organizations, with no one having a majority interest. A further degree of complexity is added where a bank puts a number of products into a vehicle and gets others to invest in this vehicle. Whilst the bank has no interest in the vehicle and gives no guarantees, it is left with tacit residual responsibility since if the vehicle fails to perform, clients may demand compensation from the bank (i.e. clients may take legal action or alternatively threaten to take their business elsewhere). Efforts are currently being made to restrict this type of activity by requiring banks to retain a carried interest.

15.4.6   Political influences

With increasing globalization, financial standards need to be internationally accepted. The 1990s Asian crisis resulted in a massive loss of confidence and acted as a catalyst, prompting the move towards international accounting standards. Companies in the Far East, that had appeared sound under local financial standards, suddenly collapsed without warning. This resulted in a dramatic increase in interest rates. Consequently, investment and growth stopped, causing unemployment to rise sharply. In order to restore confidence and attract international investment, the Far Eastern countries adopted international financial reporting standards (the alternative US standards being regarded as too complex).

Despite the virtually unanimous acceptance of the need for international accounting standards, quite what these standards should be is not always agreed on. Certainly, standards can be subject to significant political influences and pressures. Whilst the President of France, Jacques Chirac, intervened in discussions concerning accounting principles, suggesting that Europe should adopt its own standards.

There have been a number of other cases of political interference and government circumvention. Traditionally, confidence in the banking system was built upon hidden reserves (e.g. properties being valued on an historical cost basis). However, when Japanese banks were faced with insolvency in the wake of the Japanese property crash, the Japanese government and their financial regulators intervened. Thus Japanese banks were not required to show the true value of property assets on their balance sheets. As a consequence the existing Basel capital adequacy requirements were circumvented and Japanese banks were allowed to gradually trade out of their difficulties over a number of years.

For markets to perform properly, investors need to be well informed and understand the information given to them. Support from major institutional investors, globally, could significantly help the activities of the International Accounting Standards Board in improving standards, reducing political interference, and reducing implementation time.

15.4.7   Principles versus rules

The two fundamental aims of financial accounting standards are to achieve compliance with those standards and to hold accountable those responsible for their implementation. Western Europe has adopted a principles-based approach whereas the US has opted for rules-based standards. Each has its advantages and disadvantages. Under the principles-based approach, companies and auditors are required to comply with established principles but are allowed to use their best judgement regarding the application of those principles. In contrast, rules-based standards focus on adherence, whatever those rules might be. Whilst rules-based standards facilitate accountability (both of the individual and the company) and prevent judgemental variation, unfortunately, they also tend to encourage (legitimate) avoidance activities.

Principles and rules should not be considered mutually exclusive; principles provide a sound overarching framework under which rules can then be used where necessary to provide precise detailed interpretation of requirements.

15.5   RATING AGENCIES

Fundamentally, rating agencies exist to give an independent "commercial" opinion on the likelihood of default of an individual organization. Clearly, the rating agencies are not meeting the requirements of the market at present. This is due to two fundamental reasons:

1. *unrealistic market expectations;*
2. *the need for rating agencies to take a more forensic approach.*

Failure to adequately address these issues is resulting in reputational damage for the rating agencies and a growing call for greater regulatory control.

15.5.1   Unrealistic market expectations

The rating agencies have received considerable criticism from politicians and regulators, particularly in the US and the UK, some of which is unjustified and based upon a lack of understanding. This is a potentially serious situation. As Dr Edwards-Deming pointed out, to change a system without properly understanding it can lead to even greater problems. For example, the market does not like shocks and therefore wants early indication of failure.

However, simple early warnings are not possible and may lead to greater volatility and self-fulfilling prophecies of failure.

To assume that risk ratings are about predicting the future is to totally misunderstand the fundamental concept of risk and probability. A rating will not tell you when or why a particular firm will fail; indeed, the firm may never fail no matter how high or low its rating. A rating merely says that of all those firms in that category a certain percentage can be expected to fail in a given period; the higher the rating the fewer the number of failures expected in that group – i.e. ratings relate to portfolio theory.

With regard to an individual firm, complexity and contingency theories state that it is impossible to accurately predict failure since there is an infinite number of potential failure modes. A catastrophic event is typically comprised of a series of weaknesses plus a trigger event. It is relatively easy to spot weaknesses by using key indicators, but these may not lead to catastrophe. Unfortunately, a trigger event can occur with little or no warning, thus causing unexpected failure.

When a triple-A rated bank fails, this does not necessarily mean the rating was wrong, although the failure may be unexpected. It may simply be that the particular firm was unlucky (all other things being equal). However, in a non-homogeneous market, those firms running the greatest risks are likely to be the ones that fail first. The simple gambler's ruin model (as demonstrated by a roulette wheel) shows that, as risk increases, the chances of a loss event occurring increases and the time to total failure decreases. The average time to total failure can be increased by increasing the amount of capital available to absorb losses (i.e. increasing the gambler's original number of chips), whereas taking bigger risks combined with placing bigger bets will shorten the time to failure.

Various suggestions have been put forward with a view to improving the responsiveness of the rating system, including the incorporation of early warning indicators. However, a rating is merely a simplified and convenient indicator of the probability of default. The rating system is primarily designed for use by professional investors and provides a convenient method of quickly discarding those firms that fall outside a predetermined range. Where a professional investor is considering buying shares, the concept of caveat emptor always applies. A rating does not excuse an investor from reading the analyst's report relating to a particular firm, and subsequently keeping in constant contact with the firm, either directly or indirectly.

15.5.2 The need to take a more forensic approach

The assertion that rating agencies could improve the quality of their analysis is certainly true, although there would undoubtedly be a cost to this.

Knowing what challenges a business faces, how well it is likely to manage them and what the possible outcomes are likely to be, together with the associated probabilities, is important. This requires a more forensic approach than currently adopted. Clearly, modeling is an important element in a more detailed forensic analysis, although the rating agencies are at a very early stage of development in this area. However, they are increasingly moving towards an enterprise-wide risk management (ERM) assessment, which requires a detailed understanding of risks and their interrelationships. In the future, it is unlikely that a bank will be awarded a triple-A rating without having an enterprise-wide risk management system that is fully integrated and used by management at all levels (including the board of directors) as part of the decision-making process.

At the moment, a rating is determined by the rating committee after the lead analyst has given a presentation of findings and conclusions, and these have been challenged by the rating committee. The final rating awarded is based upon comparative peer assessment. This methodology is recognized as being scientifically robust. However, it fails to fully meet the expectations of investors who want to know precisely what each rating category means and how this can be expressed in terms of the mathematical probability of failure.

It would be a major step forward if a clearly defined industry-wide standard were agreed for each rating grade. Given that the regulators are concerned about the quality and accuracy of ratings, the regulators may consider setting a deminimus regarding the contents of a risk rating report. This would assist in promoting a more forensic approach and thus drive forward knowledge and understanding. In our view, rather than simply having a single overall rating, it would be more informative to also have a number of subcategories. The subcategory ratings should limit the overall rating (i.e. a low rating in any subcategory would prevent a higher overall rating being awarded). The subcategories should be those strategic factors that determine competitive advantage (i.e. that indicate the long-term winners). At the moment, a rating simply indicates the probability of default. As a minimum, we would recommend the following subcategory ratings be considered:

- **reputation** (including corporate governance, culture, ethics, and customer centricity);
- **financial stability and robustness** (including capital adequacy, the quality and stability of earnings, volatility, liquidity, and sovereign support);
- **risk management**; and
- **transparency**.

The introduction of such subcategory ratings would support the actions of long-term institutional investors in their drive to have enhanced analytical factors properly recognized and assessed. In essence, "what gets measured gets managed."

15.6   INSURANCE COMPANIES

It was originally thought that insurance companies could contribute considerably to the management of risk within banks. However, this potential has yet to be fully realized. Consequently, regulatory and governmental initiatives and support may be required.

The need to adopt a "more forensic approach" is well understood by the insurance industry, given its traditional detailed peril specific approach to the assessment of risk. Indeed, the insurance industry has considerable knowledge of risk management, supported by a significant amount of claims data extending back over many years.

It has been suggested that the management of risk in banks could potentially be enhanced by the use of insurance, since an insurer would expect to see the existence of adequate controls and would continuously monitor the situation. In addition, a number of the leading insurers themselves are well advanced in the introduction of enterprise-wide risk management, so these practices could be expected to traverse into the banking industry. However, despite the efforts of a small number of leading insurers and reinsurers in developing new products, the take-up from the banking sector has been somewhat muted. It would clearly be preferable for insurance companies to be positively involved, as this would support the activities of the regulators in overseeing the banking system. However, to-date regulatory support for insurance has been cautious.

Insurance can be regarded as a means of pooling resources with the intention of achieving balance within the portfolio and thus assisting in improving stability within the system as a whole. For an individual bank, insurance allows losses to be written-off over a long period, thus smoothing earnings and preventing sudden shocks abhorred by the market. The primarily regulatory and governmental concern is the prevention of extreme losses that pose a systemic risk, thus threatening the stability of the financial system. Extreme risks can be regarded as events that may occur very infrequently and are effectively outside the control of management. Thus, whilst a poorly managed bank should be allowed to fail, it is questionable whether an otherwise excellent firm should be allowed to fail when an extreme loss event is likely to be a matter of pure chance. Given the potential size of these losses in comparison to existing insurance capacity, regulatory and governmental support may prove essential. Central banks could consider underwriting those insurance firms offering extreme risk cover. Alternatively, a central clearing-house could be established. The issue of catastrophe bonds could be considered where this central body is acting as a guarantor or lender/insurer of last resort, depending upon the type of structure adopted. Banks would then be able to decide upon the level of protection they want, thus encouraging them to properly evaluate their risk profile and risk appetite. Knowing where risks lie and the size of those risks would assist in improving liquidity and transparency.

15.7   BANKS

Banking will remain fiercely competitive with rationalization continuing to take place. Ultimately, the winners will be those responsive banks with a sound reputation who are able to attract and retain customers. Fundamentally, the key factors that will determine which banks become long-term winners will include:

- *reputation;*
- *financial stability and robustness;*
- *risk management; and*
- *transparency.*

Rationalization is resulting in banks growing ever larger. However, there is little or no evidence of support for infinite economies of scale. Indeed, there have been calls for the break-up of Citigroup. The optimum size of a bank is governed by many factors, although it is primarily dependent upon the ability of the directors and senior management. Growth through acquisition is often based more upon the personal ambitions of senior executives rather than on the commercial realities of competitive advantage. Since investors require the ability to diversify their portfolios and reward or punish management performance as appropriate, a larger number of competing banks may be preferable to a small number of very large and powerful banks that potentially have oligopolistic powers. However, market forces may be distorted to some extent by the actions of regulators and politicians who now regard many banks as being "too big to allow to fail." Currently, as a result of the credit crunch, weak and vulnerable banks are being encouraged to merge with more robust banks.

15.7.1   Reputation

Reputational damage can have a major impact upon a bank's ability to retain and attract customers, affecting its earnings capability and hence its credit rating. Reputation once lost can be virtually impossible to restore. Reputational risk is therefore a serious consideration for all banks; consequently, some have started to actively manage reputational risk and, indeed, a few are attempting to quantify it.

Reputational risk is present in many guises and relates to customers, shareholders, regulators, and employees.

- **Customers**. Customers' perceptions of banking have changed considerably over the last three decades due in part to ongoing globalization and rationalization. In the UK, following the "big bang" in 1986 which resulted in a freeing of the financial markets, banks have moved from being regarded as pillars of society, providing advice and assistance over a client's lifetime, to a situation where they are now considered by many as somewhat unscrupulous and dangerous, self-interested, money-making machines, lacking customer empathy. Whilst these two views may be regarded as polar extremes, there is no doubt that there is a growing lack of confidence in the banking system. The possibility of a run on a bank has therefore increased, as seen with Northern Rock. Whilst government actions (such as increasing the depositor protection limit), can have some benefits, ultimately the answer lies with the banks themselves, both individually and collectively.
- **Shareholders**. From a shareholder perspective, reputation is influenced by the ability to achieve performance and growth targets, consistently, with no shocks. A credible and sustainable business strategy is essential. In the case of long-term institutional investors, factors such as ethics, corporate governance and other enhanced analytical factors affecting long-term future performance, are becoming increasingly important.
- **Regulators**. The reputation of a bank can be adversely affected by regulatory intervention. Pillar 2 of the new Basel Accord allows regulators to increase the risk capital requirement of a bank where, in effect, the level of risk management is considered inadequate. Clearly, such intervention will send a negative signal to the market. Similarly, compliance failures and fines adversely affect a bank's reputation. Put simply, regulatory intervention impacts upon the earnings capability of banks and is therefore to be minimized.
- **Employees**. High profile losses resulting from acts of fraud and unauthorized trading activities serve to damage the reputation of a bank. There are numerous examples of such events, including Barings – probably the most well known – and SocGen – one of the most recent. Because of the danger of reputational damage, many frauds are thought to go undisclosed by the banks affected.

  Another area of concern is the relatively high level of salaries and bonuses paid to deal-makers and senior executives in the banking and financial services sector. Indeed, there has been considerable criticism of what are often referred to as excessive rewards, which encourage recklessness. As a result, there have been suggestions of regulatory intervention and even of bonuses being repaid where a firm subsequently gets into difficulties (as with the recent credit crunch). However, it has been argued that enforcing salary and bonus restrictions is difficult in a global industry, where an individual is free to simply move from one firm to another and from one country to another. This has been shown to be true in practice where an individual firm embarked upon unilateral action to restrict remuneration. However, it is unlikely that in the future proactive institutional shareholders will simply turn a blind eye. A more focused performance-related pay structure is likely to be demanded, which also takes account of the contribution to longer-term enhanced analytical factors. Fundamentally, rewards for efforts will need to be more overt and transparent.

15.7.2   Financial stability and robustness

Confidence in the financial system is dependent upon financial stability and robustness. The credit crunch clearly demonstrated the need for governmental and regulatory intervention in times of stress. However, for an individual bank, the need for support is likely to be taken as a sign of weakness by the market and thus its survival may be threatened. Whilst Basel II has given the impression that financial stability and robustness are primarily concerned with capital adequacy, there are in fact a number of other issues that need to be taken into consideration, including earnings capability, volatility, and liquidity.

- **Capital**. Whilst capital is important in dealing with short-term unexpected losses, it is not a panacea. Underutilized excess capital causes underperformance and can lead to the potential risk of takeover. Consequently, regulatory capital should be minimized.
- **Earnings**. In the longer term, earnings capability is more important than capital. Whilst capital will gradually be eroded by losses, a bank with strong earnings can replenish its capital reserves, earning its way out of trouble and funding its growth and expansion.
- **Volatility**. Volatility of earnings can also create liquidity problems. Clearly, a bank should not enter markets or deal in products it does not understand; the recent credit crunch serves as a warning against complacency. In addition, a bank must manage its operational risks efficiently and effectively, since unexpected losses can impact upon the quality and stability of earnings and thus affect liquidity.
- **Liquidity**. Liquidity relates not only to assets, liabilities, and cashflow but also includes liquidity arrangements with other institutions (both short term and longer term) and the robustness of those arrangements in times of stress.

15.7.3   Risk management

Risk management affects shareholder value in two ways:

1. defensively: through preventing or mitigating losses;
2. offensively: through gaining competitive advantage.

Enterprise-wide risk management (ERM)

The fundamental idea of adopting a more forensic approach is to better understand and assess the risks faced – i.e. what those risks are, where they lie, their interactive relationships and their underlying causality. By knowing cause, management can take action to prevent or mitigate risk.

Risk management is becoming increasingly recognized as a key factor in the assessment of banks. There is growing awareness that enterprise-wide risk management enables an organization to more precisely tailor its risk appetite and risk profile. Consequently, the rating agencies are placing greater emphasis on ERM. As stated previously, in the future it is unlikely that any bank will be awarded a triple-A rating without having adopted an enterprise-wide risk management approach.

Competitive advantage

Whilst regulatory requirements are of catalytic importance, the primary driving force is competitive advantage. Informed risk-taking enables a bank to improve its responsiveness and flexibility and thus adopt a more aggressive stance. Risk management facilitates innovation and improvement, enabling a bank to gain competitive advantage.

Best practice

Despite the lack of standardization with regard to "best practice," a gradual rationalization of approaches is taking place. However, it should be recognized that many banks do not have a fully articulated comprehensive AMA framework and, indeed, such a sophisticated approach may only prove practical for a relatively small number of major banks. "Best practice" will, therefore, continue to be determined by what is appropriate, given the organization's size, sophistication, and stage of development.

Failure to properly manage operational risk can result in a misstatement of an organization's risk profile and potentially expose it to significant losses. Therefore, sound practice principles require the board of directors to regularly review a bank's operational risk framework and compare it to industry "best practice." However, "best practice" is still emerging within the banking industry, with there being a range of views existing. The "use test," as stipulated by the new Basel Accord, requires the operational risk framework to integrate the operational risk measurement system into the bank's day-to-day risk-management processes. Consequently, best practice can be regarded as that which is most appropriate (cf. complexity and contingency theories).

Quantification and modeling

In the light of Basel II, significant effort has been devoted to the development and integration of qualitative and quantitative risk-management techniques. It is now generally accepted that, given the complexity of risk assessment, an approach based upon multiple lenses of perception is necessary. This requires consideration of the past (historical data), present (key indicators), and future (scenarios).

Whilst historical data may not be perfect it provides a sound base upon which to build. Data is reality; the alternative to data is guesswork. Even predictions developed through scenario analysis need to be soundly based. Quantification and modeling are essential (although not sufficient in themselves). The fundamental strength of modeling is derived from structured consideration of alternatives, which promotes reasoned discussion. As such, it represents an important element in both the analysis and assessment of risk. Unfortunately, in many banks quantification and modeling remain poorly understood by management.

The Basel II requirement, which specifies a confidence level of 99.9 % for operational risk capital adequacy models, is unrealistic. The loss distribution models being used are unstable at this level and no greater insight is achieved by specifying a very high confidence level. Therefore, we believe this requirement should be reconsidered. In our view, development of appropriate models is the responsibility of banks, with senior management being responsible for ensuring the assumptions upon which models are based remain appropriate as business and economic conditions change. It is the responsibility of the regulators to assess the extent to which these models are used by management (i.e. do they actually meet the "use test").

Transparency

The level of transparency effectively indicates a bank's degree of cultural honesty. Internationally, it enables countries with good governance to attract funding at lower rates than would otherwise be available and thus it facilitates economic development. Similarly, individual organizations that are recognized as being ethically sound, with good corporate governance, can expect to gain competitive advantage through their shares trading at a premium.

The importance of transparency is well understood. However, there has been considerable criticism of banks due to their lack of openness and their deliberate attempts to disguise activities through the use of off-balance-sheet activities and the creation of special purpose vehicles. Analysts and institutional investors are unlikely to readily accept such practices in the future. Indeed, given the increasing complexity and length of financial statements, the International Accounting Standards Board (IASB) is taking action to improve consistency and the level of transparency.

Where transparency becomes opaque the market will react adversely since default becomes more difficult to predict. Transparency, therefore, requires adoption of a more forensic approach, encompassing risk management. A number of leading institutional investors are now taking a longer-term perspective and are actively considering enhanced analytical risk factors, with a view to gaining a better understanding of a firm's overall risk profile and increasing market awareness.

In summary, the long-term winners are likely to be those banks that gain competitive advantage and increase shareholder value by increasing responsiveness through adoption of a more forensic risk-based approach, together with improving transparency and thereby enhancing their reputation.

ENDNOTES

[1] In its simplest form the credit crisis can be said to have resulted from the original providers of mortgages failing to properly evaluate the creditworthiness of mortgagee borrowers (i.e. negligence on the part of the lender). And failure by the institutional buyers of these securitized assets to carry out adequate due diligence – caveat emptor.

[2] Davies, H. and Green, D. (2008). *Global Financial Regulation: The Essential Guide*. NY: John Wiley & Sons Inc.

[3] Financial Reporting Council, Guidance on Audit Committees (The Smith Guidance), October 2005. http://www.frc.org.uk/documents/pagemanager/frc/Smith%20Report%202005.pdf.

[4] All members of the audit committee should be independent non-executive directors. See Note 2 above.

[5] Further information is available on the IASB website (www.IASB.org).

Part II
Quantification

16
Introduction to Quantification

The adoption of a "more forensic approach" to operational risk management will necessarily involve the application of quantification techniques in order to increase understanding. However, quantification is limited by the quality and quantity of data, the appropriateness of the models used together with the underlying assumptions made, and the ability of management to properly interpret the results derived. Given the dynamic nature of the banking and financial services sector, it is unlikely that any one model will prove adequate on its own.

Traditional actuarial techniques provide a sound starting point, since they are based on real data. Whilst they can be used to give an indication of the level of capital required (at a given confidence level), they will not tell you when, where, or why the next loss will occur, nor what size it will be.

To manage risk it is necessary to know the underlying causal factors. Hence, managers are primarily interested in event-cause-effect relationships. Bayesian Belief Networks (BBNs) offer the opportunity to explore interrelationships and related probabilities. However, BBNs can become complex, and any results obtained may prove difficult to reproduce.

Scenario analysis is an attempt to overcome the primary limiting factor of historical data, its essential backward-looking feature. But identifying future possible business environments and the related performance outcome for any particular bank is difficult in a dynamic environment, becoming more so as time increases.

Primarily, the board of directors is interested in ensuring the organization achieves its aims and objectives, which are expressed quantitatively in budgets and corporate plans. It is here that dynamic financial analysis (DFA) can prove useful. However, DFA models can become overly complex and may fail to accurately represent the real world, particularly in times of stress.

Unfortunately, we are witnesses to many examples of banks using mathematical tools incorrectly. However, while it is recognized that the mathematics is sound, weakness resides with the user.

The questions you are probably hoping will be answered in this quantification section are:

- What models are available to choose from, and how is one to choose between them?
- How can one determine whether the model is well matched to the data, and how well matched?
- How can one check that the data is reliable, and the assumptions necessary for choosing the model hold?
- How are the actual problems experienced by the firm being met by loss data analysis?
- How can the regulators and senior management be confident that the models being used are giving the right answers, and under what conditions will they stop giving the right answers?

Loss data approaches to quantification cannot completely answer these questions. The objective of this methodology is to aid decision makers and decision making. At best it will make the user more sensitive to data and what it can tell us.

16.1 OBJECTIVES

This introduction to quantification aims to give the reader an understanding of the statistical methods involved in a "more forensic approach," and a broad background to the very sophisticated analytics that are being used, while keeping the mathematics at a basic level. Some of the more technical and alternative methodologies that are not open to easy application are given only brief explanatory accounts, sufficient to allow at least a small insight into this more difficult material. References are included to those areas where a more in-depth understanding may be found.

To sum up, this is an accessible, short, illustrated introduction to the statistical modeling of small samples of data such as will be collected as operational losses. Methodologies applicable to the analysis of this data will be described. The authors also hope that this book will provide the reader with a useful reference source on relevant elementary probability and statistical theory.

Special attention is given to developing and understanding of statistics, particularly to sampling fluctuations in small data sets. This is important in that the theoretical underpinning of the mathematical theory for extremes used in finance is based on asymptotics as the sample size grows infinitely large. This would require a great stream of data, when in practice operational loss data is often scarce. From a statistician's point of view, if we have only a small data set, simulating large amounts of data does not turn it into a large data set. We must look to the data we have. This data limitation has direct consequences on the accuracy of results derived from it.

16.2 MEASURING THE UNMEASURABLE

Operational risk (OR) had no name other than "unmeasurable risk" before a working group of the international banking regulators – the Basel Committee on Banking Supervision (BCBS) of the Bank of International Settlement (BIS) which meets in Basel, Switzerland – turned its attention to it after (supposedly) "solving" the problems of credit and market risks. Indeed operational risk was defined at that time as the "losses from business activity other than market risk (price variability) and credit risk (non-payment)."

In 1995, Barings, a well-respected City of London merchant bank with a proud history, collapsed from losses made by a single rogue dealer stationed in Singapore. Its assets were held in the Cayman Islands, and the Bank of England declined to bail it out. The shock of this bank failure, together with major financial institutions elsewhere in the world going under from disasterous losses, led to proposed regulations from Basel aimed at preventing systemic failure in international banking from operational risk. Can we put the global financial meltdown of October 2008 down to systemic failure from credit risk and market risk rather than operational risk? The Basel II framework occasioned a closer look at how operational risk capital might be calculated, and how OR should be managed. The proposals were to require that major banks operating across international borders prepare to use advanced measurement approaches (AMA) for operational risk. The banks were to collect operational risk loss data, and use statistical methodologies to model the data, and then use their acquired knowledge in their OR management. How was this expected to be done when there were no generally agreed mechanisms for putting these regulations into practice?

The models were to be used to supply the size of a loss that would be expected to occur "no more frequently than once in a thousand years." As an aside, we might ask how it can be sound business practice to expend risk capital on scenarios involving one in a thousand year events that spell ruin, particularly when such a company-breaking event has not been experienced by the institution asked to carry out the exercise. Unreasonable, many would say.

> How can it be sound business practice to expend risk capital on scenarios involving one in a thousand year events that spell ruin, particularly when such a company-breaking event has not been experienced?

Nevertheless, it is now widely accepted that it makes sense to collect and use data on OR losses in the management of OR, and that it has a useful role in assisting decisions on economic capital allocation, if not on averting extremely unlikely catastrophic failure.

16.3   LOSS DATA ANALYSIS: REGULATORY REQUIREMENTS UNDER BASEL II

The Basel II framework (BCBS 2006, pp. 140–151) gives an outline of three methods, in increasing complexity and risk sensitivity, for calculating OR capital charges. These are the Basic Indicator Approach (BIA), the Standardized Approach (TSA), which also has an Alternative Standardized Approach (ASA), and the Advanced Measurement Approaches (AMA). We summarize these as follows.

16.3.1   Basic Indicator Approach

The OR capital requirement is a fixed proportion α of the positive annual gross income averaged over three years. Negative income is treated as zero. The proportion α, currently 15%, will be set by the regulator.

16.3.2   The Standardized Approach

This splits the bank's activities into eight business lines (BLs). For each BL there will be an assigned capital factor (CF) β based on gross income (GI) for that BL. The βs will depend on the risk exposures from the corresponding BL. The total capital charge is the average over three years ($i = 1, 2, 3$) of the sum of products of GI and β.

$$K_{\text{TSA}} = \frac{1}{3} \sum_{i=1}^{3} \left\{ \sum_{j=1}^{8} (\text{GI})_{ij}\, \beta_{ij} \right\}$$

The Alternative Standardized Approach permits the BLs of retail banking and commercial banking to replace gross income with outstanding retail loans and advances multiplied by a fixed factor currently set at 3.5 %. It also allows the aggregation of the gross income of retail and commercial banking using the 15 % β, and aggregation of the gross income of the other six BLs using an 18 % β.

The use of the Standardized Approach further requires that the bank be actively involved in OR management with a sound risk-management system, and with the resources of control and audit to implement it with integrity.

16.3.3 Advanced Measurement Approaches

This comprises the requirements for the Standardized Approach to apply, with additional systems, audit and validation processes.

The bank must be able to show that it can identify potentially extremely serious loss events. Indeed, "a bank's risk measurement system must be sufficiently 'granular' to capture the major drivers of OR affecting the shape of the tail of the loss distribution." This is a direct quotation from BCBS (2006, para. 667(c)), and I venture to say that this requirement would be hard to comply with without very substantial quantities of data, and in the absence of a prescriptive methodology from the regulatory authorities. In particular, its OR measure must be at least as good as its internal ratings approach for credit risk which is based on a one-year holding period and a 99.9 % confidence level. The Basel Committee on Banking Supervision (2006) uses the phrase "confidence *interval*" which suggests it would be applied to both excess gain as well as excess loss, though this is clearly not what is meant. Extreme gains should in fact be a part of risk assessment – is the bank aware of any excess risk in achieving such a large profit? However AMA is concerned with loss data only, making no capital charge against profits.

> Extreme gains should also be part of risk assessment.

The Advanced Methodology Approaches allow internal measurement as well as pure loss-data analysis.

16.3.4 The Internal Measurement Approach (IMA)

The regulators require that the internally-generated standard for OR measurement must calculate the regulatory capital as the sum of *expected loss* (EL) and *unexpected loss* (UL) unless the bank can show that it is already making accurate calculations of EL. Here, EL is not the expected loss in its mathematical statistics meaning of the expectation of the severity distribution of loss, which will henceforth be written $E(L)$ or μ. It is used as a label for the upper limit of the size of loss that would be absorbed by net profit. The "expected loss" EL per transaction can easily be embedded in bank charges, so if a business unit handles 8000 transactions in a typical week, with weekly aggregate expected losses estimated at £88 000, then £11.00 per transaction would cover these. Unexpected losses are losses that might be expected to be covered by risk capital from reserves, part of the economic capital provision. The value to be set for UL is the maximum size of loss that would be characterized in this way as an unexpected loss. It might well be made to coincide with the 99.9 % confidence limit that is used for UL in the Loss Data Approach (LDA) to AMA. It is the rare but extreme stress losses in excess of UL that the institution must be most concerned with. These require core capital or hedging for cover.

The calculations use a grid of eight business lines and seven risk event types. For each of the 56 cells, the bank will provide an exposure indicator (EI), a probability of loss event (PE), and a loss-given-event (LGE). The capital charge is the sum over the cells of the product of these values times the assigned capital factor γ for the cell, averaged over three years of data:

$$K_{\text{IMA}} = \frac{1}{3} \sum_{i=1}^{3} \left\{ \sum_{j=1}^{8} \sum_{k=1}^{7} (\text{EI})_{ijk} \, (\text{PE})_{ijk} \, (\text{LGE})_{ijk} \, \gamma_{jk} \right\}$$

In providing these EI, PE, and LGE factors, it is recognized that correlations may mitigate risk, and banks may use their internally determined correlations provided that they can demonstrate that the systems are sound and take into account the uncertainty in correlation measurements (BCBS 2006, para. 669(d)). To keep correlation estimation robust with validated assumptions will demand very large amounts of data, not generally available in the one- or three-year window. Furthermore, the statistics of correlations arising in interpreting copulae, the probabilistic models, are not yet widely understood, with no guide as to which model to adopt.

> There is no clear indication currently as to which copula model is appropriate for any particular set of correlation data.

The measurement system must have elements that "include the use of internal data, relevant external data, scenario analysis and factors reflecting the business environment and internal control systems" (BCBS 2006, para. 669(e)). Scenario analysis is the use of expert opinions in conjunction with external data to evaluate exposure to high severity events.

In cases where the estimates of the 99.9 percentile would be unreliable for a heavy-tailed loss distribution with few observed losses, scenario analysis may play a more dominant role (BCBS 2006, para. 669(f)). This acknowledges the statistical problem of estimation in the absence of data, but the subjectivity in the use of external data and expert opinion creates unease in the minds of many statisticians.

> The subjectivity in using external data or expert opinion makes many statisticians uneasy.

16.3.5 Loss Distribution Approach (LDA)

This replaces the internal measures with the 99.9 % confidence limit UL. The capital charge is the sum over the cells of the product of UL with the assigned capital factor γ for the cell, averaged over three years of data.

$$K_{\text{LDA}} = \frac{1}{3} \sum_{i=1}^{3} \left\{ \sum_{j=1}^{8} \sum_{k=1}^{7} (\text{UL})_{ijk}\, \gamma_{jk} \right\}$$

16.4 WHAT COMES NEXT?

The 99.9 % level mimics the Value-at-Risk (VaR) provisions for market and credit risk. This uses quantile measures such as medians and percentiles, but the provisions that require modeling will also require moment measures such as mean, variance, skewness, and kurtosis. These are introduced in the next chapters. After that, statistical theory and methods are given which show how we approach data analysis. Then, following a wide-ranging compilation of probability models, we are ready to meet the description of risk and its measurement.

17

Loss Data

17.1 DATA CLASSIFICATION

Any statistical study begins with the selection of variables to observe and their measurement scales. Data may be quantitative or qualitative. Quantitative data is of two sorts. *Discrete* data (e.g. 1,25,99) gives frequency counts, such as the number of losses in a particular category that exceed a certain threshold on a business day. *Continuous* data gives values over an interval, such as random values between zero and one, as are used in simulating severity data. Severity data itself is of course rounded if only to the smallest unit used, but for modeling we presume that they can be measured to an infinitessimal precision. The other sort of data is *qualitative*. This gives an attribute or quality, generally coded to create a scale. These scales are of three sorts. The data may be *binary* coding 1 and 0, for yes or no, for exceeding a certain threshold or not, for being an insurable loss or not, etc. The data may be *nominal*, the codes having no natural ordering, being just labels of categories. The third sort is *ordinal*, where the data has a natural grade ordering, such as measuring loss severity on a scale of 1–5.

An operational risk database would typically show high impact events (having low frequency) among events of high frequency (having low impact). The database will also need to incorporate the Basel II AMA classification of business line/event type. Each of these BL/ET cells will need a loss threshold of OR classification below which the loss can avoid entry into the database. Each loss surviving this preprocessing will need its "where," "why," and "when." Was there a potential severe loss lurking behind the recorded loss? Was there any recovery of funds to be associated with the loss event?

17.2 DATABASE CREATION

Measuring OR begins with thorough database modeling. Events should carry details of their losses, the business activity responsible for the losses, and other risk indicators. For sound risk management the database should importantly also include near losses.

It is important that a database also includes near losses.

The creation and management of the database is key to understanding the control environment. In investment banking most losses will be from processing a high volume of transactions, and will show up as interest payments to counterparts, fees, and fines paid to exchanges, etc. Retail banks will be exposed to frauds, legal and liability problems and small claims arising from processing errors. The database should allow separate analysis for each business unit (BU) and for each potential loss-making activity. Clearly, one single model will not fit all. Aggregating losses over BUs and activities would have the potential of concealing low impact risks behind the more dramatic. "Bottom up" is thus essential to gaining an understanding of the risk environment. Aggregation at each higher level will inform management throughout the enterprise.

17.2.1 Database modeling

Operational loss databases are not generally made publicly available for reasons of business confidentiality, and OR management must rely on internal loss events and internal key risk indicators. Empowerment – giving greater authority at lower management levels within the firm – increases operational risk by fragmenting decisions, despite the obvious benefit of OR awareness throughout the firm.

There are databanks which hold anonymous but verified loss scenarios that regulators demand are used to supplement internal data in calculating capital requirements when following the Advanced Measurement Approach (AMA) set out in the Basel Accord.

Database creation involves splitting the organization into business units and operational risk categories. The Basel II guidelines suggest how this is to be done and mandate it under the AMA. For each business unit and each category the OR staff should obtain loss data, data on unrealized losses, and subjective values from questionnaires. Operational risk measurement should be at the lowest level, aggregating for higher levels.

Aggregating losses (over BUs and activities) has the potential to conceal low impact risks behind the more dramatic larger events. Thus a "bottom-up" approach is essential.

17.3 USE OF QUESTIONNAIRES

A common problem will be the absence of an historical database covering the risks under study. It may be impossible to retrieve past data for many business units, so the mechanisms for pricing the risk will not function until the collection has been going on for some time. Even with an up and running database, there may be little or no appropriate data associated with particular business units and OR risks. The use of questionnaires to establish expert opinion has been shown to provide good estimates. It is important that the responses one will potentially require are built in at the time that the questionnaire is being designed.

Cruz (2000) designed a questionnaire to derive an economic capital figure for those business units unable to provide operational loss data. It used the following headings:

- current budget of the BU;
- activities of the BU, and their percentage contributions to the total revenues;
- the percentage attributable to OR management;
- at each size on a given scale, the level of manager to whom errors and failures are reported;
- for a given list of errors, the financial cost for the current and previous year;
- rank the activities in order of risk.

The questionnaire also asks that for each activity and risk category, give the maximum impact of a single event, and the expected loss over the next 12 months (transaction risk, operational control risk, regulatory and legal risk, system risk, people risk).

17.4 ILLUSTRATIVE EXAMPLES OF DATA SETS

These data sets will be used later to demonstrate the quantitative methods. The first three data sets show frequency data, the latter two show severity data. Each data set is followed with a display of its summary statistics.

The statistics are:

- sample size n
- sample mean $\bar{x}$
- sample variance s^2
- sample standard deviation s
- sample coefficient of skewness $\hat{\beta}_1$
- sample coefficient of kurtosis $\hat{\beta}_2$
- sample first quartile Q1
- sample median x_{med}
- sample third quartile Q3

The interpretation and calculation of these statistics are shown in the subsequent sections, though brief notes comparing the data sets with Poisson distribution data for the counting (frequency) data and with normal distribution data for the continuous (severity) data sets are here given. The mean and variance of the Poisson distribution take the same value so we should expect the sample values $\bar{x}$ and s^2 to be similar. The normal distribution is symmetric about its central value which is both its mean and median so the sample values $\bar{x}$ and x_{med} should be close and the sample skewness $\hat{\beta}_1$ should be fairly close to zero. Since the kurtosis for the normal distribution is 3 we might also expect that $\hat{\beta}_2$ is fairly close to that, but there is quite large statistical variability to be expected in this kurtosis estimation.

17.4.1   Discrete data: data 1

Table 17.1 shows frauds in a commercial bank counted on 33 consecutive business days over seven weeks (Cruz 2002, p. 89).

We see that $\bar{x}$ and s^2 are so very different that we can say without reference to statistical tables that the data are not Poisson.

Table 17.1   Data 1 with summary statistics.

Week	M	Tu	W	Th	F	Total
1		4	1	6	9	20
2	9	10	2	4	8	33
3	2	3	0	1	–	6
4	2	3	1	3	4	13
5	5	4	4	4	9	26
6	5	4	3	11	8	31
7	12	3	10	0	7	32
Total	35	31	21	29	45	161

n	$\bar{x}$	s^2	s	$\hat{\beta}_1$	$\hat{\beta}_2$	Q1	x_{med}	Q3
33	4.879	11.172	3.342	0.552	2.131	2.5	4	8

Table 17.2 Data 2 with summary statistics.

Frauds	0	1	2	3	4	5	6	7	8	9	10	11	12	13	14	15	≥ 16	Total
Freq.	221	188	525	112	73	72	44	40	14	7	2	2	4	3	2	1	0	1310

n	$\bar{x}$	s^2	s	$\hat{\beta}_1$	$\hat{\beta}_2$	Q1	x_{med}	Q3
1310	2.379	4.581	2.140	1.804	7.899	1	2	3

Table 17.3 Data 3 with summary statistics, reproduced by permission of Risk Books.

1,372,513.09	91,852.83	42,313.46	23,309.66	18,671.75	17,358.62	11,938.22	7,247.95
264,444.24	50,529.47	38,502.77	23,294.31	18,460.19	16,919.05	11,901.87	5,447.41
233,378.31	48,967.00	35,778.97	21,276.85	17,690.14	14,735.85	11,195.92	3,265.99
159,662.66	46,900.45	29,885.15	20,316.38	17,595.19	14,524.10	9,529.86	553.66
118,229.12	43,043.83	27,697.06	18,995.36	17,373.52	13,641.50	8,808.65	

n	$\bar{x}$	s^2	s	$\hat{\beta}_1$	$\hat{\beta}_2$	Q1	x_{med}	Q3
39	75.583	48797.648	220.902	5.338	31.293	13.642	18.995	43.044

17.4.2 Discrete data: data 2

Table 17.2 shows the daily frequencies for 3117 frauds over 1310 days at a large retail bank (Cruz 2002 p. 94).

17.4.3 Severity data: data 3

Table 17.3 shows data for 39 legal losses, interest claims at a trading desk, each in excess of $500, given here in size order (Cruz 2003, p. 113). The summary statistics treat the data in units of $1000.

17.4.4 Severity data: data 4

Table 17.4 gives losses from legal events (Cruz 2002, p. 57) in units of $1000, here shown in size order and rounded to the nearest $1000. The summary statistics are given firstly for the

Table 17.4 Data 4 with summary statistics.

3822	907	735	556	423	395	302	260	248	220	204	193	180	160	150
2568	845	660	550	417	360	297	255	239	220	202	191	176	157	147
1416	800	650	506	410	350	295	252	232	220	200	186	176	154	146
1299	750	630	484	406	350	275	251	230	215	200	185	165	151	143
917	743	600	426	400	332	270	250	229	211	194	182	165	151	143

n	$\bar{x}$	s^2	s	$\hat{\beta}_1$	$\hat{\beta}_2$	Q1	x_{med}	Q3
75	439.726	289,879	538.404	4.303	24.633	187.5	252.0	500.4
75	439.733	289,877	538.403	4.303	24.634	187.25	252	500.5

Table 17.5   Data 5 with summary statistics.

1992	1993	1994	1995	1996
907,077.00	1,100,000.00	6,600,000.00	600,000.34	1,820,000.00
845,000.00	650,000.00	3,950,000.00	394,672.11	750,000.00
734,900.00	556,000.00	1,300,000.00	260,000.00	426,000.00
550,000.00	214,634.95	410,060.72	248,341.96	423,319.62
406,001.47	200,000.00	350,000.00	239,102.93	332,000.00
360,000.00	160,000.00	200,000.00	165,000.00	294,835.23
360,000.00	157,083.00	176,000.00	120,000.00	230,000.00
350,000.00	120,000.00	129,754.00	116,000.00	229,368.50
220,357.00	78,375.00	109,543.00	86,878.46	210,536.56
182,435.32	52,048.50	107,031.00	83,613.70	128,412.00
68,000.00	51,908.05	107,000.00	75,177.00	122,650.00
50,000.00	47,500.00	64,600.00	52,700.00	89,540.00

Year	n	$\bar{x}$	s^2	s	$\hat{\beta}_1$	$\hat{\beta}_2$	Q1	x_{med}	Q3
1992	12	419.48	82,120.20	286.57	0.428	1.863	191.9	360.0	688.7
1993	12	282.13	104,619.4	323.45	1.511	4.012	58.5	158.5	470.7
1994	12	1125.33	4,188,508	2046.58	1.896	5.024	108	188	1078
1995	12	203.46	25,774.6	160.54	1.307	3.745	84.4	142.5	257.1
1996	12	421.39	226,481.3	475.9	2.241	6.860	149	262	425

actual data and secondly for the same data rounded to the nearest $1000. We see that there are absolutely no grounds for believing that the rounding will in any way affect the quality of any statistical decisions reached.

17.4.5   Severity data: data 5

Table 17.5 shows the losses from fraud at a large UK retail bank (Cruz 2002, p. 69). Every month throughout each of the five years, the largest loss in that month is recorded. The table shows, for each year separately, the 12 values in order of size. In preparing the summary table the losses were rounded to the nearest pound with the results displayed in units of £1000.

17.5   SUMMARIZING DATA SETS WITH A PROPORTION PLOT OR HISTOGRAM PLOT

17.5.1   Discrete data

Frequency data can be displayed as a proportion plot or as a sample distribution function plot (Figure 17.1). The proportion plot is a bar chart with the frequencies scaled to proportions, representing estimates of probabilities. The sample distribution function plot gives the cumulative proportions and represents an estimate of the cumulative distribution function (cdf), the function giving the probability (y-axis) that an observation will take a value not greater than point x on the x-axis.

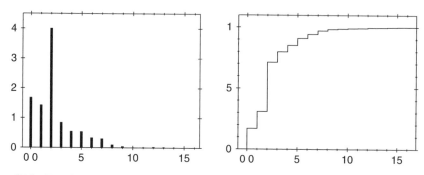

Figure 17.1   Bar chart and sample cdf for Data 2.

17.5.2   Severity data

Severity data can be displayed as a histogram and a sample distribution function plot. The boxplot is shown later as a summary in terms of quantiles.

Histogram plot

The histogram summarizes the data when sorted into bins. It gives the proportion of observations per unit of x-axis. It is *not* a plot of frequency, and the bins do not need to be constructed to have the same width. We plot $y = \dfrac{\text{proportion in bin at } x}{\text{width of bin at } x}$ against x. This scaling of the y-axis is so that the area under the plotted histogram estimates probability. The total area is one.

For Data 4 (Section 17.4.4) the histogram on the left of Figure 17.2 shows the data to be very skewed to the right, with much of it concentrated in the first few bins. The right-hand histogram of the logs of the data values gives a more informative plot (shown base 10) through spreading out the bunched-up smaller values and bringing closer in the largest ones.

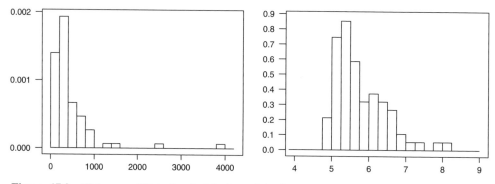

Figure 17.2   Histogram of Data 4 and of the logs of the data.

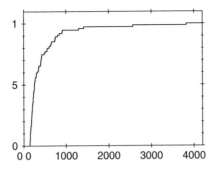

Figure 17.3   Sample cdf for Data 4.

Sample distribution function

This sample distribution function shows a jump of size $1/n$ at each of the n observations when in size order. There is no loss of information here in contrast with when data is grouped in creating a histogram (Figure 17.3).

17.6   SUMMARIZING DATA SETS WITH SAMPLE MOMENT STATISTICS

We look at statistics which provide data summaries. The statistics commonly used for this are the sample moments and sample quantiles. We review first the sample moments. The sample data is represented as a sequence of observations $x_1, x_2, \ldots, x_n$. If they are in size order, these are often written as $x_{(1)}, x_{(2)}, \ldots, x_{(n)}$. Since our interest lies mainly in the largest losses, we shall in the following take $x_{(1)}$ to be the largest value and $x_{(n)}$ to be the smallest. If the sample is of frequency data, it may already have been sorted, in which case we represent the frequency at value y as n_y.

In summarizing a data sample we are losing information, in particular the order in which the data was collected. We leave till later the important case in which changes over time of the loss process are the features of interest. Here we assume that the data was collected as a random sample, independently under identical conditions.

17.6.1   Sample moments

A statistical description of data by the first four sample moments, which indicate location, spread, skewness, and peakedness, is often used in the estimation of the parameters of a probability model we wish to fit from the data, assumed to be a random sample of size n consisting of the values $x_1, x_2, \ldots, x_n$. For a random sample the order of the data does not matter, so it does not matter if we use the size ordered data in the computations.

The statistical procedure – the *method of moments* – will be demonstrated at a later point, but it matches the sample moments to their corresponding population moments. Table 17.6 gives definitions for the population and sample moments. When the population distribution is represented by the random variable X, the population moments are written in terms of expectations of powers of X.

Table 17.6 Population and sample moments.

$\mu = E(X)$	$\mu'_k = E(X^k)$	$\mu_k = E\{(X - \mu)^k\}$
$= \displaystyle\sum_{\text{all } x} x p_x$	$= \displaystyle\sum_{\text{all } x} x^k p_x$	$= \displaystyle\sum_{\text{all } x}(x - \mu)^k p_x$
or $\displaystyle\int_{-\infty}^{\infty} x f(x)\,\mathrm{d}x$	or $\displaystyle\int_{-\infty}^{\infty} x^k f(x)\,\mathrm{d}x$	or $\displaystyle\int_{-\infty}^{\infty}(x - \mu)^k f(x)\,\mathrm{d}x$
$\bar{x} = \dfrac{1}{n}\displaystyle\sum_{i=1}^{n} x_i$	$m'_k = \dfrac{1}{n-1}\displaystyle\sum_{i=1}^{n} x_i^k$	$m_k = \dfrac{1}{n-1}\displaystyle\sum_{i=1}^{n}(x_i - \bar{x})^k$
$= \dfrac{1}{n} S'_1$	$= \dfrac{1}{n-1} S'_k$	$= \dfrac{1}{n-1} S_k$

In Table 17.6, the formulae using $p_x = P(X = x)$ are used for the frequency model, with the probability density function $f(x)$ used in the formula for severity modeling. The abbreviations $S'_k = \sum x_i^k$ and $S_k = \sum(x_i - \bar{x})^k$ simplify the formulae for the computations for sample moments.

Population moments

The kth population moment (about zero), $E(X^k)$, is the expectation of kth power of X and written μ'_k. The special case of the first moment, $E(X)$, is more usually written simply as μ. The kth population *central moment*, $E\{(X - \mu)^k\}$, is written as μ_k for $k = 2, 3, \ldots$. Obviously $\mu_1 = E(X - \mu)$ is zero, and μ_2 is the population variance σ^2. Similarly, m'_1 is just $\bar{x}$, the sample mean, and m_2 is just s^2, the sample variance. Since sums and integrals of the population moments may not converge, the population moments may not all exist. However the sample moments are built from finite sums of finite values, so they will always have finite values.

The first two population moments give measures μ of location and σ of scale. We use them to create a standardized random variable

$$Z = \frac{X - \mu}{\sigma}$$

which has expectation 0 and variance 1. We note that in some representations scale is shown as $1/\sigma$ or by σ^2. The third and fourth central moments of Z define the population coefficients of skewness and kurtosis, now independent of the location and scale.

- *Population coefficient of skewness* $\beta_1 = E(Z^3) = \dfrac{E\{(X - \mu)^3\}}{\sigma^3} = \dfrac{\mu_3}{\sigma^3}$

- *Population coefficient of kurtosis* $\beta_2 = E(Z^4) = \dfrac{E\{(X - \mu)^4\}}{\sigma^4} = \dfrac{\mu_4}{\sigma^4}$

- *Standardized scores z_i.*   The sample skewness and kurtosis are versions of the third and fourth central moments relocated to $\bar{x}$ and rescaled by factor s. These are generally expressed in terms of the sums of powers of the *standardized scores* z_i, where

$$z_i = \frac{x_i - \bar{x}}{s}.$$

Table 17.7 Computing formulae for moment measures.

Sample mean	$\bar{x}$	$=$	$\dfrac{1}{n}S_1'$
Sample variance	s^2	$=$	$\dfrac{1}{n-1}S_2$
		$=$	$\dfrac{1}{n-1}\{S_2' - (1/n)S_1'^2\}$
Sample coefficient of skewness	$\hat{\beta}_1$	$=$	$\dfrac{1}{n-1}\sum z_i^3$
		$=$	$\dfrac{1}{n-1}s^{\frac{1}{3}}\{S_3' - (3/n)S_2'\,S_1' + (2/n^2)S_1'^3\}$
Sample coefficient of kurtosis	$\hat{\beta}_2$	$=$	$\dfrac{1}{n-1}\sum z_i^4$
		$=$	$\dfrac{1}{n-1}\dfrac{1}{s^4}\{S_4' - (4/n)S_3'\,S_1' + (6/n^2)S_2'\,S_1'^2 - (3/n^3)S_1'^4\}$

That is to say, for $k = 3$ or more we have $\sum_i z_i^k = S_k/s^k$. Using the expansion of $S_k = \sum_i (x_i - \mu)^k$ in terms of $S_k' = \sum_i x_i^k$, we obtain the computing formulae shown in Table 17.7.

17.6.2 The sample mean $\bar{x}$

This tells us where the sample is centred. It is the data average, the centroid of the data set. It estimates the population mean μ, the centroid of the the population from which the data have been drawn.

17.6.3 The sample variance s^2

This measures the spread of the data about the sample mean $\bar{x}$, and is an unbiased and consistent estimator of the population variance σ^2, the spread of the population about the population mean μ. Unbiasedness avoids systematic error in application. Consistency indicates that, as the sample size increases to infinity, the sequence of estimations will approach the true value of the parameter being estimated.

The sample standard deviation is s, the square root of the sample variance. It is a biased estimator of the population standard deviation σ, but it is a consistent estimator. Its importance lies in that it is measured in the units of the data, rather than in squared units.

17.6.4 The sample coefficient of skewness $\hat{\beta}_1$

Data will often show skewness when it is only positive (or only negative) and close to zero. This is particularly true with loss data, with plenty of small and middling losses but with only a few large losses strung out. Positive skewness has the longer tail on the right, negative on the left.

From the tables of summary statistics every data set there shows positive skewness, and for the data sets representing loss data, with the exception of 1992 losses of Data 5 (Section 17.4.5) the skewness coefficient is significantly above zero.

We sometimes transform data by taking logarithms or square roots to reduce skewness, which may allow the use of statistical methods developed for symmetrically distributed data.

17.6.5   The sample coefficient of kurtosis $\hat{\beta}_2$

This measures the peakedness with values less than 3 showing a peak flatter, shoulders fatter and tails thinner when compared with the gaussian (normal) bell shaped probability density. Values greater than 3 are more peaked with thinner shoulders and thicker tails. We therefore often see the excess over the value 3 used as the measure of kurtosis.

- *Excess kurtosis*   This is $\hat{\beta}_2 - 3$.

With loss data, the flatness of the peak is generally not of major concern. For the data sets of Section 17.4, we see a wide variety of values for kurtosis.

17.6.6   The sample coefficient of correlation

This is a statistical measure of the linear relationship between two features measured on the same item. A simple example is that of height and weight. A more pertinent example might be the values of two key risk indicators within a business unit at the day's end. Within a portfolio of assets, we might wish to make pairwise comparisons of market price movements. A loss event scenario will have a number of associated measurements. Over a sequence of losses, pairwise relationships between these associated variables can be described through their correlation coefficients. Other applications might be a pairwise comparison over categories of business lines or event types, comparing their aggregate weekly frequencies of losses.

Example

The frequencies (x, y) of operational risk losses for two business lines shown over 15 weeks are given in the table below. The pattern of points in the scatter plot (Figure 17.4) indicates a positive correlation between the frequencies of losses in the two business lines.

x	19	15	35	52	35	33	30	57	49	26	45	39	25	40	40
y	12	15	15	33	25	21	25	32	28	15	22	22	19	18	28

Correlation is location-free and scale-free and measures the closeness to a straight line. *Uncorrelated* does not imply there is no dependence between the two variables, only that there is no straight line relationship. The *population correlation coefficient* is a measure of the strength of the linear relationship between the two variables.

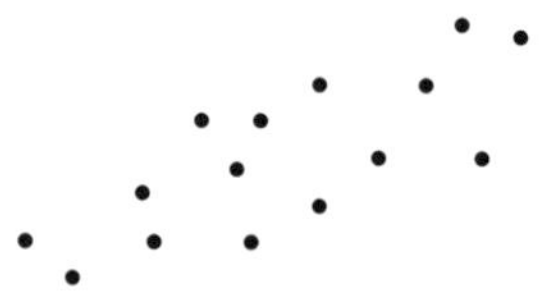

Figure 17.4   Scatter plot.

Population correlation coefficient

$$\rho = \mathrm{corr}(X, Y) = \frac{\mathrm{cov}(X, Y)}{\mathrm{sd}(X)\,\mathrm{sd}(Y)} = \frac{\sigma_{XY}}{\sigma_X\,\sigma_Y},$$

where σ_X and σ_Y are the population standard deviations of the marginal distributions of X and Y, the population random variables of the xs and ys treated separately.

Population covariance

$$\sigma_{XY} = \mathrm{cov}(X, Y) = E[\{X - E(X)\}\{Y - E(Y)\}] = E(XY) - \{E(X)\}\{E(Y)\}.$$

Sample covariance

$$s_{XY} = \sum_{i=1}^{n}(x_i - \bar{x})(y_i - \bar{y}) = \sum_{i=1}^{n} x_i\, y_i - \sum_{j=1}^{n} x_j \sum_{k=1}^{n} y_k$$

where $\bar{x}$ and $\bar{y}$ are the sample means of their corresponding samples.

Sample correlation

$$r = \frac{s_{XY}}{s_X\, s_Y},$$

where s_X and s_Y are the sample standard deviations of their corresponding samples.

The sample correlation is sensitive to outliers, those observations giving points which seem to be excessively far away from a natural straight line through the rest of the points.

17.6.7   Rank correlation statistics

For these statistics we consider the two sets of ranks of the data when ordered by their x-values and their y-values. When there are ties with more than one x or y taking equal values, we average the rankings. This complicates the statistical properties of the resulting scores.

Spearman's Rho

If each x_i is replaced by its rank x_i' and each y_i by its rank y_i', then Spearman's estimate r_S of ρ, the correlation coefficient, is just the value given by the sample correlation coefficient of these ranks. A useful computational reduction takes place if there are no ties. In this case,

$$r_S = 1 - \frac{6}{n^3 - n} \sum_{i=1}^{n} (x_i' - y_i')^2.$$

We see immediately that when the ranks match exactly the second term vanishes and $r_S = 1$.

Kendall's Tau

This measures monotonicity rather than correlation, but has the properties of correlation in that its value is zero for independence with values increasing to 1 with increasing monotonicity and decreasing to -1 for decreasing negative monotone values.

For any two pairs (x_i, y_i) and (x_j, y_j) let

$$t_{ij} = \text{sign}\{(x_i - x_j)(y_i - y_j)\} = \begin{cases} +1 & ((x_i - x_j)(y_i - y_j) > 0) \\ 0 & ((x_i - x_j)(y_i - y_j) = 0) \\ -1 & ((x_i - x_j)(y_i - y_j) < 0) \end{cases}$$

Kendall's tau is the average over every pair.

$$r_K = \binom{n}{2}^{-1} \sum_{i<j} t_{ij}.$$

17.7   SUMMARIZING DATA SETS WITH SAMPLE QUANTILE STATISTICS

17.7.1   The sample median and sample quartiles

Suppose that we have a data set consisting of n values in their size order, with the largest first. Then the *sample median* x_{med} is the value which has one half of the values smaller than it and one half larger.

The *sample first quartile* Q1 has one quarter of the values smaller and three quarters larger, the second quartile Q2 is just the sample median x_{med}, and the *sample third quartile* Q3 has three quarters smaller and one quarter larger.

The sample median is easily seen to be the middle value if n is odd, and if n is even will be just the average of the two middle values. But what about Q1 and Q3? One method is to take them to be the medians of their own halves of the data set. This is fine if n is even, but what should we do with the middle value if n is odd? Some take it to belong to both halves. A bigger problem is that the method collapses if we want to calculate for example deciles, which split the data into 10 subsets. This method will not be developed further.

Let us consider alternative methods for calculating quartiles that will carry over to any partition of the data.

Plotting points

The problem is that for continuous models $P(X < x)$ and $P(X \le x)$ are the same, since $P(X = x)$ is zero. With data the observed values which each has zero probability have actually occurred, at least when rounded to the number of significant digits recorded. The sample distribution function $\hat{F}(x)$ is the step function which is the proportion of observed values no larger than x. We have lots of choices for how to smooth out the steps.

- **Rule 1**. With n points, use the locations $\frac{3}{4}(n+1)$, $\frac{1}{2}(n+1)$ and $\frac{1}{4}(n+1)$ respectively for Q1, Q2 and Q3. Recall, the largest value comes first. Now these positions may not be integer. If so, we will need to interpolate between the pair of values on each side of the position in the correct proportions.

The generalization to plotting the 100α-percentile is to use the location $(1 - \alpha)(n + 1)$. With 50 points,

Percentile	0	10	25	50	60	75	95	100
Plotting point	51	45.9	38.25	25.5	20.4	12.75	2.55	0

- **Rule 2.** A minor problem with Rule 1 is that the spacing between the plotting points for adjacent values is the same as that at each end. The plotting points for the largest and the smallest values have only one neighbor, so the data is not treated equally. To get round this, this rule takes each value to be at the centre of its location, so we consider locations from $\frac{1}{2}$ to $n + \frac{1}{2}$, instead of from 0 to $n + 1$. The sample median is still at $(n + 1)/2$, but the location for Q1 is now at $\frac{1}{2} + \frac{3}{4}\{(n + \frac{1}{2}) - \frac{1}{2}\} = \frac{3}{4}n + \frac{1}{2}$, and Q3 is at $\frac{1}{4}n + \frac{1}{2}$.
  For the 100α-percentile we would use the location $(1 - \alpha)n + \frac{1}{2}$.
  This rule would be considered the (academically) better choice. However, Rule 1 is very widely used and taught, and was used in the summary statistics above. The differences are most prominent with small samples as will be seen in the following artificial data sets.
- **Rule 3.** Other rules have been proposed, in fact many of them. The following (Castillo 1988) has been proposed as appropriate for extremes. This puts the 100α-percentile in the location $0.32 + (1 - \alpha)(n + 0.12)$.

Examples of computations

(1) 120, 80, 52, 36, 32, 25, 24, 22, 21, 20, 18, 15, 10, 7
(2) 120, 80, 52, 36, 32, 25, 24,   21, 20, 18, 15, 10, 7
(3)   80, 52, 36, 32, 25, 24, 22, 21, 20, 18, 15, 10, 7

Example 2 differs from Example 1 only in that value 22 has been dropped, while in Example 3 the largest value has gone.
  Rule 1 applied to Example 1 gives the locations for Q1, Q2 and Q3 respectively as

$$\frac{3}{4} \times 15 = 11.25, \quad \frac{1}{2} \times 15 = 7.5, \quad \frac{1}{4} \times 15 = 3.75.$$

Interpolation between the values gives

$$Q1 = 18 - \frac{1}{4}(18 - 15) = 17.25, \quad Q2 = 24 - \frac{1}{2}(24 - 22) = 23,$$

$$Q3 = 52 - \frac{3}{4}(52 - 36) = 40.$$

Rule 2 gives the corresponding locations $(0.75)(14)+0.5 = 11$, 7.5, and $(0.25)(14)+0.5 = 4$. These give Q1 $= 18$, Q2 $= 23$ and Q3 $= 36$.
  These together with the quartile values for Examples 2 and 3 are shown in the table below.

	Example 1			Example 2			Example 3		
	Q1	Q2	Q3	Q1	Q2	Q3	Q1	Q2	Q3
Rule 1	17.25	23	40	16.5	24	44	16.5	22	34
Rule 2	18	23	36	17.25	24	40	17.25	22	40

In practice, with large data sets, the differences caused by various applications of interpolation will be of little importance. We must keep in mind that these are just descriptive statistics, not definitive measures on which decisions are reached.

The box plot

The *5-figure data summary*, x_{min}, Q1, Q2, Q3, x_{max}, is a useful set of numbers that adds the smallest and largest values to the set of sample quartiles. The box plot inserts two further values to give a graphical 7-figure data summary. The additional values are the upper and lower whiskers, which represent the "normal" range for data based on the sample interquartile range IQR = Q3 − Q1. The *lower whisker* LW is the smallest data value exceeding the *lower fence* Q1 − 1.5(IQR), and the *upper whisker* UW is largest data value smaller than the *upper fence* Q3 + 1.5(IQR). As the table below shows, in each of the three examples the lower fence is smaller than the minimum observation. This is a consequence of the data being skewed to the right. Data values outside the interval (LW, UW) are called outliers and shown individually in the plot.

For Examples 1, 2 and 3, the IQRs are 22.75, 27.5 and 17.5.

Sample	x_{min}	LF	LW	Q1	x_{med}	Q3	UW	UF	x_{max}
Example 1	7	−16.875	7	17.25	23	40	52	74.125	120
Example 2	7	−24.75	7	16.5	24	44	80	85.25	120
Example 3	7	−9.75	7	16.5	22	44	52	60.25	80

In the boxplot (Figure 17.5) the box runs from Q1 to Q3 with x_{med} shown by a line across the box. The median line being so far towards Q1 is a strong indication of positive skewness, with the data more stretched out towards the larger values. Further, we see that for Example 1 the values 80 and 120 are both outliers, while for Example 2 only value 120 is.

The sample moments are much more sensitive to tail values than the quantile measures, reflecting the fact that the latter ignore the tail values. This is demonstrated when we compare the statistics for Example 1 with those for the same data with the largest value 120 replaced

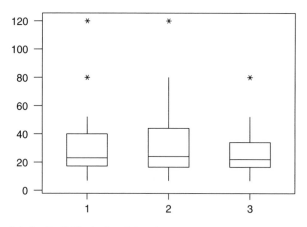

Figure 17.5   Boxplots for the 3 illustrative data sets.

by a value 420. The sample mean increases to 55.6 from 34.1. The sample standard deviation increases from 31.1 to 106.6. The sample quartiles are untouched.

This is not to say that that we cannot have robust moment measures for location and spread. The mechanism often adopted is to use a trimmed data set, excluding a fixed percentage of data points from each end of the ordered data. While this would reduce the variability in the moment measures, it would also remove the sensitivity to the data of the feature of most interest in operational risk, which just happens to be the tail containing the largest values.

17.7.2   Sample quantiles

Partitioning the data further, we have deciles – which split the data into tenths – and percentiles – which split them into hundreths. The general description is that of sample quantiles.

The *sample α-quantile* $\hat{Q}(\alpha)$ has proportion α of values smaller, and proportion $1 - \alpha$ larger. Under Rule 1 of Section 17.7.1, its location is in position $p = (1 - \alpha)(n + 1) = k + r$, where k is the integer part and r is the fractional part. Then

$$\hat{Q}(\alpha) = x_{(k)} - r(x_{(k)} - x_{(k+1)}) = (1 - r)x_{(k)} + rx_{(k+1)}.$$

The sample median is $\hat{Q}(\frac{1}{2})$, Q1 is $\hat{Q}(\frac{1}{4})$, Q3 is $\hat{Q}(\frac{3}{4})$, and the sample interquartile range is $\hat{Q}(\frac{3}{4}) - \hat{Q}(\frac{1}{4})$.

The interpretation of the sample quantile

The quantiles conjure up strange ideas. For loss data collected over a year, the 95 % is the size of a loss that would be exceeded in 5 years out of 100. It does not mean that we have to collect 100 years of data, or that decisions based on it are taking into account the next 100 years. It is a probability statement. If data was collected independently under identical circumstances hundreds of times – in parallel universes, so to speak – then in 5 percent of them the 95 % quantile value will be exceeded. In general, the probability distribution of losses is such that proportion $1 - \alpha$ of the population data will have values larger than the α-quantile $Q(\alpha)$.

17.7.3   Quantile measures of skewness and kurtosis

The mean/median examples show skewness, as data often will when it are only positive (or only negative) and close to zero.

- *Quartile difference* $QD = (Q3 - Q2) - (Q2 - Q1) = Q3 - 2 Q2 + Q1$
- *Galton skewness* $\hat{\beta}_{GS} = \dfrac{QD}{IQR}$
- *Moors kurtosis* $\hat{\beta}_{MK} = \dfrac{\hat{Q}(7/8) - \hat{Q}(5/8) + \hat{Q}(3/8) - \hat{Q}(1/8)}{IQR}$

Data 3 (Section 17.4.3) gives $QD = 18.695$, $\hat{\beta}_{GS} = 0.636$, $\hat{\beta}_{MK} = 2.910$.

An interesting generalization is the decomposition (Benjamini and Krieger, 1995):

$$Q(p) = Q(\frac{1}{2}) + \frac{1}{2}\{Q(p) - Q(1 - p)\} + \frac{1}{2}\{Q(p) - 2Q(\frac{1}{2}) + Q(1 - p)\},$$

where the three terms on the right-hand side represent location, spread, and skewness respectively. The ratio of the skewness to spread terms is called the Parzen skewness, with the Galton skewness QD/IQR being the special case of this having $p = \frac{1}{4}$. If there is sufficient data, the Parzen skewness with $p = 0.95$ is often used as a robust measure.

- *Parzen skewness* $\hat{\beta}_{PS} = \dfrac{\hat{Q}(p) - 2\hat{Q}(\frac{1}{2}) + \hat{Q}(1 - p)}{\hat{Q}(p) - \hat{Q}(1 - p)}$

A robust measure of kurtosis that is used is the ratio of the spread terms at $p = 0.95$ and $p = 0.75$.

- *Robust kurtosis* $\hat{\beta}_{RK} = \dfrac{\hat{Q}(0.95) - \hat{Q}(0.05)}{\text{IQR}},$

which is compared with the value 2.905 given by the normal distribution. Corresponding to excess kurtosis, we subtract the 2.905 from the robust measure.

17.7.4   The relationship between moment and quantile measures

Table 17.8 shows how the population moments (Table 17.6) can be written in terms of the quantile function $Q(p)$.

Table 17.8   Relation between moments and quantiles.

$$\mu = E(X) \qquad\qquad = \int_0^1 Q(p)\,dp$$

$$\mu'_r = E(X^r) \qquad\qquad = \int_0^1 \{Q(p)\}^r\,dp$$

$$\mu_r = E\{(X - \mu)^r\} \quad = \int_0^1 \{Q(p) - \mu\}^r\,dp$$

17.7.5   Probability weighted moments (PWM)

The rth *probability weighted moment* is

$$\omega_r = \int_0^1 Q(p)\,p^r\,dp\,.$$

We can interpret this formula as the expectation $E\{Q(p)\,p^r\}$, where p has a *Uniform*(0,1) distribution (Section 20.17.1).

An argument for using these moments is that they are defined explicitly in terms of the quantile function $Q(p)$ which is the direct describer of risk. Indeed, some distributions proposed for extreme loss modeling are specified only through the quantile function and have no analytic inversion into probability density functions.

We note that $\omega_0 = \mu$, the population mean. If the population moments exist as far as the $(r - 1)$st, there is a correspondence between the probability weighted moments and the population moments up to μ'_r, which enables the probability weighted moments to give an alternative description of the population distribution. Their application is essentially when we use linear combinations of the order statistics; in particular when the largest observations have an emphasized importance as we have when analyzing risk analysis loss data.

For $x_{(1)} > x_{(2)} > \cdots > x_{(n)}$, the order statistics from a random sample of size n, the corresponding sample values are

$$\hat{\omega}_r = \frac{1}{n} \sum_{j=1}^{n} x_{(j)} \, p_{(j)}^r$$

where $p_{(j)}$ are plotting points on the interval $(0,1)$. We saw in Section 17.7.1 the wide range of choices for these. Here we also need plotting points on $(0,1)$ not just for $p_{(j)}$ but for each $p_{(j)}^r$.

For $p_{(j)}$ we have for example

(1) $\dfrac{n - j + 1}{n + 1}$

This is $E(U_{(j)})$, where $U_{(j)}$ is the random variable for the jth largest value $u_{(j)}$ from a random sample of n values from $Uniform(0,1)$.

(2) $u_{(j)}$

This is the jth order statistic of a simulated random sample of size n from $Uniform(0,1)$. The order statistics are the set $\{u_{(j)}\}$, where $u_{(1)} > u_{(2)} > \cdots > u_{(n)}$.

(3) $\dfrac{n - j + \frac{1}{2}}{n}$

(1) and (3) are the special cases with $\delta = 0$ and $\frac{1}{2}$ of (4) following.

(4) $\dfrac{n + 1 - j - \delta}{n + 1 - 2\delta}$ $\quad (-\dfrac{1}{2} < \delta < \dfrac{1}{2})$

(5) With $j = n(1 - \alpha)$, (4) becomes $\dfrac{n\alpha + 1 - \delta}{n + 1 - 2\delta}$

(6) $\dfrac{n - j + 0.65}{n}$

Hosking (1990) reports that good results have been found with this for the GPD, GEV, and Wakeby distributions.

For $p_{(j)}^r$ we are confronted with an even wider set of choices.

(7) $(p_{(j)})^r$

This is a straightforward powering up of the choices for $p_{(j)}$.

(8) $E\{(U_{(j)})^r\} = \dfrac{n!}{(n + r)!} \dfrac{(n + r - 1 - j)!}{(n - 1 - j)!}$

This uses $E\{(U_{(j)})^r\}$ rather than $\{E(U_{(j)})\}^r$.

17.7.6   L-moments

L-moments are moment measures for describing distributions through probability weighted moments. They can be written in terms of the expectations of the order statistics of a random sample. This has the advantage that, whenever the expectation of a population is finite, its L-moments all exist, whereas for thick-tailed probability distributions not all the moments necessarily exist. The formulae are adapted from Hosking (1990). Let $X_{j:n}$ be the random

Table 17.9 L-moments.

$\lambda_1 = E(X) = E(X_{1:1})$	$= \int_0^1 Q(p)\mathrm{d}p$	$= \omega_0$
$\lambda_2 = \frac{1}{2}E(X_{1:2} - X_{2:2})$	$= \int_0^1 (2p - 1)Q(p)\mathrm{d}p$	$= 2\omega_1 - \omega_0$
$\lambda_3 = \frac{1}{3}E(X_{1:3} - X_{2:3} + X_{3:3})$	$= \int_0^1 (6p^2 - 6p + 1)Q(p)\mathrm{d}p$	$= 6\omega_2 - 6\omega_1 + \omega_0$
$\lambda_4 = \frac{1}{4}E(X_{1:4} - 3X_{2:4} + X_{3:4} - X_{4:4}) = \int_0^1 (20p^3 - 30p^2 + 12p - 1)\mathrm{d}p$		$= 20\omega_3 - 30\omega_2 + 12\omega_1 - \omega_0$

variable for the jth largest value in a random sample of size n from a continuous distribution having quantile function $Q(p)$ and PWMs ω_r. Table 17.9 gives the first few L-moments.

In general

$$\lambda_r = \frac{1}{r}\sum_{j=1}^{r}\binom{r-1}{j-1}E(X_{j:r}) = \sum_{k=0}^{r}(-1)^{r-k}\binom{r}{k}\binom{r+k}{r}\omega_k .$$

The first L-moment λ_1 is the expectation μ and so measures location; the second L-moment λ_2 measures scale or dispersion. These together give an L-moment coefficient of variation (L-CV) $\tau = \lambda_2/\lambda_1$ corresponding to the coefficient of variation σ/μ.

The L-skewness measure is $\tau_3 = \dfrac{\lambda_3}{\lambda_2}$.

The L-kurtosis measure is $\tau_4 = \dfrac{\lambda_4}{\lambda_2}$.

Through consideration of $E(X_{1:r})$, i.e. $E(X_{\max})$, for sample sizes $r = 1$ to 4, we get the constraints on these measures (Hosking, 1990)

$$\lambda_2 > 0, \ -1 < \tau_3 < 1, \ -\frac{1}{4}(5\tau_3^2 - 1) \leq \tau_4 < 1.$$

Furthermore, if the population can take only positive values, then the L-CV satisfies $0 < \tau < 1$.

Sample L-moments $\{\hat{\lambda}_r\}$

The unbiased estimators for the L-moments are the average of the sample order statistics for $\hat{\lambda}_1$, half the average of every difference $x_{(i)} - x_{(j)}$ ($i < j$) for $\hat{\lambda}_2$, one-third of the average of every $x_{(i)} - 2x_{(j)} + x_{(k)}$ ($i < j < k$) for $\hat{\lambda}_3$, and so on. This will be a heavy computation, mitigated by the good properties of unbiasedness and asymptotic normality. The sample second moment $\hat{\lambda}_2$ is known as the Gini mean difference statistic.

As an alternative it might be easier to substitute the estimates of the probability weighted moments $\hat{\omega}_r$, obtained using plotting points, in the second formula for λ_r above.

17.8   CHECKING DATA QUALITY

The question most frequently put by statisticians is: "Have you looked at your data?" Data should be examined before it is submitted to statistical analysis. All statistical procedures are subject to assumptions about the data or the process of acquiring the data. We cannot rely on the charts and summary statistics generated by a computer package if these assumptions are not satisfied, or if we fail to understand the consequences of their not being satisfied.

> "Have you looked at your data?" Data should be examined before it is submitted to statistical analysis.

This principle is illustrated by considering two data sets with the caveat that we have no background information on either set other than that given in Cruz (2002).

17.8.1 Data 1

Week	M	Tu	W	Th	F	Total
1		4	1	6	9	20
2	9	10	2	4	8	33
3	2	3	0	1	–	6
4	2	3	1	3	4	13
5	5	4	4	4	9	26
6	5	4	3	11	8	31
7	12	3	10	0	7	32
Total	35	31	21	29	45	161

This data set (from Section 17.4.1) is very small for modeling. There are no obvious patterns, and so it might suggest randomness. Serious fraudulent activity may be expected to relate to individuals acting independently, though this might not apply in retail banking with multiple usage of a stolen credit or debit card. The model generally used to represent this independent behaviour is the Poisson frequency model. However the Poisson distribution has the property that its expectation (population mean) and population variance are the same. With this data the summary statistics give sample estimates $\bar{x}$ and s^2 which are 4.88 and 11.17. These clearly show that the Poisson model is not appropriate.

17.8.2 Data 3

1373	264	233	160	118	92	51	49	47	43	42	39	36
30	28	23	23	21	20	19	19	18	18	18	17	17
17	15	15	14	12	12	11	10	9	7	5	3	1

These data (from Section 17.4.3) is shown again here in units of $1000 after rounding values to the nearest $1000. The largest value, 1373, is more than five times the size of the second largest, 264. It is 5.87 standard deviations ($s = 221$) from the mean ($\bar{x} = 76$), 18 times larger than the mean, and 72 times larger than the median ($x_{med} = 19$). In contrast, the second largest value is only 0.86 standard deviations from $\bar{x}$, and 13 times larger than x_{med}. Statistical tables show that if the data were from a normal distribution, a value of 4 or more standard deviations would occur with a probability of 0.00003. What we are seeing is an extreme value, an outlier. We have to ask if there is anything in the circumstances of this extremely large value that indicates that it needs a separate treatment from the rest of the data, and may require separate modeling assumptions. Outliers remain an important part of the data and should not simply be ignored (as is often found to be the case within the insurance industry). They may be the

Table 17.10 Logdata of Data 3 with summary statistics.

14.13	11.68	10.76	10.49	10.06	9.83	9.76	9.58	9.32	8.60
12.49	11.43	10.67	10.31	9.97	9.82	9.76	9.52	9.16	8.09
12.36	10.83	10.65	10.23	9.92	9.78	9.74	9.39	9.08	6.32
11.98	10.79	10.56	10.06	9.85	9.78	9.60	9.38	8.89	

n	$\bar{x}$	s^2	s	$\hat{\beta}_1$	$\hat{\beta}_2$	Q1	x_{med}	Q3
39	10.118	1.700	1.304	0.362	5.231	9.521	9.852	10.670

most important and informative part of the data. Indeed, regulatory operational risk capital is primarily concerned with potential outliers.

> Outliers require individual investigation, and must not be dropped from the data set. Their importance in risk management is obvious.

The data exhibits extreme skewness. For the symmetric normal distribution, the mean and median are the same and the skewness coefficient $\hat{\beta}_1$ is 0. For this data this latter is 5.3. The skewness is so extreme that a logarithmic scale has to be used to obtain a boxplot that is viewable. The Galton skewness $\hat{\beta}_{GS}$ is 0.64. Even after the log transformation the data shows skewness, including three outliers (Figure 17.6). These include the smallest value, 0.554, as well as the two largest values. The boxplot is shown using a log-scale to base 10 since it affords an easier identification with the unlogged values.

These logdata give QD = 0.487, $\hat{\beta}_{GS} = 0.426$, $\hat{\beta}_{MK} = 1.709$.

We see that the Galton skewness coefficient has dropped from 0.636 for the raw data to 0.426 for the logdata. These skewness coefficients ignore the values of data larger than Q3 and smaller than Q1, removing attention from the tails. The Moors kurtosis coefficient for the raw data is 2.910, and for the logdata is 1.709, though in loss data analysis kurtosis does not play a serious role.

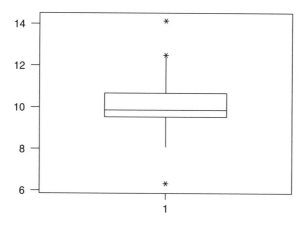

Figure 17.6 Boxplot for logarithms of Data 3.

The losses reported by Cruz are recorded to the nearest penny. Nothing in the modeling will be lost from rounding these data. Further, the small values are also untypical of the models we shall use to fit these data. Why are they so few? How did the $553.66 creep in? Was the threshold indeed $500? What would be the consequences for modeling if the threshold were upped to $3000? This problem of censorship of small losses is paradoxically of some importance in modeling the high impact tail of severity data. If we have 5 % of unrecorded low impact values, the quantiles of the loss distribution model based on the recorded data must be increased appropriately, but how do we know it is 5 %? The paradox is that the sizes of the small losses would not be expected to have any influence on the sizes of the largest losses. The estimation of the censored proportion from the recorded data is not easy and is beyond the scope of this introductory text. We must view the estimated quantiles in the knowledge of this censorship.

These questions highlight the importance of understanding the data prior to subjecting it to statistical analysis. Finally, we note that this is not typical oprisk loss data. It is financial penalties imposed by a regulatory authority.

17.9   DIFFICULTIES ARISING IN OR MODELING

The above discussion was not directed particularly to loss data. Oprisk loss data has its own specific problems. While some oprisk losses have transactions automatically logged, such as basic banking transactions of deposit and cash withdrawal at ATMs, those due to errors by personnel serious enough to merit disciplinary or other consequences may lead to underreporting. Other problems include an ambiguity of assigning the loss category or putting a precise value to the loss, particularly if it is not clear if the loss was incurred as a single event. How should the near miss be handled? Should the potential loss or the incurred loss be reported when a theft is forestalled or an erroneous transaction is reversed? These problems relate to the risk culture and policy.

Problems also arise directly from the setting of thresholds appropriate to each category of loss below which loss events are not subject to the stringent reporting discipline, with the losses treated as costs of doing business. When these censored data sets are modeled and we find from the fitted model the quantiles representing OpVaR values, how does the missing data distort these values?

Further difficulties with OR data can be categorized as follows.

17.9.1   Shortage of data

Operation risk loss data are commercially sensitive, and not publicly available. Furthermore, Basel 2 regulations ask that we sort the data collected over a single year into 56 categories and model each.

17.9.2   Unobserved extremely large losses

The losses so large that the bank could be seriously damaged have not yet occurred. Yet one purpose of the regulatory regime is to factor in provision for just such an event. A basic principle of the statistical analysis of experimental data is that we cannot presume to make inferences about properties of the matter under study far beyond the range of the data where our model assumptions may not hold. Basel 2 asks explicitly that we model losses in the extreme tail of a probability distribution, assigning a value from this region as a measure of regulatory capital.

> A basic principle of statistical analysis is that inferences should not be made about properties far beyond the range of the observed data.

17.9.3   The small sample problem

An extreme loss in a small sample is overrepresentative of its one in a hundred or one in a thousand chance. Extreme losses in a small sample are underrepresented if there are no extreme losses observed. We must conclude that we cannot, through fitting data, discern the true distribution of a heavy-tailed distribution. This is true whatever model we try to fit.

17.9.4   Unrecorded small losses

This arises from the censoring of small losses by assigning them to "expected losses" to be absorbed by net profit. Thus loss databases will generally have records of loss events only when the losses exceed some threshold value. Modeling procedures have problems compensating for this, though it will not impinge strongly on the management of the larger losses.

17.9.5   Validation

Model uncertainty arises in that many alternative models can be used to fit the bulk of the data, as can be seen from published accounts of how major financial institutions model their OR losses. Added to the problems above, the negative view of loss data analysis as backward looking amplifies its perceived backward-lookingness.

18

Introductory Statistical Theory

The basic element is the *random variable* (rv). This is the value that will be given by the outcome of a random event such as the size of a loss or the number of losses in the course of a day. The value once it is observed is called a *variate*. We use capital letters late in the alphabet to label the random variables: X, Y, Z, U, W, T, for example. We use the early part of the alphabet to represent events. Small letters are used to represent the values taken. We first look at *discrete* random variables which give counting data and frequency models. These require a different probabilistic description from *continuous* random variables, that give the size data such as lengths, weights or temperatures that can in principle be modeled to any number of decimal places and give severity models.

18.1   DISCRETE PROBABILITY MODELS

18.1.1   Notation and definitions

If the random variable X is the number of loss events recorded in a particular category during a particular day, then "$X = x$" is the event "There were x loss events that day in that category," "$X \leq x$" is "There were no more than x loss events," and "$X < x$" is "There were fewer than x."

- The *sample space* is the set of all values that X can take.
- The probability that the rv X takes the value x is written p_x or $P(X = x)$.
- The *probability distribution* of X is the set of probabilities p_x for all values of x. The set $\{p_x\}$ is also called the *probability mass function* (pmf). Its properties are $0 \leq p_x \leq 1$,   since p_x is a probability;

$$\sum_x p_x = 1, \quad \text{since a possible value is always observed.}$$

These give us the result that every set $\{p_x\}$ satisfying these two properties is a pmf, and an be used as a frequency model.

18.1.2   A short table of discrete probability models

The models in Table 18.1 are examined in detail in Chapter 19.

18.2   CONTINUOUS PROBABILITY MODELS

18.2.1   Notation and definitions

Continuous random variables give data that can in principle be modeled to any number of decimal places. With more and more data, histogram bin-widths can be reduced until, in the limit, the histogram becomes a smooth curve. If the random variable is X, then this curve $f(x)$

Table 18.1   Discrete probability models.

Distribution	$f(x)$	$x \in \mathbb{X}$	$\theta \in \Theta$
Bernoulli (θ)	$\theta^x (1-\theta)^{1-x}$	$x = 0, 1$	$0 < \theta < 1$
Binomial (n, θ)	$\binom{n}{x} \theta^x (1-\theta)^{n-x}$	$x = 0, 1, \ldots, n$	$0 < \theta < 1$
Geometric (θ)	$(1-\theta)^{x-1}\theta$	$x = 1, 2, \ldots$	$0 < \theta < 1$
Hypergeometric (N, M, n)	$\binom{M}{x}\binom{N-M}{n-x} \Big/ \binom{N}{n}$	$x = 0, 1, \ldots, n,$ $x \le M, \ x \ge M+n-N$	$N \ge n,$ $N \ge M$
Negative Binomial (ν, θ)	$\binom{x+\nu-1}{x}(1-\theta)^x \theta^\nu$	$x = 0, 1, 2, \ldots$	$0 < \theta < 1,$ $\nu > 0$
Poisson (λ)	$\dfrac{\lambda^x e^{-\lambda}}{x!}$	$x = 0, 1, 2, \ldots$	$\lambda > 0$
(Discrete) Uniform (k)	$\dfrac{1}{k}$	$x = 1, 2, \ldots, k$	$k = 1, 2, \ldots$

Distribution	$E(X)$	$var(X)$
Bernoulli (θ)	θ	$\theta(1-\theta)$
Binomial (n, θ)	$n\theta$	$n\theta(1-\theta)$
Geometric (θ)	$\dfrac{1}{\theta}$	$\dfrac{1-\theta}{\theta^2}$
Hypergeometric (N, M, n)	$\dfrac{nM}{N}$	$\dfrac{nM(N-M)(N-n)}{N^2(N-1)}$
Negative Binomial (ν, θ)	$\dfrac{\nu(1-\theta)}{\theta}$	$\dfrac{\nu(1-\theta)}{\theta^2}$
Poisson (λ)	λ	λ
(Discrete) Uniform (k)	$(k+1)/2$	$(k^2-1)/12$

is the *probability density function* (pdf). The area under the curve between a range of values measures its probability.

- $P(a < X < b) = \displaystyle\int_a^b f(x)\,\mathrm{d}x$.

The *cumulative distribution function* (cdf) $F(x)$

- $F(x) = P(X \le x) = \displaystyle\int_{x_0=-\infty}^{x} f(x_0)\,\mathrm{d}x_0$.
- $P(a < X \le b) = F(b) - F(a)$.

The cdf as a function of x is the fundamental measure for probability in probability theory. It is also meaningful with discrete probability models since, for example, the probability that a frequency takes a value not exceeding two and a half means that it takes its value as 0, 1 or 2.

The properties of continuous probability distributions are that $F(x)$ has a derivative, the pdf $f(x)$, that is non-negative and integrates to 1.

- $f(x) = \dfrac{\mathrm{d}F(x)}{\mathrm{d}x}$.
- $F(\infty) = P(X \leq \infty) = 1$.
- $P(a < X \leq b) = F(b) - F(a)$.

The *quantile function* (qf) $Q(p)$ is the inverse cumulative distribution function. If $F(x) = p$, then $Q(p) = x$ follows from solving $F(x) = p$ for p.

- $Q(p) = F^{-1}(p)$.

Graphically, the x-axis becomes the y-axis, now labelled $Q(p)$, and the y-axis, which was labelled $F(x)$, becomes the x-axis, now labelled p.

The population moments (Section 17.6.1) are, providing that the integrals converge,

- $\mu = \displaystyle\int_{-\infty}^{\infty} x f(x) \mathrm{d}x$;

- $\mu'_k = \displaystyle\int_{-\infty}^{\infty} x^k f(x) \mathrm{d}x$.

Standardized random variables

The distributions of random variables X will generally be given in terms of the the properties of the standardized random variables

$$Z = \frac{X - \mu}{\sigma}$$

where μ and σ are location and scale parameters. These do not always have $E(X) = \mu$ and $\mathrm{var}(X) = \sigma^2$, since heavy-tailed models which give rise to extreme loss values do not have all their moments existing. The property of a moment existing is the property of an infinite sum or an unbounded integral converging to a finite value. It may instead be because location is represented by a bound on the possible values that can be taken by the random variable. Thirdly, it may be when the random variable is a derived variable. For example, if X is normally distributed $N(\mu, \sigma^2)$, then the random variable $Y = e^X$ has a lognormal distribution, but generally retains the parameters μ and σ^2 of the originating distribution.

Linear transformation formulae

The standardization formula is a special case $X = \alpha + \beta Y$, with α and β (> 0) finite constants.

The relationships are based on the events '$X \leq x$' and '$Y \leq (x - \alpha)/\beta$' being the same and so having the same probabilities. This gives

$$F_X(x) = P(X \leq x) = P(\alpha + \beta Y \leq x) = P\left(Y \leq \frac{x - \alpha}{\beta}\right) = F_Y\left(\frac{x - \alpha}{\beta}\right)$$

Table 18.2　Linear transformation formulae.

	$y = (x - \alpha)/\beta$	$x = \alpha + \beta y$
cdf	$F_Y(y) = F_X(\alpha + \beta y)$	$F_X(x) = F_Y((x - \alpha)/\beta)$
pdf	$f_Y(y) = \beta f_X(\alpha + \beta y)$	$f_X(x) = (1/\beta) f_Y((x - \alpha)/\beta)$
expectation	$E(Y) = \{E(X) - \alpha\}/\beta$	$E(X) = \alpha + \beta E(Y)$
variance	$\operatorname{var}(Y) = (1/\beta^2)\operatorname{var}(X)$	$\operatorname{var}(X) = \beta^2 \operatorname{var}(Y)$
quantile function	$Q_Y(p) = (1/\beta)\{Q_X(p) - \alpha\}$	$Q_X(p) = \alpha + \beta Q_Y(p)$

The coefficients of skewness and kurtosis, β_1 and β_2, are unaltered by changes of location and scale.

and

$$f_X(x) = \frac{d}{dx} F_Y\left(\frac{x - \alpha}{\beta}\right).$$

We see from Table 18.2 that if $Q_X(p) = x$ then $Q_Y(p) = \dfrac{x - \alpha}{\beta}$.

We note that when $E(X) = \mu$ and $\operatorname{var}(X) = \sigma^2$, for $Z = (X - \mu)/\sigma$ we have the standardized variable with $E(Z) = 0$ and $\operatorname{var}(Z) = 1$.

Non-linear transformation formulae

The above argument applies directly for monotone increasing relationships between X and Y.

- **Example.** Let us find the distribution of $Y = e^X$ when X is *Uniform* (0,1). Since X takes its values in (0, 1), Y takes its values in (1, e). Then, for $1 < y < e$,

$$F_Y(y) = P(Y \le y) = P(e^X \le y) = P(X \le \ln y) = \int_0^{\ln y} 1\, dx = \ln y .$$

Then the pdf

$$f_Y(y) = \frac{dF_Y(y)}{dy} = \frac{1}{y} \quad (1 < y < e).$$

- **Example.** Let us find the distribution of $Y = -\ln X$, when X is *Uniform* (0,1). Here Y takes its values on $(0, \infty)$. Then, for $y > 0$,

$$F_Y(y) = P(Y \le y) = P(-\ln X \le y) = P(X \ge e^{-y}) = 1 - F_X(e^{-y}),$$

so $F_Y(y) = 1 - e^{-y}$, the cdf of *Exponential* (1), since $F_X(x) = x$ $(0 < x < 1)$.

The formulae for F_X and F_Y are given in the detailed descriptions of the *Uniform* and *Exponential* in Chapter 20.

18.2.2　Special integrals

Some formulae for probability distributions contain integrals that can require computers or tables for their evaluation. This arises from the property that any non-negative function which has a finite integral can, when divided by the total integral, be used as a probability density function. Integrals with well understood mathematical properties – sometimes called the special functions of mathematical physics – then become useful models as probability distributions. We give here definitions and computational formulae for the:

- gamma function;
- beta function;
- standard normal cdf and its inverse; and
- error function.

The gamma function, $\Gamma(z)$

The gamma function is generally expressed as the integral

$$\Gamma(z) = \int_0^\infty u^{z-1} e^{-u} du$$

for $z > 0$. Its main properties are

- $\Gamma(z+1) = z\,\Gamma(z)$.
- If z is a positive integer, $\Gamma(z) = (z-1)!$
- It is convenient therefore to use the factorial notation also for non-integer values $0 < z < \infty$ of $\Gamma(z)$ by writing $z!$ for $\Gamma(z+1)$.
  Using this extended factorial notation we have for example that
  $\Gamma\left(3\frac{1}{2}\right) = \left(2\frac{1}{2}\right)! = \left(2\frac{1}{2}\right)\left(1\frac{1}{2}\right)\left(\frac{1}{2}\right)\Gamma\left(\frac{1}{2}\right) = (15/8)\Gamma\left(\frac{1}{2}\right)$.
- $\Gamma\left(\frac{1}{2}\right) = \sqrt{\pi}$.
- $\Gamma(z)\Gamma(1-z) = \dfrac{\pi}{\sin(\pi z)} \quad (0 < z < 1)$.
- $\Gamma\left(\frac{1}{2}+z\right)\Gamma\left(\frac{1}{2}-z\right) = \dfrac{\pi}{\cos(\pi z)} \quad \left(-\frac{1}{2} < z < \frac{1}{2}\right)$.
- $\Gamma(2z) = 2^{2z-1}\Gamma(z)\Gamma\left(z+\frac{1}{2}\right)/\sqrt{\pi} \quad (z > 0)$.
- The derivative $d\Gamma(z)/dz$ evaluated at $z = 1$, $\Gamma'(1) = -\gamma$, where γ is Euler's constant.

Leonhard Euler (1707–1783) was a prolific Swiss mathematician who gave the labels π and e to other more familiar constants.

- *Euler's constant* $\gamma = -\displaystyle\int_0^\infty (\ln u)\, e^{-u} du = 0.5772156649\cdots$
- *Stirling's formula approximating $\Gamma(z)$ for large z*

$$\Gamma(z) = \sqrt{2\pi}\, e^{-z} z^{z-\frac{1}{2}} \left(1 + \frac{1}{12z} + \frac{1}{288z^2} + \cdots\right)$$

- *Approximation for $\ln\Gamma(z)$*

$$\ln\Gamma(z) = \ln\left(\sqrt{2\pi}\, e^{-z} z^{z-\frac{1}{2}}\right) + \frac{1}{12z} - \frac{1}{360z^2} + \cdots \quad (z \geq 10)$$

Now $\ln\Gamma(z+1) = \ln z + \ln\Gamma(z)$, so for $z < 10$ we can write

$$\ln\Gamma(z) = \ln\Gamma(z+k) - \ln z - \ln(z+1) - \cdots - \ln(z+k-1)$$

with $z + k > 10$, and then use the following approximation.

- A *computer formula for closely approximating* $\Gamma(r)$ $(0 < r < 1)$

$$\Gamma(r) = (1/r) + a_0 + a_1 r + a_2 r^2 + a_3 r^3 + a_4 r^4$$

where the coefficients are
$a_0 = -0.5748646$, $a_1 = 0.9512363$, $a_2 = -0.6998588$, $a_3 = 0.4245549$, $a_4 = -0.1010678$.
Then for $\Gamma(z)$ with $z > r$ we have

$$\Gamma(z) = z(z - 1)(z - 2) \cdots r \, \Gamma(r)$$

where $0 < r < 1$.

- *The Digamma Function* $\psi(z)$

$$\psi(z) = \frac{d}{dz} \ln \Gamma(z) = \frac{1}{\Gamma(z)} \frac{d\Gamma(z)}{dz}$$

- $\psi(1) = -\gamma = -0.57721 \cdots$ where γ is Euler's constant.
- $\psi\left(\frac{1}{2}\right) = -\gamma - 2\ln 2 = -1.96351 \cdots$.

For large z,

$$\psi(z) = \ln z - \frac{1}{2z} - \frac{1}{12z^2} + \frac{1}{120z^4} - \cdots$$

The beta function, $B(\alpha, \beta)$

The beta function is generally expressed as one or other of the integrals

$$B(\alpha, \beta) = \int_0^1 u^{\alpha-1}(1 - u)^{\beta-1} du = \int_0^\infty \frac{v^{\alpha-1}}{(1 + v)^{\alpha+\beta}} dv$$

for $\alpha > 0$, $\beta > 0$.

The second representation arises as the transformation $v = u/(1 - u)$. The beta function can be written in terms of gamma functions as

$$B(\alpha, \beta) = \frac{\Gamma(\alpha)\Gamma(\beta)}{\Gamma(\alpha + \beta)}$$

The standard normal cdf, $\Phi(x)$

The probability density function for the standard normal $N(0,1)$ probability distribution is

$$\phi(x) = \frac{1}{\sqrt{2\pi}} \exp\left(-\frac{1}{2}x^2\right)$$

with cumulative distribution function

$$\Phi(x) = \int_{-\infty}^x \phi(x_0) \, dx_0$$

- *An approximation for* $\Phi(x)$

In Tanizaki (2004) we have that, if $t = 1/(1 + cx)$ where $c = 0.2316419$, then an approximation accurate to at least seven decimal places is

$$\Phi(x) = 1 - \phi(x) \sum_{k=1}^{5} b_k t^k$$

with
$b_1 = 0.319381530, \quad b_2 = -0.356563782, \quad b_3 = 1.781477937, \quad b_4 = -1.821255987,$
$b_5 = 1.330274429.$

- *An approximation for* $x = \Phi^{-1}(p)$

If $0.5 \leq p < 1$, let $y = \sqrt{-2 \ln(1 - p)}$, then

$$x = y - \frac{a_0 + a_1 y + a_2 y^2}{1 + b_1 y + b_2 y^2 + b_3 y^3}$$

where
$a_0 = 2.515517, \quad a_1 = 0.802853, \quad a_2 = 0.010308,$
$b_1 = 1.432788, \quad b_2 = 0.189269, \quad b_3 = 0.001308,$
has an error less than 0.00045.

If $0 < p < 0.5$, let $y = \sqrt{-2 \ln p}$, and replace x by $-x$ in the formula.

The error function, $\mathrm{erf}(x)$

This is the function generally seen in mathematical tables (in contrast with statistical tables).

$$\mathrm{erf}(x) = \frac{2}{\sqrt{\pi}} \int_0^x \exp(-t^2)\, dt .$$

Let $y = \sqrt{2}\, t$ in this integral, then

$$\mathrm{erf}(x) = 2 \int_0^{\sqrt{2}x} \phi(y)\, dy = 2\,\Phi\left(\sqrt{2}\, x\right) - 1 .$$

18.2.3   A short table of continuous probability distributions

When α is a location parameter and β is a scale parameter, the standardized variate

$$z = \frac{x - \alpha}{\beta}$$

is used to simplify expressions in Tables 18.3 and 18.4. Detailed properties are given in Chapter 20.

Tabulated probability distributions

Statistical methods at an introductory level rely in the main on referring to tables of the following distributions.

- The chi-square distribution is used in testing the model fit of distributions. Also, for data from a normal distribution, we can use the chi-square to examine the variability of the sample variance s^2 as an estimate of the population variance σ^2.

Table 18.3   Continuous distribution models.

Distribution	$f(x)$	$x \in \mathbb{X}$	$\theta \in \Theta$
Beta (α, β)	$\dfrac{1}{B(\alpha, \beta)} x^{\alpha-1}(1-x)^{\beta-1}$	$0 < x < 1$	$\alpha > 0,\ \beta > 0$
Beta$_2(\alpha, \beta)$	$\dfrac{1}{B(\alpha, \beta)} \dfrac{x^{\alpha-1}}{(1+x)^{\alpha+\beta}}$	$x > 0$	$\alpha > 0,\ \beta > 0$
Cauchy (α, β)	$\dfrac{1}{\pi\beta(1+z)^2}$	$-\infty < x < \infty$	$\beta > 0$
Exponential (λ)	$\lambda \exp(-\lambda x)$	$x > 0$	$\lambda > 0$
Gamma (ν, λ)	$\dfrac{1}{\Gamma(\nu)} \lambda(\lambda x)^{\nu-1} \exp(-\lambda x)$	$x > 0$	$\lambda > 0,\ \nu > 0$
Gumbel (α, β)	$\dfrac{1}{\beta} \exp(-z)\exp\{-\exp(-z)\}$	$-\infty < x < \infty$	$\beta > 0$
Logistic (α, β)	$\dfrac{1}{\beta} \dfrac{\exp(-z)}{\{1+\exp(-z)\}^2}$	$-\infty < x < \infty$	$\beta > 0$
$N(\mu, \sigma^2)$	$\dfrac{1}{\sqrt{2\pi\sigma^2}} \exp\left\{-\dfrac{1}{2}\left(\dfrac{x-\mu}{\sigma}\right)^2\right\}$	$-\infty < x < \infty$	$\sigma > 0$
Pareto (θ, α)	$\dfrac{\theta\alpha^\theta}{x^{\theta+1}}$	$x > \alpha$	$\theta > 0,\ \alpha > 0$
Uniform (α, β)	$\dfrac{1}{\beta - \alpha}$	$\alpha < x < \beta$	$\alpha < \beta$
Weibull (α, β)	$\beta\alpha x^{\alpha-1} \exp(-\beta x^\alpha)$	$x > 0$	$\alpha > 0,\ \beta > 0$

Table 18.4   Continuous distribution models (continued).

Distribution	$E(X)$	$\mathrm{var}(X)$
Beta (α, β)	$\dfrac{\alpha}{\alpha + \beta}$	$\dfrac{\alpha\beta}{(\alpha+\beta)^2(\alpha+\beta+1)}$
Beta$_2(\alpha, \beta)$	$\dfrac{\alpha}{\beta-1}\ (\beta > 1)$	$\dfrac{\alpha(\alpha+\beta)}{(\beta-1)(\beta-2)}\ (\beta > 2)$
Cauchy (α, β)	none	none
Exponential (λ)	$1/\lambda$	$1/\lambda^2$
Gamma (ν, λ)	ν/λ	ν/λ^2
Gumbel (α, β)	$\alpha + \beta\gamma\ (\gamma = 0.5772\cdots)$	$\pi^2\beta^2/6$
Logistic (α, β)	α	$\pi^2\beta^2/3$
$N(\mu, \sigma^2)$	μ	σ^2
Pareto (θ, α)	$\dfrac{\alpha\theta}{\theta-1}\ (\theta > 1)$	$\dfrac{\alpha^2\theta}{(\theta-1)^2(\theta-2)}\ (\theta > 2)$
Uniform (α, β)	$(\alpha + \beta)/2$	$(\beta - \alpha)^2/12$
Weibull (α, β)	$\beta^{-1/\alpha}\Gamma\left(1 + \dfrac{1}{\alpha}\right)$	$\beta^{-2/\alpha}\left\{\Gamma\left(1 + \dfrac{2}{\alpha}\right) - \left[\Gamma\left(1 + \dfrac{1}{\alpha}\right)\right]^2\right\}$

Table 18.5   Distributions generally found in books of statistical tables.

Distribution	$f(z)$	$z \in \mathbb{Z}$	ξ
N(0,1)	$\dfrac{1}{\sqrt{2\pi}} \exp\left(-\dfrac{1}{2}z^2\right)$	$-\infty < z < \infty$	
Chi-square χ_k^2	$\dfrac{1}{2^{k/2}\,\Gamma(k/2)}\, z^{(k/2)-1} \exp\left(-\dfrac{1}{2}z\right)$	$z > 0$	$k = 1, 2, \ldots$
Student t_m	$\dfrac{\Gamma((m+1)/2)}{\Gamma(m/2)\sqrt{\pi m}} \left(1 + \dfrac{z^2}{m}\right)^{-(m+1)/2}$	$-\infty < z < \infty$	$m = 1, 2, \ldots$
Fisher $F_{m,n}$	$\dfrac{m^{\frac{1}{2}m}\, n^{\frac{1}{2}n}}{B\left(\frac{1}{2}m, \frac{1}{2}n\right)} \dfrac{z^{\frac{1}{2}(m-2)}}{(n + mz)^{\frac{1}{2}(m+n)}}$	$z > 0$	$m > 0,\, n > 0$

Distribution	$E(Z)$	var(Z)
N(0,1)	0	1
Chi-square χ_k^2	k	$2k$
Student t_m	$0 \;\; (m = 2, 3, \ldots)$	$\dfrac{m}{m-2} \;\; (m = 3, 4, \ldots)$
Fisher $F_{m,n}$	$\dfrac{n}{n-2} \;\; (n = 3, 4, \ldots)$	$\dfrac{2n^2(m + n - 2)}{n(n-2)^2(n-4)} \;\; (n = 5, 6, \ldots)$

- The t distribution is used in examining the variability of the sample mean $\bar{x}$ as an estimate of the population mean μ for data from a normal distribution when the population variance is unknown and estimated by s^2. It converges to the normal distribution as the sample size grows.
- The F distribution is used for testing whether the variances of a random sample from each of two normally distributed populations are the same. This is a test arising in Analysis of Variance.

18.3   INTRODUCTORY STATISTICAL METHODS

The statistical methods being introduced here are those of estimation and hypothesis testing, in particular classical parametric statistical inference, the use of data to answer questions about model parameters. The theory is concerned with finding methods that are optimal, most effective, and most economical in the amount of data required.

The methods of parameter estimation described are *method of moments* estimation (MoME) and *maximum likelihood* estimation (MLE). For many of the standard models these yield the same estimators, which can be shown to have good statistical properties such as small bias and standard error. The relative merits of different estimation methods are addressed through their sampling distributions. *Minimum variance unbiased* estimators (MVUE) are considered the best amongst unbiased estimators.

The methods of testing how well the model fits the data are graphical and the *chi-square test of fit*. More sophisticated tools will be shown in later chapters directed at loss data analysis.

The estimation and graphical techniques assume that there is no relationship with other variables. The data is then sorted and the proportions of 0s, 1s, 2s, ... are calculated. We use proportions rather than frequencies because proportions do not depend on how many values are collected and so will describe better the population the data come from.

18.3.1 Sampling distributions

Each time an experiment is repeated under identical conditions, we get a value for a statistic t, so t has a probability distribution, the *sampling distribution* of t. This is the probability distribution of a random variable T. To compare two estimators – for example the sample mean $\bar{x}$ and the sample median x_{med}, both of which estimate μ – we need to look at the properties of their respective sampling distributions.

The *standard error* of an estimate is the standard deviation of its sampling distribution, *i.e.* $se(t) = sd(T)$. To support a statistic we should aim to report its standard error.

From a random sample $x_1, x_2, \ldots, x_n$, $se(\bar{x}) = sd(\overline{X}) = \sigma/\sqrt{n}$; and we can estimate this using the sample standard deviation s, to give estimated $se(\bar{x}) = \widehat{se}(\bar{x}) = s/\sqrt{n}$.

For any random sample $x_1, x_2, \ldots, x_n$, if n is fairly large, by the Central Limit Property, $\bar{x}$ will have a sampling distribution which is approximately $N(\bar{x}, s^2/n)$.

We generally examine estimators for their bias and standard errors; the lower it is in each of these the better they are.

- **Unbiasedness**. An estimate t of parameter θ is unbiased if its sampling distribution has θ as its expectation. If $E(T) \neq \theta$, its bias bias$(t) = E(T) - \theta$.
- A parameter θ is said to be *estimable* if there is an unbiased estimator of it. The unbiased estimator with the smallest standard error is the *minimum variance unbiased estimator* (MVUE).
- A small bias and small standard error will generally be preferable to one with no bias and large standard error. There may in fact be no unbiased estimator at all.
- **Mean square error** (MSE). In choosing between estimators, for example $\bar{x}$ and x_{med}, we choose the one whose sampling distribution is more concentrated about the parameter as measured by the MSE. This balances the two properties.

$$MSE(t) = E\{(T - \theta)^2\} = \{se(t)\}^2 + \{bias(t)\}^2.$$

- **Consistency**. An estimator T is consistent if its MSE reduces to 0 as the sample size n increases to infinity.
- **Example**. A random sample of 20 observations $x_1, \ldots, x_{20}$ gave the summary data $\bar{x} = 3.905$ and $s^2 = 0.0289$. The estimate of $E(X)$ is $\bar{x} = 3.905$, and its estimated standard error $\widehat{se}(\bar{x}) = s/\sqrt{n} = 0.0373$.

18.3.2 Method of moments estimation

To obtain MoMEs we match the sample moments to the formulae for the population moments written in terms of the parameters. For single parameter models, we solve $\mu = \bar{x}$ for the parameter. For two parameter models, we solve the pair of equations $\mu = \bar{x}$ and $\sigma^2 = s^2$, and so on.

Examples:

- For *Poisson*(λ), $E(X) = \lambda$, so the MoME of λ is $\bar{x}$.
- For *Exponential*(θ), $E(X) = 1/\theta$, so the MoME of θ is $1/\bar{x}$.
- For $N(\mu, \sigma^2)$, $E(X) = \mu$ and var$(X) = \sigma^2$, so the MoME of (μ, σ^2) is $(\bar{x}, s^2)$.

18.3.3 Maximum likelihood estimation

Likelihood for a discrete distribution

The *likelihood* is the joint probability treated as a function of the unknown parameter value θ. For a random sample $x_1, x_2, \ldots, x_n$, it is the product

$$\ell(\theta \,;\, x_1, x_2, \ldots, x_n) \;=\; P(X_1 = x_1) \times \cdots \times P(X_n = x_n) \;=\; \prod_i P(X = x_i).$$

Example

Suppose that we have a random sample, $x = \{x_1, x_2, \ldots, x_k\}$, of k independent observations from *Binomial* (n, θ), where n is known. Then the likelihood is

$$\ell(\theta \,;\, x) \;=\; \prod_{i=1}^{k} \left\{ \binom{n}{x_i} \theta^{x_i}(1-\theta)^{n-x_i} \right\} \;=\; \left\{ \prod_{i=1}^{k} \binom{n}{x_i} \right\} \theta^{k\bar{x}}(1-\theta)^{k(n-\bar{x})}.$$

In this expression $\binom{n}{x}$ is 'n choose x', the number of ways of choosing x items from n.

Likelihood for a continuous distribution

The likelihood from a random sample $x = \{x_1, x_2, \ldots, x_n\}$ from a distribution having pdf $f(x|\theta)$, where θ is the parameter, is the joint pdf treated as a function of the parameter, so

$$\ell(\theta \,;\, x) \;=\; \prod_i f(x_i|\theta).$$

Examples

- For *Exponential* (θ), $f(x) = \theta e^{-\theta x}$ on $x > 0$, so

$$\ell(\theta \,;\, x_1, x_2, \ldots, x_n) \;=\; \prod_i (\theta\, e^{-\theta x_i}) \;=\; \theta^n \exp\left(-\theta \sum_i x_i\right) \;=\; \theta^n e^{-\theta(n\bar{x})}.$$

- For $N(\mu, \sigma^2)$,

$$\ell(\{\mu, \sigma^2\} \,;\, x) \;=\; \prod_i \left\{ \frac{1}{\sqrt{2\pi\sigma^2}} \exp\left(-\frac{1}{2\sigma^2} \sum_i (x_i - \mu)^2\right) \right\}.$$

Maximum likelihood

The MLE $\widehat{\theta}$ of θ is the value of θ that maximizes the likelihood. It has optimal properties, being the best asymptotically (as the sample size n becomes large), if the probability mass function or probability density function satisfies regularity conditions (dealing with differentiability and integrability). These are satisfied for a wide class of probability models, including the binomial, Poisson and negative binomial, exponential and normal.

The likelihood $\ell(\theta \,;\, x_1, x_2, \ldots, x_n)$ and its logarithm, the log-likelihood $L(\theta \,;\, x_1, x_2, \ldots, x_n)$ are maximized at the same value $\widehat{\theta}$ of θ. It is often easier to maximize the log-likelihood than the likelihood itself since it converts the product into a sum.

The MLE is the estimate of θ that maximizes the likelihood function, treating the data x as fixed.

Example

For a random sample of size n from *Exponential* (θ), the log-likelihood is

$$L(\theta ; x) = n \ln(\theta) - n\theta\bar{x} .$$

$$\frac{dL}{d\theta} = \frac{n}{\theta} - n\bar{x} ,$$

so $dL/d\theta = 0$ when $\theta = 1/\bar{x}$, Further $d^2L/d\theta^2 < 0$ for $\theta = 1/\bar{x} > 0$, giving a check that we have a maximum. This is the same estimator as the MoME.

Example

For a random sample of size n from the normal distribution $N(\mu, \sigma^2)$ the log-likelihood is

$$L(\theta ; x) = -\frac{1}{2\sigma^2} \sum_i (x_i - \mu)^2 - \frac{1}{2} n \ln(\sigma^2) - \frac{1}{2} n \ln(2\pi).$$

We have three cases to consider.

(a) If σ^2 is known, let X be $N(\theta, \sigma^2)$, then

$$\frac{dL}{d\theta} = -\frac{1}{2\sigma^2} \sum_i (-2)(x_i - \theta) = \frac{n}{\sigma^2} \left(\frac{1}{n} \sum_i x_i - \theta \right),$$

which is zero when $\theta = \bar{x}$. The MLE for $\theta = \mu$ is thus also the MoME.

(b) If μ is known, let X be $N(\mu, \theta)$, then

$$\frac{dL}{d\theta} = -\frac{1}{2} \sum_i (x_i - \mu)^2 \left(-\frac{1}{\theta^2} \right) - \frac{n}{2\theta} = \frac{n}{2\theta^2} \left(\frac{1}{n} \sum_i (x_i - \mu)^2 - \theta \right),$$

which is zero when $\theta = (1/n) \sum_i (x_i - \mu)^2$.

(c) When μ and σ^2 are both unknown, let X be $N(\theta_1, \theta_2)$, then we must maximize the likelihood with respect to both parameters simultaneously. We have

$$\frac{\partial L}{\partial \theta_1} = \frac{n}{\theta_2} (\bar{x} - \theta_1),$$

$$\frac{\partial L}{\partial \theta_2} = = \frac{n}{2\theta_2^2} \left(\frac{1}{n} \sum_i (x_i - \theta_1)^2 - \theta_2 \right).$$

These are both zero when $\theta_1 = \bar{x}$ and $\theta_2 = (1/n) \sum_i (x_i - \bar{x})^2$.

In this example the MLE $\widehat{\sigma^2}$ for σ^2 is $(n-1)s^2/n$ instead of the more usual (unbiased) s^2, so the MLE for σ^2 is biased. However, as $n \to \infty$, the bias, $E(\widehat{\sigma^2}) - \sigma^2$, converges to 0.

Example: MLE for survival data

The survival times of 10 startup companies are $13, 6, 10, 11, 7, 11, 7, 15, 12^+, 8^+,$ where the last two were censored by the end of the study (not having failed after times 12 and 8).

Looking at this in general, we suppose that k fail after times $\{t_1, t_2, \ldots, t_k\}$, and $n - k$ are censored after times $\{t_{k+1}, \ldots, t_n\}$. These are just labels for the times – the subscripts do not signify chronological order. The likelihood can be written as

$$\ell(\theta; t_1, t_2, \ldots, t_n) = \left\{\prod_{i=1}^k f(t_i)\right\} \left\{\prod_{i=k+1}^n R(t_i)\right\},$$

where $f(t)$ is the lifetime pdf, and $R(t)$ is the survivor function $P(T > t)$ at time t. If the data are *Exponential*(θ),

$$\ell(\theta; t_1, t_2, \ldots, t_n) = \prod_{i=1}^k (\theta e^{-\theta t_i}) \prod_{i=k+1}^n (e^{-\theta t_i}).$$

The log-likelihood is then

$$L(\theta; t_1, t_2, \ldots, t_n) = \sum_1^k \{\ln(\theta) - \theta t_i\} - \sum_{k+1}^n (\theta t_i) = k \ln(\theta) - \theta(\text{TTT})$$

where $\text{TTT} = \sum_1^n t_i$, the *total time on test*. This name comes from reliability analysis.

$$\frac{dL}{d\theta} = \frac{k}{\theta} - \text{TTT},$$

so $dL/d\theta = 0$ gives the MLE $\widehat{\theta} = k/\text{TTT}$.

For *Exponential*(θ) data, $\mu = E(T) = 1/\theta$, so the MLE for μ is $1/\widehat{\theta} = \text{TTT}/k$, which is the MTTF, the *mean time on test per failure*.

For the survival data, $k = 8$ and $\sum t_i = 100$, so the estimate $\widehat{\mu} = 12.5$.

Example

For a random sample of size n from the gamma distribution *Gamma*$(0, 1)$, with scale 1 and unknown index parameter θ (> 0), the likelihood function is

$$\ell(\theta; x) = \prod_i \left\{\frac{1}{\Gamma(\theta)} x_i^{\theta-1} e^{-x_i}\right\}.$$

The log-likelihood is

$$L(\theta; x) = -n \ln \Gamma(\theta) + (\theta - 1) \sum_i \ln x_i - \sum_i x_i.$$

$$\frac{dL}{d\theta} = -n \frac{d}{d\theta} \{\ln \Gamma(\theta)\} + \sum_i \ln x_i = -n \psi(\theta) + \sum_i \ln x_i,$$

where ψ is the digamma function (Section 18.2.1). Since $(d^2/d\theta^2) L = -(d/d\theta)\psi(\theta) < 0$ on $\theta > 0$, the minimum of L is the solution $\widehat{\theta}$ of $\psi(\theta) = (1/n) \sum_i \ln x_i$. This can be found from a graph or tables of $\psi(\theta)$.

We note that $E(X) = \theta$ so the MoME is $\bar{x}$. The asymptotic relative efficiency (ARE) of the MoME to the MLE is $1/\{\theta\psi'(\theta)\}$. This compares the number of observations for the same accuracy with large samples. The MLE is asymptotically efficient under regularity conditions. Here, the ARE goes to zero as θ goes to 0, and to one as θ goes to ∞.

We see also the computational problem associated with using a gamma model for survival data such as in the example above. Nevertheless, the mean time on test (MTTF), is applicable quite generally as a nonparametric method of estimating the population mean, becoming $\bar{x}$ if there is no censored data.

18.3.4   Interval estimation

As an alternative to reporting an estimate and its standard error, we can describe the location and spread of the sampling distribution through a *confidence interval*.

A 95 % confidence interval (CI) for an unknown parameter θ is an interval on the sampling distribution which contains 95 % of its probability. Its interpretation is in terms of the sampling distribution: there is a 95 % probability that θ will lie inside its 95 % CI.

If t has an $N(\theta, \sigma_T^2)$ sampling distribution, then $(T - \theta)/\sigma_T$ is $N(0, 1)$, so

$$P\{-1.96 \; < \; (T - \theta)/\sigma_T \; < \; 1.96\} \; = \; 0.95.$$

The bracketed event can be re written to give

$$P(T - 1.96\sigma_T \; < \; \theta \; < \; T + 1.96\sigma_T) \; = \; 0.95.$$

This is a probability statement about the sampling distribution, the distribution of T, and not about θ, which is an unknown constant.

The *95 % confidence interval* for θ is $(t - 1.96\sigma_T, t + 1.96\sigma_T)$.

The 99 % CI contains more of the sampling distribution and so is wider. We generally determine both the 95 % CI and the 99 % CI.

A confidence interval for θ is *best* if the probability of it containing a value of θ other than the true (unknown) value is as small as possible. This is often the shortest interval, but not always.

Reducing the width of a CI by a factor 4 requires the sample size to increase by a factor 16.

If σ^2 is estimated by s^2 from n observations, then $(\bar{X} - \mu)/(S/\sqrt{n})$ is Student t on $n - 1$ df, t_{n-1}. From the table of t_{n-1} we find $t_0 = t_{n-1, 0.05}$ for which

$$P\left\{-t_0 \; < \; \frac{\bar{X} - \mu}{S/\sqrt{n}} \; < \; t_0\right\} \; = \; 0.95$$

so $P\{\bar{X} - t_0\,(S/\sqrt{n}) < \mu < \bar{X} + t_0\,(S/\sqrt{n})\} \; = \; 0.95$.
The 95 % CI for μ is therefore $(\bar{x} - t_0\,s/\sqrt{n}, \; \bar{x} + t_0\,s/\sqrt{n})$.

Example

With $\bar{x} = 3.905$, $s^2 = 0.0289$ and estimated standard error 0.0373 from a random sample of 20 observations, the table of Student t for $m = n - 1 = 19$ degrees of freedom gives $t_{19, 0.05} = 2.093$, so the 95 % CI for μ is $3.905 \pm (2.093 \times 0.0373) \; = \; (3.827, 3.983)$.

Upper and lower confidence limits

We may require not an interval but a confidence bound. The reasoning follows the pattern for CIs. If t has an $N(\theta, \sigma_T^2)$ sampling distribution. then $P\{-1.645 < (T - \theta)/\sigma_T\} = 0.95$, giving $P(\theta < T + 1.645\sigma_T) = 0.95$. From this the *upper 95% confidence limit* for θ is $t + 1.645\sigma_T$. Similarly the *lower 97.5% CL* for θ is $t - 1.96\sigma_T$. Again, if the standard error is estimated we use the values taken from tables of the Student t distribution.

For the example above, the lower 99% CL for μ is $3.905 - (2.539)(0.0373) = 3.810$.

18.4 REGRESSION ANALYSIS

Here we seek to answer the question: how does the probability distribution of an experimental outcome Y depend on an input value or a set of input values X given by the experimenter? The input X is called the *explanatory* variable, but is also known as the *controlled* variable, the *predictor* variable, the *regressor* variable or, in econometrics, the *exogenous* variable. The output variable Y is called the *response* variable; it is random, and depends on values assigned to X. In econometrics, it is the *endogenous* variable.

The expression $E(y|x = x)$ denotes the expectation of the conditional probability distribution of the random variable Y given that X has taken the value x.

18.4.1 Linear regression models

- *Straight line regression*

$$E(Y|X = x) = \alpha + \beta x , \quad ie\ E(Y_i) = \alpha + \beta x_i$$

- *Polynomial regression*

$$E(Y|X = x) = \beta_0 + \beta_1 x + \beta_2 x^2 + \cdots + \beta_q x^q$$

$$ie\ E(Y_i) = \beta_0 + \beta_1 x_i + \beta_2 x_i^2 + \cdots + \beta_q x_i^q$$

To test for a straight line fit, we can compare it with a parabolic fit ($q = 2$).
- *Multiple regression*

$$E(Y|X_1 = x_1 , \ldots , X_q = x_q) = \beta_1 x_1 + \beta_2 x_2 + \cdots + \beta_q x_q$$

$$ie\ E(Y_i) = \beta_1 x_{1i} + \beta_2 x_{2i} + \cdots + \beta_q x_{qi} \quad (i = 1, 2, \ldots, n)$$

$(x_{1i}, \ldots, x_{qi})$ are the experimental settings, y_i is a measurement of the result.

Each of these is a linear regression, since each can be written in the linear form $E(Y_i) = \sum_i \beta_i x_i$, linear in the explanatory input settings x_i.

18.4.2 Straight line regression

When the scatterplot of y on x is approximately a straight line, we fit the model

$$y = g(x) = \alpha + \beta x.$$

- α is the intercept on the y-axis (if $x = 0$, then $y = \alpha$).

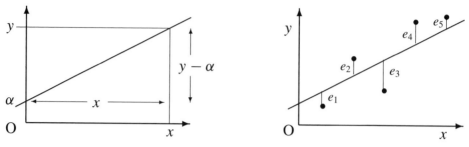

Figure 18.1   Modeling a straight line (left) and residual distances from the line (right).

- β is the slope $(y - \alpha)/x$

$$y_1 = \alpha + \beta x_1 , \quad y_2 = \alpha + \beta x_2 , \cdots , \quad y_n = \alpha + \beta x_n.$$

The method of least squares

This fits the line by choosing α and β to be the values $\widehat{\alpha}$ and $\widehat{\beta}$ that minimize the sum $T = \Sigma e_i^2$ of squared distances e_i in the y-direction from the points to the line $y = \alpha + \beta x$.

The minimization involves solving the simultaneous equations

$$\frac{\partial T}{\partial \alpha} = -2 \sum (y_i - \alpha - \beta x_i) = -2 \left(\sum y_i - n\alpha - \beta \sum x_i \right) = 0$$

$$\frac{\partial T}{\partial \beta} = -2 \sum x_i (y_i - \alpha - \beta x_i) = -2 \left(\sum x_i y_i - \alpha \sum x_i - \beta \sum x_i^2 \right) = 0$$

These become

$$n\widehat{\alpha} + \left(\sum x_i \right) \widehat{\beta} = \sum y_i ,$$

$$\left(\sum x_i \right) \widehat{\alpha} + \left(\sum x_i^2 \right) \widehat{\beta} = \sum x_i y_i .$$

In matrix notation this is

$$\begin{pmatrix} n & \sum x_i \\ \sum x_i & \sum x_i^2 \end{pmatrix} \begin{pmatrix} \widehat{\alpha} \\ \widehat{\beta} \end{pmatrix} = \begin{pmatrix} \sum y_i \\ \sum x_i y_i \end{pmatrix} .$$

To solve the equations without computer assistance, we create a table with rows x_k, y_k, x_k^2, $x_k y_k$, y_k^2, then total the rows and calculate the five values:

$$\bar{x}, \quad \bar{y}, \quad S_{xx}, \quad S_{xy}, \quad S_{yy},$$

where

$$S_{xx} = \sum x_k^2 - \frac{1}{n} \left(\sum x_k \right)^2 ,$$

$$S_{xy} = \sum x_k y_k - \frac{1}{n} \left(\sum x_k \right) \left(\sum y_k \right) ,$$

$$S_{yy} = \sum y_k^2 - \frac{1}{n} \left(\sum y_k \right)^2 .$$

The least squares fit is given by

$$\widehat{\beta} = \frac{S_{xy}}{S_{xx}} \ , \quad \widehat{\alpha} = \overline{y} - \overline{x}\widehat{\beta} .$$

The estimated regression line is $\widehat{y} = \widehat{\alpha} + \widehat{\beta}x$. This is the line with slope $\widehat{\beta}$ through $(\overline{x}, \overline{y})$ since it can be written $\widehat{y} - \overline{y} = \widehat{\beta}(x - \overline{x})$. The sample variance

$$\widehat{\sigma}^2 = \widehat{\text{var}}(Y|X = x) = \frac{1}{n-2} \sum_i (y_i - \widehat{y}_i)^2 ,$$

the bias-adjusted mean square deviation of the observations from their fitted values. In matrix notation the model is

$$E \begin{pmatrix} Y_1 \\ Y_2 \\ \vdots \\ Y_n \end{pmatrix} = \begin{pmatrix} 1 & x_1 \\ 1 & x_2 \\ \vdots & \vdots \\ 1 & x_n \end{pmatrix} \begin{pmatrix} \alpha \\ \beta \end{pmatrix} ,$$

which can be written in more general terms as

$$E(Y) = X \beta ,$$

where X is called the *design matrix*. Partial differentiation then gives the least squares equations, usually called the *normal equations:*

$$X^\top X \widehat{\beta} = X^\top y .$$

If $X^\top X$ is non-singular, then the LS estimates are

$$\widehat{\beta} = (X^\top X)^{-1} X^\top y .$$

Regression model assumptions

Least squares is a curve-fitting technique making no assumptions about the statistical properties of the data. For statistical inference we need to say something about the data variability.

- **SOA**. The *Second Order Assumptions* are that each observation y_i has the same variance, and that they are uncorrelated with each other.
- **NTA**. The *Normal Theory Assumptions* are the SOA with the addition that the observations are normally distributed.

18.4.3 The statistical properties of the parameter estimates

Under SOA,

1. $E(\widehat{\alpha}) = \alpha$, $E(\widehat{\beta}) = \beta$, and $E(\widehat{y}_x) = \alpha + \beta x$,
   where $\widehat{y}_x = \widehat{\alpha} + \widehat{\beta}x$ is the least squares predictor of y when the explanatory variable takes value x.

2. $\text{var}(\widehat{\alpha}) = \dfrac{\sum x_i^2}{n S_{xx}} \sigma^2$, $\text{var}(\widehat{\beta}) = \dfrac{\sigma^2}{S_{xx}}$, $\text{cov}(\widehat{\alpha}, \widehat{\beta}) = -\dfrac{\overline{x}}{S_{xx}} \sigma^2 .$

3. $\text{var}(\widehat{y}_x) = \left\{ \dfrac{1}{n} + \dfrac{(x - \overline{x})^2}{S_{xx}} \right\} \sigma^2 .$
   Under NTA, we have (1), (2), and (3), with the the addition of (4).

4. When $\widehat{\sigma}^2$ is used to estimate σ^2 in the expressions for $\mathrm{var}\,(\widehat{\alpha})$, $\mathrm{var}\,(\widehat{\beta})$, and $\mathrm{var}\,(\widehat{y}_x)$, then

$$\frac{\widehat{\alpha} - \alpha}{\widehat{se}\,(\widehat{\alpha})}\,, \quad \frac{\widehat{\beta} - \beta}{\widehat{se}\,(\widehat{\beta})}\,, \quad \frac{\widehat{y}_x - \alpha - \beta\,x}{\widehat{se}\,(\widehat{y}_x)}$$

are all from the Student t distribution on $n - 2$ degrees of freedom, the two degrees of freedom being lost from fitting the two parameters α and β by least squares. The estimated standard errors are the square roots of the variances when σ^2 is replaced by its estimated value $\widehat{\sigma}^2$.

18.4.4 Testing for the fit of a straight line regression

To test the null hypothesis, the one we are seeking evidence to reject, that the intercept takes specified value α_0, i.e. $H_0 : \alpha = \alpha_0$, we know that if H_0 is true, then under NTA $(\widehat{\alpha} - \alpha_0)/\widehat{se}\,(\widehat{\alpha})$ is from t_{n-2}. Similarly, to test the slope, $H_0 : \beta = \beta_0$, if H_0 then the test statistic $(\widehat{\beta} - \beta_0)/\widehat{se}\,(\widehat{\beta})$ is from t_{n-2}.

There is a simplification to the test statistic when testing for evidence of non-zero slope. In this case, with $H_0 : \beta = 0$, the test statistic can be written

$$\frac{\widehat{\beta}}{\widehat{se}\,(\widehat{\beta})} \;=\; \frac{r\,\sqrt{n-2}}{\sqrt{1-r^2}}\,.$$

Here, r is the sample correlation coefficient (of Section 17.6.6)

$$r \;=\; \frac{S_{xy}}{\sqrt{S_{xx}\,S_{yy}}}\,.$$

An alternative method is to fit a quadratic regression

$$E(Y|X = x) \;=\; \beta_0 + \beta_1 x + \beta_2\,x^2,$$

and test for evidence that β_2 is non-zero.

18.4.5 Multiple regression models

$$E(Y_i) \;=\; \beta_1 x_{1i} + \beta_2 x_{2i} + \cdots + \beta_q x_{qi}$$

These models are used in econometrics, where the x_{ki} are values given for example by key risk indicators. In practice it would be more common to see models of a greater sophistication, where the explanatory variables are themselves random and correlated with each other. This is just a starting point for models such as the Kalman Filter and State Space models.

For the least squares fit, we find $\widehat{\beta} = (\widehat{\beta}_1, \widehat{\beta}_2, \cdots, \widehat{\beta}_q)^\top$ which minimize

$$\sum_{i=1}^{n} \left\{ y_i - (\beta_1 x_{1i} + \beta_2 x_{2i} + \cdots + \beta_q x_{qi}) \right\}^2,$$

which in matrix notation is $(y - X\beta)^\top (y - X\beta)$, where $\beta = (\beta_1, \beta_2, \cdots, \beta_q)^\top$. Partial differentiation with respect to each β_i gives the normal equations

$$X^\top X \widehat{\beta} \;=\; X^\top y$$

with least squares estimates

$$\widehat{\boldsymbol{\beta}} = (X^T X)^{-1} X^T \boldsymbol{y}.$$

The expectations, variances and covariances are given by

$$E(\widehat{\boldsymbol{\beta}}) = \boldsymbol{\beta}, \quad C(\widehat{\boldsymbol{\beta}}) = (X^T X)^{-1} \sigma^2,$$

where $C(\widehat{\boldsymbol{\beta}})$ is the covariance matrix,
i.e. $[C(\widehat{\boldsymbol{\beta}})]_{ij} = \mathrm{cov}(\widehat{\beta}_i, \widehat{\beta}_j), \quad \mathrm{var}(\widehat{\beta}_i) = [C(\widehat{\boldsymbol{\beta}})]_{ii}, \quad \mathrm{se}(\widehat{\beta}_i) = \sqrt{\mathrm{var}(\widehat{\beta}_i)}.$

The fitted values are $\widehat{\boldsymbol{y}} = (\widehat{y}_1, \ldots, \widehat{y}_n)^T = X\widehat{\boldsymbol{\beta}}$.

The *Residual Sum of Squares* (RSS) is the sum of squared differences between the observed and fitted values and can be written as

$$\mathrm{RSS} = \boldsymbol{y}^T \boldsymbol{y} - \widehat{\boldsymbol{y}}^T \widehat{\boldsymbol{y}} = \boldsymbol{y}^T \boldsymbol{y} - \widehat{\boldsymbol{\beta}}^T X^T X \widehat{\boldsymbol{\beta}}$$

Then the unbiased estimator for σ^2 is

$$\widehat{\sigma}^2 = \frac{\mathrm{RSS}}{n - q},$$

where the denominator corrects the biased arising from fitting q parameters.

Under normal theory assumptions, if the null hypothesis is $H_0 : \beta_i = b_i$, then $z_i = (\widehat{\beta}_i - b_i)/\widehat{\mathrm{se}}(\widehat{\beta}_i)$ is from t_{n-q}. There is some evidence against H_0 if $|z_i|$ exceeds $t_{n-q,\,0.05}$.

For the straight line regression

$$X^T X = \begin{pmatrix} n & \sum x_i \\ \sum x_i & \sum x_i^2 \end{pmatrix} \quad C(\widehat{\boldsymbol{\beta}}) = \frac{1}{n\,S_{xx}} \begin{pmatrix} \sum x_i^2 & -\sum x_i \\ -\sum x_i & n \end{pmatrix} \sigma^2$$

18.4.6   Logistic regression

This is a regression model for zero-one events, for example when we wish to model how the chance of default depends on explanatory variables. Let $\theta(\boldsymbol{x}) = E(Y \mid \boldsymbol{x})$ be the probability of default of the binary (Bernoulli distributed) variable Y given the explanatory variables $\boldsymbol{x}$. Then for a single regressor variable x and straight line regression, the logistic regression model has

$$\theta(x) = \frac{\exp(\alpha + \beta x)}{1 + \exp(\alpha + \beta x)}.$$

The *logit transformation* is

$$g(x) = \ln\left(\frac{\theta(x)}{1 - \theta(x)}\right) = \alpha + \beta x.$$

For any probability θ, the function $\ln\{\theta/(1 - \theta)\}$ is known as the log-odds.

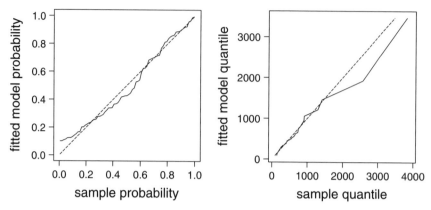

Figure 18.2   P-P and Q-Q plots for Data 4 (Table 17.4).

18.5   VALIDATION: TESTING MODEL FIT

18.5.1   Basic methods

Probability plots

The P-P and Q-Q plots Figure 18.2 for the severity data 4 (Table 17.4) show the sample values compared with the GEV model (Section 20.7) fitted using probability weighted moments (Section 17.7.5). A fuller treatment is given in Chapter 21.

The chi-squared test of fit

(1) We group the frequencies into bins so that the fitted frequency for each bin group $\widehat{n}_y$ is about 5 or more.
(2) We calculate the statistic

$$X^2 \;=\; \sum_y \frac{(n_y - \widehat{n}_y)^2}{\widehat{n}_y} \;=\; \sum_y \frac{(O_y - E_y)^2}{E_y} \;,$$

where $O_y = n_y$ is the *O*bserved frequency and $E_y = \widehat{n}_y$ is *fitted* (or *E*xpected) frequency. The *X* in the formula is the capital letter form of the Greek lower case letter χ *(chi)*.
(3) Refer to the table of χ^2_k with significance level α, where k is the number of bins, less the number of parameters fitted, less 1 for having made the fitted total the same as the actual total.
(4) If $X^2 > \chi^2_{k,.05}$ there is *some evidence* for rejecting the model.
   If $X^2 > \chi^2_{k,.01}$ there is *strong evidence*.

A disadvantage associated with this test is that evidence for rejecting the model does not point to why.

   A wider description of tests of fit is given after an introduction to statistical testing. They essentially examine ways of measuring the differences between the two curves in probability plots, and identifying when the difference is statistically significant.

Comparison with simulated data

We might create simulated data from a hypothesized model, and compare its analysis with that of the observed data. The simulation of data from continuous distributions can be done by taking independent values in (0,1) from a standard uniform random number generator and feeding them into the quantile function for the required model. This is expanded on in Chapter 21 after we have identified the quantile functions in Chapter 20.

18.5.2   Introduction to hypothesis testing

A statistical test follows the path of the scientific method. We take a hypothesis that we seek evidence for overturning. This we call the *null hypothesis,* and label it H_0. We generally also specify an *alternative hypothesis* H_1, often wider in scope than H_0, sometimes just saying "*Not* H_0." We collect evidence from experimental data. We reject H_0 if the evidence goes much more strongly in support of H_1 than H_0. Otherwise we accept H_0. There is a strong reluctance to reject the null hypothesis without good evidence, which usually requires a lot of data. This might not be available for operational risk losses in many or any of Basel II's 56 categories under loss data analysis. If H_0 is rejected, the scientific method goes on to narrow down H_1 to provide a new null hypothesis, the test of which requires fresh data. Using the same data that gave support for the new hypothesis leads to "overfitting."

Examples of hypotheses in respect of a parameter θ are

- $H_0 : \theta = 0,$ $H_1 : \theta = 1.$
  Hypotheses like these are *simple hypotheses,* with each having θ taking just one value.
- $H_0 : \theta = 0,$ $H_1 : \theta \neq 0.$
  Here H_1 is a composite hypothesis, since θ takes a set of values. It is also a *two-sided test,* since H_1 allows rejection if either $\theta > 0$ or $\theta < 0$. The scope of $H_1 : \theta \neq \frac{1}{2}$, for example, includes both $\theta = 0.49999$ and $\theta = 0.99999$.
- $H_0 : \theta = 0,$ $H_1 : \theta > 0.$
  This is a *one-sided test* since evidence supporting $\theta < 0$ would not lead us to reject H_0.

Accepting H_0 does not mean H_0 is true, only that there is no evidence for rejecting it. The *critical region R* is the rejection set, the values of the test statistic for which H_0 is to be rejected. The *decision rule* is the specification of R.

We judge a test by its error probabilities. Some definitions used in testing are

- *Type 1 Error*: rejecting H_0 when H_0 is true.
- *Type 2 Error*: accepting H_0 when H_0 is false.
- *Size*: $\alpha = P(\text{reject } H_0 | H_0 \text{ is true})$, the probability of a Type 1 error.
- *Power*: $\beta(\theta) = P(\text{reject } H_0 | H_1 \text{ is true})$.

Here are two examples which clearly show that we cannot treat the two errors as being equivalent. First, when H_0 is "*the prisoner is guilty,*" the type 1 error is "*finding a guilty prisoner innocent,*" with the type 2 error being "*condemning an innocent prisoner.*" The second example matches a surprise attack with a false alarm.

18.5.3 Likelihood ratio tests

Suppose that we have two simple hypotheses, $H_0 : \theta = \theta_0$ to be tested against $H_1 : \theta = \theta_1$. Suppose also that our data is $x = x_1, x_2, \ldots, x_n$, and our random variable is $X = X_1, X_2, \ldots, X_n$. Then the *likelihood ratio* is (for discrete probability models)

$$\lambda(x) = \frac{P(X = x|H_1)}{P(X = x|H_0)}.$$

The larger $\lambda(x)$ is, the stronger the evidence we have for rejecting H_0.

Example: A biased coin

A coin has either probability $\frac{1}{2}$ or $\frac{1}{4}$ of showing heads. In 10 tosses of a coin we observe three heads. Does this support $H_0 : \theta = \frac{1}{2}$ or $H_1 : \theta = \frac{1}{4}$?

$$\lambda(3) = \frac{\binom{10}{3} \left(\frac{1}{4}\right)^3 \left(1 - \frac{1}{4}\right)^7}{\binom{10}{3} \left(\frac{1}{2}\right)^3 \left(1 - \frac{1}{2}\right)^7} = 267 \gg 1.$$

This 267 is so very high compared with 1 that we must reject H_0, that the coin is unbiased. If we observe four heads: $\lambda(4) = 0.71 < 1$ so we have no reason to say that the coin is biased. Since we would need good reasons for rejecting H_0 in choosing the rejection threshold we must set its value to be higher than 1.

18.5.4 The five-step procedure for a composite alternative hypothesis

1. Specify the hypotheses such as "a coin is fair" i.e. $H_0 : P(H) = \frac{1}{2}$, $H_1 : P(H) \neq \frac{1}{2}$, and choose the size (significance level) α, usually 0.05 or 0.01.
2. Select a test statistic, t, for example, the observed number of Hs in 10 tosses.
3. Specify the rejection set R, for example, values well away from 5 if H_0 is true. Since, if H_0, t then has the *Binomial* $(10, \frac{1}{2})$ sampling distribution we can calculate $P(R)$.
   (a) Suppose that R_a is the rejection set $\{0, 1, 9, 10\}$, that is we would reject H_0 if we were to observe 0, 1, 9 or 10 Hs. The chance of this, $P(R_a)$ is 0.021 if H_0.
   (b) For $R_b = \{0, 1, 2, 8, 9, 10\}$, we have $P(R_b) = 0.109$ if H_0.
   Neither 0.021 nor 0.109 value matches our specified rejection probability of 0.05 under H_0. Suppose that we take a probability mixture of the two rejection sets.
   (c) For $R_c = \{2, 8\}$, we have $P(R_c) = 0.088$ if H_0.
   Now let us choose a randomized decision rule for which
   - if t is in the set R_a then we always reject H_0;
   - if it is in R_c, then we reject H_0 with probability p;
   - and if it is in neither, we don't reject H_0.
   Then $P(\text{reject } H_0) = 0.021 + 0.088\,p = 0.05$ if $p = 0.029/0.088 = 0.330$. This is very close to 1/3, so the randomization could easily be carried out by rolling a die.
4. Do the experiment. Calculate t. See if t is in the rejection set R.
5. State the conclusion.

If t is in R, then, if H_0 were true, this would happen less than 5 % of the time, and so would be unlikely. We express this by writing that the experiment provides *some evidence* for rejecting H_0, or that we reject H_0 at the 5 % level. At the 1 % level we say it provides *strong evidence*, and so it would be very unlikely. If t is not in R, then, if H_0 were true, this would happen at least 95 % of the time. The experiment therefore gives no evidence for rejecting H_0 (at the 5 % level).

Example

A product is known to be calibrated as normally distributed with expectation 154 and variance 16, i.e. $N(154,16)$. As a result of replacing some elements of the processing, we wish to test if there has been a change in output. Twenty items were selected at random and found to have an average score of 151. From past experience it is known that the variance is unchanged.

1. $H_0 : \mu = 154$, $H_1 : \mu \neq 154$, $\alpha = 0.01$.
2. $t = \dfrac{\bar{x} - 154}{\sqrt{16}/\sqrt{20}} = -3.35$.
3. t is from $N(0,1)$ under H_0
   A suitable rejection region is the 1% in the tails of $N(0,1)$, i.e. beyond ± 2.58.
4. -3.35 is beyond ± 2.58.
5. We have strong evidence for rejecting H_0.

We are not estimating σ, so the table of the normal distribution is used, and not the Student t table. Size $\alpha = 0.01$ gives wider range at ± 2.58, than the size 0.05 range of ± 1.96.

In terms of confidence intervals, the 99 % confidence interval for the expectation μ is (148.7, 153.3), so 154 lies outside.

Example

The average time for processing a loss event is 6 units. To test if the average time has gone down after a training session, 16 test items were processed and gave a sample mean time of 5.8, with a sample standard deviation of 1.2. We assume that the times are from a normal distribution.

1. $H_0 : \mu = 6$, against $H_1 : \mu < 6$. This is a one-sided test. We set the size α to be 0.05.
2. The test statistic $t = \dfrac{\bar{x} - 6}{s/\sqrt{n}} = \dfrac{5.8 - 6}{1.2/\sqrt{16}} = -0.67$.
3. Since the standard deviation is estimated from 20 observations we refer to the table of the Student t distribution with 19 degrees of freedom, which gives $t_{19,\,0.10} = 1.73$. The one-sided test has all the rejection probability in one tail so we find a value t for which $P(|T| > t) = 0.10$. Our test statistic would have to be less than -1.73 to be in the rejection region.
4. $t = -0.67$.
5. We have no evidence for rejecting H_0.

The 95 % lower confidence limit is $5.8 - 1.73\,(0.3) = 5.3$, so we would need a mean time smaller than this to provide evidence from 16 trials of a reduction in speed.

18.5.5   Testing for a difference in expectations

Analysts A and B make independent readings on samples of the same material. Analyst A has n_A samples and B has n_B. From previous work, their readings have known precisions given by variances σ_A^2 and σ_B^2. We wish to test for relative bias between the two analysts.

1. To test $H_0 : \theta = \mu_A - \mu_B = 0$, against $H_1 : \theta \neq 0$.
2. An estimate of θ is $z = \bar{x}_A - \bar{x}_B$. If n is fairly large z is from $N(\theta, \sigma_Z^2)$

   where $\sigma_Z^2 = \dfrac{\sigma_A^2}{n_A} + \dfrac{\sigma_B^2}{n_B}$
3. If H_0 is true, then $t = z/\sigma_Z$ is from $N(0,1)$. If H_1 is true, then t is from $N(\theta/\sigma_Z, 1)$. We check from tables of $N(0,1)$ whether H_0 is unlikely.

If σ_A^2 and σ_B^2 are unknown and we are prepared to assume that they have the same value σ^2 then

$$s^2 = \frac{1}{n_A + n_B - 2} \left\{ (n_A - 1)s_A^2 + (n_B - 1)s_B^2 \right\}$$

using the two separate estimates s_A and s_B of σ. The test statistic for testing $H_0 : \mu_A = \mu_B$ becomes

$$t = \frac{(\bar{x}_A - \bar{x}_B) - 0}{s\sqrt{1/n_A + 1/n_B}}$$

and we use the table of Student t on $n_A + n_B - 2$ df.

18.6   SUBJECTIVE PROBABILITY AND BAYESIAN STATISTICS

So far in this review of quantification we have looked only at classical statistical methods involving the estimation of unknown parameters of a model from collected data through likelihood-based techniques such as maximum likelihood, with measurement of the uncertainty due to sampling variability. There would be model checking, including the investigation of model change as new data is introduced, and effective decision procedures when the data is tested against the model.

Bayesian statistics assumes that the unknown parameter is random and has a probability density called the *prior probability density function*, which expresses the statistician's or client's beliefs about the parameter before any data is collected. This can involve serious introspection, particularly for models containing more than one parameter when we need beliefs about their joint randomness. After the data is collected, the *posterior pdf* is calculated using Bayes Rule. This is the formal expression for the belief we are required to accept, given that the model is true, based on the rules of probability in the light of the evidence given by the data. For reasonable prior pdfs, the evidence from the data should overwhelm the initial beliefs.

Thomas Bayes (1702–1761), a nonconformist minister, was elected in 1742 to a fellowship of the Royal Society of London for his skill in mathematics. His formula, widely known as Bayes Theorem, was presented to the Society by letter on his behalf. This is his only published contribution to probability theory. See also Figure 8.7.

18.6.1 Subjective "probability"

We begin with the formal notation expressing more or less likeliness, the likeliness ordering.

$A \preceq B$ is "event B is at least as likely to occur as A."
$A \prec B$ is "B is more likely than A to occur."
$A \approx B$ is "A and B are equally likely to occur."

With these relationships there is a "probability" function P which *agrees* with $\preceq$
   i.e. $P(A) \leq P(B)$ if and only if $A \preceq B$.
   This function P is unique if we use a *Uniform* $(0,1)$ random variable X as a scale. If we were indifferent between A and "$X \leq \lambda$" then they would have the same "probability" λ. We are calibrating the Bayesian probability function by matching it to a *Uniform* distribution.
   Consider the two gambles: You get \$100 tomorrow
   A : if there is no rain tomorrow, B : with probability λ.
   If you were to choose the value of λ so that you were indifferent between A and B, then $P(\text{no rain tomorrow}) = \lambda$ is a subjective "probability." This is a probability that does not have a frequency interpretation as a long-run proportion of successes, yet it satisfies all the axioms and rules of probability theory.

18.6.2 Bayes Rule and inverse probability

Bayes Rule (although widely called Bayes Theorem, it is not really a theorem at all) gives the inverse probability required in assessing evidence.
   Suppose that a test for state C is carried out. Let T be the event "the test result provides evidence that supports C," and let C be the event that "state C holds." For example, suppose that T is "the evidence supports the guilt of a defendant," such as a blood sample found at the crime scene matching that of the defendant, then C would be that the defendant is guilty. We want to know the value of the probability $P(C|T)$ that the defendant is guilty in the light of the test showing support for the guilt.
   From our database we have our best estimates of $P(T|C)$ and $P(T|\overline{C})$, where $\overline{C}$ is the event "C does not hold."
   Bayes Rule gives the relationship

$$P(C|T) \;=\; \frac{P(T|C)\,P(C)}{P(T|C)\,P(C) \,+\, P(T|\overline{C})\,P(\overline{C})}$$

This involves $P(C)$ (and $P(\overline{C}) = 1 - P(C)$), which often is not known. However, we can use a subjective best estimate as a prior probability here.
   We note that Bayes Rule can be written as

$$P(C|T) = P(C \cap T)/P(T)$$

which is the definition of conditional probability, where $\cap$ can be read as 'and'. The inverse probability is the representation of $P(C|T)$ in terms of $P(T|C)$ and $P(T|\overline{C})$.

18.6.3 Prior probabilities

A prior probability of 0 or 1 is not allowed since it cannot be modified by evidence.

As new test data come in, $P(T|C)$ will be updated in the light of the evidence. With sufficient test data, the resulting $P(T|C)$ will be dominated by the evidence and not our prior belief, allowing a consensus to arise regardless of differing initial beliefs.

18.6.4   The courtroom fallacy

Suppose as above that T = "the evidence supports guilt," C = "the defendant is guilty." Suppose also that $P(T|C) = 1$. The prosecutor's fallacy is to argue that $P(C|T) = 1$.

If $P(C)$ is 1 % and $P(T|\overline{C})$ is also 1 %, then from Bayes' Rule $P(C|T)$ is approximately 0.5. We see the implications for random drug testing.

In a letter to the influential journal *Nature*, Jack Good (Good, 1996) reported that the law professor, Alan Dershowitz, while assisting the defence of O.J. Simpson on trial for murdering his wife, used a version of this fallacy during a television talk show. Dershowitz argued that since only one in a thousand wife beaters actually goes on to murder his spouse, it was very unlikely that, despite Simpson being a wife beater, he was her murderer.

Let C be "the husband murdered his wife," $\overline{C}$ be "the husband didn't do it," and T be "the woman was murdered." Let all probabilities be conditional on the victim having previously been battered by her husband. Then the defence is arguing that $P(C|T) = 0.0001$.

However, by Bayes Rule, $P(T|\overline{C}) = 0.0001$, and

$$P(C|T) = \frac{P(T|C)P(C)}{P(T|C)P(C) + P(T|\overline{C})P(\overline{C})}$$

$$= \frac{1 \times 0.0001}{(1 \times 0.0001) + (0.0001 \times 0.9999)} = \frac{1}{1.9999} = 0.5.$$

This holds without any supporting evidence.

For the trial of a rape case that relied on DNA evidence, professors of statistics from the universities of Oxford and London, acting as expert witnesses for opposing sides, had jointly prepared a questionnaire by which the members of the jury might apply Bayes Theorem to obtain their assessments of the probability of guilt. However, the Lord Chief Justice, Lord Bingham, in the Court of Criminal Appeals in London, reported as *R v Adams [1998] 1 Cr App R 377*, ruled that Bayes Theorem "would confuse the jury and deflect them from their proper task", and the case was sent for retrial. Perhaps the judge felt that Bayes was not compatible with the proof beyond reasonable doubt demanded in a jury trial.

18.6.5   Testing for HIV

The data is from the US Food and Drug Administration and the Centre for Disease Control and relate to use of the standard Wellcome Elisa test. The test is known to be very accurate, with only 0.01 % of false-positives, giving a positive result to people who do not have the virus. It takes three months after catching the virus for it to show up on the test. This gives a 0.70 % of HIV+ subjects getting a false-negative indicating that they are free of the virus. Let T represent a positive result, the test indicating that the subject is HIV+, and let H represent that the subject is indeed HIV+. Then $P(T|\overline{H})$ is 0.0001, and $P(T|H)$ is 0.9930. In 1991 the

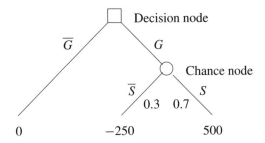

Figure 18.3   The decision tree showing a decision node and a chance node.

estimate of HIV+ in USA among those with known risk factors was 0.000025, so we take this as $P(H)$.

However, a person testing positive is more interested in the probability that, having tested positive, he or she is in fact positive. Bayes Rule gives

$$P(H|T) = \frac{P(T \cap H)}{P(T)} = \frac{P(H)\,P(T|H)}{P(H)\,P(T|H) + P(\overline{H})\,P(T|\overline{H})}$$

$$= \frac{(25)(0.993)}{(25)(0.993) + (999975)(0.0001)} = 0.198882.$$

We conclude that only one in five who test positive are HIV+. This has implications for random drug testing. A positive test result needs a further independent test.

18.6.6   An application of decision tree analysis to a product launch

The best estimates of the probability of S (a successful launch) is 0.7, and of $\overline{S}$ (failure) is 0.3. The returns from S if G (the go ahead) is 500, and from $\overline{S}$ if G is -250. The returns if $\overline{G}$ (abort the launch) is 0. The decision is made that maximizes the expected return, $E(Y)$.

We calculate the expected return at the chance node shown in Figure 18.3:

$$E(Y|G) = (-250)(0.3) + (500)(0.7) = 275, \quad E(Y|\overline{G}) = 0 < 275,$$

so the decision would be G.

If we knew for certain S or $\overline{S}$, the decision would be G if S, or $\overline{G}$ if $\overline{S}$. This would give

$$E(Y|S \text{ or } \overline{S} \text{ known}) = (0)(0.3) + (500)(0.7) = 350.$$

It is thus not worth spending more than $350 - 275 = 75$ to find out.

Market research will show H, high returns, or $\overline{H}$, low returns. Past records show

$$P(H|S) = 0.85, \quad \text{and} \quad P(\overline{H}|\overline{S}) = 0.25.$$

From   this: $P(H \cap S) = P(H|S)\,P(S) = (0.85)(0.7) = 0.595$,   and $P(H \cap \overline{S}) = P(H|\overline{S})\,P(\overline{S}) = (0.25)(0.3) = 0.075$.

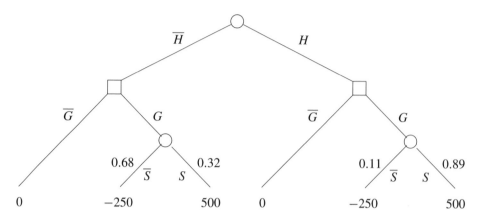

Figure 18.4 The decision tree after market research.

We draw up the probability table

	H	$\overline{H}$	Total
S	0.595	0.105	0.7
$\overline{S}$	0.075	0.225	0.3
Total	0.67	0.33	1

This gives

$$P(S|H) = \frac{P(H \cap S)}{P(H)} = 0.89, \quad \text{and} \quad P(S|\overline{H}) = \frac{P(\overline{H} \cap S)}{P(\overline{H})} = 0.32,$$

and decision tree Figure 18.4

Let Y_0 exclude the cost of the market research.
$E(Y_0|\overline{H} \cap G) = (-250)(0.68) + (500)(0.32) = -10$
$E(Y_0|\overline{H} \cap \overline{G}) = 0 > -10$, so the decision would be $\overline{G}$ if $\overline{H}$.
$E(Y_0|H \cap G) = (-250)(0.11) + (500)(0.89) = 417.5$
$E(Y_0|H \cap \overline{G}) = 0 < 417.5$, so the decision would be G if H.
   The decision is to be made whether to have market research (M) or not ($\overline{M}$).

$$E(Y_0|M) = (0)(0.33) + (417.5)(0.67) = 280$$

Let the cost of market research be c ($0 < c < 75$). Then, if $c > 5$,

$$E(Y|\overline{M}) = 275 > E(Y_0|M) - c,$$

so the decision would be $\overline{M}$ and G if $c > 5$, and M if $c < 5$ with $\overline{G}$ if $\overline{H}$ or with G if H.

18.6.7   What is Bayesian inference?

Let us go back to the classical inference problem of estimating the unknown parameter θ from data $x_1, x_2, \ldots, x_n$ from a Poisson distribution. We have the estimate $\overline{x}$ with the estimated variance $\overline{x}$ and estimated standard error $\sqrt{\overline{x}}/n$.

Bayesian inference assumes that the unknown parameter θ is a random variable Θ which has a probability density function $\pi_\Theta(\theta)$. This probability density function is called the *prior probability density function* and expresses our beliefs about θ before any data is collected. It can involve serious introspection, particularly for models containing more than one parameter when we need a joint pdf. The *posterior pdf* is calculated using Bayes Rule, and it gives the formal expression for the belief regarding the parameter that we should be arriving at in the light of the evidence given by the data.

How can decisions be validated in this environment where each is a consequence of a personal prior belief? How should advice from a Bayesian statistician be received when we know that it is based on the advisor's belief system? By using Bayes Rule, as more and more evidence is introduced, the posterior pdf will have less and less reliance on the prior pdf, leading to a consensus over all reasonable priors.

Bayes Rule is expressed through the formula

$$\pi_{\Theta|x}(\theta) = \frac{f_{X|\Theta}(x|\theta)\,\pi_\Theta(\theta)}{f_X(x)}$$

where $X = (X_1, X_2, \ldots, X_n)$, $x = (x_1, x_2, \ldots, x_n)$, $f_{X|\Theta}(x|\theta)$ is the *likelihood function*, $\ell(\theta|x)$ (Section 18.3.3). The denominator $f_X(x)$ is a constant of proportionality, making the total probability sum or integrate to 1.

How is this used? We can report the mode, mean and median of the posterior distribution. The mode is sometimes called the *Bayes maximum likelihood*, the others the *Bayes mean* and *Bayes median*. We can give a 95 % or 99 % confidence band on the posterior distribution, called a *credible region*.

The Bayesian method of using conjugate priors can simplify the computation. This uses a family of probability models for the prior that lead to the posterior staying within the same family. Updating the posterior as more data enters the system becomes a simple matter.

Much energy has been expended in trying to find priors that express having no beliefs, so-called *non-informative priors*, based on invariance behaviour under transformation of the parameters. If the values that might be taken by the parameter are unbounded, for example, saying that our belief is that it is equally likely to take any value from 0 to ∞, then the prior distribution cannot be made to have its total probability 1. We often compromise and use it anyway as long as the posterior is a true distribution.

Frequency Models

We review the frequency models in turn, tabulating their moment properties, and giving estimation methods for their parameter values.

19.1 BERNOULLI DISTRIBUTION, *Bernoulli* (θ)

This honours the Swiss mathematician Jakob (James in English, Jacques in French) Bernoulli (1654–1705). He is one of a family of distinguished mathematicians.

The distribution models events having only two possible outcomes. These might be

- success/failure   - yes/no   - 0/1   - default/not   - defective/not   - on/off.

One of the outcomes is scored 1, the other 0. The result scoring 1 is called a success, and its probability θ is called the probability of success. This applies even when the storyline counts failures, as when an item being classified unsatisfactory is scored 1.

From an experiment based on a sequence of independent Bernoulli events (called repeated Bernoulli trials) such as tosses of a coin, the sample mean $\bar{x}$ is the proportion of successes and is the MoME, MLE and MVUE estimator of $\mu = \theta$. The Law of Large Numbers, that $\bar{x}$ converges to θ as the sample size grows large, was proved by Jakob Bernoulli in 1689 though not published until 1713, eight years after his death. The mean score $\bar{x}$ is asymptotically normally distributed as the number of trials increases to infinity. This asymptotic normality was established in 1733 by Abraham de Moivre (1667–1754) and is known as De Moivre's Theorem. It is a special case of the Central Limit Theorem. De Moivre was a French-born mathematician who fled to London in 1688 to escape religious persecution. Its probability mass function shown in Figure 19.1 and its properties in Table 19.1.

19.2 BINOMIAL DISTRIBUTION, *Binomial* (n, θ)

This models the number of defective items in a batch of size n, when each independently has probability θ of being defective. It is the distribution of a random variable which is the total score in n independent *Bernoulli* (θ) trials, with each scoring $+1$ for a success, and $+0$ for

Table 19.1 *Bernoulli* (θ).

pmf	p_x	$p_0 = 1 - \theta, \quad p_1 = \theta$	$(0 < \theta < 1)$
expectation	μ	θ	
variance	σ^2	$\theta(1 - \theta)$	
skewness	β_1	$(1 - 2\theta)/\sqrt{\theta(1 - \theta)}$	
kurtosis	β_2	$\dfrac{1}{\theta(1 - \theta)} - 3$	
mode		$1 \, (\theta > 1/2), 0 \, (\theta < 1/2)$	

each failure. The pmf is shown for two examples in Table 19.1. Its descriptive measures are given in Table 19.2.

From the modeling as the total score in independent Bernoulli trials, if $X_1, X_2, \ldots, X_k$ are independent random variables with X_j having the *Binomial* (n_j, θ) distribution, then their sum, $X_1 + X_2 + \cdots + X_k$, is a *Binomial* $(\sum n_j, \theta)$ random variable. We need each Bernoulli distribution to have the same θ. From this representation, by virtue of the de Moivre theorem, the distribution of the total score is asymptotically normal.

Suppose that we have a random sample, $x_1, x_2, \ldots, x_k$, of independent observations from *Binomial* (n, θ) (same n and θ for each), then the sample mean $\bar{x} = (1/k)\sum_{j=1}^{k} x_j$ estimates $\mu = n\theta$, so the MoME of θ is $\widehat{\theta} = \bar{x}/n$.

The likelihood is

$$\ell(\theta; x_1, x_2, \ldots, x_k) = \prod_{i=1}^{k}\left\{\binom{n}{x_i}\theta^{x_i}(1-\theta)^{n-x_i}\right\} = \left\{\prod_{i=1}^{k}\binom{k}{x_i}\right\}\theta^{k\bar{x}}(1-\theta)^{k(n-\bar{x})}.$$

The log-likelihood is

$$L(\theta; x_1, x_2, \ldots, x_n) = \ln\left\{\prod_{i}\binom{k}{x_i}\right\} + n\bar{x}\ln(\theta) + n(k-\bar{x})\ln(1-\theta)$$

$$\frac{dL}{d\theta} = \frac{n\bar{x}}{\theta} - \frac{n(k-\bar{x})}{1-\theta}.$$

Then $dL/d\theta = 0$ when $\theta = \widehat{\theta} = \bar{x}/k$. We check that $d^2L/d\theta^2 < 0$ when $\theta = \widehat{\theta}$, which shows that $\widehat{\theta}$ gives a maximum and not a minimum. We conclude that $\widehat{\theta}$ is also the MLE.

Illustration

Suppose that reported events being processed by the back office staff are sorted according to the number of boxes ticked out of six features that have been identified as significant. From 100 such forms, the following data were obtained.

Number	y	0	1	2	3	4	5	6	Total
Frequency	n_y	5	14	34	29	16	2	0	100
	yn_y	0	14	68	87	64	10	0	243

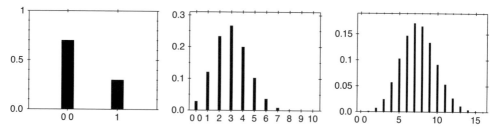

Figure 19.1 *Bernoulli* (0.3) *Binomial* (10,0.3) *Binomial* (25,0.3)

Table 19.2 *Binomial* (n, θ).

pmf	p_x	$\binom{n}{x} \theta^x (1 - \theta)^{n-x}$ $(x = 0, \ldots, n)$ $(0 < \theta < 1)$
expectation	μ	$n\theta$
variance	σ^2	$n\theta(1 - \theta)$
skewness	β_1	$\dfrac{1 - 2\theta}{\sqrt{n\theta(1 - \theta)}}$
kurtosis	β_2	$\dfrac{1}{n\theta(1 - \theta)} + 3 - \dfrac{6}{n}$
mode		x satisfying $n\theta \leq x \leq (n + 1)\theta$

$\binom{n}{x} = \dfrac{n!}{x! \, (n - x)!}$ is "n choose x" $(0! = 1)$

$x! = x(x - 1) \cdots 1$, so for example $4! = 4 \times 3 \times 2 \times 1 = 24$

We investigate how well a *Binomial* $(6, \theta)$ model fits the data. The table gives total frequency 243, with an average of $\bar{x} = 243/100 = 2.43$, so $2.43/6 = 0.405$ is the MoM and ML estimate of θ.

The fitted binomial probabilities are

$$\widehat{p}_y = \binom{6}{y}(0.405)^y(0.595)^{6-y} \quad (y = 0, 1, \ldots, 6)$$

Number	0	1	2	3	4	5	6	Total
Proportion	0.05	0.14	0.34	0.29	0.16	0.02	0	1.00
Fitted probability	0.044	0.181	0.308	0.280	0.143	0.039	0.004	0.999

The two plots are different ways of showing the same information. The first is a bar chart comparing the observed proportions with the fitted probabilities. The second is a P-P plot showing the cumulative fitted probabilities against the cumulative proportions, with a diagonal line from which we can see deviations from fitted values. There is clearly a good fit. Nevertheless, let us continue with the chi-square test of fit. The fitted probabilities for 5 and 6 do not amount to 5 %, so we group frequencies 4, 5, and 6. This gives the table

Number	y	0	1	2	3	≥ 4	Total
Frequency	O_y	5	14	34	29	18	100
Fitted frequency	E_y	4.4	18.1	30.8	28.0	18.6	99.9
	$\dfrac{\|O_y - E_y\|^2}{E_y}$	0.082	0.929	0.332	0.357	0.019	1.719

The number of bins is 5. Only one parameter, θ, has been fitted. The number of degrees of freedom, k, is therefore $5 - 1 - 1 = 3$. The 95 % and 99 % quantiles of the χ_3^2 distribution are 7.81 and 11.34 respectively. Since 1.719 does not exceed 7.81 there is no evidence for rejecting the hypothesis that the binomial distribution fits the data.

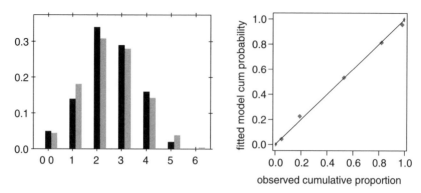

Figure 19.2 Bar chart of proportions and fitted probabilities and corresponding P-P plot.

19.2.1 Trinomial distribution

This extends the two binomial responses into three, for example, when the responses are "*yes,*" "*no,*" and "*don't know.*" The trinomial distribution gives the joint distribution for the numbers X, Y and Z of "*yes*'s," "*no*'s," and "*don't know*'s," in n independent trials, where $P(yes) = \theta_X$, $P(no) = \theta_Y$, and $P(don't\ know) = \theta_Z$, with $\theta_X + \theta_Y + \theta_Z = 1$.

If we observe x "*yes*'s," y "*no*'s" and $z = n - x - y$ "*don't know*'s," then

$$P(\{X = x\} \cap \{Y = y\}) = \frac{n!}{x!y!z!}\ \theta_X^x \theta_Y^y \theta_Z^z \quad (x = 0, 1, \ldots, n;\ y = 0, 1, \ldots, n - x)$$

Since the "*no*'s" plus "*don't know*'s" are "*not yes*'s," the marginal distribution of X is *Binomial* (n, θ_X), and similarly for Y and Z, so we obtain the expectations and variances of X, Y and Z. The covariances follow from

$$\mathrm{var}(X) = \mathrm{var}(n - X) = \mathrm{var}(Y + Z) = \mathrm{var}(Y) + \mathrm{var}(Z) + 2\,\mathrm{cov}(Y, Z)$$

giving $\quad 2\,\mathrm{cov}(Y, Z) = n\theta_X(1 - \theta_X) - n\theta_Y(1 - \theta_Y) - n\theta_Z(1 - \theta_Z)$

$$= n\theta_X(\theta_Y + \theta_Z) - n\theta_Y(\theta_Z + \theta_X) - n\theta_Z(\theta_X + \theta_Y) = -2n\,\theta_Y\theta_Z$$

The negative correlation comes from the sum $x + y + z$ being fixed. This gives Table 19.3.

19.2.2 Multinomial distribution

This generalizes the binomial/trinomial further to k distinct outcomes. It models the responses from n independent trials, with the outcome i in each trial occurring with probability θ_i, where $\sum_{i=1}^{k} \theta_i = 1$. The random variable is $(X_1, X_2, \ldots, X_k)$, where $\sum_{i=1}^{k} X_i = n$.

Table 19.3 Moments for the trinomial distribution.

	X	Y	Z
Expectation	$n\theta_X$	$n\theta_Y$	$n\theta_Z$
Variance	$n\theta_X(1 - \theta_X)$	$n\theta_Y(1 - \theta_Y)$	$n\theta_Z(1 - \theta_Z)$
	(Y, Z)	(Z, X)	(X, Y)
Covariance	$-n\theta_Y\theta_Z$	$-n\theta_Z\theta_X$	$-n\theta_X\theta_Y$

Table 19.4 Moments for the multinomial distribution.

Expectation	$E(X_i)$	$n\theta_i$
Variance	$\text{var}(X_i)$	$n\theta_i(1 - \theta_i)$
Covariance	$\text{cov}(X_i, X_j)$	$-n\theta_i\theta_j$

The probability mass function

$$P(\{X_1 = x_1\} \cap \cdots \cap \{X_k = x_k\}) = \binom{n}{x_1 \cdots x_k} \theta_1^{x_1} \cdots \theta_k^{x_k} \quad \left(\sum_{i=1}^{k} x_i = n\right)$$

where

$$\binom{n}{x_1 \cdots x_k} = \frac{n!}{(x_1!) \cdots (x_k!)}$$

is "n choose $x_1, \cdots, x_k$."

The formulae for the expectations, variances, and covariances of Table 19.4 are given by the same reasoning as for the trinomial.

19.3 GEOMETRIC DISTRIBUTION, *Geometric* (θ)

This models the number of independent Bernoulli trials (same θ) up to and including the first success. The random variable is the number of trials, not the number of successes. It is the model for return times for losses exceeding a fixed threshold in any year (Section 21.1.1). Its pmf is shown in Figure 19.3 and its properties in Table 19.5.

Success coming later than the xth trial is the same as saying each of the first x trials ended in failure so

$$P(X > x) = (1 - \theta)^x.$$

The *Geometric* distribution is characterized by its "lack of memory property," often called "no wear and tear." This can formally be stated as "future life at age $x + k$ has the same pmf

Table 19.5 *Geometric* (θ).

pmf	p_x	$(1 - \theta)^{x-1}\theta$ ($x = 1, 2, 3, \ldots$) ($0 < \theta < 1$)
expectation	μ	$\dfrac{1}{\theta}$
variance	σ^2	$\dfrac{1 - \theta}{\theta^2}$
skewness	β_1	$\dfrac{2 - \theta}{\sqrt{1 - \theta}}$
kurtosis	β_2	$\dfrac{\theta^2}{1 - \theta} + 6$
mode		1

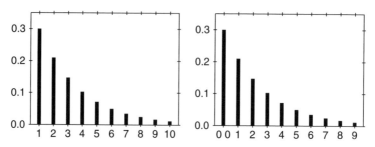

Figure 19.3 *Geometric* (0.3) and *waiting time* (0.3).

as at age x," and written as

$$P(X > x + k \mid X > k) = P(X > x).$$

This is satisfied only with $P(X > x) = (1 - \theta)^x$, since

$$\frac{P(\{X > x + k\} \cap \{X > k\})}{P(X > k)} = \frac{P(X > x + k)}{P(X > k)}$$

To validate the model we start with the expression

$$-\ln P(X > k) = -k \ln(1 - \theta).$$

For a random sample of n observations from *Geometric* (θ), with observed frequencies n_k ($k = 1, 2, \ldots$), the proportion of observations taking values exceeding k is

$$\widehat{p}_k = \frac{1}{n} \sum_{x=k+1}^{\infty} n_x .$$

Let $y_k = -\ln \widehat{p}_k$, then plotting y_k against k should give points approximately on a line through the origin with slope approximately $-\ln(1 - \theta)$. If the line through the points is clearly not a straight line through the origin, we have evidence against the data coming from the *Geometric* distribution. If we can accept that the points are approximately in a straight line through the origin, we can proceed to obtain the MoME $\widehat{\theta} = 1/\overline{x}$.

The waiting time distribution

This distribution shown in Figure 19.3 and Table 19.6. It models the number of *failures* before the first success. If the random variable X is *Geometric* (θ) then the random variable

Table 19.6 *Waiting time* (θ).

pmf	p_x	$(1 - \theta)^x \theta \quad (x = 0, 1, 2, \ldots) \quad (0 < \theta < 1)$
expectation	μ	$\dfrac{1}{\theta} - 1$
mode		0

$Y = X - 1$ has the waiting time distribution with parameter θ. The expectation drops by one, but the variance, skewness, and kurtosis are unchanged since they do not depend on location.

This waiting time distribution is the zero-truncated geometric distribution. Some care is needed in applying these two models since the names are often used the other way round.

19.4 HYPERGEOMETRIC DISTRIBUTION,
Hypergeometric (N, M, n)

This is a model for resampling from a finite binary population. An example is capture-recapture. A simple illustration of this is the problem of counting the number of fish in a pond. Fish are taken from the pond and marked and put back. After M have been marked and returned to the pond, a further n are taken, and the number x of these that carry a mark is noted. The probability distribution of this number is a function of the number N of fish in the pond.

The probability mass function is

$$p_x = \frac{\binom{M}{x}\binom{N-M}{n-x}}{\binom{N}{n}} \qquad (x = 0, 1, \ldots, n)$$

The numerator is the number of ways of choosing x out of M and the remaining $n - x$ out of the remaining $N - M$, each of which choices is equally likely from the ways of choosing n from N.

$$E(X) = \frac{nM}{N}, \qquad \mathrm{var}(X) = \frac{nM(N-M)(N-n)}{N^2(N-1)}$$

If we observe x, the method of moments estimator of N is nM/x, where n and M are known.

In sampling without replacement for quality control, a random sample of n items from a collection of N is inspected and x are found to be mis-classified, then M, the number mis-classified in the collection, can be estimated as Nx/n.

19.5 NEGATIVE BINOMIAL DISTRIBUTION,
Negative Binomial (v, θ)

This is sometimes called the Pascal distribution after the French mathematician and philosopher Blaise Pascal (1623–1662) who considered special cases.

The Negative Binomial model can arise in many different ways, but as a frequency model for loss data its two parameters give a greater flexibility in fitting data than the single parameter Poisson model. It models the frequency when the Poisson parameter λ is itself a random variable with its value taken from a gamma severity distribution. We see, from Table 19.7 of its properties, that the variance always exceeds that of the Poisson distribution.

If the index parameter $v = n$, an integer, the negative binomial random variable corresponds to the number of Bernoulli trials which fail prior to the nth success. This then is the sum of n independent *waiting time* distributed random variables, each having the same parameter θ. Confusingly, the model representing the number of trials up to *and including* the nth success, which is the sum of n independent geometric random variables, is also known as the *Negative Binomial*. The basic properties of this distribution also are given in Section 19.5.2 and Table 19.11. A pmf is shown in Figure 19.4.

Table 19.7 *Negative Binomial* (v, θ).

pmf	p_x	$\binom{v+x-1}{x} \theta^v (1-\theta)^x \quad (x = 0, 1, 2, \ldots)$ with $v > 0$, and $0 < \theta < 1$
expectation	μ	$\dfrac{v(1-\theta)}{\theta}$
variance	σ^2	$\dfrac{v(1-\theta)}{\theta^2}$
skewness	β_1	$\dfrac{2-\theta}{\sqrt{\theta(1-\theta)}}$
kurtosis	β_2	$3 + \dfrac{6}{v} + \dfrac{\theta^2}{v(1-\theta)}$

In Table 19.7, $\binom{v+x-1}{x} = \dfrac{(v+x-1)!}{x!(v-1)!}$, generally referred to as "$v+x-1$ choose x."

However, because we are not requiring that the index parameter v takes just integer values, we must take $z!$ to be the extended integral form of factorial notation for the Gamma Function $\Gamma(z+1)$ (Section 18.2.2).

The distribution is sometimes given an alternative parameterization by writing $\theta = v/(\mu + v)$. This gives $E(X) = \mu$ and $\text{var}(X) = \mu + \mu^2/v$.

19.5.1 Fitting a negative binomial model

By the method of moments, we solve $\bar{x} = v(1-\theta)/\theta$ and $s^2 = v(1-\theta)/\theta^2$ to get $\widehat{\theta} = \bar{x}/s^2$ and $\widehat{v} = \bar{x}^2/(s^2 - \bar{x})$. For these estimates to make sense, we cannot have $\bar{x} > s^2$.

The MLEs require numerical iteration methods to solve for $\widehat{v}$ and $\widehat{\theta}$. The MoMEs are generally used as starting values for the iteration. This is probably best left to statistics computer packages since the iteration process can be slow.

Fitting a negative binomial model to Data set 1

In Section 17.8.1, we noted that a visual inspection of Table 17.1 gives no indication of dependence on the date or the day of the week. We therefore treat the data as a single set of

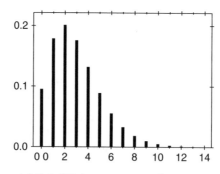

Figure 19.4 *Negative Binomial* $(5, 0.625)$ has $\mu = 3$ and $\sigma^2 = 8$.

Table 19.8 Fitting *Negative Binomial* (4, 0.450) to Data 1.

Number of frauds	0	1	2	3	4	5	6	7	8	9	
Frequency	2	3	3	5	7	2	1	1	2	3	
Percentage	6.1	9.1	9.1	15.2	21.2	6.1	3.0	3.0	6.1	9.1	
Fitted NegBin %	4.1	9.0	12.4	13.6	13.1	11.6	9.5	7.5	5.7	4.2	

Number of frauds	10	11	12	13	14	15	16	17	18	≥ 19	Total
Frequency	2	1	1	0	0	0	0	0	0	0	33
Percentage	6.1	3.0	3.0	0	0	0	0	0	0	0	100.1
Fitted NegBin %	3.0	2.1	1.4	1.0	0.6	0.4	0.3	0.2	0.1	0.2	100

33 observations. Table 19.8 shows the result of fitting a negative binomial distribution. The percentages are rounded so in this case they sum to 100.1 rather than 100.

From Section 17.4.1, we have $\bar{x} = 4.879$ and $s^2 = 11.172$. These give method of moments estimates $\widehat{\nu} = 3.782$ and $\widehat{\theta} = 0.437$. The MLEs are $\widehat{\nu} = 3.997$ and $\widehat{\theta} = 0.450$. In the table we fit *Negative Binomial* (4, 0.450).

Fitting a negative binomial model to Data set 2

The fitted distribution is *Negative Binomial* (2.576, 0.520).

The bar charts in Figure 19.6 show observed proportions against fitted *Negative Binomial* distributions. It is clear visually that in neither case is there a match between data and model, so there is no need to carry out formal tests. The *P-P plots* (P-P is short for *probability-probability plot*) match the cumulative fitted probabilities with the cumulative proportions (Figure 19.5). It is an alternative representation of the bar chart data. Sometimes P-P plots show the points joined up.

We see that the P-P plots do not show the discrepancy as well as the bar charts. This is because they plot cumulative values which smooth the variability. The clear differences at 4, 9 and 10 for Data 1 and at 1 and 2 for Data 2 the frequencies 1, 2, and 3, really need further investigation.

Testing the fit of Data 2

Despite the demonstrably poor fit shown by the bar charts, we will carry out the chi-squared test, for which we group the frequencies $\{ \geq 10\}$.

There are 11 bins. Two parameters have been fitted. The number of degrees of freedom, k, is therefore $11-2-1 = 8$. The 95 % and 99 % quantiles of the χ_8^2 distribution are 15.51

Table 19.9 Fitting *Negative Binomial* (2.576, 0.520) to Data 2.

Frauds	0	1	2	3	4	5	6	7	8
Frequency	221	188	525	112	73	72	44	40	14
Fitted	243.0	300.5	257.9	188.9	126.4	79.8	48.3	28.4	16.4

Frauds	9	10	11	12	13	14	15	≥ 16	Total
Frequency	7	2	2	4	3	2	1	0	1310
Fitted	9.2	5.1	2.8	1.6	0.8	0.4	0.3	0.2	1310.0

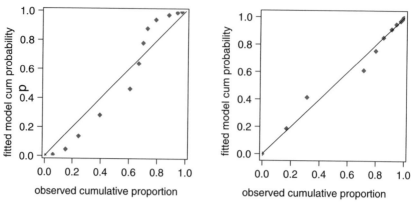

Figure 19.5   P-P plots for Data 1 and Data 2 (Tables 17.1 and 17.2) fitted by a *Negative Binomial* distribution.

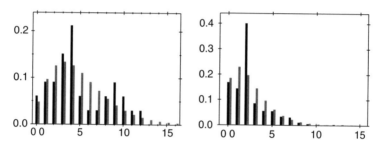

Figure 19.6   Bar charts of proportions and fitted probabilities for Data 1 and Data 2. Data (black), Negative Binomial (gray)

and 20.09 respectively. As seen in Table 19.10, 382 is way over these values so there is very strong evidence for rejecting the hypothesis that the negative binomial distribution fits the data. Further, since the Poisson distribution is a special case of the negative binomial, we can dismiss that as well.

Table 19.10   Chi-squared test of fit of Data 2.

y	0	1	2	3	4	5	6	7	8	9	≥ 10	Total
$|O_y - E_y|^2/E_y$	2.0	42.1	276.6	31.3	22.6	0.8	0.4	4.7	0.4	0.5	0.7	382.1

Table 19.11   Alternative form of the Negative Binomial model.

pmf	p_y	$\dbinom{y-1}{n-1} \theta^n (1-\theta)^{y-n}$ $(y = n, n+1, n+2, \ldots)$
		with $n = 1, 2, \ldots,$, and $0 < \theta < 1$
expectation	μ_Y	$\dfrac{n}{\theta}$

Table 19.12 *Poisson* (θ).

pmf	p_x	$\dfrac{\theta^x e^{-\theta}}{x!}$ $(x = 0, 1, 2, \ldots)$ (with $\theta > 0$)
expectation	μ	θ
variance	σ^2	θ
skewness	β_1	$1/\sqrt{\theta}$
kurtosis	β_2	$3 + (1/\theta)$
mode		the integer closest to θ

19.5.2 Alternative form of the Negative Binomial distribution

The random variable Y is $X + n$, where X is *Negative Binomial* (n, θ). This gives the number of independent Bernoulli trials up to and including the nth success. This is not a natural model for a loss data frequency distribution. We observe in Table 19.11 that $\mu_Y = \mu_X + n$, with the variance, skewness, and kurtosis unchanged by this shift in location.

19.6   POISSON DISTRIBUTION, *Poisson* (θ)

The Poisson distribution was described in 1837 by the French mathematician Siméon Denis Poisson (1781–1840). However, it was not until 1898 that it became well known. It was then that the Polish statistician Ladislaus Bortkiewicz (1868–1931) noted that rare events in a large population, such as the births of triplets, follow a Poisson distribution. He termed it the Law of Small Numbers. A particularly striking example was his demonstration, from data collected over 20 years of deaths from horse-kicks in 14 Prussian cavalry units, that it provided a good model for the annual numbers of deaths. Another popular illustration is R. D. Clark's study published in 1946 of the flying bomb hits on London during the Second World War. Counts of hits on 580 same-size regions were checked against the Poisson distribution to establish whether the doodlebugs were landing at random or had programmed guidance.

The *Poisson* (θ) distribution models the number of events in a unit time interval when they occur independently at a constant rate θ (as a *Poisson process* or *Poisson stream*). Three examples of its pmf are shown in Figure 19.7, and its properties in Table 19.12.

19.6.1 Fitting a Poisson distribution

I use the data in the following table under various storylines to illustrate the fitting of a Poisson distribution. Here, let us say that the data are 205 oprisk loss events observed over 143 days. The reason for using so-called toy data is that we would generally need far more than 143 counts to get the Poisson shape appearing.

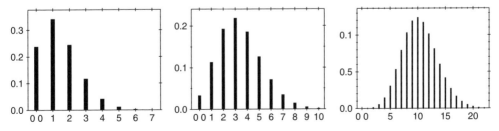

Figure 19.7 *Poisson* (1.434), *Poisson* (3.4), and *Poisson* (10.4).

Number seen	x	0	1	2	3	4	5	≥ 6	Total
Frequency	n_x	34	46	38	19	4	2	0	143
	$x n_x$	0	46	76	57	16	10	0	205

This gives the following summary statistics.

n	$\bar{x}$	s^2	s	$\hat{\beta}_1$	$\hat{\beta}_2$	Q1	x_{med}	Q3
143	1.434	1.332	1.154	0.616	3.02	1	1	2

The method of moments estimate of θ sets the sample mean $\bar{x} = \mu = 1/\theta$ so the estimate is $\hat{\theta} = 1/\bar{x}$. This has a direct interpretation as the rate at which events occur as a Poisson process. The inverse of the number of events per unit of time is the time per event. This estimate is also the MLE.

The data shows 205 losses over 143 days, giving a sample mean $\bar{x}$ of 1.434 per day. The number of oprisk events per day is the ratio $205/143 \approx 1.434$. This is just the sample mean of the data, and it estimates the expectation θ of the Poisson model. We calculate the pmf of *Poisson* (1.434) and present this as a row "Fitted probability" in the table. Note, the pmf gives positive probability values for x going all the way to infinity, so we may need to add a few extra columns until a "$\geq$" column is suitably small.

Number seen	x	0	1	2	3	4	5	≥ 6	Total
Proportion	n_x/n	.238	.322	.236	.133	.028	.014	0	1.001
Fitted prob.	$\hat{p}_x$	.238	.342	.245	.117	.042	.012	.004	1.000
Frequency	n_x	34	46	38	19	4	2	0	143
Fitted freq.	$n\hat{p}_x$	34.0	48.9	35.0	16.7	6.0	1.7	0.6	142.9

This data looks like Poisson data in the sense that, if we were to look at the proportions by dividing each frequency by 143, we can compare the proportions against the probabilities given

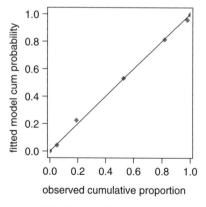
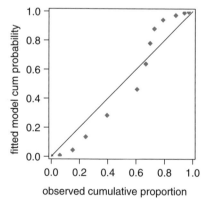

Figure 19.8 P-P plots for the data of Section 19.6.1 and for Data 1 of Table 17.1 fitted by *Poisson* distributions.

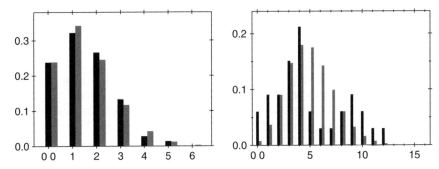

Figure 19.9 Bar charts of proportions and fitted probabilities for the data of Section 19.6.1 and Data 1 of Table 17.1. Data (black), Poisson (gray).

by the Poisson distribution having the population mean 1.434. Multiplying the proportions by 143 gives the fitted frequencies of the table. The frequency and fitted values give a very close match.

Parameter estimation uncertainty

We examine simulations of 143 values from a Poisson distribution having population mean 1.434 using two different computer packages. The simulations give the Table 19.13.

The sample means of the simulated data are 1.315 and 1.629. There is no reason to suppose that either of the two computer packages was seriously at fault for giving such poor estimates of 1.434. It is simply a consequence of taking small samples. The estimates are unbiased but the standard error of the estimates are $\sqrt{1.434/143} = 0.100$. About 95 % of the time we estimate the sample mean we can expect the result to be within a confidence band about 0.2 on either side of 1.434. Both 1.315 and 1.629 fall inside the confidence interval. This is an illustration of sampling fluctuation of small samples.

Table 19.13 Simulation of Poisson data.

	y	0	1	2	3	4	5	6	≥ 7	Total
Simulation 1	n_y	46	41	35	10	9	1	1	0	143
Simulation 2	n_y	33	42	31	24	8	5	0	0	143

	n	$\sum x_i$	$\sum x_i^2$	$\bar{x}$	s^2	s
Data	143	205	483	1.434	1.332	1.154
Simulation 1	143	188	476	1.315	1.612	1.269
Simulation 2	143	233	635	1.629	1.798	1.341

Testing the fit

Grouping $\{4, 5, \geq 6\}$ into $\{y \geq 4\}$ gives $E_{\geq 4} = 8.3 \geq 5$ and the table

Number	y	0	1	2	3	≥ 4	Total
Frequency	O_y	34	46	38	19	6	143
Fitted frequency	E_y	34.0	48.9	35.0	16.7	8.3	142.9
	$\lvert O_y - E_y \rvert^2 / E_y$	0	0.172	0.257	0.317	0.627	1.373

The number of bins is 5. Only one parameter, θ, has been fitted. The number of degrees of freedom, k, is therefore $5 - 1 - 1 = 3$. The 95 % and 99 % quantiles of the χ_3^2 distribution are 7.81 and 11.34 respectively. Since 1.373 does not exceed 7.81 there is no evidence for rejecting the hypothesis that the Poisson distribution fits the data.

A consequence of the Poisson distribution is that the frequency is such that its expectation and variance take the same value. Estimates of each give a quick indication of how well the model fits. However, this also restricts the applicability of the model. The negative binomial model allows over-dispersion, when the variance exceeds the mean. However, as seen in Section 19.5.1, this is no guarantee of a good fit.

The Poisson model fitted to Data 1

We have previously (Section 19.5.1) fitted a negative binomial to this data. The fitted distribution here is *Poisson* (4.879).

The Poisson model fitted to Data 2

Frauds	0	1	2	3	4	5	6	7	8	9	10	11	12	13	14	15	≥ 16	Total
Freq.	221	188	525	112	73	72	44	40	14	7	2	2	4	3	2	1	0	1310
Fitted	121	289	343	272	162	77	31	10	3	1	0	0	0	0	0	0	0	1309

Here the fitted distribution is *Poisson* (2.379). It is clear visually from the plots (Figures 19.8, 19.9 and 17.1) that Data 1 and Data 2 are nothing like Poisson data. Indeed the mismatch at frequencies in the fraud data tabled above is quite extreme. This was seen from the summary statistics, the sample mean and sample variance are so disparate as to make a Poisson fit inappropriate. The Negative Binomial model (Section 19.5.1) fared little better. There is no need to carry out formal tests with these data.

19.6.2 The zero-truncated Poisson frequency model

When events occur in continuous time we may be unable to identify zero counts. Also it may be that events with losses below a threshold may go unrecorded. The probabilities p_x are scaled up by a factor $(1 - p_0)^{-1}$ to restore the total probability to 1. The zero-truncated distribution is also called the *positive Poisson* distribution (Johnson *et al.*, 1993). The pmf and properties are given in Table 19.14.

Table 19.14 *Zero-Truncated Poisson* (θ).

pmf	p_x	$\dfrac{1}{1 - e^{-\theta}} \dfrac{\theta^x e^{-\theta}}{x!}$ $(x = 1, 2, \ldots)$ (with $\theta > 0$)
expectation	μ	$\dfrac{\theta}{1 - e^{-\theta}}$
variance	σ^2	$\mu(\theta + 1 - \mu)$
	μ_3	$\mu\{\theta(\theta + 3) - 3\mu(\theta + 1) + 2\mu^2\}$
	μ_4	$\mu\{(\theta^3 + 6\theta^2 + 7\theta + 1) - 4\mu\theta(\theta + 3) + 6\mu^2(\theta + 1) - 3\mu^3\}$
skewness	β_1	μ_3/σ^3
kurtosis	β_2	μ_4/σ^4

Method of moments estimation matches $\bar{x}$ with μ and this gives an estimate of θ which is the solution of

$$\theta = \bar{x}(1 - e^{-\theta}).$$

This is also the maximum likelihood estimate for this example. There are tables or graphical methods for solving this; for example, we might plot $y = 1 - e^{-x}$ and $y = tx$, where $t = 1/\bar{x}$. The lines cross when x is the estimate of θ. Alternatively, it is ready for simple iterative solution as

$$\theta_{k+1} = \bar{x}(1 - e^{-\theta_k}).$$

We might use as the starting value θ_0 the quick but poor solution given by noting that

$$p_1 = \frac{\theta}{1 - e^{-\theta}} e^{-\theta}$$

where $1! = 1$. When we substitute the proportion n_1/n of 1s in the data for p_1 and $\bar{x} = \sum x_i/n$ from the method of moments formula, we obtain the formula $n_1 = (\sum x_i)e^{-\theta_0}$. This gives estimate $\ln(\sum x_i) - \ln(n_1)$ of θ_0.

The asymptotic variance of the MLE for large n is approximately

$$\text{var}(\theta_{MLE}) \approx \frac{\theta}{n} \frac{(1 - e^{-\theta})^2}{1 - (1 + \theta)e^{-\theta}}.$$

An unbiased estimator for θ is

$$\widehat{\theta} = \frac{1}{n} \sum_{x=2}^{n} x n_x,$$

where n_x is the frequency of value x in a random sample of size n. This is proved in the general truncation case in Section 19.6.3.

$$\text{var}(\widehat{\theta}) = \frac{\theta}{n}(1 + p_{1|0}) = \frac{\theta}{n}\left(1 + \frac{\theta e^{-\theta}}{1 - e^{-\theta}}\right).$$

The asymptotic relative efficiency relative to the MLE is over 95% (Subrahmaniam, 1965).

The case in which there is an excess of zero values, more than would be given by the Poisson distribution, can be treated as a mixture distribution of zeros and the zero-truncated Poisson. We look at mixture distributions in Section 19.8, where this is treated as a special case (Section 19.8.1) and its maximum likelihood solution found.

19.6.3   The left-truncated Poisson distribution

This has the probability mass function

$$p_{x|a} = \begin{cases} p_x/\overline{F}_a & (x = a + 1, a + 2, \ldots), \\ 0 & (\text{otherwise}), \end{cases}$$

where $p_x = \theta^x e^{-\theta}/x!$ is the *Poisson* (θ) pmf, and

$$\overline{F}_a = \sum_{x=a+1}^{\infty} p_x.$$

An unbiased estimator for θ is

$$\widehat{\theta}_a = \frac{1}{n} \sum_{x=a+2}^{\infty} x n_x,$$

where n_x is the frequency of value x in a random sample of size n. The proof of unbiasedness uses the property of the Poisson pmf that $p_x = (\theta/x) p_{x-1}$ for $x > 0$. Then, since the proportion n_x/n is unbiased for $p_{x|a}$,

$$E(\widehat{\theta}_a) = \sum_{x=a+2}^{\infty} x p_{x|a} = \sum_{x=a+2}^{\infty} \theta p_{x-1|a} = \theta \sum_{x-1=a+1}^{\infty} p_{x-1|a} = \theta \sum_{y=x-1=a+1}^{\infty} p_{y|a} = \theta,$$

where $p_{y|a}$ sum to 1 since they form a probability distribution.

Subrahmaniam (1965) shows that

$$\mathrm{var}(\widehat{\theta}_a) = \frac{\theta}{n}(1 + (a+1) p_{a+1|a}).$$

He shows that for $\theta \leq 1$, the efficiency exceeds 90 %, and for $\theta > 1$ with $a \leq 5$ the efficiency exceeds 73 %, this bound reducing to 62 % at $a = 10$.

19.7   (DISCRETE) UNIFORM DISTRIBUTION, *(Discrete) Uniform (k)*

An example is *(Discrete) Uniform* (6), which models the spots showing when a die is rolled. Table 19.15 gives its properties.

19.7.1   General Uniform Distribution, *(Discrete) Uniform (k, α, β)*

This has equal probabilities $1/k$ at k points equally spaced between α to β. The spacing is $\gamma = (\beta - \alpha)/(k - 1)$. In Table 19.16, z is the serial number in increasing size from 0 to $k - 1$. That is to say, if X is *(Discrete) Uniform* (k, α, β), then

$$p_z = P(Z = z) = P(X = \alpha + \gamma z).$$

The moments in Table 19.16 are those of X.

The skewness and kurtosis coefficients do not depend on location or scale and so can be seen to be unchanged from the *(Discrete) Uniform (k)* model.

Table 19.15   *(Discrete) Uniform (k).*

pmf	p_x	$\frac{1}{k}$ $(x = 1, 2, \ldots, k)$
expectation	μ	$\frac{1}{2}(k+1)$
variance	σ^2	$\frac{1}{12}(k^2 - 1)$
skewness	β_1	0
kurtosis	β_2	$\frac{3}{5}\left(3 - \frac{4}{k^2 - 1}\right)$

Table 19.16 *(Discrete) Uniform* (k, α, β).

pmf	p_z	$\dfrac{1}{k}$ $(z = 0, \ldots, k - 1)$
expectation	μ_X	$(\alpha + \beta)/2$
variance	σ_X^2	$\dfrac{1}{12}\left(\dfrac{k+1}{k-1}\right)(\beta - \alpha)^2$
skewness	β_1	0
kurtosis	β_2	$\dfrac{3}{5}\left(3 - \dfrac{4}{k^2 - 1}\right)$

The obvious estimates of α and β are $x_{\min}$ and $x_{\max}$ respectively. Other estimates are inappropriate.

19.8   MIXTURE MODELS

Suppose that we wish to combine the frequencies over more than one business line or event type, where each has its own frequency model. This will apply also when we wish to incorporate external data. Then, if category i has the probability mass function $\{p_i(x)\}$, and they are combined as a weighted average with weights α_i summing to 1, then the probability

$$p_x = P(X = x) = \sum_i \alpha_i \, p_i(x),$$

where $p_i(x) = P(X = x \mid X \text{ has pmf } \{p_i(x)\})$. The weights themselves form a discrete probability distribution. It is as if we select a value for i with probability α_i. This tells us which distribution to sample from. We build up a sample from the mixture distribution in this way.

The moments of the mixture distribution are just weighted mixtures

$$\mu'_r = E(X^r) = \sum_i \alpha_i \, E_i(X^r),$$

where E_i is expectation with respect to the ith distribution.

A case of some importance in frequency modeling is when the counts from a frequency distribution are "contaminated" by a small amount of wrongly classified data or data that deserves its own sub-classification such as frauds.

Another case, a special case of this "contamination," is that of zeros-added mixtures.

19.8.1   Zeros-added mixtures

When the zero count of no losses has a different character from the non-zero counts of loss activity, we can write the pmf as

$$p_x = \begin{cases} \alpha_0 + \alpha_1 \, p_1(0) & (x = 0), \\ \alpha_1 \, p_1(x) & (x \neq 0), \end{cases}$$

where $\alpha_0 + \alpha_1 = 1$.

Zeros-added Poisson

This is the case in which we have added zeros to the *Poisson* (θ) distribution. Here

$$p_0 = \alpha_0 + \alpha_1 e^{-\theta}, \quad p_j = \alpha_1 \frac{\theta^j e^{-\theta}}{j!} \quad (j = 1, 2, \ldots), \quad (\alpha_1 = 1 - \alpha_0).$$

We demonstrate the derivation of the maximum likelihood equations for the parameters when we observe frequencies n_j of $x = j$ in n independent trials.

The likelihood $\ell(\alpha_0, \theta; x) = p_0^{n_0} \prod_{j \geq 1} p_j^{n_j}$.

The log-likelihood

$$L(\alpha_0, \theta; x) = n_0 \ln(\alpha_0 + \alpha_1 e^{-\theta}) + \left(\sum_{j=1}^{\infty} n_j\right) \ln \alpha_1 + \left(\sum_{j=1}^{\infty} j n_j\right) \ln \theta$$

$$- \theta \sum_{j=1}^{\infty} n_j - \sum_{j=1}^{\infty} \ln(j!).$$

We note that $\sum_1^{\infty} n_j = n - n_0$, that $\sum_1^{\infty} j n_j = \sum x_i = n\bar{x}$, and that $d\alpha_1/d\alpha_0 = -1$. Then

$$\frac{\partial L}{\partial \alpha_0} = \frac{n_0}{\alpha_0 + \alpha_1 e^{-\theta}} (1 - e^{-\theta}) + (n - n_0)\left(-\frac{1}{\alpha_1}\right) = \frac{n_0 - n(\alpha_0 + \alpha_1 e^{-\theta})}{\alpha_1(\alpha_0 + \alpha_1 e^{-\theta})},$$

so $\partial L/\partial \alpha_0 = 0$ when $\alpha_0 + \alpha_1 e^{-\theta} = n_0/n$, the proportion of zeros.

$$\frac{\partial L}{\partial \theta} = \frac{n_0}{\alpha_0 + \alpha_1 e^{-\theta}} (-\alpha_1 e^{-\theta}) + \frac{1}{\theta} \sum_{j=1}^{\infty} j n_j - \sum_{j=1}^{\infty} n_j,$$

so $\partial L/\partial \alpha_0 = 0$ and $\partial L/\partial \theta = 0$ when

$$\frac{n_0}{n_0/n} (-\alpha_1 e^{-\theta}) + \frac{1}{\theta} n\bar{x} - (n - n_0) = 0.$$

This reduces to

$$0 = n\bar{x}/\theta + n_0 - n(1 + \alpha_1 e^{-\theta}) = n\bar{x}/\theta + \{n_0 - n(\alpha_0 + \alpha_1 e^{-\theta})\} - n\alpha_1$$
$$= n\bar{x}/\theta + 0 - n\alpha_1.$$

This gives $\alpha_1 = \bar{x}/\theta$. Finally, substituting for α_1 in $n\bar{x}/\theta + n_0 - n(1 + \alpha_1 e^{-\theta}) = 0$ gives

$$\theta = \frac{n\bar{x}}{n - n_0} (1 - e^{-\theta}),$$

the equation for iterative solution for θ. We see that written in this form with $n_0 = 0$ and $\alpha_0 = 0$ we have the maximum likelihood solution already obtained for the *zero-truncated Poisson* (θ). Having obtained a value for θ we then get a value for α_1 as $\bar{x}/\theta$.

20

Continuous Probability Distributions

20.1 BETA DISTRIBUTION, *Beta* (α, β)

The Beta distribution is useful in modeling because its support is over a bounded range, and it has a variety of shapes. Both α and β are shape parameters and take positive values. The support is the interval 0 to 1, though location and scale transformation will take it into any bounded interval. Its probability density function and moments are given in Table 20.1.

Table 20.1 *Beta* (α, β).

pdf	$f(x)$	$\dfrac{1}{B(\alpha, \beta)} x^{\alpha-1}(1-x)^{\beta-1}$	$(0 < x < 1)$
expectation	μ	$\dfrac{\alpha}{\alpha+\beta}$	
variance	σ^2	$\dfrac{\alpha\beta}{(\alpha+\beta)^2(\alpha+\beta+1)}$	
$E(X^r)$	μ'_r	$\dfrac{B(\alpha+r, \beta)}{B(\alpha, \beta)} = \dfrac{\Gamma(\alpha+r)}{\Gamma(\alpha+\beta+r)} \dfrac{\Gamma(\alpha+\beta)}{\Gamma(\alpha)}$	

Γ is the Gamma Function, B is the Beta Function
β_1 and β_2 are found from the moments $E(Z^r)$ (Section 17.6.1)

20.1.1 Beta distribution of type 2

In Section 18.2.2 we had an alternative form for the Beta Function

$$B(\alpha, \beta) = \int_0^\infty \frac{x^{\alpha-1}}{(1+x)^{\alpha+\beta}} \, dx$$

for $\alpha > 0$, $\beta > 0$. Since the integrand is always non-negative, this gives rise to the pdf on $(0, \infty)$

$$f(x) = \frac{1}{B(\alpha, \beta)} \frac{x^{\alpha-1}}{(1+x)^{\alpha+\beta}} \,,$$

known as the type 2 beta pdf. Its tails are thick enough for it to have no moments. Its mode is at 0, and when $\alpha = \beta = 1$ it is a special case of the loglogistic distribution (Section 20.10.1).

20.1.2 *Beta* (ξ) (GP2)

In extreme value theory this is known as the Beta distribution. A special case of the Beta distribution above, *Beta* (λ, 1), is known as the Power function distribution (Section 20.14), and has the pdf

$$f(y) = \lambda y^{\lambda-1} \qquad (0 < y < 1).$$

Table 20.2   *Beta* (ξ) (GP2) $(\xi < 0)$.

cdf	$F(z)$	$1 - (-z)^{\alpha}$	$(-1 < z < 0)$
pdf	$f(z)$	$\alpha (-z)^{\alpha - 1}$	$(-1 < z < 0)$
expectation	μ	$-\dfrac{1}{1 - \xi}$	
variance	σ^2	$\dfrac{\xi^2}{(2 - \xi)(1 - \xi)^2}$	
$E(Z^r)$	μ'_r	$(-1)^r \dfrac{1}{1 - r\xi}$	
mode		$\begin{cases} 0 & (\xi < -1) \\ -1 \le z \le 0 & (\xi = -1) \\ -1 & (-1 < \xi < 0) \end{cases}$	
quantile function	$Q(p)$	$-(1 - p)^{-\xi}$	
prob. weighted moments	ω_r	$-B(1 - \xi, r + 1)$	
2nd L-moment	λ_2	$\dfrac{-\xi}{(2 - \xi)(1 - \xi)}$	
3rd L-moment	λ_3	$\dfrac{12 - 11\xi + \xi^2}{(3 - \xi)(2 - \xi)(1 - \xi)}$	
L-skewness	$\tau_3 = \lambda_3/\lambda_2$	$\dfrac{12 - 11\xi + \xi^2}{(3 - \xi)(-\xi)}$	

$\alpha = 1/\xi$. β_1 and β_2 are found from the moments $E(Z^r)$ (Section 17.6.1)
B is the Beta Function. The L-kurtosis is found from ω_r (Sections 17.7.5 and 17.7.6)

If we reflect this about the origin replacing a random variable Y from this distribution by X where $X = -Y$, then the pdf for X is

$$f(x) = (-\lambda)(-x)^{\lambda - 1} \qquad (-1 < x < 0).$$

If we now set $\lambda = -1/\xi$ we get *Beta* (ξ), where $\xi < 0$. Its properties are given in Table 20.2 and illustrated in Figure 20.1.

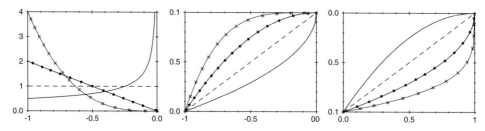

Figure 20.1   Pdfs, cdfs, and quantile functions for *Beta* (ξ) for $\xi = -2$ (line), -1 (dashes), -0.5 (dots), -0.25 (crosses).

Table 20.3 *Burr* (α, β).

cdf	$F(z)$	$1 - (1 + z^\alpha)^{-\beta}$	$(0 < z < \infty)$
pdf	$f(z)$	$\dfrac{\alpha \beta z^{\alpha-1}}{(1 + z^\alpha)^{\beta+1}}$	$(0 < z < \infty)$
$E(Z^r)$	μ'_r	$\beta B(1 + r\xi, \ \beta - r\xi)$	$(-1/\xi < r < \beta/\xi)$
mode		$\begin{cases} \left(\dfrac{\nu(1 - \xi)}{1 + \nu\xi} \right)^\xi & (0 < \xi < 1) \\ 0 & (\xi \geq 1) \end{cases}$	
quantile function	$Q(p)$	$\{(1 - p)^{-\nu} - 1\}^\xi$	

$\xi = 1/\alpha, \ \nu = 1/\beta.$ B is the Beta Function.
$\mu, \ \sigma^2, \ \beta_1$ and β_2 are found from the moments $E(Z^r)$

20.2   BURR DISTRIBUTION, *Burr* (α, β)

The Burr distributions is a system of 12 distributions based on the solutions of a system of differential equations, These solutions can be read as cdfs. The American statistician Irving W. Burr introduced the system in 1942, but studied only Burr XII in depth. This is the one usually referred to as the Burr distribution and the one most widely used because of its simple structure. It is the one described here in Table 20.3 and Figure 20.2.

Burr XII has two shape parameters, α and β, both positive, and has support on $(0, \infty)$.

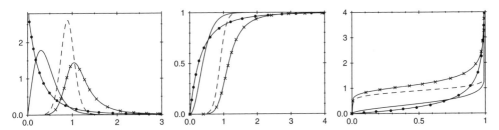

Figure 20.2   Pdfs, cdfs, and quantile functions for *Burr* (α, β) for $(\alpha, \beta) = (2, 5)$ (line), (8,2) (dashes), (1,3) (dots), (8,0.5) (crosses).

20.3   CAUCHY DISTRIBUTION

Table 20.4 and Figure 20.3 describe the standard Cauchy distribution.

20.4   EXPONENTIAL DISTRIBUTION, *Exponential* (λ)

This models the intervals between events occurring at a constant rate λ. The parameter λ is a scale parameter. If X is *Exponential* (λ), then $Z = \lambda X$ is standard exponential, *Exponential* (1). This is not a standardized distribution since $E(Z)$ is 1 and not zero. See Figure 20.4 and Table 20.5.

Table 20.4   *Cauchy* (0,1).

cdf	$F(z)$	$\frac{1}{2} + \frac{1}{\pi}\tan^{-1}(z)$	$(-\infty < z < \infty)$
pdf	$f(z)$	$\dfrac{1}{\pi(1+z)^2}$	$(-\infty < z < \infty)$
moments	μ_r	none	$(r = 1, 2, \ldots)$
mode		0	
quantile function	$Q(p)$	$\tan\{\pi\,(p - \frac{1}{2})\}$	
L-moments	λ_r	none	$(r = 1, 2, \ldots)$

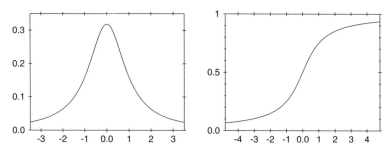

Figure 20.3   Pdf and cdf for *Cauchy* (0,1).

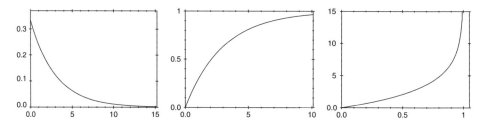

Figure 20.4   Pdf, cdf, and quantile function for *Exponential* (3).

20.4.1   Delayed exponential distribution

This is an exponential distribution on the range τ to infinity. Although τ may be negative (anticipation), it commonly takes a positive value. If the random variable X is *Exponential* (λ), then $Y = X + \tau$ is *Delayed Exponential* (λ, τ), and $Z = \lambda(Y - \tau)$ has the standard exponential distribution *Exponential* (1). See Table 20.6.

This model has a role, for example in communications, when τ is the transmission and processing time, or when τ is an insurance excess or a warranty time.

20.4.2   Checking the model assumptions

If the data is a random sample from *Exponential* (λ), then the proportion of observations with values exceeding x, $\widehat{p}_x$, estimates

$$P(X > x) = 1 - F(x) = e^{-\lambda x}.$$

Then $-\ln(\widehat{p}_x)$ estimates λx, where $\ln = \log_e$.

Table 20.5 *Exponential(λ).*

pdf	$f(x)$	$\begin{cases} \lambda e^{-\lambda x} & (x > 0) \\ 0 & (x \le 0) \end{cases}$
cdf	$F(x)$	$\begin{cases} 1 - e^{-\lambda x} & (x > 0) \\ 0 & (x \le 0) \end{cases}$
expectation	μ	$1/\lambda$
$E(X^r)$	μ'_r	$r!/\lambda^r$
variance	σ^2	$1/\lambda^2$
skewness	β_1	2
kurtosis	β_2	9
mode		0
quantile function	$Q(p)$	$-(1/\lambda) \ln(1 - p)$
second L-moment	λ_2	$1/(2\lambda)$
L-skewness	τ_3	$1/3$
L-kurtosis	τ_4	$1/6$

Table 20.6 *Delayed Exponential(λ, τ).*

pdf	$f(y)$	$\begin{cases} \lambda e^{-\lambda(y-\tau)} & (y > \tau) \\ 0 & (y \le \tau) \end{cases}$
cdf	$F(y)$	$\begin{cases} 1 - e^{-\lambda(y-\tau)} & (y > \tau) \\ 0 & (y \le \tau) \end{cases}$
expectation	μ	$\tau + 1/\lambda$
variance	σ^2	$1/\lambda^2$
skewness	β_1	2
kurtosis	β_2	9
mode		τ
quantile function	$Q(p)$	$\tau - \dfrac{1}{\lambda} \ln(1 - p)$

In this case, a plot of $y = - \ln(\widehat{p}_x)$ against x for a sequence of values of x should be approximately a straight line through the origin with slope λ. This is essentially the quantile-quantile (Q-Q) plot seen already in Figure 18.2 and later in tabular form in Table 24.1.

Example: survival data

With a starting population of 100, a count was made of the number of failures in each successive time interval of 10 units until time 500.

6 6 4 3 2 2 3 1 7 1 3 2 0 5 1 3 1 3 4 1 0 3 3 3 1 1 1 2 1 1 1 1 0 2 1 2 0 0 1 2 0 1 0 1 0 0 0 0 2

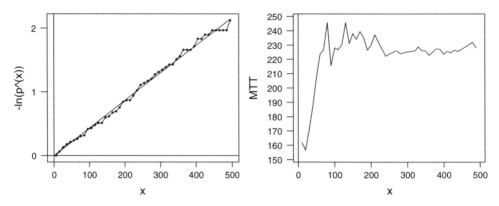

Figure 20.5 Probability plot and mean time on test plot for survival data.

For plotting purposes here we assume that the losses occurred at the midpoints of the intervals. The plot (Figure 20.5) shows the straight line fitted by least squares. We see a quite close fit. The slope gives estimate 0.004327 of λ, and 231.127 for $E(X)$. The MTT (mean time on test) estimate of $E(X)$ (Section 18.3.3) is 228.182, which gives 0.004382 for λ (Figure 20.5).

20.4.3   The relationship between the Exponential and Poisson distributions

Both distributions model the process, known as the *Poisson process*, of events occurring independently at a constant rate.

- *Poisson* models the frequency of events of the process in a fixed time interval.
- *Exponential* models the lengths of intervals between events of the process.

The event "fewer than k events occur in the time interval $(0, \ t\ ]$" is the same event as "the kth event occurs after time t."

In particular, if the events occur at a rate of λ per unit time, and X_t is the random variable for the number of events in $(0, t]$, with T_k the random variable for the time to the kth event, then

$$P(X_t = 0) \ = \ p_0 \ = \ \frac{(\lambda t)^0 \, e^{-\lambda t}}{0!} \ = \ e^{-\lambda t}$$

and

$$P(T_1 > t) \ = \ 1 - F(t) \ = \ 1 - (1 - e^{-\lambda t}) \ = \ e^{-\lambda t}.$$

20.5   FRÉCHET DISTRIBUTION, *Fréchet* (ξ, μ, σ)

The French statistician Maurice Fréchet (1878–1973) was equally distinguished as a mathematician, being a founder of the branch of pure mathematics known as functional analysis.

Table 20.7   *Fréchet* $(\xi, 0, 1)$.

cdf	$F(z)$	$\exp(-z^{-\alpha})$	$(z \geq 0)$
pdf	$f(z)$	$\alpha z^{-(1+\alpha)} \exp(-z^{-\alpha})$	$(z \geq 0)$
$E(Z^r)$	μ'_r	$\Gamma(1 - r\xi)$	$(\xi < 1/r)$
quantile function	$Q(p)$	$(-\ln p)^{-\xi}$	
mode		$\begin{cases} (1+\xi)^{-\xi} & (0 < \xi \leq 1) \\ 0 & (\xi > 1) \end{cases}$	

$\alpha = 1/\xi$, Γ is the Gamma Function
μ, σ^2, β_1 and β_2 are found from the moments $E(Z^r)$

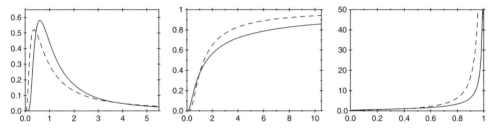

Figure 20.6   Pdfs, cdfs, and quantile functions for *Fréchet* $(0.833, 0, 1)$ (line) and *Fréchet* $(1.25, 0, 1)$ (dashes).

For a random variable X from *Fréchet* (ξ, μ, σ) where μ and $\sigma > 0$ are the location and scale parameters and $\xi > 0$ is the shape parameter, let Z be the standardized random variable $(X - \mu)/\sigma$. Let us write $z = (x - \mu)/\sigma$, and $\alpha = 1/\xi$. We note that μ and σ^2 do not represent $E(X)$ and var (X). Table 20.7 and Figure 20.6 show properties of the standarized variable.

20.6   GAMMA DISTRIBUTION, *Gamma* (ν, λ)

- ν is the index (shape) parameter $(\nu > 0)$, λ is the scale parameter $(\lambda > 0)$.
- $\nu = 1$ gives *Exponential*(λ).
- If $\nu = n$, an integer, then *Gamma*(n, λ) gives the distribution of the sum of n independent *Exponential*(λ) random variates. The shapes of the pdfs can be seen in Figure 20.7, with Table 20.8 giving the formulae.

20.6.1   LogGamma distribution

This is sometimes used as an alternative to the lognormal distribution.

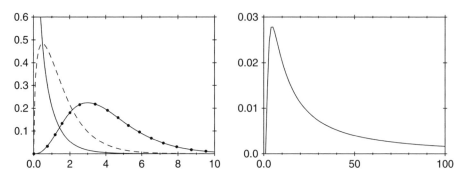

Figure 20.7   Pdfs for *Gamma* (v,1) with v = 0.5 (line), 1.5 (dashes), 4 (dots), and *LogGamma* (4,1) (right).

Table 20.8   *Gamma* (v, λ).

pdf	$f(x)$	$\dfrac{\lambda^v}{\Gamma(v)}\, x^{v-1}\, e^{-\lambda x}$ $\quad (x > 0)$
expectation	μ	v/λ
variance	σ^2	v/λ^2
skewness	β_1	$2/\sqrt{v}$
kurtosis	β_2	$3 + (6/v)$
$E(X^r)$	μ'_r	$\dfrac{1}{\lambda^r}\dfrac{\Gamma(v+r)}{\Gamma(v)}$
mode		$\begin{cases} 0 & (0 < v \le 1) \\ \dfrac{v-1}{\lambda} & (v > 1) \end{cases}$

Γ is the Gamma Function

If the random variable X is *Gamma* (v, λ), then the random variable $Y = e^X$ is *LogGamma* (v, λ). That is to say, $\ln Y$ is *Gamma*. This gives the pdf

$$f(y) \;=\; \frac{\lambda^v}{\Gamma(v)}\; y^{-\lambda-1}(\ln y)^{v-1} \qquad (y > 1).$$

This pdf with $v = 4$ and $\lambda = 1$ is shown in Figure 20.7.

20.7   GENERALIZED EXTREME VALUE DISTRIBUTION, $GEV(\xi, \mu, \sigma)$

This distribution is central to modeling the severity of operational risk loss data. It arises as the limit distribution for the largest observation of a random sample of observations from a distribution as the sample size increases (Section 23.2.2). It combines the Gumbel, Fréchet, and (Reflected) Weibull distributions.

Table 20.9   *GEV* $(\xi,0,1)$.

cdf	$F(z)$	$\begin{cases} \exp\{-\exp(-z)\} & (-\infty < z < \infty)\ (\xi = 0) \\ \exp\{-(1+\xi z)^{-1/\xi}\}\ (1+\xi z \geq 0) & (\xi \neq 0) \end{cases}$
pdf	$f(z)$	$\begin{cases} \exp(-z)\exp\{-\exp(-z)\} & (-\infty < z < \infty)\ (\xi = 0) \\ (1+\xi z)^{-1/\xi}\exp\{-(1+\xi z)^{-1/\xi}\}\ (1+\xi z \geq 0) & (\xi \neq 0) \end{cases}$
expectation	μ	$\{\Gamma(1-\xi)-1\}/\xi \quad (\xi < 1)$
qf	$Q(p)$	$\{(-\ln p)^{-\xi}-1\}/\xi \quad (\xi \neq 0)$
mode		$\dfrac{(1+\xi)^{-\xi}-1}{\xi} \quad (\xi \neq 0)$
second L-moment	λ_2	$(2^{\xi}-1)\,\Gamma(1-\xi)/\xi$
L-skewness	τ_3	$2(3^{\xi}-1)/(2^{\xi}-1)$
L-kurtosis	τ_4	$\{5(4^{\xi})-10(3^{\xi})+6(2^{\xi})-1\}/(2^{\xi}-1)$

For a random variable X from $GEV(\xi, \mu, \sigma)$, where μ and σ are the location and scale parameters and ξ is the shape parameter, let $z = (x - \mu)/\sigma$. Here μ and σ are not probability moments, merely translation and scale parameters.

The limit as $\xi \to 0$ case is the standard *Gumbel* $(0,1)$ distribution (Section 20.9, where its properties are given).

For $\xi > 0$, if Z is $GEV(\xi, 0, 1)$, then $1 + \xi Z$ has the *Fréchet* $(\xi,0,1)$ distribution (Section 20.5). If X is *Fréchet* $(\xi,0,1)$, then $Z = (X - 1)/\xi$ is $GEV(\xi, 0, 1)$.

Similarly, for $\xi < 0$, if Z is $GEV(\xi,0,1)$, then $X = -(1 + \xi Z)$ has the *(Reflected) Weibull* $(0,1)$ distribution (EV2) (Section 20.18.1), and $-X$ has the *Weibull* $(-\xi,0,1)$ distribution (Section 20.18).

Figures 20.8 and 20.9 illustrate the variety of shapes given by this class of distributions with Section 20.9 giving its properties.

20.7.1   Parameter fitting using probability weighted moments

The method of L-moment estimation of μ, σ and ξ is to match the L-moment values, $\widehat{\lambda}_1$ $(= \overline{x})$, $\widehat{\lambda}_2$ and $\widehat{\lambda}_3$ obtained from the sample L-moments, or through the estimated probability weighted moments, with their theoretical values (Section 17.7.6) and solve the three simultaneous equations.

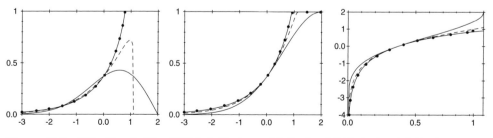

Figure 20.8   Pdf, cdf, and qf for $GEV(\xi, 0, 1)$: $\xi = -0.5$ (line), -0.9 (dashes), -1.1 (dots).

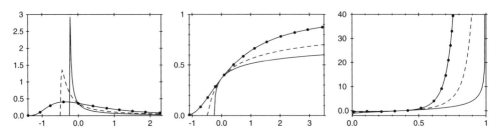

Figure 20.9   Pdf, cdf, and qf for $GEV(\xi, 0, 1)$: $\xi = 0.5$ (line), 0.9 (dashes), 1.1 (dots).

Estimating the parameter values of GEV (ξ, μ, σ)

For the GEV having its shape parameter $\xi < 1$, ξ is estimated by the solution $\hat{\xi}$ of

$$\frac{3^{\hat{\xi}} - 1}{2^{\hat{\xi}} - 1} = \frac{1}{2}(\hat{\tau}_3 + 3),$$

where $\hat{\tau}_3$ is the sample L-skewness $\hat{\lambda}_3/\hat{\lambda}_2$. A good approximation to the solution $\hat{\xi}$ is

$$\hat{\xi} = 7.8590c - 2.9554c^2,$$

where

$$c = \frac{\ln 2}{\ln 3} - \frac{2}{\hat{\tau}_3 + 3}.$$

The estimates of μ and σ are then given by

$$\hat{\sigma} = \frac{\hat{\lambda}_2 \hat{\xi}}{(2^{\hat{\xi}} - 1)\Gamma(1 - \hat{\xi})}, \qquad \hat{\mu} = \hat{\lambda}_1 + \frac{\hat{\sigma}}{\hat{\xi}} \{1 - \Gamma(1 - \hat{\xi})\}.$$

In Section 23.4, we meet the Hill and other methods of estimating ξ directly from the largest observed values.

20.8   GENERALIZED PARETO DISTRIBUTION, GPD

This distribution is central to modeling the extreme tail severity of operational risk loss data. It arises as the limit distribution for the probability of the value exceeding an increasingly high threshold.

For a random variable X from $GPD(\xi, \mu, \sigma)$, where μ and σ are the location and scale parameters and ξ is the shape parameter, let $z = (x - \mu)/\sigma$. Here μ and σ are not probability moments, merely translation and scale parameters.

The limit as $\xi \to 0$ case is the standard *Exponential* (1) distribution (Section 20.4, where its properties are given). For $\xi > 0$, $1 + \xi Z$ has the standard *Pareto* (0,1) distribution (Section 20.13). Similarly, for $\xi < 0$, $1 + \xi Z$ has the standard *(Reflected) Beta* (0,1) distribution (GP2) (Section 20.1.2). The properties and shapes can be seen in Table 20.10 and Figures 20.10 and 20.11.

Table 20.10   *GPD* (ξ,0,1).

cdf	$F(z)$	$\begin{cases} 1 - e^{-z} & (z \geq 0) & (\xi = 0) \\ 1 - (1+\xi z)^{-1/\xi} & (z \geq 0) & (\xi > 0) \\ 1 - (1+\xi z)^{-1/\xi} & (0 < z < -1/\xi) & (\xi < 0) \end{cases}$
pdf	$f(z)$	$\begin{cases} e^{-z} & (z \geq 0) & (\xi = 0) \\ (1+\xi z)^{-(1+1/\xi)} & (z \geq 0) & (\xi > 0) \\ (1+\xi z)^{-(1+1/\xi)} & (0 < z < -1/\xi) & (\xi < 0) \end{cases}$
expectation	$E(Z)$	$1/(1-\xi) \quad (\xi \neq 0)$
variance	$\text{var}(Z)$	$1/\{(1-\xi)^2(1-2\xi)\} \qquad (\xi < 1/2)$
	$E\{(1+\xi Z)^r\}$	$1/(1-r\xi) \qquad (\xi < 1/r)$
skewness	β_1	$\dfrac{2(1+\xi)\sqrt{1-2\xi}}{1-3\xi} \qquad (\xi < 1/3)$
kurtosis	β_2	$\dfrac{3(1-2\xi)(3+\xi+2\xi^2)}{(1-3\xi)(1-4\xi)} \qquad (\xi < 1/4)$
qf	$Q(p)$	$\{(1-p)^{-\xi}-1\}/\xi \qquad (\xi \neq 0)$
second L-moment	λ_2	$1/\{(1-\xi)(2-\xi)\}$
L-skewness	τ_3	$(1+\xi)/(3-\xi)$
L-kurtosis	τ_4	$\dfrac{(1+\xi)(2+\xi)}{(3-\xi)(4-\xi)}$

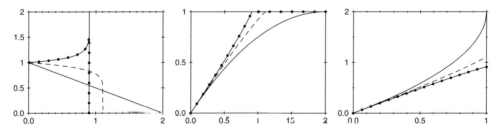

Figure 20.10   Pdf, cdf, and qf for *GPD* (ξ, 0, 1): ξ = −0.5 (line), −0.9 (dashes), −1.1 (dots).

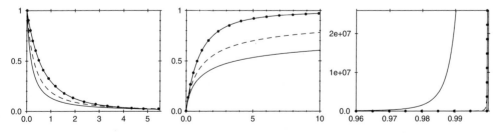

Figure 20.11   Pdf, cdf, and qf for *GPD* (ξ, 0, 1): ξ = 0.5 (line), 0.9 (dashes), 1.1 (dots).

20.8.1 Estimating the parameter values of GDP (ξ, μ, σ)

Method of moments

For $\xi < 1/3$, we solve

$$\bar{x} = \mu + \sigma/(1-\xi), \quad s^2 = \sigma^2/\{(1-\xi)^2(1-2\xi)\},$$

$$\widehat{\beta}_1 = \widehat{\mu}_3/s^3 = \frac{2(1+\xi)\sqrt{1-2\xi}}{1-3\xi}.$$

The last gives a cubic equation to solve for the estimate of ξ. The appropriate solution in the second relation gives the estimate of σ^2. These estimates in the first give the estimate of μ.

The location parameter μ is a threshold value that is often known. That being so, we would require only the first two relations to estimate σ and ξ.

Let $\bar{y} = \bar{x} - \mu$, then $\widehat{\xi} = \frac{1}{2}(1 - \bar{y}^2/s^2)$, $\widehat{\sigma} = \frac{1}{2}\bar{y}(1 + \bar{y}^2/s^2)$.

Method of L-moments

For the GPD having its shape parameter $\xi < 1$, the estimated parameter values are given by the solution of the estimate $\widehat{\xi}$ given by the expression $\tau_3 = (1+\xi)/(3-\xi)$ from the Table 20.10 for $GPD(\xi,0,1)$, since this does not depend on location and scale, i.e.

$$\widehat{\xi} = \frac{3\widehat{\tau}_3 - 1}{\widehat{\tau}_3 + 1},$$

where $\widehat{\tau}_3$ is the sample L-skewness $\widehat{\lambda}_3/\widehat{\lambda}_2$. Then

$$\widehat{\sigma} = \widehat{\lambda}_2(2-\widehat{\xi})(1-\widehat{\xi}), \qquad \widehat{\mu} = \bar{x} - \frac{\widehat{\sigma}}{1-\widehat{\xi}}.$$

In Section 23.4, we meet the Hill and other methods of estimating ξ directly from the largest observed values.

20.9 GUMBEL DISTRIBUTION, *Gumbel* (μ, σ)

German-born Emil J. Gumbel (1891–1966), an outspoken anti-Nazi, was stripped of his position as a professor of statistics, leaving Germany for a professorship in France before fleeing to the United States when France fell in 1940 to the invading Germans.

For a random variable X from *Gumbel* (μ, σ) where μ and $\sigma > 0$ are the location and scale parameters, let $z = (x - \mu)/\sigma$, and Z be the standardized random variable $(X - \mu)/\sigma$. Table 20.11 and Figure 20.12 show its properties.

20.9.1 Gompertz distribution

Benjamin Gompertz (1779–1865) was born in London to Dutch parents. A self-taught mathematician, he was a pioneer of actuarial science. He introduced his model, now known as the Gompertz distribution, in 1825. It models the logarithm of death rates as following an exponential distribution. The Gompertz distribution is thus a log-exponential distribution. If the random variable Y is Exponential, then $X = \ln Y$ is Gompertz. See Table 20.12.

Table 20.11   *Gumbel* (0,1).

cdf	$F(z)$	$\exp(-e^{-z})$
pdf	$f(z)$	$e^{-z}\exp(-e^{-z})$
expectation	μ_Z	$\gamma = 0.57721\cdots$
variance	σ_Z^2	$\pi^2/6 = 1.64493\cdots$
skewness	β_1	$1.13954\cdots$
kurtosis	β_2	$27/5$
quantile function	$Q(p)$	$-\ln(-\ln p)$
mode		0
second L-moment	λ_2	$\ln 2$
L-skewness	τ_3	0.1699
L-kurtosis	τ_4	0.1504

γ = Euler's constant

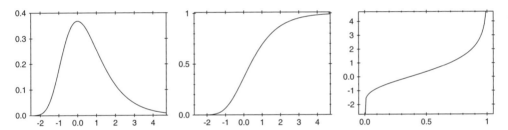

Figure 20.12   Pdf and cdf and quantile function for *Gumbel* (0,1).

It is also the Reflected Gumbel distribution, since if T is *Gumbel* (0,1), then $X = -T$ is *Gompertz* (0,1). Let Z be the standardized *Gompertz* (0,1) random variable. We observe that since the Gumbel is skewed to the right, this reflection causes the Gompertz to be skewed to the left – not what we would want when modeling severity data. To force the skewness to the right, the model is generally truncated to exclude negative values.

Table 20.12   *Gompertz* (0,1).

cdf	$F(z)$	$1 - \exp(-e^{z})$
pdf	$f(z)$	$e^{z}\exp(-e^{z})$
expectation	μ_Z	$-\gamma = -0.57721\cdots$
variance	σ_Z^2	$\pi^2/6 = 1.64493\cdots$
skewness	β_1	$-1.13954\cdots$
kurtosis	β_2	$27/5$
quantile function	$Q(p)$	$\ln\{-\ln(1 - p)\}$
bmode		0

γ = Euler's constant

Table 20.13   *(Truncated) Gompertz* $(0,1,1)$.

cdf	$F(z)$	$1 - \exp\{-(e^z - 1)\}$	$(z \geq 0)$
pdf	$f(z)$	$\exp\{-(e^z - z - 1)\}$	$(z \geq 0)$
qf	$Q(p)$	$\ln\{1 - \ln(1 - p)\}$	
mode		0	

The moments require computers for their evaluation

Table 20.14   *(Truncated) Gompertz* (τ, λ, β).

cdf	$F(x)$	$1 - e^{-g(x)}$	$(x \geq \tau)$
pdf	$f(x)$	$\lambda e^{\beta x} e^{-g(x)}$	$(x \geq \tau)$
qf	$Q(p)$	$\dfrac{1}{\beta} \ln\{e^{\beta \tau} - (\beta/\lambda)\ln(1 - p)\}$	
mode		$\begin{cases} \dfrac{1}{\beta} \ln\left(\dfrac{\beta}{\lambda}\right) & (\lambda < \beta) \\[2mm] 0 & (\lambda \geq \beta) \end{cases}$	

$g(x) = (\lambda/\beta)(e^{\beta x} - e^{\beta \tau})$
The moments require computers for their evaluation

20.9.2   Truncated Gompertz distribution, *(Truncated) Gompertz* (τ, λ, β)

The Gompertz distribution is generally used in this truncated form which restricts it to its positive values. In this case we have a random variable X from *Gompertz* (τ, λ, β) where $\lambda > 0$ is the shape parameter and $\beta > 0$ is the scale parameter, with truncation at τ. See Tables 20.13 and 20.14 and Figure 20.12.

20.10   LOGISTIC DISTRIBUTION

The logistic distribution is a symmetric distribution somewhat like the normal distribution, and the log-logistic is used as an alternative to the lognormal (Figure 20.14 and Table 20.15).

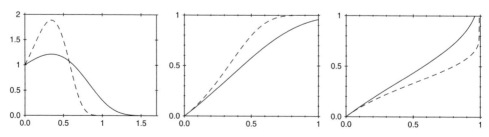

Figure 20.13   Pdfs, cdfs, and qfs for *Truncated Gompertz* $(0,1,\beta)$, $\beta = 2$ (line), 4 (dashes).

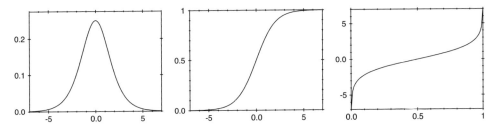

Figure 20.14   Pdf, cdf, and quantile function for *Logistic* (0,1).

Table 20.15   *Logistic* (0,1).

cdf	$F(z)$	$\dfrac{1}{1+e^{-z}}$
pdf	$f(z)$	$\dfrac{e^{-z}}{(1+e^{-z})^2}$
expectation	μ	0
variance	σ^2	$\pi^2/3 = 3.28987\cdots$
skewness	β_1	0
kurtosis	β_2	21/5
quantile function	$Q(p)$	$\ln\{p/(1-p)\}$
mode		0
second L-moment	λ_2	1
L-skewness	τ_3	0
L-kurtosis	τ_4	1/6

Table 20.16   *Loglogistic* $(\xi,0,1)$.

cdf	$F(y)$	$\dfrac{y^\alpha}{1+y^\alpha}$ $(y \geq 0)$
pdf	$f(y)$	$\dfrac{\alpha y^\alpha}{(1+y^\alpha)^2}$
$E(Y^r)$	μ_r'	$B(1+r\xi,\,1-r\xi) = \dfrac{\pi r\xi}{\sin(\pi r\xi)}$ $(0 < \xi < 1/r)$
mode		$\begin{cases}\left(\dfrac{1-\xi}{1+\xi}\right)^\xi & (0<\xi<1) \\[2mm] 0 & (\xi \geq 1)\end{cases}$
quantile function	$Q(p)$	$\{p/(1-p)\}^\xi$
prob. weighted moments	ω_r	$B(1-\xi,\,1+\xi+r)\ (0<\xi<1)$

$\alpha = 1/\xi$. B is the Beta Function.
The L-moments can be obtained from the probability weighted moments ω_r (Sections 17.7.5, 17.7.6).

20.10.1 LogLogistic distribution

If the random variable Z is *Logistic* $(0,1)$, then the random variable $Y = e^{\xi Z}$ is *Loglogistic* $(\xi, 0, 1)$. That is to say, $\ln Y$ is *Logistic* $(0, \alpha)$, where $\alpha = 1/\xi$. (Table 20.16).

20.11 NORMAL DISTRIBUTION, $N(\mu, \sigma^2)$

20.11.1 Standard normal distribution, $N(0,1)$

We standardize $N(\mu, \sigma^2)$ to the standard normal by taking $Z = (X - \mu)/\sigma$. The shape of the distribution is unchanged. The importance of the standard distribution is marked by special notation, $\phi(z)$ for the pdf and $\Phi(z)$ for the cdf. (Figures 20.15 and 20.16 and Tables 20.17 and 20.18).

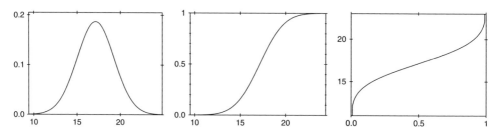

Figure 20.15 Pdf $f(x)$, cdf $F(x)$, and quantile function for $N(17.14, 4.56)$.

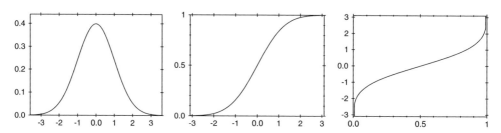

Figure 20.16 Pdf $\phi(z)$, cdf $\Phi(z)$, and quantile function for $N(0,1)$.

Table 20.17 $N(\mu, \sigma^2)$.

pdf	$f(x)$	$\dfrac{1}{\sqrt{2\pi\sigma^2}} \exp\left\{-\dfrac{1}{2}\left(\dfrac{x-\mu}{\sigma}\right)^2\right\}$	$(-\infty < x < \infty)$
expectation	$E(X)$	μ	
variance	$\mathrm{var}(X)$	σ^2	
skewness	β_1	0	
kurtosis	β_2	3	
mode		μ	
median		μ	
second L-moment	λ_2	σ/π	
L-skewness	τ_3	0	
L-kurtosis	τ_4	$(30/\pi)\arctan(\sqrt{2}) - 9 = 0.1226$	

Table 20.18 $N(0,1)$.

pdf	$\phi(z)$	$\dfrac{1}{\sqrt{2\pi}}\, e^{-\frac{1}{2}z^2}$	$(-\infty < z < \infty)$
cdf	$\Phi(z)$	$\dfrac{1}{\sqrt{2\pi}} \displaystyle\int_{-\infty}^{z} e^{-\frac{1}{2}y^2}\, dy$	
expectation	μ	0	
variance	σ^2	1	
skewness	β_1	0	
kurtosis	β_2	3	
mode		0	
median		0	

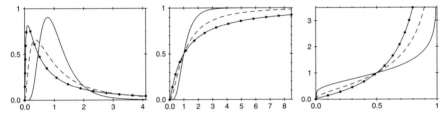

Figure 20.17   Pdf, cdf, and quantile functions for lognormal distributions.

20.12   LOGNORMAL DISTRIBUTION, *Lognormal* (μ, σ^2)

If the random variable X is $N(v, \lambda)$, then the random variable $Y = e^X$ is *Lognormal* (v, λ). That is to say, $\ln Y$ is normally distributed. The parameters of the lognormal are the moments of the underlying normal distribution. (Table 20.19).

Table 20.19   *Lognormal* (μ, σ^2).

pdf	$f(y)$	$\dfrac{1}{\sqrt{2\pi\sigma^2}\, y} \exp\left\{ -\dfrac{1}{2}\left(\dfrac{\ln y - \mu}{\sigma}\right)^2 \right\}$ $(y > 0)$
cdf	$F(y)$	$\Phi\left(\frac{\ln y - \mu}{\sigma}\right)$
expectation	μ_Y	$\exp(\mu + \frac{1}{2}\sigma^2)$
$E(Y^r)$	μ'_r	$\exp(r\mu + \frac{1}{2}r^2\sigma^2)$
variance	σ_Y^2	$e^{2\mu + \sigma^2}(e^{\sigma^2} - 1)$
skewness	β_1	$(e^{\sigma^2} + 2)(e^{\sigma^2} - 1)^{\frac{1}{2}}$
kurtosis	β_2	$e^{4\sigma^2} + 2e^{3\sigma^2} + 3e^{2\sigma^2}$
mode		$\exp(\mu - \sigma^2)$
median		e^{μ}

Φ is the standard normal cdf

Table 20.20   *Pareto* $(\xi, 0, 1)$.

cdf	$F(z)$	$1 - z^{-\alpha}$	$(z > 1)$
pdf	$f(z)$	$\alpha\, z^{-\alpha - 1}$	$(z > 1)$
expectation	$E(Z)$	$\dfrac{1}{1 - \xi}$	$(\xi < 1)$
variance	$\mathrm{var}\,(Z)$	$\dfrac{\xi^2}{(1 - \xi)^2(1 - 2\xi)}$	$(\xi < \tfrac{1}{2})$
skewness	β_1	$\dfrac{2(1 + \xi)\sqrt{1 - 2\xi}}{1 - 3\xi}$	$(\xi < \tfrac{1}{3})$
kurtosis	β_2	$\dfrac{3(1 - 2\xi)(3 + \xi + 2\xi^2)}{(1 - 3\xi)(1 - 4\xi)}$	$(\xi < \tfrac{1}{4})$
rth moment	$E(Z^r)$	$\dfrac{1}{1 - r\xi}$	$(\xi < 1/r)$
mode		1	
quantile function	$Q_\xi(p)$	$(1 - p)^{-\xi}$	
prob. weighted moments	ω_r	$B(1 - \xi,\, r + 1)$	$(\xi < 1)$
2nd L-moment	λ_2	$\dfrac{\xi}{(2 - \xi)(1 - \xi)}$	
3rd L-moment	λ_3	$-\dfrac{6 - \xi - \xi^2}{(3 - \xi)(2 - \xi)(1 - \xi)}$	
L-skewness	τ_3	$-\dfrac{6 - \xi - \xi^2}{3(3 - \xi)}$	

$\alpha = 1/\xi$.   B is the Beta function

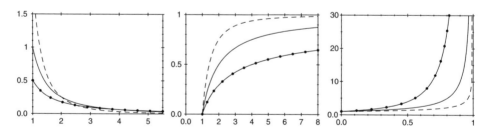

Figure 20.18   Pdfs, cdfs, and qfs for *Pareto* $(\xi, 0, 1)$ for $\xi = 0.5$ (dots), 1 (line), 2 (dashes).

20.13   PARETO DISTRIBUTION, *Pareto* (ξ, μ, σ)

The Swiss economist Vilfredo Pareto (1848–1923) introduced a so-called law dealing with family incomes which resulted in the Pareto distribution being used to model these. The shape parameter is $\xi > 0$. Some versions use the translated variable $Y = X - 1$, which changes the support from $(1, \infty)$ to $(0, \infty)$. The expectation, quantile function, and mode are each reduced by 1. The variance, skewness, and kurtosis are unchanged. (Figure 20.18 and Table 20.20).

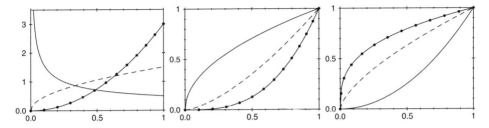

Figure 20.19 Pdfs, cdfs and quantile functions for $Power(\xi)$ with $\xi = 0.5$ (line), 1.5 (dashes), 3.0 (dots).

20.14 POWER FUNCTION DISTRIBUTION, $Power(\xi)$

The power function distribution is a special case of the Beta distribution (Section 20.1). Its support is the interval 0 to 1. The shape parameter ξ is positive. The distribution is skewed to the left if $\xi < 1$, to the right if $\xi > 1$, and is flat (the standard uniform distribution) if $\xi = 1$ (Figure 20.19, Table 20.21). If the random variable X has the $Power(\xi)$ distribution, then $-X$ is from the Beta (GP2) (Section 20.1.2).

Table 20.21 $Power(\xi)$.

cdf	$F(z)$	$z^{1/\xi}$ $(0 < z < 1)$
pdf	$f(z)$	$\alpha z^{\alpha-1}$ $(0 < z < 1)$ where $\alpha = 1/\xi$
expectation	μ	$1/(1+\xi)$
rth moment	$E(Z^r)$	$\dfrac{1}{1+r\xi}$
variance	σ^2	$\dfrac{\xi^2}{(1+\xi)^2(1+2\xi)}$
skewness	β_1	$\dfrac{2(\xi-1)\sqrt{1+2\xi}}{1+3\xi}$
kurtosis	β_2	$\dfrac{3(1+2\xi)(3-\xi+2\xi^2)}{(1+3\xi)(1+4\xi)}$
mode		$\begin{cases} 1 & (0 < \xi \le 1) \\ 0 & (\xi > 1) \end{cases}$
quantile function	$Q(p)$	p^ξ
prob. weighted moments	ω_r	$1/(\xi+r+1)$
2nd L-moment	λ_2	$\xi/\{(\xi+1)(\xi+2)\}$
3rd L-moment	λ_3	$\{\xi(\xi-1)\}/\{(\xi+1)(\xi+2)(\xi+3)\}$
L-skewness	τ_3	$\xi/(\xi+2)$

20.15   TUKEY'S g-and-h DISTRIBUTIONS

John Tukey (1915–2000) was one of the most inventive and influential statisticians of the second half of the 20th century. In 1944 he coined the words "software" and "bit" used in computer programming. In the 1950s he criticized Kinsey's research into sexual behaviour in the United States, arguing that a random sample of subjects should have been used rather than people who knew each other. In the 1970s he chaired the committee warning that aerosal sprays were damaging the ozone layer. He took a particular interest in robust statistical methods, which give credible statistical results when the data is contaminated or fails to match the modeling assumptions.

The g-and-h distributions were devised by Tukey (Tukey, 1977) for exploratory data analysis as a system that encompasses a wide class of models. Dutta and Perry (2006) show that with large amounts of data the system can be applied to loss data giving good estimation including skewness and kurtosis. Jobst (2007) reports that data from the fourth Quantitative Impact Study (QIS4) (Federal Reserve Board, 2006) was satisfactorily modeled by taking the functions g and h to be constants.

Hoaglin (1985) describes it through the following transformations. If X is $N(0, 1)$, then the random variable Y has the g-and-h distribution, where

$$Y = \frac{1}{g}(e^{gX} - 1) \exp\left(\frac{1}{2}hX^2\right).$$

In this formula g and h can be constants or any monotone functions of X^2. The g is influential in respect of skewness, the h in respect of kurtosis. Taking h to be zero, gives a g-distribution. The h-distribution is based on taking the limit as g tends to zero. This gives the transformation

$$Y = X \exp\left(\frac{1}{2}hX^2\right).$$

However the identification of models for g and h for modeling $Z = (Y - \alpha)/\beta$ is beyond the scope of this book.

20.16   TUKEY'S LAMBDA DISTRIBUTIONS

These *Tukey lambda distributions* (Johnson *et. al.* (1995), Gilchrist (2000)) are based directly on the quantile function $Q(p)$, which is the value that is exceeded by proportion $1 - p$ of the population (Section 17.7.2). Quantile functions are examined more fully in Chapter 21.

The standard quantile functions for this system of distributions is (Table 20.22)

$$Q_0(p) = \theta p^\xi - (1 - p)^\xi, \qquad \theta > 0, \ \xi \neq 0.$$

If $\xi = 0$, the limit case as $\xi \to 0$ gives a *skew logistic* distribution having

$$Q_0(p) = \theta \ln(p) - \ln(1 - p).$$

This lambda distribution was originally described with the shape parameter labeled λ. We systematically use ξ.

Table 20.22 *(Skew) Lambda* (θ, ξ).

quantile function	$Q_0(p)$	$\theta p^\xi - (1-p)^\xi$
expectation	$E(Z)$	$\dfrac{\theta - 1}{\xi + 1}$
2nd moment	$E(Z^2)$	$\dfrac{\theta^2 + 1}{2\xi + 1} - 2\theta\, B(\xi + 1, \xi + 1)$
median	$Q2$	$(\theta - 1)2^{-\xi}$
lower quartile	$Q1$	$(\theta - 3^\xi)4^{-\xi}$
upper quartile	$Q3$	$(3^\xi\theta - 1)4^{-\xi}$
Galton skewness	β_{GS}	$\left(\dfrac{\theta - 1}{\theta + 1}\right)\left(\dfrac{3^\xi - 2^{\xi+1} + 1}{3^\xi - 1}\right)$

B is the Beta Function. $E(Z^r) = \displaystyle\int_0^1 \{Q_0(p)\}^r \, dp$ (Table 17.8).

The θ parameter is a skewness parameter. The distribution is symmetric if $\theta = 1$. The case of interest when $\theta = 1$ is if $\xi < 0$. This makes the symmetric pdf unimodal with Pareto-like tails. As ξ increases to zero, the shape becomes like the logistic pdf, and with ξ increasing further it looks approximately like the normal pdf at about 0.135, and is a uniform pdf at $\xi = 1$.

Quantile defined distributions lend themselves to simulation, since we obtain values from the population by substituting *Uniform* $(0,1)$ values from a random number generator for p in $Q(p)$.

A more general form introduces a second shape parameter having

$$Q_0(p) = \theta p^{\xi_1} - (1-p)^{\xi_2}, \qquad \theta > 0, \ \xi_1 \neq 0, \ \xi_2 \neq 0.$$

20.17   UNIFORM DISTRIBUTION, *Uniform* (α, β)

This is sometimes called the rectangular distribution in view of the shape of its pdf. See Figure 20.20 and Table 20.23.

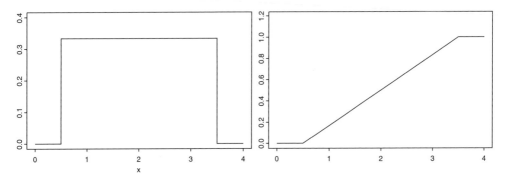

Figure 20.20   Pdf and cdf for *Uniform* $(0.5, 3.5)$.

Table 20.23   *Uniform* (α, β) and *Uniform* $(0,1)$.

		Uniform (α, β)	Uniform $(0,1)$
pdf	$f(x)$	$\begin{cases} \dfrac{1}{\beta - \alpha} & (\alpha < x < \beta) \\ 0 & \text{(otherwise)} \end{cases}$	$\begin{cases} 1 & (0 < z < 1) \\ 0 & \text{(otherwise)} \end{cases}$
cdf	$F(x)$	$\begin{cases} 0 & (x \leq \alpha) \\ \dfrac{x - \alpha}{\beta - \alpha} & (\alpha \leq x \leq \beta) \\ 1 & (x \geq \beta) \end{cases}$	$\begin{cases} 0 & (z \leq 0) \\ z & (0 < z < 1) \\ 1 & (z \geq 1) \end{cases}$
expectation	μ	$(\alpha + \beta)/2$	$1/2$
variance	σ^2	$(\beta - \alpha)^2/12$	$1/12$
$E(X^r)$	μ'_r	$\dfrac{1}{r+1} \dfrac{\beta^{r+1} - \alpha^{r+1}}{\beta - \alpha}$	$1/(r+1)$
skewness	β_1	0	0
kurtosis	β_2	$43/240 = 0.179$	0.179
mode		$\alpha \leq x \leq \beta$	$0 < z < 1$
median		$(\alpha + \beta)/2$	$1/2$
quantile function	$Q(p)$	$\alpha + (\beta - \alpha)p$	p
second L-moment	λ_2	$(\beta - \alpha)/6$	$1/6$
L-skewness	τ_3	0	0
L-kurtosis	τ_4	0	0

The obvious estimates of α and β are the $x_{\min}$ and $x_{\max}$, but $x_{\min}$ is biased too large for α and $x_{\max}$ too small for β. The unbiased estimators correct for these biases. We take

$$\widehat{\alpha} = \frac{1}{n-1}(nx_{\min} - x_{\max}), \qquad \widehat{\beta} = \frac{1}{n-1}(nx_{\max} - x_{\min}).$$

20.18   WEIBULL DISTRIBUTION, *Weibull* (ξ, λ)

The probability distribution of Waloddi Weibull (1887–1979), a Swedish engineering researcher, explaining changes in the strength of materials, was published in Sweden in 1939. However, the onset of the Second World War in Europe that year meant it did not achieve worldwide notice until it was reprinted in 1951.

Suppose that we have a random variable X from *Weibull* (ξ, λ), where $\xi > 0$ is the shape parameter and $\lambda > 0$ is the scale parameter (Table 20.24, Figure 20.21). Then the cdf is

$$F(x) = 1 - \exp\{-(\lambda x)^{1/\xi}\} \quad \text{for } x \geq 0.$$

Table 20.24   *Weibull* $(\xi, 1)$.

cdf	$F(z)$	$1 - \exp\{-z^{\alpha}\}$	$(z > 0)$
pdf	$f(z)$	$\alpha\, z^{\alpha-1} \exp\{-z^{\alpha}\}$	$(z > 0)$
expectation	μ_Z	$\Gamma(1 + \xi)$	
rth moment	$E(Z^r)$	$\Gamma(1 + r\xi)$	
quantile function	$Q(p)$	$\{-\ln(1 - p)\}^{\xi}$	
mode		$\begin{cases} (1 - \xi)^{\xi} & (0 < \xi < 1) \\ 0 & (\xi \geq 1) \end{cases}$	

$\alpha = 1/\xi$, Γ is the Gamma Function

σ^2, β_1 and β_2 are found from the moments $E(Z^r)$ (Section 17.6.1)

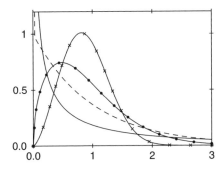

Figure 20.21   Pdf $f(z)$ for *Weibull* $(\xi, 1)$, with $\xi = 2$ (line), 1 (dashes), 2/3 (dots), 2/5 (crosses).

This model is widely used as a lifetime distribution in reliability theory and survival analysis. We can see that it is closely related to the Exponential distribution, since this cdf shows that the random variable $Y = (\lambda X)^{1/\xi}$ will be *Exponential* (1).

Let us extend the model by introducing a delay τ as was done for the Delayed Exponential (Section 20.4.1), then we have a standardized distribution for $Z = \lambda (X - \tau) = (X - \mu)/\sigma$, where $\mu = \tau$ and $\sigma = 1/\lambda$ are location and scale parameters, but which here do not represent expectation and standard deviation. The standardized distribution of Z will be denoted *Weibull* $(\xi, 1)$ and corresponds to the distribution of X when $\tau = 0$ and $\sigma = 1$. We write α for $1/\xi$ when it provides a tidier formula.

Weibull $(\frac{1}{2}, 1)$ (so $\alpha = 2$) is known as the Rayleigh distribution.

20.18.1   (Reflected) Weibull distribution, *(Reflected) Weibull* $(\xi, 1)$ $(\xi < 0)$

This is the distribution of $-Z$ where Z is *Weibull* $(\xi, 1)$. This reflected version of the Weibull is commonly called the Weibull in Extreme Value Theory. It is almost always clear which is being referred to, but the added labels "reflected" or EV2 will be used when needed. When used in reflected form we replace ξ by $-\xi$ with ξ taking negative values (Table 20.25, Figure 20.22).

Table 20.25   *(Reflected) Weibull* $(\xi, 1)$ $(\xi < 0)$.

cdf	$F(z)$	$\begin{cases} \exp\{-(-z)^{-\alpha}\} & (z \leq 0) \\ \qquad 1 & (z > 0) \end{cases}$
pdf	$f(z)$	$\begin{cases} -\alpha\,(-z)^{-\alpha-1}\exp\{-(-z)^{-\alpha}\} & (z < 0) \\ \qquad\qquad 0 & (z > 0) \end{cases}$
expectation	$E(Z)$	$-\Gamma(1 - \xi)$
rth moment	$E(Z^r)$	$(-1)^r\,\Gamma(1 - r\xi)$
quantile function	$Q(p)$	$-(-\ln p)\}^\xi$
mode		$\begin{cases} \qquad 0 & (\xi \geq -1) \\ (1 + \xi)^{-\xi} & (-1 < \xi < 0) \end{cases}$

$\alpha = 1/\xi,$ Γ is the Gamma Function
β_1 and β_2 are found from the moments $E(Z^r)$ (Section 17.6.1)

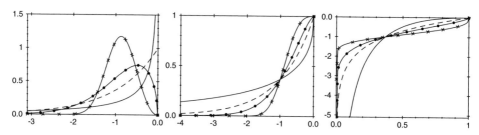

Figure 20.22   Pdfs, cdfs and quantile functions for *(Reflected) Weibull* $(\xi, 1)$ with $\xi = -2$ (lines), -1 (dashes), $-2/3$ (dots), $-1/3$ (crosses).

What is Risk and How Do We Measure It?

21.1 RETURN VALUES

Although risk is generally described in terms of median and percentiles (i.e. quantile measures), the models used to portray risk are generally described in terms of mean and variance (i.e. moment measures). Basel II proposes that a firm may simply read the total loss amount over a year horizon at the appropriate percentile, and then subtract the mean or expected losses to determine the capital required, thus mixing both systems of measurement.

21.1.1 Return values as risk measures

Nuclear plants, dams, bridges, and sea dykes are generally required to be maintained to a standard that gives them less than a 1 in 10 000 chance of catastrophic loss in any year. These are *return values* – the basic risk measure for extreme events – and return values are defined via *quantiles*. Value-at-Risk is a measure of this sort.

The probability of a loss exceeding x in any year being less than p gives (assuming independence of loss events) that the probability of no loss exceeding x in any year will exceed $1 - p$. A simple consequence is that the probability of no loss exceeding x throughout k years will exceed $(1 - p)^k$.

$$P(\text{No loss} > x \text{ over } k \text{ years}) > (1 - p)^k.$$

This is a result previously seen in Section 19.3 with the time to first success – here the first exceedance – having the Geometric distribution with parameter $1 - p$ and expectation $1/(1 - p)$.

Example: reactor safety

Suppose that the chance of meltdown in any given nuclear installation in a year is one in 20 000. Since there are 600 nuclear plants in the USA, there is a greater than 50 % chance that at least one of them will experience a meltdown sometime in the next 25 years.

We argue as follows. If the probability of no meltdown at a single plant in any year is p, then the probability of none in any of m plants operating independently is p^m. If the chance does not change from year to year, the probability of no meltdown over k years is $(p^m)^k$, so the chance of at least one meltdown in a plant over a period of k years is $1 - (p^m)^k$. Table 21.1 shows the result when $p = 0.99995$, $m = 600$, and k takes various values.

21.1.2 The k-year return level

We have k annual maximum losses independently from a distribution having cdf F. The probability of an exceedance of amount u or more in any year is $p = 1 - F(u)$. The expected number of years having exceedances u or more when taken over k years is kp. This is a

Table 21.1 Probability of a meltdown.

Years	k	1	2	4	16	20	23	24	32
P(no meltdown)	p^{600k}	0.970	0.942	0.887	0.787	0.549	0.502	0.487	0.383
P(a meltdown)	$1 - p^{600k}$	0.030	0.058	0.113	0.213	0.451	0.497	0.513	0.617

consequence of the total having a *Binomial* (k, p) distribution (Section 19.2). For the expected number of years being less than one (expectation being an average, this does not mean zero), we need $kp < 1$, i.e. $p < 1/k$. This gives $F(u) = 1 - p > 1 - 1/k$. The threshold quantile $u = Q(1 - 1/k)$.

21.2   QUANTILE FUNCTIONS

The population quantile function, $Q(p)$, is the value having proportion p of the population smaller. It treats $Q(p)$ as a function of p. We look first at some of its properties. Its importance in modeling is that we can look upon a quantile function directly as a measure of risk.

Let us look at the relationship between the value x and a continuous random variable X. Continuous is used in the sense that X has a probability density function $f(x)$. With discrete distributions (Poisson, Binomial, Negative Binomial, for example) the quantile function is non-unique at the values where there are jumps in the cumulative distribution. The cumulative distribution function $F(x) = P(X \le x)$ is a function of x. In the continuous case, the quantile function is the inverse function given by solving the equation $F(x) = p$ for x in terms of p. Graphically, the x-axis becomes the y-axis, now labelled $Q(p)$, and the y-axis, which was labelled $F(x)$, becomes the x-axis, now labelled p.

We use standardized variables $Z = (X - \mu)/\sigma$, where μ is a location variable and σ a scale variable. These are not necessarily expectation and standard deviation, probability moments that may not exist. Location may be a lower bound for example. The standard cdf $P(Z \le z)$ will be labeled $F(z)$ when there will be no confusion with the cdf for X. When the distinction is necessary, we shall use subscripts, as with $F_X(x)$ and $F_Z(z)$. The standard quantile function will be written $Q_0(p)$.

21.2.1   Examples of finding quantile functions

If $F(z)$ is cdf of a random variable and $Q(p)$ is its corresponding quantile function, we write $p = F(z)$ and solve the algebraic equation to obtain the inverse function $z = Q(p)$.

The standard exponential distribution: Exponential (1)

$$p = 1 - e^{-z} \quad \text{for} \quad z \ge 0.$$

Then

$$e^{-z} = 1 - p, \quad -z = \ln(1 - p), \quad z = -\ln(1 - p) = Q_0(p).$$

The standard gumbel distribution: Gumbel (0, 1)

$$p = \exp(-e^{-z}) \quad \text{for } z \geq 0.$$

Then

$$\ln p = -e^{-z}, \quad z = -\ln(-\ln p) = Q_0(p).$$

The standard generalized extreme value distribution: GEV (ξ, 0, 1)

$$p = \exp(-w^{-1/\xi}) \quad \text{for } w = 1 + \xi z \geq 0.$$

Then

$$w = (-\ln p)^{-\xi}, \quad z = \{(-\ln p)^{-\xi} - 1\}/\xi = Q_0(p) \quad \text{for } \xi \neq 0.$$

As $\xi \to 0$, $z \to -\ln(-\ln p)$, which is the Gumbel quantile function.

The standard generalized pareto distribution: GPD (ξ, 0, 1)

$$p = 1 - w^{-1/\xi} \quad \text{where} \quad w = 1 + \xi z \geq 0,$$

for $z \geq 0$ if $\xi > 0$, and for $0 < z < -1/\xi$ if $\xi < 0$. Then

$$w = (1-p)^{-\xi}, \quad z = \{(1-p)^{-\xi} - 1\}/\xi = Q_0(p) \quad \text{for } \xi \neq 0.$$

As $\xi \to 0$, $z \to -\ln(1-p)$, which is the Exponential quantile function.

21.2.2 A table of quantile functions

These are presented in Table 21.2 in alphabetical order in their standard forms. Location and scale transformations are easily made. In those incorporating a shape parameter, the shape parameter is ξ. The list contains most but not all of the severity distribution models that have the potential to give extreme values. The Lambda and Wakeby quantile functions incorporate a skewness parameter θ.

For the log-distributions (the lognormal, the loggamma and the loglogistic distributions), if a random variable X has a log-distribution then $Y = \ln X$ has the distribution itself. This leads to

$$Q_X(p) = \exp\{Q_Y(p)\} \quad \text{and} \quad Q_Y(p) = \ln Q_X(p).$$

In the table, the cumulative distribution function of the standard normal distribution $N(0,1)$ is represented by $\Phi(z)$, and the cumulative distribution function of the gamma distribution Gamma (ξ, 1) having shape index ξ and scale parameter 1 by $G_\xi(z)$. Neither has a representation that does not need computation or tabulation. However, good approximation formulae are available for the normal distribution (Section 18.2.2). The log-gamma computation would need considerably more effort.

Table 21.2   Quantile functions for standardized severity models.

Model	$Q_0(p)$	Shape parameter ξ
Beta (GP2)	$-(1-p)^{\xi}$	$(\xi > 0)$ ie $-(1-p)^{-\xi}$ $(\xi < 0)$
Burr (Burr XII)	$\{(1-p)^{-\xi_1} - 1\}^{\xi_2}$	$(\xi_1 > 0,\ \xi_2 > 0)$
Cauchy	$\tan\{\pi(p - \frac{1}{2})\}$	
Davies	$p^{\xi_1}/(1-p)^{\xi_2}$	$(\xi_1 > 0,\ \xi_2 > 0)$
Exponential (GP0)	$-\ln(1-p)$	
Fréchet (EV1)	$(-\ln p)^{-\xi}$	$(\xi > 0)$
Gamma	$G_{\xi}^{-1}(p)$	$(\xi > 0)$
Generalized Extreme Value (GEV)	$\{(-\ln p)^{-\xi} - 1\}/\xi$	$(\xi \neq 0)$
Generalized Logistic	$\{[p/(1-p)]^{\xi} - 1\}/\xi$	$(\xi \neq 0)$
Generalized Pareto (GPD)	$\{(1-p)^{-\xi} - 1\}/\xi$	$(\xi \neq 0)$
Gompertz	$\ln\{-\ln(1-p)\}$	
Gumbel (EV0)	$-\ln(-\ln p)$	
Lambda	$\theta p^{\xi} - (1-p)^{\xi}$	$(\theta > 0)$
Loggamma	$\exp\{G_{\xi}^{-1}(p)\}$	$(\xi > 0)$
Logistic	$-\ln\{(1-p)/p\}$	
Loglogistic	$\{p/(1-p)\}^{\xi}$	
Lognormal	$\exp\{\Phi^{-1}(p)\}$	
Normal	$\Phi^{-1}(p)$	
Pareto (GP1)	$(1-p)^{-\xi}$	$(\xi > 0)$
Power	p^{ξ}	$(\xi > 0)$
Uniform	p	
Wakeby	$\theta\{1 - (1-p)^{\xi_1}\}$ $-\{1 - (1-p)^{-\xi_2}\}$	$(\theta > 0)$
Weibull	$\{-\ln(1-p)\}^{1/\xi}$	$(\xi > 0)$
(Reflected) Weibull (EV2)	$-(-\ln p)^{\xi}$	$(\xi > 0)$ ie $-(-\ln p)^{-\xi}$ $(\xi < 0)$

21.2.3   The Davies and Wakeby distributions

These distributions are defined by their quantile functions and not through their probability density functions which do not exist as simple formulae.

The Davies distribution

Hankin and Lee (2006) describe the properties of this generalization of the loglogistic distribution. In particular they find that there is a close least squares fit of a Davies quantile function to the exponential, gamma, lognormal, Weibull, and lambda quantile functions. They conclude that it provides a flexible model for right-skewed non-negative data, which for appropriate parameter values can closely match the standard models.

The Wakeby distribution

This distribution was created as a robust and flexible model for hydrological data.

21.2.4 Properties of quantile functions

We bear in mind that quantiles are just x-values, such as may be taken by operational risk losses. Gilchrist (2000) is devoted to statistics based on quantile functions and the following list of properties reflects the selection there.

- A quantile function $Q(p)$ is a non-decreasing function.
- Any non-decreasing function can be a quantile function.
- If Ψ is any non-decreasing function, then $\Psi(Q(p))$ is a quantile function. Examples are $\ln Q(p)$ (provided that $Q(p)$ takes only positive values) and $\exp Q(p)$ as seen above in Table 21.2 for the lognormal and loggamma distributions.
- An important case of a non-decreasing function is the linear transformation $y = ax + b$ $(a > 0)$. In particular, a location parameter μ and scale parameter σ $(\sigma > 0)$ transform a quantile function $Q_0(p)$ to give

$$Q(p) = \mu + \sigma \, Q_0(p).$$

In the theory of extremes the moments of the thick tail model distributions may not exist, so μ and σ are not necessarily expectation and variance.
- If Q, Q_1, and Q_2 are quantile functions of random variables X, Y, and Z respectively, then non-decreasing transformations give, for example, the following quantile functions.
- *Addition* $Q_1(p) + Q_2(p)$
- *Multiplication* $Q_1(p) \times Q_2(p)$
  An example is *Power(ξ)* $\times$ *Pareto(ξ)* which gives the quantile function $p^\xi \times (1 - p)^{-\xi} = \{p/(1 - p)\}^\xi$ of the loglogistic distribution.
- *Logarithmic transformation* $\ln Q(p)$ $(Q(p) > 0)$
  The Exponential is the log-Gompertz.
- *Power transformation* $\{Q(p)\}^\xi$ $(\xi > 0)$
- *Reflection* $-Q(1 - p)$
  This gives the quantile function for $-X$. The Gompertz is the reflected Gumbel. The Beta (GP2) is the reflected Power. We also have reflection between the Weibull and the (Reflected) Weibull (EV2).
- *Inversion* $1/Q(1 - p)$
  This gives the quantile function for $1/X$, and is the relationship between the power function distribution and the Pareto (GP1).
- *Combining*   Combining the above gives further relationships. For example, the transformation relating X and $-1/X$ links the Pareto with the Beta (GP2) and the Fréchet with the Weibull (EV2).

21.3 SIMULATION DATA FROM CONTINUOUS DISTRIBUTIONS

Within the table of quantile functions (Table 21.2), we see applied many of the quantile transformations. In particular, every single one is a transformation of the standard uniform quantile function $Q_U(p) = p$. This mapping enables the simulation of data from any continuous distribution from randomly generated deviates of the standard uniform distribution.

- $p = F_X(x) = P(X \leq x)$, and $Q_X(p) = x$ are inverse mappings which swap the axes, reading x from p, in place of reading p from x. When we read from x to p and then back from p to x, we have $Q_X(F_X(x)) = x$, and similarly $F_X(Q_X(p)) = p$.

- If the random variable U has the *Uniform* (0,1) distribution, then, for $0 < u < 1$, $F_U(u) = P(U \le u) = u$ and $Q_U(u) = u$, so they have the same probability. Here we are just swapping the axes of $y = x$.
- If X has cdf $F_X(x)$, then the random variable U which is the transformation $F_X(X)$ of the random variable X is a *Uniform* (0,1) random variable. The reasoning goes as follows. Let Y be the random variable defined by the transformation $Y = F_X(X)$. The event $F_X(X) \le u$ for $0 < u < 1$ is the same event as $Q_X(F_X(X)) \le Q_X(u)$, ie $X \le Q_X(u)$. Then

$$F_Y(y) = P(Y < y) = P(F_X(X) \le y) = P(X \le Q_X(y)) = F_X(Q_X(y)) = y,$$

so $F_Y(y)$ is the *Uniform* (0,1) cdf.
- Arguing in reverse, if U is *Uniform* (0,1), then the transformation $Q_X(U)$ of U is an rv X with cdf F_X and quantile function Q_X. This can be shown by letting Z be the random variable $Q_X(U)$, then

$$F_Z(z) = P(Z \le z) = P(Q_X(U) \le z) = P(U \le F_X(z)) = F_X(z),$$

since $P(U \le u) = u$, so Z has the cdf F_X.
- In conclusion we have the result that: from a random sample of data $u_1, u_2, \ldots, u_n$ from *Uniform* (0,1), the values $Q_X(u_1)$, $Q_X(u_2)$, $\ldots$, $Q_X(u_n)$ are a random sample from F_X.
- From Table 21.2 we see that if u is a *Uniform* (0,1) random deviate, then $x = -\ln(1 - u)$ is an *Exponential* (1) random deviate, and $x = -\ln(-\ln u)$ is from *Gumbel* (0,1). Similarly with all the other entries in the table.

21.4 QUANTILE REGRESSION

We can consider a regression formula for the dependence of the p-quantile on a regressor variable x with the error term a multiple of a standard quantile, usually the standard normal quantile. For example

$$\hat{Q}(p|x) = a + bx + \sigma Q_0(p).$$

Here p might be a sequence of values 0.99, 0.98, $\cdots$, 0.01, a and b unknown constants, σ the scale factor to be determined alongside a and b, and $\hat{Q}(p|x)$ the observed quantiles from the data.

21.5 QUANTILE FUNCTIONS FOR EXTREME VALUE MODELS

Our modeling will focus on the extreme value models. Though these will be dealt with more fully in the modeling chapters, their quantile functions are extracted from Table 21.2 to give

Table 21.3 Quantile functions for extreme value models.

Model	$Q_0(p)$		Model	$Q_0(p)$	
Gumbel	$-\ln(-\ln p)$		Exponential	$-\ln(1 - p)$	
Fréchet	$(-\ln p)^{-\xi}$	$(\xi > 0)$	Pareto	$(1 - p)^{-\xi}$	$(\xi > 0)$
Weibull	$-(-\ln p)^{-\xi}$	$(\xi < 0)$	Beta	$-(1 - p)^{-\xi}$	$(\xi < 0)$
GEV	$\{(-\ln p)^{-\xi} - 1\}/\xi$	$(\xi \neq 0)$	GPD	$\{(1 - p)^{-\xi} - 1\}/\xi$	$(\xi \neq 0)$

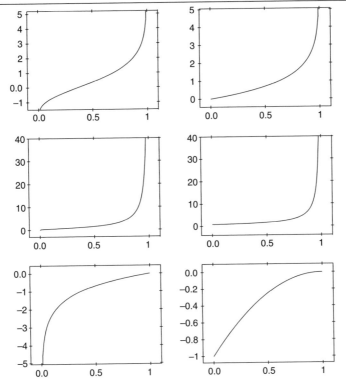

Figure 21.1   Plots of $Q_0(p)$ for Gumbel and Exponential (top row), for Fréchet ($\xi = 1$) and Pareto ($\xi = 1$) (middle row), and for Weibull ($\xi = -1$) and Beta ($\xi = -2$) (bottom row).

Table 21.3, and are shown in Figure 21.1 for ease of reference. We shall henceforth use the terminology of extreme value practice to call the Beta (GP2) and the (Reflected) Weibull (EV2) just the Beta and the Weibull.

22

Frequency Modeling from Small
Data Sets

22.1 INTRODUCTION

The first question to ask is why we should be modeling frequency, when our overriding interest is in the severity of the losses. The explanation generally given is that data from external sources will often have to be incorporated into the database. This can happen if banks merge and the new entity will not have accumulated sufficient data to model the severity distribution or satisfy regulatory requirements of several years of data collection. By fitting a frequency model independently from a severity model we are assuming an independence between the random process of times (epochs) at which the loss events occur and the random variables giving the sizes of the losses. This separation of the two seems to be an unwarranted squandering of risk information contained in the loss database. The rebuild from a fitted frequency distribution and a fitted loss size distribution and the subsequent validation is a poor and imperfect solution to the shortage of data.

> The separation of frequency and severity is an unwarranted squandering of risk information. The re-creation of a loss distribution from a fitted frequency distribution and a fitted loss size distribution is a poor and imperfect solution.

The commonly available choices are the Poisson and Negative Binomial models. Rarely will either model give a satisfactory fit to small data sets. We saw this when we fitted these distributions to the data sets 1 and 2 in Sections 19.5.1 and 19.6.1.

22.2 ASSESSING THE QUALITY OF FIT: MODEL SELECTION UNCERTAINTY

In Table 22.1, the data sets are simulations of 143 values from a Poisson distribution having population mean 1.434. This is the fitted distribution of Section 19.6.1. The data was obtained from two different computer programs.

The two sample means are 1.315 and 1.629. There is no reason to suppose that either of the two computer packages was seriously at fault for giving such poor estimates of 1.434. It is simply a characteristic of taking small samples. The estimates are unbiased but the standard error of the estimates are 0.100. Usually about 95 % of the time we estimate the sample mean we can expect the result to be in error by up to about twice that, as is the case here. This is an illustration of sampling fluctuation.

We note that a property of the *Poisson* (λ) distribution is that its variance $\sigma^2 = \mu = \lambda$. A comparison of $\bar{x}$ and s^2 is a first check on the quality of the fit.

Table 22.1 Poisson simulated data with summary statistics.

Simulation 1	n_y	46	41	35	10	9	1	1	0	143
	yn_y	0	41	70	30	36	5	6	0	188
Simulation 2	n_y	33	42	31	24	8	5	0	0	143
	yn_y	0	42	62	72	32	25	0	0	233

	n	$\sum x_i$	$\sum x_i^2$	$\bar{x}$	s^2	s
Data	143	205	483	1.434	1.332	1.154
Simulation 1	143	188	476	1.315	1.612	1.269
Simulation 2	143	233	635	1.629	1.798	1.341

22.3 SIMULATING FREQUENCY DISTRIBUTIONS

Although simulation will generally be done through the use of a computer package, it is useful to have an understanding of the pencil and paper mechanism.

22.3.1 Model method

We can often use properties of how the probability distribution arises as a model of randomness.

- *Bernoulli* (θ).   This is a particularly easy case. Here $p_0 = 1 - \theta$, $p_1 = \theta$, where $0 < \theta < 1$, so, if u_k is uniformly random between 0 and 1 we take $x_k = 1$ if $u_k \leq \theta$, otherwise take $x_k = 0$. For particular cases of θ, we may have alternative methods. For example, if $\theta = \frac{1}{2}$ we could toss a coin, or if $\theta = \frac{1}{4}$ or $\frac{3}{4}$, toss 2 coins. For one-sixth or one-third, we could roll a die.
- *Binomial* (n, θ).   Here we could count the number of 1s in n simulated *Bernoulli* (θ) values.
- *Geometric* (θ).   Here we could count the number of 0s in simulated *Bernoulli* (θ) values up to the first 1, and then add one to the count.

22.3.2 Table look-up method

Most simulation procedures make use of a *random number generator* which yields values which resemble independent values $u_1, u_2, \ldots,$ uniformly at random on the interval 0 to 1. In the old days statistics textbooks gave lists of random digits $0, 1, 2, \ldots, 9$, which, with a decimal point before a string of these, became a random number on 0 to 1.

In the continuous distribution case this was the basis for creating simulated data through substituting the values into the quantile function. However, in the frequency case in carrying out the mapping $p = F_X(x) \rightarrow x = Q(p)$, each x has a whole range of $Q(p)$ values.

The *table look-up method* uses uniform random deviates, $u_1, u_2, \ldots,$ to simulate data $x_1, x_2, \ldots$ for a tabulated probability mass function $\{p_x\}(x = \{0, 1, 2, 3, \ldots\})$.

The cumulative distribution function is

$$F_X(x) = P(X \leq x) = \sum_{j=0}^{[x]} p_j,$$

where $[x]$ is the integer part of x. If u_k takes its value in the range $F_X(m - 1) < u_k \leq F_X(m)$, then we assign value m to x_k, with value 0 if $u_k \leq F_X(0)$, where m runs from 0 to ∞. Table 22.2 illustrates obtaining the first few random deviates from *Poisson* (Section 18.15).

Table 22.2   Table look-up for simulated *Poisson* (18.15) data.

x	$F(x-1)$	$F(x)$	i	u_i	x_i
0	0.0000	0.0429	1	0.20457	2
1	0.0429	0.1778	2	0.97689	7
2	0.1778	0.3904	3	0.84244	5
3	0.3904	0.6137	4	0.71812	4
4	0.6137	0.7895	5	0.87372	5
5	0.7895	0.9002	6	0.45209	3
6	0.9002	0.9584	7	0.06513	1
7	0.9584	0.9845	8	0.31287	2
8	0.9845	0.9948	9	0.87894	5
9	0.9948	0.9984	10	0.25181	2
10	0.9984	0.9999	11	0.09640	1
11	0.9999		12	0.79476	5

22.3.3   How might we assign Poisson time points to scenarios?

For an interval of length t, the number of points of a *Poisson process* having rate λ per unit interval will be randomly from a *Poisson*(λt) distribution. The points will be located as if they had been dropped independently uniformly at random over the interval. Now the parameter of the Poisson distribution is a scale parameter so we may drop the points over a unit interval – that is to say, use the random values $u_1, u_2, \ldots$,

Why might we wish to assign Poisson time points if we are aggregating data over a fixed time period, such as a year? There seems to be little good reason for simulating an arrangement as a Poisson process in this case.

23

Severity Modeling

23.1 WHICH SEVERITY MODEL SHOULD WE USE?

The normal distribution that forms the basis of much of statistical inference needs to be replaced by a loss distribution showing a thicker upper tail.

The summary statistics, and the histograms of Data 4 (Table 17.4 and Figure 17.2) show a right-skewed shape typical of those arising from loss data.

The lognormal distribution was historically the model of choice in econometrics, and still is for some major international banks. There is a substantial view that the tail of the lognormal is insufficiently thick, failing to model the chance of extremely large losses. The Weibull distribution has a long history of use in reliability analysis to model the times to failure of systems, and in survival analysis, for example to model the times to death or recovery after surgery or disease onset or treatment. It belongs to the class of extreme value distributions, where in financial circles it is called the Fréchet distribution, with the Reflected Weibull distribution being called Weibull.

In Figure 23.1 we have examples of the probability distribution functions of four representative models which have this right-skewed shape: the lognormal, gamma, Gumbel, and GEV. From Chapter 20 and Table 21.2 we might have added to these the Burr XII, loggamma, the lambda and the Wakeby, and this is not a definitive list.

Two heavy-tailed distributions emerge as models for severity data from the theory of extreme values. These are the Generalized Extreme Value distribution (GEV) and the Generalized Pareto Distribution (GPD). We review briefly Extreme Value Theory despite the fact that the results are asymptotic, requiring the sample size to go to infinity when our data sets are generally relatively small. In many cases, the GEV and GPD offer sufficient flexibility through their three parameters to give a reasonable model fit without our relying on the asymptotic theory that gave rise to them.

23.2 EXTREME VALUE THEORY

23.2.1 The Central Limit Theorem

Extreme value theory (EVT) is a theory of limiting probability distributions for sequences of record values. However, we start with a look at the Central Limit Theorem with its normal distribution limit since it is widely known, and although not useful for recording values it illustrates the idea and terminology of the convergence of distributions.

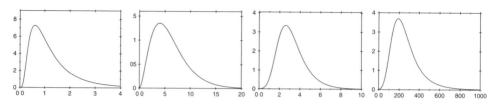

Figure 23.1   Pdfs respectively for the lognormal, gamma, Gumbel, and GEV distributions.

Theorem

For a sequence $X_1, X_2, \ldots$ of independent and identically distributed random variables having a distribution with a finite variance, the sequence of sums

$$T_n = \sum_{i=1}^{n} X_i$$

is such that there are sequences of constants μ_n and σ_n so that, when T_n is relocated and scaled,

$$T_n^* = \frac{T_n - \mu_n}{\sigma_n}$$

has in the limit as $n \to \infty$ the standard normal distribution $N(0,1)$.

We know that if each X_i is from a distribution $F(x)$ having $E(X_i) = \mu$ and $\text{var}(X_i) = \sigma^2 < \infty$ then $\mu_n = n\mu \, (= E(T_n))$ and $\sigma_n = \sqrt{n\sigma^2} \, (= \sqrt{\text{var}(T_n)})$ will achieve the result.

The choice of μ_n and σ_n are to force a non-degenerate limiting distribution. By non-degenerate we mean it does not collapse to a single point or go off to $+\infty$ or $-\infty$.

We say that the distribution F belongs to the domain of attraction of the normal distribution. We might also say that F is sum-stable, since the result of summing independent values from the limiting normal distribution preserves the normality, merely modifying the gaussianity. We can show in reverse that the normal distribution is a consequence of this property.

23.2.2   Max-stable distributions

We now turn to the limiting distribution of maxima. Again let $X_1, X_2, \ldots$ be independent and identically distributed random variables having a cumulative distribution function $F(x)$, though with no constraints on the moments. Then take

$$T_n = \max\{X_1, X_2, \ldots, X_n\},$$

and let us write $F_n(t)$ for its cumulative distribution function. Then

$$F_n(t) = P(T_n \leq t) = P(\text{each } X_i \leq t) = \prod_{i=1}^{n} P(X_i \leq t) = \{F(t)\}^n.$$

Then

$$T_n^* = \frac{T_n - \mu_n}{\sigma_n}$$

is such that there are sequences of constants μ_n and $\sigma_n > 0$ so that it has a non-degenerate limit distribution. In this case there are three possible limit distributions given by cases for which

$$F(t) = \{F(\mu_n + \sigma_n t)\}^n$$

(1) *Gumbel.*   This has $\mu_n = \ln n$ and $\sigma_n = 1$ for each n, so $T_n^* = T_n - \ln n$. The distribution F is in the domain of attraction of Gumbel and is said to be of Exponential type. It includes the normal, lognormal, and exponential distributions.

(2) *Fréchet.*   Here $\mu_n = 0$ and $\sigma_n = n^{-\xi}$ ($\xi > 0$) so $T_n^* = n^\xi T_n$. The limit distribution is on the positive values. The distribution F is in the domain of attraction of Fréchet and is said to be of Cauchy type.

(3) *Weibull (i.e. (Reflected) Weibull).*   Here $\mu_n = 0$ and $\sigma_n = n^{-\xi}$ ($\xi < 0$) so $T_n^* = n^\xi T_n$. The limit distribution is on the negative values. The distribution F is in the domain of attraction of Weibull and is said to be of Limited type.

We call distributions in these three domains of attraction *max-stable*. The three domains, the Gumbel, Fréchet, and Weibull distributions, can be combined through reparameterization as the GEV distribution (Section 20.7). This extreme value theory result makes the GEV a prime model for loss data analysis.

23.2.3 Extreme value modeling

We can fit directly a GEV distribution to a data set (Section 24.1), or take as our data the largest loss observed in each of equal time periods (Section 24.2). A criticism of this use of blocks of data is that information from clusters of large losses within a block is not being used. This can be mitigated by using rolling data sets. Suppose that we are taking as our blocks units of 20 business days. Then we refit our GEV each day as the new data comes in. The new maximum (or aggregate) loss for the day becomes the 20th observation in the last block, pushing each earlier day's observation back one place. The sequence of fitted models will highlight any changes. However, if we have records of all loss events there is an alternative to this block analysis: it is to model those losses which exceed some fixed threshold τ. This is the *peaks over threshold* (POT) method. This requires modeling the tail distribution.

23.2.4 Tail behaviour

Modeling the tail behaviour, in particular the heavy tails that model extreme loss sizes, is central to loss data analysis for regulatory operational risk capital.

What do we mean by heavy or thick tails?

Distributions classified as sub-exponential, that is, having tail pdfs thicker than those of an exponential distribution, have the property that the probability distribution of the aggregate loss above a very large threshold is close to that of the distribution of the largest loss above the threshold.

$$\frac{P(X_1 + X_2 + \cdots + X_n > x)}{P(\max(X_1, X_2, \ldots, X_n) > x)} \longrightarrow 1 \text{ as } x \to \infty.$$

The extreme value theory for tail behaviour is based on the distribution of the excess loss above the threshold value. Let $Y = X - \tau$ represent the excess over a threshold τ.

$$P(X > \tau + y \,|\, X > \tau) = \frac{P(X > \tau + y)}{P(X > \tau)} = \frac{\overline{F}(\tau + y)}{\overline{F}(\tau)}$$

for $y > 0$, where $\overline{F}(x) = P(X > x)$ is the survivor function (reliability function).

Corresponding to the three domains of attraction of the max-stable distribution, we have three domains for the tail behaviour, the Exponential, Pareto, and Beta (GP2). These combine to give the Generalized Pareto distribution (Section 20.8). If block maxima are approximately GEV then excesses over the threshold are like GPD. This makes the GPD the natural model for the tail behaviour of max-stable distributions.

The theorem giving the relationship between GEV and GPD may be interpreted as follows. For the maximum of a random sample of size n from cdf $F(y)$, with n large enough for a limiting $GEV(\xi, \mu, \sigma)$ distribution to have kicked in at least approximately, then

$$\{F(y)\}^n \approx \exp\{-(1 + \xi z)^{-1/\xi}\},$$

where $z = (y - \mu)/\sigma$ and $z > -1/\xi$. Then taking logs gives

$$n \ln F(y) \approx -(1 + \xi z)^{-1/\xi}.$$

For y large (in the tail), $\overline{F}(y) = 1 - F(y)$ will be small, giving the leading term of the expansion $\ln\{1 - \overline{F}(y)\} \approx -\overline{F}(y)$. Then

$$P(Y > \tau + x \mid Y > \tau) = \frac{\overline{F}(\tau + x)}{\overline{F}(\tau)} \approx \left\{ \frac{1 + \xi(\tau + x - \mu)/\sigma}{1 + \xi(\tau - \mu)/\sigma} \right\}^{-1/\xi} = \left(1 + \frac{\xi x}{\sigma^*}\right)^{-1/\xi},$$

where $\sigma^* = \sigma + \xi(\tau - \mu)$. But this right-hand side is the survivor function $\overline{F}(x)$ for a random variable from $GPD(\xi, 0, \sigma^*)$.

23.3   MODELING EXCESSES

Let $Y_\tau = X - \tau$ be an excess random variable having a $GPD(\xi, 0, \sigma^*)$ distribution with $\sigma^* = \sigma + \xi(\tau - \mu)$, where τ is known and $\xi < 1$. Then

$$E(Y_\tau \mid Y_\tau > 0) = \frac{\sigma + \xi(\tau - \mu)}{1 - \xi} = \frac{\sigma - \xi\mu}{1 - \xi} + \frac{\xi}{1 - \xi}\tau.$$

This is linear in τ with slope $\xi/(1 - \xi)$. If $\bar{x}_\tau$ is the mean of observations larger than τ, and $\bar{y}_\tau = \bar{x}_\tau - \tau$, the mean of the excesses, a plot of $\bar{y}_\tau$ as τ increases will become approximately straight as the tail approaches its Pareto form. The slope of the straight line will give an estimate for ξ. The straight line gives a measure for the behavior of the tail beyond the threshold, which the VaR quantile does not.

23.4   ESTIMATING THE TAIL SHAPE PARAMETER FROM THE LARGEST ORDER STATISTICS

We can exploit Pareto-like tail behavior by looking at $Pareto(\xi, 0, \tau)$; the reasoning is easier if we work from the Pareto than the GPD. We have

$$P(X > x) = \left(\frac{x}{\tau}\right)^{-1/\xi} \qquad (x > \tau).$$

We note that the scale parameter is also the threshold τ, which shows some of the ambiguity between location and scale.

The maximum likelihood estimate for Pareto $(\xi, 0, \tau)$

We first obtain the MLE for ξ when τ is known, using the information in Table 20.20,

$$f(z) = \alpha z^{-\alpha-1}, \quad \ln f(z) = \ln \alpha - (\alpha + 1)\ln z, \quad \frac{d \ln f(z)}{d\alpha} = \frac{1}{\alpha} - \ln z.$$

For log-likelihood $L(\alpha; z_1, z_2, \ldots, z_n)$

$$\frac{dL}{d\alpha} = \frac{n}{\alpha} - \sum_1^n \ln z_i, \quad \frac{d^2 L}{d\alpha^2} = -\frac{n}{\alpha^2}.$$

Since $d^2 L/d\alpha^2 < 0$ for all values of α, $dL/d\alpha = 0$ gives the MLE $\widehat{\alpha} = \{(1/n)\sum \ln z_i\}^{-1}$. Further since $\xi = 1/\alpha$ and $z_i = x_i/\tau$, and $dL/d\xi = (dL/d\alpha)(d\alpha/d\xi) = 0$ when $dL/d\alpha = 0$, the MLE for ξ is

$$\widehat{\xi} = \frac{1}{n}\sum_{i=1}^n \ln\left(\frac{x_i}{\tau}\right) = \frac{1}{n}\sum_{i=1}^n \ln x_i - \ln \tau.$$

Hill estimates

For the order statistics $x_{1:n} > x_{2:n} > \cdots > x_{n:n}$ from a random sample of size n, if we set the threshold for the MLE for ξ to be the kth largest observation $x_{k:n}$, we get a sequence of estimates of ξ known as the Hill estimates.

$$\widehat{\xi}_k = \frac{1}{k-1}\sum_{i=1}^{k-1} \ln x_{i:n} - \ln x_{k:n} \qquad (k = 2, \ldots, n)$$

Other variants are sometimes used such as

$$\widehat{\xi}_k = \frac{1}{k}\sum_{i=1}^{k} \ln x_{i:n} - \ln x_{k:n} \qquad (k = 2, \ldots, n)$$

but this is not important, as subjectivity is applied in how we use these $k - 1$ estimates in estimating ξ.

We wish to choose a value of ξ for which the values ξ_k have settled down. When I am computing on a largish scale with small data sets (as with the rolling data study in Section 24.2), I remove the first two or three and the last two or three and average the rest. The use of bootstrap resampling methods have been proposed for choosing k, but with fairly small sample sizes a subjective judgement based on plotting the values may be just as satisfactory given the large standard errors.

Pickands estimates

For finite sample sizes the Hill estimate is biased. Alternative estimators have been proposed which attempt to improve the asymptotic properties. The Pickands estimator with sample size $4n$ is

$$\widehat{\xi}_k = \frac{1}{\ln 2} \ln\left(\frac{x_{k:4n} - x_{2k:4n}}{x_{2k:4n} - x_{4k:4n}}\right) \qquad (k = 1, \ldots, n).$$

This needs considerable amounts of data.

De Haan and Resnick estimates

$$\widehat{\xi}_k = \frac{1}{\ln k}(\ln x_{1:n} - \ln x_{k:n}).$$

23.5   GOODNESS-OF-FIT TESTS

These tests assume that if parameters have been estimated from the data set, we have new data to validate them. In particular cases, simulations have shown how adjustments to the rejection set might be made to account for the over-fitting from using estimated parameter values without further data.

The chi-squared test and likelihood ratio test were described in Section 18.5. The likelihood ratio test shown there takes the following form for testing with a simple null hypothesis and a composite alternative hypothesis. If $H_0 : \theta = \theta_0$, and $H_1 : \theta \neq \theta_0$, the likelihood ratio test statistic is

$$\lambda(x) = \frac{\ell(\widehat{\theta}; x)}{\ell(\theta_0; x)}$$

with H_0 rejected if $\lambda(x)$ is too large, where x is the data set. Here $\widehat{\theta}$ is the MLE for θ. Wilks theorem proves that, as the sample size increases, $2 \ln \lambda(x)$ becomes like a chi-squared random variable on 1 degree of freedom.

A second class of tests compares the sample cumulative distribution function with the cdf for the hypothesized model. The list of these is more extensive than the following selection.

Kolmogorov-Smirnov (K-S) D^+, D^- and D
Kuiper V
Brunk B
Durbin D and M^2
Cramér-von Mises W^2
Watson U^2
Anderson-Darling A

These tests correspond in the main to measuring differences on the probability plots: the cdf against sample cdf plot, the P-P or Q-Q plots.

In these tests we suppose that the fitted model has cdf $F(x)$, and the data has the sample cdf $\widehat{F}(x) = $ the proportion of observations with values no larger than x. In practice, if the data is ordered with $x_1 \geq x_2 \geq \cdots \geq x_n$, this gives $\widehat{F}(x_i) = (n - i + 1)/n$, so we would use for $\widehat{F}(x_i)$ one of the symmetric plotting points of Section 17.7.5, such as $\widehat{p}_i = (n - i + \frac{1}{2})/n$. Let us also write p_i for $F(x_i)$.

Kolmogorov-Smirnov and Kuiper tests

If the data is $x_1, x_2, \ldots, x_n$, then

$$D^+ = \max_x \{\widehat{F}(x) - F(x)\} = \max_i \{\widehat{p}_i - p_i\},$$

$$D^- = \max_x \{F(x) - \widehat{F}(x)\} = \max_i \{p_i - \widehat{p}_i\},$$

$$D = \max(D^+, D^-), \quad \text{and} \quad V = D^+ + D^-.$$

We need check for the maxima only at the n points and not throughout the cdf. These tests reject the fit if the test statistics $\sqrt{n}D^+$, $\sqrt{n}D^-$, $\sqrt{n}D$, $\sqrt{n}V$ are too large.

Cramér-von Mises test

$$W^2 = \sum_i (p_i - \widehat{p}_i)^2.$$

The big problem is that the rejection set depends on the sampling distribution of the test statistics, and have been computed only for a small number of cases, often through simulation exercises. No significance tables have been constructed for use with the 3-parameter distributions such as the GEV and GPD, and so the value of the test statistics can only be suggestive of what the correct rejection set should be. The other problem is their conservatism, their reluctance to reject the null hypothesis. The probability plots might still be the best decision-making tool.

The Zempléni test for GEV distributions

The null hypothesis is that the data is a random sample from GEV against the alternative that they are from some other continuous distribution. This uses the max-stable property of GEV that for any integer m there are constants a_m and b_m for which the GEV cdf $F(x) = \{F(a_m x + b_m)\}^m$ for all x. From a random sample of size n, giving the sample cdf $F_n(x)$, the test statistic t takes $m = 2$.

$$t = \sqrt{n} \min_{a,b} \max_x |F_n(x) - \{F_n(ax + b)\}^2|.$$

Zempléni (1996) shows that there is an easy iterative maximization procedure, and that the test has low rejection percentages, with strong dependence on the shape parameter.

23.6   FITTING A GPD TAIL TO A GEV

We examine how we might best marry a GPD tail to a GEV body. We shall see that it would lead to very demanding computation. A short cut is offered.

We begin with minimum threshold, a, of losses recorded with full event loss detail. This is a known constant. The first *unknown* parameter, τ, is the quantile at which GEV and GPD should meet for best model fit. The GEV and GPD each have three parameters, (ξ_0, μ_0, σ_0) and (ξ_1, μ_1, σ_1) respectively. Extreme value theory suggests that we may be able to use the same shape parameter ξ for each, though this should be tested, and we adopt it in this illustration. Let us further assume that $\xi > 0$. For probability weighted moment fitting we would also need $\xi < 1$.

The pdf for GEV is

$$f_0(x) = f_0(x|\xi, \mu_0, \sigma_0) = (1/\sigma_0)(1 + \xi z_0)^{-1/\xi} \exp\{-(1 + \xi z_0)^{-1/\xi}\}$$

where $z_0 = (x - \mu_0)/\sigma_0$. That for GPD is

$$f_1(x) = f_1(x|\xi, \mu_1, \sigma_1) = (1/\sigma_1)(1 + \xi z_1)^{1+1/\xi}\}$$

where $z_1 = (x - \mu_1)/\sigma_1$.

The pdf for the joined up distribution is

$$f(x) = f(x|\tau, \xi, \mu_1, \sigma_1, \mu_2, \sigma_2) = c\{I(\tau - x)f_0(x) + I(x - \tau)f_1(x)\} \qquad (x > a)$$

where $I(u) = \begin{cases} 1 & u \geq 0, \\ 0 & u < 0. \end{cases}$

The factor c is the normalization that makes the pdf integrate to 1, i.e.

$$c = \left\{ \int_{x=a}^{\tau} f_0 dx + \int_{x=\tau}^{\infty} f_1 dx \right\}^{-1}.$$

The next step is to ensure a smooth transition between the components, since the join is an artifact with no inherent risk interpretation. We apply two constraints,

$$C_1 : \quad f_0(\tau) = f_1(\tau), \qquad C_2 : \quad \left(\frac{d f_0(x)}{dx} \right)_{x=\tau} = \left(\frac{d f_1(x)}{dx} \right)_{x=\tau}.$$

This reduces the six parametric degrees of freedom to four (or from seven to five, if we fit both ξ_1 and ξ_2), making the problem of maximum likelihood estimation more manageable in principle, despite the complexity between the parameters given by C_1 and C_2.

The MLE solution comes from maximizing the log-likelihood function

$$L((\tau, \xi, \mu_1, \sigma_1, \mu_2, \sigma_2); x_1, x_2, \ldots, x_n, C_1, C_2) = \sum_{i=1}^{n} \ln f(x_i).$$

The massive computation process has not yet been fully developed.

Compromises will generally be necessary. One alternative which can be applied to a fairly small data set is to fit a GEV. We will often be able to achieve a fairly good fit other than in the tail where we will have only sparse data – this is clearly seen in the case study in Section 24.1. We could assume the fitted values for ξ_1, μ_1 and σ_1, and use a sequence of values of τ. This will reduce the parameter estimation to ξ_2, μ_2, σ_2 and τ, with simplified constraints. The likelihood from this practice of using fitted parameter values is called the *profile likelihood*.

A serious problem with this methodology is the severe shortage of data in the tail component. Methods of using scenarios derived from experts, questionnaires, databanks or simulation to create potential tail data are widely used.

Giacometti *et al.* (2007, 2008) parameterize the model slightly differently from the one described above. They use

$$f(x) = \{\alpha / F_0(\tau)\} f_0(x)I(\tau - x) + (1 - \alpha)f_1(x)I(x - \tau).$$

An alternative modeling approach is to interpret the extreme stress losses as a contamination of the basic loss pdf. This throws in a small proportion α from a distribution representing data anomalous to the main body of data:

$$f(x) = \alpha f_0(x) + (1 - \alpha)f_1(x).$$

24

Case Studies

24.1   CASE STUDY: FITTING A LOSS DATA SET

If a model fits badly where we have data, why should we expect good estimation when we extrapolate into the tail beyond the data?

Sometimes we can agree on a model, for example between GEV and GPD depending on the way the data was collected. At other times, the choice of model will be subjective. Statistical analysis may show the subjective choice to be relatively insensitive to the model choice. This will not necessarily address the extrapolation problem.

Database of legal events: Data 4 (Table 17.4)

3822	907	735	556	423	395	302	260	248	220	204	193	180	160	150
2568	845	660	550	417	360	297	255	239	220	202	191	176	157	147
1416	800	650	506	410	350	295	252	232	220	200	186	176	154	146
1299	750	630	484	406	350	275	251	230	215	200	185	165	151	143
917	743	600	426	400	332	270	250	229	211	194	182	165	151	143

The calculations were for all three parameters of GEV and GPD using probability weighted moments (pwm), and by calculating the Hill estimate of ξ with μ and σ by probability weighted moments (pwh) (Sections 23.4 and 17.7.5). Maximum likelihood estimation gave results out of line with these, and the quantile-quantile plot confirmed visually that the fit it gave was poor.

My own calculations for all three parameters for both GEV and GPD using probability weighted moments, and by calculating ξ by Hill estimation with μ and σ by probability weighted moments gave

	GEV pwm	GEV pwh	GPD pwm	GPD pwh
μ	234	232	135	187
σ	124	72	172	75
ξ	0.53	0.70	0.435	0.70

The parameters of the fitted distributions were then tweaked, including rounding the values where it seemed to make no significant difference. The mechanism for this was the use of the sliders given by the *Xtremes* computer package that accompanied Reiss and Thomas (2007). The computer package offers, as well as maximum likelihood estimation, *minimized distance estimation*, which selects the parameters that give a minimum to the distance between the sample cdf and the model cdf, and a class of estimators based on *ratios of spacings* between loss sizes.

The fitted models

	GEV pwm	GEV pwh	GPD pwm	GPD pwh
μ	230	230	135	150
σ	130	100	165	125
ξ	0.53	0.70	0.44	0.70

These appear to have parameter values quite different from those offered by the computer package. The fitting was based on comparing the sample cdf with the cdfs given by these models as seen in the top right figure of Figure 24.2 which covers the range of the data. The pdfs, cdfs, and quantile probability density functions are shown over ranges of loss sizes. For all the data exceeding about 300, each of these models gives approximately the same curve. For loss sizes beyond the data, the areas under the pdf curves, which measure probability, are very different.

The tables of quantiles and fitted values (Tables 24.1, 24.2) show that despite a good fit throughout the range of the data, beyond that the pwm method has led to lower quantile values than when the Hill estimation is used. We see this particularly in Table 24.2 where the discrepancy with the largest observed data value is already well out of line with its corresponding quantile values. This gets worse when we view the 99.9 % fitted quantile values of Table 24.1. Identification of the models in the Figures 24.1, 24.2 and 24.3 can be seen from Tables 24.1 and 24.2.

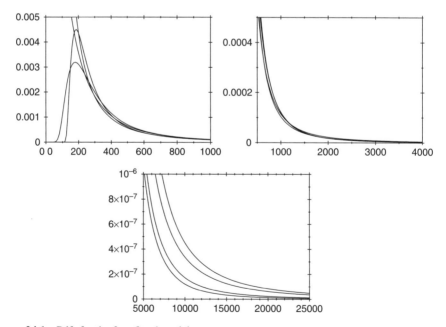

Figure 24.1   Pdfs for the four fitted models.

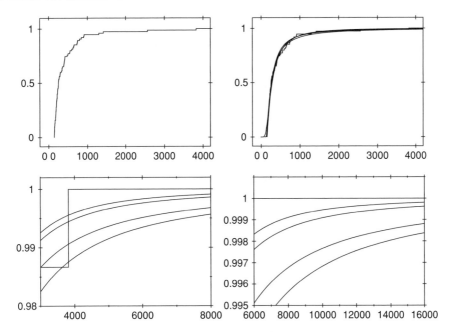

Figure 24.2   The sample cdf with the four models over various ranges.

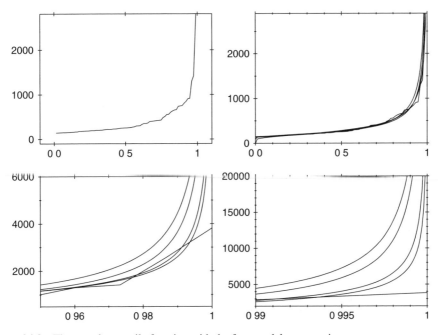

Figure 24.3   The sample quantile function with the four models over various ranges.

Table 24.1   Quantiles of the fitted distributions.

	GEV pwh	GEV pwm	GPD pwh	GPD pwm
μ	230	230	150	135
σ	100	130	125	165
ξ	0.70	0.53	0.70	0.44
Q(0.25)	201	191	190	187
Q(0.5)	272	283	262	269
Q(0.75)	429	459	443	450
Q(0.8)	495	528	522	521
Q(0.85)	597	627	645	624
Q(0.9)	777	793	866	793
Q(0.95)	1230	1169	1425	1161
Q(0.96)	1428	1321	1671	1306
Q(0.97)	1733	1545	2050	1514
Q(0.975)	1960	1706	2333	1661
Q(0.98)	2280	1925	2733	1857
Q(0.99)	3663	2794	4457	2605
Q(0.995)	5906	4046	7258	3619
Q(0.999)	18066	9525	22452	7595

Table 24.2   Data and fitted values for the 15 largest losses.

Data	GEV pwh	GEV pwm	GPD pwh	GPD pwm
μ	230	230	150	135
σ	100	130	125	165
ξ	0.70	0.53	0.70	0.44
600	506	539	536	533
630	530	563	564	558
650	557	589	597	585
660	588	619	635	616
735	624	653	679	651
743	666	692	730	691
750	716	738	791	738
800	777	793	866	793
845	854	860	961	860
907	954	945	1083	944
917	1089	1057	1251	1053
1299	1288	1214	1497	1204
1416	1614	1459	1902	1435
2568	2280	1925	2733	1857
3822	4842	3470	5929	3160

Estimated confidence intervals for the quantiles

From the estimated quantiles from 30 simulations of 75 losses from *GPD*(0.44, 135, 165), the fitted model giving the smallest estimate of the quantiles in the range 95 % to 99.9 %, standard errors and confidence limits were obtained. The estimate 99.9 percentile is seen to have an extremely large estimated error and very wide estimated confidence band.

Percentile	Fit	se	95% CI	99% CI
99.9	7595	870	(5816, 9374)	(5197, 9993)
99	2605	120	(2360, 2850)	(2274, 2936)
95	1161	32.2	(1095, 1227)	(1072, 1250)
90	793	18.8	(755, 793)	(741, 845)

Quantile estimation using L-moments

As reported in Hosking (1990), estimating high quantile values using lower order L-moments can give poor results particularly for heavy-tailed distributions. The formulae for GEV and GPD above make no sense for values of $\xi \geq 1$, and this applies also to the formulae for the quantile function when we seek to substitute the L-moment estimates of μ and ξ into it.

24.1.1   What might be done?

Despite the way that the GEV and GPD arise as consequences of extreme value theory, there is no reason why the GEV should not be used for modeling threshold exceedances, or the GPD for sample maxima, or any other heavy-tailed distribution, as we will not necessarily be approaching the asymptotic state unless we have a very large data set. In this latter case the small sample problem does not arise, and tests made for model fit can be powerful enough to identify the lack thereof.

In that Basel II required the use of a fitted 99.9 % quantile as proxy for regulatory oprisk capital, we might consider a standardization which makes prescriptive the use of any GPD or GEV severity model which fits the data as well as can be done, and then take the 99.9 % value from that. The 90 % quantile should be fairly stable in value, so it might be better still to use this with a prescribed capital factor γ of about 10. This is arbitrary at this stage but the fitted quantiles of Table 24.1 show factors of 9.6 to 25.9 between the 90 % and 99.9 % quantiles.

24.2   CASE STUDY: FITTING SEQUENTIAL LOSS DATA

24.2.1   Rolling data analysis

One mechanism for estimation is to fit a GEV distribution to the sample maxima of loss data over each of the preceding 12 months. The estimation process can be applied daily, weekly, or monthly on a rolling 12-month basis. In view of the heavy-tail characteristics – just think of the size of a potential catastrophic loss – a very high quantile such as 99 % can yield a figure which implies an economic capital allocation beyond that which would until recently have seemed unfeasibly excessive. Recall the Basel Committee proposal that a 99.9 % quantile value over a one-year holding period be calculated. Severe fraud loss events will show the fitted parameters to vary in time, since each large loss event will distort the shape of the fitted distribution. Historic data cannot be assumed to be like recent or future data, so long data series cannot be assumed to improve the estimation.

> Although no estimates will be reliable, rolling 12-month data would highlight the impact of each extreme loss, and allow its effect to decline in time. This approach would also provide a pricing mechanism that reflects the occurrence of extreme loss, and which can be compared with hedge prices, such as insurance costs.

24.2.2   Example: retail banking fraud

Data 5 (Section 17.4.5) showed separately for each year the losses from fraud at a large UK retail bank. From these, I have created a sequence of 60 values by assigning at random within each year the months January to December. Further, I have rounded the values to the nearest thousand pounds.

Month	J	F	M	A	M	J	J	A	S	O	N	D
Year 1	907	182	735	845	360	550	406	360	68	220	350	50
2	52	120	556	78	200	157	650	214	1100	50	160	48
3	350	176	110	1300	65	107	107	130	6600	200	410	3950
4	165	87	239	53	600	120	75	248	84	116	260	395
5	750	211	1820	128	230	423	295	90	426	332	123	229

For each of the 49 sequences of 12 values: January to December, then February to January, and so on, the GEV was fitted using probability weighted moments for all three parameter values and quantiles calculated (Section 20.7.1). The Hill estimation of the shape parameter was also done but could not be used to fit the parameters and quantiles since for a number of the sequences it yielded values of ξ exceeding 1.

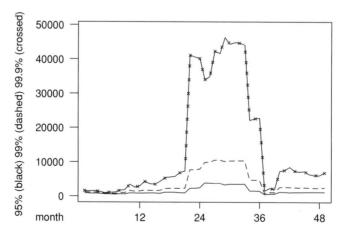

Figure 24.4   The pwm-fitted 95, 99 and 99.9 percentiles.

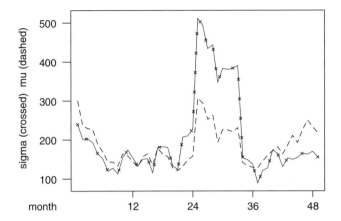

Figure 24.5   The pwm-estimates of the parameters μ and σ.

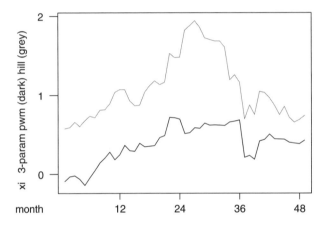

Figure 24.6   The pwm-fitted (dark) and Hill estimated (gray) shape parameter ξ.

It is important to note that just 12 values were seen to be inadequate for good estimation, but on a rolling basis they will show up changes in the model as loss values are introduced and removed from the samples. This is seen in cost-of-living and other indices where the year-on-year value is reported monthly. We might also consider weights that discount the influence of past values on the current one, such as those given by exponential smoothing.

We would not expect the model to be fixed at a constant set of parameter values throughout the five years, also not to have large jumps, so smoothing was also carried out.

Cruz (2002) uses bootstrap methods (Section 26.6.2) to determine sampling distribution properties of the parameter estimates.

25

Combining Frequency and Severity Data

Basel II asks that for the loss data approaches the frequency and severity distributions be modeled separately and then combined.

25.1 AGGREGATING LOSSES

A first step is to obtain the probability model for aggregating losses.

If X and Y are independent non-negative random variables having probability density functions f_X and f_Y, then the random variable $S_2 = X + Y$ has the pdf

$$f_{S_2}(s) = \int_0^s f_X(s - x) f_Y(x) dx = (f_X \star f_Y)(s),$$

where we use the $\star$ notation for convolution. There is also a corresponding summation formula for discrete probabilities.

The second step in the argument is to suppose that we have a sequence $X_1, X_2, \cdots$ of independent non-negative rvs each having the same pdf f_X. Then $S_3 = X_1 + X_2 + X_3 = (X_1 + X_2) + X_3$, so the convolution formula gives that

$$f_{S_3}(s) = \int_0^s f_{S_2}(s - x) f_X(x) dx = (f_X \star f_X) \star f_X(s) = f_X^{\star 3}(s).$$

Continuing with this yields the formula

$$f_{S_n}(s) = \int_0^s f_{S_{n-1}}(s - x) f_X(x) dx = f_X^{\star n}(s).$$

The next stage is to suppose that we have the sum of a random number N of losses, $S = X_1 + X_2 + \cdots + X_N$, where N has the probability mass function $\{p_n\}_{n=0,1,2,...}$, then conditional probability reasoning gives

$$f_S(s) = \sum_{n=0}^\infty P(N = n) f_{S_N}(s | N = n) = \sum_{n=0}^\infty p_n f_{S_n}(s) = E\{f_{S_N}(s)\},$$

where we are averaging with respect to the pmf. Now

$$E(S_n) = E(X_1 + X_2 + \cdots + X_n) = nE(X) = n\mu_X$$

so

$$\mu_S = E(S) = \sum_{n=0}^\infty p_n E(S_n) = \sum_{n=0}^\infty p_n(n\mu_X) = \mu_X \sum_{n=0}^\infty np_n = \mu_X \mu_N,$$

where $\mu_X = E(X)$ and $\mu_N = E(N)$. Similarly we can show that

$$\text{var}(S) = \sigma_S^2 = \mu_N \sigma_X^2 + \sigma_N^2 \mu_X^2$$

and

$$E\{(S - \mu_S)^3\} = \mu_{S3} = \mu_N \mu_{X3} + 3\sigma_N^2 \mu_X \sigma_X^2 + \mu_{N3}\mu_X^3,$$

where

$$\sigma_X^2 = \text{var}(X), \quad \sigma_N^2 = \text{var}(N), \quad \mu_{X3} = E\{(X - \mu_X)^3\}, \quad \text{and} \quad \mu_{N3} = E\{(N - \mu_N)^3\}.$$

What if we want to aggregate losses over a time interval such as a week or year? For losses over a time interval of length t, let us assume that they occur randomly at a constant rate λ. Then $N(t)$, the number of losses falling in the interval, will have a *Poisson* (λt) distribution. This has moments

$$\mu_N = \lambda t, \quad \sigma_N^2 = \lambda t, \quad \mu_{N3} = \lambda t, \quad \text{and} \quad \mu_{N4} = (\lambda t) + 3(\lambda t)^2.$$

Then

$$E(S_{N(t)}) = (\lambda t)\mu_X, \quad \text{var}(S_{N(t)}) = (\lambda t)(\sigma_X^2 + \mu_X^2),$$

and

$$E\{(S_{N(t)} - \mu_{S_{N(t)}})^3\} = (\lambda t)(\mu_{X3} + 3\mu_X \sigma_X^2 + \mu_X^2).$$

25.2   SIMULATING AGGREGATED LOSSES

We use simulation to sample from the frequency distribution, for example, from *Poisson* $(\widehat{\lambda}t)$, where λ has been estimated and t can be taken as value 1 giving a daily or weekly rate for λ. This will give a sequence of values, $n_1 = 3$, $n_2 = 0$, $n_3 = 4$, and so on. Similarly, for the severity distribution, we might simulate from $GEV(\widehat{\xi}, 0, 1)$ using an estimated ξ, and obtain a sequence of values $z_1 = 2.341$, $z_2 = 7.593$, $z_3 = 0.480$, and so on. We transform these latter values to $x_1 = \widehat{\mu} + \widehat{\sigma}z_1$, $x_2 = \widehat{\mu} + \widehat{\sigma}z_2$, ..., where we use the estimates of μ and σ. These simulated values can be generated as we need them for each sum. If $s_1 = x_1 + x_2 + \cdots + x_{n_1}$, with $s_1 = 0$ if $n_1 = 0$, then $s_2 = x_{n_1+1} + x_{n_1+2} + \cdots + x_{n_1+n_2}$.

We would most likely use the values given by the simulation process built into a statistics computer package. We must recognize that there is large variability in real data, from model choice, in the precision of estimated parameters, etc., so, although the simulations from these packages may not pass tests for quality, the accumulated error means that we should not treat the results as offering a greater reliability than they deserve. Judgement in the interpretation of results is vital.

Da Silva de Carvalho *et al.* (2008) use the Kuiper statistic V (Section 23.5) to compare the traditional classical approach and a Bayesian conditional dynamic model when the frequency data is 1000 simulated Geometric distributed variates and the severity data is 1000 Gamma distributed variates. The paper also proposes that the Metropolis-Gibbs Markov Chain Monte Carlo simulation procedure be used. This procedure is beyond the scope of this introduction to quantification.

25.3   AGGREGATION WITH THRESHOLDS

If there is a threshold separating the body and tail distributions, they will need their separate treatments. For the body, we obtain the distribution of frequencies which gave aggregate losses below the threshold, while for the tail we use those that gave aggregate losses above it.

25.4   AGGREGATION INCORPORATING EXTERNAL DATA

How do we incorporate external data? Aue and Kalkbrener (2006/7) cite evidence that the size of a bank and the severity of its loss events have no significant relationship. They adjust upwards the probabilities for small loss events and decrease those for large losses to reflect bias in the data bank's profile towards large losses.

Giacometti *et al.* (2007) integrate the internal sample with data from an external database holding data from 200 institutions, taking six times as much external data as internal data. They report that their objective is to increase statistical accuracy and account for potential losses. The minimum thresholds differ for the internal and external data sets. To align the two, the external data is rescaled so that its location and scale parameters match those of the internal data. This was done for each business line. The threshold of the pooled data was set at the larger of the two values, smaller losses than that were censored.

Brief Notes

26.1 WHAT IS VAR?

VaR is the loss on a portfolio of assets held for a fixed period T that would be exceeded with small probability $1 - q$, ie $P(L > v) = 1 - q$. That is to say VaR takes value v if v is the q-quantile, making it the $100q\%$-quantile of the distribution of loss over the holding period. If a bank were to hold the portfolio for one year (not 1000 years), its chance of having a loss in excess of VaR is one in a thousand.

Historical simulation uses past returns under the assumption that the loss distribution is constant throughout the sampling period; that is to say, the chance of a loss exceeding v is the same each day of the sampling period. It gives no information about losses that might exceed the largest loss in the sample of losses. If we have 1000 losses in the sample, our estimate could be anywhere between the largest and the second largest. If we have fewer than 1000, all we can say is that our estimate exceeds the largest value.

If we use the data to test trends, to fit a loss model, etc., we can say more, and current regulatory VaR is based on a 10-day holding period, so local features can be picked up. The one-year holding period would probably be monitored every business day on a rolling basis. This is all part of the internal measurement process that Basel is calling for.

26.2 COHERENT RISK MEASURES

Artzner *et al.* (1997, 1999) give four axioms for a mathematical theory of risk. Risk is here defined to be the future random net loss; in general terms, the worth of an unacceptable future position. The risk measure is to be the minimum capital needed to cover the loss; in general terms, the minimum capital which prudently invested would cover the loss position. If X is a non-negative risk, the risk measure is $\rho(X)$, the regulatory capital for holding X. There is no regulatory risk cover for gains.

The axioms for coherent risk are

• *Monotonicity*

$$X \leq Y \Rightarrow \rho(X) \leq \rho(Y)$$

• *Positive homogeneity*: (the currency does not change risk)

$$\rho(\alpha X) = \alpha \rho(X) \quad (\alpha \geq 0)$$

• *Translation invariance*: (charges and interest rates do not change risk)

$$\rho(\alpha + X) = \alpha + \rho(X) \quad (\alpha \geq 0)$$

- *Sub-additivity*: (without this money could be saved by allocating capital separately)

$$\rho(X + Y) \leq \rho(X) + \rho(Y)$$

This last is the key condition, though it has been argued that translation invariance and sub-additivity together imply convexity, and can be replaced with this single property (Eberlein *et al.*, 2007).

- *Convexity*: (a probability weighted mixture reduces risk)

$$\rho\{\alpha X + (1 - \alpha)Y\} \leq \alpha\rho(X) + (1 - \alpha)\rho(Y) \quad (0 \leq \alpha \leq 1)$$

26.3   DYNAMIC FINANCIAL ANALYSIS

DFA is a systematic approach based on large-scale computer simulations for modeling the full financial structure of a company. It has been likened to a flight simulator for decision makers. It uses scenario testing to project business results under specified scenarios into the future. The main tool is stochastic simulation where thousands of scenarios are randomly generated to give full probability distributions as the solutions to stochastic differential equations. DFA is a tool for comparing different strategies, not the generator of optimal solutions. The input is the key business indicator. The output paves the way for management decision making (Kaufman *et al.* (2001).)

26.4   BAYES BELIEF NETWORKS (BBN)

A BBN is a graph of nodes connected by directed links of consequential relationships having no loops, similar to a decision tree. The nodes are uncertain variables. At each node we have a "belief" table (*the nodal probability distribution table*). The BBN requires these probabilities to be specified for each nodal state given each state that might be taken by each node on each possible path to it.

The panel shows a system risk network example of Norman Fenton. All the links are directed downwards. For the node labelled SS, we would need the conditional probabilities $P(SS_i|OU_j)$, $P(SS_i|Corr_j, IC_k)$, $P(SS_i|Corr_j, QS_k)$ for every possible (higher) state SS_i, OU_j, $Corr_j$, IC_k, and QS_k.

The BBN is not complete until starting values for all these probabilities (the *prior probabilities*) are assigned. This is a mighty undertaking even when each node has only two states (on/off, yes/no, 0/1). A simple network for cheque fraud at a clearing bank can have 1000 nodes. The UK Ministry of Defence is said to have a network with more than a million nodes. However, commercial computer packages can assist with this.

Initial choice of prior probabilities can be done using best management estimates. Alternatively, a test set of scenarios can be used. These will be post hoc paths that are contained in our (or an external database), assigning values 1 to the observed nodal states. Probabilities can be set from observed proportions when there is sufficient data.

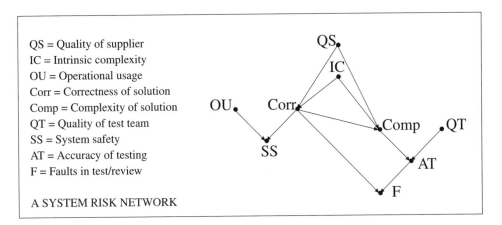

QS = Quality of supplier
IC = Intrinsic complexity
OU = Operational usage
Corr = Correctness of solution
Comp = Complexity of solution
QT = Quality of test team
SS = System safety
AT = Accuracy of testing
F = Faults in test/review

A SYSTEM RISK NETWORK

Adusei-Poku *et al.* (2007) illustrate their article with Bayes networks for failure probability and for severity.

26.4.1 Why create a BBN for OR?

The identification of the nodes, and the introspection required to offer all the prior probabilities that the methodology demands, is a powerful tool for encouraging risk managers to review every activity throughout the enterprise. Those business lines not seen as being risky will also be involved through identifying and assessing their risk profiles.

Furthermore, once the network has been up and running, stress testing can be applied by observing the consequences of feeding in extreme scenarios. Interest would center on the sensitivity of the BBN model to these scenarios.

26.5 CREDIBILITY THEORY

This is the name given to the set of statistical techniques used in insurance and actuarial calculations for setting insurance premiums.

Suppose that a policyholder experienced claims or losses to the value X (the formulation deals with either) over a fixed period. We assume that the expectation and variance of the losses of the policyholders within the group are constants, μ and σ^2 respectively, constant over time, and that the losses of different policyholders are statistically independent of each other.

The insurer has at his disposal a book value v_B from actuarial tables, and from past data the pooled average $\bar{x}$ loss from the group (called the *full credibility*). In practice the insurer would use a probability mixture

$$\text{premium} = q\bar{x} + (1 - q)v_B,$$

where q $(0 \le q \le 1)$ is called the *credibility factor*.

The insurer would like the future $\bar{x}$ to be close to its expectation μ with high probability. In statistical terms the requirement is for a relatively narrow confidence interval about μ, i.e.

$$P(|\overline{X} - \mu| \le \eta) \ge p$$

where η is small and p $(0 < p < 1)$ is fairly large. If we standardize by writing $Y = (\overline{X} - \mu)/(\sigma/\sqrt{n})$ then Y has expectation 0 and variance 1, since $E(\overline{X}) = \mu$ and $\text{var}(\overline{X}) = \sigma^2/n$. We can write the result as

$$P(|Y| \le y_p) \ge p$$

where $y_p = \eta/(\sigma/\sqrt{n})$. This is often expressed in terms of the *coefficient of variation* CV $= \sigma/\mu = \kappa\sqrt{n}/y_p$, where $\eta = \kappa\mu$.

Not all policyholders in group insurance will have the same risk profile, and some may assess their risks as deserving a reduced premium. The group behaviour information will play just one part in setting individual premium rates. Credibility theory is often given a Bayesian statistics setting, allowing the individual circumstances within the group to be expressed as a prior belief as to the policyholder's risk, and incorporated into the pricing (Klugman *et al.* 1998).

26.6   RESAMPLING METHODS

Resampling methods in statistics are based on recycling a set of observations $x = x_1, x_2, \ldots, x_n$ to give information about the robustness of an estimate $\widehat{\theta}$ or test statistic t obtained from the data. The robustness refers to the stability of the result from using the estimation formula in its repeated use. They give improved estimators of parameters when fitting distributions. It is important to remember that these methods give only information contained in the original data. No new data is created.

26.6.1   The jackknife

The jackknife was introduced in 1956 by the English statistician Maurice Quenouille (1924–1973). It is a technique that reduces bias without compromising the standard error. The simplest version is a leave-one-out process that deletes one of the sample values in turn and estimates θ or calculates t from the remaining $n - 1$. When this is done, it gives a set of estimates $\widehat{\theta}_1, \widehat{\theta}_2, \ldots, \widehat{\theta}_n$ (or $t_1, t_2, \ldots, t_n$). The values

$$w_i = n\widehat{\theta} - (n - 1)\widehat{\theta}_i$$

are then calculated and averaged to give the jackknife estimate $\widehat{\theta}_J = \overline{w}$ and its variance estimate $s_J^2 = \sum(w_i - \overline{w})^2/(n - 1)$.

The jackknife estimates are unbiased but generally inefficient (that is, they fail to give the minimum possible standard error), and the variance estimate is generally biased. Furthermore, if we are estimating a parameter that can take only positive values, it is theoretically possible for the jackknife to give a negative estimate. This is not likely, but could slip by unnoticed.

26.6.2   The bootstrap

The bootstrap, introduced in 1979 by Bradley Efron, also resamples to reduce bias and improve the standard error. Repeatedly, for a large number – usually in excess of 250 – of times, a random sample of values of the same sample size as the data is selected from the data using sampling with replacement. This will result in many values being duplicated.

From the ith of m bootstrap samples an estimate $\widehat{\theta}_i$ is obtained. These $\widehat{\theta}_i$ are used to obtain the sampling distribution function which puts an equal weight $1/m$ at each value. Sometimes just the mean and standard error are of interest, or a confidence interval.

Example (Klugman et al., 2008)

The data are simulated data from a distribution having $\mu = 0.2$ and $\sigma^2 = 0.016$.

No. of samples	$\widehat{\mu}$	$\widehat{\sigma^2}$
1000	0.1972	0.01735
2000	0.2004	0.01563
5000	0.1999	0.01566

How might we introduce extremes?

If we fit a model to the bootstrap sampling distribution, a model with a long tail of large values, we might simulate samples from the model, and use these samples in the bootstrap fashion (Efron and Tibshirani, 1993).

26.7 DATA MINING

This is the name given to the activity of trying to extract information that might be of some value but which is hidden in very large databases. Data mining is particularly applied to the search for information that was not part of the objectives of the creators of the database, not even considered by its proprietors, yet could prove to be fruitful for answering a different set of questions.

Data mining is the search for unknown structure in the data, possibly just for mis-coding at data entry. In large data sets, spurious patterns may be found that have arisen purely by chance, so one aspect of data mining is that the proprietor must be able to give a reason for the existence of the pattern.

The methodology is generally based on algorithms rather than modeling, since the latter needs a theory to support it.

By and large, it is not applicable to loss databases, though more widely it would be used to detect possible insider dealing or fraudulent activity. The databases covering credit card use or customer loyalty cards would offer greater scope for data mining.

26.8 LINEAR DISCRIMINANT ANALYSIS

Given a descriptive set of measured variables such as KRIs or key risk ratios on units from a limited number of classes, linear discriminant analysis finds the coefficients for the linear combination of variables that separates the classes most strongly. The linear combination can be used to predict the class that a new unit from an unknown class belongs to from its measured descriptive variables. It can also be used itself as a descriptive variable.

The method uses means, variances, and covariances of the measured variables.

26.9   COPULAS

These measure relationships between variates $X_1, X_2, \ldots, X_d$ of a multivariate random variable X. The joint distribution function F_X can be decomposed into its univariate marginal distributions $F_1, F_2, \ldots, F_d$ and a distribution called a *copula*. We assume that each marginal F_j is continuous.

The quantile transformation $X_j = Q_j(U_j)$ transforms the rv X_j into $U_j = F_j(X_j)$ where U_j is *Uniform* (0,1). The joint distribution function C of $U = (U_1, U_2, \ldots, U_d)$ is the copula for F_X.

$$C(\boldsymbol{u}) \; = \; P(U_1 \leq u_1, \cdots, U_d \leq u_d) \; = \; F(Q_1(u_1), \cdots, Q_d(u_d)).$$

In reverse, $F_X(\boldsymbol{x}) = C(F_1(x_1), \cdots, F_d(x_d))$.

The sampling properties require substantial quantities of data.

Some examples for bivariate data are.

- Gaussian copula, the bivariate normal cdf with correlation ρ;
- Student t copula, the bivariate t_ν on ν degrees of freedom;
- Frank copula,

$$C_\alpha(u, v) \; = \; -\frac{1}{\alpha} \ln(1 \, + \, \{g(u)g(v)/g(1)\})$$

where $g(w) = e^{-\alpha w} - 1$.

Others are the Archimedean which is a family of copulae that includes the Clayton and the Gumbel (McNeil *et al.,* 2005).

26.10   QUALITY CONTROL AND RISK MANAGEMENT

Some of the methods of quality management are being taken up in commerce and finance as tools of risk management.

A high-quality product has consistent properties that can be relied on in use. A low-quality product lacks these consistent properties and will require back-up through redundancy or other means. The link with risk management is in the need of each for statistical techniques for measurement and control. Statistical methodologies for quality control that could only be understood by mathematical statisticians were preventing their use until the likes of W. Edwards Deming adapted them through diagrams and charts. Instead of needing to rely on so-called rocket scientists for their risk computations, these would enable management to confidently take control. A caution must be expressed. The complexity of many financial products would defeat any simple risk assessment. Years after the collapse of Enron the complexity of the structure of that company's deals continues to defeat its administrators, and may let its former top management off the hook if the courts accept their defence that they could not have been expected to understand what was done in their name.

Dr William Edwards Deming (1900–1993) found Japan particularly receptive to his ideas in the 1950s, emphasizing as he did process control through everyone involved understanding the organizational flow chart.

Japan nurtured many quality control gurus. Dr Genichi Taguchi (1924–) developed tools of robust experimental design. His methodology sought to reduce sensitivity to factors that are difficult or expensive to control. Taguchi achieved the feat of getting statistical methods used without demanding an understanding of the details of how they worked. However, the

Taguchi methodology has met some criticism from statisticians, and has failed in use (often due to competing demands on resources).

The statistics-light approach to quality engineering was not entirely a Japanese phenomenon. Motorola's control chart monitoring methodology, *Six Sigma*, is extensively used in manufacturing, and the exploratory data analysis (*EDA*) of Dr John W. Tukey (1915–2000) is a methodology well-regarded by statisticians.

To the above gurus I would add Professor George E. P. Box (1919–). His skilful writings ensured that his learning process of continuous improvement by monitoring and feedback adjustment was readily understandable without compromizing the mathematical statistics. He argues that optimization methodologies can defeat this learning process since they imply that when an optimum is achieved further change can only make things worse.

Deming's mentor, Dr Walter A. Shewhart (1891–1967) had pointed out as early as 1939 that the normal distribution was inadequate for modeling statistical controls. Box, however, writes that non-normality is usually trivial when compared with non-stationarity and lack of independence. Operational risk quantification is, however, geared to the analysis of extreme non-normality, so the relevance to risk modeling of these methods is limited. A positive aspect is a new respect for statistical methods of quality control in industry, and hopefully also in business and finance (Bendell *et al.*, 1999; Box, 1993).

Bibliography

Many banks are willing to show how they tackle the loss data approaches to OR. Some of their practices may be seen in the conference proceedings and the journal articles listed below, in particular those from the *Journal of Operational Risk*.

CONFERENCE PROCEEDINGS

Leading Edge Issues in Operational Risk Management. Basel Committee on Banking Supervision's Risk Management Group (May 2003).
www.newyorkfed.org/newsevents/events/banking/2003/con052903
   New Challenges for Operational Risk Measurement and Management. Federal Reserve Bank of Boston (May 2008).
www.bos.frb.org/bankinfo/qau/conf/oprisk2008/AMA08Agenda

REFERENCES

Adusei-Poku, K., den Brink, G. J. V. and Zucchini, W. (2007). Implementing a Bayesian Network for Foreign Exchange Settlement: A Case Study in Operational Risk Management. *Journal of Operational Risk* **2**, 101–107.
Artzner, P., Delbaen, F., Eber, J. and Heath, D. (1997). Thinking Coherently. *Risk* **10**, 68–71.
Artzner, P., Delbaen, F., Eber, J. and Heath, D. (1999). Coherent Measures of Risk. *Mathematical Finance* **9**, 203–208.
Aue, F. and Kalkbrener, M. (2006/07). LDA at Work: Deutsche Bank's Approach to Quantifying Operational Risk. *Journal of Operational Risk* **1**, 49–93.
Bendell, A., Disney, J. and McCollin, C. (1999). The Future Role of Statistics in Quality Engineering and Management (Including Discussion). *The Statistician* **48**, 299–326.
Benjamini, Y. and Kreiger, A. M. (1995). Concepts and Measures for Skewness with Data Analytic Implications. *Can J Statist* **24**, 131–140.
Box, G. (1993). Quality improvement – The New Industrial Revolution *International Statistical Review* **61**, 3–19.
Castillo, E. (1988). *Extreme Value Theory in Engineering*. Academic Press.
Cruz, M. G. (2000). Practical Approaches to Quantifying Operational Risk. Unpublished proceedings from Quantifying Operational Risk Conference, London, 5 February 2000.
Cruz, M. G. (2003). Developing an Operational VaR Model using EVT. Chapter 7 in *Advances in Operational Risk: Firm-wide Issues for Financial Institutions*, 2nd ed. Risk Books.
Cruz, M. G. (2002). *Modeling, Measuring and Hedging Operational Risk*. Chichester: John Wiley & Sons Ltd.

da Silva de Carvalho, R., Migon, H. S. and Paez, M. S. (2008). Dynamic Bayesian Models as an alternative to the Estimation of Operational Risk Measures. *Journal of Operational Risk* **3**, 25–49.

Dutta, K. and Perry, J. (2006). A Tail of Tails: An Empirical Analysis of Loss Distribution Models for Estimating Operational Risk Capital. Working Paper 06-13, Federal Reserve Bank of Boston.

Eberlein, E., Frey, R., Kalkbrenner, M. and Overbeck, L. (2007). Mathematics in Financial Risk Management. *Jahresbericht der DMV* **109**, 165–193.

Efron, B. and Tibshirani, R. (1993). *An Introduction to the Bootstrap.* Chapman & Hall.

Federal Reserve Board. (2006). *Fourth Quantitative Impact Study 2006.* Federal Reserve Board, Washington, DC.

Giacometti, R., Rachev, S., Chernobai, A. and Bertocci, M. (2007). Aggregation Issues in Operational Risk. *Journal of Operational Risk* **2**, 55–90.

Giacometti, R., Rachev, S., Chernobai, A. and Bertocci, M. (2008). Heavy-tailed Distributional Models for Operational Risk. *Journal of Operational Risk,* **3**, 3–23.

Gilchrist, W. (2000). *Statistical Modeling with Quantile Functions.* Chapman & Hall/CRC.

Good, I.J. (1996). When Batterer Turns Murderer. *Nature* **381**, 481.

Hankin, R. K. S. and Lee, A. (2006). A New Family of Non-negative Distributions. *Aust N Z J Stat* **48**, 67–78.

Hoaglin, D. C. (1985). Summarising Shape Numerically: The g-and-h Distribution In: *Exploring Data Tables, Trend and Shapes.* D. C. Hoaglin, F. Mosteller and J. W. Tukey (Eds). NY: John Wiley & Sons Inc, 417–513.

Hosking, J. R. M. (1990). L-moments: Analysis and Estimation of Distributions using Linear Combinations of Order Statistics. *J R Statist Soc B* **52**, 105–124.

Johnson, N. L., Kotz. S. and Balakrishnan, N. (1995). *Continuous Univariate Distributions, Volume 2,* 2nd ed. NY: John Wiley & Sons Inc.

Johnson, N. L., Kotz, S. and Kemp, A. W. (1993). *Univariate Discrete Distributions,* 2nd ed. NY: John Wiley & Sons Inc.

Jobst, A. A. (2007). Operational Risk: The Sting is Still in the Tail but the Poison Depends on the Dose. *Journal of Operational Risk* **2**, 3–59.

Kaufmann, R., Gadmer, A. and Klett, R. (2001). Introduction to Dynamic Financial Analysis. *ASTIN Bulletin* **31 (May)**, 213–249. Available also from http://www.risklab.ch

Klugman, S. A., Panjer, H. H. and Willmot, G. E. (2008). *Loss Models: From Data to Decisions.* NY: John Wiley & Sons Inc.

McNeil, A. J., Frey, R. and Embrechts, P. (2005). *Quantitative Risk Management.* Princeton University Press.

Reiss, R-D. and Thomas, M. (2007). *Statistical Analysis of Extreme Values.* 3rd ed. Birkhäuser.

Subrahmaniam, K. (1965). A Note on Estimation in the Truncated Poisson. *Biometrika* **52**, 279–282.

Tanizaki, H. (2004). *Computational Methods in Statistics and Econometrics.* Marcel Dekker.

Tukey, J. W. (1977). *Exploratory Data Analysis.* Addison-Wesley.

Zempléni, A. (1996). Inference for Generalized Extreme Value Distributions. *J Appl Statistical Science* **4**, 107–122.

FURTHER READING

Basel Committee on Banking Supervision. (2006). International Convergence of Capital Measurement and Capital Standards: A Revised Framework. Comprehensive Version (June 2006). *Bank for International Settlements* Section V. Operational Risk, 140–151 (see http://www.bis.org).

British Bankers Association. (1999). BBA/ISDA/RMA Research Study on Operational Risk. See http://www.bba.org.uk.

Coleman, R. (2002). Op Risk Modeling for Extremes. Part 1. Small Sample Modeling. *Operational Risk* **3:12**, 7–10.

Coleman, R. (2003). Op Risk Modeling for Extremes. Part 2: Statistical Methods. *Operational Risk* **4:1**, 6–9.

Coleman, R. (2000). Using Modeling in OR Management. Operational Risk in Retail Financial Services Conference, London, June 2000. Unpublished: http://stats.ma.ic.ac.uk/~rcoleman/iir.pdf.

Coleman, R. and Cruz, M. (1999). Operational Risk Measurement and Pricing (Learning Curve). *Derivatives Week* **VIII:30**, 5–6. Revised preprint: http://stats.ma.imperial.ac.uk/~rcoleman/opriskLCV.html.

Coles, S. (2001). *An Introduction to Statistical Modeling of Extreme Values.* Springer.

Cruz, M., Coleman, R. and Salkin, G. (1998). Modeling and Measuring Operational Risk. *Journal of Risk* **1**, 63–72.

Daníelsson, J., Embrechts, P., Goodhart, C., Keating, C., Muennich, F., Renault, O. and Shin, H.S. (2001). Submitted in Response to the Basel Committee for Banking Supervision's Request for Comments. May, 2001. http://www.riskresearch.org.

Embrechts, P. (Ed.) (2000). *Extremes and Integrated Risk Management.* London: Risk Books.

Embrechts, P., Klüppelberg, C. and Mikosch, T. (1997). *Modeling Extremal Events.* Springer.

Hill, B. M.(1975). A Simple General Approach to Inference about the Tail of a Distribution. *Annals of Statistics* **3**, 1163–1174.

Hosking, J. R. M. and Wallis, J. R. (1997). *Regional Frequency Analysis: An Approach Based on L-Moments.* Cambridge University Press.

Hosking, J. R. M. and Wallis, J. R. (1987). Parameter and Quantile Estimation for the Generalized Pareto Distribution. *Technometrics* **29**, 339–349.

Jorion, P. (1997). *Value at Risk: The New Benchmark for Controlling Market Risk.* McGraw-Hill.

Kotz, S. and Nadarajah, S. (2002). *Extreme Value Theory.* Imperial College Press.

Panjer, H. H. (2006). *Operational Risk: Modeling Analytics.* NY: John Wiley & Sons, Inc.

Temnov, G. and Warnung, R. (2007/08). A Comparison of Loss Aggregation Methods for Operational Risk. *Journal of Operational Risk* **2**, 3–23.

Zwillinger, D. and Kokoska, S. (2000). *CRC Standard Probability and Statistics Tables and Formulae.* Chapman & Hall/CRC.

Index